Internet Technologies at Work

Fred T. Hofstetter

Technology Education

Boston   Burr Ridge, IL   Dubuque, IA   Emeryville, CA   Madison, WI   New York   San Francisco   St. Louis
Bangkok   Bogotá   Caracas   Kuala Lumpur   Lisbon   London   Madrid   Mexico City
Milan   Montreal   New Delhi   Santiago   Seoul   Singapore   Sydney   Taipei   Toronto

The McGraw·Hill Companies

Senior Sponsoring Editor
Chris Johnson

Senior Project Editor
Jody McKenzie

Developmental Editor
Pamela Woolf

Technical Editors
Sandra Cobb, Patricia Sine

Copy Editors
Malinda McCain, Nancy Crumpton

Proofreaders
Stefany Otis, Susie Elkind

Indexer
Valerie Perry

Composition
Peter F. Hancik
Elizabeth Jang
John Patrus

Illustrators
Kathleen Edwards
Melinda Lytle

Cover Design
James C. Korne

Series Design
Seventeenth Street Studios
Peter F. Hancik

McGraw Hill **Technology Education**

1333 Burr Ridge Parkway
Burr Ridge, Illinois 60527
U.S.A.

Internet Technologies at Work

1 2 3 4 5 6 7 8 9 0 QPD QPD 0 1 9 8 7 6 5

ISBN 0-07-222999-3

This book was composed with Corel Ventura™ Publisher.

www.mhteched.com

Dedication

To JoAnn Balingit and all our wonderful children and grandchildren.

Acknowledgments

I have many people to thank for making this project possible, but most of all, I want to acknowledge my students, who inspired this book through their enthusiastic participation in the experimental courses that were the precursors to what we now know as *Internet Technologies at Work*. I learn more from my students than from anyone else, and I look forward to every class, not so much to teach as to learn.

University of Delaware (UD) Research Professor L. Leon Campbell provided valuable service as my "intelligent agent" on the Internet. Almost daily, Leon sent me information about issues, trends, and new developments gleaned from his extensive surfing of the network. Leon is a valued friend and colleague.

I am grateful to UD networking director Dr. Dan Grim, who read an early draft of Chapter 10 and made insightful comments. Craig Prettyman, who specializes in computer security for UD user services, read Chapter 13 and made important contributions to the security auditing strategies. During the summer of 2004, 15 public school teachers worked through the final draft of this book in a course I taught as part of UD's Summer Institute in Educational and Assistive Technology. I will always be grateful for the thorough beta testing these teachers provided before this book went to press.

My virtual friend Larry Goldberg, who directs the Media Access Group at WGBH in Boston, helped me obtain the screen captures that illustrate the fine work WGBH is doing to make multimedia accessible to users with special needs. I am grateful to Larry and his talented staff not only for their contributions to Chapter 9 but also for their dedication to this vitally important cause.

My wife, JoAnn Balingit, deserves a special acknowledgment. When I reviewed with her the plans for this book, JoAnn asked how the proposed contents compared to my other three McGraw-Hill book titles (*Internet Literacy*, *Multimedia Literacy*, and *Advanced Web Design*). When I explained this book would address the NWCET and CIW foundation standards, JoAnn pointed out how this would add an important dimension for many of my professional students who have operational responsibilities to make these technologies truly work. This led to the book's title, *Internet Technologies at Work*.

At McGraw-Hill, Chris Johnson served as the editor of this book. More than just editing, Chris was an inspiration in helping decide what to include in this book and how to present it. I am especially grateful to Chris for the thorough manner in which he conducted external reviews of this text prior to its publication. I want to thank the following reviewers for their many insights and suggestions: Sandra Cobb, Pat Sine, Scott Cline, Lee Cottrell, Ron Eaglin, Shelly Hawkins, Walt Merchant, Peggy Mooney, Lewis Pulsipher, Lauran Sattler, and Paul Wilson.

About the Author

Fred T. Hofstetter was born and raised in Columbus, Ohio. A graduate of St. Joseph's College with a Ph.D. from Ohio State University, Dr. Hofstetter is professor of instructional technology at the University of Delaware, where he coordinates the ed tech master's and doctoral programs. Author of the GUIDO, PODIUM, and Serf software, he has written many books and articles about multimedia and the Internet. Winner of a Gold CINDY award, he has lectured widely throughout Africa, Australia, Canada, Europe, the United States, and the Pacific Rim. Most recently he received the School of Education's Distinguished Faculty Award.

About the Technical Editors

Sandra Cobb (MCIWD, CIW-CI, Certified Dreamweaver MX Developer) is currently the director of Instructional Technology at Mid-South Community College in West Memphis, AR. In addition, she serves as program chair for the Information Technology Systems program of study. Sandra, a graduate of Capella University, was largely instrumental in bringing the CIW program of study into the academic arena at Mid-South Community College and currently teaches online for the CIW Faculty Training Institute. She serves on the national CIW Advisory Council.

Pat Sine is the director of the Office of Educational Technology in the College of Human Services, Education and Public Policy at the University of Delaware. She regularly consults with teachers, schools, and school districts on technology integration across the curriculum. She also serves as a technical editor and Web developer for McGraw-Hill/Irwin. She holds a M.Ed. degree from the University of Delaware and has ten years of experience as a middle and high school teacher. She has taught many seminars and classes on educational uses of computers, the Internet, multimedia, and various programming languages.

Peer Reviewers

Scott Cline
Southwestern Community
College, NC

Lee Cottrell
Bradford School, PA

Dr. Ron Eaglin
University of Central Florida

Shelly Hawkins
Western Washington University

Walt Merchant
ECPI College of Technology, VA

Peggy Mooney
College of Alameda, CA

Lewis Pulsipher
Central Caroline Community
College, NC

Lauran Sattler
Ivy Tech State College, IN

Paul Wilson
DeVry University, CA

Contents

ACKNOWLEDGMENTS, III
PREFACE, XV
INTRODUCTION, XVIII

Internet Business Foundations

1 Understanding the Internet   3

Defining the Internet, 4
  Who Is Using the Internet?, 5
  How Fast Is the Internet Growing?, 5
Identifying Eleven Popular Internet Services, 6
  Electronic Mail, 7
  Listserv, 9
  Newsgroups, 9
  Chat, 10
  Instant Messaging, 12
  Videoconferencing, 12
  FTP, 13
  Multimedia Streaming, 13
  World Wide Web, 14
  Rich Site Summary (RSS), 16
  Blogging, 17
Describing the Infrastructure of the Internet, 18
  What Is Client-Server Computing?, 19
  What Is TCP/IP?, 19
  What Are Domains and Subdomains?, 20
  What Is an Intranet?, 22
  What Is an Extranet?, 23
Changing the World via the Internet, 23
  Corporate Mergers and Alliances, 23
  Telecommuting, 24
  Business and Advertising, 25
  Online Shopping, 25
  Online Banking and Investing, 26
  Government and Politics, 26
  Information Warfare and Homeland Security, 28
  Electronic Publishing, 28
  Television and Entertainment, 29
  Teaching and Learning, 30
Tracing the History of the Internet, 30
Looking into the Future of the Internet, 32
  Improving the Infrastructure, 32
  Personal Digital Assistants, 36
  Artificial Intelligence, 38
  Digital Television and Video, 40
Chapter 1 Review, 44

2   Surfing and Searching the Internet _____   **51**

Getting Connected, 52
    Internet Service Providers, 53
    Transport Medium, 54
    Telephone Modems, 55
    Ethernet, 56
    ISDN, 56
    Cable Modems, 57
    DSL, SDSL, and ADSL, 57
    Satellite, 58
    Comparing the Ways to Connect, 58
    Prepaid Internet Cards, 58
    Direct Connections, 59
Browsing the Web, 60
    What Is a Browser?, 60
    Selecting a Web Browser, 60
    Legacy Browsers, 61
    Understanding URLs, 62
    Surfing Concepts and Techniques, 64
    Managing Your Web Browser's Cache, 71
    Advanced Browser Settings, 72
    Resetting the Browser Settings, 73
    Wireless Web Browsing and the Wireless Application Protocol (WAP), 73
Handling Multimedia Objects, Plug-ins, and Viewers, 73
    Built-In Browser Support for Multimedia, 74
    Audio Controls, 74
    Video Controls, 75
    Streaming Media, 76
    What Is a Stream?, 77
    Plug-ins, 77
    Object Development and Runtime Environments, 80
    Objects and Security Issues, 83
Configuring Browser Security, 84
Finding Things with Search Engines, 85
    Subject-Oriented Searching of Directories, 86
    Keyword Searching, 87
    Advanced Boolean Searching, 87
    Concept Searching, 89
    Metasearching, 89
    Human-based Searching, 90
    Scholarly Searching, 91
    Multimedia Searches, 92
    Newsgroup Searches, 93
    File Searches, 94
    How to Find People, 95
    Finding Places, 96
    Finding Legal Information, 96
    Index of Collected Search Engines, 97
    Adding a Web Site to a Search Engine, 97
Downloading from the Internet, 98
    Commonly Found Text File Formats, 98
    Commonly Found Graphics File Formats, 100
    Commonly Found Audiovisual File Formats, 104
    Video Formats, 106
    Downloading Software and Data from the Internet, 108
    Safeguarding Against Viruses, 110
Chapter 2 Review, 112

3   Communicating Over the Internet _____ **119**

Internet Etiquette (Netiquette), 120
  Netiquette Guidelines, 120
  Computer Ethics, 121
  Spam, 122
  Hoaxes, 123
  Viruses, 124
  Lurking, 125
  Flames, 125
  Firefighters, 126
  Smileys and Emoticons, 126
  Three-Letter Acronyms (TLAs) and Jargon on the Net, 126
Electronic Mail, 127
  Getting an E-mail Account, 127
  Selecting an E-mail Client, 128
  Deciding on POP vs. IMAP and HTTP, 128
  Advanced E-mail Configuration Settings, 130
  Answering and Forwarding Mail, 133
  Filing and Retrieving E-mail Messages, 133
  Sending Mail Attachments, 134
  Addressing E-mail to Groups of People, 136
  Searching E-mail Messages, 136
  Dealing with Unwanted E-mail, 136
  Using Mail Filters, 137
  Detecting Fake Mail IDs, 137
  Encrypting Your Mail, 137
  E-mail Priority Settings, 138
  Return Receipt Requested, 138
  Spell Checking, 138
  Web-based E-mail, 138
  Sending Mail as HTML, 139
Listserv Mailing Lists, 139
  How to Subscribe to a Listserv Mailing List, 140
  Receiving Listserv Messages: Remember to Lurk, 141
  Responding to a Listserv Message, 142
  Sending a New Message to a Listserv, 143
  Filing Messages Received from Listservs, 143
  Pausing a Listserv, 143
  Finding Out Who Belongs to a Listserv, 143
  Receiving Messages in Digest Mode, 144
  Unsubscribing from a Listserv, 144
  Listserv Archives, 144
  Listserv Command Summary, 145
  Setting Up Your Own Listserv, 145
Newsgroups and Forums, 146
  Computer Conferencing, 146
  Universe of USENET Newsgroups, 146
  USENET Hierarchy, 146
  Configuring Your Newsgroup Client, 147
  Choosing a Newsgroup, 147
  Reading a Newsgroup, 149
  Responding to a Newsgroup, 149
  Creating a New Topic in a Newsgroup, 151
  Finding Newsgroups in Your Profession, 151
  Web-based Discussion Forums, 151

Blogging,   152

Reading RSS Channels and Feeds,   152

IRC Chat Rooms,   153

Instant Messaging,   154

   ICQ,   155

   AOL Instant Messenger,   156

   Microsoft MSN Messenger Service,   156

   Yahoo! Messenger,   157

Whiteboarding, Audioconferencing, and Videoconferencing,   159

Logging on to Legacy Systems via Telnet,   163

   Running a Telnet Client,   164

   Setting the Local Echo Option,   164

   Freeing Up the Remote Connection,   164

Transferring Files via Legacy FTP Commands,   165

Chapter 3 Review,   168

4   Commercializing the Internet _____   **175**

Defining E-Commerce,   177

   Who Is Using E-Commerce?,   178

   The Different Kinds of E-Commerce,   178

   Business-to-Consumer (B2C),   179

   Business-to-Business (B2B),   179

Enabling E-Commerce Technologies,   180

   Electronic Data Interchange (EDI),   181

   Secure Electronic Transactions (SET),   182

   XML Web Services,   182

Processing Payments Online,   185

   Cash Model,   185

   Check Model,   185

   Credit Model,   186

   Smart Card Model,   187

   Person-to-Person Payment Model,   187

Choosing an E-Commerce Solution,   188

   Instant Storefronts,   188

   Auctions,   189

   Case Study: Microsoft bCentral Commerce Manager,   189

Developing an In-House E-Commerce System,   195

   ADDIE Software Development Cycle,   196

   Project Management Fundamentals,   198

Regulating Copyrights, Licenses, Patents, and Trademarks,   199

   Copyright,   200

   Licensing,   203

   Patents,   204

   Trademarks,   207

Trading Internationally,   207

   Multiple Currencies,   208

   Shipping Overseas,   208

   Language Issues,   209

Chapter 4 Review,   210

Web Page Authoring Fundamentals

5   Creating Web Pages _____   **221**

Adopting a Web Page Creation Strategy,   222

   Text Editors,   223

   HTML Editors,   223

HTML Translators, 225
WYSIWYG Editors, 228
Defining the Elements of Web Page Design, 230
Headings, 231
Paragraphs, 231
Horizontal Rules, 231
Lists, 232
Images, 233
Backgrounds, 233
Bookmarks, 233
Links, 234
Special Characters, 234
Tables, 234
Frames, 234
Understanding Screen Design Principles, 236
Layout, 236
Font Selection, 238
Text Sizing, 239
Foreground vs. Background Colors, 239
Photographic Backgrounds, 240
Tiled Backgrounds, 240
Navigational Icons, 240
Scrolling, 241
Usability, 241
Consistency, 242
Analyzing the Layout of a Web Page Résumé, 242
Chapter 5 Review, 244

6   HTML Coding _____ **251**

How HTML Works, 252
Understanding Markup, 253
HTML Tag Formats, 253
Versions of HTML, 254
Taxonomy of HTML Tags, 255
Tags Used in the Web Page Creation Tutorial, 255
Creating Your Web Page Résumé, 256
Starting the Page, 256
Creating the Page Title, 257
Writing the Heading, 257
Saving the Page, 258
Viewing the Page with a Web Browser, 259
Writing Paragraphs, 259
Creating a List, 260
Horizontal Rules, 261
Remember to Save the File, 261
Inserting a New Heading, 262
Creating Named Anchor Bookmarks, 262
*Creating Hypertext Links to Named
   Anchor Bookmarks, 263*
Returning to the Table of Contents, 264
Linking to URLs, 265
Identifying the Web Page Owner, 265
Mailto Links, 266
Creating White Space on Web Pages, 266
Character Attributes on Web Pages vs. Word Processors, 266
HTML Graphics and Animated GIFs, 267
Obtaining Images to Use on a Web Page, 267
Preparing Images for a Web Page, 268

Configuring Paint Shop Pro,   269
Capturing Images,   270
Converting Images,   271
Resizing Images,   272
Color Adjustments,   272
Inserting an Image into Your Web Page Résumé,   273
Tiling an Image into the Background of a Web Page,   274
Creating Transparent Images,   274
Creating Animated Images,   275
Clip Art for Web Pages,   276
HTML Tables and Web Page Layout,   276
What Is a Table?,   276
Why Use Tables on Web Pages?,   277
Creating a Table,   278
Adjusting the Attributes of a Table,   280
Indenting to Document the Structure of a Table,   284
Subdividing Table Cells,   285
Making Cells That Span More Than One Row or Column,   287
HTML Hyperlinks and Web Design,   287
How Links Form Webs,   287
Hypermedia Design Paradigms,   289
Chapter 6 Review,   292

7   Interacting with Users _____ **301**
Creating HTML Forms,   302
Getting Information from Users,   303
Designing the Prompts,   303
Coding the Form,   303
Coding the Text Field Input Controls,   304
Coding the Radio Button Input Controls,   305
Coding the Submit and Reset Buttons,   306
Processing the Response,   307
Creating Check Boxes,   308
Creating Single and Multiple Item Selection Menus,   309
Creating Text Areas,   310
Creating Password Fields,   311
HTML Web Form Control Summary,   311
Making a PayPal Buy Now Button,   312
Hidden Fields,   312
Image Buttons,   313
Coding a PayPal Buy Now Button,   313
Using the PayPal Button Factory,   315
Designing HTML Image Maps,   316
Analyzing a Client-Side Image Map,   316
Defining the Map and Area Tags,   316
Visualizing the Coordinates,   317
Applying the Usemap Attribute,   317
Creating Nonrectangular Areas,   317
Creating HTML Frames,   319
What Is a Frameset?,   319
Creating Frameset Layouts,   320
Frame Targeting,   325
When Should You Use or Not Use a Frameset?,   328
Publishing a Web Site via FTP,   328
Getting Your Web Space,   329
Your Web Space Address,   329
Choosing an FTP Client,   330
Installing the FTP Software,   330

How to Configure a New FTP Connection, 330
How to FTP Files to the Web, 331
How to Delete and Rename Files at a Web Site, 332
Coping with Case-Sensitive File Servers, 333
Correcting Problems and Updating Published Web Pages, 333
Relative vs. Absolute Links, 333
Maintaining a Good Directory Structure, 334
How to Create New Folders on the Web, 334
Setting the File Permission Attributes, 335
Chapter 7 Review, 336

8 Creating Active Web Pages _____ 343

Introduction to Scripting, 344
What Scripting Languages Are There?, 345
Where Do Scripts Go?, 345
Where Do Scripts Run?, 346
When Should You Use JavaScript?, 346
JavaScript "Hello, World!" Project, 346
Variables and Assignments, 348
Objects, Methods, and Properties, 355
JavaScript Clock Project, 356
Document Object Model (DOM), 359
Popular JavaScript DOM Objects, 359
Intrinsic Events, 362
Accessing DOM Objects via Dot Notation, 362
Accessing DOM Objects by Arrays, 364
Accessing DOM Objects by Name, 365
Debugging JavaScript via the Alert Box, 366
JavaScript Code Sources, 368
Maintaining State in Cookies, 369
What Is a Cookie?, 369
Why Does the Internet Need Cookies?, 369
How to Read and Write the Value of a Cookie, 370
Cookie Cutter Code Analysis, 372
Cascading Style Sheets, 374
Three Kinds of Cascading Style Sheets, 375
Creating an Inline CSS, 375
Creating an Embedded CSS, 376
Creating an External CSS, 377
When to Use the <span> and <div> Tags, 378
When to Create Style Classes and IDs, 379
What Is Absolute Positioning?, 380
Dynamic HTML, 382
Dynamic Animation Effects, 382
Dynamic Gradient Effects, 384
Dynamic Page Transitions, 384
XML and XHTML, 388
What Is XML?, 388
What Is the Extensible Stylesheet Language (XSL)?, 389
What Are the Flavors of XHTML?, 391
What Is an XML Module?, 392
Chapter 8 Review, 395

9 Making Web Pages Accessible _____ 403

Defining Web Accessibility, 404
Accessibility Is a Right, 405
W3C Web Accessibility Initiative (WAI), 405
WAI Web Content Accessibility Guidelines, 405
Section 508 Accessibility Standards, 406

Coding to the Section 508 Web Accessibility Standards,   406
  Textual Equivalents for Nontext Elements,   406
  Synchronized Alternatives for Multimedia Presentation,   408
  Conveying Color-Coded Information from Context or Markup,   409
  Making Web Pages Readable Without Requiring Style Sheets,   409
  Text Links for Active Regions of Server-Side Image Maps,   410
  When to Use Client-Side vs. Server-Side Image Maps,   411
  Table Row and Column Headers,   412
  Related Table Row and Column Headers,   412
  Frame Titling,   413
  Avoiding Screen Flicker in the Range of 2 Hz to 55 Hz,   414
  Providing Text-Only Page Alternatives for Noncompliant Pages,   414
  Describing Scripts with Functional Text,   415
  Applet and Plug-in Accessibility,   415
  Form Elements, Directions, and Cues,   416
  Skip Navigation,   417
  Timed Responses,   418
Making Applets, Helpers, and Plug-ins Accessible,   418
  Flash Accessibility,   418
  PDF Accessibility,   419
  Multimedia Accessibility Showcase,   420
Designing Style Sheets for Accessibility,   421
  Font Selection and Spacing,   422
  Color and Contrast,   423
  Layering and CSS Page Layout,   425
Tools for Assessing Web Site Accessibility,   426
  Bobby,   427
  LIFT,   427
  WebKing,   427
  STEP508,   428
  Learning More about Web Accessibility,   428
Chapter 9 Review,   429

Networking Fundamentals

10 Introduction to Networking _____ 437

Understanding Networks,   438
  Mainframe/Terminal Model,   439
  Client-Server Model,   440
  Peer-to-Peer Model,   441
  Enterprise Model,   441
  Push vs. Pull Technology,   442
  Network Operating Systems,   442
Classifying Network Topologies,   445
  Bus Topology,   445
  Ring Topology,   445
  Star Topology,   446
  Hybrid Topology,   447
  Mesh Topology,   448
Adopting Network Protocols,   448
  Defining the Seven Layers of the OSI Reference Model,   449
  OSI/RM Protocol Suite Examples,   452
Creating LANs, MANs, and WANs,   454
  IEEE Project 802 Networking Standards,   455
  IEEE 802.2 Standard: Logical Link Control (LLC),   456
  IEEE 802.3 CSMA/CD (Ethernet),   456
  IEEE 802.5 Token Ring,   457

IEEE 802.12 Demand Priority Access LAN (100VG-AnyLAN),   457
Fiber Distributed Data Interface (FDDI) Networks,   457
Wide Area Networks (WANs),   458
X.25,   458
Frame Relay,   459
Asynchronous Transfer Mode,   459
Network Access Points (NAPs),   460
Wireless Access Points (WAPs),   461
Network Address Translation (NAT),   461
Physical Network Components,   461
Physical Connection Media,   463

Chapter 10 Review,   468

11   Architecting the Internet _____ **475**

Understanding TCP/IP,   476
Internet Architecture,   476
Internet Engineering Task Force (IETF),   477
Application Layer Protocols,   478
Transport Layer Protocols,   479
Internet Layer Protocols,   480
Network Access Layer Protocols,   480
Demultiplexing,   481
Routing,   481
Static vs. Dynamic Routers,   482
Routing Protocols,   482
Port Numbers,   483

Internet Addressing,   484
Internet Address Classes,   484
IP Addressing Rules,   485
Subnet Masks,   487
Configuring TCP/IP on a Personal Computer,   488

Configuring Networks for Optimum Performance,   489
ping,   489
traceroute,   490
netstat,   491
ipconfig,   492
winipcfg,   492
arp,   492
Network Analyzers,   493

Internetworking Servers,   494
DNS Servers,   495
Proxy Servers,   498
Caching Servers,   499
Mirrored Servers,   500
Certificate Servers,   500
Directory Servers,   500
Catalog Servers,   501
Transaction Servers,   502

Serving Internet Resources,   502
Web Servers,   502
Mail Servers,   506
Mailing List Servers,   507
Streaming Media Servers,   507
FTP Servers,   508
News Servers,   508
Popular Server Products,   508
UNIX and Linux,   509
Microsoft Windows Server,   510

Chapter 11 Review,   513

12 Database Connectivity and Server-Side Scripting _____ **521**

Providing Web Access to Server-Side Databases, 522

Common Gateway Interface (CGI), 523

Server Application Programming Interfaces (SAPIs), 523

Active Server Pages (ASP), 524

Java Servlets and Java Server Pages (JSP), 525

PHP Hypertext Preprocessor (PHP), 526

ColdFusion, 526

ASP.NET, 526

Understanding Databases, 527

Designing a Relational Database, 528

Normalizing a Database, 529

Indexing a Database, 529

Database Design Principles, 529

Accessing Server-Side Databases, 531

Connectivity Options, 532

OLE DB Data Sources, 533

ActiveX Data Objects (ADO), 533

Creating an ADO Connection Object, 533

Using the Structured Query Language (SQL), 534

Creating Data-Driven Web Pages, 537

Reading Data from a Recordset, 537

Using Logic to Make Decisions, 538

Chapter 12 Review, 542

13 Securing the Internet _____ **549**

Identifying Internet Security Issues, 550

User-level Issues, 551

Physical Access Security, 551

Network Security Threats, 551

Identifying Assets, 552

Viruses and the Hacker Process, 553

Applying Internet Security Safeguards, 556

Microsoft Security Newsletters, 556

Microsoft Windows Update Service, 557

Defeating Attacks, 558

Security Auditing and Intrusion Detection, 559

Firewall Strategies, 560

Firewall Topologies, 561

Transmitting Network Data Securely, 566

Symmetric Cryptography and Secret-Key Encryption, 566

Asymmetric Cryptography and Public Key Infrastructure (PKI), 567

Digital Signatures and Hash Encryption, 567

Using a Digital ID with Microsoft Outlook, 569

Secure Sockets Layer (SSL) Handshake Protocol, 571

Transport Layer Security (TLS) Handshake Protocol, 572

IPSec and Virtual Private Networks (VPN), 572

Pretty Good Privacy (PGP), 573

Publishing a Web Securely, 573

Using a Secure Shell (SSH) Protocol, 573

Making a Secure FTP (SFTP) File Transfer, 574

Chapter 13 Review, 575

Glossary _____ **581**

Bibliography _____ **601**

Index _____ **603**

Preface

Information Technology Skill Standards and Your Curriculum

Students in today's increasingly competitive IT career market are differentiated not only by their technical skills, but by their communication, problem solving, and teaming skills. These professional skills are the ones that guarantee career longevity and success. The National Workforce Center for Emerging Technologies (NWCET) and McGraw-Hill Technology Education have partnered in an effort to help you build technical *and* employability skills in the classroom.

Skill standards–aligned curriculum is becoming a *de facto* requirement for schools everywhere in the United States today. Programs are required to be standards aligned in order to show clearly that students are being taught and assessed consistently and to an agreed upon set of skill and content standards. For those programs preparing students to enter the workforce, skill standards provide an excellent skeleton upon which to build courses.

Research has shown improved learning and retention of knowledge when learning takes place in a rich learning context. Students who learn in a real-world context are also better equipped to transfer their skills to the real world. IT skill standards provide the kind of real-world data that educators can use. Educators can draw from the skill standards to develop contextually rich assignments that help students to situate their learning in specific work contexts with complex and real-world problems to solve.

IT skill standards provide a common language between industry and education so that building bridges between these two groups can be more efficient. The more industry recognizes what educational programs are doing, the easier it is for education to gain industry support. Schools that use a skill standards–aligned program are better prepared to gain support from industry for technical advisory boards, student internships, job shadows, faculty internships, and a host of other support resources.

IT skill standards provide increased portability of skills because of the common language. Other institutions can clearly identify the content and skills that graduates of a skill standards–aligned curriculum have acquired. Programs that are skill standards based will effectively oil the wheels of articulation between programs that traditionally may have difficulty agreeing on what has been taught and assessed.

NWCET and McGraw-Hill in Partnership

National Workforce Center
for Emerging Technologies

McGraw-Hill Technology Education and the NWCET have partnered with the goal of helping IT educators meet these demands by making the IT skill standards more easily available and ready to use. McGraw-Hill Technology Education and the NWCET have developed four different products that will help you to address the IT skill standards in your web development programs and courses. You will find these great resources in the textbook's instructor's resource kit:

- A summary crosswalk that highlights the aspects of NWCET's Information Technology Core addressed by McGraw-Hill's *Internet Technologies at Work.*

Chapter 1	Chapter 2	Chapter 3	Chapter 4	Chapter 5
IT Core: *Computer Trends in Business and Society*—Demonstrate the ability to present and discuss how computer systems impact the operation and management of business and society	IT Core: *Internet*—Demonstrate the ability to use the Internet as a research tool in an efficient manner	IT Core: *Email*—Demonstrate a basic understanding of e-mail system components and organization Demonstrate the ability to use e-mail effectively and appropriately	IT Core: *Computer Trends in Business and Society*—Demonstrate the ability to discuss the issues affecting the selection of a computer system for a specific environment Demonstrate the ability to present current computer technology and systems trends	IT Core: *Internet*—Demonstrate the ability to develop, deliver, and manage content

Chapter 6	Chapter 7	Chapter 8	Chapter 9	Chapter 10
IT Core: *Programming*—Demonstrate the ability to perform Web programming	IT Core: *Internet*—Demonstrate the ability to implement and maintain site and applications	IT Core: *Internet*—Demonstrate the ability to implement and maintain site and applications	IT Core: *Analytical and Logical Thinking*—Demonstrate the ability to apply analytical and logical thinking to gathering and analyzing information, designing and testing solutions to problems, and formulating plans	IT Core: *Network*—Demonstrate an understanding of the overall design and components of a LAN and WAN system

Chapter 11	Chapter 12	Chapter 13
IT Core: *Network*—Demonstrate an understanding of the overall design and components of a LAN and WAN system Demonstrate the ability to perform basic setup and configuration of network hardware and software	IT Core: *Database Applications*—Demonstrate the ability to define and use the basic terminology of relational databases *Principles of Programming*—Describe the required formats for and explain the purpose of data types, variables, and arrays	IT Core: *Internet Information Assurance*—Demonstrate the ability to ensure infrastructure and network security

- A detailed crosswalk listing Technical Knowledge, Employability Skills, and Performance Indicators addressed by the compliant curriculum (textbook, lab manual, and learning activities in the instructor's resource kit)

- Thirteen skill standards–based activities with associated assessment tools

- A training document that helps instructors understand and use the features of teaching a skill standards–aligned curriculum

NWCET Background and Mission

In 1995, the National Science Foundation (NSF) designated and funded the NWCET as a National Center of Excellence in Advanced Technological Education. The Center was created to advance IT education and improve the supply, quality, and diversity of the IT workforce.

The National Workforce Center for Emerging Technologies has since become a leader in new designs for Information Technology (IT) education developing products, services, and best practices that provide timely, relevant, and lasting solutions to meet the needs of IT educators and the IT workforce. The NWCET translates the rapidly changing demands of the technology workplace into programs, curricula, courseware, and assessments that prepare students for current and future IT careers.

The NWCET is perhaps best known for its IT skill standards. Skill standards provide an agreement of what is expected to be successful in a given career area. They provide a validated, industry-derived framework upon which educators can build curricula. Using industry skill standards as the foundation for curricula will result in a closer alignment between educational programs and workplace expectations, and result in a better-skilled workforce.

To support new and innovative IT programs and degrees, the NWCET (www.nwcet.org) provides other professional development opportunities for high school teachers and community college and university faculty. The Educator-to-Educator Institute (E2E), the training branch of the NWCET, is dedicated to helping IT educators achieve excellence in IT instruction. NWCET provides IT career education through its CyberCareers pages, a Web site oriented toward middle and high schools students and teachers, offering a wide variety of career education materials such as job descriptions and an IT Interest Inventory. NWCET also provides consulting and assistance in developing and implementing new IT programs aligned to skill standards. You can try out some of the NWCET curriculum development and alignment tools online at www.bcc.ctc.edu/wcit/Toolkit/index.asp.

Instructor and Student Web Site

For instructor and student resources, check out www.mhteched.com\itaw, where you'll find a wide range of online materials that will help you learn more about internet technologies. On the Web site you'll find:

- Web links to additional resources and information
- Student quizzes
- Study outlines
- Chapter summaries

Additional Resources for Teachers

Resources for teachers are provided via an instructor's resource kit that maps to the organization of the textbook. This resource kit includes the following:

- Answer keys to the end-of-chapter activities in the textbook
- ExamView® Pro testbank software that generates a wide array of paper- or network-based tests, and features automatic grading
- Hundreds of test questions, written by experienced IT instructors
- A wide variety of question types and difficulty levels, allowing teachers to customize each test to maximize student progress
- Engaging PowerPoint slides on the lecture topics
- NWCET IT skills standards guide with activities that supplement each chapter in the book
- WebCT e-Packs and Blackboard cartridges

Introduction

This may be the most strategic book you have ever purchased. Why? Because no matter what role you will eventually play in the information society, this book will provide you with a working knowledge of the Internet technologies employers are looking for across virtually all sectors of the knowledge economy. These skills are so vitally important in all kinds of business today that the National Science Foundation awarded a grant to the National Workforce Center for Emerging Technologies (NWCET) for the purpose of creating nationally validated IT skills standards. This book teaches to the NWCET foundation standards. More information about NWCET is available at www.nwcet.org.

The title of this book, *Internet Technologies at Work*, has a double meaning. Through the book's hands-on, step-by-step tutorials, you will not only acquire conceptual knowledge about how the Internet works, but you will also get hands-on experiences in actually making it work. These experiences come from walkthroughs, labs, and problem-solving exercises that are situated in the workplace. As you work through the 13 chapters in this book, you will learn tools and techniques that you can immediately apply to solving problems at work.

Some of the students using this book are working toward obtaining one of the Certified Internet Webmaster (CIW) certifications. All students working toward earning their Webmaster certifications need to take the CIW foundations exam. Upon passing the foundations exam, students earn the designation of Certified International Webmaster Associate. The foundations exam has three modules that cover (1) Internet business foundations, (2) site development foundations, and (3) network technology foundations. This book has three parts that correspond to these three modules of the CIW foundations exam.

Each part of this book is divided into chapters designed to teach you the concepts and give you the hands-on experience that will enable you to pass the foundations exam. At the end of each chapter you will find practice exam questions and standards-based labs designed to help you master the certification objectives. Even if you are not seeking to earn a formal certification, completing these end-of-chapter materials will reinforce the concepts and provide you with a true working knowledge of *Internet Technologies at Work*. More information about CIW certification is online at www.ciwcertified.com.

This book is much more than a CIW cookbook, however. It goes beyond teaching just what you need to know to pass the exam. If your objective is to pass the CIW foundations exam, you should certainly read the chapters, study the end-of-chapter summaries, and practice the sample test questions. But the goal of this book is to take you further. This book has you do the Internet, not just study it.

In a speech that World Wide Web inventor Tim Berners-Lee delivered at the Royal Society in London on September 22, 2003, he complained that one of his greatest obstacles is that most people think the Web is finished. This book seeks to remove that obstacle by presenting the Internet from a dynamic perspective. Besides teaching you how the Internet works today, this book considers how the network is evolving and encourages you to reflect on how the emerging technologies will empower you to do more with the Internet in the future.

This educational philosophy makes this book appropriate for use as a college or university textbook that reflects as well as instructs. Besides teaching what students need to know to pass the CIW foundations exam, this book will encourage college students to reflect on why they are doing what they are doing, what they will be able to do better as the Internet continues to evolve, and what the Internet means in their lives and in their workplace and in society. I believe that every professional who works in the information economy needs to have this perspective if we are to keep the Internet open and evolving. By reflecting on what we are doing and considering how to do it better, we create the kind of mindset that enables new technologies to emerge.

—*Fred T. Hofstetter*

part

I

Internet Business Foundations

Many people have a cloudy understanding of the Internet. Technical network diagrams often use the symbol of a cloud to represent large portions of the Internet, rather than depicting all the switches, routers, signal boosters, and wiring that wind their way across the Net. This cloud is not meant to imply, however, that the Internet is elusive or hard to understand.

This part of the book will enable you to see through the clouds by defining what the Internet is, describing what you can do with it, and demonstrating how it has changed the world. Rather than just reading about Internet fundamentals, you step through hands-on exercises that reinforce the key concepts and provide you with real experience implementing best practices across a broad range of business and industry.

If you are working toward obtaining your Webmaster certification, completing this part of the book will prepare you to answer the questions in the first module of the CIW Foundations exam.

chapter

1

Understanding the Internet

"What do you want the Internet to be?"

—*Nortel Networks TV advertisement*

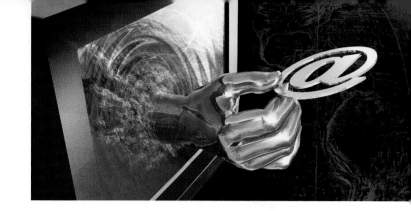

In this chapter, you will learn how to:

▪ Define the Internet, describe how large it is, and compare its explosive growth rate to the relatively slower pace of adoption of other communications media.

▪ Identify the most popular Internet services and clarify the relationship between the Internet and the World Wide Web.

▪ Describe underlying technological concepts that enable the Internet to work.

▪ Define how the Internet impacts everyday activities.

▪ Provide a brief history of the Internet, explaining how it grew from its humble origins into the worldwide network that we enjoy today.

▪ Describe efforts that are underway to improve the infrastructure of the Internet.

Y

O U may expect a book about Internet technologies to begin by defining a lot of technical terms. In order to understand the Internet, however, you need to know more than the meanings of terms. You need to know who is using the Internet, explain why it grew so fast, and understand how it has changed the world. This chapter introduces the Internet and defines the necessary terms in the broader context of who is using the Internet, what the Internet services mean to society, and why business will never be the same as it was prior to the commercialization of the Internet.

As you work your way through this chapter, I hope you will follow the suggested links and complete the Try This! exercises. Besides reinforcing the concepts that help you understand the Internet, these exercises take you online and bring the book to life. Please immerse yourself and enjoy this journey.

At the end of the chapter is a list of key terms and practice quizzes that will help students who are preparing to take the CIW Foundations exam. These are followed by lab projects that are situated in the workplace to help you apply these concepts to solving real-world problems.

Defining the Internet

The **Internet** is a worldwide connection of more than 171 million computers that use the Internet Protocol (IP) to communicate. The Internet Protocol was invented for the Advanced Research Projects Agency (ARPA) of the U.S. Department of Defense. The goal was to create a decentralized network that would continue to function if a bomb destroyed one or more of the network's nodes; information would get rerouted automatically so it could still reach its address. As a result of this bomb-proof design, any user on the Internet can communicate with any other user, regardless of their locations.

Figure 1-1 illustrates the web that is formed by the interconnections of computers on the Internet in the United States. Nearly 200 countries and territories around the world are similarly connected to the Internet, forming a worldwide telecommunications network.

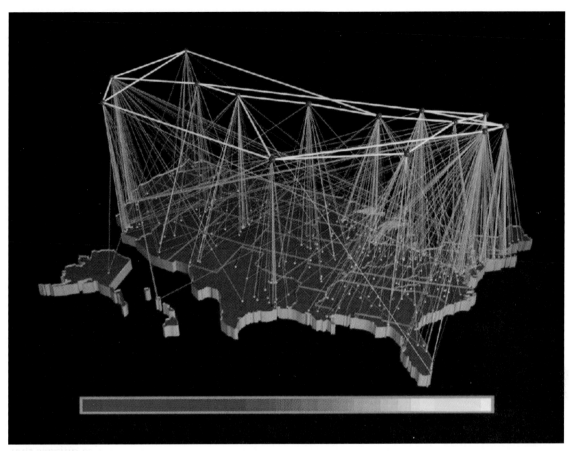

FIGURE 1-1   *This image is a visualization study of traffic on the Internet. The traffic volume range is depicted from purple (zero bytes) to white (100 billion bytes). Move your eye along the white lines to get a sense of how very high-speed lines called the backbone carry Internet traffic to distribution points that route the packets toward their destinations.* ■

Source: "NSFNET T1 Backbone and Regional Networks." Rendered by Donna Cox and Robert Patterson, National Center for Supercomputing Applications/University of Illinois.

Who Is Using the Internet?

People from all walks of life are using the Internet. Business professionals, stockbrokers, government workers, politicians, doctors, teachers, researchers, students, monks, kids, elderly people, soldiers, parents, entertainers, police, social workers, pilots, waiters, disk jockeys, and movie stars—virtually everyone who wants to succeed in the information society is using the Internet.

According to the CIA's *World Factbook*, 604.1 million people were online worldwide in August 2003. To find out how many people are online today, follow this book's Web site links to the Internet usage surveys.

How Fast Is the Internet Growing?

Figure 1-2 shows how fast the Internet is growing. The number of pages on the Web has increased dramatically from about 300 million in 1998 to more than three billion in 2003. According to Nielsen Media Research, the number of people who are banking online nearly doubled, from 13 million in 2001 to 23.2 million in 2003. For more information, follow this book's Web site links to the Nielsen NetRatings and to Hobbes' Internet Timeline.

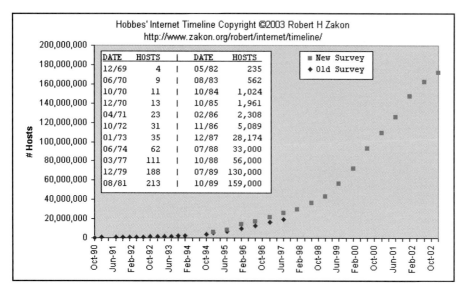

Hobbes' Internet Timeline Copyright ©2003 Robert H Zakon
http://www.zakon.org/robert/internet/timeline/

DATE	HOSTS		DATE	HOSTS
12/69	4		05/82	235
06/70	9		08/83	562
10/70	11		10/84	1,024
12/70	13		10/85	1,961
04/71	23		02/86	2,308
10/72	31		11/86	5,089
01/73	35		12/87	28,174
06/74	62		07/88	33,000
03/77	111		10/88	56,000
12/79	188		07/89	130,000
08/81	213		10/89	159,000

■ New Survey
◆ Old Survey

FIGURE 1-2 *Follow the dots on this growth chart to see how fast the Internet is growing. Notice how the shape of the growth curve is beginning to follow the proverbial S-curve, whereby innovations such as the Internet tend to grow slowly at first and then ramp up sharply. Then the curve begins to taper as the innovation achieves widespread adoption.* ■

Source: Hobbes' Internet Timeline at http://www.zakon.org/robert/internet/timeline/#Growth. Used by permission of Robert H. Zakon.

Identifying Eleven Popular Internet Services

What people do on the Internet is organized according to services defined by protocols that specify how information moves across the **Net**. The most popular services include electronic mail (e-mail), listserv, newsgroups, chat, videoconferencing, File Transfer Protocol (FTP), multimedia streaming, the World Wide Web, the Rich Site Summary (RSS), and blogging. Figure 1-3 shows that you have access to all these services when you are connected to the Internet.

FIGURE 1-3

An Internet Protocol (IP) connection provides you with access to Internet services all over the world. ■

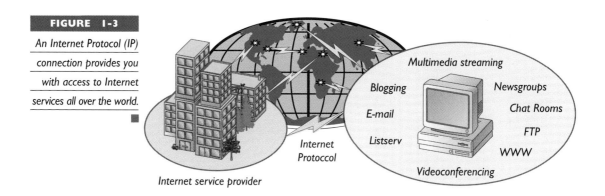

Internet service provider

Internet Protoccol

Multimedia streaming
Blogging
E-mail
Listserv
Newsgroups
Chat Rooms
FTP
WWW
Videoconferencing

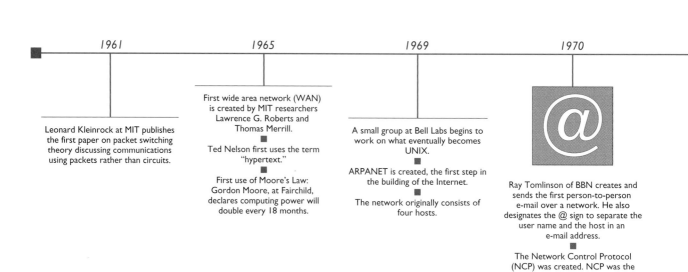

| 1961 | 1965 | 1969 | 1970 |

1961 — Leonard Kleinrock at MIT publishes the first paper on packet switching theory discussing communications using packets rather than circuits.

1965 — First wide area network (WAN) is created by MIT researchers Lawrence G. Roberts and Thomas Merrill. ■

Ted Nelson first uses the term "hypertext." ■

First use of Moore's Law: Gordon Moore, at Fairchild, declares computing power will double every 18 months.

1969 — A small group at Bell Labs begins to work on what eventually becomes UNIX. ■

ARPANET is created, the first step in the building of the Internet. ■

The network originally consists of four hosts.

1970 — Ray Tomlinson of BBN creates and sends the first person-to-person e-mail over a network. He also designates the @ sign to separate the user name and the host in an e-mail address. ■

The Network Control Protocol (NCP) was created. NCP was the first standardized network protocol used by ARPANET.

Try This!

How Large Is the Internet?

Robert H. Zakon is an Internet evangelist who created and maintains a Web page called Hobbes' Internet Timeline. More than just a timeline, this page is full of charts and graphs that illustrate many different ways of measuring the size of the Internet. Perusing the facts and figures at this site is a good way to develop your perspective on the size and significance of the Net. To visit this site, follow these steps:

1. Launch your Web browser and type the following Web address into the browser's address field:
www.zakon.org/robert/internet/timeline#growth

2. Press the ENTER key to open the site, and the page appears onscreen.

   Note: Another way to open the site is to pull down the browser's File menu, choose Open or Open Location, type the Web address, and click the button to open the page.

3. Scroll down a little until the Internet Hosts growth chart appears. Compare it to Figure 1-2, which pictures how the chart appeared when this book went to press.

4. Many other statistics about the Internet are on this page. Scroll up and down to peruse interesting facts and figures that appear onscreen.

Electronic Mail

The most often used Internet service is electronic mail, which is also known as **e-mail**. Every registered user on the Internet has an e-mail address. E-mail is a great way to communicate, because it avoids the delays caused by playing telephone tag. As depicted in Figure 1-4, mail queues up in your "inbox," and you read and respond to it at your convenience. Many users read their electronic mail several times a day. You will learn how to use advanced electronic mail features in Chapter 3.

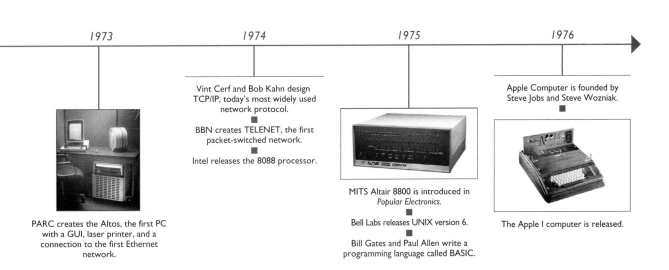

1973   1974   1975   1976

Vint Cerf and Bob Kahn design TCP/IP, today's most widely used network protocol.

BBN creates TELENET, the first packet-switched network.

Intel releases the 8088 processor.

Apple Computer is founded by Steve Jobs and Steve Wozniak.

MITS Altair 8800 is introduced in *Popular Electronics*.

Bell Labs releases UNIX version 6.

Bill Gates and Paul Allen write a programming language called BASIC.

The Apple I computer is released.

PARC creates the Altos, the first PC with a GUI, laser printer, and a connection to the first Ethernet network.

Mail queues up in your inbox, where you click to select the message you want to read.

The preview pane displays the message currently selected in the Inbox.

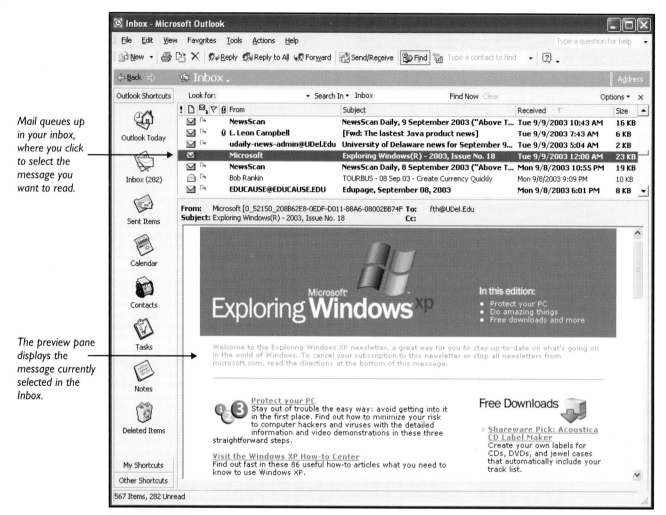

FIGURE 1-4   *E-mail clients, such as the Microsoft Outlook program shown here, display the incoming queue of e-mail messages in your inbox. When you click a message to select it, the client displays the message and provides you with options to reply, forward, file, or delete the message.* ■

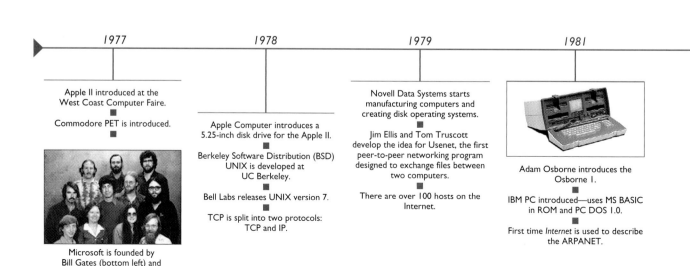

1977

Apple II introduced at the West Coast Computer Faire.

■

Commodore PET is introduced.

■

Microsoft is founded by Bill Gates (bottom left) and Paul Allen (bottom right).

1978

Apple Computer introduces a 5.25-inch disk drive for the Apple II.

■

Berkeley Software Distribution (BSD) UNIX is developed at UC Berkeley.

■

Bell Labs releases UNIX version 7.

■

TCP is split into two protocols: TCP and IP.

1979

Novell Data Systems starts manufacturing computers and creating disk operating systems.

■

Jim Ellis and Tom Truscott develop the idea for Usenet, the first peer-to-peer networking program designed to exchange files between two computers.

■

There are over 100 hosts on the Internet.

1981

Adam Osborne introduces the Osborne 1.

■

IBM PC introduced—uses MS BASIC in ROM and PC DOS 1.0.

■

First time *Internet* is used to describe the ARPANET.

Listserv

Listserv stands for "list server" and is built on top of the e-mail protocol. Listservs work like electronic mailing lists, sending e-mail messages to people whose names are on the list. You join a listserv by e-mailing a message to it, saying you want to subscribe. Many listservs also let you subscribe by filling out a Web form at the listserv's Web site. After you subscribe, whenever someone sends e-mail to the listserv, you receive a copy in your e-mail. Likewise, when you send e-mail to the listserv, everyone on the listserv receives a copy of your message, as depicted in Figure 1-5. Thus listserv is a simple way for groups of people to communicate with one another through e-mail.

There are thousands of listservs on the Internet. Listservs are used, for example, to deliver many of the Internet's **e-zines** (electronic magazines) via e-mail. You will learn how to find out about listservs and join them in Chapter 3.

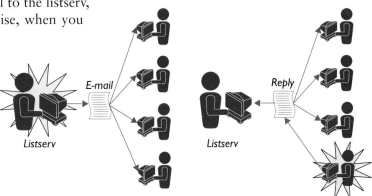

FIGURE   1-5   *Listservs distribute messages to people whose names are on an electronic mailing list. When you send a message to a listserv, everyone on the list receives a copy via e-mail.* ■

Newsgroups

A more highly organized way for groups of people to communicate is through **USENET**, which is an electronic bulletin-board service consisting of newsgroups, newsfeeds, and newsreaders. Once you subscribe to a newsgroup, you use a newsreader to access the group's newsfeed. Figure 1-6 shows how information in the newsfeed is organized according to topics. In addition to reading information on existing topics, you can add your own comments and create new topics, thereby participating in a virtual conference on the Internet.

Do not be confused by the use of the word *news* in the term *newsgroup*. Although some newsgroups are devoted to what is traditionally known as news, a newsgroup can contain discussions on any topic. In Chapter 3, you will learn how to find out what newsgroups exist and how to join them.

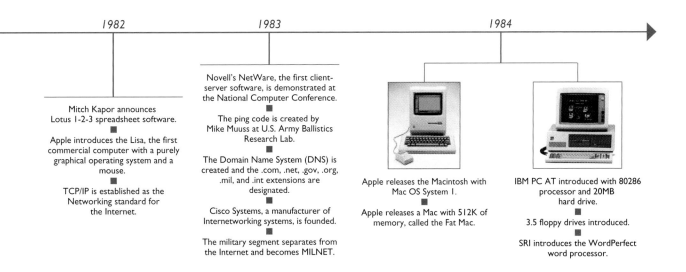

1982

Mitch Kapor announces
Lotus 1-2-3 spreadsheet software.
■
Apple introduces the Lisa, the first commercial computer with a purely graphical operating system and a mouse.
■
TCP/IP is established as the Networking standard for the Internet.

1983

Novell's NetWare, the first client-server software, is demonstrated at the National Computer Conference.
■
The ping code is created by Mike Muuss at U.S. Army Ballistics Research Lab.
■
The Domain Name System (DNS) is created and the .com, .net, .gov, .org, .mil, and .int extensions are designated.
■
Cisco Systems, a manufacturer of Internetworking systems, is founded.
■
The military segment separates from the Internet and becomes MILNET.

1984

Apple releases the Macintosh with Mac OS System 1.
■
Apple releases a Mac with 512K of memory, called the Fat Mac.

IBM PC AT introduced with 80286 processor and 20MB hard drive.
■
3.5 floppy drives introduced.
■
SRI introduces the WordPerfect word processor.

Click the plus sign to expand a topic and see the responses.

Click the minus sign to contract a topic and hide the responses.

The preview pane displays the message currently selected in the hierarchy.

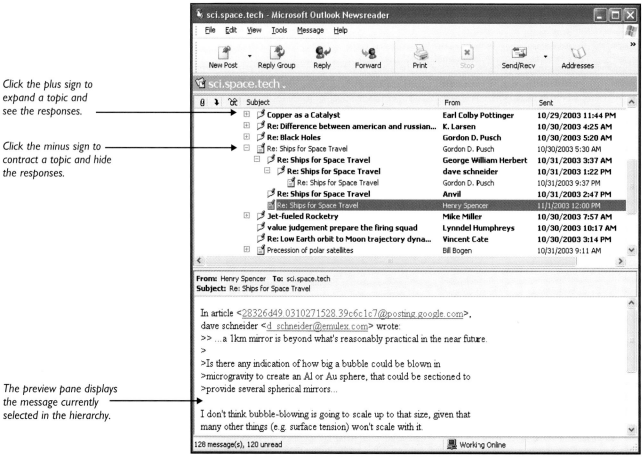

FIGURE 1-6 USENET newsgroups organize information according to a hierarchy of topics. You navigate through the hierarchy via onscreen controls that enable you to scroll up or down and expand or contract the menu of messages to reveal something that interests you. ∎

Chat

A very popular form of real-time communications is **chat**, which enables people to converse with one another over the Internet. As you type a message on your computer keyboard, the people you are chatting with see what you type almost immediately, and you can simultaneously see what

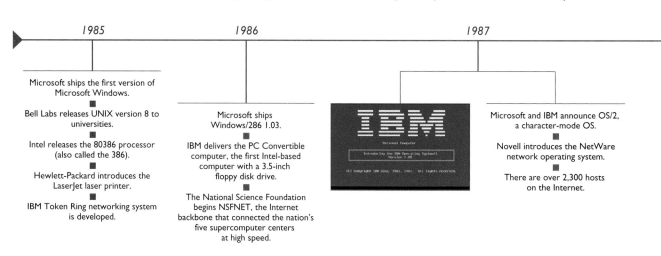

1985

Microsoft ships the first version of Microsoft Windows.
∎
Bell Labs releases UNIX version 8 to universities.
∎
Intel releases the 80386 processor (also called the 386).
∎
Hewlett-Packard introduces the LaserJet laser printer.
∎
IBM Token Ring networking system is developed.

1986

Microsoft ships Windows/286 1.03.
∎
IBM delivers the PC Convertible computer, the first Intel-based computer with a 3.5-inch floppy disk drive.
∎
The National Science Foundation begins NSFNET, the Internet backbone that connected the nation's five supercomputer centers at high speed.

1987

Microsoft and IBM announce OS/2, a character-mode OS.
∎
Novell introduces the NetWare network operating system.
∎
There are over 2,300 hosts on the Internet.

they type in reply. Figure 1-7 shows a conversation in progress. Users with microphones and speakers can speak verbally to one another if their chat software supports audio.

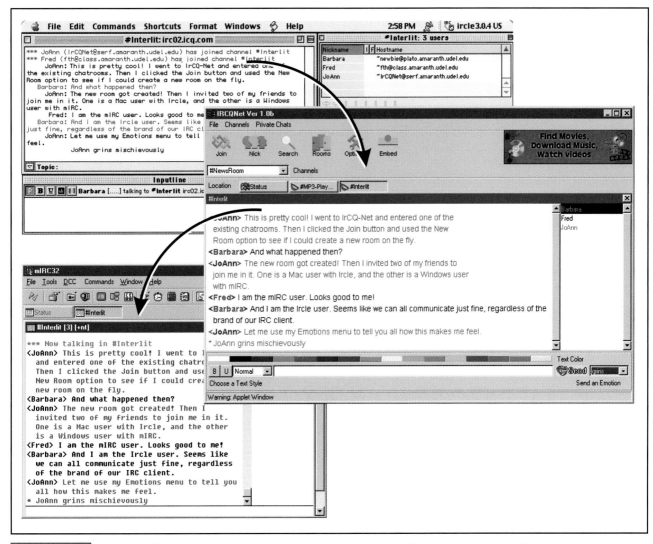

FIGURE 1-7 *Several different brands of clients support the Internet's chat protocol. Here you see a conversation in progress between three users who are using a Windows client, a Macintosh client, and a browser-based Java client.* ■

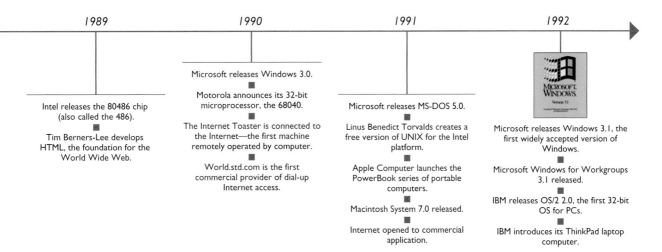

1989

Intel releases the 80486 chip (also called the 486).
■
Tim Berners-Lee develops HTML, the foundation for the World Wide Web.

1990

Microsoft releases Windows 3.0.
■
Motorola announces its 32-bit microprocessor, the 68040.
■
The Internet Toaster is connected to the Internet—the first machine remotely operated by computer.
■
World.std.com is the first commercial provider of dial-up Internet access.

1991

Microsoft releases MS-DOS 5.0.
■
Linus Benedict Torvalds creates a free version of UNIX for the Intel platform.
■
Apple Computer launches the PowerBook series of portable computers.
■
Macintosh System 7.0 released.
■
Internet opened to commercial application.

1992

Microsoft releases Windows 3.1, the first widely accepted version of Windows.
■
Microsoft Windows for Workgroups 3.1 released.
■
IBM releases OS/2 2.0, the first 32-bit OS for PCs.
■
IBM introduces its ThinkPad laptop computer.

The conversations take place in virtual spaces called chat rooms or channels; each chat room or channel is a different conversation that is going on. There are thousands of chat rooms where you can join a conversation, or you can create your own chat room. In Chapter 3, you will learn how to find and enter existing chats or create your own free chat room.

You can click this arrow to change your status from online to offline in case you want to hide from your buddies.

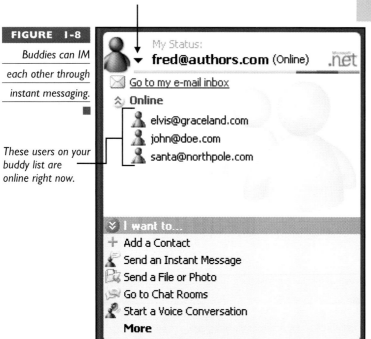

FIGURE 1-8

Buddies can IM each other through instant messaging.

These users on your buddy list are online right now.

Instant Messaging

Most people have a circle of friends or working associates with whom they like to keep in close contact. A service called **instant messaging (IM)** enables you to do that. Figure 1-8 depicts how you can put your friends on a buddy list that identifies who is allowed to contact you. When someone on your buddy list asks to talk with you, an instant message appears on your screen, letting you know that someone wants to chat, something just happened that you wanted to know about, or an important message just arrived in your e-mail.

Instant messaging has become so popular that its acronym "IM" has become a verb, which is pronounced eye-emm. To IM someone means to send them an instant message over the Internet. Chapter 3 covers instant messaging in more detail.

Videoconferencing

Videoconferencing is the use of a video camera and a microphone to enable people conversing over the Internet to be able to see and hear each other. Because of the higher bandwidth or data rate required to transmit video over the Internet, videoconferencing has not yet become as popular as text-only chat. As data rates increase, however, more people will be able to participate in videoconferences. Chapter 2 explains your options for

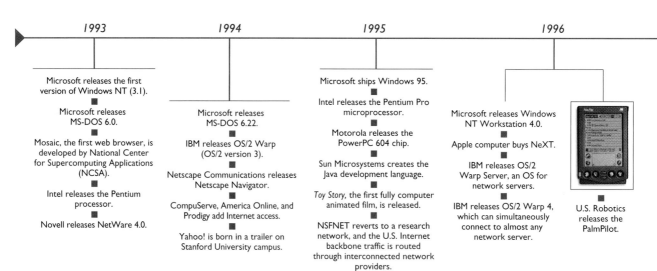

1993	1994	1995	1996

Microsoft releases the first version of Windows NT (3.1).

Microsoft releases MS-DOS 6.0.

Mosaic, the first web browser, is developed by National Center for Supercomputing Applications (NCSA).

Intel releases the Pentium processor.

Novell releases NetWare 4.0.

Microsoft releases MS-DOS 6.22.

IBM releases OS/2 Warp (OS/2 version 3).

Netscape Communications releases Netscape Navigator.

CompuServe, America Online, and Prodigy add Internet access.

Yahoo! is born in a trailer on Stanford University campus.

Microsoft ships Windows 95.

Intel releases the Pentium Pro microprocessor.

Motorola releases the PowerPC 604 chip.

Sun Microsystems creates the Java development language.

Toy Story, the first fully computer animated film, is released.

NSFNET reverts to a research network, and the U.S. Internet backbone traffic is routed through interconnected network providers.

Microsoft releases Windows NT Workstation 4.0.

Apple computer buys NeXT.

IBM releases OS/2 Warp Server, an OS for network servers.

IBM releases OS/2 Warp 4, which can simultaneously connect to almost any network server.

U.S. Robotics releases the PalmPilot.

connecting to the Internet at different data rates, and Chapter 3 describes the leading videoconferencing programs.

FTP

FTP stands for **File Transfer Protocol**. It is the standard method for transferring files over the Internet from one computer to another. "FTP" can be used as a verb as well as a noun. For example, if you want someone to send you a file, you can ask them to FTP it to you. FTP comes in handy, especially when files are too large to attach to an e-mail message.

Figure 1-9 shows how I used FTP to transfer this book's chapters to McGraw-Hill for production and publication. You will learn how to use FTP in Chapter 7.

The right pane shows this book's folder on McGraw-Hill's FTP server.

The left pane shows the Word processor files on my computer.

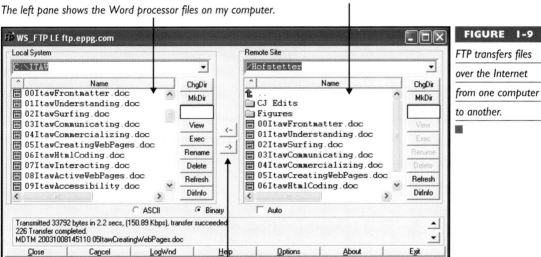

FIGURE 1-9

FTP transfers files over the Internet from one computer to another.

I click this button to FTP a file from my computer to McGraw-Hill.

Multimedia Streaming

Streaming is the digital transmission of multimedia content in real time over the Internet. Streaming enables a large multimedia file to begin playing as soon as your computer has received enough of the information to

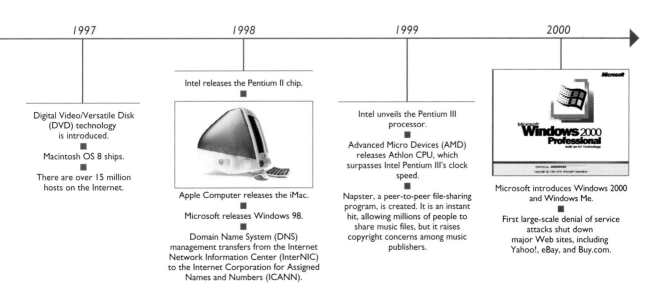

1997
1998
1999
2000

Intel releases the Pentium II chip.

Digital Video/Versatile Disk (DVD) technology is introduced.

Macintosh OS 8 ships.

There are over 15 million hosts on the Internet.

Apple Computer releases the iMac.

Microsoft releases Windows 98.

Domain Name System (DNS) management transfers from the Internet Network Information Center (InterNIC) to the Internet Corporation for Assigned Names and Numbers (ICANN).

Intel unveils the Pentium III processor.

Advanced Micro Devices (AMD) releases Athlon CPU, which surpasses Intel Pentium III's clock speed.

Napster, a peer-to-peer file-sharing program, is created. It is an instant hit, allowing millions of people to share music files, but it raises copyright concerns among music publishers.

Microsoft introduces Windows 2000 and Windows Me.

First large-scale denial of service attacks shut down major Web sites, including Yahoo!, eBay, and Buy.com.

begin playing it, without waiting until it all downloads. Instead of swamping your hard drive with all the data in the file, your computer stores in a memory buffer only the amount of data needed for the media to continue playing. Once played, the data is erased from the buffer. Thus broadcasters can use multimedia streaming to send out copyrighted material without fear that it will be reproduced.

Many radio stations, for example, use real-time streaming to broadcast shows live over the Internet. Television networks often archive important video streams after the broadcast, enabling you to access the broadcast stream later if you were unable to view the show live. The CNN Web site at www.cnn.com, for example, has links you can click to play video streams of the day's leading news broadcasts. Chapter 3 covers multimedia streaming and plugs you in to the key multimedia resources on the Internet.

World Wide Web

Invented by Tim Berners-Lee in 1989, the **World Wide Web (WWW)** is a networked hypertext system that allows documents to be shared over the Internet. Developed at the European Particle Physics Center (CERN) in Geneva, Switzerland, the Web's original purpose was to let researchers all over the world collaborate on the same documents without needing to travel anywhere physically.

The word **hypertext** was coined by Ted Nelson in 1965 and refers to text that has been linked. When you click a linked word, your computer launches the object of that link. The links give the text an added dimension, which is why it is called hyper.

When the Web was released in 1991, it was purely text-based. In 1993, the National Center for Supercomputer Applications (NCSA) released **Mosaic**, a graphical user interface that made the Web extremely easy to use. Thanks to Mosaic, Web pages could contain pictures, with links to audio and video as well. This led to the Web's becoming the most popular service on the Internet. As depicted in Figure 1-10, the Web enables you to follow links to documents and resources all over the world.

In 1994, Netscape Communications Corporation was started by some of Mosaic's developers, and over the next few years, a program called **Netscape Navigator** became the most popular Web browser. Microsoft

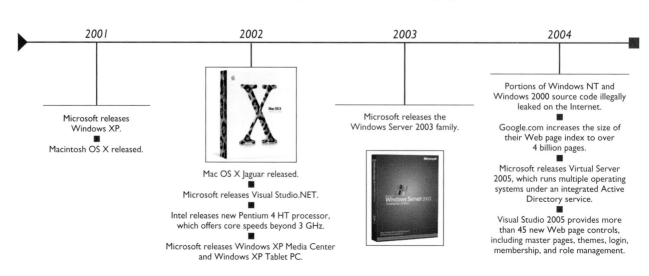

2001 — Microsoft releases Windows XP. ■ Macintosh OS X released.

2002 — Mac OS X Jaguar released. ■ Microsoft releases Visual Studio.NET. ■ Intel releases new Pentium 4 HT processor, which offers core speeds beyond 3 GHz. ■ Microsoft releases Windows XP Media Center and Windows XP Tablet PC.

2003 — Microsoft releases the Windows Server 2003 family.

2004 — Portions of Windows NT and Windows 2000 source code illegally leaked on the Internet. ■ Google.com increases the size of their Web page index to over 4 billion pages. ■ Microsoft releases Virtual Server 2005, which runs multiple operating systems under an integrated Active Directory service. ■ Visual Studio 2005 provides more than 45 new Web page controls, including master pages, themes, login, membership, and role management.

FIGURE 1-10

The World Wide Web is the most popular service on the Internet. The U.S. Department of State uses the Web to communicate all over the world via printed text, audio, and video.

also created a Web browser called Microsoft **Internet Explorer**, which now ships as part of Windows. The popularity of Netscape Navigator and Microsoft Internet Explorer diminished the need for Mosaic, and in 1997, the NCSA quietly discontinued work on it, opting instead to work on other advanced Internet technologies. In the meantime, Netscape and Microsoft grew their browsers into suites of programs that enable users to access almost all the Internet's services and resources without needing any other software.

You can learn more about the history of the Web by following this book's Web site links to the **W3C World Wide Web Consortium**, which coordinates the research and development of new standards and features for the Web. By following the links to Tim Berners-Lee, you can read papers about the past, present, and future of the Web written by the person credited with inventing the Web.

Visiting the W3C

The best way to find out the status of current issues and news related to the Web is to visit the World Wide Web Consortium (W3C) site at www.w3.org. The W3C site is organized according to working initiatives, called activities, that cover a broad range of exciting topics. The technologies that are emerging from the W3C will have a profound impact on the information society in the years ahead.

Rich Site Summary (RSS)

The World Wide Web has become so popular that it has spun off some Internet services of its own. One of these Web-inspired services is **Rich Site Summary (RSS),** which is an XML format for syndicating the content of a Web site in a form that can be registered with an RSS publisher. Other sites can subscribe to the Web site in order to access the RSS feed and display its content onscreen. RSS has become a very popular format for distributing news headlines, project updates, and events listings. As illustrated in the example in Figure 1-11, users can quickly read the headlines and news summaries and click to follow links to more detailed information.

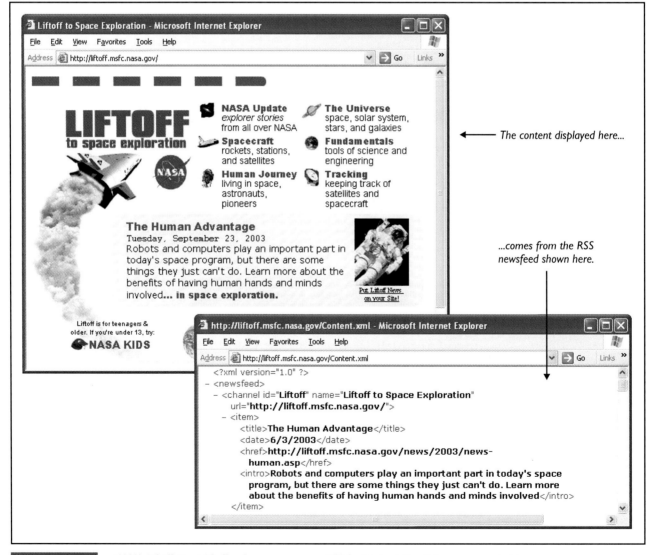

← *The content displayed here...*

...comes from the RSS newsfeed shown here.

FIGURE 1-11 NASA's Liftoff site at liftoff.msfc.nasa.gov uses an RSS feed to keep the site's news current. ■

RSS is an example of how the eXtensible Markup Language (XML) can add functionality to the Web. You will learn more about this kind of markup in the XML section of Chapter 8. RSS is part of the Resource Description Framework (RDF) developed through the World Wide Web Consortium at www.w3.org/RDF. In addition to Rich Site Summary, the acronym RSS also stands for RDF Site Summary.

Blogging

As the Web becomes a mass market utility, new ways of using the Web are emerging to address the needs and preferences of the masses. One of the most popular ways of using the Web is blogging. The term **blog** is short for Web log, which is a Web-accessible log written by an individual who wants to chronicle activity related to a given topic that is often personal. "Blog" can be used as a noun to refer to what gets written or as a verb that means the act of writing these kinds of messages. Through blogging, people are essentially keeping their diaries online. The mass-market appeal of blogging teaches us that people like to make these kinds of diaries public. In response to this mass-market appeal, a wide range of blogging tools have arisen. At sites such as www.blogger.com, you can create your own public blogs. You can also license blogging tools for private use, such as to keep track of a worker's progress toward meeting a project milestone or target date. Figure 1-12 shows how the campaign to reelect President Bush used a blog to chronicle their activities. For a list of blog directories, go to Google or Yahoo! and search for "blog directory." For tools, search for "blog tools."

Cross Check

Matching Internet Services

Okay, now it's time to test your knowledge. See if you can match the Internet services on the left with their service descriptions on the right.

____ e-mail	**A.** Participate in an online conference consisting of hierarchically organized topics and subtopics.
____ listserv	**B.** Transfer a file from one computer to another.
____ instant messaging	**C.** Converse with one or more people in real time over the Internet.
____ USENET newsgroups	**D.** Web-accessible chronicle of activity related to a given topic that is often personal.
____ chat	**E.** A global hypertext system.
____ stream	**F.** An XML format for syndicating the content of a Web site in a form that can be registered with a publisher. Other sites can subscribe to the Web site in order to access the feed and display its content onscreen.
____ FTP	**G.** Send an e-mail message to a single address that routes the message to a list full of people.
____ World Wide Web	**H.** Send a message to an individual.
____ Rich Site Summary	**I.** Contact your buddies whenever they are online to chat or trade files.
____ blog	**J.** Watch a movie without first having to download it completely to your computer.

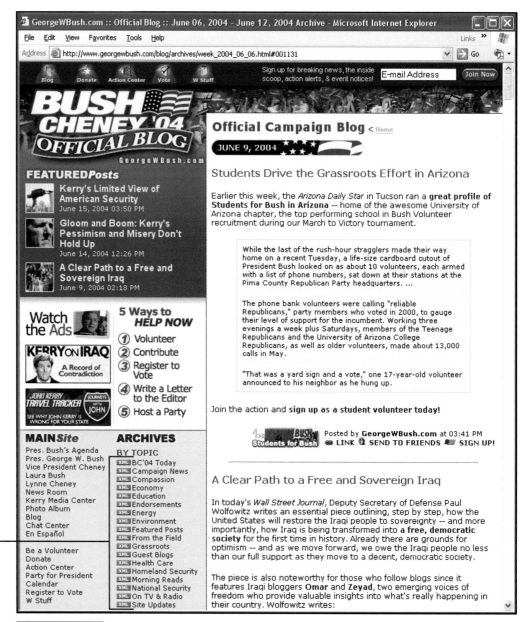

Click a topic to view messages in the Blog that deal with particular categories.

FIGURE 1-12   *When you visit a blog, you scroll down to peruse the entries, which appear in reverse chronological order. Pictured here is the official blog of the campaign to reelect President George W. Bush at www.georgewbush.com/blog. Democratic candidates Wesley Clark, Howard Dean, John Kerry, and Dennis Kucinich also used blogs in their campaigns.* ■

Describing the Infrastructure of the Internet

Several key concepts enable the Internet to work. These concepts include (1) client-server computing, which describes the roles that computers play in sending and receiving information over the Internet; (2) TCP/IP, which is the networking protocol that enables this communication to take place; (3) the domain name system (DNS), which provides a way of naming the computers on the Internet; (4) intranetworking, which is what enables a private network to hide from users on the public Internet; and

(5) extranetworking, which enables authorized users to access an intranet from outside its normal boundaries. Each of these concepts is discussed in turn in this section.

What Is Client-Server Computing?

Client-server computing is an important concept on the Internet. Think about what the Internet is: a worldwide connection of millions of computers. Think about what these computers do: they send and receive information. That is what client-server computing is all about. When a computer sends information, the computer is a server. When a computer receives information, the computer is a client. The term client-server computing refers to the manner in which computers exchange information by sending it (as servers) and receiving it (as clients).

In client-server networks, end-user workstations are called clients because they primarily receive information. For example, when you surf the World Wide Web with a browser such as Microsoft Internet Explorer, your computer is a client, because you are receiving information from other computers on the World Wide Web. The computers that are devoted primarily to sending information are called **servers**; computers devoted to serving Web pages are called Web servers.

Sometimes a server needs to obtain additional information in order to answer a request from a client. At the moment when the server requests information from another computer, the server becomes a client. When the server obtains the information it needs, it routes the information back to you, fulfilling its role as your server.

tip *You will encounter the terms client and server a lot. The key to understanding them is to remember that client means "receive" and server means "send." If you play tennis, this will be easy to remember, because when you serve a tennis ball, you send it—hopefully very fast—to your opponent!*

What Is TCP/IP?

On the Internet, information gets transmitted from place to place in logical units called **packets**. In order to send these packets to the right place in the correct order, two protocols are required. The first protocol, which is called TCP, handles the routing. The second protocol, which is called IP, governs the addressing. Because both protocols are needed to make the Internet work, the Internet is said to use the **TCP/IP** protocol suite. Let us take a closer look at what TCP and IP do.

TCP stands for the **Transmission Control Protocol**, which defines the rules and procedures for transmitting information across the Internet. The information gets transmitted in packets. If a message is too long to fit in one packet, the data gets divided into more than one packet. Each packet contains addressing that identifies which computer sent the packet and which computer will receive it. The packets also contain sequencing information that specifies the order in which they must be reassembled when the packets arrive at their destination.

IP stands for **Internet Protocol**, which defines the addressing system TCP uses to transmit packets over the Internet. Every computer on the Internet has a unique Internet Protocol (IP) address. Each packet of information that gets transmitted over the Internet contains the **IP address** of the computer that sent it and the IP address of the computer to which it is being sent. An IP address consists of four numbers separated by periods.

The numbers are 8-bit bytes that range in value from 0 to 255. The smallest address is 0.0.0.0 and the largest is 255.255.255.255. The number of IP addresses this scheme allows is 256^4, which is 4,294,967,296. This provides room for adding more computers as the network grows.

The format of an IP address that has four 8-bit bytes separated by periods is known as **dotted quad notation**. When the Internet was invented, people thought dotted quad notation would provide enough unique addresses for every computer to have its own IP address. The proliferation of computers all over the world, however, will eventually exceed this number. A new version of IP addressing, called IPv6, will have eight numbers instead of four, and each number will be a 16-bit value ranging from 0 to 65,535. The number of IP addresses this scheme allows is $65,536^8$, which is a huge number that provides thousands of addresses per square meter of the earth's surface. Why are so many new addresses being created when the world will most likely never have that many computers? One of the reasons is to permit computers to contain multiple interfaces, with each interface having a unique IPv6 address. As you will learn later in this chapter, IPv6 is being used in a new version of the Internet called Internet2.

note *Chapter 11 explains how TCP/IP makes the Internet work. The section entitled "Introduction to TCP/IP" will walk you through the TCP/IP protocol suite, and the section about "Internetworking" will explain the various kinds of servers and routers that use TCP/IP to power the internet.*

What Are Domains and Subdomains?

IP addresses can be hard to remember. For example, the Web server at the Library of Congress has the IP address 140.147.249.7. The National Aeronautics & Space Administration (NASA) is at 198.116.142.34. The Smithsonian is 160.111.252.106. If you had to remember numbers like these, the Internet would not be very user-friendly.

To make IP addresses easier for human beings to remember, a **domain name system (DNS)** was invented to permit the use of alphabetic characters instead of numbers. For example, instead of having to remember that the Library of Congress is at 140.147.249.7, you can use its domain name, www.loc.gov. NASA is www.nasa.gov, and the Smithsonian is www.si.edu. Thus DNS is a method of resolving names that humans understand into IP addresses that the network understands.

A complete DNS address is called a **fully qualified domain name (FQDN)**. Fully qualified domain names have the following format:

hostname.registered-domain-name.top-level-domain

In the United States, the **top-level domain (TLD)** normally consists of one of the following:

Code	Top-Level Domain Name	Code	Top-Level Domain Name
.aero	aerospace	.int	international treaty organizations
.biz	business	.mil	military
.com	commercial	.museum	museums
.coop	cooperatives	.name	individual's names
.edu	educational	.net	network support centers
.gov	government	.org	other organizations
.info	public use information	.pro	professionals

In the rest of the world, top-level domains are usually country codes, such as *fr* for France. The **domain** refers to the network to which a computer is connected, and the host name refers to the computer itself. For example, in the domain name www.louvre.fr, which is the World Wide Web server at the famous Louvre museum in Paris, the top-level domain *fr* indicates that the server is located in France, the domain *louvre* tells you that the server is on the Louvre's network, and the host name *www* identifies this computer as the Louvre's World Wide Web server.

Top-level domains can be further subdivided. In Canada, for example, the Humber College server is at www.humberc.on.ca. Notice that the top-level domain *ca*, which stands for Canada, has the second-level domain *on*, which stands for Ontario. This reflects the fact that Humber College is located in the province of Ontario in Canada. The format is

hostname.registered-domain-name.second-level-domain.top-level-domain

A domain can also be subdivided. In the FQDN of the Web server located at webs.oet.udel.edu, for example, the domain has two parts that reflect the division of the udel domain into **subdomains**. The subdomain *.oet* indicates that the server is located in the Office of Educational Technology, and *.udel* is the registered domain name that places the office at the University of Delaware. The format is

hostname.subdomain-name.registered-domain-name.top-level-domain

Regardless of how many periods are in an FQDN, everything after the host name is collectively referred to as the server's domain. Thus, if someone asks "What is the domain of the server at webs.oet.udel.edu," you would answer *oet.udel.edu*.

There are more than 200 registered country codes for use in top-level domains. Some common country codes you should recognize are as follows:

Code	Country	Code	Country
.au	Australia	.de	Germany
.ca	Canada	.fr	France
.ch	Switzerland	.us	United States
.cn	China	.mx	Mexico
.cz	Czech Republic	.uk	United Kingdom

The Internet Corporation for Assigned Names and Numbers (ICANN) is in charge of the assignment of domain names, IP address numbers, and protocol parameter and port numbers. ICANN has established a process for creating new top-level domain names. Several new names are being considered. You can find out the status by following this book's Web site link to ICANN.

Register a Domain Name

Registering a domain name costs so little that many users are beginning to register their own domain names on the Internet. If your family name has not already been registered as a domain name, for example, you should consider grabbing it before someone else registers it. To find out whether you can register your family name and to find out how little it will cost to do so, follow these steps:

1. Browse to www.verisign.org. This brings you to the ICANN-accredited registrar for .com and .net domains. If you want to choose a different registrar, go to www.icann.org and follow the link to the registrar of your choice.

2. At the Verisign site, you'll find a domain registration blank into which you can type any name to find out whether it has been taken. Enter the domain you want to register, such as your last name, into this blank. It will not cost you anything to find out if the name is taken.

3. Check the boxes corresponding to your choice of top-level domains.

4. When you click the submit button, Verisign responds by telling you whether the name is taken. If the name is available, you will be offered an opportunity to register it.

5. If you want to reserve a domain name for future use, you can register the name without yet having an IP address to connect it to.

What Is an Intranet?

So far, this book has touted the public nature of the Internet. Certain kinds of businesses and government agencies, however, do not want their computers to be so publicly available. Instead of connecting their computers to the public Internet, institutions that want their computers kept private connect them to an intranet.

In order to understand the difference between the public Internet and a private intranet, you need to understand the meaning of the two Latin words *inter* and *intra*. The word *inter* means "between," and the word *intra* means "within." An **intranet**, therefore, is a network that uses the TCP/IP protocols to provide private services within an organization whose computers are not publicly accessible on the Internet.

An example of a corporation that has an intranet is JPMorgan Chase. The privacy of the financial information JPMorgan Chase deals with is so vital to their business that they run their own private intranet. Not connecting to the public Internet helps JPMorgan Chase protect its most sensitive computers from crackers (someone who maliciously tries to break into a computer system), viruses, and other kinds of information attacks. When I taught an online Internet technologies course at JPMorgan, for example, I had to travel physically to computers on the JPMorgan campus in order to grade student projects that had been created inside this private intranet. In Part III of this book, you will learn more about setting up an intranet and securing computers on the Internet.

What Is an Extranet?

Now it is time for another tiny Latin lesson: The Latin word *extra* means "outside" or "beyond." Thus, the term **extranet** refers to Internet resources such as Web sites that are beyond the public's reach and require authorized users to do something extra, such as type a logon name and password, in order to obtain access.

Imagine that you are the network administrator of an intranet that contains highly sensitive information. Suppose you need to provide dial-in access to high-ranking executives who need to connect to this intranet from remote locations when the executives travel to distant cities. You are worried that over the public-switched telephone network, a cracker could sniff the packets that are being transmitted through this extranet connection to your private intranet. What you can do in this case is require that authorized users have special client software that encodes the packets by using very strong encryption. By periodically changing the encryption method, you can make it practically impossible for unauthorized users to gain access to the intranet's private resources. In Part III of this book, you will learn the best-practice methods of properly securing an extranet.

Cross Check

Inter! Intra! Extra!

Keeping your Latin prefixes straight can help you understand the underlying concepts of the Internet. See if you can match the following terms to check your knowledge of network infrastructure:

_____ Internet   **A.** Private network formed by running TCP/IP inside a firewall that prevents public access.

_____ intranet   **B.** Access provided to a private network outside its normal boundaries; normally requires authentication.

_____ extranet   **C.** Worldwide public network of computers running the TCP/IP protocol suite.

Changing the World via the Internet

If you had to summarize in one word how the Internet is changing the world, that word would be **convergence**. No matter how you want to encode your message—whether through text, image, video, audio, print, or speech—you can communicate it digitally over the Internet. Convergence is the process of unification that digitalization causes by enabling all the world's traditional ways of communicating to work over a common communications medium on the Internet. Digitalization is changing the kind of world we live in. It is becoming an instantaneously connected world, highly productive and without bounds.

Because the Net cannot see racial differences, age, gender, or physical handicaps, it does not discriminate. It does perhaps discriminate against the unconnected, because in an information society, to be cut off from the network is to be disenfranchised. **Digital divide** is a term used to refer to the barriers faced by the unconnected. To understand what needs to be done to achieve universal access, follow this book's Web site link to the Digital Divide.

Corporate Mergers and Alliances

Bane, Bradley, and Collis (1995:2) compare the forces of digitalization to the gravity of a wormhole in *Star Trek,* pulling recognizable industries through it and merging them into newly converged companies. Indeed, these forces have caused an unprecedented number of mergers and alliances as corporations jockey for position in the converged world. Viacom's $48.9 billion buyout of CBS, for example, merged a movie studio, cable networks, the Blockbuster video chain, and the UPN and CBS television networks.

Why are media companies forming alliances with computer vendors? Because they want to grow their markets by offering digital information and entertainment services that can be displayed either on a TV set or on a computer screen. NBC partnered with Microsoft, for example, to create the MSNBC network at www.msnbc.com, which uses the brand power of a TV network to transition people to become online users. Motorola bought cable set-top box maker General Instrument for $11.4 billion, positioning Motorola to become a leading manufacturer of equipment for both cable TV and wireless Internet services. To set the stage for launching a new travel-oriented cable TV company, USA Networks purchased the travel Web site Expedia.com.

Telecommuting

For a large percentage of the population, the Internet is becoming the workplace. Because tens of millions of workers have Internet access at home, the home is a potential place to work online. As depicted in Figure 1-13, **telecommuting** is the act of working from home by using computers, dial-up modems or broadband network connections, and fax machines to perform work that formerly required a person to travel physically to work. According to TeleWork America (2000) survey results, there were 16.5 million **teleworkers** in the United States in the year 2000. Of workers not telecommuting, 39 percent expressed an interest in working from home, and 13 percent said the ability to telework would be an important decision in accepting another job. TWA estimates that by the year 2005, there will be 30 million teleworkers in the United States. Look to see these estimates reflected in the next U.S. Census, which tracks the number of Americans who are telecommuting.

By reducing the need for people to drive to work, telecommuting results in fewer automobiles on highways. In addition to relieving traffic congestion, this improves air quality by reducing the number of cars emitting pollutants. To hasten the adoption of telecommuting, the Environmental Protection Agency and the Department of Transportation have established a voluntary National Standard of Excellence for employer-provided commuter benefits that not only reduce pollution but also lower expenses and taxes for employers and employees alike. For more information, follow this book's Web site link to EPA telecommuting programs.

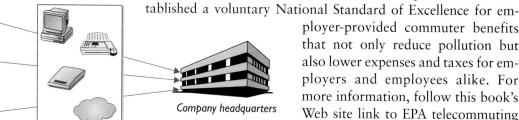

Telecommuting workers

Company headquarters

FIGURE 1-13   *Telecommuting is the act of working from home by using computers, dialup modems or broadband network connections, and fax machines.* ■

Business and Advertising

The Internet has become a mass-market utility, and businesses are using it to advertise and market their products. To attract users who will see their ads, commercial Web sites are offering an increasingly wide range of free Internet services. For example, to expand the popularity of its Web site, Yahoo! wanted to offer free Web space, so it bought the popular GeoCities community and Web-hosting site for $5 billion. As a result, you can go to www.yahoo.com and follow the link to GeoCities to get a free Web site. Other free services at Yahoo! include keeping your address book, photo album, and personal calendar, which can send you e-mail reminders as important dates approach.

If you follow the links to My Yahoo, you can set up a personal Yahoo! home page, including weather reports for your favorite cities, stock quotes for your stock portfolio, news reports from your favorite newsfeed, showtimes at local movie houses, and scores from your favorite sports teams. As if all this were not enough, you can also use Yahoo! to get driving instructions, search the yellow pages, go shopping, read and post classified ads, and get a personal Web-based e-mail account. By the time you read this, more free services will be at Yahoo!, all intended to make you spend more time there. Every time you use one of these services, you will see one or more ads. Thus, the frequency with which you visit the site increases the value of the commercial advertising you see there.

More pervasive forms of Internet advertising seek to capture your attention while you're browsing. So-called pop-under ads persist onscreen in their own windows after you close the Web site that created them. Saunders (2001) reports that pop-under ads can backfire, however, because consumers are quick to click to eliminate the unwanted window. Pop-up ads, on the other hand, are more than twice as likely to engage users in shopping, because these ads appear on top of the window the user is trying to look at. The user must move or close the pop-up ad in order to see what it is hiding. During the process of dismissing the pop-up, the user is likely to notice what is in it. Pop-under ads are not visible until the user closes the main window. Once the main window is gone, users are quick to delete a pop-under ad without paying much attention to it.

Online Shopping

The goal of all this advertising is not just to get you to see the ads; vendors also want you to purchase products over the Net, which is changing how the world shops. Instead of wearing yourself out trek-

> **Inside Info**
>
> ## Car Buying and the Internet
>
> *In 2003, 49 percent of new car buyers reported that their buying decisions were influenced by the Internet, which affected significantly the make and model purchased. This was up 9 percent from the year before, when 40 percent of new car buyers felt this way. (J.D. Power and Associates, New Autoshopper.com Study, 2003)*

king from store to store, trying to find the size and style you like, and then waiting in line to pay for it, teleshopping services let you shop from home. According to market research firm TNS Interactive (2001), 57 percent of adults in the United States shopped online in 2001, representing a 50-percent growth from the year before. The most popular items are books, clothes, and music. The most frequent reason given for not wanting to shop online is the fear of providing credit-card information over the Web. As the financial industry works to improve security, the number of online shoppers will continue to increase.

Follow this book's Web site links for evaluations and rankings of online shopping sites. To find out if there are any consumer complaints against your potential shopping sites, follow the link to the Better Business Bureau Online.

Online Banking and Investing

The Internet is changing the face of business. Online shopping and banking are creating a cashless society by eliminating the need for printed money. When this book went to press, more than 27 million Americans were paying their bills online.

During the past few years, online brokers have captured a third of the retail investor market. By following this book's Web site links, you can visit some of the more popular online brokerages, including Charles Schwab, E*trade, Fidelity, Ameritrade, Morgan Stanley Online, and Quick & Reilly. In addition to investing online, you can use the Web to help manage your portfolio. At Yahoo! Finance, for example, you can track the value of each stock or mutual fund in your portfolio. If a stock goes down in value, you can read news reports explaining why. Research informs you of recommended stocks, and profiles give insight into the nature of the business and financial summaries of the company.

At InfoBeat Finance, you can subscribe to news alerts for the companies in which you are invested. If late-breaking events affect the value of one of your investments, you receive an e-mail message informing you of the news, hours before it appears in the newspapers. To learn more about investing online, follow this book's Web site links to Yahoo! Finance, InfoBeat Finance, and the Gomez Scorecard site, where you will find ratings of online banks and brokerages and other consumer services.

Government and Politics

Government officials have turned increasingly to the Internet for solutions to problems inherent in governance. The Net makes services more widely available and enables municipalities to respond more quickly to emergencies and disasters. You can access a wealth of information by following this book's Web site links to the U.S. Government Consumer Information Center in Pueblo, Colorado. At the Internal Revenue Service Web site pictured in Figure 1-14, you can learn about the tax code, download tax forms, and file your income tax return over the Internet.

Videoconferencing and the Internet provide ways for politicians to reach, canvass, and broaden their constituencies. The Internet has become so important in getting elected to public office that almost every political candidate has a Web site. For example, Figures 1-15 and 1-16 show the Democratic and Republican Web sites, respectively. For an index of political candidate Web sites, follow this book's Web site links to Political Candidates.

tip *If you still write checks by hand, follow this book's Web site links to learn how you can pay bills online through AOL, Yahoo!, the U.S. Postal Service, American Express, or Citibank.*

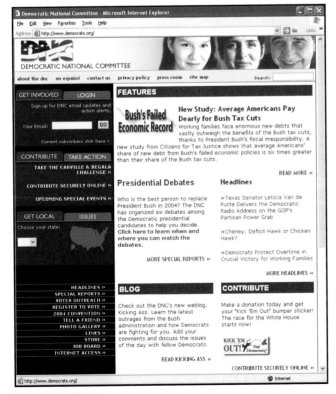

FIGURE 1-15 *The Democrats' Web site* ■

FIGURE 1-16 *The Republicans' Web site* ■

Information Warfare and Homeland Security

The United States relies heavily on the Internet. Perhaps even more devastating than a nuclear attack would be an electronic invasion of the computer networks without which this country would grind to a halt. Such a form of electronic attack is known as **information warfare**. To protect against a global large-scale attack on the Internet, the Pentagon has prepared a failsafe whereby the Department of Defense could disconnect its entire global network from the Internet if security threats arise that warrant so doing.

As President of the United States, George Bush Senior criticized the CIA for being so slow to issue reports that the White House learned more about world developments by watching commercial TV. The government now uses the Internet to provide officials with newsfeeds from online news services such as cnn.com and msnbc.com.

Especially challenging is the use of the Internet by terrorists who hide secret messages in graphics, video, or audio files. The process is called steganography, from the Greek word for hidden writing. A terrorist arrested for planning to blow up the U.S. Embassy in Paris, for example, communicated with the Al Qaeda terrorist organization through pictures posted on the Internet.

To intercept messages from terrorists and criminals, the FBI is using a system called **Carnivore** that can scan the Internet's e-mail traffic, looking for key words and phrases related to terrorist plots and criminal investigations. Messages containing suspicious content get routed to an FBI agent to investigate. The **USA Patriot Act**, signed into law in October 2001 in the aftermath of the 9/11 attacks on America, gives the federal government wide latitude in using Internet surveillance systems, including Carnivore and its successors. For more information about the use of information technologies in defense applications, follow this book's Web site links to Carnivore, the USA Patriot Act, and the Defense Advanced Research Projects Agency (DARPA).

Electronic Publishing

During the past decade, virtually every newspaper has created a Web site. By following this book's Web site link, you can peruse the Newslink index of more than 4,000 online newspapers, magazines, broadcasters, and news services. The Internet enables people to go online and quickly see headlines and search through articles printed in the newspapers. Most of the news services keep online archives of past stories, making the Web a valuable resource for searching past as well as current events. News programs broadcast by cable news services, such as CNN and MSNBC, often refer you to their Web sites for more in-depth coverage or to conduct public opinion polls. People who are online frequently can subscribe to a news service that e-mails you when important news breaks.

Electronic book (eBook) technology enables publishers to sell books in an electronic format. Consumers download the eBook into a portable reading device, such as a Palm Pilot or a PocketPC. Not only does the eBook become as portable as a printed book; it also overcomes one of the greatest disadvantages of books printed on paper. How many times have you been frustrated by trying to find a quote or a passage you know you read in a certain book, but try as you might, you just cannot find it? The eBook solves this problem by rendering books in a full-text searchable format.

Besides purchasing eBooks from commercial publishers, you can also create eBooks of your own. If you have Microsoft Word, for example, you can create an eBook with the Microsoft Reader Add-In. The free service eBook Express enables you to create eBooks online from almost any text document. These books are formatted according to the Open eBook standard, which provides an industry-wide format for eBooks. The Open eBook standard is based on XML, which stands for eXtensible Markup Language. Electronic books contain hidden XML codes that enable eBook viewers to display the books and provide users with a rich set of reading features. The XML section of Chapter 8 takes you behind the scenes and shows you how the markup works. For more information about electronic books, follow this book's Web site links to Microsoft Reader, eBook Express, and Open eBook.

Television and Entertainment

The Internet is competing with television for people's free time. According to a Nielsen survey, the turn of the century marked the point at which more than half of U.S. households had obtained Internet access. Nearly 144 million people in the United States logged on to the Internet during July of 2000, for example. A survey of 3,000 households indicated that these users were spending an average of 10 hours a month online, up 26 percent from the year before (*Financial Times* 18 Aug 2000).

As you might expect, the Internet can also help you find what is worth viewing on television. At www.tvguide.com, for example, you will find the leading independent TV entertainment guide on the Internet. You can create and search free TV listings by day, time, program category, or specific channel up to seven days in advance, in either a traditional grid or a scroll-down list format. So-called top picks, movie picks, and sports picks recommend what is worth viewing on TV.

Microsoft's MSN TV (formerly called WebTV) is making substantial progress toward making television more interactive. Interactive TV merges the Internet and television so you can participate in your favorite shows. On *Wheel of Fortune* and *Jeopardy*, for example, you can play along and match wits with other contestants. While watching *Judge Judy*, you can vote in live polls taken during the show. Tens of thousands of people are participating. During a recent NFL football game, the referees made a disputed call. The announcers invited the TV audience to log on to the program's Web site and cast a vote either agreeing or disagreeing with the call. Within five minutes, more than 75,000 viewers had voted.

MSN TV receivers are sold at Wal-Mart, Best Buy, and Circuit City. For the latest information, follow this book's Web site links to MSN TV.

Teaching and Learning

The benefits of computer-based learning are well documented by Professor James Kulik (1985, 1986, 1991, 1994, 1998, and 2002) and his associates at the University of Michigan. During the past 25 years, Kulik has analyzed hundreds of controlled experiments on the effectiveness of computer-based learning. Overall, the findings indicate that average learning time has been reduced significantly (sometimes by as much as 80 percent) and achievement levels are more than a standard deviation higher (a full letter grade in school) than when computers are not used.

The Internet is enabling educators to make use of computer-based learning strategies online. By linking universities, colleges, schools, and homes into a worldwide network, the Internet is helping break down the distinctions between grade levels. The Internet is enabling students of all ages to collaborate on worldwide projects, share discoveries, and develop strategies for acquiring knowledge in a social context.

Providing this kind of environment for each student in a traditional classroom is difficult. Because there is only one teacher for many students, supporting each student's individual needs is physically impossible. The World Wide Web helps by providing students with an interconnected world of knowledge to explore. Screen capture and downloading enable students to collect what they discover and construct a framework for organizing and understanding. Because the learner is portrayed as an active processor who explores, discovers, reflects, and constructs knowledge, the trend to teaching from this perspective is known as the constructivist movement in education. As you work through this book, you will benefit from learning how to use the Internet this way in your own learning.

Tracing the History of the Internet

The Internet originated when the Advanced Research Projects Agency (ARPA) of the United States Department of Defense began a network called **ARPANET** in 1969. Its goal was to support military research about how to build a network that could continue to function in the midst of partial outages that could be caused by bomb attacks. Instead of giving the network the responsibility for routing the information, the computers on the network shared equally in the responsibility for ensuring that the communication was accomplished. The messages were divided into packets that wound their way through the network on an individual basis. Each packet contained some information and the address of the destination to which it was to be delivered. If one of the computers along the way stopped functioning, such as in a bomb attack, the packets would automatically find an alternate route to their destinations. Thus, every computer on the network was treated as a peer. That is why, to this day, no computer on the Internet is more important than any other, and no one computer is in charge.

During the 1970s, universities began using the Internet Protocol to connect their local networks to the ARPANET. Access to the Pentagon's computers on the ARPANET was tightly controlled, but university computers were permitted to communicate freely with one another. Because the IP software was public-domain and the basic technology made joining the network relatively simple, the Internet became more diverse. Joining the Internet did not cost much, because each local network simply paid for its connection to the nearest node. As the network grew, it became more valuable as it embraced larger user populations, social groups, and resources. Diversity posed security risks, however, and in 1983 the military segment broke off and became **MILNET**.

In 1986, the National Science Foundation (NSF) began the **NSFNET**, a backbone that connected the nation's five supercomputer centers at high speed. NSF upgraded the network repeatedly, setting a blistering pace for technical advancement. In 1991, NSF lifted the restriction that prohibited commercial entities from using the backbone. By 1994, the NSFNET was carrying 10 trillion bytes of Internet traffic per month. In 1995, NSFNET reverted to a research network, and the U.S. Internet backbone traffic is now routed through interconnected network providers.

Prior to 1998, the U.S. government sponsored a company called Network Solutions to manage the domain name system (DNS) through an organization called the Internet Network Information Center (InterNIC). In 1998, the responsibility for managing the domain name system (DNS) was transferred from InterNIC to the Internet Corporation for Assigned Names and Numbers (ICANN), which is an international not-for-profit organization.

During the late 1990s, use of the Internet exploded as costs declined, access increased, and new companies such as amazon.com, ebay.com, and yahoo.com pioneered the commercial potential of the Internet. When this book went to press, online ad spending in the United States had grown to 9.5 billion dollars annually. By the time you read this, online business-to-business (B2B) activity is projected to top $6.3 trillion annually.

To support this kind of growth, attempts to expand and speed up the Internet continue. A consortium of research universities is working in partnership with industry and government to create an even faster network named Internet2. The White House has pledged financial support to help build it. To learn more, follow this book's Web site link to Internet2. For a complete chronology of the Internet, follow the link to the Hobbes' Internet Timeline.

Cross Check

Internet History Timeline

To check your knowledge of Internet history, match the following events to the dates when they happened.

____	1969	**A.** NSFNET began a backbone to connect the nation's five supercomputer centers.
____	1983	**B.** NSFNET reverted to a research network, and the backbone was routed through interconnected network providers.
____	1986	**C.** Responsibility for managing the domain name system transferred from InterNIC to ICANN.
____	1991	**D.** The military part of the Internet broke off and became MILNET.
____	1995	**E.** NSF lifted the restriction that prohibited commercial entities from using the backbone.
____	1998	**F.** The U.S. Department of Defense began a network called ARPANET.

Looking into the Future of the Internet

Because the Internet is the communications infrastructure of the twenty-first century, its future is vitally important. From a technological standpoint, this future promises to be bright indeed because of some exciting new technologies. Newly emerging technologies follow a cycle that includes (1) invention, (2) prototyping, (3) proof of concept, (4) productizing, and (5) manufacture. During the planning stage, users who communicate effectively with product planners can influence how the technologies emerge. In order to provide you with such an opportunity, this chapter concludes by looking into the future of the Internet.

Improving the Infrastructure

You have undoubtedly experienced some problems with the Internet's physical transport layer. Network delay is the most obvious problem. You click a hypertext trigger to go to a Web site, and you wait, and you wait, and you wait. Sometimes it seems that WWW stands for World Wide Wait. The delays can be particularly long if the transmission carries multimedia content.

Multimedia MBONE

Multicast Backbone (MBONE) is a network of computers on the Internet specially designed for the transmission of simultaneous live video and audio broadcasts. In a traditional packet-switched network, if you send a video to four different people, four identical copies of the information are sent over the network. Multicasting the video over the MBONE sends only one copy of the message and replicates the information only at branch points in the network.

As the television, telephone, and computer industries continue to converge, real-time audio and video will grow in importance on the Internet. Look for IP multicasting on the MBONE to have a significant impact on the Web in the years ahead.

FIGURE 1-17

On the MBONE, audio and video streams propagate across the Internet from the server that initiates the broadcast.

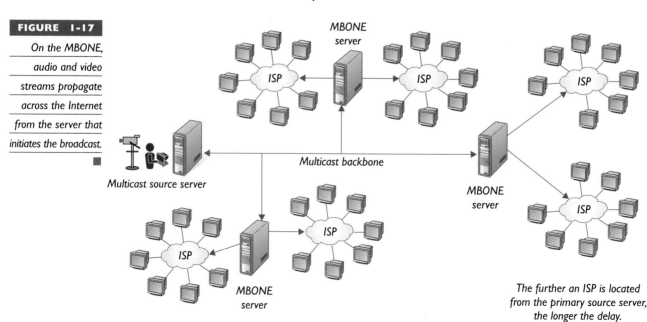

Multicast source server

MBONE server

Multicast backbone

MBONE server

MBONE server

The further an ISP is located from the primary source server, the longer the delay.

Connecting to the MBONE requires your Internet service provider (ISP) to have special routing and switching equipment. Follow this book's Web site link to Multicasting and the MBONE for a technical description of how the MBONE works.

Streaming Media Networks

Streaming Media Network (SMN) vendors are applying MBONE concepts to bring uninterrupted audio and video streams to end users. For example, iBeam is an SMN that uses satellites to feed streaming media directly to servers located at or near local ISPs. Akamai is another SMN that locates streaming media content on server farms that are physically closer to an ISP network than the streams would normally be on the public Internet. Akamai refers to these locations near the ISP as the "edge" of the Internet. Relative to the users connected to that local ISP, the local Akamai server is on their edge of the Internet. In Europe, an SMN named Servecast has built a similar edge-delivery network.

Figures 1-17 and 1-18 illustrate the difference between a typical MBONE multicast network and an edge-delivery system. In Figure 1-17, streams move across the MBONE and eventually reach their ISPs, who distribute them over the quintessential "last mile" to end users. The further an ISP is from the primary server, the longer the delay. In Figure 1-18, edge servers mirror the content on the primary source server. Multimedia streams get delivered more efficiently because the edge servers are located physically closer to the ISPs. In many cases, SMNs locate their servers within the local ISP's server farm. To learn more about this emerging SMN technology, follow this book's Web site links to Streaming Media Networks.

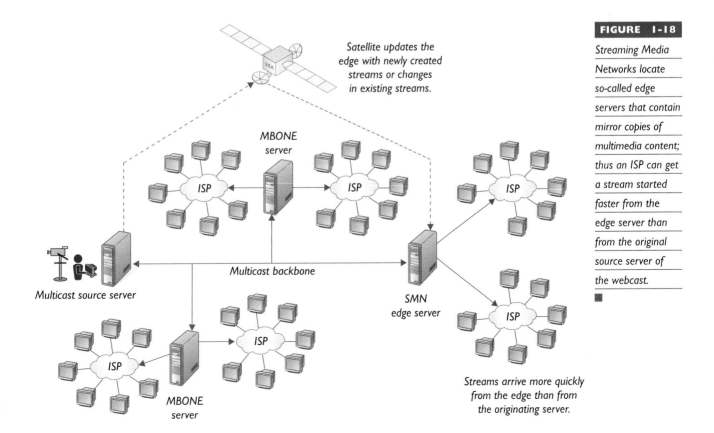

Satellite updates the edge with newly created streams or changes in existing streams.

MBONE server

ISP

ISP

Multicast source server

Multicast backbone

SMN edge server

ISP

ISP

ISP

MBONE server

Streams arrive more quickly from the edge than from the originating server.

FIGURE 1-18

Streaming Media Networks locate so-called edge servers that contain mirror copies of multimedia content; thus an ISP can get a stream started faster from the edge server than from the original source server of the webcast.

Internet2

A consortium of more than 180 universities is leading a project called **Internet2**. The goal is to create a higher-speed version of the Internet that revolves around high-speed connection points called **gigapops**. Strategically placed throughout the network, gigapops guarantee high-speed bandwidth between universities, schools, and companies that are implementing the Internet2 standards.

Internet2 uses three protocols to provide high-speed transmission and guaranteed bandwidth:

- Resource Reservation Protocol (RSVP) permits users to reserve bandwidth from the workstation to the network host computer.

- Internet Protocol version 6 (**IPv6**) is a packet-delivery protocol that lets users assign priority to certain kinds of information. You may want your Web search traffic to have a higher priority than your e-mail traffic, for example, so your searches get completed faster.

- Multicast uses IP tunneling and multithreading to increase multimedia throughput.

The K20 project extends Internet2 participation to all levels of education, from K–12 (pre-college) to 16 (college) and 20 (doctoral level study)—hence the name, K20. To find the current status, follow this book's Web site link to Internet2.

Wireless Communications

In the twentieth century, most Internet use occurred at the end of a wire or cable that connected the user's computer to the Internet. Today, emerging wireless technologies are enabling mobile users to remove the tether.

By the time you read this, for example, AT&T Wireless will be offering Internet service on the Motorola Smartphone pictured in Figure 1-19. In addition to letting you make ordinary phone calls, the Smartphone will provide you with access to e-mail and a mobile Web browser with which you can do online shopping; get news, weather, sports, and stock quotes; make flight reservations and check arrival times; and even trade online. ActiveSync software synchronizes your phone with personal information managers such as Microsoft Outlook or Lotus Notes. You can read e-mail via your wireless phone from AT&T WorldNet, AOL, or Yahoo! mail services. To learn more about the wireless phone's features, follow this book's Web site link to Smartphone. For more about new products that enable you to access the Internet without needing a conventional telephone line or network cable, follow this book's Web site links to Wireless Design and Development.

FIGURE 1-19 *Motorola's MPX 200 Smartphone runs the Windows Mobile operating system, bringing the Internet literally into the palm of your hand.* ■

Bluetooth

Bluetooth is an emerging standard for high-speed wireless communications. All the major telecomm vendors and computer companies are supporting it, including Ericsson, IBM, Nokia, 3COM, Lucent, Microsoft, Motorola, Apple, Toshiba, Agilent, Tektronix, and Intel. Bluetooth enables the synchronization and exchange of information between mobile computers, telephones, portable handheld devices, and the Internet. Bluetooth transmits a short-range radio signal intended to replace the cables connecting electronic devices. It offers wireless connections to local area networks (LANs), the public switched telephone network, and the Internet.

Figure 1-20 depicts how a Bluetooth-enabled device such as a PC can communicate with up to seven other devices at once. Because Bluetooth communicates over radio frequencies (RF), it does not need the line-of-sight required by infrared devices. There are a wide array of applications in home automation, security systems, network access in public places, and wireless headsets. The Bluetooth specification is available royalty-free at www.bluetooth.com. To learn more, follow this book's Web site links to Bluetooth and the Bluetooth tutorial.

Bluetooth devices communicate via short-wave radio links called Piconet.

FIGURE 1-20 *Bluetooth-enabled devices can communicate with up to seven other devices at once.* ∎

Wi-Fi

Wi-Fi is the industry trade name for products based on the IEEE 802.11 specification for wireless local area networking. The Wi-Fi Alliance is a nonprofit international association that formed in 1999 to certify interoperability of these products. When this book went to press, the Wi-Fi Alliance had 205 member companies from around the world, and 903 products had received Wi-Fi certification.

Wi-Fi networks operate over a radius of up to 300 feet, depending on local conditions and equipment. Wi-Fi access points are called HotSpots. When you bring a Wi-Fi equipped computer or PDA into the range of a HotSpot, you can tap into the network, which uses 128-bit encryption to keep your data secure. Unless you are at a FreeSpot, you must have a Wi-Fi provider account in order to connect. There is a FreeSpot directory that lists Wi-Fi HotSpots offering free wireless Internet access. FreeSpot locations include hotels, coffee shops, restaurants, shopping malls, airports, and downtown business districts. To learn more, follow this book's Web site links to Wi-Fi and the FreeSpot directory.

IP Telephony

Imagine making a long-distance telephone call from your PC without having to pay toll charges. Imagine a virtual help desk that brings a live person onscreen to help when you have trouble using your computer. Imagine being able to place a phone call to your computer and remote-control your PC via voice commands. Microsoft's Telephone Application Program Interface (TAPI) is enabling Windows users to do all these things and more by converging the public switched telephone network (PSTN) with

Internet Protocol (IP) telephony. IP telephony converges voice, video, and data into a common Internet protocol, effectively collapsing three networks into one. Using TAPI, a Web site can have a push-to-talk button that instantly establishes a **Voice-over IP (VoIP)** link between, for example, the user at a microphone-equipped PC and a customer service representative at a Web site.

TAPI is evolving as the technology progresses and Microsoft adds more features. For example, Microsoft is developing a telephone markup language that will enable Web pages to contain telephony tags. This will enable Web site developers to create pages to which users can dial up and talk over the phone. Speech recognition will be used to translate the user's voice into commands that the browser will use to surf the Web. Speech synthesis will render the Web's response as a voice the user will hear in reply. For more on the future of TAPI, follow this book's Web site link to Microsoft Internet Telephony. To learn more about the telephony markup language, follow the link to the World Wide Web Consortium's Voice Browser activity.

As Internet telephony services emerge, traditional long-distance telephone companies will see revenues begin to fall. To place an IP telephone call, you dial a local access number that brings up a second dial tone. Then you dial the long-distance number and key in a personal access code that charges you for the call. The savings can be substantial. According to an International Telecommunication Union survey, a one-minute call from the United States to Australia over a traditional phone line costs 17 cents as compared to only 8 cents through a Net-based service (*Hollywood Reporter 7 Mar 2001*). Sprint has begun a project that will replace its conventional telephone network with packet-switching technology over the next 12 to 15 years. Sprint's approach will enable a person to use the same phone number at multiple locations (*San Jose Mercury News 27 May 2003*). Follow this book's Web site links to visit IP telephony sites and learn more about their services.

Personal Digital Assistants

Personal digital assistants (PDAs) are portable, handheld computers that you can take with you to work, school, or anyplace where a PC might come in handy. You can easily synchronize a PDA with your personal computer and take almost any information with you, such as your address book, calendar, and key Web sites. If you have enough memory in your PDA, you can even download music and videos to view while you are away from your PC. There are two main families of PDAs: Windows CE and Palm. Both have taken on exciting new capabilities as PDA technology continues to emerge.

Windows CE

Windows CE is a compact modular version of the Microsoft Windows operating system designed for use on consumer electronic devices. If you know how to use Windows, you know how to use Windows CE. Consider, for example, the user interface on Toshiba's **PocketPC**. As illustrated in

Figure 1-21, you use the Windows Start button to choose programs, which include special pocket versions of Microsoft Office apps—MS Word, MS Excel, and MS Schedule—as well as e-mail, Pocket Windows Media, Pocket MS Reader, and the Pocket Internet Explorer Web browser. Instead of using a mouse, you choose things onscreen with a stylus via Microsoft's pen-computing interface.

One of the advantages of using Windows CE is that it contains modular versions of the Microsoft Windows application programming interfaces. Windows CE supports TAPI, for example, which was described in the section on Internet telephony. If you have a PDA that runs the Phone Edition of Windows CE, you can use that PDA to connect to the Internet. If your PDA and your cell phone both have Bluetooth, for example, your PDA can use your cell phone as a wireless modem to dial up to the Internet. To learn more about these emerging technologies, follow this book's Web site links to Windows CE and the PocketPC Web site.

n o t e *PocketPC is the trade name for palm-sized PDAs based on the Windows CE operating system.*

Palm OS

Palm, Inc., has traditionally been the market leader in personal digital assistants, and Palm is continuing to innovate in order to stay ahead of its biggest competitor, the PocketPC family of products from Microsoft. Palm established its early lead by being first to market, in 1996, with an operating system developed specifically for a small device. Palm handhelds began as personal organizers designed to make people's lives easier through built-in programs, including a date book, an address book, a note-taker, and a to-do list. Today the Palm OS offers Internet connectivity enabling people to access all kinds of information, from stock quotes for investors to driving instructions for travelers. Figure 1-22 illustrates that the latest model has Wi-Fi connectivity built in.

When this book went to press, however, the Palm OS was losing market share. Palm's 70-percent market share in 2000 had slipped to about 40 percent in 2003. Windows enthusiasts feel that the PocketPC will begin to sell even better as larger memories and faster processors permit Windows CE to work more like the familiar desktop computer. This will not necessarily make PocketPCs outsell Palm de-

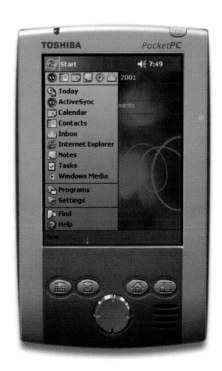

FIGURE 1-21 *Toshiba's PocketPC uses the Windows CE operating system. Notice the Windows Start button in the upper-left corner of the screen.* ■

FIGURE 1-22 *The Palm OS combines built-in personal productivity programs with Internet connectivity.* ■

vices, however, because the challenge is not so much trying to make Windows run on a PDA as it is figuring out what works best on a PDA. Look for exciting competition between the Pocket PC and the Palm OS in the years ahead. For the current status, follow this book's Web site links to Palm OS, PocketPC, and CNET's comparative reviews of the different brands of PDAs that are available today.

Artificial Intelligence

Artificial intelligence (AI) is for real—not just a theoretical science for researchers. As handheld technologies reduce the size of computers, for example, AI researchers are developing more effective ways for people to use them. Featured here are several AI technologies that promise to improve your use of the Internet in years to come.

Voice Recognition

Many people do not type very fast, and even fast typists wish for an easier way to enter information into a computer. Voice recognition is rapidly emerging as a solution to this problem. Apple Speech Recognition, for example, lets developers incorporate speech recognition into any Macintosh application. Among the first to take advantage of this new technology was the *Star Trek Omnipedia* CD-ROM from Imergy, a voice-activated guide to a galaxy of *Star Trek* facts, characters, and movies. Imergy was amazed at how accurate the recognition is, even for such phrases as "Denibian Slime Devil." Apple Speech Recognition enables application developers to define how many words are active and to build custom vocabularies or language models. Apple Speech Recognition is built into Mac OS X. To learn more, follow this book's Web site link to Apple Speech Recognition.

On the Windows platform, IBM's speech division is dueling with Dragon Systems, and all users will benefit from the resulting breakthroughs. The IBM product is ViaVoice, and the Dragon product is NaturallySpeaking. Both products can recognize tens of thousands of words, and they are trainable, meaning that you can teach them new words. Applications include voice-controlled Web surfing, legal dictation, environmental control systems, and word processing by persons with physical disabilities such as repetitive stress injuries. ViaVoice is also available in Macintosh and Linux versions. For more information, follow this book's Web site links to ViaVoice and NaturallySpeaking.

Text-to-Speech Conversion

In Chapter 3 you will learn about a virtual chat environment, which is called the Palace on the Internet. If you have a Macintosh, Apple's text-to-speech extension enables you to hear the conversations as well as see them onscreen in the cartoon talk balloons. Called PlainTalk, Apple's text-to-speech product can speak in Mexican Spanish as well as English.

On the Windows and Unix platforms, IBM has a product called DirectTalk that is a text-to-speech system for building interactive voice response systems. There is also a library of DirectTalk JavaBeans for use in creating Java applications that can talk. Chant Corporation makes a SpeechKit consisting of speech-synthesis and text-to-speech components developers can use when developing Web sites with C/C++, Delphi, Java, JavaScript, VBScript, and Visual Basic. For more information about text-to-speech technology, follow this book's Web site links to PlainTalk, DirectTalk, and the Chant SpeechKit.

Foreign Language Translation

IBM's WebSphere Translation Server can translate Web pages, e-mail, and chat from English into a host of languages, including French, Italian, German, Spanish, Chinese, Japanese, and Korean. It can also translate into English from French, Italian, German, and Spanish. Translation speeds range from 200 to 500 words per second. Slot grammars are used to parse complex sentences that might fool less capable translation engines. Idiomatic expression-handling can be fine-tuned for specific domains and contexts.

Foreign language translation technology is used at the Google.com search engine, which has language tools that can translate English language Web pages into German, French, Italian, Portugese, or Spanish, and vice versa. In addition to these languages, the search site at AltaVista.com adds Chinese, Japanese, Korean, and Russian. To learn more, follow this book's Web site links to Google language tools, AltaVista translator, slot grammars, and the IBM WebSphere Translation Server.

Image Recognition

If you have ever tried to find a specific image in a database, you know how difficult it is to locate an image via keywords. Virage has developed software that can compare images with a visual template, which is how the human brain recognizes images. The Virage software reduces the image into a 1-kilobyte file called a feature vector, which is based on the placement, color, and texture of shapes in the image. You search for images by describing the visual properties of what you are seeking. Virage's product, which is called VIR, for Visual Image Recognition, is protected by U.S. Patent 5,893,095. The VIR Image Engine has been licensed for use in databases from Oracle, Informix, Sybase, Object Design, and Objectivity.

Try This!

Virage VIR Patent

You can read any patent by going to the U.S. Patent and Trademark Office at http://www.uspto.gov and following links to perform a patent search. To read the Visual Image Recognition (VIR) patent, follow these steps:

1. Use your Web browser to open the site www.uspto.gov.

2. Follow the link to perform a patent search.

3. Under issued patents, choose the option to search via patent number.

4. When the search form appears, type the following patent number into the blank: 5,893,095

5. Click the button to perform the search and view the patent.

Bots

Bots, short for robots, are software applications programmed to act as intelligent agents that go out on the network to find or do things for you. You tell a bot what you want, and it worms its way through the Internet, finding all the relevant information, digesting it, and reporting it to you succinctly.

Likening them to robotic librarians, Krol (1996: 418) refers to bots as "software worms that crawl from source to source, looking for answers to your question. As a knowbot looks, it may discover more sources. If it does, it checks the new sources too. When it has exhausted all sources, it comes crawling home with whatever it found."

This book's Web site links to several bot repositories. At FerretSoft, for example, you will find search utilities for locating Web pages, utilities, e-mail addresses, files, chat channels, phone numbers, and news. At BotSpot you will find bots that can help you shop, invest, learn, research, and game. StreetPrices, MSN eShop, Priceline, mySimon, and BottomDollar are online shopping sites that use agents to help you find the best prices. For books, an interesting bot is AddALL, because you can see it working for you when you click to compare prices. Also linked to this book's Web site are the Software Agents Group and the Multi-Agent Systems Laboratory.

Digital Television and Video

Computer technology is creating fundamental changes in the way televisions are made and videos are distributed. Almost everyone reading this book will be purchasing one of the new TVs during the next few years. Because the new TV signal is digital, computer data and Web pages can be transmitted along with the television broadcast to enhance the user experience. By the end of the decade, this convergence will enable most users to surf the Internet and watch TV on the same high-resolution display screen.

High-Definition Television (HDTV)

The new digital television signal is called **HDTV**, which stands for **high-definition television**. HDTV is intended to replace NTSC (National Television System Committee standard) as the television standard for the United States. HDTV is based on four technologies:

- MPEG digital video compression
- Transmission in packets that permit any combination of video, audio, and data
- Progressive scanning for computer interoperability up to 60 frames per second (fps) at 1920 x 1080 pixels
- CD-quality digital surround sound using Dolby AC-3 audio technology

During the 1990s, the major television studios began recording shows in HDTV so reruns can be broadcast in HDTV when the standard changes. To find out how many television stations are broadcasting in HDTV today, follow this book's Web site link to HDTV Group—Reception Maps.

How soon will your analog TV become obsolete? The FCC had planned to order all analog TV transmitters off the air in the year 2006, but Congress is lobbying to delay that until most Americans have either new HDTV sets or digital adapters for their analog sets. There is a lot of intrigue involved in the rollout of high-definition television. To find out the current status of HDTV, follow this book's Web site link to *Current* newspaper's briefing on digital television.

MPEG Digital Video

MPEG stands for **Motion Picture Experts Group**, which is the name of the ISO standards committee that created this digital video standard. MPEG compresses video by using a discrete cosine transform algorithm to eliminate redundant data in blocks of pixels on the screen. MPEG compresses the video further by recording only changes from frame to frame; this is known as *delta-frame encoding*. MPEG is emerging as the digital video standard for compact discs, DVD, cable TV, direct satellite broadcast, and high-definition television. MPEG is the standard for the DirecTV system. Direct satellite broadcasts have become so popular as an alternative to videotape that Blockbuster has begun selling DirecTV in its home video stores. For the DirecTV dealer nearest you, follow this book's Web site links to DirecTV.

MPEG is also being used to bring digital video to handheld wireless devices. The PocketTV movie player, for example, can play MPEG movies on certain models of Windows CE PocketPCs, including Casio's Cassiopeia, HP's Jornada, and Compaq's iPAQ line of pocket computers. Due to the present-day memory limitations of handheld computers, different versions of MPEG are being worked on to enable movies to play on devices that have different bandwidth and memory capabilities. A special version of MPEG is being created, for example, to permit video streaming over wireless connections to the Internet. For more information, follow this book's Web site links to MPEG and PocketTV.

MSN TV Internet Receiver

The MSN TV Internet Receiver is one of the hottest set-top boxes on the planet, and emerging technology promises to keep it that way. As illustrated in Figure 1-23, the MSN TV Internet Receiver is a device that essentially combines your telephone with the video signal on your TV or VCR. When you start up the MSN TV Internet Receiver, it dials up to your Internet service provider, and you see the Web pages on your TV screen. As depicted in Figure 1-24, a cleverly designed hand control lets you do one-thumb surfing on the Internet, but to take advantage of all the features, you need to use the wireless computer keyboard that comes as part of MSN TV.

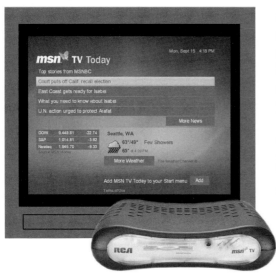

FIGURE 1-23 *MSN TV connects your telephone to your TV for access to the World Wide Web and e-mail.* ■

In order to use the MSN TV receiver, you must subscribe to the MSN TV service. The MSN TV service provides access to MSN Messenger, MSN News, and Hotmail. Your mail messages can include pictures and audio clips, and you can build personal Web pages. There is a $10 per month discount if you already have an ISP; otherwise, you use MSN as your ISP.

Through products such as MSN TV, you can see how emerging technology is integrating the television, the telephone, and the computer into a networked supermedium. Withrow (1993) credits technology prophet George Gilder with coining the term *telecomputer* to describe such a device.

UltimateTV

Microsoft offers a more high-end service called UltimateTV. Through a DirecTV satellite dish, UltimateTV lets you record your favorite shows without a VCR, pause live television, create your own TV program line-up, and instantly replay anything you see on TV. Everything you watch is digitally recorded onto a digital video recorder that uses an internal hard drive to record up to 35 hours of your favorite shows. You can make your own slow-motion instant replays during sporting events. You can also participate in interactively enhanced TV programs such as *Who Wants to Be a Millionaire, Judge Judy, Wheel of Fortune,* and *Jeopardy!*

Microsoft is working actively to continue enhancing its digital television products. During the keynote at the 2002 Consumer Electronics Show, for example, Bill Gates used a PocketPC with a wireless connection to demonstrate how consumers will be able to set up TV recordings by using the UltimateTV Web site remotely.

If UltimateTV subscribers get caught in traffic on the way home from the office, they will be able to record a show they might otherwise miss. To learn more about UltimateTV and how Microsoft plans to keep enhancing it, follow this book's Web site links to UltimateTV.

FIGURE 1-24 *MSN TV comes with a set-top box, a computer keyboard, and a universal remote that features "one-thumb" surfing.* ■

Digital Hubs

Start thinking of your home PC not so much as a personal computer but rather as a **digital hub** that will eventually coordinate all the electronic devices in your home. According to Forrester Research, 10 million U.S. homes will use digital hubs in 2003, and that number will grow to 25 million by 2006. Very aware of this trend, Microsoft created a digital hub version of Windows called Windows XP Media Center Edition, which a dozen leading brands are using as the operating system for their digital entertainment hubs. In the meantime, Apple is working to position the Macintosh as the center of your home entertainment system. At the 2002 Consumer Electronics Show, Moxi Digital won best of show with a digital hub called the Moxi Media Server. Its inventor is Moxi founder Steve Perlman, who created WebTV back in the 1990s and sold it to Microsoft for $425 million in 1997. As digital hub technology evolves, it will be interesting to watch how the Moxi competes for market share with Windows Media Center PCs and the Macintosh.

Features that you will see emerging in digital hubs over the next few years will include the following:

- Wireless transmission of multimedia objects to devices located in various places in the house. This will enable you to play, for example, music stored on a PC in your study on the surround sound system in your family room.

- Distribution of video streams from the digital hub to receivers located in different parts of the house. While Dad watches *Monday Night Football,* Mom can watch *Absolutely Fabulous* and the kids can watch the Discovery Channel.

- Printing of photos taken by your digital camera without having to plug anything in.

- Downloading of music into your PDA or other portable listening device.

- Uploading of a movie from your camcorder to edit on the PC in your den and play on the HDTV set in the living room.

- Capturing of images from wireless cameras located about the house and out in the yard so you can see your house over the Web when you are not at home.

- Paging you if someone jumps or falls into your swimming pool when it is supposed to be closed.

- Remote control of all home appliances and electronic devices, both inside the house when you are home and via the wireless Web when you are away.

To quote the Apple digital hub Web site, these are the kinds of features that will "make your digital lifestyle possible." To learn more about digital hubs, follow this book's Web site links to Windows XP Media Center, Moxi, and Apple digital hubs.

Chapter 1 Review

Chapter Summary

After reading this chapter and completing the Try This! exercises, you should understand the following facts about the Internet:

Defining the Internet

- The Internet is a worldwide connection of more than 171 million computers that use the TCI/IP protocol suite to communicate.

- According to the CIA's *World Factbook,* 604.1 million people were online worldwide as of August 2003.

- The number of pages on the Web has increased dramatically from about 300 million in 1998 to more than three billion in 2003.

- Up-to-date Internet growth charts can be found online as part of Hobbes' Internet Timeline.

- Client-server computing refers to the manner in which computers exchange information by sending it (as servers) and receiving it (as clients).

- TCP/IP is the suite of wide area networking protocols that make the Internet work. TCP stands for the Transmission Control Protocol, which is in charge of routing packets of information across the Internet. Every computer on the Internet has a unique Internet Protocol (IP) address. Each packet of information that gets transmitted over the Internet contains the IP address of the computer that sent it and the IP address of the computer to which it is being sent. TCP ensures that the packets get routed to the proper destination and reassembled in the correct sequence.

- The domain name system (DNS) allows alphabetical names to substitute for numbers in IP addresses on the Internet; for example, the Library of Congress, which has the IP address 140.147.249.7, can also be addressed by its domain name, which is www.loc.gov.

- An intranet is a network that uses the TCP/IP protocols to provide private services within an organization whose computers are not publicly accessible on the Internet. An extranet refers to Internet resources, such as Web sites, that are beyond the public's reach and require authorized users to do something extra, such as type a logon name and password, in order to obtain access.

Identifying Eleven Popular Internet Services

- Electronic mail (e-mail) is a store-and-forward method of sending people messages over the Internet. Messages queue up in your Inbox, permitting you to read and respond to them at your convenience.

- Listserv, which stands for list server, is a mailing list service that enables users to send a message to a particular mailing list, which then e-mails a copy of the message to each member of the list.

- USENET is a distributed bulletin board system hosting more than 10,000 newsgroups. Once you subscribe to a newsgroup, you use a newsreader to access the group's newsfeed. In addition to reading information on existing topics, you can add your own comments and create new topics, thereby participating in a virtual conference on the Internet.

- Chat is a very popular form of real-time communication that enables people to converse with one another over the Internet. As you type a message on your computer keyboard, the people you are chatting with see what you type almost immediately, and you can simultaneously see what they type in reply. Users with microphones and speakers can speak verbally to one another if their chat room software supports audio.

- Instant messaging is a real-time communication protocol that lets you send and receive instant messages over the Internet. You put onto a buddy list the names of users who are permitted to contact you. Only the people on your buddy list can IM you.

- Videoconferencing is the use of real-time video and audio streaming to enable people conversing over the Internet to be able to see and hear each other.

- FTP, which stands for File Transfer Protocol, is the standard method for transferring files over the Internet from one computer to another.

- Multimedia streaming is the digital transmission of a real-time feed from an audio or video source, encoded in such a way that the media can begin playing steadily without making users wait for the entire file to download to their computers.

- The World Wide Web (WWW) is a networked hypertext system that allows multimedia documents to be shared over the Internet without requiring people to travel anywhere physically in order to obtain the information.

- Rich Site Summary (RSS) is an XML format for syndicating the content of a Web site in a form that can be registered with an RSS publisher to which other sites can subscribe in order to access the RSS feed and display its content onscreen.

- A Web log (blog) is a Web-accessible log written by an individual who wants to chronicle activity related to a given topic that is often personal.

Describing the Infrastructure of the Internet

- The term client-server computing refers to the manner in which computers exchange information by sending it (as servers) and receiving it (as clients).

- Transmission Control Protocol/Internet Protocol (TCP/IP) is the suite of protocols that enable the Internet to work.

- To make IP addresses easier for human beings to remember, a domain name system (DNS) was invented to permit the use of alphabetic characters instead of numbers. A complete DNS address is called a fully qualified domain name (FQDN).

- An intranet is a network that uses the TCP/IP protocols to provide private services within an organization whose computers are not publicly accessible on the Internet.

- The term extranet refers to Internet resources, such as Web sites, that are beyond the public's reach and require authorized users to do something extra, such as type a logon name and password, in order to obtain access.

Changing the World via the Internet

- Digitalization is the process of encoding messages into a digital format that can be transmitted over the Internet.

- Convergence is the process of unification that digitalization causes by enabling all the world's traditional ways of communicating to work over a common communications medium on the Internet.

- The forces of digitalization have caused an unprecedented number of mega-mergers in the communications field.

- The Internet is changing the face of business. Online shopping and banking are creating a cashless society by eliminating the need for printed money.

- Through telecommuting, a growing number of companies are permitting employees to work from home by using computers, dialup modems or broadband network connections, and fax machines to perform work that formerly required a person to travel physically to work.

- Government officials have turned increasingly to the Internet for solutions to problems inherent in governance. The Net makes services more widely available and enables municipalities to respond more quickly to emergencies and disasters.

- To intercept messages from terrorists and criminals, the FBI is using a system called Carnivore, which can scan the Internet's e-mail traffic, looking for key words and phrases related to terrorist plots and criminal investigations. The USA Patriot Act gives the federal government wide latitude in using Internet surveillance systems, including Carnivore and its successors.

- Electronic book (eBook) technology enables publishers to sell books in an electronic format that consumers can download into portable reading devices.

- The Internet is enabling educators to make use of computer-based learning strategies online. By linking universities, colleges, schools, and homes into a worldwide network, the Internet is helping to break down the distinctions between grade levels.

- The digital divide is the barrier that disenfranchises citizens who are not connected to the Internet and therefore cannot participate fully in the converged digital economy.

Tracing the History of the Internet

- The Internet originated when the Advanced Research Projects Agency (ARPA) of the United States Department of Defense began a network called ARPANET in 1969.

- ARPANET was the first network based on packets and packet switching. The packets contained IP addresses that enabled the information to get routed to their intended destination. If one of the computers on the network got wiped out in an attack, the packets would find their way by another route.

- During the 1970s, universities began using the Internet Protocol to connect their local networks to the ARPANET.

- In 1983, the military segment broke off and became MILNET.

- In 1986, the National Science Foundation (NSF) began the NSFNET, a backbone that connected the nation's five supercomputer centers at high speed.

- In 1991, NSF lifted the restriction that prohibited commercial entities from using the backbone. By 1994, the NSFNET was carrying 10 trillion bytes of Internet traffic per month.

- In 1995, NSFNET reverted to a research network, and the U.S. Internet backbone traffic was routed through interconnected network providers.

- In 1998, the responsibility for managing the domain name system (DNS) was transferred from the Internet Network Information Center (InterNIC) to the Internet Corporation for Assigned Names and Numbers (ICANN), which is an international not-for-profit organization.

Looking into the Future of the Internet

- The Multicast Backbone (MBONE) is a network of computers on the Internet specially designed for the transmission of simultaneous live video and audio broadcasts. Instead of sending multiple copies of these transmissions, multicasting sends only one copy of the message and replicates the information only at branch points in the network.

- A consortium of research universities is working in partnership with industry and government to create an even faster network named Internet2. The goal is to create a higher-speed version of the Internet that revolves around high-speed connection points called gigapops.

- Wi-Fi is the trade name for products based on the IEEE 802.11 specification for wireless local area networking. Wi-Fi networks operate over a radius of up to 300 feet, depending on local conditions and equipment. Wi-Fi access points are called HotSpots, which use 128-bit encryption to keep your data secure. A FreeSpot directory lists Wi-Fi HotSpots offering free wireless Internet access in selected hotels, coffee shops, restaurants, shopping malls, airports, and downtown business districts.

- Voice-over IP (VoIP) is converging the public switched telephone network (PSTN) with IP telephony. This enables a Web site to have a push-to-talk button that instantly establishes a VoIP link between, for example, the user at a microphone-equipped PC and a customer service representative at a Web site.

- Voice recognition promises to provide an easier way for people who do not type very fast to enter information into a computer. Text-to-speech extensions enable you to hear as well as see printed text onscreen.

- Bots, short for robots, are software applications programmed to act as intelligent agents that go out on the network to find or do things for you. You tell a bot what you want, and it worms its way through the Internet, finding all the relevant information, digesting it, and reporting it to you succinctly.

- During the coming decade, high-definition television (HDTV) will replace NTSC as the television standard for the United States. The signal is MPEG digital, transmitted in packets and displayed at up to 1920 x 1080 pixels of graphical resolution.

- Start thinking of your home PC not so much as a personal computer but rather as a digital hub that will eventually coordinate all the electronic devices in your home. According to Forrester Research, 25 million U.S. homes will be using digital hubs by 2006.

■ Key Terms

ARPANET *(30)*
blog *(17)*
Bluetooth *(35)*
bot *(40)*
Carnivore *(28)*
chat *(10)*
client-server computing *(19)*
convergence *(23)*
digital divide *(23)*
digital hub *(42)*
domain *(21)*
domain name system (DNS) *(20)*
dotted quad notation *(20)*
e-mail *(7)*
extranet *(23)*
e-zine *(9)*
File Transfer Protocol (FTP) *(13)*
fully qualified domain name (FQDN) *(20)*
gigapop *(34)*
high-definition television (HDTV) *(40)*

hypertext *(14)*
information warfare *(28)*
instant messaging (IM) *(12)*
Internet *(4)*
Internet2 *(34)*
Internet Explorer *(15)*
Internet Protocol (IP) *(19)*
intranet *(22)*
IP address *(19)*
IPv6 *(34)*
listserv *(9)*
MILNET *(31)*
Mosaic *(14)*
Motion Picture Experts Group (MPEG) *(41)*
Multicast Backbone (MBONE) *(32)*
Net *(6)*
Netscape Navigator *(14)*
NSFNET *(31)*
packet *(19)*
Personal Digital Assistant (PDA) *(36)*

PocketPC *(36)*
Rich Site Summary (RSS) *(16)*
server *(19)*
streaming *(13)*
subdomain *(21)*
TCP/IP *(19)*
telecommuting *(24)*
telecomputer *()*
teleworker *(24)*
top-level domain (TLD) *(20)*
Transmission Control Protocol (TCP) *(19)*
USA Patriot Act *(28)*
USENET *(9)*
videoconferencing *(12)*
Voice-over IP (VoIP) *(36)*
Wi-Fi *(35)*
Windows CE *(36)*
World Wide Web (WWW) *(14)*
World Wide Web Consortium (W3C) *(15)*

■ Key Terms Quiz

1. The Internet protocol suite is called _____, which stands for _____ / _____.

2. IP addresses that have four numbers separated by periods are said to have _____ notation.

3. FTP stands for _____.

4. The first popular Web browser, which was created by the National Center for Supercomputer Applications, was called _____.

5. W3C stands for _____.

6. In the Web address www.loc.gov, gov is the _____.

7. In the Web address www.humberc.on.ca, www is the _____.

8. Using computers, dialup modems or broadband network connections, and fax machines to work from home is known as _____.

9. In the aftermath of the 9/11 attacks on America, the _____ was signed into law, giving the federal government wide latitude in using Internet surveillance systems.

10. _____ is the industry trade name for products based on the IEEE 802.11 specification for wireless local area networking.

▧ Multiple-Choice Quiz

1. Which one of the following networks was invented first?
   a. Internet2
   b. MILNET
   c. ARPANET
   d. USENET

2. Which one of the following descriptions best fits the design of the Internet?
   a. Centrally controlled with a single point of failure
   b. Centrally controlled with no single point of failure
   c. Decentralized control with a single point of failure
   d. Decentralized control with no single point of failure

3. Text that has been linked such that when you click the text, you trigger the link is called:
   a. Rich text
   b. Hypertext
   c. Clear text
   d. Active text

4. An IP address consists of how many numbers that are separated by periods?
   a. 2
   b. 3
   c. 4
   d. 5

5. Prior to 1998, the responsibility for managing the domain name system (DNS) was vested in an organization called:
   a. InterNIC
   b. ICANN
   c. Interpol
   d. W3C

6. In 1998, the responsibility for managing the domain name system (DNS) was transferred to an organization called:
   a. InterNIC
   b. ICANN
   c. Interpol
   d. W3C

7. The barriers faced by the unconnected are known as:
   a. Viruses
   b. Firewalls
   c. The digital divide
   d. Wormholes

8. Web sites that are beyond the public's reach and require authorized users to do something extra, such as type a logon name and password, in order to obtain access are called:
   a. Public domain
   b. ARPANETS
   c. TAPI
   d. Extranets

9. Wi-Fi access points that offer free wireless Internet access are called:
   a. HotSpots
   b. FreeSpots
   c. BotSpots
   d. OpenSpots

10. Software applications programmed to act as intelligent agents that go out on the network to find or do things for you are called:
    a. Librarians
    b. Bots
    c. Spies
    d. Scripts

▧ Essay Quiz

1. How large is the Internet today? When this book went to press, just over 109 million computers were using the Internet Protocol (IP) to communicate. To find out how much the Internet has grown since then, follow the *Interlit* Web site links to one of the Internet surveys. Tell how large the Internet is today, and state which survey you used to obtain this data. Also tell which kind of data you think best measures how large the Internet is.

2. Follow this book's Web site links to Voice Recognition, and explore the material you find there. Then reflect on how voice recognition might help make computers easier to use. What ways can you think of? How would you use voice recognition in your daily life? List at least three ways in which voice recognition could improve operations at your school or workplace.

3. Follow this book's Web site link to BotSpot and peruse the range of intelligent agents available there. Which one of the bots would be most useful to you in your daily life? Name the bot, describe what it does, and tell why it would be useful for you. In addition to naming the bot that would best serve you personally, tell whether you found any bots that would improve the efficiency of your school or workplace. Name the bots, describe what they do, and tell how they would make things better at work or school.

4. Go to your local computer store and ask to see demonstrations of a PocketPC running Windows CE and a Palm device running the Palm OS. Compare the Windows CE to the Palm OS operating systems. Were you able to launch programs from the Windows Start button on the PocketPC? Do you feel that is more intuitive for a Windows user than the custom interface on the Palm OS, or does the Palm interface work better for a handheld device? What was the nicest feature you found on the PocketPC? What did you find to be the best feature of the Palm OS? If you had to choose one over the other for use in your school or workplace, which family of PDAs would you recommend: one of the PocketPCs based on the Windows CE or a Palm device running the Palm OS? Give at least three reasons why you chose this particular brand.

5. Go to your local computer store and ask for a demonstration of the Tablet PC. Use the pen to write a message onscreen. How well does the Tablet PC recognize your handwriting? Do you think it works well enough for use in your school or workplace? Give at least three reasons for or against using the Tablet PC in your school or workplace. Also tell what brand and model of Tablet PC you used for this exercise.

Lab Projects

• Lab Project 1-1: Planning Internet Services

Imagine that you are employed in a school or small company that is planning its information technology infrastructure. Your employer has asked you to consider the basic Internet services and plan how they can function in the workplace to improve productivity and communication on a daily basis. You will submit your plan in the form of a matrix. To create the matrix, follow these steps:

1. Use your word processor to make an outline of the basic functions of your school or business.

2. Consider how each function in the outline could make use of one or more of the basic Internet services you studied in this chapter.

3. Using the table feature of your word processor, create a matrix that lists the eleven basic Internet services across the top and the functions in your outline along the side.

4. In each cell of the matrix, put a check mark if the Internet service in that column can help achieve the task in that cell's row.

This matrix constitutes a functional analysis that will inform how and where your school or company would apply the different Internet services. Save the matrix on your hard drive. If your instructor has asked you to hand in the matrix, make sure you put your name at the top of the matrix; then save it on a disk or follow the other instructions you may have been given for submitting this assignment.

• Lab Project 1-2: Adopting a PDA Platform

As you learned in this chapter, the PDA market is divided into two camps: PocketPC and Palm. The operating systems are very different, as is the software needed to use these devices. Because of these differences, most schools or companies will probably choose to adopt one or the other instead of trying to support them both. Imagine that your superior has asked you to recommend which PDA platform your school or company should adopt. In developing this recommendation, consider these issues:

■ The marketplace for PDAs is volatile. From 2000 to 2003, for example, Palm's market share dropped from more than 70 percent to about 40 percent of the market for personal digital assistants. Use the search engines at google.com or yahoo.com to find the latest reports on PDA market share.

■ Consider the extent to which your coworkers use Windows. If they are diehard Windows users, for example, they may prefer the PocketPC platform. Macintosh users may prefer the Palm.

■ Get personal experience with both operating systems before you make a recommendation. You can try them in the PDA departments at Circuit City, Best Buy, Staples, Office Depot, and many other retail stores.

■ Functionality should be your guiding light in deciding on a PDA platform. Consider the applications available on the various brands, and match these applications to the daily tasks faced by your coworkers.

Use a word processor to write a brief essay telling what PDA you recommend and why. Report the brands of PDA you considered. Discuss the relative pluses and minuses of the PocketPC and Palm platforms as they relate to daily activities in your workplace. If it seems necessary to support both the PocketPC and the Palm, state the reasons for this. Also state what the current market share is for the Palm versus the PocketPC brands of PDA. If your instructor has asked you to hand in this assignment, make sure you put your name at the top of your PDA recommendation; then save it on a disk or follow the other instructions you may have been given for submitting this assignment.

chapter

2

Surfing and Searching the Internet

"On the Internet, there is no there."

—Anna Paquin, MCI Commercial

In this chapter, you will learn how to:

- List and define the six things you must have in order to connect to the Internet.

- Use a Web browser to go surfing on the Internet, bookmark important sites, and share bookmarked favorites with coworkers.

- Download and install multimedia plug-ins and viewers that are not built into the browser.

- Configure the browser's advanced security settings to help guard against malicious code such as viruses, worms, and Trojans that can be harmful to your computer.

- Use the appropriate search engine to conduct subject-oriented as well as full-text searches by keyword or concept, including multimedia searches that can find pictures, audio, and video as well as text.

- Download found objects from the Internet and define the types of files that are commonly found.

E

VERYONE reading this book has most likely been on the Internet. You have probably surfed the Web, for example, and you may consider yourself pretty good at surfing. But do you understand the theory of surfing well enough to truly glide across the Net and find things quickly? Do you know the proper way to download and handle the different kinds of resources you can find on the Internet? Are you sure you know the most cost-effective way to connect to the Internet? Do you know the best way to configure your security settings to safeguard against viruses, worms, Trojans, and other kinds of Internet attacks?

So you can get more out of the Internet, this part of the book helps you understand how best to connect and surf the Net safely, productively, and cost effectively. To get the most out of your online experience, you learn how to download and configure the latest multimedia plug-ins. Then you will be ready to use the search engines not only to find but also to play the multimedia objects of your desire. Before you can do any of these things, however, you need to learn about getting connected, so that is where this chapter begins.

Getting Connected

To get connected to the Internet, you need the following six things:

- **Internet-Ready Computer**   A computer is Internet ready if it has the physical hardware needed to connect to the Internet, such as a modem or a network interface card.

- **Operating System**   Most computers come with an operating system preinstalled. The most popular operating systems are Microsoft Windows, the Macintosh OS, UNIX, and Linux.

- **TCP/IP**   In Chapter 1, you learned that computers communicate with the Internet through a protocol suite called TCP/IP. To get on the Internet, therefore, the computer must have TCP/IP installed.

- **Client Software**   Client software is the application program you run when you access services on the Internet. The most popular examples of Internet clients include programs that let you read your e-mail, browse the Web, and IM (i.e., instant message) your friends and colleagues.

- **Internet Connection**   The connection from your computer to the Internet is called your *Internet connection*. The next part of this chapter covers different ways of creating this physical connection to the Internet.

- **Internet Address**   To go somewhere on the Internet, you need to know the destination address of the service or resource you are planning to access. This destination could be the address of a Web site, the e-mail address of a person to whom you are sending a message, or the FTP address of a server from which you want to download a file.

Internet Service Providers

Most users get their Internet connection from an **Internet Service Provider (ISP)**. An ISP is a networking company that connects you to the Internet and provides you with Internet services, including access to the World Wide Web, e-mail, listserv, chat, and newsgroups.

In the past, some ISPs charged an hourly fee. If you use the Internet a lot, however, paying by the hour can be very expensive. Listed here are four of the most popular ISPs, all of which provide unlimited dialup usage for a flat fee of about $24 per month.

America Online

America Online, also known as AOL, is the largest Internet Service Provider. The number of AOL subscribers has skyrocketed to 32 million users. Each user gets up to seven e-mail accounts and an allotment of 2MB of personal Web space for each account. AOL uses a channel-style of presentation to make it easy to navigate its many offerings. A huge amount of AOL content is not otherwise available on the Internet. Parental controls enable parents to limit access to adult content. To find out more about AOL, go to www.aol.com.

AT&T WorldNet

AT&T WorldNet Service provides fast, reliable Internet access nationwide. You get six e-mail accounts, each of which has 10MB of personal Web space. For more information about AT&T WorldNet Service, go to www.att.net.

Microsoft Network

The Microsoft Network (MSN) provides up to nine e-mail accounts, the MSN Messenger service for talking with your friends online, and up to 30MB of space for your photos and personal Web pages. To find out more about the Microsoft Network, go to www.msn.com.

EarthLink

In 2000, EarthLink merged with Mindspring to become the nation's second-largest ISP (Bloomberg News, 2000). Its partnership with the Snap! Portal provides EarthLink users with an intuitive user interface. Every user gets an allotment of Web space with a personal start page including an e-mail indicator, a search engine, headline news, stock quotes, weather, and personal reminders. You can find EarthLink on the Web at www.earthlink.net.

Regional and Local Networks

By looking up "Internet Services" in the yellow pages of your telephone directory, you will probably find some regional and local ISPs listed in addition to the nationwide service providers discussed so far. For example, a regional ISP called *Starpower* offers Internet services in Washington, DC, northern Virginia, and Maryland. Starpower can also provide telephone and cable TV services. To contact Starpower, go to www.starpower.net.

An excellent source for finding out about other ISPs in your area is on the Web at thelist.internet.com.

School and College Networks

Schools and colleges commonly operate computer networks that provide Internet services for free to their faculty, staff, and students. If you are lucky enough to belong to such a user community, your local school or college serves as your ISP. Because these services are free, however, the resources are sometimes inadequate to meet the demand, and it is not uncommon for members of school and college networks to also subscribe to one of the commercial ISPs. Some campuses have even negotiated deals with commercial ISPs to get a lower price for individuals to subscribe to the commercial service.

User Satisfaction

Consumer Reports magazine rates ISPs in terms of customer satisfaction. In a survey of 1,640 dialup modem users, for example, AT&T WorldNet, BellSouth, and EarthLink were highly rated. AOL and MSN users, on the other hand, reported problems with interruptions during dialup sessions. Both AOL and MSN have pledged to work to correct these problems. For the latest rankings of Internet service providers, go to consumersearch.com/www/computers/internet_service_providers.

Transport Medium

The transport medium is the physical connection over which information travels on the Internet. Very high-speed transmission lines carry the backbone of the Internet across the country and over the world. Most often these backbone lines are fiber-optic cables or copper transmission lines. The major ISPs have very high-speed connections to the Internet's backbone.

The physical connection between your computer and your ISP is often the most critical part of the transport medium, because it determines the bandwidth of your connection to the Net. Most Internet connections use wires or cables you can see and touch. It is also possible to use wireless connections such as cell phones and satellites that communicate via radio signals. Depending on the medium you choose, you need to have specific hardware installed in your computer to handle the communication.

Telephone Modems

The most common means of connecting to the Internet from home is via plain old telephone service, also known as *POTS*. To communicate with the Internet over an ordinary telephone line, your computer must have a modem. The term **modem** is a combination of the terms *mo*dulate and *dem*odulate, which describe how your computer sends and receives digital information over analog phone lines. Modems are so popular that most computers being sold today come with modems built in. Other models require the addition of external modems that connect to your computer's serial port or modem cards that plug into one of your computer's expansion slots. Figure 2-1 contains a block diagram that describes how modems work.

Modems have gotten steadily faster as computer technology has advanced. Modem speed is important because it determines how long you have to wait for information to arrive. Modem speed is often expressed in units known as **bits per second (bps)** or kilobits per second (**Kbps**). A **kilobit** is a thousand bits. Common speeds are 14,400 bps (14.4 Kbps), 28,800 bps (28.8 Kbps), 33,600 bps (33.6 Kbps), and 56,000 bps (56 Kbps). For example, information traveling at 14,400 bps takes twice as long to arrive as it would at 28,800 bps.

Just because you have a superfast modem, such as 56 Kbps, does not necessarily mean information actually travels that fast to and from your computer. The telephone lines and the equipment (routers and switches) the lines pass through on their way to your ISP may preclude your superfast modem from using its highest speed. Many modems have built-in compression and decompression features that enable them to pack information more tightly in the communication packets, thereby achieving an actual transmission rate higher than their advertised data rate. This feature only works, however, for data that have not already been compressed.

As data communications technology continues to advance, modems will continue to increase in speed. Someday, the so-called high speeds discussed in this book will seem slow.

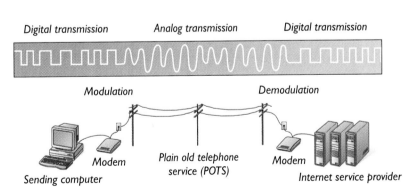

Digital transmission   Analog transmission   Digital transmission

Modulation   Demodulation

Modem   Plain old telephone   Modem
Sending computer   service (POTS)   Internet service provider

FIGURE 2-1   *Follow the signal to see how modems work by modulating the computer's digital signal into an analog signal that can be transmitted over plain old telephone service (POTS) to your ISP, where the signal is demodulated into a digital signal.* ∎

PPP vs. SLIP

The two most popular protocols for telephone modems are **Point to Point Protocol (PPP)** and **Serial Line Internet Protocol (SLIP)**. True to its name, SLIP handles the Internet Protocol only. PPP, which is the more modern of the two, supports not only TCP/IP but also NetBEUI and IPX/SPX, which are communication protocols you will study in the networking part of this book. SLIP has faded in popularity due to the superiority of PPP, which has better error checking and supports user ID and password authentication. Another reason PPP has become the telephone modem protocol of choice is that PPP can assign IP addresses automatically, whereas SLIP requires a preassigned IP address. PPP is built in to the Windows XP operating system, which uses PPP when modem users dial up to the Internet.

Ethernet

The invention of **Ethernet** (pronounced *ee-thur-net*) in Bob Metcalfe's Harvard Ph.D. thesis in 1973 was a data communications breakthrough that fueled the explosion of local area networks (LANs) throughout academia and industry. Ethernet networks transmit data at high speed, typically up to 10 megabits per second (**Mbps**). (Mega means a million, so 10 **megabits** means 10 million bits.) At Ethernet speeds, a file that takes 10 minutes to transmit over a 14.4 Kbps modem arrives in just 1 second. Actual downloading times may vary, depending on compression schemes, network traffic, and the number of users sharing the Ethernet.

If you work at a school or company that has its PCs connected to the Internet at high speeds, chances are the communications medium is an Ethernet. At first, Ethernet required the use of coaxial cable, the kind of wire used in cable TV. Now there is a so-called **10BaseT** Ethernet that can use category 5 twisted-pair telephone wiring. A faster **10/100BaseT** Ethernet can move data at rates up to 100 megabits per second. There is also a 10 gigabit Ethernet standard known as **10GbE**. Officially ratified in the summer of 2002, the 10GbE standard uses fiber optics to push Ethernet into speeds ranging up 10 gigabits per second (**Gbps**). The prefix giga means billion; a **gigabit** is one billion bits and 10 Gbps is therefore 10 billion bits per second.

ISDN

ISDN stands for **Integrated Services Digital Network**. It is the digital telephone system the regional Bell companies are installing in most of the United States; when this book went to press, about 80 percent of the country could get ISDN.

ISDN signals are carried over two or more 64-Kbps (64,000 bits per second) circuit-switched channels to carry voice and data and a lower-speed packet-switched channel that carries control signals. The Basic Rate Interface (BRI) service of ISDN is 144 Kbps, made up of two 64-Kbps data channels and one 16-Kbps control channel. A special version of PPP called *multilink PPP* combines the two 64-Kbps data channels to create an effective data rate of 128 Kbps. The Primary Rate Interface (PRI) service uses 23 data channels and a 64-Kbps control channel to boost the data rate to 1,544 Kbps (1.544 Mbps), which is capable of real-time videoconferencing in addition to more traditional data services.

To use ISDN to connect to the Internet, you need to contact both your local telephone company and your Internet Service Provider to find out whether ISDN is available in your area and to make sure your ISP supports it. ISDN lines cost more than ordinary phone lines, so be prepared to pay more for the higher data rate.

Cable Modems

A **cable modem** is a network adapter used to connect PCs to TV cables in neighborhoods where cable TV companies offer Internet services over TV cables. Cable modems are potentially faster than telephone modems because TV cables, being coaxial, are capable of carrying high-speed Ethernet signals in addition to conventional television signals. The term **broadband** is used to refer to this type of connection that carries multiple channels of information over a single cable.

To find out if cable modems are available in your neighborhood, follow this book's Web site link to the cable modem Zip code search.

DSL, SDSL, and ADSL

DSL stands for **Digital Subscriber Line**, which is a broadband method of connecting to the Internet over existing telephone lines. There are two kinds of DSL: synchronous and asynchronous. Synchronous DSL (SDSL) supports the same high-speed data rate for both upstream and downstream traffic. Asynchronous DSL (ADSL) lowers the cost of DSL connections by using a high-speed data rate for downloads but a slower rate for uploads. Download speeds range from 384 Kbps to 8 Mbps, and upload speeds range from 128 Kbps to 1 Mbps. The faster the speed, the higher the cost.

The typical home user spends a lot more time downloading than uploading. When you click to play a movie, for example, very little information goes up from your computer to the movie site to trigger the playing of the movie. When the movie comes down to your PC, on the other hand, the amount of bandwidth required is huge. ADSL models itself after this trend of home users downloading much more information than they upload. Another advantage of ADSL is that you can use the same telephone line for voice as well as data transmissions. SDSL, on the other hand, cannot operate simultaneously with voice transmissions on the same wire.

When this book went to press, DSL was available in about 75 percent of the United States. To find out whether you can get DSL at your home or business, follow this book's Web site link to the DSL area code search and use the menus to find out if access is available in your locale, and how much it costs to connect at different speeds. Be prepared to see some pretty high prices for the faster speeds.

To learn more about DSL and compare the relative merits of SDSL and ADSL, follow the link to the DSL Resource Center.

Satellite

Where cable or DSL is not available, satellite Internet service is an attractive alternative in areas that have a clear view of the southern sky. Like ADSL, satellite Internet service has a faster download than upload speed. Typical transmission speeds are 500 Kbps downstream and 150 Kbps upstream. In extremely bad weather, the speeds can decline due to the obstructed view. Whereas most DSL vendors permit subscribers to connect more than one computer, satellite providers normally restrict usage to a single computer per subscription. To learn more, follow this book's Web site links to satellite Internet providers.

Comparing the Ways to Connect

To summarize the many alternatives presented in this chapter, Table 2-1 compares the different ways to connect to the Internet. By studying this comparison, you should be able to select an option that suits your needs and budget.

To test the bandwidth your connection actually provides, follow this book's Web site link to the bandwidth meter.

Prepaid Internet Cards

Computer users who travel may be interested in prepaid Internet calling cards. Manufactured by Sprint and AT&T, the prepaid Internet cards let you purchase a number of hours of Internet connection time in advance of using it.

Transport Medium	Time to Download 100KB Picture	Time to Download 900KB Audio	Time to Download 10MB Movie	Estimated Monthly Communications Cost
14.4 Kbps modem	55 seconds	500 seconds	93 minutes	$23
28.8 Kbps modem	28 seconds	250 seconds	46 minutes	$23
33.6 Kbps modem	24 seconds	214 seconds	40 minutes	$23
56 Kbps modem	14 seconds	128 seconds	24 minutes	$23
128 Kbps ISDN	6 seconds	56 seconds	10 minutes	$35
256 Kbps DSL	3 seconds	28 seconds	5 minutes	$129
500 Kbps satellite downstream, 159 Kbps upstream	1.6 seconds	14.4 seconds	2.6 minutes	$70
1.5 Mbps DSL	0.54 seconds	4.8 seconds	54 seconds	$309
1.5 Mbps ADSL downstream, 128 Kbps upstream	0.54 seconds	4.8 seconds	54 seconds	$49
3 Mbps cable modem	0.27 seconds	2.4 seconds	27 seconds	$35-50

Note: Cable modem speeds vary depending on the number of simultaneous users of the local cable network.

TABLE 2-1 *Internet Connection Comparison Matrix* ■

The prepaid Internet card may also be of interest to people who seldom connect to the Internet and wish to avoid paying a regular monthly fee. The prepaid Internet market is expected to grow from $10 million in 2001 to $280 million in 2005. To learn more, follow this book's Web site links to prepaid Internet cards.

Direct Connections

An Internet connection that is always on is called a **direct connection**. To use the Internet over a direct connection, you simply begin using the client software with which you wish to access the Internet. Of the various ways this chapter has presented for connecting to the Internet, the following provide you with a direct connection:

- Ethernet
- ISDN
- Cable modem
- DSL
- Satellite

Connections that are not direct, on the other hand, require you to do something special to get connected. To use a dialup connection, for example, you must dial up to your ISP to get connected.

Sometimes even a direct connection can stop working. When hurricane Isabel hit the mid-Atlantic United States, for example, my ISDN line was out of service for several days. To work online in the meantime, I used a modem to dial up, which enabled business to continue, albeit at a lower speed. Many users with direct connections keep a prepaid Internet card on hand for emergency use during such outages.

Cross Check

Comparing the Ways to Connect

As you have learned so far in this chapter, there are many ways to connect to the Internet. Keeping them straight in your own mind is important if you want to advise people regarding the appropriate way to connect to the Internet in their particular circumstances. See if you can match the ways of connecting on the left with their operational descriptions on the right.

_____ telephone modem	**A.** Broadband coaxial connection that carries high-speed Ethernet signals as well as conventional television
_____ Ethernet	**B.** Typical transmission speeds are 550 Kbps downstream and 150 Kbps upstream
_____ ISDN	**C.** Broadband method of connecting to the Internet over existing telephone lines
_____ cable modem	**D.** Basic service is 144 Kbps, made up of two 64-Kbps data channels and one 16-Kbps control channel
_____ DSL	**E.** Operates over category 5 twisted-pair telephone wiring at speeds up to 10 Mbps
_____ satellite	**F.** Modulates the computer's digital signal into an analog signal that can be transmitted over POTS

Browsing the Web

Most of the people reading this book have probably already had their first surfing experience. Many may consider themselves adept at surfing, and some could even be addicted to it.

Whether or not you have surfed the Net, studying the concepts in this chapter will enable you to become a better surfer than if you "just do it." If you have become addicted, the techniques you learn here will help you gain control over the Net instead of allowing it to control you.

In telecommunications, the term **surf** means to browse by going from place to place in search of something that interests you. On TV, you surf by changing channels continually until you find a program you want to watch; this is known as *channel surfing*. On the Net, surfing means to use a program called a browser to go from site to site in search of information that interests you.

The most popular place to surf on the Internet is the World Wide Web. As you learned in Chapter 1, the Web is a worldwide hypertext system that interconnects millions of documents. The connections are made through links, which can be textual or graphical. A **link** is a hot spot that, when selected, triggers the object of the link. You select the link by clicking on the word or picture that triggers it. Progressively clicking through the Web by triggering the links that interest you is known as **browsing**, a term synonymous with surfing the Net.

What Is a Browser?

The program you run when you surf the Web is called a **browser**. Because you surf the Web to receive content, the browser is an example of client software. As this chapter proceeds, you will learn how to use a browser not only to surf Web pages but also to search for and download pictures, audio, and video content. You will learn how to configure the browser to display multimedia content by using the plug-in of your choice. To keep your computer safe, you will also learn how to configure the browser's security settings to protect your computer from Internet attacks.

Selecting a Web Browser

Microsoft makes the most popular browser, called **Internet Explorer (IE)**. More than 90 percent of Internet users browse the Web with Internet Explorer. It is an excellent choice for computers that run the Windows operating system. Internet Explorer comes in both desktop and handheld versions. The handheld version is called Pocket Internet Explorer and runs under Windows CE on the Pocket PC family of handheld computers. Internet Explorer is preinstalled on most computers sold today. Users who do not have Internet Explorer can download it freely from www.microsoft.com/windows/ie, where the latest updates are also available. If you have trouble downloading the browser, ask your Internet Service Provider to help you get a setup disk that will install the browser for you.

On the Macintosh, an important Web browser change occurred in 2003. Before then, the default browser was the Macintosh version of Internet Explorer. In 2003, however, Microsoft announced that it was discontinuing work on the Macintosh version of IE. Apple now produces its own Web browser, which is called **Safari** and ships on every Macintosh as the default Web browser. Macintosh users can download the latest version or get updates at www.apple.com/safari. To run Safari, Macintosh users need to be running the Mac OS X operating system.

Another popular Web browser is **Netscape Navigator**. In 2003, however, Netscape's parent company, America Online, officially stopped all work on the Netscape Navigator product. Work continues on an open source version called **Mozilla**. The term **open source** refers to software for which the source code is available to the general public free of charge. Anyone can download the source code, use it freely, and make enhancements. People who make enhancements to Mozilla can submit them to the Mozilla Foundation, which maintains the official master copy of the Mozilla software. You can download the Windows, Linux, or Macintosh version of Mozilla from www.mozilla.org.

Legacy Browsers

In computing, the term legacy refers to something old. The term **legacy browser** refers to old versions of Web browsers. You need to be aware that some people have not upgraded to the latest version and are using a legacy browser. Some Web page elements may display differently or may not work at all in the older browsers. In Chapter 8, for example, you learn how cascading style sheets (CSS) provide you with some powerful new ways of formatting and laying out Web pages. Legacy browsers, however, do not support all the CSS features. Web pages that use CSS, therefore, may display differently, depending on the age of the browser. Internet Explorer did not support style sheets prior to version 3, and Netscape began supporting CSS with version 4. Chapter 8 provides you with a link to a chart that shows which CSS features are supported in which versions of the legacy browsers.

The legacy browsers you will encounter most often are the earlier versions of Internet Explorer and Netscape Navigator. Table 2-2 compares the features they support. The Web authoring tutorial in Part II of this book shows you how to create Web pages using all these features. In my opinion, users who have legacy browsers should upgrade to the latest versions rather than expect Web developers to shy away from the newer features.

Try This!

Update Your Browser

To make sure you have the latest version of your Web browser, you should go to the download site for the brand of Web browser you are using primarily on your computer. Check to see if a new version of your browser is available. If so, follow the onscreen instructions to download and install the update. Here are the sites to check:

- To update Internet Explorer, go to www.microsoft.com/windows/ie.

- To update Netscape, go to www.netscape.com.

- To update Mozilla, go to www.mozilla.org.

- To update Safari, go to www.apple.com/safari.

Browser	Frames	Inline Frames	Plug-ins	JavaScript	Style Sheets	Dynamic HTML	XML
IE 6.0	Yes	Yes	Yes	Yes	Yes	Yes	Yes
IE 5.5	Yes	Yes	Yes	Yes	Yes	Yes	Yes
IE 5.0	Yes	Yes	Yes	Yes	Yes	Yes	Some
IE 4.0	Yes	Yes	Yes	Yes	Yes	Yes	No
IE 3.0	Yes	Yes	Yes	Yes	Yes	No	No
IE 2.0	No	No	No	No	No	No	No
IE 1.0	No	No	No	No	No	No	No
Netscape 7.0	Yes	Yes	Yes	Yes	Yes	Yes	Yes
Netscape 6.1	Yes	Yes	Yes	Yes	Yes	Yes	Yes
Netscape 6.0	Yes	Yes	Yes	Yes	Yes	Yes	Yes
Navigator 4.7	Yes	No	Yes	Yes	Yes	Yes	No
Navigator 4.5	Yes	No	Yes	Yes	Yes	Yes	No
Navigator 3.0	Yes	No	Yes	Yes	No	No	No
Navigator 2.0	Yes	No	Yes	Some	No	No	No
Navigator 1.1	No	No	No	No	No	No	No

TABLE 2-2 *Windows Legacy Browser Comparison Chart* ■

Understanding URLs

Every place you can go on the Web has a global address known as a **Uniform Resource Locator (URL)**. Most often the resources are hypertext documents, but they can also be pictures, sounds, movies, animations, or application software. URLs can also bring up newsgroups, chat rooms, search engines, and real-time audio and video streams.

Elements of a URL

A URL can have several parts, which always appear in this order:

- Protocol
- Server name
- Port number (optional)
- Path/filename (optional)
- Anchor (optional)

Here is what the different parts of a URL mean:

protocol	Protocols include HTTP, FTP, mailto, and news; the Web's protocol is HTTP, which stands for *hypertext transfer protocol*.
server name	The server name is the Internet address of the computer or file server on which the resource resides.
port number	Port numbers rarely appear in URLs, because almost every file server is on the Web's default port, which is port 80.

path/filename	The filename is the name the file has on the server. If the file is in a folder or subfolder on the server, the filename includes the path to the file as well as the name of the file. If a URL that begins with http does not contain a filename, the default filename (usually index.html) gets served.
anchor	The anchor is a named bookmark within an HTML file. Anchors are optional. If a URL does not contain an anchor, the browser begins display at the start of the file.

The following analysis shows how the various parts of a URL get combined into a specific address on the World Wide Web. This example is the URL for the professional experience section of my résumé.

http://www.udel.edu/fth/resume.html#professional

protocol	**http**
server name	**www.udel.edu**
path/filename	**fth/resume.html**
anchor	**professional**

Web Sites

Every hypertext document on the World Wide Web resides on one of the computers connected to the network. The place where the hypertext document is stored on that computer is known as its **Web site**. Every Web site has a URL.

For example, Sony's Web site is http://www.sony.com. CNN's Web site is http://www.cnn.com. Netscape is at http://www.netscape.com. Microsoft is at http://www.microsoft.com. Do you notice the similarity in these corporate Web site addresses? Almost every company in the world has a Web site address in the form of http://www.*company_name*.com.

HTTP is the default protocol for Web pages. It is not necessary to type http:// because the browser assumes this is the protocol and inserts it automatically. Typing www.cnn.com takes you to the same place as typing http://www.cnn.com, for example. You need to type the protocol only if it is not HTTP.

Web Pages

Like books, each site on the Web consists of one or more pages. Each page at a Web site is known as a **Web page**. Unlike the pages in books, however, Web pages can contain more information than you can see at once. Scrollbars let you move the page up and down inside your browser window, which displays the text and graphics on the Web page.

Every Web page has a URL. As mentioned earlier, the URL of my résumé is http://www.udel.edu/fth/resume.html. By analyzing this URL, you can see that this Web page is stored in the *fth* folder (*fth* are my initials) at the University of Delaware's Web site. The filename of the Web page is *resume.html*. The filename extension *html* is the standard format used for documents on the Web. HTML stands for *h*ypertext *m*arkup *l*anguage. You will learn HTML in the Web page authoring tutorial in Part II of this book.

Surfing the Net is a lot more involved than channel surfing television. Instead of just flipping through the relatively limited number of channels available on a TV, surfing the Net enables you to navigate a world full of interconnected information, discover new sites you did not know about, keep track of where you have been so you can easily get there again, and download things that interest you. By practicing the surfing concepts and techniques presented here, you can master the art of navigating the Net so you can get where you want quickly and accomplish your purpose for going there. Even if you consider yourself an accomplished surfer, studying these concepts will probably teach you some new techniques that will make you even more productive in surfing the Net.

Entering URLs

Oftentimes you will have been given a specific URL or Web address that you want to go to. For example, you may have seen an ad for a Sony product that told you to go to the Web site www.sony.com for more information. To go there (or to any other site for which you know the URL), you simply type the URL into your Web browser's address or location field, and press the ENTER key. If your browser's address or location field is not visible, follow these steps to get the URL field onscreen and go to a URL with Microsoft Internet Explorer:

1. Microsoft Internet Explorer calls the URL field the Address field.

2. If the Address field is not visible, pull down the View menu, select Toolbars, and if the Address Bar is not checked, select the Address Bar to display it. If the Address field still is not visible, click your right mouse button on the toolbar and select Address Bar.

3. Click once inside the Address field to position your cursor in it.

4. Type the URL you want to go to. In this example, type **www.sony.com**.

5. Press ENTER.

To activate the URL field so you can type a URL into it, click once inside the URL field to position your cursor there. Erase any URL that might be there currently by dragging your cursor over the URL to select it and then pressing the DELETE key to delete it. Or you can just position your cursor at the end of the URL and backspace over the URL to delete it. Now type **www.sony.com** and press ENTER. Your browser takes you to the Sony site.

Home Pages

Home is a relative concept. For example, a person from London considers England to be home. To fly to Hawaii, that person takes off from London's Heathrow airport. When someone from Los Angeles flies to Hawaii, however, the plane takes off from the Los Angeles airport. So it is on the Web, where your **home page** is your taking-off point. Many people create their own home page, to which they link documents and resources they want people who visit their home page to be able to access. Almost every company has a home page, as do government offices, schools, and colleges. Home pages organize the information at that site and help you access it. If you were considering going to graduate school at Princeton University, for example, you could find out a lot about it by going to their home page at www.princeton.edu.

A huge mass of information is out there on the Net. Other people's home pages help you make sense out of their stuff. Eventually, after you complete the Web page creation tutorial in Part II, your home page will organize your stuff and help other people make sense out of it.

Default Pages

If you go to a Web site without requesting a specific document, you view that site's **default page**. For example, when you went to www.sony.com, you were taken to the default page of the Sony site. The default page is often the home page of the company or person who owns the site. In Chapter 6, you learn how to make your home page function as the default startup page for your Web site.

Links

Links are perhaps the most important surfing concept, because without links, there would be no Web! Links form the pathways that interconnect the documents and resources on the Web. You activate a link by clicking it. There are two kinds of links: hypertext and hypergraphic.

Hypertext Links

A **hypertext link** consists of one or more words that you click to trigger the events that are linked to the text. Hypertext links are also known as **hot words,** because they make things happen when you click them. So you can tell which words are hot, the hypertext links are underlined or printed in a different color than the rest of the text. Usually, links you have not visited are colored blue and visited links dark pink. When you move your cursor over a hypertext link, the cursor shape changes from an arrow to a hand pointer.

You can change the default color of the hot words by modifying your browser's preferences. To change the color of the hypertext links in Netscape Navigator, pull down the Edit menu, choose Preferences, click Colors, and click the color swatches for Visited Links and Unvisited Links. In Microsoft Internet Explorer, pull down the Tools menu, choose Internet Options, click Colors, and click the color swatches for Visited and Unvisited links. Even though you can change the colors, however, it is recommended that you not modify them unless you have a special reason for doing so.

Sometimes the color selections you make have no effect on the colors you see on a Web page. That is because the Web page author may have preset the hypertext links to specific colors that you cannot change. Unless the author has preset the colors on the Web page, the color preferences you choose will take effect.

Hypergraphic Links

note   *In Chapter 8, you learn how to use cascading style sheets to change the appearance of unvisited and visited hyperlinks. Chapter 8 also teaches you how to make the link's appearance change when users move their cursors over the link. When you mouse over a link, you are said to hover over it. The color of a moused-over link is called its hover color.*

Hypergraphic triggers are pictorial hot spots you click to trigger events linked to images on the screen. The images can be little icons or larger graphics.

Well-designed Web pages make it obvious where to click to make different things happen. Poorly designed pages can be confusing if they're not clear what will happen when you trigger a link. In Chapter 5, you will learn how to design Web pages that make it clear what will happen when users trigger a link.

Figure 2-2 shows a Web page with an interesting combination of hypertext and hypergraphic links. Its URL is http://www.loc.gov. Point your browser there (to "point" your browser means to go to the URL) and try triggering the different hypertext and hypergraphic links.

FIGURE 2-2   *Analysis of a Web page with a combination of hypertext and hypergraphic links. When you mouse over these links, notice that your cursor changes shape to indicate that you are hovering on a hot spot.* ■

Image Maps

A graphic may have more than one hot spot; if so, clicking different parts of the graphic triggers different links. Consider the question being asked in Figure 2-3. The user is being asked to click Middle C on a piano keyboard. The image has triggers on the region of the keyboard below C, above C, and on Middle C itself. Depending on where the user clicks, the appropriate feedback is given.

Figure 2-4 maps the triggers in Figure 2-3. The technique used to map multiple triggers onto an image is known as an *image map*. In Chapter 7, you learn how to create image maps.

Image Map   **Where's Middle C?**
Can you find Middle C on the music keyboard below? Click the key that you think is Middle C, and then I'll tell you if your answer is too low, too high, or just right.

Image Map   **Where's Middle C?**
Can you find Middle C on the music keyboard below? Click the key that you think is Middle C, and then I'll tell you if your answer is too low, too high, or just right.

FIGURE 2-3   The student is asked to click Middle C on a music keyboard. ■

FIGURE 2-4   Mapping of the triggers in Figure 2-3. ■

Try This!

Can You Find Middle C on an Image Map?

Now you can have a little fun trying out the Middle C image map illustrated in Figure 2-3. This image map is a little game that teaches users how to find Middle C on a music keyboard. To play the game, follow these steps:

1. Go to www.udel.edu/fth/middle-c. Your browser displays the music keyboard illustrated in Figure 2-3.

2. Try clicking different places on the keyboard, and observe the feedback you get.

3. If you do not know where Middle C is, the feedback will eventually teach you.

4. You can also look up the answer by studying Figure 2-4.

5. In Chapter 7, you learn the HTML codes for creating this kind of an image map. By using these codes, you can create an image map for any conceivable image you would like to present onscreen for users to interact with and make different things happen depending on where the user clicks.

Navigation Buttons

At the top of your browser you should see a row of navigation buttons with names such as Forward, Back, Home, and Stop. Figure 2-5 shows how the buttons appear in Microsoft Internet Explorer.

One of the most useful navigation buttons is the Back button. If you end up someplace you did not want to go, clicking the Back button returns you to the page from which you triggered the ill-chosen link. Conversely, the Forward button moves you ahead to pages you visited earlier in your current browsing session. Right-clicking on Back or Forward pops out a menu that shows the whole path you covered, and you can click a site to jump directly to it.

note *Macintosh users, you trigger the menu on a Mac by holding down CONTROL during the click or by holding down the mouse button until the menu pops out.*

FIGURE 2-5 *Navigation buttons in Microsoft Internet Explorer. If these buttons are not visible, pull down the View menu, choose Toolbars, and select Standard Buttons. If the navigation buttons still do not appear, right-click the toolbar and choose Standard Buttons.* ■

Any time you want to return to your browser's default home page, just click the Home button. If you want to change the Internet Explorer's default home page, follow these steps:

1. Pull down the Tools menu and choose Internet Options.

2. Click the General tab, if it is not already selected.

3. In the Address field, type the URL of your desired home page.

4. Click OK to close the dialog.

Manipulating URLs

You can play some tricks with URLs to help find information. For example, suppose you have been told to go to the URL http://www.microsoft.com/windows/ie/enthusiast/default.asp for a list of tips to help you learn more about the features in Microsoft Internet Explorer. You find the list helpful, and you are curious to see what else is available at this site. By progressively stripping off the subfolder names of the path to the original document you were given, you can go to the higher levels of the Web site and use them as surfing-off points. For example, http://www.microsoft.com/windows/ie/ takes you to a menu of other links related to Microsoft Internet Explorer. Stripping off the last part of the URL (i.e., /ie) and trying http://www.microsoft.com/windows/ brings up a list of feature articles related to Windows technologies. Going all the way back to http://www.microsoft.com takes you to the Microsoft default page.

Stripping off parts of the URL in this manner normally brings you to the home page of the Web site where the page is hosted. Taking a look at the hosting site's home page reveals the source of the information, which can help you judge how reliable the information is. Remember that anyone can publish pages to the Web. If you discover that one page about airplanes, for example, came from the Smithsonian's air and space museum and another page came from a four-year-old child learning how to build paper airplanes, you would consider the page from the Smithsonian to have greater authority. Going to the source of the information can also help you find related information available at the site and correct errors in the URL if the original file could not be found.

Manipulating the URL Field

Try This!

You can easily manipulate URLs by using your browser's Address field. If your browser's Address field is not visible, pull down the View menu and select Toolbars; if the Address Bar is not checked, select the Address Bar to display it. Click once inside the Address field to position your cursor there and erase anything that already appears in the field. Then type the URL **http://www.loc.gov/exhibits/flw/flw03.html** and press ENTER to go there. Next complete the following steps, which will help you learn how to manipulate a URL:

1. Position your cursor at the end of the Address field and use the backspace key to erase the last part of the URL, which is /flw03.html. Press ENTER. Your Web browser displays the Web page of the manipulated URL.

2. Once again, position your cursor at the end of the Address field and use the backspace key to erase the last part of the URL, which is /flw. Press ENTER to go to the manipulated URL.

3. Repeat this process for each part of the URL until all you have in the Address field is http://www.loc.gov—this is the URL of the Library of Congress Web server. LOC stands for Library of Congress.

Bookmarking Favorite Sites

Web browsers have built-in support for bookmarks, which make it quick and easy for you to take note of your favorite Web pages and return to them later on. In a Web browser, a **bookmark** is a pointer to a Web page that enables you to jump directly to that page, without having to navigate the Web to get there.

As you surf the Net and become familiar with the wealth of resources available, you will begin to favor certain sites over others. To save time getting to your favorite sites, you can bookmark them. To bookmark a site on the Web, simply pull down the Favorites menu and click Add to Favorites. To jump to any site you bookmarked, pull down the Favorites menu and select the bookmark you want. Your browser will take you to the bookmarked Web page.

Bookmark Folders

You can organize your bookmarks in folders. This is recommended if you have a lot of bookmarks so you can organize them according to topics. You might make a folder called SearchEngines, for example, to hold bookmarks to your favorite search engines. Similarly, you might create a folder called Shopping in which you bookmark your favorite shopping sites. To create a bookmark folder, follow these steps:

1. Pull down the Favorites menu and choose Add to Favorites; the Add Favorite dialog appears.

2. Click the Create In button to expand the dialog to appear as shown here.

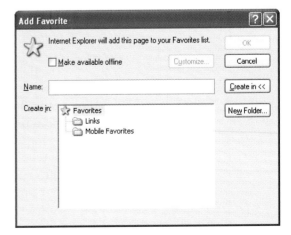

3. Click the New Folder button to make the Create New Folder dialog appear.

4. In the Folder Name field, type the name you want the new folder to have.

5. Click OK to close the Create New Folder dialog, and click OK to close the Add Favorite dialog.

6. To bookmark a Web site in a folder, pull down the Favorites menu, choose Add to Favorites, click Create In, select the desired folder, and click OK.

Importing and Exporting Bookmarked Favorites

Bookmarked favorites are so important that the browser has a built-in mechanism for importing and exporting them. Suppose you just bought a new computer. Its browser will not have any knowledge of the bookmarked favorites on your old computer. You can use the export/import mechanism to move your bookmarks from your old browser to your new computer's browser. Another situation in which you need to be able to export bookmarks is when you want to share your bookmarks with other users, such as at home, at school, or in your workplace. At the end of this chapter, Lab Project 2-2 gives you practice exporting bookmarks.

Retracing Your Steps: The History Folder

The IE browser remembers your most recently visited sites and makes it possible for you to jump back to a previous site without having to press the Back button repeatedly to back through the sites one by one. To jump back to a site you previously visited, follow these steps:

1. Click the History button; a History pane opens up to provide a visual display of the sites you visited.

2. Click a category in the history to expand it, and then click a Web site to go there.

3. If you want to hide the history, click the X in the upper-right corner of the History pane to close it.

Auto Completion

The IE browser has a feature called *Auto Completion*. If you begin typing into the browser's URL field the address of a Web site you visited previously, the browser auto-completes the entry to save you time. If you do not mean to go exactly to the address that gets auto-completed, just keep on typing, and the auto-completed address adjusts to what you type.

When you begin typing a Web address you visited previously, IE pops out a menu of similar addresses you visited. If you see the address you want in the menu, just click the address to go to it.

Try This!

Creating More Screen Space

No matter how large your computer screen is, you will sometimes wish it were larger so more information would fit into it. You can increase the viewing area of your Web browser by turning off some of the options that make your browser use extra screen space. For example, turning off the display of the URL field saves a little screen space and increases the viewing area inside the browser. Turning off the navigation buttons frees even more screen space. You can still navigate by using your browser's shortcut navigation keys, or you can turn the navigation buttons back on again when you want them to reappear. To create more screen space with the IE browser, follow these steps:

1. Pull down the View menu, choose Toolbars, and see if the Standard Buttons option is checked; if so, click Standard Buttons to turn the buttons off.

2. Pull down the View menu, choose Toolbars, and see if the Address Bar option is checked; if so, click Address Bar to turn it off.

3. Pull down the View menu and see if the Status Bar option is checked; if so, click Status Bar to turn it off.

4. To turn the toolbars back on, pull down the View menu, select Toolbars, and click the toolbars to turn them back on.

5. To turn the status bar back on, pull down the View menu and select Status Bar.

6. Another way to create more screen space is to click the IE browser's full-screen button, which is the F11 function key. To return to normal view, press F11 again. This full-screen option is also found on the View menu.

Managing Your Web Browser's Cache

When you surf the Web, your browser keeps copies of the most recently visited Web sites in a place on your hard disk called the **cache** (pronounced *cash*). As you navigate back and forth around the Web and revisit one of the sites in the cache, your browser checks to see if the timestamp on the Web site has changed since your local copy was cached. If the site has not changed, the browser redisplays the site from the cache instead of downloading it again. Thus the cache speeds your use of the Web and reduces traffic on the Net.

If you want to increase the number of pages your cache can hold, you can change the size and location of the browser's cache. You can also purge (i.e., delete) the cache, which you might want to do if you have been reading sensitive information that you would not want someone else using your computer to find. Purging the cache can also fix problems when Web pages do not work properly, especially Web pages with Java, for which purging the cache causes the Java to reload. To manipulate your cache in the IE browser, follow these steps:

1. Pull down the Tools menu and choose Internet Options; the Internet Options dialog appears.

2. If the General tab is not already selected, click the General tab.

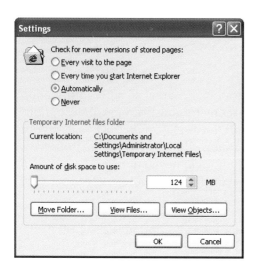

3. The Temporary Internet Files group contains your cache controls. Click the Settings button to make the cache settings appear, as shown to the left.

4. You can change the amount of your hard disk that is used for the cache by dragging the slider. Do not change this unless you're sure you want to modify this setting; most users never need to change this.

5. To move the cache to a different folder, click the Move Folder button. Do not do this unless you know what you are doing. Most users never need to change the location of the cache.

6. To view the contents of your cache, click the View Files button. This opens a file window, which you can close when you are done viewing the file window's contents.

7. Click OK to close the Settings dialog.

8. To purge the cache, click the Delete Files button in the Temporary Internet Files group.

9. Click OK to close the Internet Options dialog.

Advanced Browser Settings

IE comes with scads of settings that let you adjust all kinds of things. Earlier in this chapter, for example, you learned how to set the home page and change the browser's cache settings. Here, we take a look at advanced settings that affect how the browser works behind the scenes.

To reveal the advanced settings, you pull down the Tools menu and choose Internet Options. When the Internet Options dialog appears, you click the Advanced tab to reveal the advanced options. There are so many advanced options that you will see a scrollbar that you can move down and up to reveal all the settings. Some of the settings are self-explanatory. The setting that says "Automatically check for Internet Explorer updates," for example, is self-explanatory. If you check it, the browser will automatically check to see if newer versions or security patches are available. If you do not check this option, you'll need to run Windows Update to check for updates. You can run Windows Update by pulling down the Tools menu and choosing Windows Update.

Some of the other options will not make as much sense until you complete the later chapters in this book. In the Accessibility section of the browser settings, for example, the option to always expand ALT text will not make sense unless you know what the ALT tag does. In Chapter 9, "Making Web Pages Accessible," you will learn that the ALT tag creates alternate text, which is an accessibility feature that does not otherwise appear unless the user mouses over the image that has alternate text. Chapter 9 teaches how to create alternate text and experience how it works onscreen.

Many of the advanced options are there for security reasons, to help protect you from downloading viruses, worms, Trojans, or other kinds of Internet attacks. The option to warn about invalid site certificates, for example, is a setting you will want to leave on. You will learn about certificates and other advanced security settings in Part III, Networking Fundamentals.

Resetting the Browser Settings

Should a situation arise in which you want to reset the browser to its factory settings, IE has a feature built right in to handle this. Follow these steps:

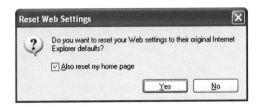

1. Pull down the Tools menu and click Reset Web Settings.

2. The Reset Web Settings dialog appears as shown here.

3. If you do not want to reset the home page, click the box to unselect the option that resets your home page.

4. Click Yes to reset the browser settings, or click No if you decided not to do it.

Wireless Web Browsing and the Wireless Application Protocol (WAP)

The **Wireless Application Protocol (WAP)** was invented to provide mobile telephone users with a way of accessing the Internet by routing requests through a WAP server that translates Web pages into a format appropriate for display on mobile phones. Depending on the capabilities of the phone being used, the WAP server may strip off the graphics and send to the phone only the textual portions of the Web page. The text is formatted according to the rules of a markup language called WML, which stands for **Wireless Markup Language**.

As this book goes to press, mobile phones are coming out with multimedia capabilities that will diminish the need for a WAP server. As the phone takes on more of the capabilities of a personal computer, the need for translating the Internet's TCP/IP signal into a specially formatted WAP signal will diminish. To learn more about the evolving mobile Internet technologies, go to www.openmobilealliance.org. To see how a Web site will appear when viewed on a mobile phone via WAP, go to www.gelon.net and use the Wapalizer. Type in the URL you want to view, and then click the Wapalize button to see how the site will appear on the phone.

Handling Multimedia Objects, Plug-ins, and Viewers

As defined in my *Multimedia Literacy* textbook, "**multimedia** is the use of a computer to present and combine text, graphics, audio, and video with links and tools that let the user navigate, interact, create, and communicate" (Hofstetter, 2001:2). More simply stated, multimedia brings the Web to life with stereo sound, colorful movies, and alluring animations. To hear the sound or see the video on a Web page, your Web browser must be configured to handle the multimedia resource contained on the Web page. Multimedia is an emerging technology that is undergoing a lot of research and development. As a result of this research, there are a lot of different ways to do multimedia.

Web browsers use a clever approach to handling this diversity. First, the browsers have built-in support for the most common kinds of multimedia.

You do not need to do anything special to get these to work as long as you have a multimedia computer that is capable of making sound and showing movies. Second, multimedia companies make plug-ins and add-ins that install inside the browser to play their company's brand of multimedia files. Third, some browsers enable you to define so-called helper apps that the browser launches to handle other kinds of multimedia files.

This chapter shows you how to do all three kinds of multimedia browsing. You will learn how to use built-in support and define helpers for file types that are not built in. You can go to this book's Web site to download the most popular plug-ins and add-ins for handling proprietary multimedia file types. Then you will be ready to visit some of the hottest multimedia Web sites in the world.

Built-In Browser Support for Multimedia

The first browsers had no support for multimedia built in. Everything had to be handled through a so-called **helper app**, an application the browser launches to help it handle something for which a player is not built in. Today, the trend is for browsers to contain built-in support for the most common multimedia file types.

Audio Controls

Internet Explorer comes preset to play audio through the Windows Media Player shown in Figure 2-6. If you want to install the latest version, go to www.microsoft.com/windows/windowsmedia and follow the link to download Windows Media Player. To find out whether your browser is configured to use the Windows Media Player, you can simply browse to some audio to find out what application launches to play it. On this book's Web site, you'll find an example of an audio file you can play. It is a waveform audio file of me greeting you. To hear this greeting, go to Chapter 2 of the Web site and click the link to my audio greeting. If the Windows Media Player is configured to play your audio, you will get controls like those displayed in Figure 2-6. Another popular player is Apple QuickTime. If your browser is configured to play audio via Apple QuickTime, the controls will appear as illustrated in Figure 2-7.

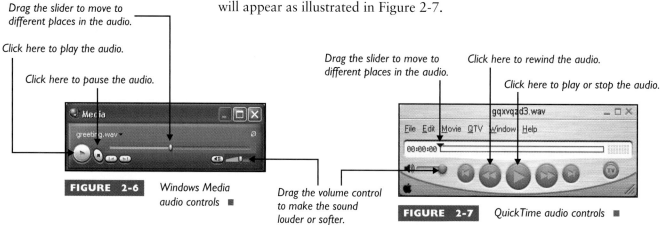

Drag the slider to move to different places in the audio.

Click here to play the audio.

Click here to pause the audio.

FIGURE 2-6   *Windows Media audio controls* ■

Drag the slider to move to different places in the audio.

Click here to rewind the audio.

Click here to play or stop the audio.

Drag the volume control to make the sound louder or softer.

FIGURE 2-7   *QuickTime audio controls* ■

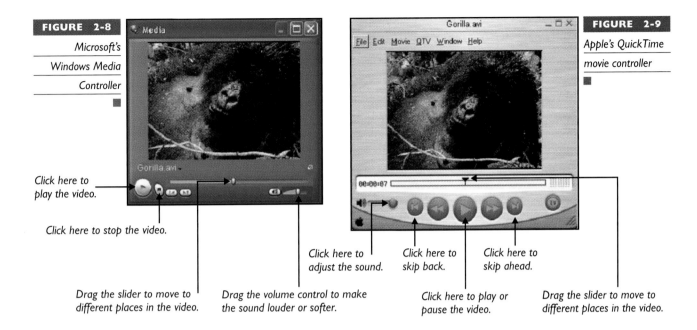

FIGURE 2-8

Microsoft's Windows Media Controller

FIGURE 2-9

Apple's QuickTime movie controller

Click here to play the video.

Click here to stop the video.

Drag the slider to move to different places in the video.

Drag the volume control to make the sound louder or softer.

Click here to adjust the sound.

Click here to skip back.

Click here to skip ahead.

Click here to play or pause the video.

Drag the slider to move to different places in the video.

Video Controls

The IE browser is preset to play video by the Windows Media Player, illustrated in Figure 2-8. Another popular video player is QuickTime for Windows, shown in Figure 2-9. The next part of this chapter teaches you how to configure the IE browser on Windows computers to play the video via QuickTime for Windows, should you wish to do so. You can download the latest version from www.apple.com/quicktime.

Step-by-Step 2-1

Windows Filename Associations for Internet Explorer

In the Windows operating system, Microsoft Internet Explorer uses the Windows filename associations to determine what application will be used to handle different multimedia file types. When you trigger the playing of a multimedia file, your browser looks to see what application is associated with that type of file on your computer, and the associated app then plays the file. If you want to inspect or change the filename associations on your computer, you can do so with the Windows Explorer. Follow these steps:

Step 1   Get the Windows Explorer running, pull down the Tools menu, and choose Folder Options.

Step 2   Click the File Types tab, scroll the list to find the filename whose association you want to see, and click once on the filename to select it. Figure 2-10 shows the setting for an MPEG movie file.

Step 3   To change the filename association, click the Change button; the Open With dialog appears.

Step 4 In the Open With dialog, click one of the recommended programs or click the Browse button to choose a different program.

Step 5 Make your changes, and then click OK. Do not make any changes, however, unless you are sure the program you are choosing can handle this type of file properly. In this example, the QuickTime player would be a reasonable choice if you want MPEG movies to play in QuickTime instead of in Microsoft Media Player.

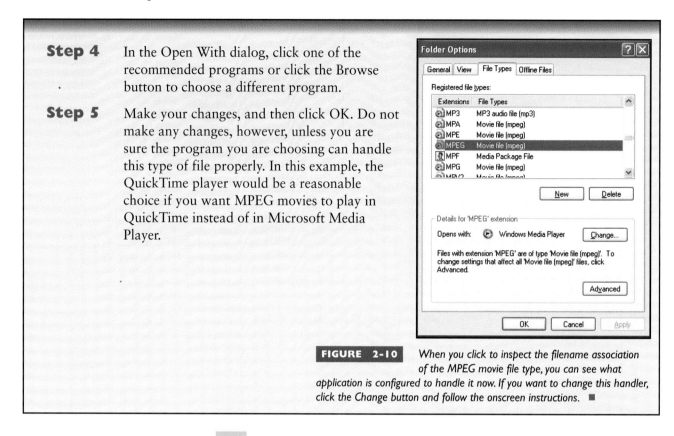

FIGURE 2-10 *When you click to inspect the filename association of the MPEG movie file type, you can see what application is configured to handle it now. If you want to change this handler, click the Change button and follow the onscreen instructions.* ■

Streaming Media

As you learned in Chapter 1, the process of digitalization is changing the world by converging the world's communications media into a digital data stream that can be delivered over the Internet. No matter what you want to say, and no matter how you want to say it—text, speech, graphics, animations, music, video—it can all be digitized and published to the Web. When a user clicks to access your content, it gets delivered over the Internet to the user's Web browser.

When content gets digitized, however, some of the media create larger data files than others. Consider this paragraph, for example. If you type it into a word processor, this paragraph takes up 989 bytes of file space. That is a relatively small amount of data that can be transmitted over the Internet very quickly. Because it is a small amount of data, we say it is low bandwidth, meaning not much time or space is needed to send it over the Web. When the user clicks to see the paragraph, the text appears very quickly. If you read this paragraph aloud and record it with your computer's microphone, on the other hand, the resulting audio file is many times larger. It has higher bandwidth, and it takes longer to transmit over the Internet. Add a webcam to record video while you speak into the microphone, and the file becomes very large. Its bandwidth is now so high that the user may lose interest while waiting for the video to arrive and the content to start playing.

Streaming was invented to avoid this kind of delay. Multimedia content creators are using streaming to deliver high-bandwidth media quickly and efficiently over the Internet. This enables you to visit Web sites where audio and video recordings are standing by, ready to begin streaming on demand to your computer as soon as you click them. In addition to playing prerecorded streams, you can also visit real-time sites, such as news channels and radio stations that are playing right now, using streaming media to deliver what is happening right now to your desktop.

What Is a Stream?

A **stream** is a real-time feed from an audio or video source, encoded in such a way that the media can begin playing steadily without making users wait for the entire file to download to their computers. Streaming media, therefore, is the simultaneous transfer and display of the sounds and images on the World Wide Web. Streaming media enables users to watch and listen to a movie while it is being sent to their browsers, for example, instead of waiting minutes or hours to download and then play it.

Streaming media can also be used to broadcast real-time events over the Internet. **Webcasting** is the term used to describe the simultaneous broadcast of a live event over the Web. Webcasting software gives you the option to make an archive, which means to save the Webcast in a computer file from which you can replay the broadcast sometime after the event. On the Web, the commercial news sites such as cnn.com, msnbc.com, cbs.com, and abc.com make news archives available. When you click to play an archive, you see the same video as the audience that viewed the stream live.

When this book went to press, the three most popular platforms for streaming media were Apple QuickTime, Microsoft Media Player, and RealNetworks. All three of these products plug in seamlessly to the leading Web browsers.

Plug-ins

A **plug-in** is a software component that adds functionality when installed into an existing computer application. The advantage of plug-ins over helper apps is that the plug-in usually gives you better integration of the media. Plug-ins normally make multimedia play in the browser's window, whereas helper apps often launch a separate window to play the file.

Apple QuickTime

One of Apple Computer's greatest gifts to the world is **QuickTime**, Apple's brand of multimedia. Originally for the Macintosh only, QuickTime is now one of the finest cross-platform tools available for multimedia creation and delivery. It plugs in seamlessly to Microsoft Internet Explorer, and it works on Windows as well as Macintosh computers.

The QuickTime player is free. For a modest fee, you can upgrade the free player to QuickTime Pro, which lets you edit audio and video clips as well as play them. To download either the free player or the more fully featured QuickTime Pro, go to www.apple.com/quicktime.

Microsoft Media Player

Microsoft is aggressively pursuing the market for streaming video and has created its own product line of streaming media servers. The player, which is free, is called the **Microsoft Media Player**. If you have Windows, there is probably a version of the Microsoft Media Player installed on your computer. To find out, click your computer's Start button, select Programs, and look under Accessories or Multimedia for the Microsoft Media Player. To check whether a more recent version is available, go to www.microsoft.com/windows/windowsmedia.

RealNetworks

RealNetworks is one of the best-known multimedia streaming companies on the Internet. Marketed under **RealOne**, which is the RealNetworks brand name, the two main families of products are RealOne Music and RealOne Player. True to its name, RealOne Music provides more than 75,000 songs by top artists plus more than 2,000 radio stations. RealOne Player adds moving pictures to the audio experience. Best of all, the basic player is free. According to RealNetworks, the RealOne Player can play more than 85 percent of the multimedia content on the Web.

The free RealOne Player includes the media player, a music jukebox, and a built-in media browser to play a wide variety of streaming media formats on the Web. The free RealOne Player does not include access to exclusive RealOne channels or programming, premium player features, or RealOne member services.

To start listening or watching live streaming content, go to www.real.com and follow the link to the Real Guide, which connects you to networks and channels that use the RealOne Player. If your computer does not have the RealOne Player installed or if your player is outdated, you will be prompted to install the latest version of the player. There is also a more fully featured version of the player called RealOne Player Plus, for which you pay a small fee to download.

To learn more about RealOne Player and RealOne Player Plus and to download the player of your choice, go to www.real.com and follow the link to free downloads. RealNetworks has proposed that its streaming protocol become an Internet standard. The name of the protocol is Real Time Streaming Protocol (RTSP). If you want the technical background, go to www.ietf.org/rfc/rfc2326.txt.

Flash

Flash is a very popular multimedia plug-in. Distributed by Macromedia, the Flash Player is freely downloadable from www.macromedia.com. According to Macromedia, the Flash Player is installed on more than 97 percent of the Internet's end-user computers. Macromedia Flash is so popular, in fact, that the Flash Player is built right into the latest browsers.

Web designers create Flash applications with a tool called Macromedia Flash MX Professional. Figure 2-11 shows that this tool uses a timeline

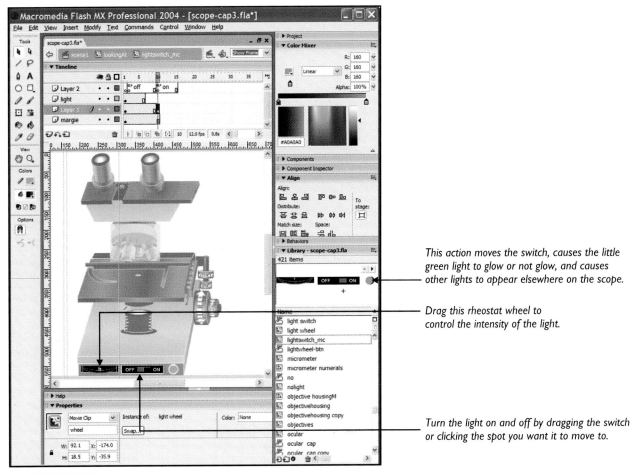

This action moves the switch, causes the little green light to glow or not glow, and causes other lights to appear elsewhere on the scope.

Drag this rheostat wheel to control the intensity of the light.

Turn the light on and off by dragging the switch or clicking the spot you want it to move to.

FIGURE 2-11 *Flash developer Becky Kinney created this light-switch animation for use in a microscope simulation at the University of Delaware. You can run this application by browsing to www.udel.edu/Biology/ketcham/microscope/scope.html. To contact Becky, send e-mail to becky@moonlightmultimedia.org. Her company's Web site has a section devoted to "Flash for Educators" at http://moonlightmultimedia.org/f4e, which offers free tools and templates. ∎*

metaphor. Authors create rich media content by dragging media objects and behaviors onto the timeline. In addition to creating animated slides, movies, and sound tracks, the latest version lets authors import Adobe PDF documents, design Web forms, and use CSS to create a common style for the Flash plug-in and the surrounding Web page.

To experience some examples of award-winning Flash applications, go to www.macromedia.com, click Showcase, and follow the link to the Flash Showcase.

Browser Support for Plug-ins

Both Netscape and Microsoft have special support for plug-ins. If you have Netscape Navigator, you can pull down the Tasks menu and choose About Plug-ins to find out what plug-ins are installed in your browser. Then you follow the links to Netscape's Index of Plug-ins to download other plug-ins you want.

If you have Microsoft Internet Explorer, pull down the Tools menu and choose Windows Update. This takes you to the Windows Update Center, which will take a look around your computer, see what options you have, and give you a list of new items you can add. Especially useful is the notification of new drivers that may be available for devices connected to your computer.

Security Risks

Every user needs to be aware that whenever you download code that executes on your computer, you run the risk of getting a virus that could cause serious problems on your PC. If you are downloading code from reputable vendor sites, such as Microsoft, Apple, and Macromedia, the chance of your getting a virus is highly unlikely. Downloading code from unknown sources, however, could open the door to trouble.

Even if the code you download is virus-free, it could contain back doors and loopholes through which malicious programmers called _crackers_ could send you viruses or cause other problems on your computer. For example, a security hole in one of the major vendor's plug-ins allowed malicious Web page developers to create a movie that could read a user's e-mail messages and upload them to a server, without the user knowing anything about it. Instructions on how to do this were published on the Internet, where any malicious programmer could learn how to do it.

The vendors respond quickly to plug such loopholes by providing fixes called _patches_. To make sure you have the latest patches, check the download center for your brand of Web browser. If you have Microsoft Internet Explorer, for example, pull down the Tools menu and choose Windows Update.

Object Development and Runtime Environments

In computing, an **object** is a software entity that is programmed to perform certain tasks or behave in certain ways depending on the context in which it is used. Objects can be used on Web pages to provide dynamic content. A page that tells you what the current time is, for example, uses a Date object to determine the current date and time to print onscreen. You will learn how to use the Date object in the JavaScript Clock tutorial in Chapter 8. Objects can also be used to display animations onscreen and provide users with controls that can calculate, simulate, and illustrate real-time data onscreen.

Java

Java is an object-oriented programming language invented by Sun Microsystems. Its main advantage over other programming languages is machine independence. Instead of creating code that can run only on a specific machine (such as a Macintosh or a Windows PC), Java creates an intermediate code that can run on any computer that knows how to interpret it. As a result, Java runs under Windows, Macintosh, UNIX, Linux, and many other operating systems, such as the OS9 system used to program set-top boxes for the Internet. Machine independence has made Java one of the hottest languages on the planet. For more information about the Java programming language, go to java.sun.com.

Java Applets

Java can be used to create a little application called an **applet** that can be transmitted over the Internet as part of a Web page. Applets bring Web pages to life in several ways. For example, scrolling tickers can move information across the screen. You can use a mouse to rotate three-dimensional objects that would otherwise appear flat on a static Web page. Active spreadsheets let users manipulate data right on the Web page.

With Java, Web pages can even contain graphics editors that enable users to create their own graphics. Applets can contain games, such as Hangman or Tic-Tac-Toe, or more complex simulations. By following this book's Web site link to the Tokamak Nuclear Reactor, for example, you can run the same nuclear reactor simulation that Princeton University scientists use to determine optimal settings for tokamak fusion reactors. Figure 2-12 shows how the tokamak applet lets you manipulate sliders that control the plasma density, heating power, and magnetic field. By letting you play with these parameters, the applet enables you to develop an intuitive feel for the process scientists go through in designing tokamak reactors. To explore a wide range of Web pages that use Java applets, go to java.sun.com/applets.

JavaScript

Developing applets in Java is time-consuming and requires advanced programming skills. Does this mean Web page programming is beyond the scope of the typical Web page author? No, thanks to **JavaScript**, a client-side object-based programming language that enables you to create dynamic Web pages without having to become a full-fledged Java programmer. JavaScript has become so popular that virtually all browsers support it, including IE, Mozilla, and Safari. Thus, JavaScript has become the best way for nonprogrammers to create dynamic Web pages that will work in the latest versions of the browsers. JavaScript runs differently on different platforms, however, so you need to test any scripts you create with any browsers that will be used to execute them. Chapter 8 steps you through a little tutorial to get you started with JavaScript.

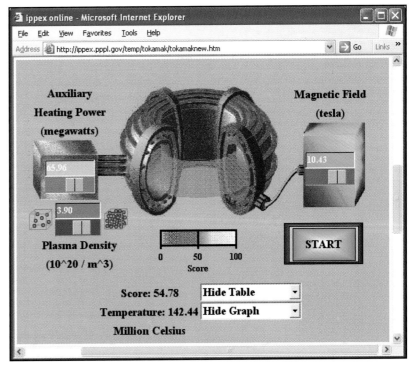

FIGURE 2-12 *A fascinating virtual field trip awaits you at the Internet Plasma Physics Education eXperience (IPPEX) online, where the tokamak nuclear reactor applet lets you manipulate sliders that control the plasma density, heating power, and magnetic field. By dragging the three sliders and clicking the Start button, you can observe the effects different settings have on the reaction onscreen and thereby discover how these parameters interact.* ■

For more information about the origins and applications of JavaScript, follow this book's Web site link to JavaScript Developer Central. There you will find sample code for creating rollovers, graphs, menus, dialogs, calendar pop-ups, and layering effects. Figure 2-13 shows one of the rollover effects you can create with JavaScript. For even more JavaScript resources, go to www.cnet.com and search for JavaScript.

C#

The C# (pronounced C sharp) programming language is the latest in a series of languages that have progressed from the original C through versions called C+ (pronounced C plus) and C++ (C plus plus). The C# language was invented by Microsoft for use in the .NET (pronounced dot net) Framework, the software architecture that underlies the Windows 2003 operating system. You can use the C# language to create native Windows applications as well as Web applications that use the browser window as the display surface.

J#

J# (pronounced J sharp) is Microsoft's version of the Java programming language. Like C#, the J# language was created for the .NET Framework. A development environment called Visual Studio .NET provides programmers with a powerful set of tools for building applications for Microsoft Windows, the Web, and mobile devices. To learn more about Visual Studio .NET, go to msdn.microsoft.com/vstudio.

JScript

True to its name, Microsoft's JScript language is very similar to JavaScript. If you know one, it is easy to learn the other. Where the two languages differ, however, is in where they run. As you learned earlier in this chapter, JavaScript is a client-side language, which means the scripts run in the browser itself. JScript, on the other hand, was invented as a server-side lan-

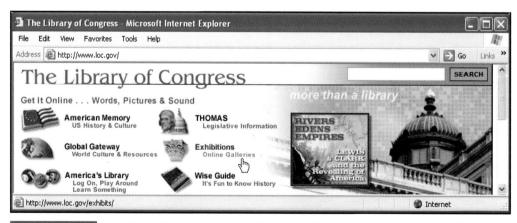

FIGURE 2-13   *A rollover effect created with JavaScript at the Library of Congress. To try this effect, go to www.loc.gov and move your cursor over the menu choices. Notice that the photo on the right changes as you mouse over the choices.* ∎

guage, which means the scripts run on the server. On the server, scripts can access databases and file systems that, primarily for security reasons, are not accessible in JavaScript. JScript began as one of Microsoft's Active Server Page (ASP) languages. There is also an ASP.NET version that is called JScript.NET.

VBScript

Visual Basic (VB) is one of Microsoft's legacy languages. It lives on in the form of VBScript, which is one of the ASP scripting languages, and VBScript.NET, which is the .NET Framework version. You can use VBScript to program virtually anything you can script in JScript, and for that reason, my *Advanced Web Design* textbook splits into columns to show tutorial examples in both JScript and VBScript.

ActiveX

ActiveX was begun by Microsoft as a way to create and distribute information over the Internet, using existing software applications and data. At first, developers were somewhat reluctant to embrace the ActiveX technology because it was not an open standard, as was Java. In 1996, Microsoft released ActiveX to The Open Group, an industry consortium experienced in promoting cross-platform technologies. As a result, ActiveX is widely accepted by Windows developers across the industry today.

ActiveX involves three concepts: controls, scripts, and documents. ActiveX controls enable a wide variety of applications and content to be embedded in HTML documents. Through Microsoft's object linking and embedding technology, you can use ActiveX controls to incorporate any supported data type directly into the window of an ActiveX-enabled Web browser such as the Microsoft Internet Explorer. More than a thousand ActiveX controls are available, from multimedia sound and video players to spreadsheets, charts, graphs, calculators, and paint programs. The Microsoft Internet Explorer itself is an ActiveX control that can be embedded inside other applications. For more information, follow this book's Web site link to ActiveX. To see dozens of controls you can download and use, follow the link to the CNET ActiveX Control Library.

Objects and Security Issues

Because embedded objects cause software to be downloaded to your computer at runtime, you run the risk of downloading viruses, worms, and Trojans. A **virus** is malicious or unwanted code that installs itself on your computer without your knowledge by hiding inside other programmed objects. Viruses are dangerous because they can consume all the memory on your computer, destroy data, and spread across the network to other computers that are connected to yours. A **worm** is a special kind of virus that can replicate itself without hiding inside other objects. A **Trojan** (also called a *Trojan horse*) is a malicious application that masquerades as a desired object that you download knowingly to your computer. When the Trojan executes, it can take over or destroy the data on your computer.

Inside Info

The Story of the Trojan Horse

The term Trojan horse comes from a story in Homer's *Iliad* in which the Greeks gave a giant wooden horse to their enemies, the Trojans, who thought the horse was a peace offering. After the Trojans brought the horse inside their city walls, however, Greek soldiers sneaked out of the horse's hollow belly and opened the city gates, allowing the rest of the Greek army to come in and capture the city of Troy.

The next part of this chapter covers the steps you can take to configure the browser's security settings to minimize the risk of downloading these kinds of attacks.

Configuring Browser Security

Anyone who has been the victim of an Internet attack will understand why browser security is important. Attackers who gain access to your computer can corrupt or destroy data, rendering the computer useless except perhaps as a very expensive paperweight. Over the years, I have been the victim of two attacks so severe that my computer had to be totally reformatted and rebuilt from the ground up. Thankfully, no data was lost, because I have learned to keep backups of all essential data. Everyone reading this book must also form such a religious habit of backing up all data, anything you wouldn't want to lose. Even if you have complete backups, however, you can lose a lot of precious time if you need to rebuild a corrupted system. That is why the browser has built-in ways of helping to safeguard against these kinds of attacks.

Step-by-Step 2-2
Configuring Security Zones

One of the ways the browser helps you safeguard against attacks is by letting you configure different security settings for different zones. On the Internet, a **zone** is a predefined range or selection of Web sites or addresses. The IE browser lets you configure different security settings in four different zones. As illustrated in Figure 2-14, these four zones are called

- **Internet**, which contains all Web sites you haven't placed in other zones

- **Local intranet**, which contains all Web sites on your organization's intranet

- **Trusted sites**, into which you place Web sites you trust not to damage your computer or your data

- **Restricted sites**, into which you place Web sites you believe could cause damage to your computer or your data.

To set the security settings for any one of these zones, follow these steps:

Step 1   Pull down the IE Tools menu, choose Internet Options, and click the Security tab to make the security zones appear, as illustrated in Figure 2-14.

Step 2   Click the name or icon of the zone you want to change.

Step 3   To set the security level to Microsoft's recommended settings, click the Default Level button.

Step 4   To change the security level, move the slider up to make the settings more restrictive or down to make the settings less restrictive. If you move the slider lower than Microsoft recommends, you will get a warning to that effect.

Step 5   When you are in the Local intranet, Trusted sites, or Restricted sites zone, the Sites button is activated. To put specific sites into one of those zones, click the Sites button when you are in that zone and follow the onscreen instructions.

Step 6   If you want to customize the IE security settings, you can do so by clicking the Custom Level button to bring up a detailed list of security settings. To change a setting, click to select the option you want and then click OK to make the changes take effect or click Cancel to ignore the changes.

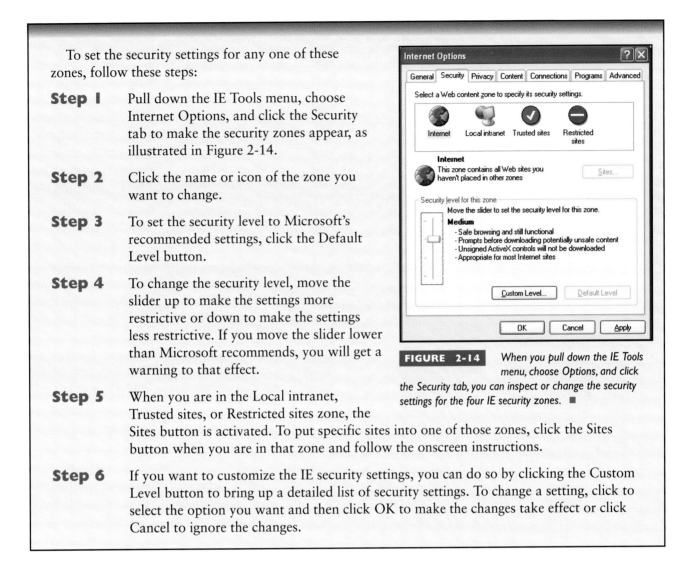

FIGURE 2-14 *When you pull down the IE Tools menu, choose Options, and click the Security tab, you can inspect or change the security settings for the four IE security zones.* ■

Finding Things with Search Engines

The Internet is the richest source of information on the planet. According to Bergman's (2001) white paper on the deep Web, more than 100,000 searchable databases exist, containing nearly 550 billion documents, 95 percent of which are publicly available.

Just about anything you could ever want to know is available online. Especially for students and scholars conducting research, the Internet is a fantastic resource for finding out what has been done in your field.

Although so much information is available online, finding what you want to know is not always easy because knowledge gets organized and stored in different ways. To find what you want, you need to understand how the different kinds of search engines work. Then you will be ready to conduct a search that has a better chance of finding what you seek.

When you research a topic, it is wise to begin by conducting a subject-oriented search of one or more of the Web's directories. This will tell you how much information is available about your topic as a subject that other people have written about. The subject-oriented directories use a combination of human beings and robots called **spiders** that search the Web continually, organizing what is found into a hierarchical directory of topics. When you conduct a subject-oriented search, the search engine searches this directory and provides you with a list of items related to your topic. To retrieve the item, you simply click it.

Step-by-Step 2-3

Searching Yahoo!

As this book goes to press, Yahoo! is the most popular subject-oriented directory. Its Web address is www.yahoo.com. There is also a version for kids at www.yahooligans.com, whose directory indexes materials appropriate for the needs and interests of children. To perform a Yahoo! search, follow these steps:

Step 1   Point your Web browser at www.yahoo.com; the Yahoo! home page appears.

Step 2   If you want to search all of Yahoo!, type your search term(s) into the blank search field and click the Search button.

Step 3   If you want to search within a Yahoo! subject area, scroll down through the subjects listed on the Yahoo! home page, and click the subject area you want—the Yahoo! subject area page appears.

Step 4   If subtopics are listed on the subject area page, scroll down through the subtopics and select the one you want. Repeat this process until you have narrowed the subject area of your search.

Step 5   When you are ready to conduct a search, type your search term(s) into the blank search field.

Step 6   Click the option to search all Yahoo! or just the subject area you have chosen.

Step 7   Click the Search button; Yahoo! performs the search and displays the items that match your search terms.

Step 8   Scroll down through the matches to see what Yahoo! found. All the matches are hot-linked; to see an item, click a highlighted word.

Step 9   If there are more matches to be displayed, you will find "Next 20 matches" printed at the bottom of the search results. Click "Next 20 matches" if you want to see more.

Step 10   By default, Yahoo! combines your search terms with the Boolean AND, which means you will get a match only when all the search terms are found together in an item. If you want a Boolean OR done instead, click the Advanced Search option that you see printed next to the Search button.

Step 11   In addition to letting you perform the Boolean OR option by searching for "any of these words," the advanced options also let you search for an exact phrase. I find this very helpful in troubleshooting technical problems. If some process gives you a cryptic error message, for example, you can use the Yahoo! exact phrase option to search for that reported error. Chances are someone else has already encountered this error and has written on the Internet about how to solve the problem.

Keyword Searching

Like subject-oriented directories, keyword search engines have spiders that are constantly combing the Web and feeding information into a database. Instead of organizing the Web according to subject areas, however, keyword search engines let you search for keywords in documents, regardless of the subject of the documents. Therefore, keyword search engines are likely to find more than subject-oriented searches, but what is found may not be as relevant to your subject.

AltaVista

The AltaVista search engine was invented by the Digital Equipment Corporation as the Web's first full-text keyword search engine. Now a freestanding company, AltaVista's Web address is www.altavista.com. AltaVista has been awarded more search-related patents than any other company. According to Digital, AltaVista is the fastest search service available (0.4–0.5 seconds average response time), with the most up-to-date content (refreshed every 28 days). When this book went to press, AltaVista's index included 350 million Web pages.

Because you are likely to get thousands of hits when you search AltaVista for a keyword, AltaVista sorts the hits according to the relevance or level of importance of the information found. This is done through statistical analysis that organizes pages with similar content into groups.

While conducting searches at the AltaVista site, you may notice that the commercial ads that appear onscreen often relate to your keywords. This is done by matching the content of the ads to the concept analysis of your keywords. This kind of concept mapping is used at many commercial search sites. Advertisers pay to have their ads come onscreen when someone conducts a search in the product's concept area.

Advanced Boolean Searching

Boolean logic is named after the nineteenth-century mathematician George Boole, who invented a form of algebra in which all values reduce to either TRUE or FALSE. The Boolean operators AND, OR, and NOT are widely used in computer programming and in search engines to construct queries that narrow a search to find precisely what you are looking for. The simplest form of a Boolean query uses AND to find things that contain two items that must be found together in the same document, such as

> hot AND cold

Such a search will find fewer documents than the following search, which is less exclusive:

> hot OR cold

The opposite of that search is

> hot AND NOT cold

More complex searches can be done by using parentheses to create more complex queries:

> sunny AND NOT (hot OR cold)

To search for exact phrases, you can use quotation marks, as in

> sunny AND NOT ("too hot" or "too cold")

Try This!

Conducting a Boolean Search

Learning how to conduct a Boolean search will make you very powerful because the Boolean logic enables you to narrow your search down to find just what you are looking for. The best way to learn to do a Boolean search is to simply try one. Follow these steps:

1. Browse to www.altavista.com; the AltaVista home page appears.
2. Click the Advanced Search option to make the advanced search screen appear.
3. Click the option to search with a Boolean expression.
4. In the Boolean Expression field, type:
   "Martin Luther"
   Be sure to type the quote signs, which force the search engine to look for the words *Martin* and *Luther* appearing next to each other. Click the Find button, and make note of the number of hits you get.
5. In the Boolean Expression field, type:
   "Martin Luther" AND NOT "Martin Luther King"
   Click the Find button, and make note of the number of hits you get. Can you explain why you get fewer hits than when you searched for "Martin Luther" by itself?
6. In the Boolean Expression field, type:
   "Martin Luther King" AND ("I Have a Dream" OR "Letter from a Birmingham Jail")
   Click the Find button. Notice that this search finds documents mentioning Martin Luther King and either his famous *I Have a Dream* speech or his *Letter from a Birmingham Jail*.
7. Almost anything in the world you want to know is retrievable once you develop skill at using the advanced search syntax. For more information about advanced searching, click the AltaVista Help option and follow the link to free-form Boolean queries using special search terms.

Concept Searching

Some users are better at keyword searching than others. Finding the right combination of keywords and logical operators (AND, OR, NOT) to get a search engine to find the kind of information you seek can be time-consuming and tedious. Concept-oriented search engines can help users who have difficulty with keyword searching.

Excite

Excite is a concept-based search engine that you will find at www.excite.com. It uses a search technology called Excite Precision Search to analyze more than 250 million Web pages in the Excite search index. Evaluations of link authority and Web page popularity combine with text indexing, semantic matching, and link analysis to select the most relevant and popular Web pages that match your search query.

But Excite is much more than a search engine. It also provides customizable newsfeeds and stock reports, shopping and weather, live chats and bookmarks. Quick Tools include a personal address book, a calendar, horoscopes, maps/directions, and yellow pages. Excite also offers a free start page that includes e-mail, clubs, chat, and your own personal portfolio. Perhaps even more than being a search engine, Excite wants to become your personal portal to the Internet. To check out its wide range of Internet services, go to www.excite.com.

Google

The Google search engine adds a new twist to searching by using an automated method that ranks relevant Web sites based on the link structure of the Internet itself. When you conduct a search, Google sorts the results in order of importance, based on how the site is linked to and referred to by other sites. The assumption is that the more a site is linked, the more of an authority it is. Google certainly takes a lot of Web pages into consideration; when this book went to press, Google indexed more than three billion Web pages. To search them, go to www.google.com.

Metasearching

By now you may be getting overwhelmed by the number of search engines and the subtle distinctions in how they work. **Metasearching** provides an alternative to trying many individual search engines to find the information you seek. Metasearching is the searching of searching, which you perform with a metasearch engine that invokes the other search engines automatically. Behind the scenes, the metasearch engine conducts different kinds of searches for you, collates the results into one list of hits, and reports back to you.

MetaCrawler

MetaCrawler conducts searches by sending your queries to several Web search engines, including AltaVista, FindWhat, Yahoo!, Ask Jeeves, LookSmart, Google, About, and Overture. MetaCrawler organizes the results into a uniform format and displays them in the order of the combined confidence scores given to each reference by the services that return it. You also have the option of scoring the hits, enabling what is found to be sorted in a number of different ways, such as by date, locale, and organization. MetaCrawler supports the advanced search syntax explained in the section on Boolean searching. MetaCrawler is on the Web at www.metacrawler.com.

Dogpile

Research attorney Aaron Flin created Dogpile when he became frustrated with finding too few results with subject-oriented directories such as Yahoo!, and then trying keyword search engines such as AltaVista that returned 30,000 or more documents in response to the same query. Dogpile is a metasearch engine that sends your Web queries to the Internet's top search engines, including Google, Yahoo!, AltaVista, Ask Jeeves, About, FAST, FindWhat, and LookSmart. Dogpile also searches FTP sites, newsfeeds, yellow pages, white pages, classifieds, auctions, audio, and image files. You can find Dogpile on the Web at www.dogpile.com.

CNET Search.com

CNET's Search.com is a metasearch engine that searches more than 800 engines, including Yahoo!, AltaVista, Magellan, Lycos, Inktomi, Direct Hit, and Snap. A special feature is the channel, which lets you customize the search engines used to look for information in different content areas. Channels include categories such as automotive, business, computing, entertainment, government, music, people, shopping, and travel. To search these channels and more, go to www.search.com.

Human-based Searching

When you do not have time to wade through the tens of thousands of documents that a keyword search engine can return in response to a search, you may wish to consider using a human-based search service. A person skilled in searching published information sources, proprietary databases, and the Internet will find an answer and e-mail you the results.

Ask An Expert

Pitsco's Ask An Expert site is a free searching service that connects you to hundreds of real-world experts, ranging from astronauts to zookeepers. You can ask questions in 14 different categories, including Science/Technology, Animals, Education, Career/Industry, Health, Internet/Computer, Recreation/Entertainment, International/Cultural, Resources, Money/Business, Arts/Humanities, Law, Home Improvement, and Repair/Trades.

The answers come to you from real-world experts who have volunteered to answer your questions. The Ask An Expert site is on the Web at www.askanexpert.com.

Scholarly Searching

One of the problems with searching for information on the Internet is that the Web is a public resource. Anyone can create a Web page about any topic, regardless of how much (or how little) the Web page author knows about the subject. When you use a search engine such as AltaVista to find information about that topic, the results contain a mix of pages written by people who know a lot about what they are talking about along with people who may not know much and may even write misleading or false information.

One way of filtering out the bad information is to use a search engine that restricts itself to scholarly information that has been published in refereed journals.

ERIC

ERIC stands for Educational Resources Information Center. The ERIC database includes more than a million abstracts of articles from education journals and other scholarly documents, including books, conference proceedings, symposia, studies, and tests. Figure 2-15 illustrates accessing ERIC at www.eric.ed.gov, where you can search the database by keyword, author, title, or topic. If you are unsure of your topic, you can use the ERIC thesaurus to select a topic.

About.com

Formerly known as The Mining Company, About.com takes a unique approach to providing access to scholarly sources. It hires real scholars to serve as guides in more than 700 subject areas. (I was invited to be the educational technology guide, for example, but had to decline due to other writing commitments, such as this book.) The guides at About.com organize the links, keep them updated, write new articles, host discussions and chats, and answer questions online. To find out more and to search your subject area, go to www.about.com.

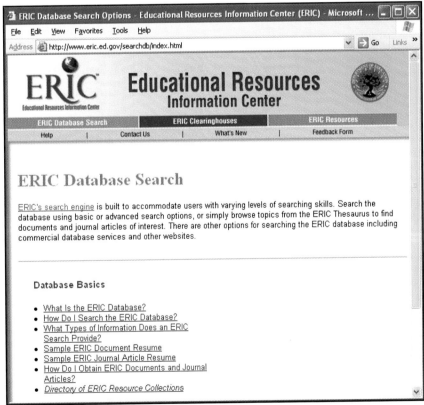

FIGURE 2-15 *The ERIC database at www.eric.ed.gov lets you freely search the world's largest source of educational information, which contains more than a million abstracts of journal articles and education documents.* ∎

Britannica.com

Britannica.com is a Web-based knowledge and learning center that includes the complete, online version of the *Encyclopaedia Britannica*. The obvious advantage of the online version is that you have access to all the latest information at once, without needing to conduct separate searches through the 32 printed volumes and the annual *Book of the Year*. The online version also includes hundreds of articles not found in the printed encyclopedia, including selected articles from *Newsweek, Discover,* and *The Economist*. There are also thousands of links to Web sites selected by Britannica editors.

To search the *Encyclopaedia Britannica* online, go to www.britannica .com. Although you can search the encyclopedia for free, you must pay a subscription fee to view the full text of encyclopedia articles over the Internet. Free-trial subscriptions are available that permit you to try out the service before you begin paying for it.

XanEdu

XanEdu offers access via the Web to thousands of publications indexed by ProQuest, a global leader in the collection, organization, and distribution of value-added information to researchers, faculty, and students in libraries, government, universities, and schools in more than 160 countries. In addition to providing a search tool for the entire ProQuest database, XanEdu has created a ReSearch Engine for General Studies, Education, and MBA business majors. These three ReSearch Engines provide access to thousands of the world's best newspapers, magazines, and scholarly journals. The education engine keys these materials to education standards and textbooks. A special section on "Teaching as a Profession" helps teachers keep up with the latest news and issues including school reform, labor issues, and certification standards. For more information, visit www.xanedu.com, where you can get a free trial subscription to try out the service.

Multimedia Searches

Multimedia is becoming increasingly popular on the Internet. You can find millions of pictures, audio files, animations, and videos to play on your computer. The challenge is to find the ones you are interested in. Happily, most of the search engines provide ways for you to search for multimedia.

Lycos Multimedia

At the Lycos Web site at www.lycos.com, you can click the multimedia option, or you can go directly to multimedia.lycos.com. After you enter your keywords, select the kind of media you are looking for, and press the Search button, the Lycos search engine returns a list of pictures, movies, streams, or sounds dealing with your topic. You then preview the objects and download the ones you want.

If your intended use of a picture or a sound found on the Internet is not a fair use, you will need to seek copyright permission by contacting the administrator of the Web site where the object was found. Chapter 4 provides detailed information and guidelines regarding the fair use of multimedia.

AltaVista Multimedia

AltaVista has a multimedia section where you can search for images, audio, and video. The audio search includes the popular MP3 audio file format for sharing music over the Internet and downloading it to play on your computer or a portable digital audio device. To perform a multimedia search, go to www.altavista.com. Depending on what you are looking for, click either Images, MP3/Audio, or Video.

With the Images search, you can look for photos, graphics, or buttons and banners, either in color or in black and white. The audio search lets you specify whether you want MP3, WAV, Windows Media, or Real audio, lasting for more or less than a minute. The video search finds movies lasting more or less than a minute in AVI, MPEG, QuickTime, Windows Media, or Real video formats. You learn more about these file formats in the last part of this chapter, which covers the types of files you are likely to find when downloading from the Internet.

Singingfish

Singingfish specializes in the development and delivery of search engines that can find streaming media content on the Web. Included is access to music, news, movies, sports, TV, radio, finance, and live events. Singingfish is a wholly owned subsidiary of Thomson multimedia. To check out their services, or to conduct a multimedia search, go to www.singingfish.com.

Newsgroup Searches

Newsgroups are a rich source of information about current research in progress. Most disciplines have active newsgroups where current research topics are discussed. Some of the keyword-oriented search engines discussed earlier in this chapter have options for searching newsgroups as well as Web pages. AltaVista, Dogpile, Excite, Google, InfoSeek, and Yahoo! all provide a newsgroup search option.

At groups.google.com, for example, you can perform keyword searches of information written in more than 700 million USENET messages over the past twenty years. The search terms can include the names of the people who wrote the messages. You can also search only on a name, to get an index of all the topics and messages a given person may have written in a newsgroup.

Some users have expressed surprise upon learning that users can now search through newsgroups and find out what has been written by specific people about specific topics. Some consider this to be a retroactive invasion of privacy. If you want to prevent messages you write in newsgroups from being visible to search engines, you must set the x-no-archive flag when you write the message. You can set this flag by making the first line in the body of your message read as follows:

```
x-no-archive: yes
```

File Searches

As you learned in Chapter 1, FTP stands for File Transfer Protocol. There are millions of files you can download to your computer from FTP sites all over the Internet. Many of these files are Web pages you can find with the Web-based search engines discussed earlier in this chapter. Some files, however, are not in Web page format. To find these other kinds of files, you need to use a search engine that can do FTP file searches.

Archie

Archie is a search tool for FTP servers. It was written by the Archie Group (Peter Deutsch, Alan Emtage, Bill Heelan, and Mike Parker) at McGill University in Montreal, Canada. The name Archie is easy to remember because it is very close to the word *archive*, which refers to the collection of files in the FTP database. The Archie program searches the names of the files in this archive, which consists of the millions of files that are available on anonymous FTP sites.

You can search the Archie database in two ways. You can either telnet to a server that hosts the Archie program, or you can use an ArchiePlex, which is a Web page that provides Web access to the Archie search engine. **Telnet** is a network service that enables you to log on remotely to other networks on the Internet. You will learn how to use telnet in Chapter 3.

Archie is a legacy tool that is waning in popularity as many other Internet search engines have acquired more efficient ways of helping you find the files you want. When this book went to press, there was a working ArchiePlex at www.usgs.gov/Mosaic/cgi-bin/archie.html. To find others, search Google or Yahoo! for ArchiePlex. To learn about the current status of FTP searches, go to www.ftpsearchengines.com.

Gopher, Veronica, and Jughead

Another legacy tool on the Internet is **Gopher**, a protocol for organizing information hierarchically on the Internet. Gopher was the rage in the early 1990s, prior to the release of the graphical Web browser. Gopher was invented in 1991 at the University of Minnesota, home of the Golden Gophers. Its function on the Internet is to help you "go fer" things; thus, the term Gopher is a play on words. Some related tools are Veronica, a search tool for finding Gopher files, and Jughead, which added keyword search and Boolean operator capabilities to Gopher search. Veronica was Archie's girlfriend in the classic Jughead comic strip. As an acronym, Veronica stands for Very Easy Rodent-Oriented Net-wide Index to Computerized Archives, and Jughead stands for Jonzy's Universal Gopher Hierarchy Excavation and Display.

Although the Gopher is used little in actual practice today, it earned its place in history as one of the first killer applications on the Internet. Although most people who used the Internet in the early 1990s used the Gopher, hardly anyone uses it today. To find out about its current status, go to www.searchenginewatch.com and search for Gopher.

Download.com

CNET's Download.com is a handy site for finding and downloading useful files to your computer. The file categories include MP3/audio, business/finance, desktop enhancements, development tools, games, Internet, multimedia/design, Web authoring, utilities, and drivers. The menus make it easy to drill down to the file you want to download. There are in-depth reviews and spotlight articles highlighting featured downloads of the day. To peruse the latest list of downloads, go to download.com.

How to Find People

In addition to helping you find Web pages, newsgroups, files, and scholarly documents, the Internet can also help you locate people.

Bigfoot

Located at www.bigfoot.com, Bigfoot offers a huge catalog of e-mail addresses and white page directories. These catalogs enable you to search for someone's e-mail address or white-page street address.

WhoWhere

WhoWhere lets you look up e-mail addresses, residential listings, toll-free 800 numbers, and millions of businesses, including maps and directions. Now that WhoWhere has become part of the Lycos network, you will find WhoWhere at www.whowhere.lycos.com.

Switchboard

You can use the Switchboard white pages service to find people and businesses. It handles more than 5 million lookups for people and businesses each week. You can find Switchboard at www.switchboard.com.

People.yahoo.com

There is a free online white pages search and listing service at people.yahoo .com. You can search by the person's name, city, or state to find out the person's e-mail address or street address. You can also search thousands of public databases with one click to find addresses, property records, licenses, and court records.

Finding Places

Have you ever gotten lost when driving somewhere? Have you encountered road closings or construction delays that you wish you had known about in advance? The next time you plan a trip, treat yourself by getting a map and a list of specific driving instructions before you take to the roads.

MapQuest

You can visit the most popular interactive mapping service on the Web at www.mapquest.com. MapQuest can help you find more than three million locations worldwide, print driving directions, and create and save personalized maps. Live traffic updates are a popular feature that can save you time when roads close or traffic snarls.

As one of the busiest sites on the Internet, MapQuest serves on the average more than 10 million maps per day. MapQuest's tools provide maps and directions tailored to different types of travelers. MapQuest's clients include Yahoo!, Lycos, the National Geographic Society, the American Auto Association, Fodor's, and many yellow page directories. As a personal user of MapQuest, I can attest to the quality and accuracy of its maps and driving instructions. Best of all, MapQuest is free.

Finding Legal Information

If you know where to look, the Web is an excellent source of legal information. By visiting the sites that follow, you will see why the Web has become the legal profession's primary source of news and information.

Law.com

American Lawyer Media (ALM) is one of the leading sources of news and information for the legal industry in the United States. ALM sponsors a Web site at Law.com, where many legal professionals go to get their news. The search engine at Law.com enables you to search the wire services for news about current legal cases. You can also read or search the full text of more than 20 legal publications, including *The National Law Journal*, *The American Lawyer*, *New York Law Journal*, and *Legal Times*. To peruse these and other ALM services, go to www.law.com.

FindLaw

True to its name, the FindLaw site enables you to search for all kinds of legal information. It can also match you up with a lawyer, if you need legal help or advice. FindLaw has channels for legal news, professionals, students, businesses, and the public at large. The search engine enables you to perform keyword searches of the U.S. Constitution, the Supreme Court, government sites, legal sites, the legal news channel, a legal dictionary, and an online library of legal articles. To visit the FindLaw site, go to www.findlaw.com.

LexisONE
....

Sponsored by LexisNexis, the LexisONE Web site brands itself as "The Resource for Small Law Firms." It features a free legal headline news service and provides free keyword searches of the news, case law, and legal forms. To perform these free searches, however, you must first register at the site. To do so, go to www.lexisone.com. To find out about other LexisNexis services, go to www.lexisnexis.com.

Index of Collected Search Engines

Search engines are undergoing a lot of research and development on the Internet. By the time you read this, new search engines will be announced that were not available when this book went to press. You can use Yahoo! to find the latest information about new search engines and what they do. At www.yahoo.com, go to the section on Computers and Internet, and do a search for the keyword *search*.

Another good place to learn about search engines is the Search Engine Watch, where you will find announcements of the latest search services and Web searching tips. Hosted by Internet.com, you will find the Search Engine Watch at searchenginewatch.internet.com.

Adding a Web Site to a Search Engine

In Part II of this book, you learn how to create a Web site and publish it on the Internet. Automatically, spiders will begin finding your site and listing it in selected search indexes. There is no guarantee, however, that your site will be listed by all the search engines. To help ensure that it gets included in a certain index, you can go to the desired search engine site and follow that site's procedure for adding your site to its search engine. Here are some examples:

- **Yahoo!**   At www.yahoo.com, go to the appropriate subject category and click the option to Suggest a Site. You will get an online form to fill out and submit, along with an explanation of how much it will cost to list your site.

- **AltaVista**   At www.altavista.com, near the bottom of the page, click the menu option to Submit a Site. You will get a screen explaining the different listing services. The free service is called Basic Submit; the other services cost money. The amount you spend will depend on the level to which you want AltaVista to promote your site.

- **Lycos**   At www.lycos.com, click Site Submit to bring up the search engine submission screen. Follow the links to learn about the different kinds of site listings and ad services that are available. There is a free site submission option, but you must register to use it.

- **bCentral** There is a Web page listing service at www.bcentral.com called Submit It, where you can submit Web pages to about 400 different search engines and indexes. You pay an annual fee for this listing service. To check it out, go to www.bcentral.com and follow the link to Search Engine Submissions.

Downloading from the Internet

You need to know how to download five basic types of files from the Internet, namely, text, graphics, audio, video, and software. After showing you how to download and handle these files, this chapter concludes by teaching you how to download and unpack a zipped (i.e., compressed) archive, which can contain any combination of these five file types.

Commonly Found Text File Formats

There are three families of text formats: plaintext, hypertext, and word processor files. Plaintext means just that—the text and nothing but the text. Hypertext contains the text intermingled with markup codes called *tags* that determine how the text is to appear and which words in the text serve as triggers that launch things when clicked. Word processors such as Microsoft Word and WordPerfect use proprietary formatting to encode the text and its properties, including font, size, margins, borders, headings, and pagination.

Step-by-Step 2-4
Downloading Text from the Internet

The quickest way to download text from the Internet is to copy the text onto your computer's Clipboard, from which you can paste the text into any other window on your screen. To perform this copy-and-paste method of downloading text from the Internet, follow these steps:

Step 1 Use your browser to display the text you want to download.

Step 2 Drag your mouse to select the text you want to copy; the selected text appears highlighted. Or, if you want to select all the text on the Web page, pull down the browser's Edit menu and choose Select All.

Step 3 Press the Copy keys (CTRL-C on Windows or ⌘-C on a Macintosh) or pull down the Edit menu and choose Copy.

Step 4 If the application into which you want to paste the text is not already running, get it running now.

Step 5 Position your cursor at the spot in the window to which you want to want to paste the text.

Step 6 Press the Paste keys (CTRL-V on Windows or ⌘-V on a Macintosh) or pull down the application's Edit menu and choose Paste.

TXT (Plaintext)

Plaintext files are identified by the filename extension *.txt*. When you see a filename such as *history.txt*, you know it is a plaintext file because of its *.txt* filename extension. In computer jargon, plaintext files are known as *ASCII files*. ASCII (pronounced *askee*) stands for American Standard Code for Information Interchange. Every text editor and word processor has an option for reading and writing files in ASCII format. Sometimes the format is called plaintext or DOS text instead of ASCII text.

Because plaintext files are so common on the Internet, the Web browsers have a built-in ability to display them. To download a copy of a plain-text file you are viewing with a Web browser, simply pull down the browser's File menu, choose Save As, and use the Save controls to save a copy in the plaintext file format.

HTML (Hypertext)

HTML stands for hypertext markup language. Files in HTML format have the filename extension *.html* or *.htm*. HTML is the most prevalent file format on the World Wide Web, because most Web pages are encoded in HTML. True to its name, an HTML file contains the text that gets displayed on a Web page, along with special codes known as *markup* that define (1) how the text should appear on-screen, (2) which words in the text are hyper, and (3) what gets triggered when the user clicks the hypertext. For example, Figure 2-16 shows how a Web page displays an HTML file, and Figure 2-17 shows how the same file appears when viewed with a text editor. The codes inside <brackets> are the markup that tells the Web browser how to interpret the text. You learn more about the HTML codes in the Web page creation tutorial in Part II of this book.

Whenever you want to download a Web page that you are viewing with your Web browser, simply pull down the browser's File menu, choose Save As, and use the Save controls to save a copy in the HTML format.

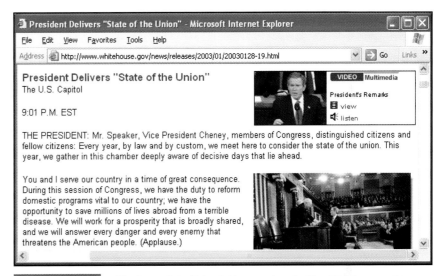

FIGURE 2-16 *The State of the Union Address as viewed with a Web browser* ■

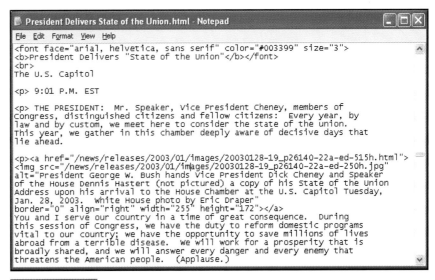

FIGURE 2-17 *The State of the Union Address as viewed with a text editor* ■

DOC (Microsoft Word) and WPD (WordPerfect)

Among the many word processor formats, the most common are Microsoft Word's DOC format and WordPerfect's WPD format. DOC stands for *document*, and WPD stands for *WordPerfect document*. Web browsers do not usually contain built-in support for word processor file formats. Instead, your browser calls on a helper application to display the file on demand. There are two ways to download this kind of file. First, you can wait for the helper app to display the file, pull down the helper app's File menu, and use the Save option to make yourself a local copy of the file. Second, you can right-click (Windows) or CONTROL-click (Macintosh) the link that otherwise launches the file. When the quick menu pops out, choose the option to save the file.

Portable Document Format (PDF)

Adobe realizes that a huge amount of printed text is not yet accessible on the Web. To provide a way to digitize printed text into a format that can be viewed on any computer platform, Adobe created the **Portable Document Format (PDF)**, for which the filename extension is *.pdf*. A quick way of creating PDF files is to scan printed documents into your word processor. If you have a lot of pages to scan, you can use a sheet feeder to speed the scanning process. Then you can print the scanned pages to a PDF file.

You view PDF files with the Adobe Acrobat Reader, a free plug-in that any user can get from the Adobe Web site. You will make some pretty amazing discoveries when you use the Adobe Acrobat Reader to view a PDF document. Because you are looking at what appears to be pictures of the original document, you do not expect to be able to select, copy, paste, and search for text as you could on a regular Web page. You will be pleasantly surprised to find, however, that all these functions are available unless the author disabled them. Perhaps your biggest surprise will come when you choose to print the document. Instead of printing the bitmap version of the image you see onscreen, Acrobat prints the document using the fonts on your printer. As a result, the printed version may appear better than the original.

To learn more about the PDF file format, go to www.adobe.com and follow the link to Adobe PDF.

Commonly Found Graphics File Formats

The computer industry has produced so many graphics formats (more than 30 at last count) that there is no true standard across the industry. Table 2-3 lists a few of the more popular graphics file formats and describes what they are used for. On the Web, however, there are only two file formats that every Web browser can be guaranteed to support: GIF and JPEG.

Filename Extension	Intended Purpose
.bmp	Windows bitmap. The *.bmp* file is the most efficient format to use with Windows.
.gif	Graphics Interchange Format. Invented by CompuServe for use on computer networks, GIF is the most prevalent graphics format for images on the World Wide Web.
.pcd	Kodak's Photo CD graphics file format; contains five different sizes of each picture, from "wallet" size to "poster" size.
.jpg or .jpeg	JPEG image, named for the standards committee that formed it: Joint Photographic Experts Group. Intended to become a platform-independent graphics format, this is arguably the best choice for publishing full-color photographs on the Web.
.pict	Macintosh graphics format.
.png	Portable Network Graphics format. Pronounced *ping*, PNG is the patent- and license-free format approved by the W3C (World Wide Web Consortium) to replace the patented GIF format. Because the PNG format is not yet fully supported by all browsers, Web authors typically convert graphics to GIF or JPEG for use on Web pages.
.tga	Truevision Targa format; *tga* stands for Targa, which is a video capture board.
.tif	TIFF file; stands for Tagged Image File Format. Known as "the variable standard" because there are so many kinds of TIFF subformats.
.wpg	WordPerfect graphics format.

TABLE 2-3   *The Most Common Computer Graphics Formats* ■

Step-by-Step 2-5
Downloading Images from the Internet

The quickest way to download an image from the Internet is to use your Web browser's option for saving the image to a file. When you save the image to a file, you have the option of changing its name. If you change the filename, make sure you keep the filename extension the same as the original filename's, because that is how other programs recognize it as the type of file it is. For example, if the image you are saving is in GIF format, make sure the filename extension on the file to be saved is *.gif*.

If the image you are saving is in JPEG format, make sure the filename extension on the file to be saved is *.jpg*. Renaming the filename extension of a *.gif* file to *.jpg* does not change the format of the file. If you want to change the format of the file, you must use a file-conversion program such as Paint Shop Pro, which you learn how to use in Chapter 6. To download an image from the Internet, follow these steps:

Step 1   Use your browser to display the image you want to download.

Step 2   Right-click (Windows) or CONTROL-click (Macintosh) the image you want to download, and a menu will pop out. On a Mac, you can also trigger the menu by holding down the mouse button until the menu pops out.

Step 3   The popout menu provides you with options you can do with the image; choose the option to "Save image as" or "Save picture as." The Save As dialog appears.

Step 4   In the File name field, you should see the name of the file this image has on the Internet. You can change the name if you want, but make sure you leave the filename extension the same as in the original.

Step 5   You can use the Save As dialog to navigate to a different drive or folder on your computer, or you can type a complete path onto the beginning of the filename to specify exactly where you want the image file to be saved on your computer.

Step 6   Click the Save button when you are ready to save the file.

Warning: Although you can easily download files from the Web, you should not do so without permission. Under U.S. copyright law, Web content is the legal property of its author and is not automatically free for the taking. Unless the material is in the common domain or is clearly marked as being free, you may need to seek permission to use it lawfully in other works. Chapter 4 provides you with guidelines for determining when you need to ask for permission.

GIF

GIF stands for **Graphics Interchange Format**. Invented by CompuServe for use on computer networks, GIF is highly efficient. Instead of containing the RGB (red, green, blue) value of every pixel (picture element) in the image, a GIF file contains a table defining the different pixel patterns found in the image, with pointers into the table indicating where the patterns go onscreen. It is important to understand that although GIF files are compressed, none of the original information in the graphic gets lost in the compression process. The decompressed image you see onscreen is exactly the same as the one that got compressed into the GIF file. Because nothing gets lost, this kind of encoding process is known as **lossless** compression. GIF files are limited to a palette of 256 colors; however, if you need more than 256 different colors in a picture, you should use the JPEG format.

JPEG

JPEG (pronounced *Jay-peg*) stands for **Joint Photographic Experts Group**, which is the name of the international standards committee that created it. JPEG was invented as a platform-independent graphics format. JPEG images can contain millions of colors, whereas GIF images are limited to a palette of 256 colors. JPEG uses a lossy compression algorithm to reduce the amount of space it would otherwise require to store so many colors. **Lossy** means that some of the image data can become lost, depending on how much compression is used when the image gets saved. JPEG compresses the image by dividing it into tiny cubes and averaging the color values within the cubes. Most people are unable to notice the tiny cubes in the image. One of the settings you can vary when saving a JPEG image is the size of the cubes. The larger the cubes, the more compression you will get, but the cubes will also be more noticeable.

PNG

The World Wide Web Consortium is working on a new graphics format called **Portable Network Graphics (PNG)**. The goal is to create a fast, lossless, patent-free file format that can handle pictures containing up to

Cross Check

Downloading a Picture from the Internet

Now that you have completed the section on images and graphical file formats, this would be a good time to test your ability to download a picture from the Internet. The Library of Congress Web site, for example, has many interesting pictures. Follow these steps:

1. Use your Web browser to go to www.loc.gov, and download one of the pictures to your computer. If you have trouble, refer to the instructions in the previous section, "Downloading Images from the Internet."

2. If you change the filename before you save the file, make sure the filename extension of the file you save matches the filename extension of the original.

3. Use the Windows Explorer or the Macintosh Finder to locate the file you saved in the preceding step, and double-click the file to launch it.

4. If the image appears properly, you have succeeded in learning how to download images to your computer; congratulations! If your computer tells you there is no program available to display the image, follow the steps in Chapter 6 to install Paint Shop Pro.

48 bits of color information per pixel. The screen captures in this book, for example, were transmitted in PNG format from my PC to the publisher's typesetter. You can monitor the progress of the creation of PNG at www.w3.org/Graphics/PNG.

Step-by-Step 2-6

Downloading Audio and Video from the Internet

To download audio and video, you follow a process very similar to the method you learned earlier for downloading graphics. You right-click (Windows) or CONTROL-click (Macintosh) on the link that triggers the audio or video, and you use the quick menu to save a local copy on your computer. Detailed instructions are provided as follows:

Step 1 Use your browser to display the link that triggers the audio or video you want to download.

Step 2 Right-click (Windows) or CONTROL-click (Macintosh) the trigger. A pop-up menu provides you with options you can do with the object linked to the trigger; choose the "Save link as" or "Save target as" option to make the Save As dialog appear.

Step 3 In the File name field, you should see the name of the file that this object has on the Internet. You can change the name if you want, but make sure you leave the filename extension the same as in the original.

Step 4 Click the Save button when you are ready to save the file.

Commonly Found Audiovisual File Formats

Every sound has a waveform that describes its frequency, amplitude, and harmonic content. Waveform audio digitizers capture sound by sampling this waveform thousands of times per second; the samples are stored in a computer file. Figure 2-18 shows a waveform in the process of being sampled. For each sample, a number gets written into the corresponding waveform audio file. The number tells how far the sample rose above or fell below the zero amplitude line. When you click to play the file, the samples play back through your computer's sound chip, and you hear the waveform audio. Waveform audio can be transmitted over the Net in several file formats.

WAV

On computers running Windows, the native waveform audio filename extension is *.wav,* which stands for waveform. When the Web started, you needed helper applications to play audio, because the first browsers lacked built-in support for *.wav* files. Happily, all the major browsers now contain native support for playing *.wav* files, on Macintosh as well as Windows operating systems.

AU and SND

The Sun audio format filename extension is *.au,* and *.snd* is the audio format that started on the NeXT workstation. These formats are essentially the same except that *.au* files do not have file headers to specify different sampling rates and compression formats. Thus an *.au* file gets recorded and played back at a "standard" rate, whereas *.snd* files can have different settings, depending on the nature of the sound and the purpose of the recording. The Macintosh has built-in support for *.snd* files. On the Java platform, *.au* is the native audio format.

RA and RAM

Real-time audio streaming used in Internet radio broadcasts requires a special file format optimized for real-time transmission over the Internet. The RealAudio filename extensions are *.ra* and *.ram,* which stand for RealAudio metafile. A RealAudio metafile is a text file that contains the Web address (URL) of a RealAudio file. RealAudio files cannot be referenced directly by the Web page because this would cause them to be downloaded in their entirety before playback. For a RealAudio file

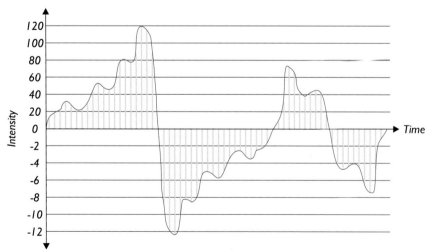

FIGURE 2-18 *A waveform in the process of being sampled; the vertical lines show the points at which samples are taken. Follow along the timeline, and imagine a number being written into a sound file to indicate how far each sample is above or below the zero line. That is how the process of sampling works.* ■

to be played in real time, it must be played through a RealAudio player and served by a RealAudio server. To accomplish this, you need a link between the Web server and the RealAudio server. The link is contained in the metafile.

AIF, AIFF, AIFC

AIFF stands for Audio Interchange File Format. Apple invented this file format to create and play audio files on the Macintosh. AIFC is a compressed version; the C stands for compressed. When you find an AIF file on the Web, chances are it was recorded on a Macintosh.

MP3

MP3 is one of the most popular audio formats on the Internet. **MP3** stands for MPEG audio layer 3. It is an audio file format that uses an MPEG audio codec to encode (compress) and decode (decompress) recorded music. MP3 can compress a CD audio track into a substantially smaller file requiring significantly less bandwidth (about 10 percent) to transmit over the Internet, without degrading the original sound track's quality.

To download a free MP3 player, find MP3 Web sites, and create MP3 files from your favorite audio CD, follow this book's Web site links to MP3. If you do not personally own the CD and/or if the MP3 files are not for your own personal use, please observe the copyright and fair use guidelines presented in Chapter 4. Because the MP3 technology makes copyright violation so easy, the kind of software used to create an MP3 file from an audio CD is called a *ripper*. Please be aware, however, that MP3 has many legitimate uses on the Web. Some recording artists are choosing to distribute their own songs in the MP3 format, for example, and some hit songs have appeared in MP3 format first before being distributed on CD. Little known artists use MP3 as a way to gain fans who may eventually want to hear them in concert or buy their CDs.

MIDI Synthesizer Format (MID)

Musical Instrument Digital Interface (MIDI) is a music synthesizer file format that requires very little bandwidth to transmit because the sound chip inside your multimedia PC does the work of generating the waveform you hear. What gets transmitted is the performance information required for your computer's sound chip to play the music. Accordingly, a MIDI file consists of a stream of codes that tells your computer when to turn notes on and off, how loud to make them, what instrument should make the sound (such as trumpet, flute, or drum), and whether to bend the notes or add other special effects. Compared to the amount of storage required for waveform audio recordings, MIDI takes up so little space that it is a very popular format for transmitting music over the Internet. MIDI files have a *.mid* filename extension.

This book's Web site provides some incredible indexes of MIDI files you can listen to. Follow the links to the MIDI archives, and you will get a list of indexes that contain thousands of songs in a wide variety of styles, ranging

MIDI vs. Wave

Imagine a situation in which you have a waveform audio recording of a symphony orchestra playing a piece of classical music and a MIDI file of the same composition. Which file will take more time to transfer from the Web to your computer? To help you answer this exercise, there is a Waveform audio file and a MIDI file for you to compare at this book's Web site. Follow the links to MIDI versus Wave, and listen to the two files. Both files are the same size, 17 kilobytes. Which one lasts longer? How do you explain the difference in the length of the music you hear, when the file size is the same?

from classical to modern and from funk to rock. You will also find music listed by artist, from Abba to Frank Zappa. You need to realize, however, that MIDI does not record the singer's voice. Thus, you will hear the synthesized instruments, but you will not hear the lyrics.

Video Formats

When a movie is digitized into a computer file, the digital data stream is enormous. To conserve file space and thereby reduce the bandwidth required to transmit the movie, the video gets compressed, down to as little as $1/200^{th}$ of its original size. One or more of the video compression schemes explained in Table 2-4 may be used.

AVI

The most common video format in the Windows world is Microsoft's AVI, which has the *.avi* filename extension. AVI stands for audio/video interleave, a clever scheme in which audio frames are interleaved with the video. The sound track plays without interruption because the audio always takes priority. Then your computer shows as many frames of video as it has time to process. If it is too late to show a given frame, the player just skips it and goes on to the next frame. Because the audio has priority, you get the aural illusion of uninterrupted playback.

MOV and QT

One of Apple Computer Corporation's greatest gifts to the field of multimedia is the QuickTime audio/video format. QuickTime is so robust and popular that it exists in both Macintosh and Windows versions. Because of its cross-platform

Method	How It Works
YUV subsampling	Divides the screen into little squares and averages color values of the pixels in each square.
Delta-frame encoding	Shrinks data by storing only the information that changes between frames; for example, if the background scene does not change, there is no need to store the scene again.
Run-length encoding	Detects a "run" of identical pixels and encodes how many occur instead of recording individual pixels.

TABLE 2-4   *Video Compression Schemes* ■

capabilities, QuickTime has become very popular on the Internet. The file-name extensions of QuickTime movies are *.qt* and *.mov*. For the latest information, go to www.apple.com/quicktime.

MPG, MPEG, and MPE

MPEG is emerging as the digital video standard for the United States and most of the world. MPEG stands for **Motion Picture Experts Group**, the International Standards Organization committee that created the standard. Endorsed by more than 70 companies, including IBM, Apple, JVC, Philips, Sony, and Matsushita, MPEG compresses video by using a discrete cosine transform algorithm to eliminate redundant data in blocks of pixels on the screen. MPEG compresses the video further by recording only changes from frame to frame; this is known as *delta-frame encoding*. MPEG is becoming the digital video standard for compact discs, DVD, cable TV, direct satellite broadcast, and high-definition television (HDTV).

Four versions of MPEG have been worked on:

- **MPEG-1** is the noninterlaced version designed for playback from CD-ROMs.

- **MPEG-2** is the interlaced version intended for the all-digital transmission of broadcast-quality TV. Adopted by the U.S. Grand Alliance HDTV specification, the European Digital Video Broadcasting Group, and the Digital Versatile Disc (DVD-ROM) consortium, MPEG-2 features surround sound. RCA's DirecTV service uses MPEG-2.

- **MPEG-3** was to be the HDTV version of MPEG, but then it was discovered that the MPEG-2 syntax could fulfill that need by simply scaling the bit rate, obviating the need for the third phase.

- **MPEG-4** is a low-bit-rate version of MPEG that is being invented for transmitting movies over mobile and wireless communications.

For more information, follow this book's Web site links to MPEG.

RM

One of the greatest challenges on the Internet is to deliver to your PC full-motion video in an uninterrupted real-time data stream. First to market with a product that does this was RealNetworks, the same company that brought you the RealAudio technology discussed earlier in this chapter. The name of the product is RealVideo, and the filename extension is *.rm*, which stands for Real metafile.

RealVideo follows the Real Time Streaming Protocol (RTSP) that RealNetworks invented for streaming audio and video over the Internet. To read about this and other technical details, go to www.rtsp.org.

Downloading Software and Data from the Internet

To download software and data from the Internet, you should begin by reading any special instructions that might appear onscreen explaining what will happen when you trigger the download. Almost all these instructions fall into one of three categories: documents, archived files, and self-extracting archives. Each kind is discussed in turn as follows.

Documents

When a document is linked to a Web page, you have two options. You can either click to view the document or, if you want to download it, you can right-click (Windows) or CONTROL-click (Macintosh) the link to pop out the menu that lets you save the document on your computer. The biggest problem beginners report is knowing where to save the downloaded document. If you have Windows, a good place is the folder called My Documents or My Downloads. On the Macintosh, beginners normally download a document onto the desktop, from which you can move it later to another folder if you want to file it away.

To download the document your Web browser is currently displaying, you pull down the browser's File menu, choose Save As, and use the Save dialog to save the file to a folder on your computer's hard drive. As always, please remember not to alter the filename extension when you save the file. If the file has a *.doc* filename extension, for example, do not change it to a *.txt* filename extension. Remember that your computer looks at the filename extension to determine what application will handle the file. Renaming the filename extension will confuse your computer when someone tries to access the file.

Compressed Archives

A popular method of distributing software and data over the Internet is via archived files. An **archive** is a container into which one or more files has been compressed to save space and packed into a single file that can be transmitted easily over a network. When you receive such a file, you need to use an extractor to unpack the archive and restore its contents onto your computer. Windows users normally unpack archived files with a product known as PKZIP for Windows or with a similar product such as WinZip, NetZip, or EasyZip. Macintosh users unpack archived files with Stuffit Expander, which is also available in a Windows version. Each of these products is described as follows.

PKZIP for Windows   PKWARE, Inc., is the industry leader in compression and decompression technology. Their product, PKZIP for Windows, takes its name from the *.zip* filename extension that archived files normally have on Windows-based machines. PKZIP for Windows makes it easy to zip and unzip files. After you download a zipped file from the Internet, you simply open it with PKZIP for Windows. As illustrated in Figure 2-19, PKZIP for Windows displays the contents of the zipped file.

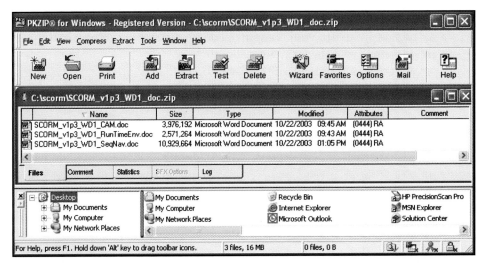

FIGURE 2-19 *When you open a .zip file, PKZIP for Windows displays the contents of the zipped archive. To expand the files into their original uncompressed format, you pull down the Extract menu, choose Extract Files, and follow the onscreen instructions to save the files in the folder of your choice.* ■

PKZIP for Windows is **shareware**, meaning you can download it for free, try it out for a limited time period (usually 30 to 60 days), and then, if you decide to keep using it, pay a reasonable fee (usually $29 to $39) to the vendor. To download a copy of PKZIP for Windows, go to www.pkware.com. If you have Windows XP, however, you may also wish to consider using the zipped option that is built in to the Windows XP File Manager. To learn about the built-in zipped option, click the Windows XP Start button, click Help, and search for the following phrase: zipped compressed folder. Installing PKZIP for Windows replaces the built-in Windows XP support with PKZIP support.

Stuffit Expander   On the Macintosh, compressed archives are handled with a freeware program from Aladdin Systems called Stuffit Expander, which is also available in Windows and Linux versions. True to its name, Stuffit Expander can extract files from archives you download from the Internet. If you are using a Macintosh and you do not have Stuffit Expander, you can download it for free from www.stuffit.com.

When you ask Stuffit Expander to expand a file, it opens a new folder on the desktop and decompresses each file into that folder. As the files are expanded, a status bar shows the progress of the decompression. When Stuffit Expander is finished extracting the files of many applications, you need only to click the app's icon in the new folder to make it run. Other apps create an install program that you must run separately to set up the application.

Self-Extracting Archives

Another popular method of distributing software and data on the Internet is the **self-extracting archive**, which is a compressed executable file into which the files that comprise an application or set of data have been packed. On the Windows operating system, self-extracting archives typically have the *.exe* executable filename extension. After you download a self-extracting archive to your computer, you simply run the archive to unpack the files and store them on your computer.

Most of the downloads at the CNET download.com site are distributed in self-extracting archives. When you click to download one of them, your browser asks whether you want to save the archive to disk or open it directly from the Web. If you choose the option to save to disk, a Save dialog appears. Use the Save dialog to save the archive in the folder of your choice, such as your computer's *temp* folder. Then run the self-extracting archive. If the archive's icon is not visible, follow these steps to start a program when its icon is not visible:

For Windows

1. Click the Windows Start button and choose Run to make the Run dialog appear.

2. Click the Browse button; the Browse dialog appears.

3. Use the browse controls to select the filename of the program you want to run.

4. Click Open; the filename of the program to be run appears in the Open field of the Run dialog.

5. Click OK to run the file.

6. If you are unable to locate the file by using this method, click the Windows Start button and use Search to locate the file. Then double-click the file to run it.

For Macintosh

1. If you have OS X, get Sherlock running by clicking Sherlock in the Dock. Set the option to search for Applications, enter the name of the program you are looking for, and click the find button.

2. Otherwise, click the Apple icon in the upper-left corner of the screen to pull down the menu, and then choose Find File.

3. Set the two drop-down menus to "Name" and "Contains" if they do not say that already.

4. In the blank field, type the name of the program you are looking for.

5. Press the Find button to make your computer find the file.

6. Double-click the file to run it.

To conserve space on your computer's hard disk after you run the self-extracting archive, you can delete the archive after extracting the files from it.

Safeguarding Against Viruses

Unfortunately, some geeks get their jollies from finding ways to send people viruses over the Internet. When you open files that you get from the Internet, you run the risk of infecting your computer with viruses that can attach or embed themselves in certain kinds of files. The most vulnerable types of files are the executables, which cause code to run on your computer. Before you download an executable file, you need to check carefully the source from which you are downloading it. If the file is coming from a reputable site, such as Microsoft or Netscape or CNET's download.com, the file is most probably virus-free. The executable filename extensions to be most careful about are *.exe, .bat, .vbs,* and *.class.* Viruses can also be transmitted through macros in *.doc* and *.xls* files.

Whenever you download files from the Internet, you should run a virus scan on your computer to make sure you have not received a virus. You can make virus-scanning happen automatically if you set your antivirus software to scan incoming and outgoing mail and file transfers. It is important to remove viruses promptly, because letting them remain on your computer can cause disruptive things to happen, such as files disappearing, unwanted messages coming onscreen, software acting strangely, and even your entire hard disk losing its contents. Make sure your virus scanner is up-to-date so it will recognize the latest viruses. When a new virus hits the Net, updates are normally available within the day, and you should install the update promptly. For the latest information about viruses and how to remove them from your computer, go to antivirus.about.com, www.mcafee.com, and www.sarc.com.

Chapter 2 Review

■ Chapter Summary

After reading this chapter and completing the step-by-step tutorials and Try This! exercises, you should understand the following facts about connecting to the Internet, surfing the Web, and finding what you are looking for:

Getting Connected

■ To connect to the Internet, you must have six things: (1) an Internet-ready computer that has (2) an operating system with (3) TCP/IP installed, along with (4) client software you use to access the Internet over (5) an Internet connection that connects you physically to the (6) Internet address of your targeted service or resource.

■ The speed at which you connect to the Internet determines bandwidth, which is the amount of information your computer can send and receive.

■ Users who connect to the Internet via plain old telephone service (POTS) must have a modem. Named by a combination of the first syllable from the terms *mo*dulate and *dem*odulate, the modem is a communications device that enables a computer to send and receive digital information over analog phone lines. Many computers have modems built in.

■ The Point to Point Protocol (PPP) is the telephone modem protocol of choice, because PPP supports not only TCP/IP but also NetBEUI and IPX/SPX. An older Serial Line Internet Protocol (SLIP) supports only TCP/IP and requires a preassigned IP address.

■ Ethernet is a high-speed local area network (LAN) standard that is widely used across industry and academia. Originally requiring coaxial cables, Ethernet now can use category 5 twisted-pair telephone wiring in a so-called 10BaseT configuration. A faster 10/100BaseT Ethernet can move data at rates up to 100 megabits per second. There is also a 10 gigabit Ethernet standard known as 10GbE.

■ The Integrated Services Digital Network (ISDN) is the digital telephone system that the regional Bell companies are installing in most of the United States. The Basic Rate Interface (BRI) service of ISDN is 144 Kbps, made up of two 64-Kbps data channels and one 16-Kbps control channel. The Primary Rate Interface (PRI) service uses 23 data channels and a 64-Kbps control channel to boost the data rate to 1,544 Kbps (1.544 Mbps).

■ A cable modem is a network adapter used to connect PCs to TV cables in neighborhoods where cable TV companies offer Internet services over TV cables. The term broadband is used to refer to this type of connection that carries multiple channels of information over a single cable.

■ DSL stands for Digital Subscriber Line, a broadband method of connecting to the Internet over existing telephone lines. Synchronous DSL (SDSL) supports the same high-speed data rate for both upstream and downstream traffic. Asynchronous DSL (ADSL) lowers the cost of DSL connections by using a high-speed data rate for downloads but a slower rate for uploads. Download speeds range from 384 Kbps to 8 Mbps, and upload speeds range from 128 Kbps to 1 Mbps. The faster the speed, the higher the cost.

■ An Internet connection that is always on is called a direct connection. Ethernet, ISDN, cable modem, DSL, and satellite all use direct connections.

Browsing the Web

■ On the Internet, surfing means to use a program called a browser to go from site to site in search of information that interests you.

■ A link is a hot spot that, when clicked, triggers the object of the link.

■ Progressively clicking through the Web by triggering the links that interest you is known as browsing, a term synonymous with surfing the Net. The program you use when you surf the Web is called a browser.

■ Microsoft makes the most popular Web browser, which is called Internet Explorer (IE). Other browsers include Netscape Navigator and Safari, the default browser that ships with every new Macintosh.

- The open source version of Netscape Navigator is called Mozilla.

- Old versions of Web browsers are called legacy browsers; in computing, the term legacy refers to something old.

- Every place you can go on the Web has an address known as a URL, which stands for Uniform Resource Locator.

- The first part of a URL is called the protocol. The Web's protocol is HTTP, which stands for hypertext transfer protocol. Other protocols include FTP, mailto, news, telnet, and Gopher.

- On the Web, the page you define as your take-off point or start page is called your home page. Almost every company has a home page, as do government offices, schools, and colleges.

- If you go to a Web site without requesting a specific document, you view that site's default page, which is often the home page of the company or person who owns the site.

- If you request a specific document that cannot be found, you get the error 404: file not found. If you strip the filename off of the URL and browse to the part of the site that formerly contained the document, you can sometimes find what you are looking for or get a clue as to what happened to the missing file.

- In a Web browser, a bookmark is a pointer to a Web page that enables you to jump directly to that page, without having to navigate the Web to get there. In the Internet Explorer, bookmarks are called favorites.

- When you surf the Web, your browser keeps copies of the most recently visited Web sites in a place on your hard disk called the cache. You can purge (i.e., delete) the cache if you have been reading sensitive information that you would not want someone else using your computer to find.

- The Wireless Application Protocol (WAP) was invented to provide mobile telephone users with a way of accessing the Internet by routing requests through a WAP server that translates Web pages into a format appropriate for display on mobile phones. The pages are formatted according to the rules of the Wireless Markup Language (WML).

Handling Multimedia Objects, Plug-ins, and Viewers

- Helpers are applications known as helper apps that the browser launches to handle certain kinds of multimedia files. In the Windows operating system, you can change the helper apps by redefining the filename associations in the Windows File Manager.

- Plug-ins are software modules that enable computer applications, such as browsers, to play media objects directly instead of launching a helper app to handle the file externally. Macromedia Flash is the most popular multimedia plug-in on the Internet.

- Java is an object-oriented programming language invented by Sun Microsystems. Java can be used to create little applications, called applets, that can be transmitted over the Internet as part of a Web page.

- JavaScript is a client-side object-based scripting language that enables you to create dynamic Web pages without having to become a full-fledged Java programmer.

- An Active Server Page (ASP) is a Web page that can execute on the server scripts written in either VBScript or JScript, which is very similar to JavaScript.

- C# and J# are newly invented server-side programming languages that are part of the Microsoft .NET Framework, which also contains .NET versions of JScript and VBScript.

- Invented by Microsoft, ActiveX is a plug-in technology that enables a wide variety of Windows controls to be embedded in HTML documents. The ActiveX Flash control, for example, enables Flash objects to be downloaded and executed as part of a Web page at runtime.

Configuring Browser Security

- On the Internet, a zone is a predefined range or selection of Web sites or addresses. The IE browser lets you configure different security settings in four different zones called (1) Internet, (2) Local intranet, (3) Trusted sites, and (4) Restricted sites.

- Into the Restricted sites zone, you place Web sites that you believe could damage your computer or data. You put sites you trust into the Trusted sites zone. The Local intranet zone contains Web sites on your organization's intranet. By definition, all other sites are in the Internet zone.

- Windows users should periodically pull down the IE Tools menu and run Windows Update to download and install the latest security patches that help safeguard against being attacked by viruses, worms, and Trojans. Setting Windows Update to run automatically is the best way to make sure you always have the latest updates.

- A virus is malicious or unwanted code that installs itself on your computer without your knowledge by hiding inside other programmed objects. A worm is a special kind of virus that can replicate itself without hiding inside other objects. A Trojan (also called a Trojan horse) is a malicious application that masquerades as a desired object that you download knowingly to your computer.

Finding Things with Search Engines

- Yahoo! is the Web's most famous subject-oriented search directory. Like most of the Internet's search engines, Yahoo! also now contains full-text keyword searching.

- AltaVista was one of the Web's first and finest full-text search engines. It is now being challenged by Google, which features full-text as well as subject-oriented searching.

- Most search engines support the advanced search syntax, which lets you use quote signs, parentheses, and the Boolean operators AND, OR, and NOT to refine a search that may not be finding what you are looking for.

- Metasearching is the searching of searching, which you perform with a metasearch engine that invokes the other search engines automatically, synthesizes the results, and reports back with a single integrated list of hits. MetaCrawler, Dogpile, and Search.com are the most popular metasearch engines.

- Scholarly search engines restrict a search to reputable sources of information that are more trusted and reliable than the public Internet. Examples of scholarly search engines are ERIC, About.com, Britannica.com, and XanEdu.

- Multimedia searches enable you to find pictures, audio, animations, and videos. Lycos, AltaVista, and Singingfish were the pioneers in multimedia searching.

- Newsgroups are searchable at several search sites, including AltaVista, Dogpile, Excite, Google, InfoSeek, and Yahoo! If you write messages in newsgroups, you need to realize that your messages are keyword searchable unless you set the x-no-archive flag when you write the message.

- Archie is a legacy tool that can search the filenames of the millions of files that are available on anonymous FTP sites.

- Gopher is another legacy protocol for organizing files in hierarchical menus on the Internet. Some related tools are Veronica, a search tool for finding Gopher files, and Jughead, a program that added keyword search and Boolean operator capabilities to Gopher search. Gopher, Veronica, and Jughead are legacy tools that do not have much practical use on the Internet today. In the early 1990s, however, Gopher was the killer application of the Internet.

- Good search engines for finding people are Bigfoot, WhoWhere, Switchboard, and Yahoo!'s people search.

- The best place to find places is MapQuest, which serves an average of more than 10 million maps per day.

- The best places to find legal information are Law.com, FindLaw.com, and LexisONE.com. These are the sites where lawyers go to get breaking legal news and conduct legal searches.

- Search engines are undergoing a lot of research and development on the Internet. A good place to keep up with what is happening is searchenginewatch.internet.com.

Downloading from the Internet

- The quickest way to download text from the Internet is to copy the text onto your computer's Clipboard, from which you can paste the text into any other window on your screen. You can also open a text file with your browser, pull down the File menu, and use the Save option to save the file on your computer.

- The Adobe Acrobat Reader is a free plug-in that reads files in the Portable Document Format (PDF), which Adobe created as a platform-independent mechanism for sharing documents across the Internet.

- To download an image from the Internet, use your browser to display it. Then right-click (Windows) or CONTROL-click (Macintosh) the image to pop out the quick menu, and choose the option to save the image or picture to your hard drive.

- On the Web, there are only two file formats that every Web browser can be guaranteed to support: GIF and JPEG. The World Wide Web Consortium, however, has created a Portable Network Graphics (PNG) format intended to replace the patented GIF format.

- To download audio and video, you right-click (Windows) or CONTROL-click (Macintosh) the link that triggers the audio or video, and use the quick menu to save a copy on your hard drive.

- MPEG is emerging as the digital video standard for the United States and most of the world. MPEG stands for Motion Picture Experts Group, the International Standards Organization committee that created it.

- An archive is a container into which one or more files have been compressed to save space and packed into a single file that can be transmitted easily over a network. When you receive such a file, you need to use an extractor to unpack the archive and restore its contents onto your computer. Windows users normally unpack archived files with a product known as PKZIP for Windows. Macintosh users unpack archived files with Stuffit Expander, which is also available in a Windows version.

- A self-extracting archive is an executable file which, when executed, automatically extracts the files that are contained in the archive.

- Whenever you save a downloaded file on your computer, make sure the file you save has the correct filename extension for the type of file it is.

- Whenever you download files from the Internet, you should run a virus scan on your computer to make sure you have not received a virus. You can make virus-scanning happen automatically if you set your antivirus software to scan all incoming and outgoing mail and file transfers.

▧ Key Terms

10BaseT *(56)*	**Flash** *(78)*	**Joint Photographic Experts Group (JPEG)** *(102)*
10/100BaseT *(56)*	**Gbps** *(56)*	**Kbps** *(55)*
10GbE *(56)*	**gigabit** *(56)*	**kilobit** *(55)*
ActiveX *(83)*	**Gopher** *(94)*	**legacy browser** *(61)*
applet *(81)*	**Graphics Interchange Format (GIF)** *(102)*	**link** *(60)*
Archie *(94)*	**helper app** *(74)*	**lossless** *(102)*
archive *(108)*	**home page** *(65)*	**lossy** *(102)*
bits per second (bps) *(55)*	**hot word** *(65)*	**Mbps** *(56)*
bookmark *(69)*	**hover** *(66)*	**megabit** *(56)*
Boolean *(87)*	**HTML** *(99)*	**metasearching** *(89)*
broadband *(57)*	**hypergraphic trigger** *(66)*	**Microsoft Media Player** *(78)*
browser *(60)*	**hypertext link** *(65)*	**modem** *(55)*
browsing *(60)*	**Integrated Services Digital Network (ISDN)** *(56)*	**Motion Picture Experts Group (MPEG)** *(107)*
cable modem *(57)*	**Internet Explorer (IE)** *(60)*	**Mozilla** *(61)*
cache *(71)*	**Internet Service Provider (ISP)** *(53)*	**MP3** *(105)*
default page *(65)*	**Java** *(80)*	**multimedia** *(73)*
Digital Subscriber Line (DSL) *(57)*	**JavaScript** *(81)*	**Musical Instrument Digital Interface (MIDI)** *(105)*
direct connection *(59)*		
Ethernet *(56)*		

Netscape Navigator *(61)*

object *(80)*

open source *(61)*

plug-in *(77)*

Point to Point Protocol (PPP) *(56)*

Portable Document Format (PDF) *(100)*

Portable Network Graphics (PNG) *(102)*

QuickTime *(77)*

RealOne *(78)*

Safari *(61)*

self-extracting archive *(109)*

Serial Line Internet Protocol (SLIP) *(56)*

shareware *(109)*

spider *(86)*

stream *(77)*

surf *(60)*

telnet *(94)*

Trojan *(83)*

Uniform Resource Locator (URL) *(62)*

virus *(83)*

Web page *(63)*

Web site *(63)*

Webcasting *(77)*

Wireless Application Protocol (WAP) *(73)*

Wireless Markup Language (WML) *(73)*

worm *(83)*

zone *(84)*

Key Terms Quiz

1. A networking company that connects you to the Internet is called a(n) _____.

2. The invention of _____ in Bob Metcalfe's Harvard Ph.D. thesis in 1973 was a data communications breakthrough that fueled the explosion of local area networks.

3. DSL stands for _____.

4. The term _____ refers to the type of connection that carries multiple channels of information over a single cable.

5. When you surf the Web, your browser keeps copies of the most recently visited Web sites in a place on your hard disk called the _____.

6. A(n) _____ is a real-time feed from an audio or video source, encoded in such a way that the media can begin playing steadily without making the user wait for the entire file to download to their computer.

7. A(n) _____ is a software module that adds functionality when installed into an existing computer application.

8. Distributed by Macromedia, _____ is a very popular multimedia plug-in that is installed on more than 97 percent of the Internet's end-user computers.

9. In computing, a(n) _____ is a software entity that is programmed to perform certain tasks or behave in certain ways depending on the context in which it is used.

10. AND, OR, and NOT are _____ operators used in constructing a search with advanced search syntax.

Multiple-Choice Quiz

1. Which of the following things do you need to get connected to the Internet?
   a. Internet-ready computer
   b. Operating system
   c. TCP/IP
   d. Client software
   e. Internet connection
   f. Internet address
   g. All of the above

2. Which of the following ways of connecting to the Internet theoretically has the most bandwidth?
   a. Dialup modem
   b. ISDN Basic Rate Interface
   c. Cable modem
   d. Tin cans and a string

3. What kind of link triggers when you mouse over a hot word and click to follow the link?
   a. Hypergraphic
   b. Image map

   c. Inline

   d. Hypertext

4. The simultaneous broadcast of a live event over the Web is called a:

   a. Cablecast

   b. Intercast

   c. Webcast

   d. Newscast

5. Microsoft's plug-in technology is called:

   a. Flash

   b. Java

   c. ASP

   d. ActiveX

6. Java applications that can be transmitted over the Internet as part of a Web page are called:

   a. Beans

   b. Modules

   c. Applets

   d. Servlets

7. A malicious application that masquerades as a desired object that you download knowingly to your computer is called a:

   a. Virus

   b. Worm

   c. Trojan

   d. Patch

8. Into which zone do you place Web sites that you believe could cause damage to your computer or your data?

   a. Internet

   b. Local intranet

   c. Trusted sites

   d. Restricted sites

9. Which of the following is a metasearch engine?

   a. Yahoo!

   b. Google

   c. Dogpile

   d. ERIC

10. Which audio file format records a stream of performance information that tells your computer's sound chip when to turn notes on and off, how loud to make them, and what instrument should make the sound?

   a. AIFF

   b. MP3

   c. RAM

   d. MIDI

▢ Essay Quiz

1. Follow this book's Web site link to the DSL lookup site, and find out whether DSL is available in your neighborhood. If DSL is available, what data rates are available in your neighborhood, and what do they cost?

2. Contact your cable TV company to find out if cable modems are available. If so, how much does it cost to get connected, and what is the ongoing cost? If your cable TV company tells you cable modem service is not available, follow this book's Web site link to the Cable Modem Area Code Search to find out if any other companies offer cable modems in your area.

3. Survey ten or more of the homes in your neighborhood to find out how they are connected to the Internet. List the kinds of connections you find (such as dialup modems, ISDN, cable modems, or DSL) and tell what percentage of your neighbors use each type of connection. If any of your neighbors are not connected, include on your list the percentage of homes you surveyed that are not on the Internet.

4. Flash can make your Web browser do some really neat stuff. Follow this book's Web site links to the Flash showcase. View some of the demonstrations you find there. Make a list of the features you find Flash supporting that you have not seen on Web pages that don't use Flash. What is your favorite Flash feature?

   Note: If you do not have the latest version of Flash, you will be prompted to install it. Go ahead and do so.

5. At this book's Web site, follow the links to the people-finder search engines listed in the section on how to find people. Look yourself up in the different directories. Does Bigfoot find you? How about WhoWhere? Do you find yourself listed in Switchboard and Yahoo! People Search? How do you feel about being included or excluded from these people finders? If you are not included and you would like to be, follow the onscreen instructions for getting yourself listed.

Lab Projects

• Lab Project 2-1: Connectivity Planning

For the employees of a company or school to work online, they need to be able to connect to the Internet. Imagine that you work for a small company or school that has decided to begin permitting its employees to do some of their work from home. Your employer has asked you to recommend the best method or strategy for your fellow employees to connect from home so they can telecommute over the Internet. In developing this recommendation, you will need to consider the following factors:

- **Time** How many hours per week will the typical employee spend telecommuting?
- **Bandwidth** Does your school or company require high bandwidth for some or all of its computing activities?
- **Geography** Do the employees live within a local calling distance, or are they spread out over a broader space?
- **Cost** In almost every school or company, you need to stay within a budget. Refer to the cost comparison in Table 2-1, and consider the cost of the telecommunication solutions you recommend.

Use a word processor to write up your telecommuting recommendation in the form of a brief essay describing the network strategy that seems appropriate for your coworkers to connect to the Internet from home. If your instructor has asked you to hand in the recommendation, make sure you put your name at the top and then save it on disk or follow any other instructions you may have been given for this assignment.

• Lab Project 2-2: Sharing Bookmarks and Favorites

One of the most valuable resources a school or company can have is a list of good, reliable, recommended Web sites where employees can go to accomplish the kinds of tasks typical of the workplace. In this chapter, you learned that the Internet Explorer contains a Favorites mechanism for accessing such sites quickly.

Imagine that your employer has asked you to create a common list of bookmarked favorites that your fellow employees can use to enhance productivity in your workplace. Follow these steps:

1. Use the IE Web browser to visit the sites you want included in the list of bookmarked favorites.
2. While you are at each site, follow the steps you learned in this chapter to bookmark it.
3. Your list should contain at least seven bookmarks. If you need help finding seven appropriate sites, use the search engines you learned in this chapter.
4. Pull down the File menu and choose Import and Export; the Import/Export wizard appears.
5. Click Next to begin the wizard, and follow the onscreen instructions.
6. When the wizard asks what you want to import or export, choose Export Favorites.
7. When the wizard asks what folder or subfolder of the favorites you want to export from, click what you want and click Next.
8. When the wizard asks where you want to save the exported folder, click the Browse button to choose the folder of your choice. Your bookmark.htm file will be copied into the folder you designate. Click Next.

If your instructor has asked you to hand in the exported bookmark file, the file to submit will be named bookmark.htm. Copy that file to a disk, or follow the other instructions your instructor gave you for submitting this assignment. If you have trouble finding the bookmark file, click the Windows Start button and use the Search option to locate the file. Later in this book, after you learn how to publish files on the Web, you will be able to publish this bookmark file to a location from which your users can easily access it over the Web or import it into their browser's bookmarks or favorites.

chapter

3

Communicating Over the Internet

"We have got to start meeting this way."

—*Lily Tomlin as Ernestine,*
WebEx Commercial

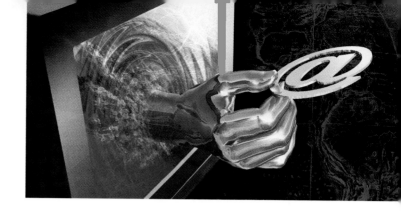

In this chapter, you will learn how to:

- Define the rules of Internet etiquette (Netiquette) for being a good citizen of the Net.

- Configure an e-mail client and use it to send, receive, answer, forward, and file e-mail; filter out unwanted mail; and detect fake mail IDs.

- Subscribe to, participate in, and set up your own listserv mailing lists.

- Configure a newsgroup reader, participate in USENET newsgroups, and create your own Web-based discussion forum.

- Set up a blog to keep an online diary or weblog of events.

- Configure an RSS reader to feed you news about new content posted at Web sites of interest.

- Enter an IRC chat room where you can participate in meaningful, real-time conversations.

- Configure an instant messaging client to IM your buddies on the Internet.

- Configure your computer for videoconferencing and participate in conversations that let you see and hear your conversants.

- Use the telnet protocol to connect to remote host computers on the Internet.

- Use text-based FTP commands to upload and download files on legacy systems that do not have graphical FTP clients.

THE most powerful use of the Internet is for communicating with other users. Never before has a communications medium made it so quick, easy, and cost-effective to communicate with tens of millions of users all over the world. So great is the benefit that the Internet can truly be called a supermedium for communicating.

In this chapter, you will learn about *electronic mail*, an asynchronous message transmission medium between two people; *listserv*, a way of communicating ideas to a specific group of people; *newsgroups*, online discussion groups in which the topics are organized hierarchically, enabling users to read and write messages and converse about the topics in a manner comparable to attending a conference; *blogs*, weblogs that users keep online to inform each other about what they are doing; *RSS*, which feeds you news headlines so you can keep up with what is happening at other Web sites; and the real-time technologies of *Internet Relay Chat (IRC)*, *instant messaging* (IM), and *videoconferencing*, which enable you to converse with other users who are online. As a bonus, this chapter will conclude by teaching you how to log on to a remote computer via telnet and use text-based FTP commands to prepare you for the possibility that you may someday need to communicate from a legacy system that does not have the latest protocols.

Before you begin communicating on the Information Superhighway, however, you should learn some of the rules of the road. Therefore, we begin with a discussion of Internet etiquette.

Internet Etiquette (Netiquette)

The term **Netiquette** was coined by combining the words "Internet etiquette" into a single name. Netiquette is the observance of certain rules and conventions that have evolved to keep the Internet from becoming a free-for-all in which tons of unwanted messages and junk mail would clog your Inbox and make the Information Superhighway an unfriendly place. By following the Netiquette guidelines, you can become a good citizen of the Net.

Netiquette Guidelines

In the "Netiquette Guidelines" section of this book's Web site, you will find links to the official rules of etiquette and ethics for responsible use of the Internet. Chief among these is RFC 1855, which was developed by the Responsible Use of the Network (RUN) Working Group of the Internet Engineering Task Force (IETF). This document consists of a bulleted list of specifications organizations can use to create their own guidelines. For example, Arlene Rinaldi's award-winning Netiquette Home Page, which is titled "The Net: User Guidelines and Netiquette," contains the Netiquette guidelines used at Florida Atlantic University. The introduction explains that use of the Internet is a privilege, not a right:

> The use of the network is a privilege, not a right, which may temporarily be revoked at any time for abusive conduct. Such conduct would include, the placing of unlawful information on a system, the use of abusive or otherwise objectionable language in either public or private messages, the sending of messages that are likely to result in the loss of recipients' work or systems, the sending of "chain letters" or "broadcast" messages to lists or individuals, and any other types of use which would cause congestion of the networks or otherwise interfere with the work of others.

Another example of Netiquette guidelines was developed by Frank Connolly in conjunction with the American Association for Higher Education and EDUCAUSE. Connolly's *Bill of Rights and Responsibilities for Electronic Learners* is a succinct and eloquent statement of Netiquette guidelines. To read these guidelines, follow the links to the *Bill of Rights* at this book's Web site, where you will also find a link to a related article by Connolly entitled "Intellectual Honesty in the Era of Computing." The most commonly known Netiquette rules are as follows:

- Use business language and write professionally in all work-related messages.
- Remember that your message may be printed or forwarded to other people.
- Proofread and correct errors in your message before sending it.
- Do not use all capital letters, because this connotes shouting.
- Keep in mind that your reader does not have the benefit of hearing your tone of voice and facial clues.
- Remember that the time, date, and reply address are added automatically to your e-mail message; therefore, you do not need to type this information.
- Always include an appropriate subject line in an e-mail message.
- Respond promptly to e-mail.

Computer Ethics

Whenever you use the Internet, you should observe the ethics principles illustrated in Figure 3-1, which lists the Ten Commandments of Computer

1. Thou shalt not use a computer to harm other people.

2. Thou shalt not interfere with other people's computer work.

3. Thou shalt not snoop around in other people's computer files.

4. Thou shalt not use a computer to steal.

5. Thou shalt not use a computer to bear false witness.

6. Thou shalt not copy or use proprietary software for which you have not paid.

7. Thou shalt not use other people's computer resources without authorization or proper compensation.

8. Thou shalt not appropriate other people's intellectual output.

9. Thou shalt think about the social consequences of the program you are writing or the system you are designing.

10. Thou shalt always use a computer in ways that ensure consideration and respect for your fellow humans.

FIGURE 3-1 *Whenever you use the Internet, you should observe the Ten Commandments of Computer Use, which were developed by the Computer Ethics Institute at www.cpsr.org/program/ethics/cei.html.* ■

Use. These principles were developed by the Computer Ethics Institute in Washington, DC. Computer Professionals for Social Responsibility (CPSR) maintains a list of other current links to Web sites devoted to computer ethics on the Internet. To peruse them, go to www.cpsr.org/program/ethics/ethlink.htm.

Spam

On the Internet, the term **spam** refers to unwanted messages posted to newsgroups or sent to a list of users through e-mail. The term can be used as either a verb or a noun. To spam means to send unwanted messages to a list of users on the Internet. Likewise, unwanted messages you receive are called spam.

Perhaps the most obnoxious form of spam is unwanted commercial advertising. The Coalition Against Unsolicited Commercial Email (CAUCE) has done the math, and the outlook is daunting. As CAUCE chairman Scott Hazen Mueller explains, "There are 24 million small businesses in the United States, according to the Small Business Administration. If just one percent of those businesses sent you just one e-mail advertisement a year, that's 657 e-mail advertisements in your inbox each day" (CAUCE, 2001). To prevent this from happening, Congress is working on legislation that will create a national "Do Not Spam" list. Follow this book's Web site link to learn the latest about anti-spam legislation.

There are other forms of spam besides unwanted commercial advertising. A lot of chain letters, for example, are circulating on the Internet. Chain letters are spam; do not send or forward them. If you get one, you may consider sending a message to the originator stating that chain letters are an unethical use of the Internet and that the sender should be ashamed of so littering the Information Superhighway. Be aware, however, that responding to spam lets the spammer know that your e-mail address is valid, thereby increasing the likelihood that you may receive more spam.

There is an example of a chain letter at this book's Web site. The title of this letter is "Share the Wealth of the Internet!" Not only did this chain letter use e-mail as its transmission medium, but it blatantly advocated the use of newsgroups to spread the message. Such use of the Internet is improper and highly unethical. Be a good Netizen; never originate or participate in such a spam, and discourage anyone who spams you from ever doing so again.

Some useful suggestions for fighting spam are found at this book's Web site. If you follow the links to "Fight Spam on the Internet," you will find a tutorial entitled "How to Complain to Providers About Spam." By following the link to the blacklist of Internet advertisers, you can see the worst offenders and read how they have violated the rules of Netiquette.

Hoaxes

Some pretty incredible hoaxes have been propagated across the Internet. The hoaxes are designed to prey on people's fears and sensitivities or their desires to keep the hoax spreading to other users over the Net. An example is the Netscape-AOL giveaway hoax. It was sent all over the Internet via e-mail by the following chain letter:

> Netscape and AOL have recently merged to form the largest Internet company in the world. In an effort to remain at pace with this giant, Microsoft has introduced a new email tracking system as a way to keep Internet Explorer as the most popular browser on the market. This email is a beta test of the new software and Microsoft has generously offered to compensate those who participate in the testing process. For each person you send this email to, you will be given $5. For every person they give it to, you will be given an additional $3. For every person they send it to you will receive $1. Microsoft will tally all the emails produced under your name over a two week period and then email you with more instructions. This beta test is only for Microsoft Windows users because the email tracking device that contacts Microsoft is embedded into the code of Windows 95 and 98. I know you guys hate forwards. But I started this a month ago because I was very short on cash. A week ago I got an email from Microsoft asking me for my address. I gave it to them and yesterday I got a check in the mail for $800. It really works. I wanted you to get a piece of the action. You won't regret it.

Another hoax that surfaces from time to time is the sulfnbk.exe virus hoax. The message comes from one of your friends telling you that a previous e-mail may have infected your computer with a nasty virus called sulfnbk.exe. The message tells you to delete the file sulfnbk.exe from your computer and then send e-mail to all your friends warning them to do likewise because your messages may have infected their computers.

In reality, the file sulfnbk.exe is part of the Windows operating system. Fortunately, deleting this file does not render your computer inoperable. As it turns out, sulfnbk.exe is needed only to resolve long filename extensions during file recovery operations after a catastrophic system crash.

Figure 3-2 shows the sulfnbk.exe hoax message. The author will keep secret the name of the distinguished professor who sent it. The danger is that someday, such a hoax could entice people to do something that could result in data loss or a computer crash. If you receive a message you suspect may be a hoax, follow this book's Web site link to the catalog of hoaxes at the U.S. Department of Energy's Computer Incident Advisory Capability (CIAC) Web site, where you can look to see whether the hoax is a recognized one. For many of the hoaxes, the CIAC will recommend actions you can take to discourage the spreading of the hoax. To look up a hoax and find out what to do about it, follow this book's Web site link to the CIAC Internet hoaxes page. Printed there are dozens of hoaxes, along with an analysis of how each hoax worked. At the CIAC site you will also find links to Web pages warning you about the major chain letters and viruses you need to watch out for on the Internet.

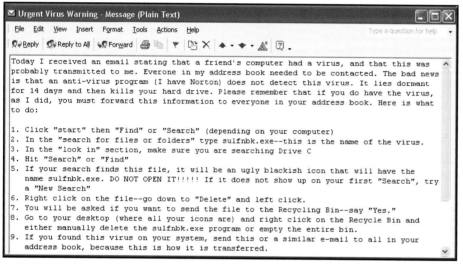

FIGURE 3-2   The sulfnbk.exe virus hoax, as sent to me by a distinguished professor colleague. Before you follow such instructions, check the antivirus centers to find out whether the message is a hoax. ∎

Viruses

Some of the more harmful chain letters and hoaxes have transmitted viruses across the Internet. Although it is not possible for your computer to catch a virus from an e-mail message directly, the mail message can contain attachments which, if you open them, can give your computer a virus. One of the most harmful such e-mail viruses was the Love Bug virus. It spread as an attachment to an e-mail message titled "I Love You" and asked you to open the attachment, which was named LOVE-LETTER-FOR-YOU.TXT.VBS. If you were using the Microsoft Outlook and Outlook Express e-mail programs, opening the attachment sent copies of the message to all the users in your computer's address book. The messages appeared to come from the person who owned the sending computer, serving as further enticement to open the attachment, because it appeared to come from someone you knew. In addition to spreading itself to your friends, the message also deleted certain kinds of files from your computer and replaced them with more copies of the virus.

The best way to guard against catching a virus through e-mail is never to open an attachment to an e-mail message, especially if the attachment has an executable filename extension such as *.exe*, *.vbs*, or *.class*. Macros in MS Word DOC files and MS Excel XLS files can also transmit viruses. Before you open any e-mail attachment, make very sure that the source of the message is one you trust and that the message actually came from that person. If you have any doubts, follow this book's Web site link to the CIAC Virus page to see if the message you received is part of an officially recognized virus attack.

A message may appear to come from a trusted acquaintance when in fact it came from a worm. Recently some viruses spread via e-mail that did not require the recipient to open the attachment. In addition, there are malicious virus programs that mimic the e-mail addresses of people from your address book. It is very important to keep current antivirus protection software on your computer. Most virus scanners have an option to scan incoming mail messages automatically; setting this option can help you avoid opening a malicious message. To keep yourself informed of the latest viruses, follow this book's Web site links to About.com's antivirus site, McAfee's antivirus center, Symantec's Antivirus Research Center (SARC), and CNET's antivirus help site.

Lurking

To **lurk** means to participate in a conversation on the Internet without responding to any of the messages. You receive and read the messages, but you do not say anything in return. Thus, you are lurking!

It is not unethical to lurk. To the contrary, lurking is often a good idea at first. For example, suppose you join a listserv that has been going on for a while. Instead of jumping right in and writing something that may make you seem really out of touch with what is going on, it is smarter to lurk for a while so you can pick up the gist of the conversation before joining in.

The same guideline applies to newsgroups. Before you begin writing messages in a newsgroup, spend some time looking around at what has been written previously in that newsgroup. When you write something, you want to sound as though you know what is going on. Writing messages that waste the time of other users on the Net is inconsiderate.

Ditto for chat rooms. When you enter a chat room in which other people are talking, spend some time listening to get the gist of the conversation before you chime in.

Flames

On the Internet, a **flame** is a message written in anger. The term flame can be used either as a verb or a noun. To flame someone is to send them an angry message. Angry messages that people send you are known as flames.

You need to be careful, especially if you have a temper. Form the habit of thinking carefully about what you write, and proofread messages several times before you send them. Make sure the message truly conveys the emotions you want to communicate. If you are extremely angry and send a hastily written flame, you may regret it later on. When you cool off a few minutes later, you may wish you could tone down the message a little, but it will be too late. The message has already been sent, and unfortunate damage may be done to your relationship with the receiving party.

Firefighters

Sometimes flaming can get out of hand, especially when it occurs in a newsgroup or a listserv with a lot of users. People start sending messages with more heat, and things can get ugly. Someone has to step in and write a message intended to restore peace. Because that puts an end to the flames, such peacemakers on the Internet are known as **firefighters**.

Smileys and Emoticons

One of the problems inherent in text messages is that you cannot see the body language or facial expression of the person sending the message. Not knowing for sure whether something is said in jest can lead people to make false assumptions about the intent of a message. You need to be careful, because miscommunication can cause serious problems.

To give the person reading your message a clue to what your emotions are, emoticons were devised. **Emoticons** are combinations of a few characters that, when turned sideways, conjure a facial expression. The most common form of emoticon is the smiley, which conveys a happy facial expression. Turn your book clockwise, and you will see that the characters :) convey a happy face. The smiley often has a nose :-) and sometimes winks ;-) at you. Left-handed people can use a left-handed smile (: which can also have a nose (-: and can wink (-; at you.

Emoticons are not always happy. For example, :(is a frown, and :-(is a frown with a nose. Someone really sad may be crying :~~(and someone obnoxious may stick out the tongue :-P at you. You can even convey drooling :-P~~ with an emoticon. There are hundreds of these faces. For a more complete list, go to this book's Web site and follow the links to smileys and emoticons.

Three-Letter Acronyms (TLAs) and Jargon on the Net

To shorten the amount of keyboarding required to write a message, some people use three-letter acronyms, appropriately known as TLAs. A **three-letter acronym (TLA)** is a way of shortening a three-word phrase such as "in my opinion" by simply typing the first letter of each word, such as *imo*. I'm not a proponent of three-letter acronyms, because life on the Internet is already filled with enough jargon, abbreviations, and technical terms. TLAs are so common, however, that no book about Internet fundamentals would be complete without mentioning them.

For a complete list of Internet jargon, go to this book's Web site and follow the links to the Web's official "Jargon File" site. You can also get a printed copy of the Jargon File, which is called *The New Hacker's Dictionary* (MIT Press, ISBN 0-262-68092-0).

Electronic Mail

Electronic mail has revolutionized the way people communicate when they cannot talk in person. No longer must people wait for traditional postal mail delivery, which has become known as "snail mail" due to its comparative slowness. On the Internet, if both the sender and the receiver log on frequently, it is possible to exchange several messages with someone in a single day.

Electronic mail is highly efficient. Compared to other forms of communication, e-mail is probably the greatest time-saver in the world. Because you must initiate the reading of your e-mail by running your e-mail software, you read e-mail only when you decide to do so; thus, e-mail does not interrupt your workday. If you are too busy to read e-mail, or if you are on vacation, your e-mail queues up in your Inbox, waiting patiently for the next time you log on. When you travel, you can dial up and read your e-mail, using almost any telephone line anywhere in the world. You can even avoid the need for a phone line if your computer is equipped for wireless communications or if you have a cell phone that supports wireless e-mail.

Getting an E-mail Account

Before you can begin using e-mail, you must have an **account**. An account enables you to log on to the computer that hosts your e-mail service. The computer that hosts your account is known as your mail server. On the mail server, your account consists of file space where your e-mail queues up waiting for you to read it and a login procedure that enables you to log on and access your files.

You get the account from your Internet service provider (ISP). Chapter 2 tells you how to select an ISP. When the ISP sets up your account, you will be told the name of your account. Usually this is your own name (such as fred.hofstetter) or your initials (such as fth) or a nickname (such as freddy). If your account name is something impersonal such as a number (such as 02737), ask your ISP how to go about changing the number to something more user-friendly. Be careful, because once you choose a name, many computers will not allow you to change it.

In addition to being told the name of your account, you will be given a password you must enter each time you log on to your account. The password prevents unauthorized users from logging on under your name and gaining access to your mail. Most host computers permit you to change your password. Choose a password you will remember, but do not select one that is easy to guess, because you do not want someone malicious to guess your password and log on under your name. That person could send offensive mail under your name and cause problems for you. Do not use your first or last name as your password, for example. If you are known to love Corvettes, do not make *Corvette* your password. Choose something unlikely to be guessed. Include a combination of letters, numbers, and special characters. If you ever suspect that someone has guessed your password, change it immediately. Above all, remember your password. ISPs do not like it when you forget your password and they have to reset it for you.

Your ISP will also tell you the IP address of the mail server that hosts your e-mail account. The IP address will be in domain-name format, such as mail.udel.edu. You will need to know all three items—your account name, your password, and the mail server's IP address—to complete the tutorial exercises in this chapter.

Selecting an E-mail Client

The software program that you use to read your e-mail is known as an **e-mail client**. The most popular e-mail client is Microsoft Outlook, which is the e-mail program that ships as part of Microsoft Office. If you use the Microsoft Internet Explorer (IE) browser but not Office, you'll have a free version of Outlook called Outlook Express. This chapter contains detailed instructions on how to use the Microsoft Outlook Express e-mail client. If you are an AOL user and you have AOL mail, you can do the exercises in this chapter by using the AOL mail client that is built in to your AOL account. You can also install Microsoft Internet Explorer and follow the instructions in this chapter by using Outlook Express for mail.

Organizations that install a Web browser other than Internet Explorer often use the mail program that ships as part of that browser for mail. Netscape users, for example, often use the built-in Netscape mail program, which is called Netscape Messenger. Mozilla users get Mozilla Messenger or Mozilla Thunderbird. On the Macintosh, most users read mail with the built-in e-mail client that simply is called Mail. Regardless of the particular software you use, the concepts covered in this chapter apply to all e-mail clients.

The e-mail tutorial in this chapter is written for Microsoft Internet Explorer and Outlook Express. It is possible that your copy of Microsoft Internet Explorer may be set to bring up some other e-mail client, such as Microsoft Exchange or Microsoft Outlook. If that happens when you work through the exercises in this chapter, you can change mail packages by following these steps:

1. Pull down Microsoft Internet Explorer's Tools menu and choose Internet Options; the Internet Options dialog appears.

2. Click the Programs tab.

3. Pull down the E-mail menu and choose Outlook Express mail.

4. Click OK to close the Internet Options dialog.

Deciding on POP vs. IMAP and HTTP

When you configure an e-mail client, you must specify whether the mail delivery protocol is POP, IMAP, or HTTP. Knowing how to set this option is important, because you must choose a protocol that your mail server supports.

Post Office Protocol (POP) was invented for delivering mail post-office style from the server to your PC. When a person logs on to read mail, the mail gets moved physically from the server to the PC, where the user reads the mail without needing to remain online.

You can use **Internet Message Access Protocol (IMAP)** when you want the mail to remain on the server instead of being delivered physically to your PC. This enables you to read your mail from different computers. IMAP is therefore the strategic choice for someone who is on the move and needs to be able to read mail from different locations, such as at home, in the office, in a classroom, or in a branch office.

HTTP is the Web's protocol, which is used for Web-based e-mail servers, the most famous of which is Hotmail. If you are setting up a mail reader to access your Hotmail account, you use the HTTP protocol.

The distinction among these ways of receiving your mail is no longer as clear as it was in the beginning. It now is possible, for example, to configure a POP client to leave the mail on the server. You can also configure an IMAP client to download the mail post-office style so you can read the mail offline.

The best idea is to use the protocols for the purpose for which they were designed. If you need a client to access a Web-based e-mail server such as Hotmail, use HTTP. If your mail server supports POP and you want to have your mail delivered to your PC, use POP. If your mail server supports IMAP and you want the mail to reside on the server, use IMAP. For a more detailed comparison, follow this book's Web site link to POP versus IMAP.

Step-by-Step 3-1
Configuring Your E-mail Client

You must configure your e-mail client before you can begin reading mail. Configuring an e-mail client means telling it the essential information it needs to know, such as the name of your e-mail account, your password, and the IP addresses of your ISP's incoming and outgoing mail servers. You can also set preferences that determine whether the mail will get deleted from the host or stay there after the mail gets downloaded to your computer. To configure your e-mail client, follow these steps:

Step 1   Get Internet Explorer running if it is not already onscreen.

Step 2   Select the Mail icon to drop the menu down, and select Read Mail.

Step 3   If you get a dialog asking you to select a folder for your mail, select the Inbox folder unless you want your mail kept somewhere else.

Step 4   If you have not set up Internet Explorer for mail, the Internet Connection Wizard launches. The wizard asks you several questions.

Step 5   First, the wizard asks for your Internet mail account name, as shown in Figure 3-3. I typed **Fred T. Hofstetter** here.

Step 6   Second, the wizard asks for your e-mail address. Your e-mail address is your account name followed by an @ sign, followed by the domain name of your ISP's host computer. For example, if your account name is SantaClaus and your host computer is northpole.com, you should type **SantaClaus@northpole.com** here.

Step 7   Third, the wizard asks whether you want the mail server to be set up as POP3, IMAP, or HTTP. If you are not sure how to set this, see the previous section of this chapter, titled "Deciding on POP vs. IMAP and HTTP." Then you enter the name of your incoming mail server and your outgoing mail server, which in the case of Santa Claus would be **mail.northpole.com**. Figure 3-4 shows how Santa would complete this step.

Step 8   The wizard asks you to enter your e-mail logon name and password.

Step 9   The wizard asks for your Internet mail account name; type the name you want this to be. Santa Claus would type something like **North Pole mail** here, for example.

Step 10   Next, the wizard asks whether you are using a phone line or a network connection; answer accordingly.

Step 11   If you have multiple connections to the Internet, the wizard asks what Internet connection to use. You should choose the same connection you made when you configured your Web browser, unless you have a reason for doing otherwise.

Step 12   When the wizard finishes, Outlook Express is ready to fetch your mail.

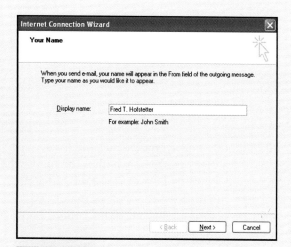

FIGURE 3-3   *The Internet Connection Wizard asks you a series of questions and uses your answers to configure your connection. When the wizard asks for your display name, type your name as you want it to appear in the From field of the messages you will send to people.* ∎

Pulling down this menu gives you the choice of POP3, IMAP, or HTTP.

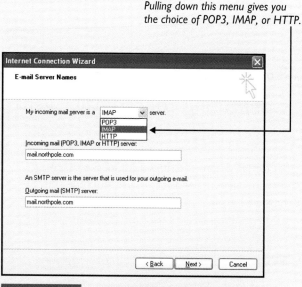

FIGURE 3-4   *When the Internet Connection Wizard prompts you for the domain names of your incoming and outgoing mail servers, you also get a menu to pull down to select the POP, IMAP, or HTTP protocol. If you are not sure how to set this, read the section of this chapter about POP versus IMAP and HTTP.* ∎

Advanced E-mail Configuration Settings

Advanced configuration settings enable you to customize the handling of your mail. The typical user may never need to change the settings, but an IT professional should know where the settings are and what the different options do.

To access these advanced configuration settings, you begin by getting your e-mail client running. If you have IE, for example, you click the e-mail button or pull down the Tools menu and choose Mail and News | Read mail. When your e-mail client appears onscreen, you pull down its Tools menu and choose E-mail Accounts. In Outlook Express, you select the account you want to change and click the Properties button. If you are using the full-fledged version of Outlook, you select the account you want to change and click the More Settings button.

The configuration settings will appear in a dialog box that has tabs labeled General, Servers, Connection, and Advanced. Clicking these tabs reveals options you can review or alter if you want to make changes in the configuration. The settings are explained here:

- **General tab**   Settings on the General tab let you change the name of the e-mail account and alter general information about the user who owns this account. You can change the user's display name, the organization with which the user is affiliated, and the reply e-mail address.

- **Servers tab**   Here you can change the addresses of the incoming and outgoing mail servers and change the incoming server's delivery protocol to POP, IMAP, or HTTP. You can also supply a user name and password and set the mail program to log on automatically when you read mail. You should choose the automatic logon option, however, only if you are the only person who has access to this computer.

- **Connection tab**   True to its name, the Connection tab lets you specify the way your computer will connect to the mail server. Depending on how the computer is connected to the Internet, the choices may include local area network, telephone modem, or dialup networking.

- **Advanced tab**   Here you can inspect the port numbers used for incoming and outgoing mail, and you can change the timeout, which is the amount of time the client will wait for the server to respond to a request to read or send mail. You should not change the port numbers unless your network administrator has told you to do so. POP normally uses port 110, IMAP uses port 143, and the outgoing server uses port 25, which is the default Simple Mail Transfer Protocol (SMTP) port. POP also has a secure version that uses port 995, and the secured version of IMAP uses port 993.

Step-by-Step 3-2

Sending and Reading Mail

Having configured the e-mail client, you are now ready to send and receive mail. This exercise steps you through the process of sending a message to yourself so you will be sure to have a message waiting to be read later in this chapter. Follow these steps:

Step 1   In Internet Explorer, click the Mail icon and choose New Message; the New Message window appears as shown in Figure 3-5.

Step 2 Your cursor will already be in the To field, so enter the e-mail address of the person to whom you want to send a message. The first time you do this, send a message to yourself so you will be sure to have a message waiting to be read in the "Reading Mail" part of this tutorial.

Step 3 Click once in the Subject field and enter a short phrase telling what this e-mail is about. If this is your first message, you might type **My first mail message** for the subject.

Step 4 Click in the large blank area beneath the subject field to position your cursor in the composition area. Here is where you type the message you want to send. If this is your first message, type something like **Hello, world! This is my very first e-mail message.**

Step 5 Click the Send button to send the message. It may take a minute or two for the message to get sent and delivered.

Step 6 Whenever you want to check your mail, click the Mail icon to drop the menu down, and then select Read Mail; the Outlook Express window appears.

Step 7 In Outlook Express, select your Inbox by clicking it once. If you chose IMAP when you configured your mail account, your Inbox is a subfolder of the Messages folder on your mail server; if you chose POP3, click the Inbox in your Outlook Express folder.

Step 8 If new mail has arrived, the Inbox window displays a menu of your incoming mail messages, as shown in Figure 3-6.

Step 9 To preview a message, click its title once, and the message appears in the window at the bottom of the screen. To read the message, double-click its title; the message appears in a Message window. When you finish reading the message, close the message window.

Step 10 In your Inbox, the mail message will now be marked as having been read. The message will stay on your computer unless you delete it.

Step 11 If you want to delete the message, click its title once to select it, and then click the Delete button.

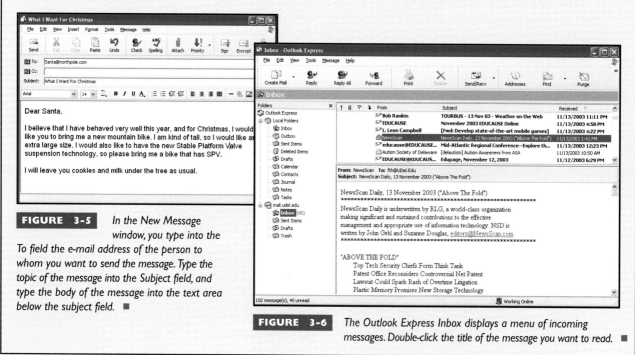

FIGURE 3-5 *In the New Message window, you type into the To field the e-mail address of the person to whom you want to send the message. Type the topic of the message into the Subject field, and type the body of the message into the text area below the subject field.* ■

FIGURE 3-6 *The Outlook Express Inbox displays a menu of incoming messages. Double-click the title of the message you want to read.* ■

Answering and Forwarding Mail

While you are viewing a message onscreen, you can respond to it by clicking either the Reply button to reply to the sender or the Reply All button to reply to the sender and all of the recipients. A shortcut for replying to the sender is to press CTRL-R; to reply to all, press SHIFT-CTRL-R.

At some point you will want to send someone a copy of mail you receive. Instead of going through all the steps needed to copy and paste the message into a new message window, you can simply forward the message by clicking the Forward button, which brings up a new Message window containing the message to be forwarded. In the To field, enter the e-mail address of the person to whom you want to forward the message. In the body of the message, enter anything more that you want to send along with the message, such as a few words indicating why you are forwarding this. Then send the message as usual.

Filing and Retrieving E-mail Messages

Occasionally you will receive an important message that you want to keep so you can refer to it later on. Instead of deleting it, you can file it. To file an e-mail message means to move it into a folder on your hard drive from the Inbox folder where your incoming mail accumulates. There are three processes to learn related to filing e-mail messages: creating an e-mail folder to hold your messages, filing mail into an e-mail folder, and retrieving filed mail whenever you want to read it again.

Creating an E-mail Folder

To file mail, you can create different folders regarding different topics. If you are using Microsoft Outlook or Outlook Express, you create the new folder in the Folders pane. First you click the place where you want to create the new folder. For example, click Local Folders. Then you pull down the File menu and choose New | Folder to bring up the Create Folder dialog. Enter a name for the new folder and click on the folder into which you want to insert the new folder. When you click OK to close the dialog, you will see the new folder in the list of folders in the Folder pane.

Filing Mail into an E-mail Folder

You can file mail in any e-mail folder on your computer. Get your Outlook window onscreen and select your Inbox to reveal the titles of your messages. To file one of the messages, click and drag the title of the message and drop it into the folder you want to file the message in. Another way to file a message is to click the title of the message you want to file, pull down the Edit menu, and choose Move to Folder. This brings up a Move dialog where you can select the folder you want to file the message in.

Retrieving Mail from an E-mail Folder

Filing mail would serve no purpose without a way to retrieve it when you want to refer to it again. To retrieve a filed e-mail message, you click one of

Try This!

Creating an E-mail Signature

When you send someone an e-mail message, it is nice to include information about yourself so the person receiving the message will know something about you, such as your street address, where you work or go to school, and your telephone number. To keep from having to enter this information each time you send an e-mail message, you can create an **e-mail signature**, which is a block of text that is automatically appended to the e-mail messages you originate. To create an e-mail signature, follow these steps:

1. In Outlook Express, pull down the Tools menu and choose Options to bring up the Options dialog.

2. Click the Signatures tab, click the New button, and type your signature into the text box, as illustrated in Figure 3-7.

3. To make the signature appear automatically at the bottom of all your messages, click the option to add signatures to all outgoing mail messages.

4. Click OK to close the Signature dialog; then click OK to close the Options dialog.

Check this box to add your e-mail signature to all outgoing messages.

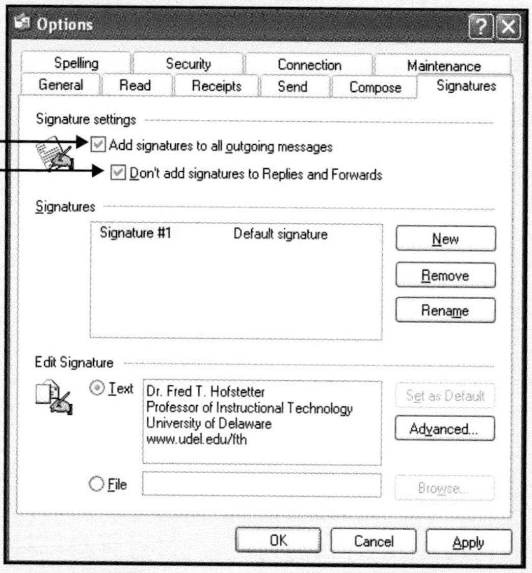

FIGURE 3-7 *When you edit your e-mail signature, keep it short. Four to seven lines is about right. Signatures that are too long are bad Netiquette.* ■

Uncheck this box if you want signatures on replies and forwards.

the folders shown in the Folders pane on the left of the Microsoft Outlook or Outlook Express window. If the Folders pane is not visible, pull down the Microsoft Outlook View menu and choose Folder List or pull down the Outlook Express menu and click the Push Pin to keep the folder list open. When you click to select one of the folders, the Inbox window displays the titles of the mail messages filed in this folder. To retrieve a message, double-click its title.

Sending Mail Attachments

A mail attachment is a file you attach to an e-mail message. When you send the message, the attached file is sent along with it. File attachments can be text documents, pictures, audio recordings, movies, spreadsheets, or virtually any kind of file you are accustomed to using on your computer.

To attach a file to an e-mail message, you compose the message as usual. Before sending the message, you click the Insert File button to make the Insert Attachment dialog appear. Use the controls to locate the file and click its name to enter it into the File name field. Then click the Attach button to complete the process. When you send the message, a copy of the attached file goes along with it.

Try This!

Using an E-mail Address Book

Before you can send e-mail to someone, you must know the person's e-mail address. To avoid having to look up a person's e-mail address every time, you can record it in an **address book**, which is an index of the e-mail addresses you want to keep for future use. To address an e-mail message to someone in your address book, you simply go into your address book, click the person's name, and choose the Send Mail option. This makes an e-mail composer screen appear with the person's e-mail address filled in automatically. The following exercise gets you started using your address book. Follow these steps:

1. Click the Outlook Express Addresses button  to make the Address Book window appear, as illustrated in Figure 3-8.

2. To add a name to the address book, click the New button; when the menu pops out, click New Contact. The Properties dialog appears, as shown in Figure 3-9.

3. In the blanks provided, fill in the person's first name, last name, e-mail address, and a nickname.

4. If you know that the person reads mail with a plaintext (i.e., non-HTML) mail reader, click the option to send e-mail using plaintext only. These days, most people read mail with HTML-enabled mail readers, so leave this option unchecked if you are unsure.

5. Click OK to close the Properties dialog box, and check to see that the person has been added to your address book. If you ever want to change any of this information you added in steps 3 and 4, double-click the user's name in your address book.

Click the New button to add a new contact to the address book.

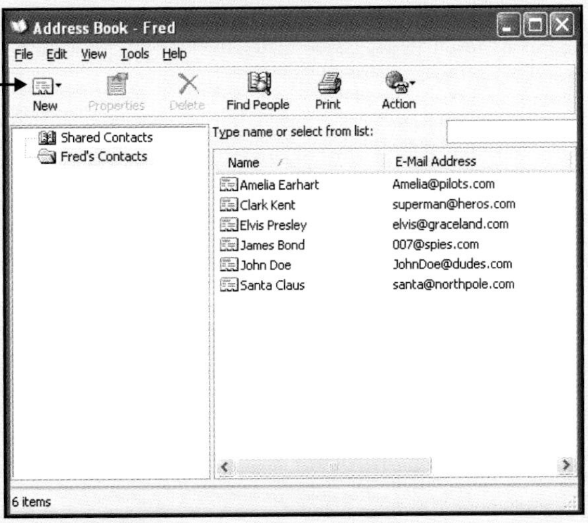

Check this plain-text only box if the person cannot receive HTML e-mail.

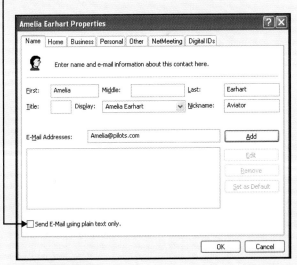

FIGURE 3-8 *An address book consists of an index of e-mail addresses. To send someone a message, click to select the person's name; then click the Action button and choose Send Mail.* ■

FIGURE 3-9 *Fill out this form to create a new entry in an address book. Type the person's name and e-mail address on the Name tab. If you also want to record the person's home or business address and phone number, click the Home tab or the Business tab.* ■

Try This!
continued

After you have entered a person's name into the address book, you can address an e-mail message by selecting that person's name from the address book. Follow these steps:

1. From your Outlook Express Inbox window, pull down the Message menu and choose New Message to make the New Message window appear.

2. In the To and Cc fields, notice the address-book icons at the left. Click the address-book icon in the To field to bring up the Select Recipients dialog.

3. Click once on the name of the person to whom you want to address the message.

4. Click the To, Cc, or Bcc button, depending on whether you want the person to receive the original message, a carbon copy, or a blind carbon copy (the Bcc recipient's address is hidden from the other recipients).

5. Click OK to close the Select Recipients dialog; the person's name appears in the address part of your message.

Addressing E-mail to Groups of People

As social beings, it is natural for computer users to want to communicate with groups of people. You might be working on a project at work or at school, for example, and you would like to send a message to all the people working on that project with you. Instead of having to enter each person's e-mail address each time you want to send the group a message, you can use your address book to create mailing lists consisting of as many users as you like. To create a mailing list, go to the Outlook Express menu and click the Addresses button to make the Address Book window appear. Click the New button to pop out the menu, and choose New Group. In the Properties dialog box, fill in a name for the group, and click the Select Members button to bring up the list of names you can add to the group. Double-click each name you want to add to the group. When you have finished, click OK.

To send e-mail to this group of people, you simply address an e-mail message to the name of the group.

Searching E-mail Messages

When you have a lot of accumulated mail, you will eventually lose track of where everything is. Happily, you can search your mail messages to find things. To search an e-mail message, pull down the Outlook Express Edit menu and choose Find | Message to bring up the Find Message dialog. Type the word or phrase you want to find; fields are provided for searching the From, To, Subject, or Message categories.

Click the Find Now button to begin the search. The results of your search appear in a listbox beneath the search controls. Double-click a title in the listbox to bring up its message.

warning *Junk mail may invite you to click an Unsubscribe link to remove yourself from the list. Clicking that link can trigger malicious code. It is better to block the mail with a filter than to click the Unsubscribe link.*

Dealing with Unwanted E-mail

There are two ways to deal with unwanted e-mail: just delete it or send a reply indicating your disdain for the unwanted mail. Be aware, however, that if the message is unwanted commercial advertising, sending a reply will tell the sender that yours is a valid e-mail address, and you may receive even more spam as a result.

If you believe the unwanted mail is illegal, such as a mail message containing child pornographic material or other criminal activity, you can report the transmission by forwarding it to the appropriate authorities. For example, you can find out how to contact your local FBI office at www.fbi.gov. It may help to forward the message to the postmaster at your Internet service provider, informing your ISP of the unwanted activity and asking for it to be stopped. To send mail to your postmaster, assuming your ISP is northpole.com, you would address the mail to **postmaster@northpole.com**.

You may also wish to support legislation to stop the unwanted mail, especially if it is unwanted commercial advertising. In that case, follow this book's Web site link to the Coalition Against Unsolicited Commercial Email (CAUCE), the Forum for Responsible and Ethical E-mail (FREE), and the Spam Recycling Center. When this book went to press, 18 states had anti-spam laws.

Using Mail Filters

You can block mail from unwanted sources by using mail filters. A mail filter blocks mail coming from any e-mail address that you forbid. You can also block mail by filtering keywords in the subject line. To set a mail filter, pull down the Outlook Express Tools menu and choose Message Rules | Mail. When the Message Rules dialog appears, click the New button to create a new rule. When the New Mail Rule dialog appears, enter the criteria for the messages you want to block. For example, Figure 3-10 shows how to block junk mail from cyberpromo.com.

FIGURE 3-10 *You can use the New Mail Rule dialog to filter incoming mail. You can move, copy, delete, or forward the filtered mail. In this example, because your goal is to block spam, you set the action to delete the message.* ■

Detecting Fake Mail IDs

If you get mail saying it is from someone that you doubt actually wrote the message (such as a message from your boss giving you a million-dollar raise), someone may have used a bogus From field when they sent you the message. You can get more information about where the message came from by revealing the headers of the mail message. To reveal the headers of the message you are viewing, pull down the File menu, choose Properties, and click the Details tab.

note *The Message Rules apply only to POP3 accounts. If you are using an IMAP or HTTP mail account, these instructions do not apply.*

Encrypting Your Mail

If you are concerned about privacy, you may want to consider encrypting your e-mail messages. To **encrypt** a message means to run it through an encoder that uses an encryption key to alter the characters in the message. Unless the person wanting to read the message has the encryption key needed to decode it, the message appears garbled.

Consider a simple example of an encryption key "123" that shifts each successive character in the message by 1, 2, or 3 characters in the alphabet. Encrypted, the message *Hello world* appears as *Igomq zptoe*. In practice, encryption keys are much longer and the encoding process is so complex you would need a supercomputer to crack the key to an encrypted message.

Outlook Express has an Encrypt icon you can click when you want a message to be sent encrypted. For this to work properly, however, you need to have a Digital ID, which consists of a public key, a private key, and a digital signature. Chapter 13 explains these Internet security concepts and provides you with detailed instructions for encrypting and digitally signing your mail.

E-mail Priority Settings

Outlook has a priority-setting option that lets you set the priority of an e-mail message. You set this option when you send a message, and when the message arrives at its destination, a priority flag indicates how important it is. The person receiving the messages can sort them in order of priority and read the most important ones first. To set the priority for an e-mail message, you click the arrow alongside the Priority button in the New Message window. This pops out a quick menu that enables you to set the priority to high, normal, or low. Click the setting you want and then send the mail as usual.

Return Receipt Requested

For a really important message, you may want to be sure the person you sent it to has received it. To verify the receipt of a message, you can set an option for the person's e-mail client to send you a return receipt when the person opens the message. To request a return receipt on a message you are composing with Outlook Express, you pull down the Tools menu and select Request Read Receipt. There is no guarantee, however, that the person who receives the message will choose the setting that acknowledges receipt. Many users, in fact, say no when asked if they want the receipt sent.

Spell Checking

As a final touch, before you send an e-mail message, you may want to spell-check it and correct any spelling mistakes. To check the spelling, pull down the Tools menu and choose Spelling or click the Spelling button in the New Message window.

Web-based E-mail

Several Internet service providers make it possible for you to read your mail on the Web, using a Web browser instead of an e-mail program. Reading mail on the Web is convenient because you can access your e-mail from any computer that has a Web browser and an Internet connection.

Several Internet portal sites offer Web-based e-mail services. You can register at the portal to receive a free Web-based e-mail account. Then you can read and send mail with your browser. Popular Web-based e-mail services are at hotmail.com and mail.yahoo.com. Setting up an account like this comes in handy when you travel, for example, because your e-mail can be delivered to any PC connected to the Internet, such as at a public library or an Internet café.

America Online has a Web-based e-mail service that lets AOL users read their AOL mail from a browser as an alternative to reading it with the AOL mail program. Microsoft Network users can read their MSN mail with Hotmail.

Follow this book's Web site links to learn more about the Web-based e-mail services available from Hotmail, Yahoo!, AOL, and other Web-based e-mail providers.

Sending Mail as HTML

In the Web-page authoring part of this book (Part II), you learn how to use HTML, which stands for hypertext markup language. You can use HTML when you want your e-mail messages to include bolding, italics, underlining, colors, fonts, and special symbols that do not get transmitted in plaintext messages. If you know that the person to whom you are sending an e-mail message is using an e-mail program that can handle HTML, you may wish to consider sending the mail as HTML instead of plaintext.

E-mail programs that can handle HTML include Netscape Messenger, Microsoft Outlook, and Outlook Express. Web-based e-mail programs such as Microsoft Hotmail and Yahoo! mail also understand the HTML option. On the other hand, if you know that the person reads mail with a text-based e-mail program such as PINE, which is popular on UNIX systems, you should not set the HTML option, because HTML mail does not display properly in a text-based e-mail reader. To send Outlook mail as HTML, pull down the Format menu and select Rich Text (HTML). After you select this option, you can put pictures in your e-mail messages. Be aware, however, that including pictures in HTML mail messages makes the files considerably larger and therefore take longer to send and receive, especially for users with dial-up access.

Listserv Mailing Lists

Now that you know how to send and receive electronic mail, you are ready to take advantage of the powerful capabilities of listserv, an Internet service that uses e-mail protocols to distribute messages to lists of users. The messages get served to everyone whose name is on the list, hence the name *listserv*.

There are tens of thousands of listserv mailing lists that you can join. Almost every subject imaginable has a mailing list already set up for people to receive and exchange information about that topic. When someone sends a message containing new information to the mailing list, everyone on the list receives a copy of the message.

Some listserv mailing lists are moderated, meaning that someone screens incoming messages before they get distributed to the list. Most mailing lists are not moderated, meaning that you can freely send messages. Some lists are used only to distribute messages from the list's owner to the members of the list, and others let the members of the list participate in the discussion. Listservs can be used to distribute electronic magazines called **e-zines**, in which each new issue gets e-mailed to all the members of the list periodically. You can easily set up your own listserv mailing list, for example, through which you could publish your own e-zine.

How to Subscribe to a Listserv Mailing List

Because a listserv uses e-mail protocols that virtually every user of the Internet already knows, listserv is easy to learn and use. There are two ways to subscribe to a listserv mailing list. First, many listservs have a Web page where you sign up by filling out a form that prompts you for your name and e-mail address. When you click the Submit button to submit the form, your name gets added to the list. The second way to join a listserv mailing list is to send its host computer an e-mail message saying you want

Try This!

Subscribing to Listservs in Your Profession

Joining the right listserv is one of the most strategic ways you can keep up with what is happening in your profession. Following are instructions for joining some of the best listservs about the Internet.

- **NewsScan**   Instructions for joining NewsScan are provided in the section, "How to Subscribe to a Listserv Mailing List." If you have not already joined NewsScan, please do so. I consider it the best single source for keeping up with what is happening.

- **Tourbus**   The best listserv for someone new to the Internet is Tourbus. Two times a week you will receive in your e-mail a message giving you the scoop on search engines, spam, viruses, cookies, urban legends, and the most useful sites on the Net. When this book went to press, 90,000 users from 130 countries were riding the Tourbus. To subscribe, go to www.tourbus.com and follow the onscreen instructions.

- **LockerGnome**   At lockergnome.com, you can subscribe to lists that will send you newsletters containing tips, updates, and industry news for Windows, OS X, or Linux users. A list called *Mobile Lifestyle* will send you news of MP3 releases, streaming video sites, online radio stations, media player skins, Webcam pages, DVD reviews, and new multimedia hardware and software. *Tech News Watch* includes the latest technology reviews, press releases, news, subscriber feedback, and stuff that does not fit into any of the other LockerGnome newsletters. To subscribe, go to www.lockergnome.com and follow the onscreen instructions.

- **Listservs in Your Discipline**   You can use the Web to find out about listservs across a broad range of disciplines and professions. To search for listservs that interest you, go to the Liszt Directory at www.topica.com, the CataList Catalog at www.lsoft.com/lists/listref.html, and the Tile.Net directory at tile.net/lists.

to subscribe. For example, suppose you want to join NewsScan, a listserv that sends out news about new technology five times each week. To subscribe to NewsScan, follow these steps:

1. Use your e-mail client to create a new message window.

2. Address the message to **NewsScan@NewsScan.com**.

3. Enter the word **Subscribe** into the subject field of the message.

4. Send the message.

Although most listservs send you a reply right away, do not expect to receive an instant reply because it may take a while for your new subscription to get processed. Before too long, however, you will receive an e-mail reply from the server letting you know that you are now subscribed to the NewsScan mailing list. Read the first message carefully. If you subscribed via the Web, the first message may instruct you to send a confirming e-mail message. This confirmation prevents other people from impersonating you and signing you up to the listserv. The first message also normally contains the instructions for how to unsubscribe from the list. Therefore, you may wish to file the first message to save these instructions for future use.

Because hundreds of thousands of people subscribe to NewsScan, it is tightly controlled by the people who moderate it. NewsScan's purpose is to distribute technology news e-zine style rather than to host discussions via the listserv. Therefore, if you try to post messages to the NewsScan listserv after you join it, you will probably receive a reply that NewsScan does not enable discussions among the members of the listserv.

Receiving Listserv Messages: Remember to Lurk

The easiest part of belonging to a listserv is receiving the messages it sends you. The messages sent by the listserv appear automatically in your e-mail Inbox, where you read them like any other e-mail message. As illustrated in Figure 3-11, the From field of your e-mail message will indicate that it came from the listserv.

If you join a listserv that allows you to send as well as to receive messages, remember the advice that was provided in the Netiquette section at the beginning of this chapter. Before you jump in and start originating your own messages, remember to lurk for a while by reading without responding until you get the gist of the ongoing conversation. When you start sending messages, make sure each message fits the topic or purpose of the listserv. If the topic does not fit the purpose of the listserv, you should not send it there.

If you do not want the messages from a listserv arriving in your daily e-mail, you can use an e-mail filter to collect them and place them in a separate file for reading later. To do this, follow the instructions presented previously in this chapter in the section on using mail filters.

This message came from the NewsScan listserv.

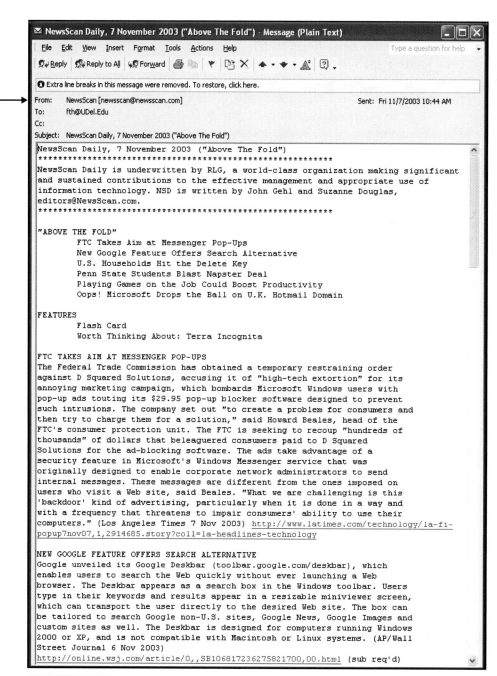

FIGURE 3-11 *You can tell that this message came from a listserv by looking at the From field, which identifies the name of the listserv that sent this newsletter.* ∎

Responding to a Listserv Message

Responding to a listserv message is easy because the address of the listserv is already in the From field or the Reply field of the listserv message. To respond, simply press your Reply button, and enter your response just as you would send an ordinary e-mail message. Remember that your reply will be sent to lots of people, however, so make sure that what you write pertains to the purpose of the listserv.

If you want to respond only to the individual who sent the message, remember to edit the To field so the reply will go to the sender instead of to everyone on the list. It can be embarrassing when a private message intended for an individual gets copied to an entire list full of people.

Sending a New Message to a Listserv

When you join a listserv mailing list, you will be told how to address new messages you want to send to the list. Because listserv addresses can be technical and hard to remember, it is a good idea to enter this address in your e-mail client's address book so you will not forget it. To send a new message to the listserv, you send e-mail to this address just as if you were sending mail to an individual user. Once again, please remember that your message will be sent to lots of people; make sure it is a proper use of the listserv.

Filing Messages Received from Listservs

Occasionally you may receive a message from a listserv that you want to file for later reference. Because messages from listservs arrive as e-mail messages, you can click your File button and file them just like any other e-mail message.

Pausing a Listserv

If you plan to be away from your computer for a while, such as on a vacation, you may want to send a command to the listserv to make it stop sending messages to you. To pause a listserv, send it the following command in the body of an e-mail message, leaving the subject blank:

SET NOMAIL

To resume the listserv, send the following command:

SET MAIL

Because there are several software packages listserv owners can use to manage their listservs, not all listservs respond to the same set of commands. If a listserv does not respond to the SET NOMAIL command, for example, you may need to unsubscribe to get the listserv to stop sending you messages and then subscribe again when you want to resume. If the listserv has a Web site, look there for documentation of the features you can use to control the sending of messages.

Finding Out Who Belongs to a Listserv

It is natural to be curious about who belongs to a listserv. When you send messages to a listserv, everyone on the list gets a copy of your message. To find out who is getting a copy, send the listserv the following command in the body of an e-mail message, leaving the subject blank:

REVIEW *listname*

If that does not work, try:

WHO *listname*

note *Each listserv has two addresses you will want to keep track of. First is the listserv address, the address to which you send your Subscribe command. Second is the list address to use when you want to send messages to everyone on the list. The listserv will tell you the list address in response to your Subscribe command.*

note   *The Review and Who commands must be sent to the listserv address, not the list address. If you send a command to the list address, every member of the list will get it; this can be embarrassing, and it marks you as a newbie on the Net.*

Replace *listname* with the name of the list. The listserv will respond by e-mailing you a list of its members, unless the list has a privacy policy not to reveal the members of the list.

If the listserv does not respond to the Review and Who commands or if you do not know the e-mail address of the listserv, try going to the listserv's Web site and looking there for documentation of the features you can use.

Receiving Messages in Digest Mode

Digest mode is a way of receiving several messages packaged in one e-mail with an index at the top summarizing the subject and sender of each message. If a listserv is full of activity, for example, and sends you several messages a day, you may prefer to receive one digest message instead of many individual messages. To tell a listserv you want to receive the messages in digest mode, send it the following command:

SET *listname* **MAIL DIGEST**

Replace *listname* with the name of the list. The listserv will begin sending you a digest of each day's messages. To end digest mode and make the list send each message in a separate e-mail, send the listserv the following command:

SET *listname* **MAIL**

Unsubscribing from a Listserv

Sometimes you join a listserv only to find that its content does not meet your needs, or you get sent so many messages that you just cannot keep up with them. In either case, you will probably want to unsubscribe from the listserv. To unsubscribe, follow the steps in the message you got from the listserv. Many listservs write unsubscribe instructions at the bottom of every message so you can always find out how to unsubscribe.

note   *Do not send the signoff message to the list address. Doing so will not unsubscribe you from the list. Rather, your signoff message will go to every member of the list, marking you as a novice who does not fully understand how to use a listserv.*

If you subscribed from a Web site, you can probably fill out a form at the Web site that will unsubscribe you. Otherwise, try sending an e-mail message to the listserv address, which is the address you used when you joined the listserv. Leave the subject line blank, and as your message, type **SIGNOFF** followed by the name of the listserv.

Listserv Archives

Many listservs have archives in which the messages sent to the list are filed. You can read and in many cases search the archives online. You can send listserv commands to see the archives, or if the listserv keeps archives on the Web, you can use your Web browser to inspect them. There is a Web-based archive of the messages at the NewsScan listserv, for example; to see them, follow this book's Web site link to the NewsScan archive. Likewise, there is an archive of the Tourbus listserv; follow the link to the Tourbus archive to see the archived Tourbus messages.

Listserv Command Summary

Table 3-1 contains a summary of some of the commands you can send a listserv. For a more complete list, send the listserv the command **LISTSERV REFCARD**. Remember that if you joined the listserv from the Web, the easiest way to send commands is probably by clicking the controls at the listserv's Web site. The trend is to put commands at the listserv's Web site instead of requiring you to send them via e-mail.

Setting Up Your Own Listserv

If you want to set up your own listserv, you can do so for free at a Web site such as topica.com or groups.yahoo.com that offers free list creation. This is one of the perks to keep people coming back to the site where they see the commercial ads that pay for the "free" service. On the other hand, if you want to avoid the commercial ads that appear on messages sent in a free listserv, you can pay a fee to get an advertisement-free list. You can also check to see if ad-free listservs are available from your ISP.

To set up a listserv you can get for free, follow this book's Web site link to setting up your own free listserv.

Listserv Command	What the Command Does
SUBSCRIBE listname *full_name*	Subscribes you to the list or changes the name under which you were previously subscribed; replace *full_name* with your name.
SUBSCRIBE listname ANONYMOUS	Subscribes you to the list anonymously, if the listserv allows that for this list.
REVIEW listname	Requests information about a list, including who owns it and who belongs to it.
SET NOMAIL	Makes the listserv stop sending you messages. (To resume, send the command SET MAIL.)
RELEASE	Find out information about the listserv software being used to run this listserv, and who maintains the server.
SIGNOFF listname	Unsubscribes you from the list.
SET listname CONCEAL	Hides your listing from REVIEW.
SET listname NOCONCEAL	Lets you be listed by REVIEW.
SET listname MAIL DIGEST	Makes the listserv send a day's messages in a single e-mail with a table of contents at the top.
SET listname MAIL	Ends digest mode and makes the listserv send you separate messages.
SHOW STATS	Shows statistics about the listserv.
SEARCH listname keyword1 <keyword2...>	Search the listserv archives; for more search options, send the LISTSERV REFCARD command.
QUERY listname	Queries your set of options on the listserv; use SET to change them.
LISTSERV REFCARD	Asks the listserv to e-mail you a reference card listing commands users can send the listserv.

TABLE 3-1 *Listserv Commands* ■

Newsgroups and Forums

Wonderful as they may be, e-mail and listserv have some shortcomings. E-mail is a great way for individuals to exchange messages with one another, and listserv makes it easy to send mail to lists of people. But it is not easy to maintain your train of thought in a conversation conducted via e-mail. That is because e-mail queues up in your Inbox on a variety of topics, requiring your mind to shift gears continually as you read mail on different subjects.

Enter the USENET newsgroup, which is a resource invented in the late 1970s by students who wanted a better way to converse over the Internet on specific topics. In the following tutorial, you learn how USENET newsgroups enable users to hold virtual conferences over the Internet. You will find out what newsgroups exist in your profession, learn how to join and participate in a newsgroup, and know how to go about creating a new newsgroup.

For more background on how USENET started, follow this book's Web site link to USENET history.

Computer Conferencing

USENET newsgroups are based on the concept of computer conferencing. Just as physical conferences are held on different topics around the country, so does a USENET newsgroup concentrate on a given subject. Just as physical conferences consist of a series of meetings dealing with different topics within the subject of the conference, so newsgroups divide into topics that make it easy for you to participate in the discussion that interests you. The main difference between a physical conference and a newsgroup is that the Internet is bounded neither by time nor by space—anyone can participate in any discussion at any time from any place where there is an Internet connection. Another advantage of newsgroups is that you can participate simultaneously in various discussions of different topics. At a physical conference, on the other hand, you can attend only one session at a time.

Universe of USENET Newsgroups

There are more than 50,000 USENET newsgroups on the Internet. Newsgroups have dotted names such as rec.bicycles.racing that describe what the groups are about. The part of the name up to the first dot is known as the prefix. Common prefixes are *news* for newsgroups that actually deal with news, *comp* for discussions about computers, *sci* for science, *soc* for social issues, *talk* for debates on controversial subjects, *rec* for recreation, and *misc* for miscellaneous topics that do not fit into the other categories.

USENET Hierarchy

USENET newsgroups are organized hierarchically. Each newsgroup has a list of topics. Under each topic is a list of subtopics. Under each subtopic comes a list of messages that users have written in response to that subject. By traversing this hierarchy with a newsgroup reader, you can quickly go to any part of a newsgroup and participate in the topic of your choice.

Messages written in a newsgroup are called *postings* or *articles*. The articles look like e-mail between one user and another, but instead of just being sent between people, the postings can be read by anyone in the world through a news server that provides access to those newsgroups.

Configuring Your Newsgroup Client

Before you can read news, you need to configure your newsgroup client. To do this, you need to know the name of your newsgroup server. It will be a domain name; if you were Santa Claus, for example, the newsgroup server would be named something like news.northpole.com. If you do not know the name of your newsgroup server, ask your Internet service provider. Then get Outlook Express running, click the Tools button, choose Accounts, click the News tab, and click Add | News. Figure 3-12 shows that the Internet Connection Wizard begins to ask you a series of questions.

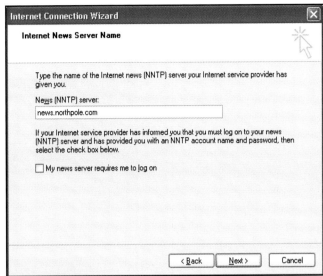

FIGURE 3-12   *The Internet Connection Wizard helps you configure your newsgroup client. In this step, the wizard is asking you to type the name of your news server. If you do not know what the name is, ask your Internet service provider to tell you.* ∎

1. The wizard asks you to type your name as you want it to be displayed when you write a newsgroup message; type your name and then click Next.

2. The wizard asks you to type your e-mail address. Do so and then click Next.

3. The wizard asks you to enter your Internet news server name. Type the name of the newsgroup server you received from your Internet service provider and click Next.

4. Depending on how you are connected to the Internet, the wizard may ask you some other questions; follow the onscreen instructions to answer the questions.

5. When the wizard is finished, it asks you to click Finish to complete the configuration. Click Finish.

6. When the wizard asks if you want to view the list of available newsgroups, click Yes.

To learn how to choose a newsgroup from this list, proceed to the next part of this tutorial, "Choosing a Newsgroup."

Choosing a Newsgroup

Your Internet service provider subscribes to a number of newsgroups from which you can choose one or more that you would like to read. To select a newsgroup, you need to make Outlook Express list the names of the available newsgroups. If you just ran the Internet Connection Wizard in the previous section of this chapter, the list is already on your screen; otherwise, in Outlook Express, click the icon next to the name of your news server in the left-hand column, as shown in Figure 3-13. Then click the Newsgroups button.

First select a newsgroup in the account tree.   *Then click the Newsgroups button.*

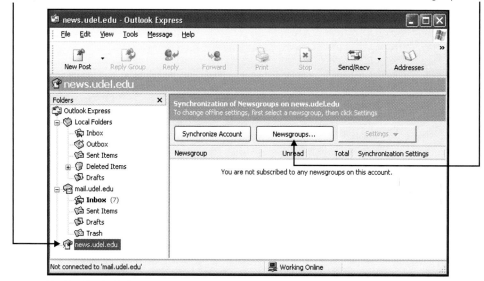

FIGURE 3-13 *When Outlook Express displays the newsgroup options, click to select a news server in the account tree, and then click the Newsgroups button to see the groups on that server.* ■

When you click the Newsgroups button, Outlook Express downloads all the available newsgroups and displays them for you, as illustrated in Figure 3-14. To subscribe to a group, select it by clicking on it, and then click Subscribe. You can narrow the list by entering a keyword in the box labeled *Display newsgroups which contain*. To get the full list back, remove the keyword. If you want to unsubscribe from a group, you can select it from the list and click Unsubscribe.

You can narrow the list by entering a keyword here.

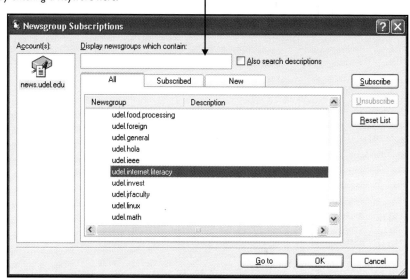

FIGURE 3-14 *When Outlook Express displays the list of available newsgroups, you click to select the name of the group to which you want to subscribe and then click the Subscribe button.* ■

To subscribe to a group you already know the name of, start typing the name of the group to shrink the list. When you see the group you want, select it by clicking on it, and then click Subscribe. Click OK when you finish choosing newsgroups.

In the list of newsgroups, you will see that the names of newsgroups are grouped by title, using compound names such as *rec.sport.basketball.college.* Here *rec* specifies recreational topics, *sport* specifies a subgroup of recreation, and so on.

Good newsgroups to join first are news.newusers.questions and news.announce.newusers, where you can read the articles about newsgroup technique and Netiquette before you begin posting your own messages to any newsgroups. If you have trouble using newsgroups, you can ask questions in news.newusers.questions.

Reading a Newsgroup

Newsgroups are threaded. Each thread represents a different topic being discussed in the newsgroup. To read a newsgroup, double-click the icon next to your newsgroup server to reveal the list of newsgroups to which you are subscribed.

In the list of newsgroups, click to select the name of the newsgroup you want to read. Your computer contacts your ISP and downloads a directory of the messages in the newsgroup; then the directory of messages appears onscreen.

If a message has a plus sign alongside it, that means the message has a hierarchy of other messages beneath it; click the plus sign to reveal the hierarchy. Click the minus sign if you want to collapse the hierarchy.

New messages you have not read yet are printed in bold. To read a message, double-click it. Outlook Express downloads the message and displays it in a message window. To read the next message in the newsgroup, click the Next button (up arrow); to read the previous message, click the Previous button (down arrow).

To help you find your way through the newsgroup, Outlook Express lets you sort the messages in a variety of ways, as shown in Figure 3-15. To sort by subject, click the subject button; to sort by who sent the message, click the From button; to sort by date, click the Sent button.

Responding to a Newsgroup

Responding to a newsgroup is a lot like responding to an e-mail message. The main difference is that instead of being sent to an individual, your response gets posted to the newsgroup. Some newsgroups are moderated, meaning that someone looks over the messages you send to the newsgroup and makes sure the messages fit the purpose of the newsgroup before they get posted to the newsgroup. Many newsgroups are unmoderated, meaning that users can freely write messages without any form of review or censorship.

The rules of Netiquette dictate that when you are first learning to use newsgroups, you should write your test messages in the newsgroup news.test. Subscribe to news.test now. If you have trouble, refer to the instructions in the previous section on choosing a newsgroup. Other practice

The plus sign means you can click here to reveal additional items.

Click here to sort by the name of the sender.

Click here to sort the newsgroup by date.

Click a minus sign to collapse the directory listing.

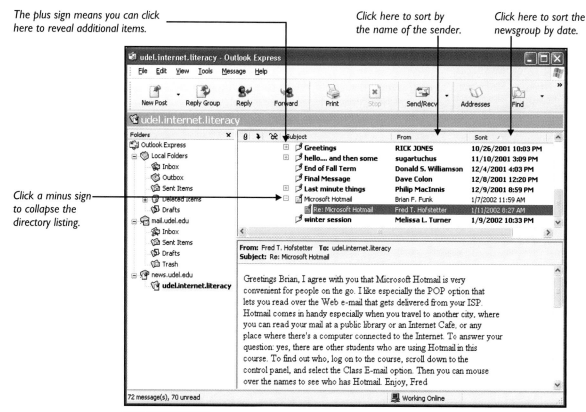

FIGURE 3-15 *Outlook Express lets you sort newsgroup messages by subject, author, and date. Click a plus sign to expand the hierarchy of messages, or click a minus sign to collapse it.* ■

newsgroups are at alt.test and misc.test. Following are the steps for writing a message:

 1. While reading the newsgroup message to which you want to respond, click the Reply Group button.

 2. If you want to reply to just the author, click the Reply button. The mail composition window appears, with a blank message automatically addressed.

 3. Complete the message as if you were creating an e-mail message, and then click the Send button to send the message.

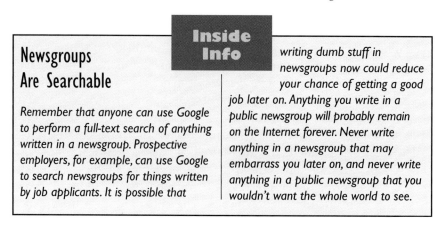

Inside Info

Newsgroups Are Searchable

Remember that anyone can use Google to perform a full-text search of anything written in a newsgroup. Prospective employers, for example, can use Google to search newsgroups for things written by job applicants. It is possible that *writing dumb stuff in newsgroups now could reduce your chance of getting a good job later on. Anything you write in a public newsgroup will probably remain on the Internet forever. Never write anything in a newsgroup that may embarrass you later on, and never write anything in a public newsgroup that you wouldn't want the whole world to see.*

Creating a New Topic in a Newsgroup

While participating in a newsgroup, you may want to start a conversation on a new topic. To create a new topic, enter the newsgroup in which you want to create a new topic of conversation. Click the New Post button; a mail composition window appears with a blank message automatically addressed to the newsgroup. Complete the message as if you were sending electronic mail, and click the Send button to send the message.

The next time you read the newsgroup, you should find your new topic listed in the newsgroup's hierarchy. If your topic is not there yet, it is possible that the server has not yet processed it, or in the case of a moderated newsgroup, the newsgroup's owner may have disallowed the topic. If your posting is rejected, Netiquette calls for the newsgroup's moderator to send you an e-mail message to let you know why your message was not accepted into the newsgroup.

Finding Newsgroups in Your Profession

Go to cyberfiber.com for a comprehensive listing of USENET newsgroups. Click the subject you are interested in to see an outline of newsgroups devoted to that topic. To join a newsgroup, just click it, and your Web browser will automatically subscribe you and take you there.

Another way to find out about newsgroups in your profession is to use the Google USENET search engine, which can perform full-text searches of the Internet's newsgroups. Chapter 2 provides detailed information on how to use Google to find out about information written in newsgroups. When you find the information you are looking for, Google identifies the name of the newsgroup it came from. Then you can subscribe to that newsgroup to explore more of the information it contains. Google finds groups aligned to your topic as well as threads and articles in other groups containing your search words.

> **Inside Info**
>
> ## Microsoft Technical Support Newsgroups
>
> *An invaluable technical resource for IT professionals who are working with Microsoft products is the hierarchy of newsgroups hosted on Microsoft's newsgroup server at news.microsoft.com. To access the Microsoft newsgroups, pull down the Outlook Express Tools menu, choose Accounts, click News, and click the Add button to bring up the Internet Connection Wizard. Follow the wizard's instructions to create your news.microsoft.com account. Then you can click that account to peruse the Microsoft newsgroups and subscribe to the groups of your choice.*

Web-based Discussion Forums

Web-based discussion forums are an alternative to newsgroups. Like newsgroups, forums have discussions that are organized according to topic and subtopic in which users can participate much like a newsgroup. Unlike newsgroups, however, forums are not cataloged as part of the public USENET service on the Internet. What you write in a forum, therefore, does not get searched by the USENET search engine described in the previous section.

Several examples of Web-based forums are linked to this book's Web site. Follow the links to some of the forums you will find recommended there to experience what Web-based forums are like. Some of the more popular forums reside at the Motley Fool at boards.fool.com, where you can search the forums for topics that interest you.

If you would like to host your own Web-based discussion, you can do that at sites such as DelphiForums.com, where you can create your own discussion forums on the Internet. Another popular free discussion host is Yahoo! Groups at groups.yahoo.com. For others, do a Google search for the keywords *forum hosting*.

Blogging

As you learned in Chapter 1, keeping a weblog through blogging has become one of the most popular ways of using the Web. There are two reasons for its popularity. First, people like to keep diaries full of chronological entries describing events that have taken place. Second, blogs are very quick and easy to create. People who would become frustrated learning HTML, for example, can easily create a blog, because the blogging tools prompt users to type in their news and click a Submit button to trigger a server-side process that automatically stores the content and creates the HTML needed to display it onscreen. One of the most popular blogging sites at www.blogger.com refers to this process as "push-button publishing for the people."

The popularity of blogging has given rise to a large number of blogging sites. When this book went to press, there were 38,379 channels cataloged at www.syndic8.com, which is a directory of XML- and RSS-driven weblogs and syndicated newsfeeds. The mass-market popularity of these channels has given rise to a large number of authoring tools. You can peruse these tools by following this book's Web site link to blogging. One of the leading tool providers is blogger.com, which is owned by Google. Taking a look at the tools and services available at blogger.com provides a good overview of the kinds of services that blogging enables. At blogger.com you will find

- A template you fill out specifying where you want your postings to appear and what style they should appear in.

- A form you fill out to make a posting. This form-driven design makes it possible for people who do not know HTML to create weblogs. People who do know HTML can use it nonetheless.

- A Publish button which, when clicked, FTPs the posting to the site of your choice.

- Free hosting services if you do not already have a Web site.

Reading RSS Channels and Feeds

Depending on who defines it, RSS can stand for different things. In Chapter 1, for example, you learned that RSS stands for Rich Site Summary. In a more technically correct sense, RSS stands for RDF Site Summary, where

RDF stands for Resource Description Framework and specifies the XML syntax from which RSS is derived. Not everyone likes these highly technical terms, however. Less technical people say that RSS stands for Really Simple Syndication. Whatever you call it, RSS has become very popular. It provides a quick and easy way for Web developers to summarize what is happening at their sites into a feed that can be channeled to other sites that want to display the news headlines with links to follow for more information.

RSS readers are available for all the major operating systems. Under Windows, popular RSS readers include BlogExpress and SharpReader. On the Macintosh, there is NetNewsWire. Linux users have an RSS reader called Lifera. This book's Web site provides links to these and other popular RSS readers. There is also a Web-based RSS reader called BlogLines that enables you to read RSS feeds from your browser.

RSS files are sometimes called channels or newsfeeds. Whatever you call them, they normally have either XML or RDF filename extensions. To subscribe to an RSS feed or channel, you simply copy its link into your RSS reader. You can often find a Web site's RSS feed by looking for the icon alongside a link to such a feed. To copy the link, right-click (Windows) or CONTROL-click (Macintosh) this icon to pop out the quick menu; then choose Copy Shortcut or Copy Target Address. To subscribe, paste the link into the appropriate section of your RSS reader. In some readers, you can drag the link from your browser to your RSS reader.

RC Chat Rooms

Chat rooms are places on the Internet where you can go to talk with other users in real time. Following the metaphor for which this technology is named, you imagine yourself entering a room in which you can converse with other users you will find there.

One of the oldest and most established chat-room protocols is Internet Relay Chat (IRC), which consists of several networks of IRC servers that support chat on the Internet. The largest IRC networks are EFnet (the original IRC net, often having more than 32,000 people chatting at once), Undernet, IRCnet, DALnet, and NewNet.

IRC conversations are organized into channels. You can join one or more communication channels and converse with other users who are subscribed to the same channel. EFnet often has more than 12,000 channels. Conversations may be public, allowing everyone in a channel to see what you type, or private between only two people who may or may not be on the same channel.

To connect to an IRC server, you must run an IRC client program. The most popular clients for Windows are mIRC and PIRCH. On the Macintosh, the IRC client is Ircle. You can download the client of your choice by following this book's Web site links to IRC.

It is also possible to join an IRC chat through your Web browser. When you enter an IRC chat through your browser, a Java-based IRC client is downloaded automatically, without requiring you to set up anything special in advance.

IRC is not a game. The users you will meet there are real people, and you should treat them with the same courtesy as if you were talking to them in person. You should be aware that it is possible, however, for robots to enter chat rooms and lead you to believe they are human.

This book's Web site links to an IRC Help site. One of its subsites is an IRC Prelude site for people new to chat rooms. Before you begin using Internet Relay Chat, you should follow the links to the IRC Help site and the IRC Prelude site and learn the rules of the road and the principles of IRC Netiquette you will find there. Then you will be ready to visit CityLive, IrCQ-Net, and other chat networks linked to this book's Web site.

Instant Messaging

Instant messaging (IM) is a real-time communication protocol with which you can send and receive instant messages over the Internet. An instant message is an electronic notification that appears on your computer screen automatically to notify you that an important message just arrived in your e-mail or someone wants to talk with you now or something just happened that you wanted to know about, such as the value of one of your stocks moving up or down on the stock market.

To prevent instant messaging from becoming a free-for-all in which anyone on the Internet could interrupt your work instantly, you use a buddy list to identify the people who are allowed to contact you. When you are online, your buddies can send you instant messages, and you can chat with them live over the Internet. If you are busy working on something that you do not want interrupted by an instant message, however, you can set your busy flag. If someone sends you an instant message while your busy setting is on, the person will be told you are busy, while you continue working uninterrupted.

Instant messaging has become so popular that its acronym *IM* has become a verb, which is pronounced eye-emm. To IM someone means to send them an instant message over the Internet.

There are four major brands of instant messaging: ICQ, AOL Instant Messenger (AIM), Microsoft's MSN Messenger, and Yahoo! Messenger. When this book went to press, AOL dominated instant messaging with 100 million users worldwide. The AOL-owned ICQ had 68 million users, MSN Messenger had 66 million, and Yahoo! Messenger 36 million. According to Nielsen/NetRatings, MSN Messenger had the highest growth rate, having grown 21 percent over the previous year, while Yahoo! Messenger grew by 11 percent and AOL increased 2 percent.

As audio and video technology progresses, IM clients are beginning to support multimedia. In a multimedia chat, users who have microphones and speakers can talk out loud to each other and hear what the participants are saying. Users with cameras attached to their computers can appear on the screen of the people they are chatting with. Multimedia chat requires a much higher bandwidth than text-based chat, however, and many users do not have fast enough connections for real-time video. Not to worry, because text-based chat offers a lot of functionality for getting your message across. Even if you have a slow connection that does not have enough bandwidth for multimedia, you will be happy to discover how effective a plaintext-based chat can be for conversing with other users over the Internet.

When you are deciding which brand of instant messenger to use for your own chatting, you need to consider the fact that the different brands do not interoperate with each other. AOL Instant Messenger chatters, for example, cannot use AIM to chat with Microsoft's MSN Messenger users. When you choose an instant messenger, therefore, you need to use the brand where your friends are or convince your friends to get the brand you choose.

ICQ

True to its name, ICQ (pronounced I Seek You) is an instant messaging service that lets you contact people you want to chat with on the Internet and create peer-to-peer communication channels that are quick and easy to use. The latest version adds a file-sharing option for setting up a folder on your PC in which you can share files with your buddies.

ICQ provides a contact list in which you keep the names of the ICQ users with whom you want to be in contact. You can add more friends or business associates to your contact list at any time, or you can remove people when you no longer want them to contact you. Figure 3-16 shows how ICQ displays the names of your buddies who are online. You can use the rich set of Send options in Figure 3-17 to send messages, files, Web pages, or greeting cards to your friends. Figure 3-18 shows that you can TXT your friends via the Short Message Service (SMS), which is a protocol for sending text messages to mobile phones. ICQ also lets you keep a to-do list and set alarms that will remind you to perform a task or help you remember something important, such as your wedding anniversary. When this book went to press, a tool was being tested that would permit ICQ users to communicate with AOL Instant Messenger users. For more information, go to www.icq.com.

FIGURE 3-16   *ICQ displays the names of your buddies who are online. In addition to IMing your buddies, you can press a button to search Google. This is but one of many ways in which instant messaging vendors are extending the scope of what you can do from an IM window.* ■

FIGURE 3-17   *ICQ has a rich set of send options. To TXT friends on their mobile phones, click the option to send an SMS message.* ■

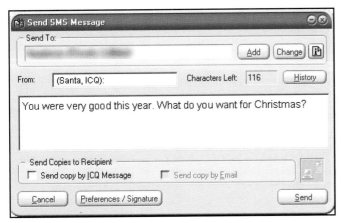

FIGURE 3-18   *When you type an SMS message, try to fit what you have to say in a single transmission instead of sending lots of shorter messages. The sentences illustrated here, for example, could have been sent in separate messages, but that would have created an extra round trip, making the transmission take longer than a single message.* ■

AOL Instant Messenger

As you might expect, AOL, which is the largest Internet service provider, has the largest instant messaging network. AOL subscribers access it via the Buddy List feature. Other users can participate via the AOL Instant Messenger (AIM) product, which is available to anyone, not just AOL members. Especially popular is the AIM Express version, a Web-based AIM client with which you can IM from any Web-connected computer. You can use AIM to accomplish the following tasks over the Internet:

- Receive instant notification when you have mail, your stocks move up or down, or a specific friend or family member comes online.
- Send instant messages.
- Share pictures, sounds, and animation with people on your AIM buddy list.
- Talk live with your friends and family through your computer.
- Chat with friends and family or people with similar interests.
- Stay on top of the news and stocks.
- Use IM Forwarding to deliver messages to your cell phone when you are away from your PC.

The latest version of AIM has an encryption feature so you can send encrypted messages and files. The chat in Figure 3-19 is using this encryption option. Notice that the messages are digitally signed.

When this book went to press, AIM was beginning to support interactive game-playing as a way to increase its popularity. Figures 3-20 and 3-21 show that you can AIM your mobile buddies. Go to www.aim.com if you want to get started using AOL Instant Messenger.

Microsoft MSN Messenger Service

Microsoft markets its MSN Messenger Service as a great way to make free phone calls to your friends and family. All you need are a Passport or Hotmail account, a multimedia PC, a 28.8 Kbps modem or faster, a sound card, speakers,

This icon indicates that the conversation is encrypted.

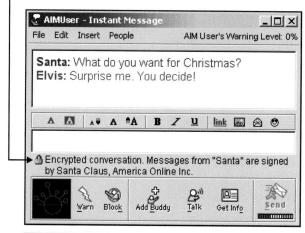

FIGURE 3-19 *AIM gives you the option of encrypting and digitally signing your messages. You should consider using this option whenever you send a message that needs to be kept private. Chapter 13 shows you how to get your own digital signature.* ∎

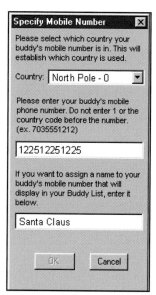

FIGURE 3-20 *You can use AIM to send a message to a mobile phone number. If you assign a name to the mobile phone number, it appears in your buddy list, as illustrated in Figure 3-21.* ∎

FIGURE 3-21 *Mobile buddies appear in your AIM buddy list. Hovering over a mobile buddy pops out an alert showing how long your buddy has been online.* ∎

a microphone, and Internet access. MSN Messenger Service supports the following features:

- **Voice calls with microphones**   Call PC to PC or PC to phone anywhere in the United States or Canada. This feature is not available, however, to users who are behind a firewall or a router that blocks these kinds of binary transmissions.

- **Online status and instant message exchange**   See when your friends are online and exchange instant messages with them. You can chat with up to four friends in the same message window.

- **File sharing**   Trade pictures, music, documents, and more—right from MSN Messenger Service.

- **Reaching beyond computers**   You can send messages to pagers and cell phones.

- **Automatic typing indicator**   To help keep you from interrupting, MSN Messenger Service shows you when one of your friends is typing a response.

- **Customization**   Change font styles and colors. Choose your own system sounds.

- **Emoticons**   Express yourself with pictures like 😊 , 😦 and 😀 .

- **Games**   The latest version has free games, including tic-tac-toe and checkers.

- **Information On Demand**   There are tabs to display MSNBC news, weather, and traffic reports.

- **Webcam**   Users with high bandwidth can use a video webcam option powered by Logitech.

Figure 3-22 shows an MSN Messenger chat in progress. MSN Messenger has built-in support for COPPA, the Child Online Privacy Protection Act, which allows you to control whether or not your children can use the service. For more information, go to messenger.msn.com.

Yahoo! Messenger

If you are a Yahoo! devotee, you may wish to consider using its brand of instant messenger, called Yahoo! Messenger. It lets you access information throughout the Yahoo! portal, and it supports multiparty voice conference calls with hands-free full-duplex conversation. Full-duplex means you can talk and listen at the same time. Users with high bandwidth can use a Super Webcam feature to engage in broadband video messaging at speeds up to 20 frames per second. The search tool enables IM users to look up movie listings and restaurant addresses, which display as clickable links in the chat

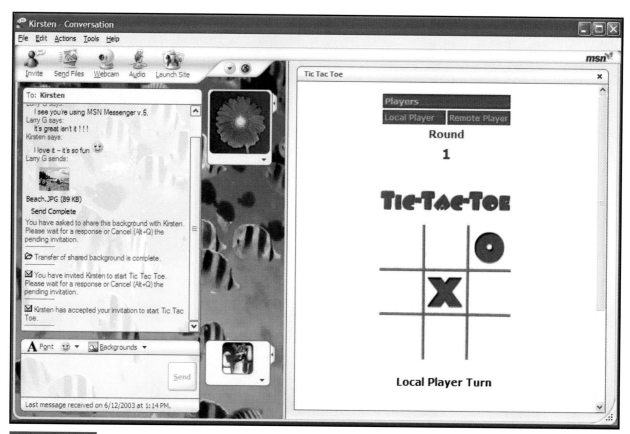

FIGURE 3-22   *MSN lets you play fast-paced games with your buddies. In this example, two users have decided to play a game of Tic-Tac-Toe over an aquarium background. Other games include Solitaire Showdown and Mindsweeper Flags.* ■

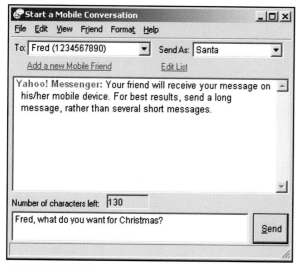

FIGURE 3-23   *When a PC user initiates a mobile phone conversation, Yahoo! Messenger advises that for best results, you should send a long message rather than several short messages.* ■

window. Windows users can download IMVironments and create themed backgrounds for the chat window. One of the IMVironments, for example, lets you get "in the zone" with Britney Spears.

You can also use Yahoo! Messenger to send messages to buddies who have mobile phones. Figure 3-23 shows a message being sent from a PC, for example, and Figure 3-24 shows how the message appears on the phone. For more information, go to messenger.yahoo.com.

FIGURE 3-24   *On the mobile phone, the buddy sees the message (top), chooses to reply (middle), and answers appropriately (bottom).* ■

Whiteboarding, Audioconferencing, and Videoconferencing

It is not always enough just to see what the other users are typing in a conversation. Sometimes you want to see other information that is on their screen as well. For example, a group of professionals collaborating on an economic model might want the conversants to be able to see a spreadsheet, play what-if games, and work together to evolve the best business plan. Distance-learning students collaborating on a scientific research project could similarly benefit from being able to contribute data from remote locations and view the results on a screen shared across the network. The type of computer program that enables remote users to share a common screen across the network is called **whiteboard** software, and the act of sharing such a screen is called *whiteboarding*.

Audioconferencing adds an aural dimension by enabling you to hear what people are saying into a microphone during a conversation, and with videoconferencing, you can see them as well. Virtually every computer sold today comes with a microphone and speakers that can be used for audio conferencing. For less than $50, you can add a camera to your computer so participants can see as well as hear you during a conference. In a videoconference, each person's PC has a video camera and a microphone attached to video and audio adapters that digitize what the camera sees and the microphone hears. Because digital audio and video transmissions contain many more bits of information than textual communications, you need a faster connection to the Internet than is required for text-based chat. A lot of research and development is being done on compressing audio and video to make them require less bandwidth, however, and hopefully videoconferencing will become more widespread when the cost of transmitting it decreases.

In the meantime, if you try to use more bandwidth than your local communication line can handle, you will notice your service degrade. Some day, as the Internet continues to develop, everyone will probably be able to use audio and video without worrying about bandwidth limitations. Until then, a good rule of thumb is to use text-based chat unless you really need audio and not to use video unless the participants really need to be able to see what you are doing on camera. If you need to use a camera but do not have enough bandwidth for the audio to work uninterruptedly, try turning off the audio channel and use text-based chat in combination with the video. Although the video frame may not update very often under these conditions, it will not be as disturbing as an audio channel that keeps dropping out due to low bandwidth. Many corporate intranets, on the other hand, have high-speed connections that permit the use of high-quality videoconferencing. If you are fortunate enough to be on such a LAN, you can enjoy today the full benefits of the emerging videoconferencing technology.

WebEx

More than 8,000 companies are using a Web-based whiteboard and computer-conferencing service created by WebEx. Based on industry standards for scalable distributed networks, the WebEx platform has grown rapidly because it integrates well with any Web-based environment. Features include the real-time sharing of applications, presentations, or documents as well as Web co-browsing, live chat, record and playback, remote control, and file transfer. Figure 3-25 shows that files and applications on any participant's desktop can be opened and shared in real time during a WebEx meeting. Figure 3-26 shows that you click the WebEx Video tab to view live video images of the participants who have cameras.

Because the system is Web-based, WebEx can be used by Windows, Macintosh, and UNIX users to collaborate on applications running on different platforms. Spontaneous presenter delegation enables any one of the participants to become the presenter and share applications and data resident on their desktop. For more information, go to www.webex.com.

CUseeMe and CUworld

One of the first videoconferencing applications on the Internet was called CUseeMe. CU stands for Cornell University, where the software

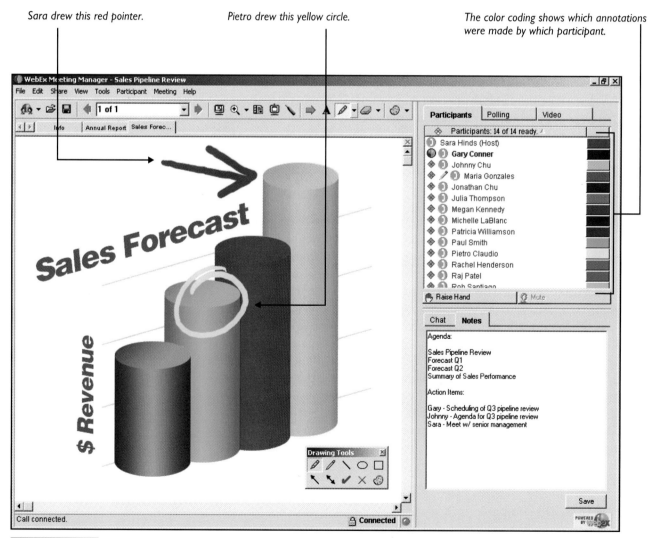

FIGURE 3-25   *With WebEx, presenters can show documents, run applications, and remotely control the participants' computers. During a meeting, you can use the drawing tools to make annotations that all the participants will see.* ∎

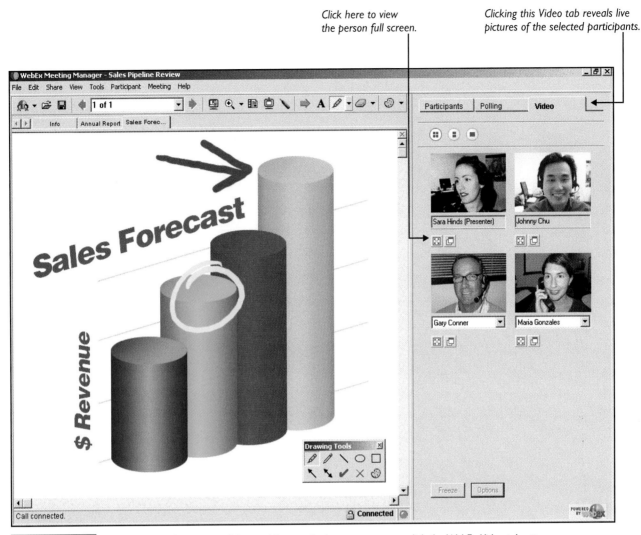

Click here to view the person full screen.

Clicking this Video tab reveals live pictures of the selected participants.

FIGURE 3-26 *To view live video images of the participants who have cameras, you click the WebEx Video tab.* ∎

was developed. Since then, CUseeMe grew into a large family of products aimed at a broad range of users from homes to schools and businesses. In 2003, a company called CUworld was formed through acquisition of the consumer business of the former CUseeMe Networks. The new CUworld service is found online at www.cuworld.com, where anyone can get a free guest membership.

At CUworld, videochats are organized in channels around a central interest theme such as Family, Relationships, Sports, Teens, Travel, and Women. Within each channel you can visit existing videochat rooms or create your own room to discuss a topic that may not already be listed.

Because video requires high bandwidth, CUworld uses a network of Internet reflector sites that handle routing and trafficking problems. The frame rate depends on traffic, and rarely do you get the smooth, full-motion video you are used to on TV, but a new frame comes often enough to give you a good idea of the other person's appearance and body language. To learn more, go to www.cuworld.com and check it out.

Take WebEx for a Free Test Drive

Try This!

You can experience the power of WebEx first-hand by getting a free demo delivered live by WebEx representatives. You do not need a video camera to do this. Follow these steps:

1. Go to www.webex.com and follow the link to join a live demo.

2. When you get a screen asking you to choose a region, such as North America, Europe, Australia, or Asia, click the region that represents your locale.

3. You will be given the option of joining a live demo now, which repeats every 30 minutes, or you can sign up for a more detailed overview at a specific date and time. For the purpose of this exercise, choose the option to join a live demo.

4. You are served a form on which you must enter your first name, last name, and e-mail address. Fill out that information and click the Join Now button.

5. At the prompt to install the WebEx client on your computer, follow the online instructions to install this browser plug-in. On my computer, this installation took three minutes over an ISDN line.

6. When the WebEx Meeting Manager appears, follow the onscreen instructions to join the demonstration, and enjoy your journey into videoconferencing!

NetMeeting and LiveMeeting

When this book went to press, Microsoft was in the process of transitioning from NetMeeting to LiveMeeting for its videoconferencing software. Introduced in 1996, NetMeeting worked its way into the Windows operating system, where it became part of Windows 2000 and Windows XP. For earlier versions of Windows, NetMeeting was freely downloadable. Known especially for its integration with the Microsoft Office programs, NetMeeting enabled users to call each other over the Internet, using the H.323 calling protocol. Figure 3-27 shows a NetMeeting session in which three users are discussing the design of a PowerPoint presentation.

In 2003, Microsoft purchased a videoconferencing company named Placeware and renamed the product LiveMeeting. By the time you read this, LiveMeeting will be integrated throughout the Microsoft Office suite, much as NetMeeting was in previous versions of Windows. To learn more, go to www.microsoft .com/livemeeting.

H.323 Multimedia Communication Standard

Inside Info

H.323 is a standard for transmitting multimedia communications, such as audiovisual conferences, across a packet-switched network. Ideally, such a standard should enable Internet users to participate in the same conference, regardless of their specific brands of videoconferencing software. With today's products, however, you generally need to be using the same brand to participate in a videoconference. As videoconferencing products continue to emerge, it is hoped that the vendors will make them truly interoperative, although the market-driven pressures that cause vendors to differentiate their products may make this interoperability impractical to achieve. You can read the H.323 standard by going to the International Telecommunications Union (ITU) at http://www.itu.int and searching for H.323.

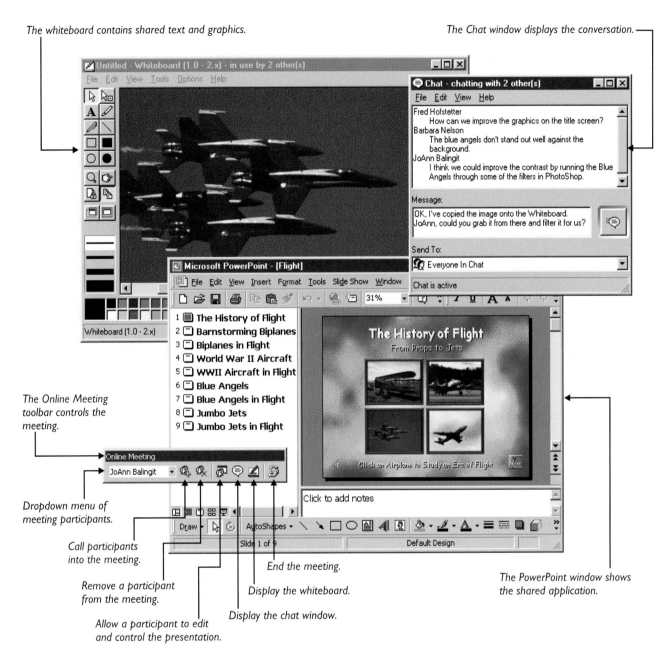

FIGURE 3-27   *You can use Microsoft Office to make audiovisual conference calls when you want to collaborate with colleagues over the Internet. In this example, three developers in remote locations are consulting on the design of a PowerPoint presentation. Each developer sees the Whiteboard window, the Chat window, and the PowerPoint window. The moderator uses the Online Meeting toolbar to control the meeting.* ■

Logging on to Legacy Systems via Telnet

If your career goal is to become an IT professional, you need to be prepared for the possibility that you may someday need to log on to a legacy system that does not have the multimedia communication capabilities presented previously in this chapter. To log on remotely to such a legacy system, you use the **telnet** protocol, which enables individual users to log on to remote host computers on the Internet. Once you are logged on, you can access the services provided by the remote host.

When you telnet to a remote host computer, it prompts you for your user name and your password. Some hosts allow an anonymous login. When prompted for your user name, you type **anonymous** or **guest**, and when prompted for a password, you either type nothing, you type **guest**, or you follow the procedure specified wherever you found out about the site. After you log on as an anonymous user, you can access the remote host's public resources. To access private resources, on the other hand, you need to log on as a specific user in an account that is permitted to access the desired resource.

Telnet can save you money on long-distance telephone charges. Suppose you live in Philadelphia and you want to log on to a remote host computer in Los Angeles. Instead of dialing up to the remote host in Los Angeles, you can telnet there to avoid the cost of the long-distance telephone call. You pay only for your existing Internet connection from your Internet service provider.

Running a Telnet Client

The software that enables your computer to telnet to other computers on the Internet is known as a *telnet client*. Your computer may already have a telnet client program installed on it. For example, all Windows users have a telnet client program called telnet.exe. To run it, you click the Start button, choose Run, and then type **telnet** and press ENTER. If your computer does not have a telnet client, contact your ISP and ask about getting a telnet client for your computer at little or no cost.

As the Web increases in popularity, telnet is becoming less important as a way to find information because it's easier to query databases by using graphical tools on the Web than to type commands at a telnet prompt. Nevertheless, telnet remains an essential Internet resource, especially for programmers and developers who use telnet to log on remotely and perform operational tasks to manage Web sites and keep servers running properly.

Setting the Local Echo Option

When you visit a telnet site, you might not see printing on your screen when you type keys on your computer keyboard. This happens when telnet sites do not echo the keys you type. To solve this problem, pull down your telnet client's Preferences or Settings menu and choose the Local Echo option. If your telnet client is command-line based, type the command **set localecho** and press ENTER.

Freeing Up the Remote Connection

When you finish using the remote computer, you should close your telnet connection to free up resources for other users who may want to connect there. To close a telnet session, type **logout** (or **quit**, **close**, **exit**, or **bye**, depending on the conventions followed at the remote host) and press ENTER.

Try This!

Telnetting to the Weather Underground

You can use telnet to log on remotely to any other computer on the Internet. All you need to know is the computer's IP address or domain name. If the remote host does not support anonymous login, you also need an account (i.e., user name) and password to log on.

Suppose you want to log on remotely to rainmaker.wunderground.com to get your local weather report. Follow these steps:

1. Get your telnet software running. If you have Windows, for example, click the Start button, choose Run, and then type **telnet** and press ENTER.

2. To see a list of the telnet commands, type **Help** and press ENTER. Peruse the list of commands to see the kinds of things you can do, but do not enter any commands yet.

3. The command that connects you to a remote host is called *open*. To telnet to rainmaker, type the following command, and press ENTER:

   open rainmaker.wunderground.com

4. When the remote host responds, it provides instructions telling how to proceed. In this example, follow the onscreen instructions to get a menu of the rainmaker options.

5. Choose the option to print the forecast for a selected city, and follow the onscreen instructions to determine your state's two-letter code and your city's three-letter code. You need to know the city's three-letter code to print out its forecast.

6. The three-letter code for Philadelphia, for example, is PHL. New York City is NYC. Los Angeles is LAX.

7. When you finish checking the weather, follow the onscreen instructions to exit the program. To make sure you are logged off, type **close** and press ENTER.

8. Now use your browser to go to http://rainmaker.wundergound.com and compare the difference between accessing your local weather information via the legacy telnet program and accessing it via the modern graphical Web interface.

Transferring Files via Legacy FTP Commands

In Chapter 1, you learned that FTP is the protocol for transferring files over the Internet. The program you use to FTP files is called an *FTP client*. There are two basic kinds of FTP clients: text-based command-line clients and graphical user interface (GUI) clients. Prior to the invention of GUI clients, the only way to FTP files was to use the text-based commands. Today most Webmasters use GUI clients, which enable you to FTP files by clicking and dragging onscreen controls. In Chapter 7, you learn how to use a graphical FTP client to publish a Web site. This graphical FTP client is all most users will ever need to know.

If you are studying for the CIW Foundations exam, however, you should also learn the text-based commands, which you may encounter on the exam. The reason Webmasters still need to know the text-based FTP commands is that GUI clients may not be usable in some situations. If you telnet to a legacy system from which you need to transfer a file, for example, you might not be able to make the transfer with a modern GUI client.

Instead, you may need to type text-based FTP commands to transfer the files. This chapter concludes, therefore, by teaching you the text-based FTP commands. If you are not studying for the CIW exam, you can skip over the text-based commands and proceed to the Chapter 3 review.

Step-by-Step 3-3

FTPing a File on a Legacy System

Transferring a file via text-based FTP commands is a nine-step process. The following example steps you through using these commands to download a copyright form from the Library of Congress. After you work through this process, you can follow the same procedure to download other kinds of files from other FTP servers on the Internet. Remember that command-line FTP is needed for legacy systems only. If you are studying for the CIW exam, or if your career goal is to become an IT professional, you can learn how to use command-line FTP by following these steps:

Step 1   Bring up a command prompt on the computer from which you plan to issue the FTP commands. If you have Windows, for example, you can get to a command prompt by clicking Start | Programs | Accessories | Command Prompt. Do this now if you want to work through this example on your computer.

Step 2   Go into the folder or directory into which you want to download or upload a file. To go into a folder at the Windows command prompt, you use the command *cd*, which stands for change directory. For help in using this command, type **help cd** and press ENTER.

Step 3   Type **FTP** and press ENTER to start the command-line FTP client. You should see an FTP prompt onscreen. Type **Help** and press ENTER to see the available FTP commands. Table 3-2 guides you in the most common uses of these commands.

Step 4   Use the Open command to connect to the FTP host on which you want to upload or download a file. The command syntax is *open* followed by a space, followed by the domain name or IP address of the FTP host. In this example, type **open ftp.loc.gov** and press ENTER to connect to the FTP server at the Library of Congress.

Step 5   Log on to the FTP server. In this example, type the username **anonymous** and press ENTER. You will be prompted to type your e-mail address as the password. Do this as instructed.

Step 6   Navigate to the directory in which you want to upload or download a file. In this example, type the command **dir** and press ENTER to list the available directories. To enter one of these directories, you use the command **cd**, which stands for change directory. In this example, type **cd pub/copyright/forms** and press ENTER. This takes you into the folder that contains downloadable copyright forms from the Library of Congress. Type **dir** and press ENTER to see the available forms.

Step 7   You need to set the mode to ASCII or binary, depending on the kind of file you want to transfer. ASCII is the default, which you use for text files such as TXT, HTML, and XML documents. Use binary for images, audio, software, PDF, and DOC files. In this example, type **binary** and press ENTER to set the mode to binary, because you will be transferring a PDF file.

Step 8   Use the Get command to download (or use the Put command to upload) the file you want to transfer. In this example, type **get formtxs.pdf** and press ENTER. After the file gets downloaded, use the Windows Explorer to open it. What you downloaded is the Library of Congress copyright form for registering nondramatic literary works, including computer programs. If you ever write a computer program that you want to copyright, you can use this form to register your copyright.

Step 9   When you finish transferring files, go to your FTP prompt, type **close**, and press ENTER to log off.

Command	Description	Example
open	Open an FTP connection	open ftp.loc.gov
close	Close an FTP connection	close
dir	Print an index of the contents in the current directory	dir
cd	Change to a different directory	cd pubs
cd ..	Go up one level of the directory hierarchy	cd ..
cd /	Go to the root directory of the FTP server	cd /
ascii	Set the transfer mode to ASCII, which is for plain text file types such as TXT, HTML, and XML	ascii
binary	Set the transfer mode to binary, which is for non plaintext files such as DOC, EXE, GIF, JPG, PDF, and ZIP	binary
get	Download a file	get formtxs.pdf
put	Upload a file	put formtxs.pdf
mget	Get multiple files from the current directory of the FTP server	mget *.* mget *.pdf
mput	Upload multiple files to the current directory of the FTP server	mput *.* mput *.pdf
help	Print a list of all FTP commands or get help regarding a specific command	help help ascii

TABLE 3-2   *Legacy System FTP Commands* ■

Chapter 3 Review

■ Chapter Summary

After reading this chapter and completing the step-by-step tutorials and Try This! exercises, you should understand the following facts about communicating over the Internet:

Internet Etiquette (Netiquette)

■ Netiquette is the observance of certain rules and conventions that have evolved to keep the Internet from becoming a free-for-all in which tons of unwanted messages and junk mail would clog your Inbox and make the Information Superhighway an unfriendly place to be.

■ On the Internet, the term spam refers to unwanted messages posted to newsgroups or sent to a list of users through e-mail.

■ The best way to guard against catching a virus through e-mail is never to open an attachment to an e-mail message, especially if the attachment has an executable filename extension.

■ To lurk means to participate in a conversation on the Internet without responding to any of the messages. It is good to lurk until you pick up the gist of the conversation.

■ On the Internet, a flame is a message written in anger. Peacemakers who work to diminish the flames are known as firefighters.

■ Messages written on the Internet are normally written in lowercase letters, with capital letters appearing only at the start of the first word of each sentence and on proper nouns, such as the term Internet. WHEN YOU WRITE IN ALL CAPS, ON THE OTHER HAND, YOU ARE SHOUTING! On the Internet, shouting is almost always considered poor taste, so do it sparingly, if at all.

■ Emoticons are combinations of a few characters which, when turned sideways, conjure a facial expression. The most common form of emoticon is the smiley, which conveys a happy facial expression.

■ To shorten the amount of keyboarding required to write a message, some people use three-letter acronyms, appropriately known as TLAs.

■ The Web's official Jargon File site can teach you how to understand some of the more commonly used Internet jargon. In printed form, the Jargon File is published as a book titled *The New Hacker's Dictionary*.

Electronic Mail

■ Before you can begin using e-mail, you must have an account on the computer that hosts your e-mail service. On the host computer, your account consists of file space where your e-mail queues up waiting for you to read it and a login procedure that enables you to log on and access your files.

■ The software program you use to read your e-mail is known as an e-mail client. The most popular e-mail client is Microsoft Outlook, which ships as part of Microsoft Office. If you use the Microsoft Internet Explorer (IE) browser but not Office, you'll have a free version of Outlook called Outlook Express.

■ POP stands for Post Office Protocol. True to its name, POP was invented for delivering mail post-office style from the server to your PC.

■ IMAP stands for Internet Message Access Protocol. You can use IMAP when you want the mail to remain on the server, instead of being delivered physically to your PC. This enables you to read your mail from different computers.

■ An e-mail signature is a block of text that is automatically appended to the e-mail messages you originate.

■ A mail attachment is a file you attach to an e-mail message. When you send the message, the attached file is sent along with it. You need to be careful to avoid catching viruses from e-mail attachments that people send you. Most virus scanners have an option to scan incoming mail messages and file attachments automatically; setting this option can help you avoid opening a malicious message.

■ An e-mail address book can help you keep track of the e-mail addresses of people to whom you send mail. You can use a mailing list to send a message to several people at once.

- To encrypt a message means to run it through an encoder that uses an encryption key to alter the characters in the message. Unless the person wanting to read the message has the encryption key needed to decode it, the message appears garbled.

- Several Internet portal sites offer Web-based e-mail services that enable you to read your mail via the Web. Reading mail on the Web is convenient because you can access your e-mail from any computer that has a Web browser and an Internet connection.

Listserv Mailing Lists

- Listserv is an Internet service that uses e-mail protocols to distribute messages to lists of users. The messages get served to everyone whose name is on the list, hence the name *listserv*.

- Joining the right listserv is one of the most strategic ways you can keep up with what is happening in your profession. Some of the best listservs for keeping up with what is happening on the Internet are NewsScan, Tourbus, and LockerGnome.

- You can use the Web to find out about listservs across a broad range of disciplines and professions. To search for listservs that interest you, go to the Liszt Directory at www.topica.com, the CataList Catalog at www.lsoft.com/lists/listref.html, and the Tile.Net directory at tile.net/lists.

- If you want to set up your own listserv, you can do so for free at a Web site such as topica.com or groups.yahoo.com that offers free list creation. If you want to avoid the commercial ads that appear on messages sent in a free listserv, you can pay a fee to get an advertisement-free list.

Newsgroups and Forums

- USENET newsgroups originated as a grassroots effort by students who wanted a better way to organize conversations over the Internet. The hierarchical structure of a newsgroup mirrors the manner in which physical conferences are organized.

- Newsgroups have dotted names such as rec.bicycles.racing that describe what the groups are about. The part of the name up to the first dot is known as the prefix. Common prefixes are *news* for newsgroups that actually deal with news, *comp* for discussions about computers, *sci* for science, *soc* for social issues, *talk* for debates on controversial subjects, *rec* for recreation, and *misc* for miscellaneous topics that do not fit into the other categories.

- Messages written in a newsgroup are called *postings* or *articles*. The articles look like e-mail between one user and another, but instead of just being sent between people, the postings can be read by anyone in the world through a news server that provides access to those newsgroups.

- Responding to a newsgroup is a lot like responding to an e-mail message. The main difference is that instead of being sent to an individual, your response gets posted to the newsgroup. Some newsgroups are moderated, meaning that someone looks over the messages you send to the newsgroup and makes sure the messages fit the purpose of the newsgroup before they get posted to the newsgroup. Many newsgroups are unmoderated, meaning that users can freely write messages without any form of review or censorship.

- Be aware that when you delete a message from a public newsgroup, this will not necessarily prevent it from going around the world, because newsgroups get copied from node to node as they make their way over the Internet. When you delete a message, it gets deleted from your ISP's copy of the newsgroup, but that may be too late to keep it from going around the world, and some servers do not honor canceled messages.

- You can find out about newsgroups in your field of study or line of work by going to cyberfiber.com or by conducting a Google USENET search.

- Web-based discussion forums are an alternative to newsgroups. Like newsgroups, forums have discussions that are organized according to topic and subtopic in which users can participate much like a newsgroup. Unlike newsgroups, however, forums are not cataloged as part of the public USENET service on the Internet.

- You can set up your own Web-based discussion forum at DelphiForums.com and Yahoo! Groups at groups.yahoo.com.

Blogging

- Keeping a weblog through blogging has become one of the most popular ways of using the Web.

Tens of thousands of channels are cataloged at www.syndic8.com, which is a directory of XML- and RSS-driven weblogs and syndicated newsfeeds.

- The mass-market popularity of these channels has given rise to a large number of authoring tools. One of the leading tool providers is blogger.com, which is owned by Google.

Reading RSS Channels and Feeds

- RSS stands for RDF Site Summary, where RDF stands for Resource Description Framework and specifies the XML syntax from which RSS is derived.

- RSS has become very popular. It provides a quick and easy way for Web developers to summarize what is happening at their sites into a feed that can be channeled to other sites that want to display the news headlines with links to follow for more information.

- RSS readers are available for all the major operating systems. Under Windows, popular RSS readers include BlogExpress and SharpReader. On the Macintosh, there is NetNewsWire. Linux users have an RSS reader called Lifera. There is also a Web-based RSS reader called BlogLines that enables you to read RSS feeds from your browser.

- RSS files are sometimes called channels or newsfeeds. They normally have either XML or RDF filename extensions. To subscribe to an RSS feed or channel, you simply copy its link into your RSS reader.

IRC Chat Rooms

- One of the oldest and most established chat-room protocols is Internet Relay Chat (IRC), which consists of several networks of IRC servers that support chat on the Internet.

- The largest IRC networks are EFnet (the original IRC net, often having more than 32,000 people chatting at once), Undernet, IRCnet, DALnet, and NewNet.

- IRC conversations are organized into channels. You can join one or more communication channels and converse with other users who are subscribed to the same channel.

- Conversations may be public, allowing everyone in a channel to see what you type, or private between only two people who may or may not be on the same channel.

Instant Messaging

- Instant messaging (IM) is a real-time communication protocol that lets you send and receive electronic notifications that appear onscreen automatically to notify you that an important e-mail just arrived, someone wants to talk with you now, or something just happened that you wanted to know about, such as the value of one of your stocks moving up or down on the stock market.

- To prevent instant messaging from becoming a free-for-all in which anyone on the Internet could interrupt your work instantly, you use a buddy list to identify the people who are allowed to contact you.

- There are four major brands of instant messaging: ICQ, AOL Instant Messenger (AIM), Microsoft's MSN Messenger, and Yahoo! Messenger.

- The Short Message Service (SMS) is a protocol for sending text messages to mobile phones. Through SMS, you can IM a TXT message to a mobile buddy.

Whiteboarding, Audioconferencing, and Videoconferencing

- The type of computer program that enables remote users to share a common screen across the network is called whiteboard software, and the act of sharing such a screen is called whiteboarding.

- More than 8,000 companies are using a Web-based whiteboard and computer-conferencing service created by WebEx. Because the system is Web-based, WebEx can be used by Windows, Macintosh, and UNIX users to collaborate on applications running on different platforms.

- One of the first videoconferencing applications on the Internet was called CUseeMe. The service now is called CUworld, which was formed through a corporate acquisition of the consumer business of the former CUseeMe Networks. The new CUworld service is found online at www.cuworld.com, where anyone can get a free guest membership.

- In 2003, Microsoft purchased a videoconferencing company named Placeware and renamed the product LiveMeeting. By the time you read this, LiveMeeting will be integrated throughout the Microsoft Office suite, much as NetMeeting was in previous versions of Windows.

- H.323 is a standard for transmitting multimedia communications, such as audiovisual conferences, across a packet-switched network. Ideally, such a standard should enable Internet users to participate in the same conference, regardless of their specific brands of videoconferencing software. With today's products, however, you generally need to be using the same brand to participate in a videoconference. You can read the H.323 standard by going to the International Telecommunications Union (ITU) at www.itu.int and searching for H.323.

Logging on to Legacy Systems via Telnet

- To log on to a remote host, you use the telnet protocol, which enables individual users to log on to remote host computers on the Internet.

- As the Web increases in popularity, telnet is becoming less important as a way to find information, because it's easier to query databases by using graphical tools on the Web than it is to type commands at a telnet prompt. Nevertheless, telnet remains an essential Internet resource for programmers and developers who use telnet to log on remotely and perform operational tasks needed to manage Web sites and keep servers running properly.

- When you visit a telnet site that does not echo the keys you type, you will not see printing on your screen when you type keys on your computer keyboard. To solve this problem, type the telnet command **set localecho** and press ENTER.

Transferring Files via Legacy FTP Commands

- Webmasters still need to know the text-based FTP commands because GUI clients may not be usable in some situations. If you telnet to a legacy system from which you need to transfer a file, for example, you may not be able to make the transfer with a modern GUI client. Instead, you may need to type text-based FTP commands to transfer the files.

- Before you start your FTP program, change into the directory in which you want to transfer or upload a file.

- Typing the Help command at an FTP prompt prints a list of all the FTP commands you can enter. For more help about any specific command, type **Help** followed by a space and the name of the command.

- You need to set the mode to ASCII or binary, depending on the kind of file you want to transfer. ASCII is the default, which you use for text files such as TXT, HTML, and XML documents. Use binary for images, audio, software, PDF, and DOC files.

Key Terms

account *(127)*	**firefighter** *(126)*	**Post Office Protocol (POP)** *(128)*
address book *(135)*	**flame** *(125)*	**spam** *(122)*
e-mail client *(128)*	**instant message (IM)** *(154)*	**telnet** *(163)*
e-mail signature *(134)*	**Internet Message Access**	**three-letter acronym (TLA)** *(126)*
emoticon *(126)*	**Protocol (IMAP)** *(129)*	**whiteboard** *(159)*
encrypt *(137)*	**lurk** *(125)*	
e-zine *(140)*	**Netiquette** *(120)*	

Key Terms Quiz

1. Coined by combining the words "Internet etiquette" into a single name, _____ is the observance of certain rules and conventions that have evolved to keep the Internet from becoming a free-for-all in which tons of unwanted messages and junk mail would clog your Inbox and make the Information Superhighway an unfriendly place to be.

2. Unwanted messages posted to newsgroups or sent to via e-mail are called _____.

3. To _____ means to participate in a conversation on the Internet without responding to any of the messages. You receive

and read the messages, but you do not say anything in return.

4. An electronic message written in anger is called a(n) _____.

5. _____ are combinations of a few characters which, when turned sideways, conjure a facial expression.

6. To log on to the computer that hosts your e-mail service, you must have a(n) _____ on that computer.

7. The software program you use to read your e-mail is known as a(n) _____.

8. The _____ was invented for the purpose of delivering mail post-office style from the server to your PC.

9. The _____ was designed for situations in which you want the mail to remain on the server instead of being delivered physically to your PC.

10. _____ is the protocol that enables individual users to log on to remote host computers on the Internet.

Multiple-Choice Quiz

1. On the Internet, chain letters are considered to be a form of:
   a. Advertising
   b. E-commerce
   c. Flame
   d. Spam

2. Which of the following was a hoax?
   a. Love Bug
   b. Netscape-AOL giveaway chain letter
   c. Nimda
   d. rotfl

3. The best way to guard against catching a virus through e-mail is never to open an e-mail:
   a. Attachment
   b. Client
   c. Message
   d. Address book

4. Which of the following file types, upon simple opening, cannot by itself infect your computer with a virus?
   a. DOC
   b. EXE
   c. TXT
   d. VBS

5. On the Internet, it is unethical to:
   a. Emote
   b. Firefight
   c. Lurk
   d. Spam

6. In configuring an e-mail client, what protocol should you use to read incoming Web-based e-mail?
   a. HTTP
   b. IMAP
   c. POP
   d. SMTP

7. On the Internet, what protocol does an e-mail client's outgoing server use?
   a. IMAP
   b. POP
   c. SMPT
   d. SOAP

8. In the Windows operating system, if you do not have the Windows Explorer set to display the entire filename, an e-mail attachment named HAPPY.JPG.SCR will appear as follows:
   a. HAPPY.JPG
   b. HAPPY.JPG.SCR
   c. HAPPY.JPG Warning: This Could Carry a Virus
   d. HAPPY.JPG.SCR Warning: This Could Carry a Virus

9. To block mail from unwanted sources, you set up a:
   a. Blog
   b. Digital signature
   c. Mail filter
   d. Mail folder

10. Which Internet service uses e-mail as its transmission protocol?
    a. Blog
    b. Listserv
    c. Newsgroup
    d. Telnet

▮ Essay Quiz

1. Go to the Coalition Against Unsolicited Commercial Email (CAUCE) at www.cauce.org. What is the latest news in their fight against spam? Follow the link to see how you can help, and consider whether you should join CAUCE. Do you think you should join the organization? Would joining CAUCE be strategic for either you or your employer? Why or why not?

2. Go to the CIAC hoaxes page at hoaxbusters.ciac.org, and scroll down to read about the latest hoaxes. Which hoax do you think is the most dangerous to have circulating about the Internet? What kind of damage could it do to the Internet and/or to your computer?

3. Go to the Bill of Rights and Responsibilities site by following the links in the "Netiquette" section of this book's Web site. Read carefully the Bill of Rights and Responsibilities for Electronic Learners that you find there. Do you agree with all the items covered in this Bill of Rights? What do you disagree with? Do you plan to abide by these guidelines? Do you think they leave out anything important? What else should be covered in terms of policies and procedures for electronic communications in your school or workplace?

4. Reveal the full headers on an e-mail message that someone sends you. What additional information can you glean from the complete headers as to who sent the message and how it was routed to your computer? Do you think this could help you identify an attacker who sends harmful messages to you or to your co-workers?

5. This chapter warns against viruses that can be transmitted in e-mail attachments. When this book went to press, the most harmful virus that had appeared to date was the Love Bug virus. Follow this book's Web site link that monitors the latest viruses. What is the name of the latest virus to have appeared to date? How does the virus work; that is, how is it transmitted, what triggers it, and what effect does it have on the user's files or computers? Do you think it is worse than the Love Bug virus? Why or why not? What impact would this latest virus have on your coworkers if it attacked your school or workplace?

Lab Projects

• Lab Project 3-1: Creating a Listserv

A listserv provides any school or company with an easy way of communicating or discussing issues of common concern to fellow employees via e-mail. Imagine that your employer has assigned you the task of creating a listserv for your workplace. To create such a listserv, follow these steps:

1. Follow this book's Web site links to one of the recommended sites that host listservs on the Web.

2. Peruse the site's features and policies. If you do not like what you see, return to step 1 and choose another site.

3. Set up the listserv, following the instructions at your chosen listserv hosting site.

4. Using your word processor, draft an invitation to send to your fellow employees, inviting them to join the list. In this message, write step-by-step instructions for the employees to follow in joining your list. Save the message on your hard drive.

5. Following the step-by-step instructions you wrote in step 4, join the list you created in step 3.

6. Test the listserv and make sure it works properly. To test the list, e-mail it a message. Use your e-mail client's Send feature to send the mail now instead of having it queue in your Outbox. Soon the message you sent should appear in your Inbox. Open the message to make sure it arrived correctly.

If your instructor has asked you to hand in this assignment, what you will submit is the draft invitation you created in step 4. Make sure your name is at the top of it; then save it on disk or follow the other instructions you may have been given for submitting this assignment.

• Lab Project 3-2: Creating a Discussion Forum

Web-based discussion forums provide one of the most powerful yet easiest ways for the employees of a workplace to communicate on topics of mutual concern. Imagine that your employer has just found out about forums and has asked you to set up a Web-based forum your fellow employees can use to discuss issues of common concern with your employer. To set up such a forum, follow these steps:

1. Follow this book's Web site links to one of the recommended sites that host forums on the Web.

2. Peruse that site's features and policies. If you do not like what you see, return to step 1 and choose another site.

3. Set up the forum, following the instructions at the forum site you chose in steps 1 and 2.

4. Using your word processor, draft an invitation to send your fellow employees, inviting them to join the forum and participate in the discussion. In this message, write step-by-step instructions teaching your coworkers how to participate in the forum. Save the message on your hard drive.

5. Test the forum and make sure it works properly. To test the forum, create a new topic in it. The first message in a forum is normally a Welcome message that welcomes users to the discussion and states the forum's purpose.

6. Invite one of your fellow students or coworkers to the forum and ask him or her to write a response to the message you wrote in step 5. Log on to the forum and see if you can read this response properly.

If our instructor has asked you to hand in this assignment, what you will submit is the draft invitation you created in step 4. Make sure your name is at the top of it; then save it on disk or follow the other instructions you may have been given for submitting this assignment.

chapter
4

Commercializing the Internet

"Show me the money!"

—*Cuba Gooding, Jr.*
in "Jerry Maguire"

In this chapter, you will learn how to:

▨ Define e-commerce, describe the demographics of who is using it, and compare e-commerce to traditional commerce.

▨ List the technological components required for e-commerce to take place over the Internet securely and define the features of electronic data interchange (EDI) and secure electronic transactions (SET).

▨ Define the payment models for collecting money when people buy things or when companies transact business online.

▨ Differentiate the types of e-commerce solutions appropriate for various kinds of large and small businesses.

▨ Define the concept of an in-house e-commerce solution, list the stages involved in managing the development of a successful e-commerce project, and define the project management principles of scheduling, budgeting, evaluating risks, preparing contingency plans, preventing scope creep, defining roles, piloting, reporting, and cutover.

▨ Differentiate the roles that licenses, trademarks, copyrights, and patents play in regulating e-commerce projects on the Internet.

▨ List the issues involved in trading internationally over the Internet.

T H E commercialization of the Internet requires us to revise the old adage that life has only two inevitabilities—death and taxes. E-commerce is fast becoming just as inevitable. When this book went to press, for example, there were already 70 million online customers. By the time you read this, that figure will be well on its way to becoming 700 million and could reach 7 billion by the next millennium. Anyone who plans to be in business during the twenty-first century must come to grips with e-commerce and develop a plan for conducting business online.

Deciding how to architect your e-commerce infrastructure is one of the most important decisions you will ever make. Hundreds of e-commerce service providers present you with options to consider. How can you tell them apart? How do you know which vendors to trust? Should you adopt an instant storefront solution that does everything for you, or should your company undertake to develop a customized in-house e-commerce application? What kinds of customization are possible, and how do you go about managing this kind of project development? How can a multi-tiered application strategy help you streamline this development by taking advantage of business-to-business Web services that are already online? What legal challenges will you encounter related to copyrights, trademarks, and patents?

This chapter prepares you to answer these vital questions by teaching you the underlying technologies that enable e-commerce to happen over the Internet. After studying the basic kinds of e-commerce models businesses are using online, you will understand how these models break down into a series of components. Some of these components are essential for any kind of online business. First, customers must be able to find out what you have for sale. Second, customers must have a way to weigh the relative merits of these products. Third, you need to keep track of what the customers decide to buy. Fourth, you must conduct the financial transaction through which the customer will pay for the purchases. Fifth, you fulfill the order. Sixth, you keep careful records of your users' browsing and buying habits that you can analyze to determine how to improve your business.

Throughout this process, keeping customer information secure is paramount. The last thing you want is to have your customer database hacked. This chapter presents best-practice strategies the computer industry is using to accept online payments and keep electronic transactions secure.

A case study, later in this chapter, steps you through a turnkey solution offered by the world's largest e-commerce provider.

Defining E-Commerce

Electronic commerce (**e-commerce**) is the integration of digital communications, data management, and security capabilities that allow organizations to exchange information related to the sale of good and services. The three elements of e-commerce are (1) digital communications, which support the transfer of data between the buyer and the seller; (2) data management, whereby the trading partners exchange information through a common digital language; and (3) security, which guarantees the authenticity, integrity, and privacy of the transactions.

In the most common scenario, a shopper browses an online catalog and selects items to purchase. Online stores typically use the metaphor of a **shopping cart**, which is the virtual basket into which the customer places each item selected for purchase. At any time, the customer can review the contents of the shopping cart and add or subtract items from the pending sale. When the customer finishes shopping, another metaphor comes into play: the **checkout**, which is the process of paying for the merchandise and any related shipping costs. During the checkout process, the customer typically selects from a variety of shipping methods, which may include regular mail or various express delivery options, depending on the product.

After the shipping costs have been determined, the final cost is computed, and the customer is presented with a choice of payment options. Once again, traditional metaphors come into play. In the cash model, **digital cash** or e-cash is a payment method whereby customers pay for the product via tokens drawn from a **digital wallet**. Like the serial numbers on printed money, these tokens are digital certificates that represent a specified sum of real money drawn from the customer's bank account. To date, however, the digital cash payment method has not gained the popularity hoped for by those who conceived it. The most popular payment option is the credit card, such as the customer's Visa, MasterCard, or American Express card. Using credit cards over the Internet can be risky, however. Unless the vendor is using the best-practice methods of Internet security presented in Chapter 13, it is possible for hackers to sniff the packets as they wind their way over the Internet. Security best practices are also needed to prevent hackers from accessing customer information stored in the vendor's back-office system. Digital cash avoids this risk because, like the printed currency from which this metaphor arose, the serial number cannot be traced back to the individual who paid the money. It is also possible to pay with a **digital check**, which is a token transmitted from your digital checkbook. As with a printed check, the merchant does not get paid until the digital check clears your bank.

Most online vendors do not ship the products until the customer has paid. Because the transactions are occurring online, however, the digital check-clearing or credit card processing occurs very fast. Indeed, credit card processing is an online business to begin with.

Who Is Using E-Commerce?

The United States Department of Commerce began to report statistics on e-commerce in the fourth quarter of 1999, when 0.69 percent of retail sales occurred online. Within four years, that percentage nearly tripled to 1.52 percent in the third quarter of 2003. The top applications were nonstore retailers and mail-order houses who conducted 75 percent of their business online and the automotive parts industry, which made 15 percent of its sales online.

According to a poll taken in 2003 by the Direct Marketing Association, there are some demographic differences in terms of the ages at which users shop online. Table 4-1 shows that the highest incidence of online shopping occurs between the ages of 25 and 34, when 61 percent buy products online, while only 14 percent of users over the age of 65 shop online. Look for this elderly percentage to rise as the general population continues to age and the baby boomers enter the 65+ age bracket.

The Different Kinds of E-Commerce

Two models define the basic forms e-commerce can take. The **business-to-consumer (B2C)** model occurs when an end user buys something from a company's online storefront. This kind of sale normally occurs for single products that are sold at a retail price. The second basic form of e-commerce is the **business-to-business (B2B)** model: transactions that occur when companies conduct business electronically between themselves. B2B sales typically have a high volume in which many products are purchased at once for a wholesale price. These two models can also be combined into a B2B2C situation in which a consumer purchases a product ostensibly in a B2C model; behind the scenes, however, the online retailer uses a B2B transaction to obtain the item from a wholesaler. Hence the acronym, B2B2C.

Age	Percent Who Shop Online
18–24	59%
25–34	61%
35–44	57%
45–54	48%
55–64	41%
65+	14%

Source: 2003 poll by the Direct Marketing Association's Shop-at-Home Information Center

TABLE 4-1   *Online Shopping Tendencies by Age Group* ■

Business-to-Consumer (B2C)

The B2C model is the form of e-commerce that end users experience when they buy a product online. Figure 4-1 shows the seven steps typically involved in the B2C process. First, the customer visits an online store and browses the products available for sale. After putting the desired products into a virtual shopping cart and selecting a shipping and payment method, the customer places the or-

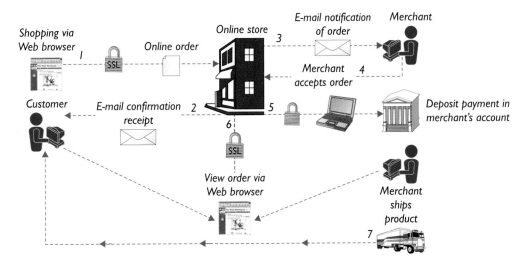

FIGURE 4-1 *The Business-to-Consumer (B2C) model describes the kind of e-commerce in which an end user buys a product online from a virtual storefront. Whenever sensitive information is transmitted, best-practice security measures are used. Many stores use an encryption method known as the Secure Socket Layer (SSL), depicted in this figure by the icon of a lock. You learn how SSL works in Chapter 13.* ∎

der. Second, the online store sends the customer an e-mail verification that the order has been received. I recommend that you save e-mails from your online shopping in an e-mail folder. I save my online shopping correspondence, for example, in an e-mail folder called shopping. Chapter 3 contains detailed instructions for creating this kind of an e-mail folder.

Steps 4–6 occur on the merchant side of the B2C model. The online store sends an e-mail message notifying the merchant that your order has been received. If the merchant accepts the order, the store processes the customer's payment. Throughout this process, both the customer and the merchant can use their browsers to view the status of the order. When the product finally ships in step 7, most online stores send an e-mail message notifying the customer of the product's estimated arrival date and linking to tracking tools, such as FedEx or UPS tracking. Many of the steps on the merchant side of the B2C model can be automated. The merchant can set an option, for example, that automatically accepts orders from financially qualified customers.

Business-to-Business (B2B)

The B2B model describes transactions that happen electronically between businesses. Using the Internet as the communications medium, any company in the world can transact business with any other company, provided they recognize each other as online trading partners and provide B2B access to each other's computers. Figure 4-2 illustrates the typical scenario, in which businesses use B2B communications to list products, highlight new products, query inventories, handle potential sales leads, negotiate pricing, place orders, arrange for shipping, and handle customer complaints.

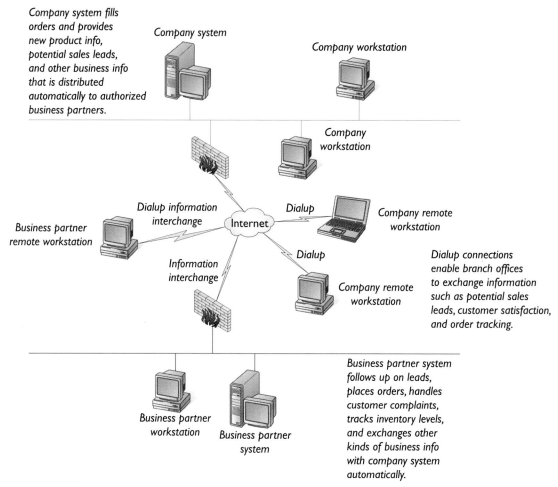

Company system fills orders and provides new product info, potential sales leads, and other business info that is distributed automatically to authorized business partners.

Company system

Company workstation

Company workstation

Dialup information interchange

Dialup

Internet

Company remote workstation

Business partner remote workstation

Information interchange

Dialup

Company remote workstation

Dialup connections enable branch offices to exchange information such as potential sales leads, customer satisfaction, and order tracking.

Business partner workstation

Business partner system

Business partner system follows up on leads, places orders, handles customer complaints, tracks inventory levels, and exchanges other kinds of business info with company system automatically.

FIGURE 4-2   The Business-to-Business (B2B) model describes the kind of e-commerce in which companies exchange information and buy products and services from online business partners. Businesses that recognize each other as online trading partners can provide access to one another's computers. Each business's firewall blocks communication from unauthorized sources. ■

Enabling E-Commerce Technologies

The underlying technologies must address three critical elements of e-commerce: communications, security, and data management.

- **Communications**   The communications must use a common digital language that can be understood by the computers involved in the transaction. EDI, SET, and UDDI are three such languages that are achieving widespread adoption. These languages are described in the next part of this chapter.

- **Security**   The security of these communications must follow the necessary safeguards to build the trust consumers need to feel confident in trading online. Secure Socket Layer (SSL) technology ensures that information packets exchanged over the Internet cannot be sniffed by unauthorized parties. Added encryption such as PGP and GNUGP can provide further security. Online business partners can enforce server- and client-side authentication by using X.509 certificates. Chapter 13 covers these kinds of security measures in detail.

- **Data management**   The data exchanged in B2C and B2B transactions must be stored in such a way that e-commerce transactions can be audited and can recover from outages that may occur during power or equipment failures. Chapter 12 covers the relational database technology that makes this possible.

Electronic Data Interchange (EDI)

In 2003, according to the U.S. Department of Commerce, 88.3 percent of all wholesale B2B e-commerce transactions occurred over **electronic data interchange (EDI),** which is the computerized exchange of business information between trading partners over computer networks. This information can include purchase orders, invoices, shipping schedules, inventory inquiries, claim submissions, or any other kind of information the trading partners need to exchange.

Prior to the invention of the Web, trading partners did their EDI over value-added networks (VANs) that were created by setting up direct links over dedicated communication lines between their computers. Because these VANs tended to be industry specific, different flavors of EDI evolved for specific industries. The heaviest users of EDI were health-related wholesalers of drugs and medical supplies and automotive and commercial equipment suppliers.

Now that the Web is enabling all businesses to interact with each other over the Internet, EDI is being standardized across industries. Known as the X12 standards, the EDI protocols are coordinated by the X12 committee that the American National Standards Institute (ANSI) created in 1979. The Internet Engineering Task Force (IETF) has an EDI Internet working group called EDIINT that has created ways for companies to communicate in X12 securely over the Web's hypertext transfer protocol (HTTP).

In 2003, the world's largest retailer, Wal-Mart, adopted the Applicability Statement 2 (AS2) method of implementing the EDI Internet standards. AS2 is a real-time EDI that uses 128-bit encryption with digital signatures, enabling businesses to transact B2B securely over HTTP. Wal-Mart's adoption of AS2 is causing thousands of trading partners to transition their legacy EDI networks over to the new Web EDI standard. By the time you read this, all these trading partners will be using Web EDI to conduct their B2B transactions over HTTP.

These companies are using EDI to accomplish the following three goals:

- **Saving cost**   By standardizing and simplifying the process of electronic data interchange, companies save time and reduce costs. This is especially important at a time when profit margins are small.

- **Reducing errors**   Streamlining the transactions into a common protocol eliminates translation errors.

- **Speeding up** Thanks to higher efficiency, transactions take less time and business is more efficient.

Secure Electronic Transactions (SET)

Developed by MasterCard and also adopted by Visa, the **secure electronic transactions (SET)** specification is an open standard for conducting secure payment card transactions over the Internet. Digital certificates create a trust chain that verifies cardholder and merchant validity throughout the transaction. To display the SET Mark on their products, e-commerce vendors must pass SET Compliance Testing, which ensures that the software is following the required security best practices. In addition to using certificates, which enforce server and client side authentication, the SET protocol uses cryptography to prevent unauthorized users from sniffing the confidential information transmitted in packets across the Internet.

Cardholders and merchants obtain their SET certificates from financial institutions, which get them from a Certificate Authority (CA). The certificates are electronic documents that enable an institution to determine whether a given encryption key belongs to the individual or entity that is purporting to own it. The SET environment establishes a hierarchy of CAs that extends all the way to the SET Root CA that is owned and operated by SET Secure Electronic Transaction LLC. Chapter 13 teaches you more about encryption and digital certificates, also referred to as Digital IDs and Electronic Credentials.

Another advantage of SET is that merchants never see the purchaser's credit card number. When it comes time to pay, the merchant directs customers to their financial institutions, which process the credit cards and inform the merchant that the payment succeeded or failed. In addition to handling payments, SET also contains methods for credits, returns, chargebacks, and reversals if a product is not available.

For more information about SET, go to www.setco.org.

XML Web Services

A **Web Service** is a software system that uses an XML protocol to support interoperable machine-to-machine interaction over a network. One of the greatest advantages of a Web Service is that the computers do not need to be programmed in the same language. Applications written in COBOL, for example, can use XML Web Service protocols to communicate with servers programmed in C#, Java, or Visual Basic. Because the communication takes place in XML, the computer does not even need to know what language the other process was written in. Because of this flexibility, all the major players in the IT industry have embraced XML Web Services, which are fast becoming the world's e-commerce infrastructure.

The World Wide Web consortium coordinates the development and standardization of the programmatic interfaces that enable Web Services to communicate with each other. For the latest news, go to www.w3.org and follow the link to Web Services.

Universal Description, Discovery, and Integration (UDDI)

Universal Description, Discovery, and Integration (UDDI) is an online yellow pages directory of Web Services that business computers can use to discover and learn how to use the B2B services offered by various companies over the Internet. UDDI is important because it is a cross-industry effort to address the interoperability problems that are limiting the growth of e-commerce. Figure 4-3 illustrates the four components of UDDI. Stage 1 is a directory service that registers Web Services intended for public consumption. Stage 2 is called discovery and is a process through which a Web Service announces its availability and tells where to find its XML service description. In stage 3, the client obtains this service description, which identifies the methods and protocols the client can use to make requests of the Web Service. In stage 4, the client uses the HTTP wire format to post the XML request and receive the XML response from the Web Service.

Trading partners who want secrecy can run a private UDDI directory that is not visible to unauthorized clients. To learn more about UDDI, go to www.uddicentral.com.

Web Service Description Language (WSDL)

The **Web Service Description Language (WSDL)** is an XML language for identifying the methods in a Web Service, defining how those methods

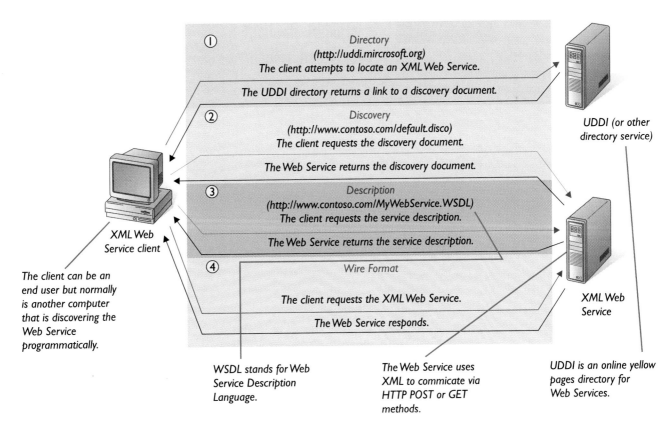

FIGURE 4-3 *The Internet's UDDI Web Services Directory Infrastructure consists of four layers, which are (1) directory, (2) discovery, (3) description, and (4) wire format.* ∎

behave, and instructing clients how to interact with the service. The filename extension for documents written in the Web Service Description Language is .wsdl. Every published Web Service has a WSDL file describing what the service does and how to interact with it.

Simple Object Access Protocol (SOAP)

The **Simple Object Access Protocol** (SOAP) is an XML language for exposing the methods and properties of a Web Service to a consumer, which is any Web client authorized to interact with the Web Service. The consumer can be, and often is, another Web Service. Because the SOAP messages can use the Web's HTTP protocol, SOAP can be used anywhere the Web is, which is essentially everywhere. The W3C is in charge of coordinating work on the SOAP language. To learn more about it, go to www.w3.org and follow the link to SOAP.

Microsoft has integrated Web Service development capabilities throughout Visual Studio .NET, which is Microsoft's premier application

Try This!

Exploring Amazon.com's XML Web Services

E-commerce industry leader Amazon.com has integrated XML Web Services throughout its enterprise. Anyone can apply for a free developer's token that identifies who you are when you use that token to access Amazon's Web Services. A Web site developer can, for example, query the Amazon catalog, advertise products for sale, and earn referral fees for sales driven through links to purchase these products from Amazon. Third-party sellers can use Web Services to manage their inventory at the Amazon site and download the latest product information to ensure that these products are competitively priced. There are some exciting demonstrations of Web Services in action at the Amazon site. To peruse these demos, follow these steps:

1. Go to www.amazon.com/webservices and read the opening paragraph in which Amazon states its vision for Web Services.

2. Look for a link to click to apply for a developer token. You do not need to click that link unless you are a developer and you really want an Amazon token. You do not need a token for this exercise.

3. Scroll down the page and read about the different ways in which Web developers and businesses can use Amazon Web Services.

4. Follow the links to the featured applications. When I did this, one of the featured applications was iPilot.net, where there was a fascinating demonstration showing how you can hang the iPilot scanner on your keychain to take along with you when you go shopping in a traditional store. Whenever you find a product you like, you use the iPilot to scan the product's barcode. Then you beam the scans to your mobile PDA or desktop computer to upload your selections to your live Amazon seller's page, which shows the latest competitive offerings of the products you scanned. If this demo still is online at iPilot.net, follow the link to run the demo, which is fascinating.

5. In the Tools section of the Amazon Web Services page, follow the links to explore the various Amazon Web Services tools. Most of these tools are for Web developers. At this point in your studies, you are not expected to download and use any of these tools. Instead, simply read the descriptions of what the various tools do. This will get you started thinking about some of the possibilities Web Services might play in future e-commerce ventures of your own.

development suite. The tools in Visual Studio make SOAP transparent to the developer. Visual Studio automatically creates the SOAP messages needed for your Web Service to communicate over the Internet. My book *Advanced Web Design* contains a step-by-step tutorial in creating Web Services with Visual Studio.

Processing Payments Online

There are three main e-commerce payment models: cash, check, and credit cards. Each of these payment models is based on a metaphor that is very familiar to mass-market consumers. A fourth model called the smart card is emerging in an attempt to bolster security and add functionality to transactions made with cards. The goal of these four models is to enable a merchant to receive payment from a customer in return for some product or service that the merchant has provided. Besides connecting customers to merchants, however, the Internet also makes it possible for people to communicate directly with each other. When customers begin transacting directly with each other, a customer-to-customer (C2C) model emerges that enables online users to bypass the storefronts and pay each other directly for goods or services that people want to sell to each other.

The following sections will discuss the relative merits of these online payment models. We begin with the three primary models, which are cash, check, and credit cards.

Cash Model

The cash model uses the metaphor of a digital wallet residing on the customer's computer. The digital wallet contains digital cash or tokens with which the customer pays for goods and services purchased online. From the vendor's perspective, the primary advantage of the cash model is that the merchant receives instant payment. The main customer advantage is that you can pay for products online without having to provide the vendor with your credit card number.

Formerly known as digicash, the electronic cash model is now called eCash. It is a legal form of online currency that you can pay for by credit card, check, or money order. Sites you can visit to see eCash in action are www.cryptologic.com/ecash and www.ecashdirect.co.uk. For other sites, search Google or Yahoo! for *eCash*.

Check Model

The check model uses the metaphor of a digital checkbook residing on the customer's computer. This checkbook contains digital checks with which the customer can pay for goods and services online. As in the cash model discussed earlier, the main customer advantage is that you do not need to provide the vendor with your credit card number. The vendor, however, does not receive payment instantly, because the check still needs to clear your bank before the vendor gets paid. Because the vendor can cash a digital check electronically, however, checks clear much more quickly online than in a paper-based system.

The digital checkbook model is especially appropriate for paying bills online. If you are still paying your bills via printed checks, do yourself a favor and begin using a digital checkbook service. To learn more, go to www.checkfree.com, a digital checkbook service that powers the online payment services at the U.S. Postal Service, Bank of America, NetBank, Charles Schwab, SouthTrust, SunTrust, U.S. Bank, USAA, and Wells Fargo. A good place to see this technology in action is at www.usps.com/paymentservices. For other digital checkbook sites, search Google or Yahoo! for *payment service*.

Credit Model

The credit card model is well established both in traditional commerce and on the Web. If you think about it, credit card processing was already electronic from the point at which the sales clerk swiped your card. What e-commerce has done is to enable you to enter your card number by typing it into a Web form instead of swiping your card through a store's card reader.

Every consumer needs to beware of the risk of having your credit card number hacked as part of an unauthorized break-in to a merchant's computer. Every online merchant has the responsibility to employ the best-practice security methods described in Chapter 13. If the online merchant is using SSL, HTTPS, and the digital certificates in Chapter 13, you can be confident that your credit card number will not get revealed to crackers who may be trying to sniff the packets your computer exchanges with merchants. If a merchant stores your credit card number in a database, however, a cracker could break in and obtain access to your confidential records on the merchant's computer.

Such a break-in occurred at America Online during the summer of 2000, for example, when more than 500 screen names were hacked, along with their owner's names, addresses, and the credit card number under which their AOL account was opened. Since then, AOL has taken steps to minimize or eliminate the possibility of such a hack from recurring. In February 2003, however, cardcops.com reported that a hacker broke into a DPI database containing around eight million Visa, MasterCard, and American Express credit card numbers. DPI is one of the companies that process credit card transactions. All three of these credit card companies notified their customers that they would automatically be credited for any unauthorized purchases. The FBI launched an investigation, and you can bet that DPI shored up this vulnerability. Anyone who understands the nature of computers, however, knows that weaknesses must still exist out there somewhere. That is why consumers need to keep a careful watch on their credit card statements and report suspicious activity promptly.

To reduce the cracker's payoff for hacking into credit card databases, some banks offer single-use credit card numbers whereby the customer has a different credit card number for each purchase. To learn more about this, search Google or Yahoo! for *single-use credit card*.

Smart Card Model

A **smart card** is a credit-card sized plastic card with an embedded computer chip and memory that can store digital information. Because the computer chip can handle digitally signed and encrypted transactions whenever the card is used, the smart card enables the cardholder to take advantage of the best-practice security measures you will be studying in Chapter 13. Moreover, the smart card typically has about 4 megabytes of storage, which is more than a hundred times as much as the magnetic strip on a credit card. Another advantage of the smart card is that its computer chip can handle currency conversions when purchases involve international transactions.

The Smart Card Alliance is on the Web at www.smartcardalliance.org. MasterCard, Visa, IBM, and Bank of America serve on the Alliance's leadership council, and several branches of the U.S. government belong to the Alliance. The Federal Aviation Administration, the General Services Administration, and several transit authorities belong as well. Electronic passports and next-generation phone services are among the applications that are emerging for smart cards.

One of the key partners on the smart card leadership council is Oberthur Systems, the world leader and number-one supplier for Visa and MasterCard payment cards. Oberthur has created a megabyte Subscriber Identity Module (SIM) card for mobile phones, thereby setting the stage for third-generation (3G) mobile phones to become e-commerce clients. Although SIM cards are an essential component of all mobile phones, previous SIM cards have not contained enough memory to serve as mobile smart cards. Look for the megabyte SIM to power the convergence of e-commerce with mobile phones. For more on this and other emerging smart card applications, go to www.smartcardalliance.org or search Google or Yahoo! for *smart card*.

Person-to-Person Payment Model

In 1998, a company called PayPal started a person-to-person payment model that enables any individual or business with an e-mail address to send and receive payments online. This model became so popular at the eBay auction site that eBay acquired PayPal in 2002. When customers use PayPal to buy and sell products from each other, a **customer-to-customer (C2C)** form of e-commerce emerges. PayPal's popularity led to its winning the Webby People's Voice Award for Best Finance Site in 2003. When this book went to press in 2004, PayPal had 35 million account members worldwide. In addition to enabling eBay buyers and sellers to transact business directly with each other, PayPal has become popular as a payment method for online retailers and offline businesses, which need only an e-mail address to participate.

PayPal enables you to pay money to anyone who has an e-mail account, even if they do not have a PayPal account. The buyer, however, must have a PayPal account. To get a PayPal account, you go to www.paypal.com and fill out a form to register. As part of the registration process, you choose whether to pay for purchases via credit card, debit from a bank account, or stored balance.

PayPal makes its money by charging sellers a percentage of the transaction as a processing fee. The charge for most purchases is either 2.2 percent plus thirty cents to 2.9 percent plus thirty cents per transaction, depending on volume. There is also a micro-payment processing fee that enables high-volume online digital music companies to sell downloads at a charge of 2.5 percent plus nine cents for each transaction.

The HTML coding needed to put a PayPal payment button at a Web site is relatively straightforward. One of the step-by-step exercises in Chapter 7 walks you through the process of creating a PayPal "Buy Now" button.

Choosing an E-Commerce Solution

There are two basic ways to go about setting up an e-commerce site. You can either develop your own or you can use an **instant storefront**, which is a preprogrammed e-commerce system into which you enter your catalog of products and begin conducting business online. The advantage of the instant storefront is its timeliness. Because the instant storefront is preprogrammed, everything is already set up for you. If a problem arises in the back-end processing at an instant storefront, the responsibility for fixing that problem vests in your instant storefront provider. If you develop your own e-commerce solution, on the other hand, the problem is yours to fix. Depending on your technical skills, this may be an advantage in that you might be able to fix the problem sooner than the instant storefront provider. On the other hand, if the glitch causes your customers to lose large sums of money, you may wish you had never decided to roll your own solution.

Instant Storefronts

Instant storefront solutions come in two kinds, namely, online and offline. In an online instant storefront solution, you do all your development online. In an offline solution, you develop the storefront on your PC and upload it for delivery on the Web. Many instant storefront vendors offer both online and offline solutions.

Searching Google for the keyword "storefront" brings up dozens of sponsored instant storefront solutions. The slogans hype the instant storefront advantages. The following are some typical catchphrases:

- In just 5 minutes you'll be selling online—
  www.shoppingcartsplus.com

- Anyone can create an ecommerce Storefront in minutes using the Storefront Wizard—www.storefront.com

- Everything you need to sell online, only $19.95 per month—
  www.ThriftEstore.com

- Low cost ecommerce shopping cart, no programming—
  www.aacard.com

- We charge, you deliver—www.kagi.com

- Putting e-commerce in your control—www.digibuy.com

These claims are mostly true. If you select a good instant storefront solution, you can be selling products online very quickly and easily, although five minutes may be a stretch. Anyone who is considering the adoption of an e-commerce solution will spend more than five minutes analyzing the relative costs and features of the various systems.

If you have a very small business and you want a quick solution, it is a no-brainer to go with one of the industry leaders such as Microsoft bCentral, Amazon, or Yahoo! These companies offer instant storefront solutions that are backed by some of the largest companies in the industry. You can rest assured that by adopting one of the frontrunners, you will have the industry's best practices working for you in the background. If you shop around, on the other hand, you may be able to find a less well-known storefront that costs you less and still offers the reliability and security your business requires. Just beware that if problems arise, an industry leader may be quicker to solve them than smaller outfits.

Auctions

Industry leader eBay has made it as easy as 1–2–3 to buy goods at an online auction over the Internet. In step 1, you search or browse for the item you are looking for. In step 2, you buy the item or place a bid. A "buy it now" option lets you purchase the item instantly. If you place a bid, on the other hand, eBay bids for you, up to the limit you specified. In step 3, you pay for the item when eBay sends you an e-mail message explaining how to pay the seller. Most sellers accept PayPal, which is free for buyers. Many sellers also accept payment by check or money order.

There are many online auctions besides eBay, such as auctions.yahoo .com, creativeauction.com, and auctionaddict.com. For more, see internetauctionlist.com or search Google or Yahoo! for *auctions*.

Case Study: Microsoft bCentral Commerce Manager

I own a small business called Serfsoft Corporation, which markets an eLearning solution called Serf. When customers began asking for a way to purchase products online, I decided to add a storefront page to the serfsoft.com Web site. Time was of the essence, because any time spent fussing with e-commerce details would be time taken away from developing Serf and writing books. To provide customers with a secure storefront, I wanted to go with an industry leader that is employing best practices on the Internet.

I developed the serfsoft.com Web site with Microsoft FrontPage, which is the Web authoring program in Microsoft Office. While considering the various instant storefront alternatives, I discovered the Microsoft bCentral e-commerce add-in, which adds to FrontPage a toolbar for creating an instant storefront. Deciding to use bCentral became a no-brainer,

n o t e *By using Serf as the example in this case study, I am not attempting to interest you in buying the Serf product. Rather, the purpose is to provide a working example of what it is like to set up an instant storefront.*

because (1) it could snap right into the existing site and (2) it is backed by Microsoft, the world's largest developer of e-commerce solutions.

This case study takes you on a guided tour of the steps I went through in adding a bCentral instant storefront to the Serfsoft site. You can visit the storefront by going to www.serfsoft.com and following the link to the on-line store. Feel free to browse the product catalog and put items into your shopping cart. As long as you do not click the Purchase button, you will not be committed to buying anything. Thus, you can follow along at the site as you read the following case study, which shows you what it is like to create an instant storefront.

Setting Up a bCentral E-Commerce Account

Microsoft bCentral's e-commerce product is called Commerce Manager. When I got my Commerce Manager account, bCentral was charging an annual fee of $249 or a monthly fee of $24.95 beginning with a 30-day free trial. I chose the annual fee, which saves $50 per year as compared to the monthly cost. If you would like to try bCentral before committing to spending anything, on the other hand, you can step through this case study and choose the 30-day free trial option.

To get a bCentral E-commerce account, you go to www.bCentral.com and follow the link to E-commerce. Figure 4-4 shows how you click the option to sign up for either the monthly or the annual plan. You are then guided through a series of screens that prompt you for information required to set up your account. Later on, if any of this information changes, you can edit your settings via the controls on the Commerce Manager menu.

Creating a Product

n o t e *SKU stands for stock-keeping unit, which is a unique alphanumeric code you assign to each product in your catalog.*

You keep your product catalog online at the bCentral Web site. To add a product to the catalog, you log on to your bCentral account, choose Commerce Manager, click Product Catalog, and choose the option to add a new product. Figure 4-5 shows how the Add Single Product screen consists of sections that let you enter the standard product information, set shipping charges, upload product images, define the product's details, and add product options. When you fill in the standard product information, be sure to include the product's name, summary, SKU, and price.

Every product in your catalog must belong to a department. By default, products are entered in the top-level department. If you click to change or edit the department, a special window opens for managing your departments. At my storefront, for example, I have two departments, one for nonprofit academic customers and one for businesses.

When you click to add an image, a Select Images window opens to help you select or upload an image to depict this product in your catalog. You should provide an image for each product.

If your product has special options that the customer needs to choose—for example, the color or size of the desired product—click the link to *Add*

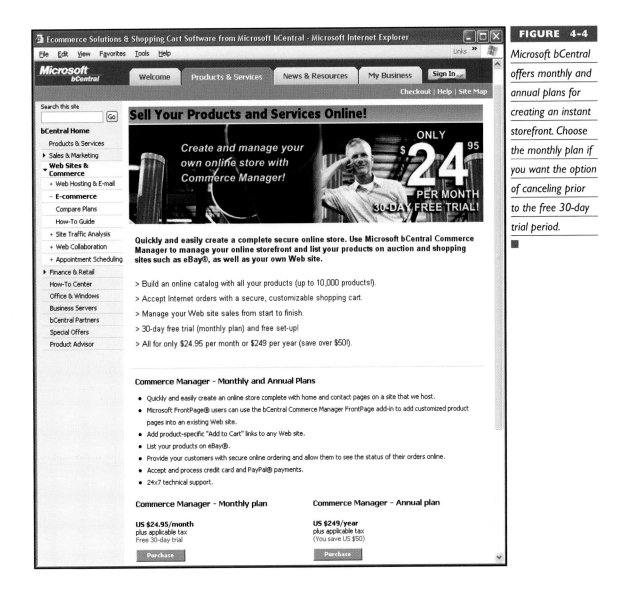

product options. This causes a special window to open where you can add options.

When you finish filling out the Add Single Product form, click Save to enter this item into your catalog. If you ever need to change this information, choose the View/Manage Products option in the Products section of the Commerce Manager.

Choosing a Marketplace

A marketplace is a virtual trading area in which products are listed for sale. After you create your product catalog at bCentral, you need to select at least one marketplace in which your products will be listed. One of the options is to make your FrontPage Web site a marketplace. I chose this option because my business's Web site is a FrontPage site. There are other marketplaces, however, where you can list your products without needing to host your own Web site. These include the Product Gallery, the MSN

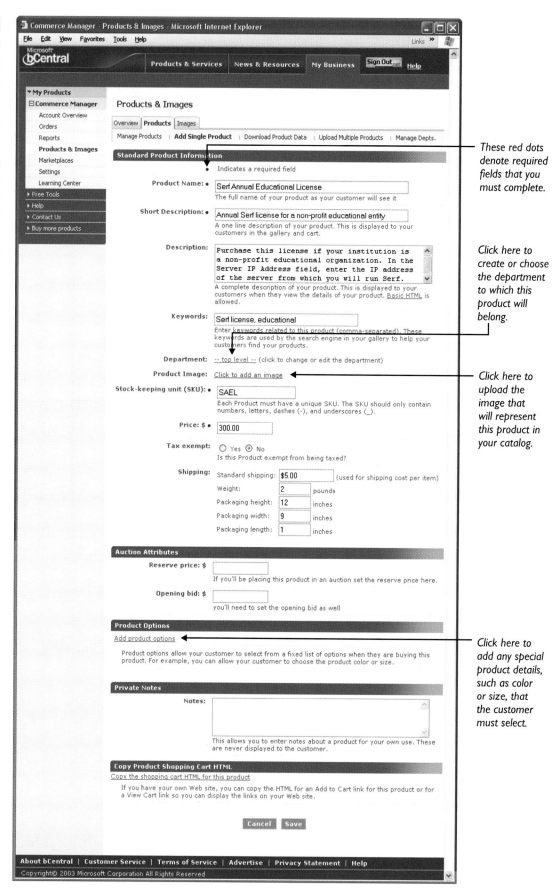

These red dots denote required fields that you must complete.

Click here to create or choose the department to which this product will belong.

Click here to upload the image that will represent this product in your catalog.

Click here to add any special product details, such as color or size, that the customer must select.

Marketplace, the bCentral marketplace, and the eBay auctions. Figure 4-6 shows how I chose to list my products in these marketplaces.

Installing the FrontPage E-Commerce Wizard

Remember that I chose bCentral because of the E-Commerce Wizard that can create automatically at a FrontPage Web site a product catalog that customers can browse to buy products online. To download this wizard, you go to www.bcentral.com and search for FrontPage Wizard. This brings up a link to the bCentral Commerce Manager Add-In for FrontPage customers. I followed the onscreen instructions to download and install this add-in.

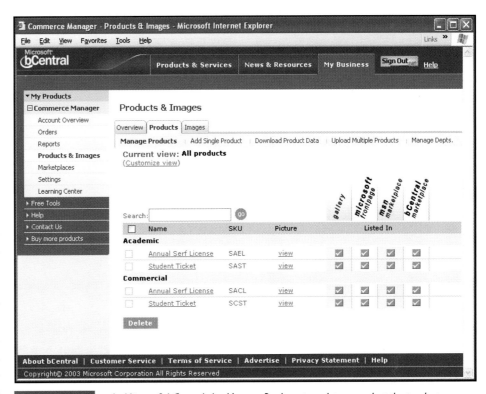

FIGURE 4-6 *At Microsoft bCentral, the Manage Products page lets you select the products you want to list in various marketplaces. I chose to list all my products in the gallery, FrontPage, MSN, and bCentral marketplaces. A nice feature of the gallery is that it creates an instant storefront to which you can send customers even if your company does not have a Web site.* ■

Running the Wizard

The simplest and most rewarding part of the bCentral process is running the wizard. To run the wizard, you click the E-commerce icon on the E-commerce toolbar pictured in Figure 4-7. When the wizard runs, it prompts you to log on to bCentral. Automatically, the wizard takes a look around and prompts you to do anything you may not have done yet at your bCentral account. If you have not yet listed your products in a marketplace, for example, you will be prompted to do so.

FIGURE 4-7 *The E-Commerce toolbar empowers the FrontPage author to insert lists, fields, images, and links to any product in the company's bCentral account. Clicking the Wizard icon at the end of the toolbar creates the FrontPage catalog pages and synchronizes them with any updates the business may have made in its bCentral account.* ■

Last but not least, the wizard asks you to select the departments you want in your FrontPage catalog. Figure 4-8 shows that I chose not to select the top level, because all my products are in either the academic or commercial departments. When you click Next, the

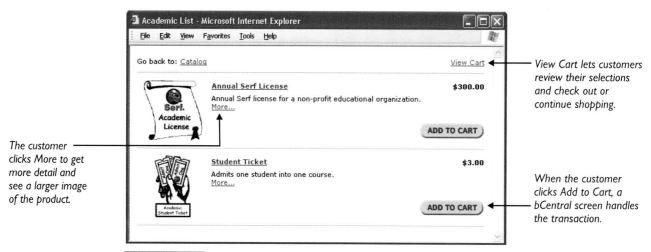

The customer clicks More to get more detail and see a larger image of the product.

View Cart lets customers review their selections and check out or continue shopping.

When the customer clicks Add to Cart, a bCentral screen handles the transaction.

FIGURE 4-8 *A catalog page created by the E-Commerce Wizard. You can stylize these catalog pages by using a FrontPage theme to create a common look and feel for your company's pages. If you visit the online store at www.serfsoft.com, for example, you will see that I used the same theme in FrontPage and at bCentral to give the storefront a seamless fit with the company pages.* ■

wizard generates the templates and creates the pages for your catalog. Then the wizard provides a button users can click to view the catalog. Any time you make a change to your products at bCentral, you simply run the wizard again, and the wizard automatically updates everything for you. This truly is a turnkey process that enables a small business to have a world-class e-commerce storefront with a minimum of effort.

Payment Settings

Last, but certainly not least, I set up my bCentral Commerce Manager account to accept and process credit card payments online. There are several ways of doing this. You will want to familiarize yourself with the options before deciding which one to choose. Figure 4-9 shows that I chose to set up a Cardservice Nanomerchant account to process Visa and MasterCard payments online. I chose this option because my business is small, and the Nanomerchant account has no monthly fee. If the business grows, on the other hand, I will switch to a monthly plan, which has a lower service fee per purchase than the free Nanomerchant account.

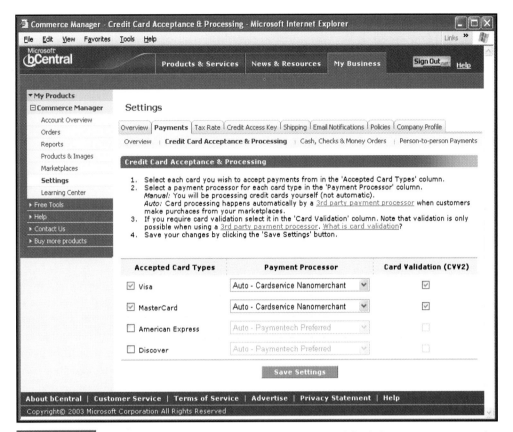

FIGURE 4-9 *The bCentral Commerce Manager payment settings. I decided to accept payments online via Visa and MasterCard. You can also configure bCentral to accept person-to-person payments via PayPal, as well as cash, checks, and money orders.* ■

Developing an In-House E-Commerce System

If your company needs or wants to customize its online business operations to work in ways that the turnkey solutions are not programmed to handle, you may wish to consider developing an in-house e-commerce system. The Internet's open standards make it technologically possible to create virtually any kind of a system you can imagine. If you need to set up a way for other businesses to conduct online transactions with your company, for example, you could create a Web Service that would provide authorized businesses with methods for making these transactions over the Internet. If you want to create a customized storefront at which consumers can buy your products directly, you can program your own product catalog and shopping cart and implement the payment models you want to offer your customers when they check out.

One of the advantages of programming your own storefront is that you do not need to pay commissions to a third party to front the store for you. If you have a large sales volume, avoiding these commissions can potentially save you a lot of money. On the other hand, developing your own e-commerce solution is a lot of responsibility. You need to create a team to do this development, because the task is larger than one person can handle alone. This team needs to include (1) a Web designer to create the look and feel of the Web forms through which customers will interact with your storefront, (2) a database designer to create the relational database that will keep track of your customers and their interactions with your site, (3) one or more application programmers to develop the software consisting of the business objects that power your site, and (4) a security officer to ensure that everyone on the team is following best-practice methods of preventing unauthorized access to the company's information all the way from customer to storefront as well as from business to business.

Because of the continually evolving nature of the Internet, the work of this team will be ongoing. The security officer needs to keep up with best practices and make sure your network stays protected from the latest security vulnerabilities and attacks. You need more than one programmer to understand your application's code so that if one person should happen to become ill or otherwise unavailable, another programmer can step in to create new features that may be needed and implement new security measures that may be required.

ADDIE Software Development Cycle

For an in-house e-commerce project to succeed, it is essential for the team to understand that software development projects follow a cycle of **analysis, design, development, implementation, and evaluation.** These five stages are easy to remember because of the acronym they form: ADDIE.

Stage 1: Analysis

The wise developer begins by conducting a thorough analysis of the company's business and customer needs. Writing down the goals of the project is a very good place to start. Follow this by articulating each goal's subgoals. This process of organizing a project into goals and sub-goals is called **task analysis.**

Stage 2: Design

Informed by the task analysis completed in stage 1, the design phase plans the work to be done. Useful design tools include storyboards and flow diagrams. A **storyboard** consists of a series of sketches that depict what will appear on each screen of the application. At the bottom of each sketch, you specify in writing any features that are not obvious in the sketch. The flow diagram depicts the logical order in which customers will work their way through the screens depicted in the storyboard. It is important to standardize the look and feel of the icons and buttons the customer will use to navigate through the application. If the user interface is not intuitive, customers will become frustrated and leave your site without buying anything.

Stage 3: Development

Artists create the icons, button shapes, banners, logos, and other kinds of graphics that will appear on the screens designed in the previous stage. Application programmers write the computer code, or scripts, that power the solution by bringing these screens to life. Large projects divide this application programming into tiers. Database programmers create the data tier, Web designers create the user interface tier, and application programmers create the business tier, which receives requests from customers and handles interactions with the data tier. Projects developed in such a manner are said to have a multi-tiered application design.

Stage 4: Implementation

Putting the software into production is often the most exciting part of a project, because this is when you learn how well your design works in practice. It is wise to pilot a new application with a small number of users before rolling out the project into large-scale production. Large projects often use two testing phases called alpha and beta testing. Alpha testing is done in-house by people close to the project, such as your fellow employees. Beta testing happens with a small group of real users to test your software before releasing it.

Stage 5: Evaluation

At the fifth stage, you conduct an evaluation to assess how well the project met its goals, how customers feel about the solution you provided, and what improvements are needed. Site statistics come in handy during this stage. Analyzing logs of customer activity can enable you to determine who bought what under different kinds of conditions. Smart companies base enhancements on strategic information that can be mined by studying customer activity at your site.

ADDIE as a Model for Continuous Improvement

You must avoid the temptation to think of these five stages as a serial process in which a project progresses in order from stage 1 through stage 5, when the project is complete. Software is never finished. As long as people are using your software, you will find yourself going back in to work on new features and troubleshoot problems. Especially on the Internet, where new capabilities are continually being invented, you will find yourself wanting to take advantage of the new features and to make sure you are following the latest security best-practices to thwart crackers.

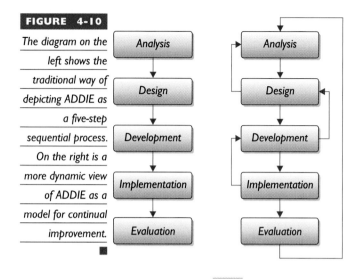

Figure 4-10 illustrates how this kind of feedback loop transforms the five-step ADDIE process into a model of continuous improvement. If the designers notice a logical flaw in the task analysis, for example, the company can save a lot of time and effort by correcting that flaw before proceeding to the more expensive development stage. Likewise, if the developers notice a problem in the design, they can ask the designers to fix it to avoid the costly need for reprogramming a faulty design. At the end of the process, the cycle repeats as the evaluation informs the analysis of what the company should work on next.

Project Management Fundamentals

Software development projects are complex. Without good management, projects can run into delays and cost overruns that will not make you very popular with your employer. Printed below is a list of project management principles designed to help you avoid things that can go wrong in any project. At the end of this chapter, three labs put these principles into practice by providing you with a framework for planning the project, allocating resources, and establishing a project review cycle.

- **Scheduling** The schedule establishes a targeted completion date for each milestone to be accomplished on the way to completing the project. Make the schedule as detailed as you can. Under each milestone, list the subtasks and identify who will accomplish them. At the end of this chapter, Lab Project 4-1 illustrates how you can lay out these tasks on a timeline that enables you to visualize the project's workflow.

- **Budgeting** The budget allocates resources for accomplishing the project's goals. To avoid cost overruns, make sure the budget contains a realistic estimate of what it will take to accomplish the tasks on the project schedule.

- **Evaluating risks** Make a list of all the risks your project is taking. Alongside each risk, write a paragraph explaining its impact on the project as a whole.

- **Contingency planning** If something goes wrong or fails to be accomplished, having a contingency plan can save you valuable time in correcting the situation. Hold a brainstorming session with your coworkers and make a list of everything you think could go wrong. For each pitfall, write a paragraph explaining how you plan to cope if it happens.

- **Preventing scope creep** During the software development process, new ideas will arise. Programmers may suggest ideas for additional features, or your employer may want the software to meet new business needs that were not articulated in project planning. Broadening the purpose of the software during project development is called scope creep. You need to minimize this to keep the project from slipping its schedule. A well-defined project plan is the best defense against scope creep.

- **Defining roles**   Most software is developed by teams consisting of one or more Web designers, artists, programmers, and database developers. Define the roles of your project's personnel and assign to each task the team member(s) playing the role(s) needed to accomplish it.

- **Piloting**   Testing the software and making sure it works properly is important before turning it over to production. Make sure you test the software with people who were not part of the development team to see if it works with users who were not privy to the design. Test the software under heavy loads, with different browsers, and at different connection speeds. Click all the links and make sure there are no dead ends. You want to find and fix any problems before production cutover.

- **Reporting**   Every member of the development team should keep logs and report regularly regarding progress toward accomplishing assigned tasks. It is especially important to report any problems that may jeopardize the schedule by causing tasks to take longer than expected.

So important is project management that the International Organization for Standardization (ISO) developed quality management standards known as the ISO 9000 family. ISO 9000 defines the vocabulary and fundamentals of quality management systems. ISO 9001 lists the certification requirements. ISO 9004 presents guidelines for performance improvements. Companies that follow these quality management standards can apply to be ISO 9001 certified. Registration procedures are online at www.iso.org.

Regulating Copyrights, Licenses, Patents, and Trademarks

Anyone who conducts business online must become educated about regulatory issues related to software licensing, intellectual property rights, patented inventions, and trademarks for two reasons. First, you want your online business practices to be ethical. Second, you want to avoid costly lawsuits that may arise if you violate the rights of another company or individual.

You need to realize that in a courtroom, ignorance is no defense. Everyone conducting business online has the responsibility to learn about these laws and observe them both in spirit and in practice. Just as the Internet is a work in progress, so are the legal interpretations that are emerging as new laws are enacted and tested in the courts. In the following sections, this

n o t e *This chapter is not intended as a substitute for legal advice. You should consult a lawyer or a campus copyright official before taking action in specific cases, because your circumstances may differ from what is described here.*

book introduces you to legal principles involving copyrights, fair use, licensing, trademarks, and patents. Equally as important are the links provided in each section to lead you to further information. Every company, no matter how large or small, should identify someone to monitor these sites and review your business practices on an ongoing basis to make sure you do not violate a statute or infringe the rights of another.

Copyright

Article I, section 8 of the United States Constitution grants Congress the power "to promote the progress of science and useful arts, by securing for limited times to authors and inventors the exclusive right to their respective writings and discoveries." Congress used this power to pass the Copyright Act of 1976, which defines and allocates rights associated with "original works of authorship fixed in any tangible medium of expression, now known or later developed, or otherwise communicated, either directly or with the aid of a machine or device" (U.S. Constitution, 17 § 102). This means that all the downloadable elements presented in Chapter 2 of this book—including illustrations, text, movies, video clips, documentaries, animations, music, and software—are protected by copyright. There are stiff penalties for copyright offenders. If a company is sued for civil copyright infringement, for example, the penalty ranges up to $100,000 per software title. If the company is charged with a criminal violation, the fine goes up to $250,000, plus up to five years in prison. The stakes are high because the Software & Information Industry Association (SIIA) reports that its members lose more than $12 billion annually due to software piracy. That is why the SIIA sues organizations that pirate commercial software or circumvent copyright protection, resulting in millions of dollars in fines. Whenever you plan to publish a Web page on the Internet, you must make sure you have the right to use every object in it. To learn about recent actions taken against copyright infringers, go to www.siia.org.

Although Web pages, like any other form of writing, are considered to be copyrighted by default, you should register a copyright for your Web pages to be fully protected. To copyright a Web page, include the following copyright notice on the page, replacing xx by the current year:

Copyright © 20*xx* by *your_name_goes_here*. All rights reserved.

Although this notice legally suffices to protect your copyright, it is also a good idea to register the copyright with the U.S. Copyright Office. If someone infringes your copyright and you take legal action to defend it, copyright registration can help your case. To register a copyright, follow these steps:

1. Go to the U.S. Copyright Office Web page at www.copyright.gov. In the section on how to register a work, choose Literary Works.

2. Read the instructions for registering a literary work. The instructions tell you that computer programs and databases are considered to be literary works for copyright purposes.

3. Find the link for downloading either the long or the short version of Form TX, and download the form you need.

4. Complete the application form and make a copy to retain in your files.

5. Mail the application along with a printout of the work and the $30 registration fee to the Library of Congress, Copyright Office, 101 Independence Ave., S.E., Washington, D.C. 20559-6000.

If you want a receipt, have the Post Office mail your application as "return receipt requested." It will take several weeks for the Library of Congress to process your application and send you the registration number. For more information, follow the link to Copyright Basics at www.copyright.gov.

Fair Use

Fair use is described in the Fair Use section of the U.S. Copyright Law that allows the use of copyrighted works in reporting news, conducting research, and teaching. The law states:

> Notwithstanding the provisions of section 106 [which grants authors exclusive rights], the fair use of a copyrighted work, including such use by reproduction in copies or phonorecords or by any other means specified by that section, for purposes such as criticism, comment, news reporting, teaching (including multiple copies for classroom use), scholarship, or research, is not an infringement of copyright. In determining whether the use made of a work in any particular case is a fair use the factors to be considered shall include:
>
> **1.** the purpose and character of the use, including whether such use is of a commercial nature or is for nonprofit educational purposes;
>
> **2.** the nature of the copyrighted work;
>
> **3.** the amount and substantiality of the portion used in relation to the copyrighted work as a whole; and
>
> **4.** the effect of the use upon the potential market for or value of the copyrighted work.

If you feel that these four tests are vague, you are correct, in that the law goes on to state that "although the courts have considered and ruled upon the fair use doctrine over and over again, no real definition of the concept has ever emerged. Indeed, since the doctrine is an equitable rule of reason, no generally applicable definition is possible, and each case raising the question must be decided on its own facts."

If you are an educator who is teaching in a classroom, you may be able to claim Fair Use. To help educational institutions interpret the Fair Use law with regard to multimedia and the Internet, the CCUMC (Consortium of College and University Media Centers) spearheaded the creation of the Fair Use Guidelines for Educational Multimedia. You can read these guidelines online by following the link to Fair Use and Multimedia at fairuse.stanford.edu.

If you are creating an e-commerce site, on the other hand, you will rarely qualify for Fair Use because you will fail the first test, which asks whether the use is of a commercial nature.

World Intellectual Property Organization (WIPO) Treaties

Because the Web is worldwide, any company conducting business online must consider the international ramifications of its e-commerce activities. As described at www.wipo.org, the **World Intellectual Property Organization (WIPO)** is in charge of administering 23 treaties comprising an international Intellectual Property (IP) system. When this book went to press, 179 countries belonged to WIPO, including the United States, which is a major stakeholder in this attempt to protect intellectual property rights throughout the world. To resolve conflicts, there is a WIPO Arbitration and Mediation Center. If someone in a WIPO member country infringes the copyright of someone in another member country, WIPO provides a mechanism for that infringement to be prosecuted in both countries. For the latest on WIPO, go to www.wipo.org.

Digital Millennium Copyright Act (DMCA)

In 1998, the **Digital Millennium Copyright Act (DMCA)** was enacted into law in the United States. One of the primary purposes of this complex act was to bring the United States into conformance with the World Intellectual Property Organization (WIPO) treaties. The DMCA includes the following:

- New rules prohibiting the circumvention of Technological Protection Measures (TPM), with stiff penalties for infringers

- Prohibition of the removal from a copyrighted work of information related to ownership, copyright, and licensing

- Limitation of liability of Online Service Providers if someone using their service infringes a copyright

- Promoting distance education over digital networks while maintaining an appropriate balance between the rights of copyright holders and the needs of teachers and students making fair use of copyrighted works

TEACH Act

In late 2002, the Technology Education and Copyright Harmonization (TEACH) Act was signed into law. This act extends the concept of Fair Use beyond the classroom to "anytime, anywhere" distance learning courses, permits educational institutions to use "reasonable and limited" portions of audiovisual works and sound recordings in distance learning courses without needing to request permission, and permits educators in certain instances to digitize and make Fair Use of works that are not already available in digital form. The TEACH Act also clarifies a point that has been in dispute since the passage of the DMCA, namely, that the temporary "buffer" copies created on networked file servers to transmit content over the Web also are covered under the exemption.

While extending the concept of educational Fair Use to digitally transmitted works, the TEACH Act also requires the transmitting institution to ensure that the performance can be received only by students who are enrolled in the course. To learn more, search Google or Yahoo! for the TEACH Act and the TEACH Act primer.

Licensing

A **license** is a permission to use a good or service provided by a third party who owns the good or provides the service. Many people have the mistaken impression that when you buy a computer application, you are buying a copy of the software. What you buy is not the software itself; rather, you purchase a license to use the software. This is why you need to read carefully the license to any software your company is using. Before you purchase additional software, be sure to study carefully the terms of the license. There are three main kinds of software licenses: single-user licenses, site licenses, and open source licenses.

Single-User Licenses

Most licenses are single-user, meaning that the individual who purchases the license thereby acquires the right to use the software. Many single-user licenses give an individual the right to use the software on more than one machine, such as on a desktop computer and on a laptop, so long as only that one person is using the software.

Site Licenses

Schools and companies often buy a **site license**, which permits the software to be used on multiple computers located in the workplace. Many site licenses exclude employees from taking the software home to use on personal computers. Before you take software from school to home or from office to home, read the license to make sure this is permitted.

Open Source Licenses

So-called **open source** licenses, on the other hand, make freely available to the public the source code from which the computer software is compiled. As described by the Open Source Initiative at www.opensource.org, the basic idea behind open source software is as follows:

> When programmers can read, redistribute, and modify the source code for a piece of software, the software evolves. People improve it, people adapt it, people fix bugs. And this can happen at a speed that, if one is used to the slow pace of conventional software development, seems astonishing (source: www.opensource.org, January 2, 2004).

The most famous example of open source software is the Linux operating system, which Microsoft's competitors are touting as an alternative to Windows. Before you consider adopting Linux, however, beware that few things in life are truly free. Open source programmers make a lot of money consulting for companies who adopt the "free" software but later find out that to make it work properly, you need support and advice, which the programmers will happily provide you for a fee. Microsoft's competitors make billions of dollars each year in Linux-related consulting services. By making you aware of this, I am not necessarily recommending against Linux, which may be a good choice if your company is prepared to pay for supporting it. What I am cautioning, however, is that you need to understand the full ramifications of the licensing. To read the open source licenses, go to www.opensource.org/licenses.

Patents

The U.S. Patent and Trademark Office defines the term **patent** as the granting to an inventor of a property right for an invention to exclude others from making, using, offering for sale, or selling the invention in the United States or "importing" the invention into the United States. The purpose of the patent is to provide the inventor an opportunity to profit from the invention for a reasonable period of time (i.e., 20 years) before the patent expires. It is the responsibility of the inventor to enforce the patent if someone infringes on it. Monetary penalties awarded in patent infringement suits can range into the tens of millions of dollars. Therefore, companies need to be careful not to infringe the patents of others. In a patent suit, ignorance is no defense. All patents are online, and you can search them at www.uspto.gov.

What causes problems in the computer industry is when a company applies to patent an invention for which there is prior art, meaning that the so-called "invention" pre-existed. There have been several cases in which computer companies have fooled the patent office into granting patents for technology that pre-existed. When these cheaters began suing other companies for infringing, there was such an industry-wide outcry that the patent office overturned the patents. The danger is that in less high-profile cases, it may cost a company less to pay for the right to use the mistakenly issued patent than to undergo the lengthy legal proceeding needed to overturn the patent.

Compton's Multimedia Search Patent

One of the most blatant cases of patent abuse occurred when Compton's announced at the 1993 Fall COMDEX convention that they had been awarded a patent that would require all multimedia developers to pay them royalties. As Compton's CEO Stanley Frank said, "We helped kick start this industry. We now ask to be compensated for our investments. We will do whatever it takes to defend our patent."

The Compton's patent is very broad. It covers any type of computer-controlled database system that allows a user to search for mixed media that includes text with graphics, sound, or animation. Compton's did not limit their claims to CD-ROM products; they also claimed rights to any type of database involving interactive TV or the Internet. Thus, the patent includes the searching of product catalogs that contain text and graphics advertising products for e-commerce purposes.

The title of the Compton's patent is "multimedia search system using a plurality of entry path means which indicate interrelatedness of information." It claims:

> A computer search system for retrieving information, comprising:
> means for storing interrelated textual information and graphical information;
> means for interrelating said textual and graphical information;
> a plurality of entry path means for searching said stored interrelated textual and graphical information, said entry path means comprising:
> textual search entry path means for searching said textual information and for retrieving interrelated graphical information to said searched text;
> graphics entry path means for searching said graphical information and for retrieving interrelated textual information to said searched graphical information;
> selecting means for providing a menu of said plurality of entry path means for selection;
> processing means for executing inquiries provided by a user in order to search said textual and graphical information through said selected entry path means;
> indicating means for indicating a pathway that accesses information related in one of said entry path means to information accessible in another one of said entry path means;
> accessing means for providing access to said related information in said another entry path means; and
> output means for receiving search results from said processing means and said related information from said accessing means and for providing said search results and received information to such user.

Compton's demanded that all multimedia developers pay back royalties of 1 percent of net receipts from sales before June 30, 1994, and 3 percent thereafter. To say the least, developers reacted negatively to Compton's demands. Some suggested that users should burn all Compton's CD-ROMs and refuse to purchase future titles from any company that would try to force such a Machiavellian proviso on the multimedia industry. As a result of public hearings held by the U.S. Patent and Trademark Office to review its handling of software patents, the Compton's patent was rescinded, and the patent office initiated reforms that include publicizing patent applications, hiring software specialists as examiners, revamping the examiner bonus program so it does not encourage superficial review, and requiring more information about patent applications before decisions are made. In fairness to the government, industry leaders such as Compton's (who know better) should stop trying to profit from patenting prior art; instead, they should concentrate on improving their products and moving the industry forward.

Unisys GIF Patent

Unisys owns the patent on the compression scheme used in the GIF file format, which is one of the most popular image formats in the world. In 1994, Unisys decided to begin charging developers a licensing fee for using the GIF file format. This resulted in a backlash of harsh opposition from developers and users who felt Unisys had acted unfairly, and Unisys backed down. Toward the end of the twentieth century, Unisys began to try again to charge for the use of GIF images. Unisys asked all Webmasters to pay $5,000 if their Web site uses one or more GIF images created by a program that is not licensed by Unisys to use GIF images.

By trying a second time to make users pay for something they thought was free, Unisys caused another uproar among GIF users and developers who, instead of paying the $5,000 fee, have begun converting their graphics to the PNG format. PNG stands for Portable Network Graphics. It's a format created largely in response to the Unisys patent fiasco. The World Wide Web consortium's PNG Web site at www.w3.org/Graphics/PNG refers to the format as "a patent-free replacement for GIF."

Happily, the U.S. version of the GIF patent expired on June 20, 2003. Unisys continues to warn developers, however, that the patent continues in some other countries. For this reason, the "Burn All GIFs" Web site at burnallgifs.org continues to urge developers to refrain from using GIFs. The recommended alternative is PNG, which is the graphics format I used when making the screen captures that illustrate this book.

Eolas '906 Patent

In 2003, Microsoft was ordered to pay $520 million for allegedly infringing U.S. patent number 5,838,906 issued to the University of California, which formed a company named Eolas to handle the licensing. The so-called Eolas '906 patent covers the technology used by browsers to launch automatically the appropriate applet or plug-in to display embedded content, such as a Flash animation, within a hypermedia document. When Eolas won the $520 million settlement against Microsoft, the World Wide Web Consortium (W3C) asked for a review of the patent. The W3C provided evidence that the Eolas patent was based on prior art and therefore should be overturned. The W3C further pointed out that enforcing this patent could cause "substantial economic and technical damage to the operation of the World Wide Web." As this book goes to press, the U.S. Patent and Trademark Office is reevaluating the Eolas '906 patent. By the time you read this, I hope the patent will be overturned. For the latest, go to the Eolas FAQ at www.w3.org/2003/09/public-faq.html. If that link does not work, go to www.w3.org and search for Eolas. To read the patent itself, go to www.uspto.gov and search for patent number 5,838,906.

I believe that the actions taken in these kinds of patent cases by Compton's, Unisys, and Eolas are unethical and self-defeating. In the Compton's and Eolas examples, technologists were taking advantage of the U.S. Patent and Trademark Office by obtaining patents for prior art of which the patent office was unaware. Unisys, on the other hand, appears to have waited until its GIF technology spread throughout the world before enforcing the patent in an attempt to cash in on its widespread adoption. In all three cases, I believe that the technologists working within these companies knew this kind of activity was unethical. Corporations need to be more honest and up-front if the patent system is to function as intended. The purpose of the patent system is to give an inventor an honest period of time in which to profit from an invention. High-tech companies are not acting in the best interests of the Internet when they abuse the patent system to rip people off.

Trademarks

The U.S. Patent and Trademark Office defines the term **trademark** as a word, phrase, symbol, or design, or a combination of words, phrases, symbols, or designs, that identifies and distinguishes the source of the goods of one party from those of others. The word Microsoft, for example, is a registered trademark of Microsoft Corporation. In the United States, you register trademarks via the Trademark Electronic Application System (TEAS) at www.uspto.gov/teas. If you want international protection for your trademark, follow the special instructions WIPO provides for the worldwide protection for trademarks. Any company that registers a trademark in a WIPO country's official trademark office has worldwide protection for that mark among all the other WIPO nations.

Trading Internationally

By definition, the Web is worldwide. Even if you do not plan to trade with customers outside the country when you begin your e-commerce activities, it may be just a matter of time before you begin trading internationally. To prepare, you need to be able to handle multiple currencies, overseas shipping, and language differences.

Multiple Currencies

If a customer purchases a product in a country that differs from that of the merchant, the customer may need to pay in a foreign currency. Depending on how your online business handles its transaction processing, you may need to use a currency converter. Most of the major turnkey systems, such as Microsoft bCentral, handle the currency conversion for you. If an international customer pays with MasterCard or Visa, for example, the credit card company handles the currency conversion by charging the customer the appropriate amount in the local currency and depositing to your bank account the converted sum in your currency. If you have developed your own in-house system, on the other hand, you may need to use a currency converter to calculate the cash conversions.

Try This!

International Currency Converter

There is an international currency calculator at www.bankrate.com. Imagine that you are in charge of an in-house e-commerce site that does not normally conduct business outside the United States. Someone from Germany wants to pay for one of your products in Euros instead of in the dollars to which you are accustomed. In U.S. dollars, the product costs $129.99. To find out how much the product costs in Euros, follow these steps:

1. Go to www.bankrate.com and follow the link to Calculators. On the Calculators page, choose the Currency calculator, and follow the link to get the currency converter onscreen.

2. Notice that there are two menus onscreen. You use the menu on the left to set the currency from which you want to convert. Set that menu to U.S. dollars.

3. You use the menu on the right to set the currency into which you want to calculate the conversion. Set the menu on the right to EUR for Euro.

4. In the blank where you enter the amount to be converted, type **129.99**. Leave the date field set to the current date.

5. Click the Convert Now button to perform the calculation.

6. For other currency converters, search Google or Yahoo! for *currency converter.*

Shipping Overseas

When you sell products in other countries, you need to be careful not to violate any customs regulations. Some products are outlawed in certain countries. The U.S. government, for example, forbids the sale of cryptology software to certain countries and terrorist organizations.

You will probably need to charge more for shipping overseas than for distributing products within your country's borders. You need to tell customers what the shipping will cost and build that cost in when the customer pays for the product. Otherwise, the customer may refuse the delivery of your product if you later add on a shipping charge that seems too high. To reduce the high cost of shipping products internationally, large vendors maintain overseas warehouses from which products can be shipped locally in countries with which they do a lot of business. Small companies, on the other hand, usually cannot afford the cost and overhead of maintaining multiple warehouses.

FedEx can ship your products to more than 213 countries. For a demonstration, go to www.fedex.com. Another premier worldwide shipping company is DHL, which you can find at www.dhl.com. For other companies that ship overseas, search Google or Yahoo! for *international shipping*.

Language Issues

Fortunately for U.S. businesses, English is the most universal language in the world. If you are marketing products to well-educated people, chances are they can read your site if the pages are written in English. If, on the other hand, you are selling mass market products that you want everyone in the world to buy, you need to create alternate language versions of your Web site so people who do not know English can browse your site and understand how to buy your products online.

When you create Web pages intended for international consumption, you should use the Unicode option for character encoding. Unicode was invented to solve the problem of displaying international characters correctly. In the Unicode standard, every character in the world has a unique code; hence the term, Unicode. The Web authoring tutorial in Part Two of this book shows you how to select Unicode for your Web pages.

You need to beware of the temptation to use automatic translation software to create international versions of your Web pages. If you search Google or Yahoo! for translation software, you will find several sites where you can enter the text of a Web page in English and have the page automatically translated into a variety of foreign languages. The field of artificial intelligence, however, has not progressed to the point at which automatic translation software can translate Web pages with 100 percent accuracy. Especially when you are conducting business online, you need your pages to be accurate. If you should happen to use an automatic translator, therefore, make sure someone who truly understands the foreign language checks to make sure your translated page says what you intend to convey.

Chapter 4 Review

Chapter Summary

After reading this chapter and completing the step-by-step tutorials and Try This! exercises, you should understand the following facts about the Internet:

Defining E-Commerce

■ E-commerce is the use of the Internet to conduct the sale of goods and services online.

■ The highest incidence of online shopping occurs between the ages of 25 to 34, when 61 percent buy products online, while only 14 percent of users over the age of 65 shop online. This elderly percentage will rise when the baby boomers enter the 65+ age bracket.

■ There are two models that define the basic forms e-commerce can take. The business-to-consumer (B2C) model occurs when an end user buys something from a company's online storefront. The business-to-business (B2B) model describes transactions that occur when companies conduct business electronically between themselves.

Enabling E-Commerce Technologies

■ There are three critical elements of e-commerce that the underlying technologies must address: communications, security, and data management. The communications must use a common digital language that can be understood by the computers involved in the transaction. The security of these communications must follow the necessary safeguards to build the trust consumers need to feel confident in trading online. The data exchanged in B2C and B2B transactions must be stored in such a way that e-commerce transactions can be audited and can recover from outages that may occur during power or equipment failures.

■ Electronic data interchange (EDI) is the computerized exchange of business information between trading partners over computer networks. This information can include purchase orders, invoices, shipping schedules, inventory inquiries, claim submissions, or any other kind of information that the trading partners need to exchange.

■ Developed by MasterCard and also adopted by Visa, the Secure Electronic Transactions (SET) specification is an open standard for conducting secure payment card transactions over the Internet. Digital certificates create a trust chain that verifies cardholder and merchant validity throughout the transaction.

■ A Web Service is a software system that uses an XML protocol to support interoperable machine-to-machine interaction over a network. Through this XML protocol, the Web Service exposes methods whereby a business process running on a primary company's computer can interact with processes running on a business partner's computer over the Internet.

■ Universal Description, Discovery, and Integration (UDDI) is an online yellow pages directory of Web Services that business computers can use to discover and learn how to use the B2B services offered by various companies over the Internet.

Processing Payments Online

■ There are three main e-commerce payment models: cash, check, and credit cards. A fourth model called the smart card is emerging in an attempt to bolster security and add functionality to transactions made with cards.

■ The cash model uses the metaphor of a digital wallet residing on the user's computer. The digital wallet contains digital cash or tokens with which the user pays for goods and services purchased online.

■ The check model uses the metaphor of a digital checkbook residing on the user's computer. This checkbook contains digital checks with which the user can pay for goods and services online. The digital checkbook model is especially appropriate for paying bills online.

■ The credit card model is well established both in traditional commerce and on the Web. Credit card processing has always been electronic from the point at which the sales clerk swiped your card. What e-commerce has done is to enable you to enter your card number by typing it into a Web form, instead of swiping your card through a store's card reader.

- A smart card is a credit-card sized plastic card with an embedded computer chip and memory that can store more than a hundred times as much digital information as the magnetic strip on a credit card. Because the chip can handle digitally signed and encrypted transactions, the smart card enables the cardholder to take advantage of the Internet's best-practice security measures.

- In 1998, a company called PayPal started a person-to-person payment model that enables any individual or business with an e-mail address to send and receive payments online. When customers use PayPal to buy and sell products from each other, a customer-to-customer (C2C) form of e-commerce emerges.

Choosing an E-Commerce Solution

- There are two kinds of instant storefront solutions: online and offline. In an online instant storefront solution, you do all your development online. In an offline solution, you develop the storefront on your PC and upload it for delivery on the Web.

- The advantage of the instant storefront is its timeliness. Because the instant storefront is pre-programmed, everything is already set up for you.

- The disadvantage of the instant storefront is flexibility. If you want to be able to customize totally the look and feel of your e-commerce screens, you should consider developing your own in-house storefront.

Developing an In-House E-Commerce System

- One of the advantages of programming your own storefront is that you do not need to pay commissions to a third party to front the store for you. If you have a large sales volume, avoiding these commissions can potentially save you a lot of money.

- On the other hand, developing your own e-commerce solution is a lot of responsibility. You will need to create a team to do this development, because the task is larger than one person can handle alone.

- For an in-house e-commerce project to succeed, it is essential for the team to understand that software development projects follow a cycle of analysis, design, development, implementation, and evaluation. These five stages are easy to remember because of the acronym they form: ADDIE.

- You must avoid the temptation to think of these five stages as a serial process in which a project progresses in order from stage 1 through stage 5, when the project is complete. Software is never finished. As long as people are using your software, you will find yourself going back in to work on new features and troubleshoot problems.

Regulating Copyrights, Licenses, Patents, and Trademarks

- Computer programs and databases are considered to be literary works for copyright purposes. To register such a copyright in the United States, you use form TX, which you can download from www.copyright.gov.

- Fair Use is a section of the U.S. Copyright Law that allows the use of copyrighted works in reporting news, conducting research, and teaching. Due to their commercial nature, however, Web pages at an e-commerce site do not qualify for Fair Use. Make sure you have written permission to use anything at your Web site that you do not already own.

- The World Intellectual Property Organization (WIPO) administers 23 treaties comprising an international Intellectual Property (IP) system among 179 member countries. The United States belongs to WIPO. One of the purposes of the Digital Millennium Copyright Act (DMCA) was to bring the United States into conformance with the WIPO treaties.

- A license is a permission to use a good or a service provided by a third party who owns the good or provides the service. Many people have the mistaken impression that when you buy a computer application, you are buying a copy of the software. What you buy is not the software itself; rather, you purchase a license to use the software.

- There are three main kinds of software licenses: single-user licenses, site licenses, and open source licenses. Most licenses are single-user, meaning that the individual who purchases the license thereby acquires the right to use the software. Schools and companies often buy a site license, which permits the software to be used on multiple computers located in the workplace.

- Open source licenses make freely available to the public the source code from which the computer software is compiled. The most famous example of open source software is the Linux operating system.

- A patent is a property right granted to an inventor for the purpose of excluding others from making, using, offering for sale, or selling the invention to provide the inventor an opportunity to profit from the invention for a reasonable period of time (i.e., 20 years) before the patent expires.

- A trademark is a word, phrase, symbol, or design, or a combination of words, phrases, symbols, or designs, that identifies and distinguishes the source of the goods of one party from those of others.

Trading Internationally

- If a customer purchases a product in a country that differs from that of the merchant, the customer may need to pay in a foreign currency. Depending on how your online business handles its transaction processing, you may need to use a currency converter to inform the buyer how much the purchase will cost in the customer's currency.

- When you sell products in other countries, you probably need to charge more for shipping than when you distribute products within your country's borders. You need to tell the customer what shipping will cost and build that cost in when the customer pays for the product.

- When you sell products in other countries, you need to be careful not to violate any customs regulations. Some products are outlawed in certain countries.

- Because English is the most universal language in the world, well-educated people will be able to read your site if the pages are written in English. If you are selling mass-market products that you want everyone in the world to buy, however, you will need to create alternate language versions of your Web site so people who do not know English can browse your site and understand how to buy your products online.

- Unicode is a character encoding scheme invented for the Internet to create a unique code for every character in all the different languages used throughout the world.

■ Key Terms

analysis, design, development, implementation, and evaluation (ADDIE) *(196)*

business-to-business (B2B) *(178)*

business-to-consumer (B2C) *(178)*

checkout *(177)*

customer-to-customer (C2C) *(187)*

digital cash *(177)*

digital check *(177)*

Digital Millennium Copyright Act (DMCA) *(202)*

digital wallet *(177)*

e-commerce *(177)*

electronic data interchange (EDI) *(181)*

fair use *(201)*

instant storefront *(188)*

license *(203)*

open source *(204)*

patent *(204)*

secure electronic transactions (SET) *(182)*

shopping cart *(177)*

Simple Object Access Protocol (SOAP) *(184)*

site license *(203)*

smart card *(187)*

stock-keeping unit (SKU) *(190)*

storyboard *(196)*

task analysis *(196)*

trademark *(207)*

Universal Description, Discovery, and Integration (UDDI) *(183)*

Web Service *(182)*

Web Service Description Language (WSDL) *(183)*

World Intellectual Property Organization (WIPO) *(202)*

Key Terms Quiz

1. _____ is a payment method whereby customers pay for the product via tokens drawn from their digital wallet.

2. The _____ model occurs when an end user buys something from a company's online storefront.

3. The _____ model occurs when companies conduct business electronically between themselves.

4. _____ is the computerized exchange of business information between trading partners over computer networks.

5. Developed by MasterCard and also adopted by Visa, the _____ specification is an open standard for conducting secure payment card transactions over the Internet.

6. A(n) _____ is a computer application that uses an XML protocol to expose methods whereby a business process running on a primary company's computer can interact with processes running on a business partner's computer over the Internet.

7. _____ is an XML language for exposing the methods and properties of a Web Service to a consumer, which is any Web client authorized to interact with the Web Service.

8. A(n) _____ is a pre-programmed e-commerce system into which you enter your catalog of products and begin conducting business online.

9. International copyright treaties are administered by the _____.

10. A(n) _____ is the granting to an inventor of a property right for an invention to exclude others from making, using, offering for sale, or selling the invention in the United States, or "importing" the invention into the United States.

Multiple-Choice Quiz

1. In a seemingly B2C situation, when a retailer obtains a product from a wholesaler behind the scenes, what kind of an e-commerce model emerges?
   a. B2B
   b. B2C
   c. B2B2C
   d. C2C2B

2. What is not one of the three critical elements that underlying e-commerce technologies must address?
   a. Communications
   b. Data management
   c. Project management
   d. Security

3. Health-related wholesalers of drugs and medical supplies, automotive, and commercial equipment suppliers have historically been the heaviest users of:
   a. ASCII
   b. EDI

   c. SET
   d. Unicode

4. One of the most important advantages of SET is that merchants never see the customer's
   a. Street address
   b. Credit card number
   c. E-mail address
   d. Phone number

5. What is the name for the XML language that is used to identify the methods in a Web Service, define how those methods behave, and instruct clients how to interact with the service?
   a. HTTP
   b. SOAP
   c. UDDI
   d. WSDL

6. Which company won a Webby for establishing the person-to-person model of e-commerce on the Internet?
   a. American Express
   b. bCentral

   c. MasterCard
   d. PayPal

7. Microsoft's e-commerce company is called:
   a. bCentral
   b. FrontPage
   c. MarketPlace
   d. Serfsoft

8. The process of organizing a project into goals and sub-goals is called:
   a. Flow charting
   b. Resource allocation
   c. Storyboarding
   d. Task analysis

9. If you want to secure your right of ownership over a Web page that you have created, you should apply for a:
   a. Copyright
   b. License
   c. Patent
   d. Trademark

10. What kind of license permits commercial software to be used on multiple computers located in the workplace?
   a. Open source
   b. Patent
   c. Single-user
   d. Site

■ Essay Quiz

1. Search Google for an instant storefront. What are the top three sponsored sites that Google brings up? Go to one of these instant storefront sites and peruse the services it offers. Compare these services to the features offered by Microsoft bCentral, which was illustrated in this chapter's case study. Name the instant storefront vendor you visited, and give at least two or three examples of ways in which its claimed features either exceed or fail to match the capabilities of bCentral.

2. When this book went to press in 2004, the World Intellectual Property Organization (WIPO) was overseeing 23 treaties that govern worldwide intellectual property rights in 179 countries belonging to WIPO. Go to www.wipo.org and find out whether any new treaties have been enacted. How many treaties is WIPO currently administering? How many nations currently belong to WIPO?

3. As you learned in the patent section of this chapter, the Eolas '906 patent threatens the future of the Web by attempting to steal the technology used by browsers to launch automatically the appropriate applet or plug-in to display embedded content, such as a Flash animation, on a Web page. Go to www.w3.org/2003/09/public-faq.html and find out the latest news regarding this patent. If that link does not work, go to www.w3.org and search for Eolas. Have the courts and/or the patent office decided whether to uphold or overturn the patent? If not, what is the latest estimate about when a decision is expected?

Lab Projects

Under a grant from the National Science Foundation, the National Workforce Center for Emerging Technologies (NWCET) has created a framework identifying key activities that successful project managers employ to develop in-house solutions. The following lab projects take you through a series of situations designed to give you practice performing these key activities. If you are considering whether to become a project manager, perusing these labs will give you a good idea of the kinds of things managers do. Completing these labs will enable you to assemble a portfolio of project plans demonstrating that you have the technical knowledge and employability skills that companies look for when recruiting a project manager.

• Lab Project 4-1: Project Planning Fundamentals

Imagine that you have been hired by a medium-sized chain of retail hobby shops that sell O-gauge model trains in traditional brick-and-mortar storefronts. These hobby shops do not sell anything online, but they are beginning to have a hard time competing with other hobby shops that have online storefronts. The problem is that many people who come into the store to handle the products and seek advice end up buying the trains online from electronic storefronts that sell the same products at discounted prices. You have been hired to solve this dilemma by creating an online store through which your employer can sell the trains online as well as in the chain of traditional stores. Your first assignment is to develop a project plan that defines the scope of work to be done, estimates how long it will take, and informs your new employer of the steps you will be taking to accomplish your objective. In creating such a plan, you should address the following issues:

- *Define the scope of the project.* At the outset of any project, you should write a goal statement that explains the project's contribution to your company's overall business needs. To ensure that the goal statement is comprehensive, make a list of the criteria you will use to determine whether the outcome of the project will meet customer needs. Then estimate the size of the project and document the e-commerce standards, regulations, and laws you will follow as you develop the solution.

- *Identify stakeholders, decision makers, and escalation procedures.* Every project has risks. You need to state what those risks will be and identify the people who will be notified if a problem arises. Explain how problems that are not solved promptly will escalate up through the company's hierarchy to be resolved by higher authorities.

- *Develop a detailed task list.* In any project, it is important to identify the tasks that need to be accomplished. As you make this list, document any special aspects the developers will need to be aware of.

- *Estimate time requirements.* Estimate how much time it will take to accomplish each task identified in the previous step. Be realistic. Avoid the temptation to please management by making time estimates you cannot realistically meet.

- *Develop the initial project management flow chart.* Some of the items on your task list can be worked on simultaneously; others will need to wait until previous steps have been completed. Create a flowchart that diagrams the simultaneous versus the sequential aspects of the project you envision. On this chart, identify the project milestones, approval points, and go/no-go decision points at which you will decide whether sequential tasks have been completed well enough to proceed to the next step. To avoid project delays, note any tasks requiring long lead times.

Use a word processor to write up your project plan. Feel free to use spreadsheet software to create your task list and add up the time estimates for each phase of your project. If your company has Microsoft Project or some other brand of project management software, you may use it as you see fit. Figure 4-11 shows how Microsoft Project enables you to create a task list, organize the tasks into phases, and schedule the tasks. (To learn more about Microsoft Project, go to www.microsoft.com/office/project.) Do not worry if you do not have this kind of project management software right now, however, because you can also create your chart with a word processor. If your instructor has asked you to hand in the recommendation, make sure you put your name at the top; then save it on disk or follow the other instructions you may have been given for submitting this assignment.

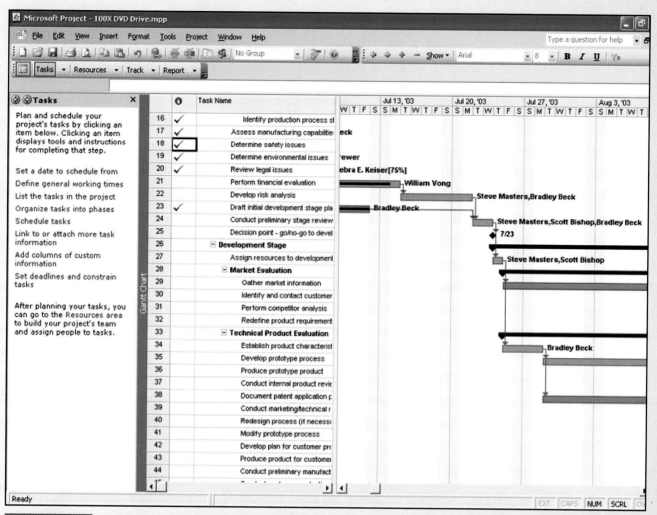

FIGURE 4-11   *Microsoft Project is the project management program in Microsoft Office. The project guide illustrated in the left pane steps you through the process of creating the task list in the middle pane, organizing the tasks into phases, and scheduling the tasks, as shown on the right.* ■

• Lab Project 4-2: Securing Resources for Project Development

Imagine that your employer was intrigued by the project plan you created in Lab Project 4-1. To determine whether to move forward, your employer wants to know how much it will cost for you to proceed with project development. In creating a cost estimate, you will need to take the following issues into account:

■ *Identify required resources and budget.* To convince your employer to fund items in your budget, you need to document them in a budget explanation that provides the rationale for the resources you recommend. The better you support your budget requests with relevant data, the more chance you will have of getting your project approved.

■ *Evaluate project requirements.* You need to explain any overlap that may exist among the resources you are requesting. Otherwise, your employer may think you are requesting more funding than you need to complete the project.

■ *Identify and evaluate risks.* You may get different advice from customers than you get from your superiors and fellow employees. You need to take these conflicting viewpoints into account when you write your budget explanation. Your employer will feel more confident about approving your budget if the risk identification is complete and considers the impact on the whole system.

■ *Prepare a contingency plan.* According to Murphy's Law, if anything can go wrong, it will. Although I hope Murphy's Law will not apply to your project, your resource allocation plan must specify alternate methods of completing any tasks that could become troublesome. A special trait of successful managers is their ability to foresee things that can go wrong and have alternate plans ready in case of a failure.

■ *Identify interdependencies.* To control costs, every member of your project team needs to be aware of any interdependencies related to their work on the project. The project will fall behind schedule if things get out of phase because members of the team did not realize the interdependent nature of their tasks and subtasks.

Use a word processor to write up your cost estimate. Feel free to use spreadsheet software to create your list of required resources and total the costs for each phase of your project. If your company has Microsoft Project or some other brand of project management software, you may use it as you see fit. If your instructor has asked you to hand in this cost estimate, make sure you put your name at the top; then save it on disk or follow the other instructions you may have been given for submitting this assignment.

• Lab Project 4-3: Establishing the Project Review Cycle

Imagine that your employer is pleased by the cost estimate you created in Lab Project 4-2. Although money is tight, your employer feels that moving forward with this project is going to be a strategic investment in your company's future. Before allocating the money, however, your employer wants to know how you will ensure that the beginning phases of the project will be done correctly before you proceed to subsequent phases that depend on earlier work. To answer this concern, you need to establish a project review cycle that will make your employer feel confident that you can manage effectively the project staging and ensure that each task meets its objective before spending money on dependent tasks. To create a project review cycle, you need to take the following issues into account:

■ *Identify and track critical milestones.* You need to establish a method for tracking the progress toward achieving the project's critical milestones. If you have Microsoft Project or its equivalent, you can use your project management software to do the tracking. Otherwise, you can use a spreadsheet or word processor to create a grid on which to track critical milestones.

■ *Participate in the project phase review.* You should schedule meetings for appropriate members of the team to review the phases of the project for which they are responsible or upon which they are dependent. Include these project review meetings in the project's master schedule.

■ *Secure needed resources.* You will have a greater chance of getting your project approved if your employer feels confident that the people, equipment, supplies, and services will be available when your project needs them. In your project review cycle, therefore, include appropriate checkpoints for making sure these resources are available on schedule.

■ *Manage the change control process.* Implementing e-commerce will cause many changes in how the company operates. Make the necessary parties aware of the impact of these changes, and build checkpoints into the review cycle to make sure the required changes are documented and implemented in the company's operating procedures.

■ *Report the project status.* To bring problems promptly to the attention of your employer, the project review mechanism needs to keep an updated report on the project's status. This report should include an explanation of lessons learned in the event that something goes wrong and the project needs to be modified. It is hoped that the report will be mainly positive, stating the extent to which each task and subtask met its goals.

Use a word processor to write up your project review cycle. If your company has Microsoft Project or some other brand of project management software, you may use it as you see fit. If your instructor has asked you to hand in this project review cycle, make sure you put your name at the top; then save it on disk or follow the other instructions you may have been given for submitting this assignment.

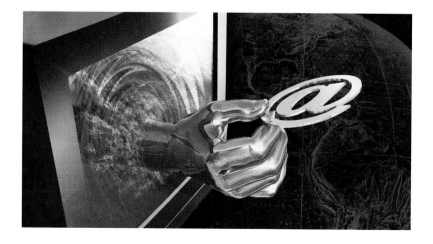

part

II

Web Page Authoring Fundamentals

How to create a Web site is one of the most empowering skills you will ever learn. Because the Internet is ubiquitous, Web page creation gives you a worldwide reach that enables you to communicate your message virtually everywhere. This part of the book teaches you how to put any form of media, including text, pictures, audio, and video, onto your Web pages. After studying Web page creation strategies, you learn how to create a résumé you can use to apply for a job. Creating a résumé on the Web provides you with the strategic advantage of being able to give prospective employers the World Wide Web address of your résumé. This shows you have network savvy that can benefit an employer in an information society.

You also learn how to create your home page—the Web page that establishes your identity on the Web. By linking things to your home page, you can create a hierarchy that makes it easy for people to access resources you put on the Web. For example, you will link your Web page résumé to your home page.

Next, you learn how to interact with users by creating Web forms that enable your visitors to make choices as you keep track of each user's preferences. You will be pleasantly surprised by how easy it is to create a Buy Now button you can use to sell things at your Web site. Then you learn how to write little computer programs called scripts, which you can use to create more highly customized interactions.

Studying cascading style sheets (CSS) and the document object model (DOM) will reveal all of the dynamic objects and methods that are at your command. These are the raw materials of the digital age that companies such as Amazon, eBay, Google, and Yahoo! have used to build their empires. Learning these technologies will place the same potential for invention into your hands. Whether you end up creating something new or just studying to pass the CIW Foundations exam, Web creation is an exciting journey you are sure to enjoy.

chapter

5

Creating Web Pages

"If you can dream it, you can do it."

—*Adobe slogan*

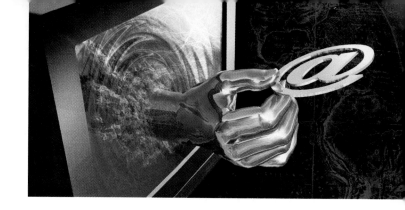

- Identify the Web page creation strategies and adopt a strategy that is appropriate for your workplace.

- Define the HTML Web page elements and explain what they do on a Web page.

- Describe the principles of good screen design and give examples of each principle in action on a Web page.

- Analyze the layout of a Web page résumé by diagramming the HTML elements the page comprises.

ACCORDING to the Adobe slogan quoted at the beginning of this chapter, "If you can dream it, you can do it." This adage implies that you have the proper tools for doing what you dream. Enabling you to acquire these tools is what this chapter is about. First, this chapter takes you on a guided tour of the approaches various authors use when creating Web pages. Some of these approaches are surprisingly simple and cost-effective. Others are more expensive but may save you time or money in the long run. By reflecting on these choices, you can get a sense of what the proper tool is for different situations.

No matter what tool you adopt, every Web author needs to understand the HTML elements a Web page comprises. The second part of this chapter defines and illustrates those elements at work on actual Web pages. Then the third part helps you understand the screen design principles you should follow to make appropriate use of HTML elements onscreen.

Finally, this chapter concludes by analyzing the layout of a Web page that uses these elements to create a résumé, an important document that potential employers expect you to show them when you are looking for a job. This chapter enables you to dream up the content and visualize the appearance on the screen of your Web page résumé. In the next chapter, you will actually create such a résumé, which will come in handy whenever you are looking for a job.

Adopting a Web Page Creation Strategy

There are four ways to create Web pages. First, you can use a plaintext editor to type the HTML code of your Web page by hand. Doing this requires that you know the HTML tags, because a plain text editor does not have any built-in help for HTML coding. Second, you can use an HTML editor that contains toolbars and menus that help you insert the codes. This built-in help makes it easier to create a Web page, but still it is technical and requires that you have a good understanding of how HTML works. Third, you can use the Save As Web Page option to convert word-processed documents into Web pages. This is the most productive way to create Web pages from term papers and other forms of scholarly writing. Fourth, you can use a what-you-see-is-what-you-get (WYSIWYG) editor to create Web pages through a graphical user interface that lets you enter text and graphics directly onto the screen exactly as you want them to appear. As you create the screen, the WYSIWYG editor automatically generates the HTML codes that make the Web page.

Text Editors

You may be surprised to hear that some of the Web's most successful authors create their pages with a text editor. Because HTML is a textual encoding language, you can use a plaintext editor to create HTML Web pages. This book saves you some money by taking advantage of this fact. Instead of requiring you to buy a fancy tool, this book is written so you can complete all the HTML exercises with a simple text editor that you already own. If you have one of the fancier tools, on the other hand, you can also work through this book's tutorials with your more high-end tool. Before discussing more high-end tools, however, let us review the text editors you can use to create Web pages without needing to purchase any other software.

Notepad   All Windows computers have a built-in text editor called **Notepad**. To get the Notepad running, you double-click its icon, which looks like the notepad after which it is named.

   If the Notepad's icon is not visible, use the Windows Start | Programs | Accessories menu. If you have a Macintosh, use the Finder to locate the Notepad's launch icon. If you have OS X, the Macintosh text editor is called *TextEdit*.

WordPad   In addition to the Notepad, the Windows operating system has a more powerful text editor called the WordPad.

   The choice of which text editor to use is totally yours. Beginners might find the Notepad less confusing because there are some rich text format (RTF) tools in the WordPad that are not applicable to HTML Web page creation. You cannot, for example, create HTML italics or bolding by clicking the italics or bold options on the WordPad's toolbar. Instead, you must type the HTML codes, which you will learn later in the next chapter.

HTML Editors

As you learned in the first part of this book, Web pages are encoded in the hypertext markup language (HTML). This language consists of the text of the Web page plus special codes called **tags** that mark up the text. The tags determine how the text will flow onto the screen, whether it will contain pictures and where they will appear, and what will happen when the user triggers items linked to the document. An editor that lets you create Web pages by working directly with the HTML tags is known as an **HTML editor**. The advantage of creating Web pages with an HTML editor is that it gives you more control over the Web page than WYSIWYG editors and HTML translators, which create the HTML for you. The disadvantage is that for less technically inclined authors, editing HTML tags can seem tedious and time-consuming. The latest versions of the HTML editors, however, contain helpful dropdown menus so you can choose tags from a list as you type your code.

HomeSite

note   *HomeSite was used to create the color-coded examples of HTML code that appear in the rest of this book's tutorials. This coloration is especially helpful for beginners who are learning HTML syntax.*

HomeSite is a popular HTML editor for creating Web pages under the Windows operating system. As shown in Figure 5-1, HomeSite lets you edit the HTML in one window and view how it will appear on the Web in another. HomeSite is a product of Macromedia, which sells it as a standalone package or in bundles with Macromedia's Dreamweaver software. For more information, go to www.macromedia.com/homesite, where you can get a 30-day free trial version.

The Edit tab shows the HTML editor.

The Browse tab shows the resulting Web page.

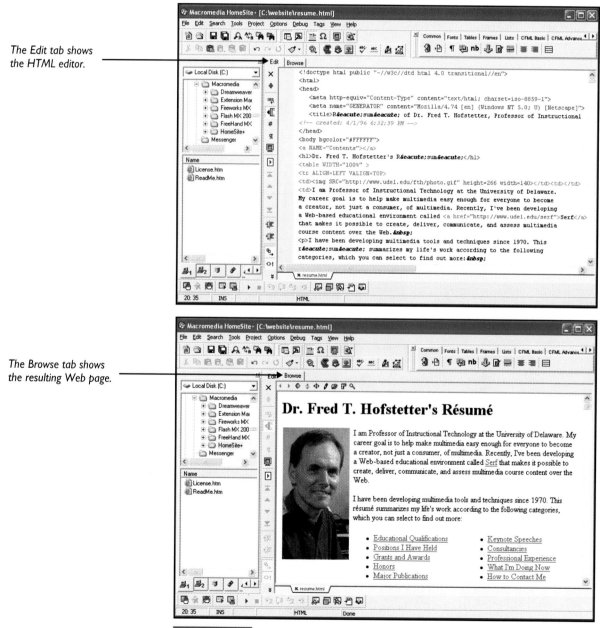

FIGURE 5-1   *HomeSite lets you edit the HTML source code in the Edit window. To see the resulting Web page, you click the Browse tab.* ∎

BBEdit

On the Macintosh, the most popular HTML editor is Bare Bones Edit (BBEdit). As illustrated in Figure 5-2, BBEdit uses menus and buttons to make it easy to input HTML tags, choose colors, and enter special symbols. For more information, go to www.barebones.com/products/bbedit, where you can get a free demo version.

Other HTML Editors

There are dozens of other HTML editors that help you create Web pages by working directly with HTML tags. For information about the others, follow this book's Web site links to the Google and Yahoo! directories of HTML editors.

HTML Translators

An **HTML translator** is a tool that can convert an existing document into the HTML format. Microsoft Word, Excel, Access, and PowerPoint have HTML translators built in. If you have an existing document that you want to turn into a Web page, the most efficient way to create the page is to pull down the File menu and choose the Save As Web Page option.

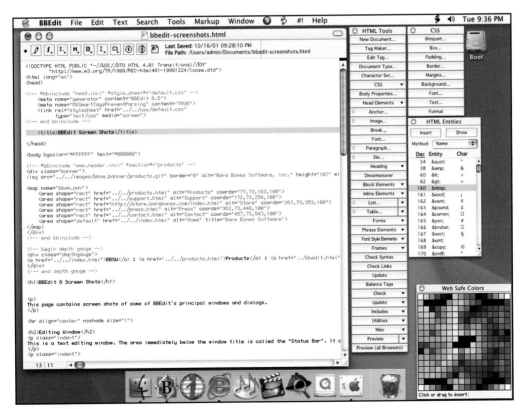

FIGURE 5-2 *BBEdit uses menus and buttons to make it easy to input HTML tags, choose colors, and enter special symbols.* ■

Word

Microsoft Word is a word processor that has an HTML translator built in. After you create a document with MS Word, you can easily translate it into a Web page. Simply pull down the File menu and choose Save As Web Page. This creates an HTML version of your document with the *.htm* filename extension. To see what the translated document will look like on the Web, you can use the browser's File menu to open the file you just saved.

Excel

Imagine being able to publish your spreadsheets to the Web. You can do this with Microsoft Excel. Simply pull down the File menu and choose Save As Web Page. This creates an HTML version of the spreadsheet with the *.htm* filename extension. To preview what the spreadsheet will look like on the Web, you can use your Web browser's File menu to open the HTML version you just saved. The information in your spreadsheet lines up neatly formatted in rows and columns on the Web page. HTML table tags are used to create the rows and columns. You will learn how to create tables with HTML in Chapter 6.

Access

Access is the name of the database program in Microsoft Office. To create a Web page version of a data table, you first select the table to view it. Then pull down the File menu and choose Export. When the Export dialog appears, set the Save As Type field to HTML Documents. Then click the Save button. This creates an HTML version of the data table that has the *.htm* filename extension. To preview how the data will appear on the Web, you can use your Web browser's File menu to open the HTML version you just saved. In Chapter 7, you learn how to publish the file to the Web.

PowerPoint

Microsoft's presentation software is called PowerPoint. It has a very powerful Web page creation capability. When you choose the option to save a presentation as a Web page, PowerPoint goes through your presentation and creates a separate HTML file for each one of your slides. The filename of your first slide is the name of your presentation followed by the *.htm* file extension. The HTML files for the rest of your slides get placed into a supporting folder that also includes any sounds and graphics used in your presentation. When you view the presentation with a Web browser, a menu of your slides appears alongside the startup screen, as shown in Figure 5-3. To navigate the Web site, the user can either click items on your presentation screen or use the menu to go to any slide at any time.

One of my other books, titled *Multimedia Literacy,* has a complete tutorial on creating multimedia applications and publishing them to the Web with PowerPoint. For more information, go to www.mhhe.com/cit/hofstetter.

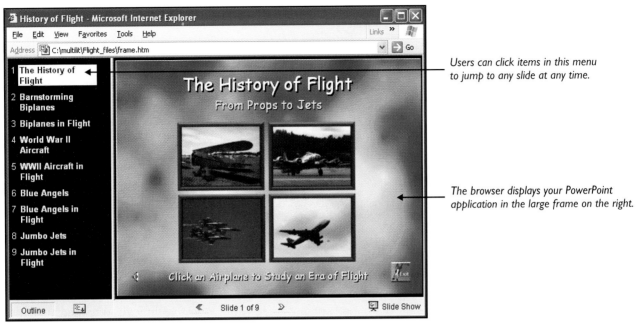

Users can click items in this menu to jump to any slide at any time.

The browser displays your PowerPoint application in the large frame on the right.

FIGURE 5-3 *When you save a PowerPoint application as a Web page, PowerPoint creates a menu that lets the user jump to any slide at any time. You learn how to create this kind of menu in the frameset section of Chapter 7. PowerPoint does all this work for you, saving you the time you would otherwise need to spend creating such a menu.* ■

Try This!

Using a Word Processor to Make a Web Page

Both Microsoft Word and WordPerfect have HTML translators built in. Whenever you need to create an HTML version of a word-processed document, using this built-in translator will come in handy. To experience the power of an HTML translator, follow these steps:

1. Use Microsoft Word or WordPerfect to open a document you have written recently, such as a term paper or an essay.

2. Pull down the File menu and choose the option to Save As Web Page or Save As HTML. When the Save dialog appears, name the file whatever you want, but make careful note of what you name it. The filename extension will be either *.htm* or *.html*.

3. Get your Web browser running. Pull down the File menu, choose Open, click the Browse button, and use the controls to open the Web page you saved in the preceding step.

4. Compare how the document appears in your browser to how it looks in your word processor. Can you see any differences? If so, what are they? Did anything happen in the translation process that you would like to change in the Web page version of your document? You will be able to make these kinds of changes in your HTML documents after you complete this book's Web page creation tutorial.

WYSIWYG Editors

WYSIWYG is an acronym that stands for **what you see is what you get**. In a WYSIWYG editor, you create Web pages by typing your text directly onscreen, where it appears exactly as it will look on the Web. To change a font, size, color, or other text attribute, you select the text you want to change and then click a button or icon that makes the change. You do not need to know the HTML tags, because the WYSIWYG editor inserts them into the document automatically, depending on what you do with the WYSIWYG controls.

Dreamweaver

This chapter began by quoting the Adobe slogan, "If you can dream it, you can do it." The title of Macromedia's Dreamweaver software plays on this theme by implying that you can weave your Web via graphical tools that can do a lot of the work for you. Figure 5-4 shows how Dreamweaver appears onscreen. For authors who are less technically inclined, using a WYSIWYG tool such as Dreamweaver is easier than using a tag-oriented HTML editor. When you work with WYSIWYG tools, however, you do not have as much control over the appearance of the Web page as when you work directly with the HTML tags. To overcome this limitation, Dreamweaver provides a Code window where you can edit the tags directly. Figure 5-4 shows a Split view in which Dreamweaver simultaneously displays both the Code window and the WYSIWYG window. Any change you make in the Code window takes effect immediately in the WYSIWYG window, and vice versa. Thus, Dreamweaver provides you with the best of both worlds. A free-trial version of Dreamweaver is available at www.macromedia.com/dreamweaver.

FrontPage

Designed for use with Microsoft Office, the FrontPage Web page editor combines a WYSIWYG tool with an HTML editor. You can use the WYSIWYG tool to create a Web page in one window, and, at any time, you can switch to an HTML window where you can view and edit the HTML tags. Changes you make in the HTML window take effect instantly in the WYSIWYG window, and vice versa. FrontPage also includes support for creating advanced Web pages that use databases and scripts. Figure 5-5 shows a Web page being edited by Microsoft FrontPage. A free-trial version is available at www.microsoft.com/frontpage.

Display the WYSIWYG Design view.

Split the screen to display both the code and the design.

This is the Code window.

Display the Code view.

This is the Design window.

You can edit aspects of the selected element in the property manager.

The Reference tab puts at your fingertips all the documentation you need.

The Files tab makes it easy to find resources that you can drag and drop onto your page.

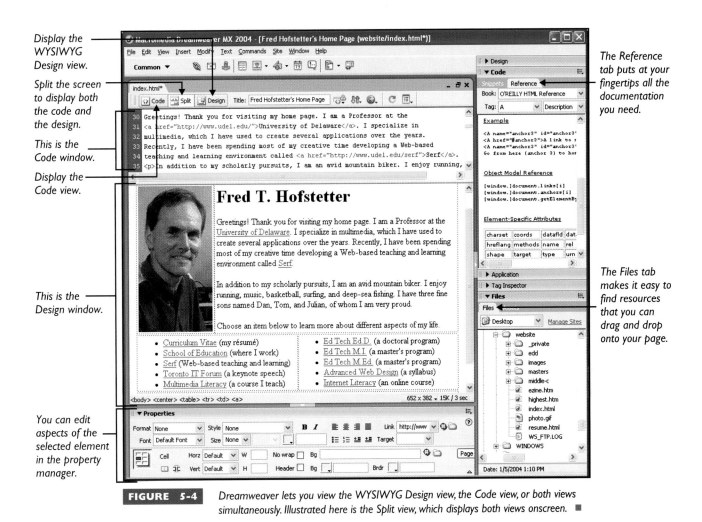

FIGURE 5-4 *Dreamweaver lets you view the WYSIWYG Design view, the Code view, or both views simultaneously. Illustrated here is the Split view, which displays both views onscreen.* ∎

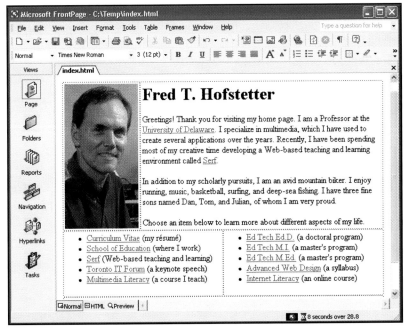

FIGURE 5-5 *Microsoft FrontPage is editing my home page. At any time, I can click the HTML button to view the code, or I can click the Preview button to see how the page will appear on the Web.* ∎

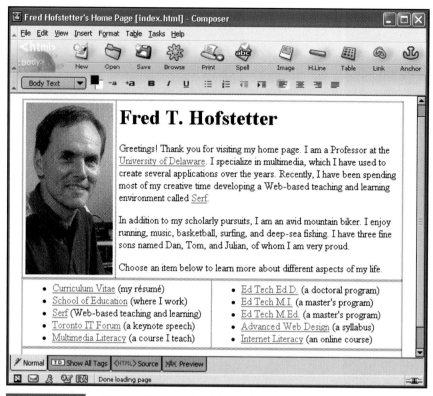

FIGURE 5-6   *Netscape Composer is editing my home page. At any time, I can click the HTML Source button to view the code, or I can click the Preview button to see how the page will appear in the Netscape Web browser.* ■

Netscape Composer

Netscape Composer is the name of the WYSIWYG Web page editor that comes as part of the suite of tools in Netscape Navigator. Figure 5-6 shows what Composer looks like onscreen. An HTML Source button lets you edit the code, and a Preview button shows you how the page will appear in the Netscape Web browser. Netscape Navigator is freely downloadable from www.netscape.com. To launch the Composer, you pull down the Netscape browser's Tasks menu and choose Composer.

Defining the Elements of Web Page Design

World Wide Web pages consist of elements defined in the HTML language that is used to create Web pages. As illustrated in Figures 5-7 to 5-15, these elements include the following:

- Backgrounds
- Bookmarks
- Frames
- Headings
- Horizontal rules
- Images
- Links
- Lists
- Paragraphs
- Special characters
- Tables

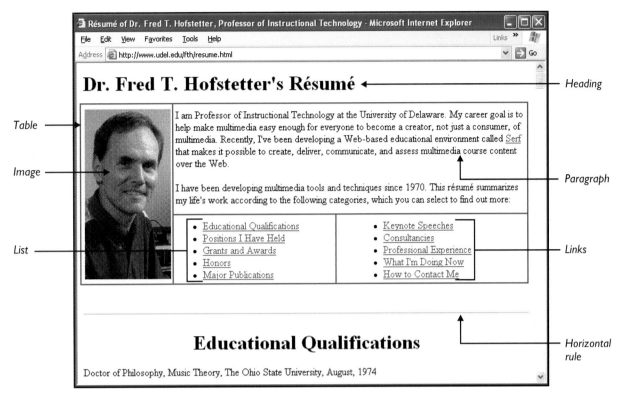

Table

Image

List

Heading

Paragraph

Links

Horizontal rule

FIGURE 5-7 *Web page elements in action on my Web page résumé. The user can click any item in the bulleted list to jump to that section of the résumé. The next chapter shows you how to create your own Web page résumé, which will come in handy any time you are looking for a job.* ■

Headings

As illustrated in Figure 5-8, there are six HTML **heading** styles, numbered from H1 to H6. The smaller the number, the bigger the heading. H1 is the biggest or most important heading, and H6 is the smallest. Headings can be left justified, centered, or right justified. Although it is possible to create the same visual effect by simply enlarging and bolding the text, you can use heading styles to create a structure within a document that programs such as Microsoft Office can use to generate an outline or a table of contents. Therefore, it is a good idea to form the habit of using heading styles for the headings of sections and subsections within a Web page.

Paragraphs

Paragraphs consist of plaintext that flows onto the screen in a continuous stream of characters. Paragraph text automatically wraps at the right margin and adapts to changes in window size.

Horizontal Rules

A **horizontal rule** is a design element used to create a divider between sections of a Web page. As illustrated in Figure 5-9, horizontal rules appear with a neat three-dimensional effect. It is possible to vary the length, thickness, and shading of a horizontal rule, but the default settings look pretty good.

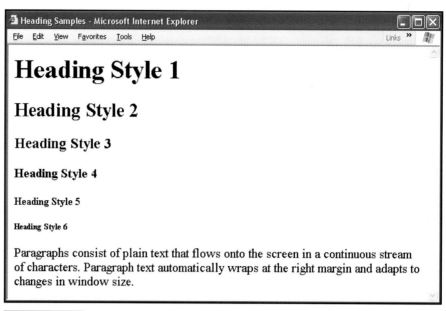

FIGURE 5-8 *There are six HTML heading styles that you can put onto a Web page. Onscreen, the headings appear larger or smaller, depending on their level of importance. Behind the scenes, the headings create a document structure that programs such as Microsoft Office can use to generate an outline or a table of contents.* ■

Lists

Lists can be ordered or unordered. In an **ordered list**, the items are numbered automatically; in an **unordered list**, the items are bulleted. Figure 5-9 shows examples of both types of lists.

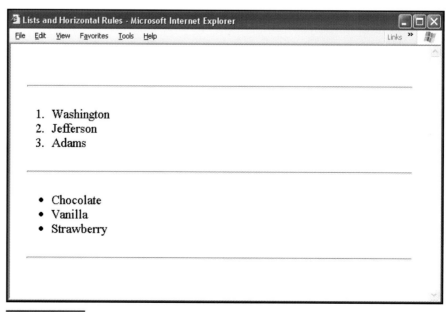

FIGURE 5-9 *Horizontal rules and lists help organize and delimit information on a Web page.* ■

Images

Images enhance the visual appeal of Web pages. Images can be left justified, right justified, or centered on the screen. Text can be made to flow around the left or the right side of an image, as illustrated in Figure 5-10.

Backgrounds

Backgrounds can be filled with a solid color, or you can tile a bitmap into the background to create a textured appearance. It is important to choose a background that does not detract from the readability of the text. For this reason, black text on a white background is the most frequent color choice on the Web.

When the Web started, the default background color was defined as gray. When the default black text color displays on a gray background, the screen is not as readable as black text on a white background, which provides better contrast. Figure 5-11 compares the black-on-gray color combination to the more readable black-on-white color scheme.

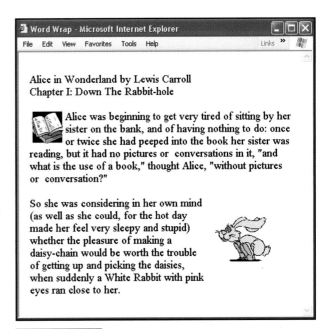

FIGURE 5-10 *Text can flow around the left or the right side of an image.* ■

Bookmarks

A **bookmark** is a named anchor to which you can link a hot word or menu item so users can jump around to different places within a Web page. For example, you might create a bookmark anchor named "education" at the start of the education section of your résumé. In your résumé's bulleted table of contents, you would link the education bullet to the bookmark anchor named "education" to provide a quick way of jumping to your educational qualifications.

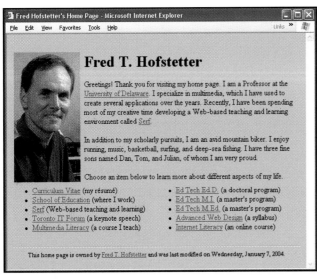
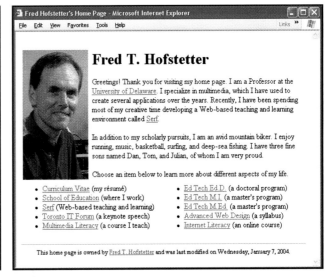

FIGURE 5-11 *When the Web started, the default background color was defined as gray, as illustrated on the left. Notice how much harder it is to read the text when it appears on the gray background as compared to the white background illustrated on the right.* ■

Links

Links are the most essential element in Web design, because links create webs. Without links, there would be no webs! On World Wide Web pages, links can be textual or pictorial. Any word or picture on the screen can be linked to any resource on the Web. Most **links** connect you to other Web pages or to bookmarks on the current Web page, as shown in Figure 5-12. As you learned in Chapter 2, however, any multimedia file or application can be the object of a link on the World Wide Web. For example, your term papers, scholarly publications, software, and multimedia applications can all be mounted on the World Wide Web and linked to your résumé so potential employers can review samples of your work. It is also common to find e-mail addresses linked to Web pages in a so-called mailto link; when you click the mailto link, an e-mail window opens, addressed to the person whose address is in the mailto. You learn how to create mailto links in Chapter 6.

FIGURE 5-12 *Named anchors work like bookmarks to provide easy access to sections within a Web page.* ■

Special Characters

Web pages can contain special symbols such as the Greek characters used in scientific notation, as well as mathematical functions, operators, delimiters, accents, arrows, and pointers.

Tables

Normally, the text of a Web page flows evenly onto the screen, aligning itself automatically with the left and right edge of your browser's window. The **table** is a design element that provides a way of dividing the screen into rectangular regions into which you can lay out text and graphics on a Web page. Text flows inside the rectangles of the table, creating a columnar appearance much like the columns of text that appear in printed newspapers. Graphics can also be made to flow into tabular columns. The borders of the rectangles in the table can be visible, creating onscreen dividing lines between the table elements, as shown in Figure 5-13, or the border can be invisible, as illustrated in Figure 5-14. Chapter 6 provides a lot of practice using tables to lay out Web pages.

note *When HTML was invented, there was no support for tables, and all Web pages looked pretty much the same in terms of design and layout. HTML was enhanced to provide this support, and today, tables are the most powerful way of positioning items on a Web page to create more interesting designs.*

Frames

Have you ever seen a TV that supports a feature called *picture in a picture*? While viewing one television program full-screen, you can watch another

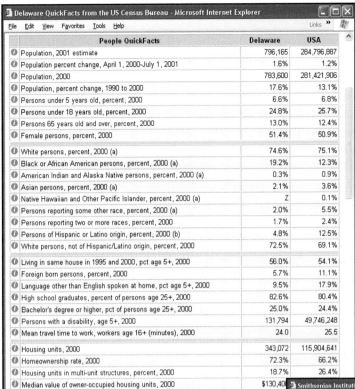

Visible table borders help users follow data across the table. You should turn the borders on when you are displaying this kind of data. ▪

program in a smaller onscreen window. On Web pages, frames serve a similar purpose. The term **frame** refers to the border that appears around windows on your screen. When Web pages contain frames, more than one window appears on your Web page, and you can interact with the information in the windows independently. The collection of these inner windows is called a **frameset**.

You can try out frames for yourself by following this book's Web site link to the presentation entitled "Emerging Technology and the Future of Education." This presentation was authored in Microsoft PowerPoint. The Web version was created by PowerPoint's Save As Web Page feature. Figure 5-15 shows how the Save As Web Page feature uses frames to provide you with three windows in the Web browser. The big window shows the slides. The window on the left displays an outline of the presentation. The window at the bottom displays the speaker notes that go with each slide.

Invisible borders permit a table to govern subtly the positioning of Web page elements. You make the borders invisible by setting their width to 0. ▪

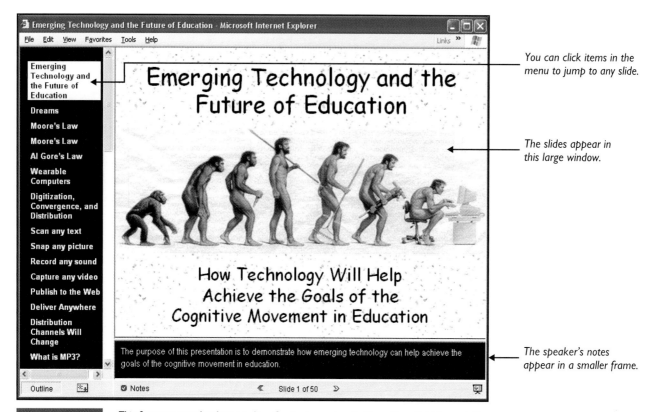

The following annotations appear beside the figure:

You can click items in the menu to jump to any slide.

The slides appear in this large window.

The speaker's notes appear in a smaller frame.

FIGURE   5-15   *This frameset provides three windows for viewing and controlling a PowerPoint presentation on the Web. PowerPoint created this frameset automatically when I used the PowerPoint option to save the presentation as a Web page. You learn how to create framesets in Chapter 7.* ■

Understanding Screen Design Principles

The hands-on tutorial in this part of the book teaches you how to create a Web page résumé. You will flow text onto the screen, create bulleted lists, and link items in the list to the different parts of your résumé. Then you will put pictures on the screen, either as backgrounds that appear behind the text or as design elements around which text flows. Before you begin, it is important to understand a few principles of Web page design that will help you make good layouts for your screens.

Layout

As you learned earlier in this chapter, Web pages consist of several design elements, including headings, paragraphs, horizontal rules, lists, images, backgrounds, bookmarks, links, special characters, tables, and frames. The relationship among these elements on the screen is called **layout**. When you create a Web page, you should plan its layout so your content is presented with good balance. Think of dividing the screen into regions, of which some will be pictorial, with others consisting of blocks of text. You must also think about how the user will interact with your screen and include the appropriate navigational buttons and hypertext links.

Figures 5-16 through 5-21 analyze the screen layouts of some example Web pages. Notice how some rely heavily on text, and others are more graphical. All the sample screens provide intuitive ways to navigate that make these Web pages user-friendly. Chapter 6 will show you how to use tables to lay out Web pages in rectangular regions such as these.

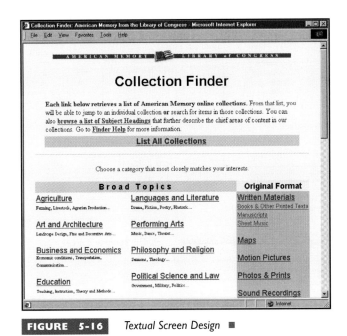

FIGURE 5-16   *Textual Screen Design* ■

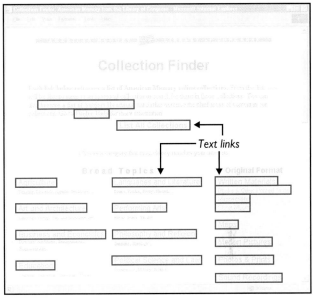

FIGURE 5-17   *Layout analysis of Figure 5-16* ■

FIGURE 5-18   *Graphical screen design* ■

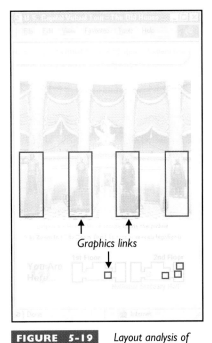

FIGURE 5-19   *Layout analysis of Figure 5-18* ■

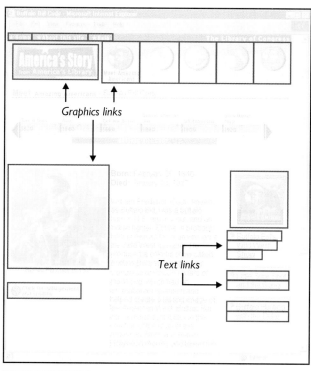

note *For a font to appear on a Web page, that font must be installed on your computer.*

Font Selection

Most Web browsers support the fonts listed in Figure 5-22. Web pages can either set these fonts specifically or leave the choice of the font up to the user. When no font is specified, the browser displays text in the default font. Most people have the default font in their browser set to Times New Roman. The Arial font, however, is generally considered to be more readable on Web pages.

All of the fonts illustrated in Figure 5-22 are proportionally spaced except Courier. Proportional spacing means that fat letters like *m* and *w* take up more space than thin letters like *l* and *i*. Normally you will want to use a **proportional font**, because proportional spacing is easier to read than nonproportional fonts. However, if you want to make columns of numbers line up precisely on the screen, such as in a spreadsheet, you will need to use the nonproportional Courier font. Figure 5-23 illustrates the difference between proportional and nonproportional spacing.

Times New Roman	ABCDEFG abcdefg 1234567
Courier New	ABCDEFG abcdefg 1234567
Arial	ABCDEFG abcdefg 1234567
Book Antiqua	ABCDEFG abcdefg 1234567
Comic Sans MS	ABCDEFG abcdefg 1234567
Century Gothic	ABCDEFG abcdefg 1234567
Century Schoolbook	ABCDEFG abcdefg 1234567
Garamond	ABCDEFG abcdefg 1234567
Impact	**ABCDEFG abcdefg 1234567**
Tahoma	ABCDEFG abcdefg 1234567
Verdana	ABCDEFG abcdefg 1234567

Times New Roman	Courier New
Proportional fonts are pleasing to the eye; their characters are varied in width and easier to read. You cannot use spaces to achieve vertical alignment:	`Nonproportional, or monospaced, fonts are regimented and somewhat graceless, but make vertical alignment much easier:`

Sales:	$100,000	$85,000	$43,614	`Sales:`	`$100,000`	`$85,000`	`$43,614`
Taxes:	54,521	3,425	6,921	`Taxes:`	`54,521`	`3,425`	`6,921`
Fees:	231,947	41	324	`Fees:`	`231,947`	`41`	`324`
Total:	$386,468	$88,466	$50,859	`Total:`	`$386,468`	`$88,466`	`$50,859`

FIGURE 5-23   *Compare the proportional spacing on the left to the nonproportional spacing on the right. Because nonproportional spacing appears regimented, save it for situations in which you need things to line up, such as the columns in a spreadsheet.* ■

Times and Arial are the most popular proportionally spaced fonts. The primary difference between the Times and Arial fonts is that Times has serifs, whereas Arial does not. A *serif* is a decorative line stemming at an angle from the upper and lower ends of the strokes of a letter. Figure 5-24 compares a few characters from the Times and Arial fonts, pointing out the serifs in the Times font.

Much of the fancy, stylized text you see on the Web is actually a graphic that was made from a font on a graphic artist's computer. This book's Web site links to some cool sites where you can make fancy text for use in banners and other places where you might want highly stylized text. In Chapter 6, you learn how to put these kinds of images onto your Web pages.

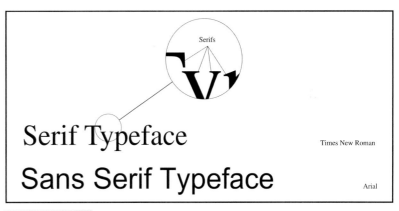

FIGURE 5-24   *When you compare the Times New Roman and Arial fonts, you notice that Times New Roman characters have special effects called serifs, which are not used in Arial. This may help explain why the Arial font is generally regarded as easier to read on a Web page, especially when the text is small and there is not as much room for the serifs.* ■

Text Sizing

Text size is measured in points, which tell how high the text is. In print media, a point is one seventy-secondth (1/72) of an inch. On a typical computer screen, a point is about the height of a single pixel. Because monitors are different sizes, the actual size of the text varies somewhat, depending on the physical height of the screen. Figure 5-25 illustrates different **point sizes** used on the Web.

Foreground vs. Background Colors

You can select from a wide range of colors for the text and the background of a Web page. Some color combinations work better than others. Figure 5-26 illustrates recommended color combinations as well as colors to avoid.

There are sites on the Web where you can see what different color combinations look like. To explore different foreground/background combinations, follow this book's Web site links to Color Pickers.

4 Point

8 Point

10 Point

12 Point

14 Point

16 Point

20 Point

24 Point

36 Point

FIGURE 5-25   *Comparison of point sizes. The higher the point size, the larger the font.* ■

Background Color	Recommended Foregrounds	Foregrounds to Avoid
White	Black, DarkBlue, Red	Yellow, Cyan, LightGray
Blue	White, Yellow, Cyan	Green, Black
Pink	Black, White, Yellow, Blue	Green, Red, Cyan
Red	Yellow, White, Black	Pink, Cyan, Blue, Green
Yellow	Red, Blue, Black	White, Cyan
Green	Black, Red, Blue	Cyan, Pink, Yellow
Cyan	Blue, Black, Red	Green, Yellow, White
LightGray	Black, DarkBlue, DarkPink	Green, Cyan, Yellow
Gray	Yellow, White, Blue	DarkGray, DarkCyan
DarkGray	Cyan, Yellow, Green	Red, Blue, Gray
Black	White, Cyan, Green, Yellow	DarkRed, DarkCyan
DarkBlue	Yellow, White, Pink, Green	DarkGreen, Blue, Black
DarkPink	Green, Yellow, White	Black, DarkCyan
DarkRed	White, LightGray, Yellow	Black, DarkBlue
Brown	Yellow, Cyan, White	Red, Pink, DarkGreen
DarkGreen	Cyan, White, Yellow	DarkBlue, DarkRed
DarkCyan	White, Yellow, Cyan	Brown, Blue, Gray

FIGURE 5-26 *Compare the recommended colors on the left with the color combinations to avoid on the right. You will probably agree that the colors on the right are not as easy to read as those on the left.* ■

tip *As you explore the use of colored backgrounds, keep in mind that the most readable combination is black text on a white background. Because you want the bulk of your text to be readable, save the razzle-dazzle colors for special effects.*

Photographic Backgrounds

Exercise care when placing text on photographic backgrounds. Some photos are so busy that text placed atop them is difficult to read. Bolding can improve the readability of text placed on photographic backgrounds. Figure 5-27 illustrates text printed on top of a background photo in different colors and sizes, with and without bolding.

Tiled Backgrounds

A **tiled background** is a graphical effect created when a bitmap smaller than the screen is drawn repeatedly up, down, and across the screen until the entire screen surface has been covered. As illustrated in Figure 5-28, a tiled background can create a special effect on a Web page. You must be careful, however, to select a tile that does not interfere with the readability of the text printed on top of it.

Tiles should be **seamless**, meaning that when the bitmap replicates itself up and down the screen, you cannot perceive the edges of the bitmap or detect a regular interruption in the pattern caused by the edges of the bitmap not fitting against each other smoothly. Figure 5-29 shows an example of a bad tile, in which you can clearly see a rectangular interruption around the edges of the bitmap. It is also difficult to read the text on top of this tile, making it a doubly bad choice on a Web page.

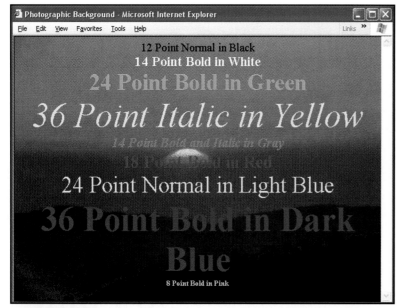

FIGURE 5-27 *Sizing, bolding, and coloring affect the readability of text on a photographic background. Notice how the color combinations with greater contrast are more readable than the colors that blend.* ■

Navigational Icons

Some Web pages contain navigational icons that give the user the option to page forward or backward, go to a menu, or return to a home page. Navigational icons normally work best when they appear lined up in the same region of the screen instead of scattered about the screen. Try to position the icons in a logical order. For example, it is logical to place the page-back icon in the lower left corner of the screen and the page-forward icon in the lower right. Here is a suggested sequence of icons that gives the user the option to page back, return to the menu, go to a home page, or page forward:

FIGURE 5-28   *Example of a seamless tile in the background of a Web page. This tile image is* ▪

FIGURE 5-29   *Example of a bad tile that is not seamless and interferes with the readability of the text. This tile image is* ▪

Scrolling

When you design a Web page, keep in mind that the user can scroll up and down through the information in it. Imagine what the user will see on each screen of your Web page document, and plan the layout accordingly. If your document is long, provide navigation options periodically in the midst of the document instead of putting them only at the end. Otherwise, the user will have to scroll all the way down to find the navigation options.

When you have a long document, organize it into sections divided by horizontal rules, and put the navigation options at the end of each section. You learn how to do this in Chapter 6 by providing navigation options at the end of each section of your Web page résumé.

As a general rule, it is best to keep the front page of a Web site short if you can, and use it to provide links to the longer pages. My home page at www.udel.edu/fth is very short, for example, and some of the documents it links to are quite long.

Usability

Web pages need to be easy to use. When you plan your layout and decide where you will place pictures and text on your screen, make sure you include navigational buttons, icons, or hypertext to clarify what the navigational options are and where the user should click to navigate.

Word your hypertext links to make it clear what will happen when the user clicks them. Descriptive phrases are better than single words. A descriptive phrase such as "table of contents" tells what will come onscreen when the link is clicked. Try to avoid the temptation to include the word "click" in your instructions. Telling users to click this to go here and click that to go there gets old after a while and sounds overly technical.

Iconic navigation is often more effective than words, takes up less screen space, and works better with international audiences because the icons can be understood regardless of what language the user speaks.

Be consistent. If you adopt navigational icons, use them consistently throughout your Web site. If you use hypertext navigation, be consistent in how you word the directions.

Consistency

Avoid the temptation to demonstrate every trick you know when you design a Web page. Keep it simple. Do not make every screen look and work a different way. Rather, adopt a common look and feel so the user will be able to navigate through your Web site intuitively.

It is frustrating to use a Web site with mixed metaphors and icons that change their meaning on different screens. Be consistent.

Analyzing the Layout of a Web Page Résumé

Figure 5-30 contains a layout analysis of a Web page résumé. Notice how the text, fonts, sizes, and colors enhance the readability of the text. Each item in the menu serves as a hypertext that links to different sections of the résumé. The navigation options at the end of each section make it clear how to move around on the page. The common look and feel of each section makes it easy for a prospective employer to find out about your job skills and work experience.

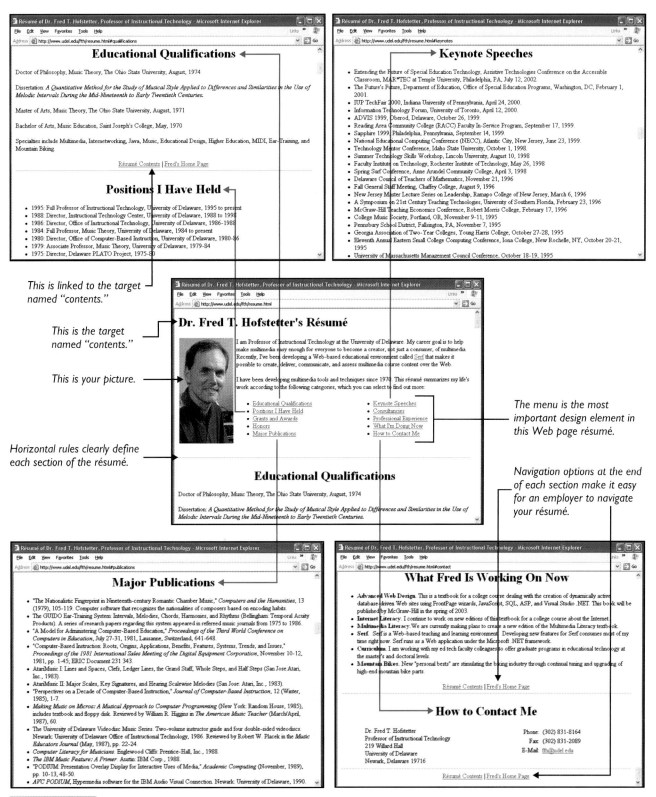

This is linked to the target named "contents."

This is the target named "contents."

This is your picture.

Horizontal rules clearly define each section of the résumé.

The menu is the most important design element in this Web page résumé.

Navigation options at the end of each section make it easy for an employer to navigate your résumé.

FIGURE 5-30 *Layout analysis of a Web page résumé. This is my résumé, which you can visit on the Web at www.udel.edu/fth/resume.html. The HTML tutorial in Chapter 6 steps you through the process of creating your own Web page résumé, which will come in handy whenever you are looking for a job.* ■

Chapter 5 Review

Chapter Summary

After reading this chapter and completing the step-by-step and Try This! exercises, you should understand the following facts about Web page authoring:

Adopting a Web Page Creation Strategy

- There are four ways to create Web pages. First, you can use a plaintext editor to type the HTML code of your Web page by hand. Second, you can use an HTML editor that contains toolbars and menus that help you insert the codes. Third, you can use the Save As Web Page option to convert word-processed documents into Web pages. Fourth, you can use a WYSIWYG editor to create Web pages through a graphical user interface that lets you enter text and graphics directly onto the screen exactly as you want them to appear.

- Because HTML is a textual encoding language, you can use a plaintext editor to create HTML Web pages. All Windows and Macintosh computers have a built-in text editor called Notepad, which you can use to create HTML Web pages.

- An editor that lets you create Web pages by working directly with the HTML tags is known as an HTML editor. HomeSite is the most popular HTML editor for Windows. On the Macintosh, the most well-known HTML editor is BBEdit.

- An HTML translator is a tool that can convert an existing document into the HTML format. Microsoft Word, Excel, Access, and PowerPoint have HTML translators built in.

- WYSIWYG is an acronym that stands for *what you see is what you get*. WYSIWYG editors let you create Web pages by typing your text directly onscreen, where it appears exactly as it will look on the Web. Dreamweaver, FrontPage, and Netscape Composer are three popular WYSIWYG Web page editors.

Defining the Elements of Web Page Design

- World Wide Web pages consist of elements defined in the HTML language that is used to create Web pages. These elements include headings, bookmarks, paragraphs, links, horizontal rules, special characters, lists, tables, images, frames, and backgrounds.

- There are six heading styles, numbered from H1 to H6. The smaller the number, the bigger the heading.

- A horizontal rule is a design element used to create a divider between sections of a Web page.

- Lists can be ordered or unordered. In an ordered list, the items are numbered automatically; in an unordered list, the items are bulleted.

- Images can be left justified, right justified, or centered on the screen. Text can be made to flow around the left or the right side of an image.

- Backgrounds can be filled with a solid color, or you can tile a bitmap into the background to create a textured appearance. It is important to choose a background that does not detract from the readability of the text. For this reason, black text on a white background is the most frequent color choice on the Web.

- A bookmark is a named anchor to which you can link a hot word or menu item to provide a way for the user to jump around to different places within a Web page.

- Links are the most essential element in Web design, because links create webs. Without links, there would be no webs.

- Tables provide a way of dividing the screen into rectangular regions into which you can lay out text and graphics on a Web page.

- The term frame refers to the border that appears around windows on your screen. When Web pages contain frames, more than one window appears on your Web page, and you can interact with the information in the windows independently. The collection of these inner windows is called a frameset.

Understanding Screen Design Principles

- The relationship among the elements that appear onscreen is called layout. When you create a Web page, you should plan its layout so your content is presented with good balance. Think of dividing the screen into regions, of which some will be pictorial, with others consisting of blocks of text. You must also think about how the user will interact with your screen, and include the appropriate navigational buttons and hypertext links.

- When no font is specified, the browser displays text in the default font. Most people have their browser's default font set to Times New Roman, although the Arial font is generally considered to be more readable on Web pages, especially when the text is very small. Book Antiqua creates a schoolbook effect, and the Comic font creates a handwritten look for less formal situations.

- Proportional spacing means that fat letters like *m* and *w* take up more space than thin letters like *l* and *i*. Normally you want to use a proportional font, because proportional spacing is easier to read than nonproportional fonts. If you want to make columns of text line up precisely on the screen, you need to use the nonproportional Courier font. Because nonproportional spacing appears regimented, save it for situations in which you need things to line up, such as the columns in a spreadsheet.

- Text size is measured in points, which tell how high the text is. In print media, a point is one seventy-secondth (1/72) of an inch. On a typical computer screen, a point is about the height of a single pixel. Because monitors are different sizes, the actual size of the text varies somewhat, depending on the physical height of the screen.

- Sizing, bolding, and coloring affect the readability of text on colored or photographic backgrounds. Color combinations with greater contrast are more readable than colors that blend.

- A tiled background is a graphical effect created when a bitmap smaller than the screen is drawn repeatedly up, down, and across the screen until the entire screen surface has been covered. You must be careful to select a tile that does not interfere with the readability of the text printed on top of it. Tiles should be seamless, meaning that when the bitmap replicates itself up and down the screen, you cannot perceive the edges of the bitmap or detect a regular interruption in the pattern caused by the edges of the bitmap not fitting against each other smoothly.

- Navigational icons normally work best when they appear lined up in the same region of the screen instead of scattered about the screen. Try to position the icons in a logical order. For example, it is logical to place the page-back icon in the lower left corner of the screen and the page-forward icon in the lower right.

- Imagine what the user will see on each screen of your Web page document, and plan the layout accordingly. If your document is long, provide navigation options periodically in the midst of the document instead of putting them only at the end. Otherwise, the user will have to scroll all the way down to find out the navigation options.

- Word your hypertext links to make it clear what will happen when the user triggers them. Descriptive phrases are better than single words. A descriptive phrase such as "go to the table of contents" tells what will happen when the icon is clicked.

- Iconic navigation is often more effective than words, takes up less screen space, and works better with international audiences because the icons can be understood regardless of what language the user speaks.

- It is frustrating to use a Web site with mixed metaphors and icons that change their meaning on different screens. Be consistent. If you adopt navigational icons, use them consistently throughout your Web site. If you use hypertext navigation, be consistent in how you word the directions.

Analyzing the Layout of a Web Page Résumé

- Layout analysis diagrams the positional and navigational relationships among the textual and graphical elements of a Web page.

- When you design a Web page, think about the menu choices and navigational options you want to provide for your site's visitors.

- Plan the layout according to what you want the user to see on each screen of your Web site. Visualizing the layout prior to creating the pages can save you a lot of time in Web development.

- Remember to be consistent and avoid mixing metaphors. Use navigational icons consistently, and make hypertext links intuitive by wording the text in such a way that users know what will happen when they click.

■ Key Terms

bookmark *(233)*	**layout** *(236)*	**table** *(234)*
frame *(235)*	**link** *(234)*	**tags** *(223)*
frameset *(235)*	**Notepad** *(223)*	**tiled background** *(240)*
heading *(231)*	**ordered list** *(232)*	**unordered list** *(232)*
horizontal rule *(231)*	**point size** *(239)*	**what you see is what you get**
HTML editor *(223)*	**proportional font** *(238)*	**(WYSIWYG)** *(228)*
HTML translator *(225)*	**seamless** *(240)*	

■ Key Terms Quiz

1. The special codes that mark up the text of an HTML document are called _____.

2. WYSIWYG is an acronym that stands for _____.

3. There are six _____ styles, which are numbered from H1 to H6.

4. The Web page design element that creates a divider between sections of a Web page is called a(n) _____.

5. On a Web page, lists can be ordered or unordered. In a(n) _____ , the items are numbered automatically; in a(n) _____ , the items are bulleted.

6. Normally, the text of a Web page flows evenly onto the screen, aligning itself automatically with the left and right edges of your browser's window. The _____ provides a way of dividing the screen into rectangular regions into which you can lay out text and graphics on a Web page.

7. When Web pages contain frames, more than one window appears on your Web page, and you can interact with the information in the windows independently. The collection of these inner windows is called a(n) _____.

8. Web pages consist of several design elements, including headings, paragraphs, horizontal rules, lists, images, backgrounds, bookmarks, links, special characters, tables, and frames. The relationship among these elements on the screen is called _____.

9. In print media, a(n) _____ of 1 is one seventy-secondth (1/72) of an inch. On a typical computer screen, this is about the height of a single pixel.

10. A bitmap that repeats up, down, and across the screen until the entire screen surface has been covered creates a(n) _____.

■ Multiple-Choice Quiz

1. What kind of a tool lets you create Web pages by working directly with the HTML tags?
   a. HTML editor
   b. HTML translator
   c. Layout analyzer
   d. WYSIWYG

2. What is the most popular HTML editor for Windows?
   a. BBEdit
   b. HomeSite
   c. Notepad
   d. WordPad

3. What is the name of the Macromedia program you can use to create Web pages from a Code view, a Design view, or a Split view that combines both the Code and Design views?
   a. Composer
   b. Dreamweaver
   c. FrontPage
   d. WebEdit

4. Which Web page editor was designed for use with Microsoft Office?
   a. Composer
   b. Dreamweaver
   c. FrontPage
   d. WebEdit

5. Which Web page editor ships freely as part of Netscape Navigator?
   a. Composer
   b. Dreamweaver
   c. FrontPage
   d. WebEdit

6. What is the most frequent color choice on the Web?
   a. Black text on a white background
   b. Black text on a blue background
   c. White text on a red background
   d. Yellow text on a brown background

7. Which color combination provides the most contrast onscreen?
   a. Black text on a gray background
   b. Black text on a white background
   c. Gray text on a black background
   d. Gray text on a white background

8. What kind of link causes an e-mail window to open onscreen?
   a. FTP
   b. Hypertext
   c. Mailto
   d. News

9. Which of the following fonts uses nonproportional spacing?
   a. Arial
   b. Book Antiqua
   c. Courier
   d. Times Roman

10. When you cannot perceive the edges of the background tile or detect a regular interruption in the pattern caused by the edges of the tile not fitting against each other smoothly, the background tile is said to be:
   a. Aligned
   b. Proportional
   c. Repetitive
   d. Seamless

Essay Quiz

1. In your own words, describe when it is best to use an HTML editor, a WYSIWYG tool, or an HTML translator to create a Web page.

2. Go to Macromedia's HomeSite page at www.macromedia.com/homesite. What is the version number of the latest HomeSite update? What is the hottest new feature you see advertised for the latest update?

3. Using the design elements presented in this chapter, plan the layout of your Web page résumé. Think about the menu choices you want to provide prospective employers who visit your Web page to find out about your experience and qualifications. Include this menu as one of the design elements in your résumé. Possible menu items include:

- Educational Qualifications
- Work Experience
- Computer Skills
- Grants and Awards
- Honorary Societies

- Professional Association Memberships
- Publications
- Software
- Presentations
- How to Contact Me

If you are just starting out, you may not have this many items, but remember not to be shy on a résumé. Think about all the things you have done, the part-time jobs you have had, the organizations for which you have volunteered, the sports teams on which you have played, and the clubs you joined. You probably have more things to list on a résumé than you can think of at first. You do not want to go overboard, however, because a résumé should be succinct, but if you cannot fill a screen or two, think harder about the things you have done in life.

4. Because you can link any document, audio, picture, movie, or software application to your Web page, you can link your résumé to examples of your work to prove your worth to a prospective employer. What examples would you like to link to your résumé? Include these links in the design of your résumé.

5. There is a knack to writing hypertext in such a way that the wording makes it clear what will happen when the user triggers the link. Write three examples of text containing a word or a phrase which, when clicked, takes the user to your home page.

6. Draw three different ways of providing an icon that moves forward to the next screen of an application.

Lab Projects

• Lab Project 5-1: Web Page Creation Strategy

When employees can create their own Web pages and publish them to the Web, a school or company becomes much more efficient in posting and sharing information. Hyperlinking enables the Web page author to link items on the page to other information that a coworker, student, or customer might be expected or encouraged to access as related information. Search engines enable users to search via keyword for any other page at the site to which they have access. This kind of information-publishing, linking, and search capability is the very reason Tim Berners-Lee gives for inventing the Web back in 1989. In his 1989 proposal for creating the Web, Berners-Lee (1989, ¶ 5) said his goal was to help his coworkers keep track of things in a large project. Imagine that your employer wants to empower your coworkers to take advantage of the power of publishing, linking, and searching school or company information on the Web. Your employer wants you to recommend a Web page creation strategy that is appropriate for your workplace. In developing a recommendation for the best approach for your school or company to take in creating Web pages, consider these issues:

- **Technical support** How much technical support is available to coworkers in your school or company? If your company has an IT organization with a support staff that helps employees troubleshoot technical problems, you may be able to recommend a more technical solution than for a small company or school that does not have a lot of technical support staff, if any.

- **Other software products** Take into account other software products that your school or company is already using. If all your coworkers are using Microsoft Office, for example, that might direct your choice toward a FrontPage solution. If your school or company has adopted Netscape as its standard browser, on the other hand, Netscape Composer may be the obvious choice.

- **Training** How will your coworkers learn how to use the Web page creation software you recommend? If you recommend FrontPage or Netscape Composer, you could use the Web page creation tutorial in McGraw-Hill's *Internet Literacy* textbook as training material.

Use a word processor to write up your answer to this assignment in the form of a two-part essay. In the opening paragraph, tell what Web page creation strategy you recommend and briefly state the reason for choosing it for use in your workplace. Then write another paragraph or two describing the other approaches you considered, and state your reasons for rejecting them. Conclude your recommendation with a paragraph describing how empowering you feel your recommended strategy will be, and give examples of a few ways in which creating Web pages in this manner will empower your coworkers and improve operations in your workplace. If your instructor has asked you to hand in this assignment, make sure you put your name at the top; then save it on disk or follow the other instructions you may have been given for submitting this assignment.

• Lab Project 5-2: Adopting a Common Look and Feel

Whether or not the Web page author is aware of it, every Web page has a certain look and feel. If the look and feel is consistent from page to page, coworkers and others who visit the site frequently get used to looking in certain places on the page to find such things as menus, link bars, headlines, different kinds of content, and navigation buttons. If the look and feel is not consistent from page to page, the user must spend more time finding where things are on the page. This is inefficient at best and can be frustrating as well. Imagine that your employer has decided that your school or company Web site needs to adopt a common look and feel. Your employer has asked you to create a design specification recommending a common look and feel for Web pages created in your workplace. In creating this design spec, address the following issues:

- **Templates**   What kinds of pages do your coworkers typically create? The pages probably fall into a few basic types, such as home pages for different projects or products, search pages for finding things, catalog pages for listing products for sale, and document pages containing reports, product information, or scholarly papers.

- **Design elements**   What are the design elements that are likely to appear on the kinds of pages you identified? Make an outline that lists the basic kinds of pages typically used in your workplace. Under each kind, list the design elements that appear on that kind of page. Consider all the different elements that can appear on your workplace Web pages, such as banners, menus, search buttons, quick links, newsfeeds, headlines, navigation buttons, pictures, icons, logos, prose, products, catalogs, advertisements, and bibliographies.

- **Positioning**   Add to this outline an indication of where each element will go on the Web page. If you are not sure where things should go, visit some Web sites of organizations like yours and study their Web page designs. If you have FrontPage, you can look at the built-in templates there. Pull down the File menu, choose New | Page, and click the option to see the templates. As you click each template, a preview pane shows the layout. There is also a template gallery at officeupdate.microsoft.com/templategallery. Surf these templates and visit other Web sites in your industry or subject matter to get more design ideas.

- **Navigation**   Include in your design spec a strategy for placing navigational elements at consistent places onscreen.

Use a word processor to write up your answer to this assignment in the form of a three-part essay. In the first part, describe the overall approach you recommend. Mention the three or four basic kinds of templates you feel your school or company needs. In the second part, present the outline of design elements that will typically appear on each template. Conclude by describing where onscreen these design elements will appear.

If you are graphically inclined, you can use your word processor's table feature to create a prototype of the screen designs you envision. Otherwise, you can describe the layout prosaically. Make sure you specify where the navigational elements will be onscreen. If your instructor has asked you to hand in this assignment, put your name at the top; then save it on disk or follow the other instructions you may have been given for submitting this assignment.

chapter

6

HTML Coding

"From then on, when anything went
wrong with a computer, we said it had
bugs in it."

—*Grace Murray Hopper, on the removal of
a moth from a computer in 1945*

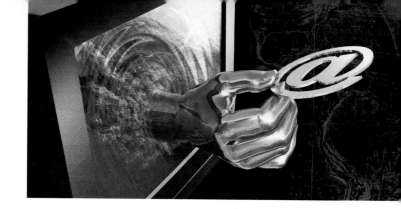

- Explain the concept of a markup language and define the HTML tags you will use to create your Web page résumé.

- Create a new HTML file and use paragraph, list, and anchor tags to format the text and create the bookmark links on your Web page résumé.

- Capture and convert images into a file format suitable for display on a Web page, and use the HTML image tag to put a graphic on your Web page résumé.

- List the HTML table tags, create a table-driven page layout, and flow text and graphics into the cells of the table onscreen.

- Define the hypermedia design paradigms you can use to link pages into well-structured Webs that enable users to navigate efficiently.

THIS may be the most empowering chapter in the book because it steps you through the process of creating an HTML Web page. After defining the HTML codes and understanding how they mark up the content of a Web page, you use these codes to create a very strategic Web page—your résumé, which will come in handy any time you are looking for a job.

To make your résumé easy to navigate, you will learn how to divide a page into sections and create a table of contents. By linking the items in this table to the various sections of your résumé, you will enable potential employers to navigate your page and learn about your job skills. In the process, your well-constructed résumé will demonstrate your Web creation skills, which employers consider strategic in the twenty-first century information economy.

To illustrate your résumé, you learn how to put graphics onto a Web page. If you do not have these graphics already at hand, the chapter teaches you how to capture graphics and convert them into a format suitable for displaying on a Web page.

Then you use tables to control the positioning of text and graphics onscreen. You learn HTML tags that enable you to create layouts consisting of any conceivable pattern of table cells onscreen. These are the same table tags that all the major sites use to create their screen layouts, such as Amazon, CNN, eBay, Google, Yahoo!, and the Library of Congress.

After learning how to design individual pages, you learn how to form Webs by hyperlinking the pages together. By creating different patterns in your links, you create hypermedia design structures that enable users to navigate your Webs efficiently. By learning how to create different kinds of hypermedia design patterns, you will become very powerful as a Web page designer.

How HTML Works

Hypertext markup language (HTML) is the markup language used to create hypertext documents for the World Wide Web. The key to understanding how HTML works is to know what it means to mark up a text. Once you understand the markup concept, you will be ready to learn the HTML tags.

Understanding Markup

To **mark up** a text means to insert special codes called **tags** into the text. The tags control how the text appears on a Web page. For example, compare Figures 6-1 and 6-2. In Figure 6-1, you see how a text appears on a Web page; notice the different-sized heading, the paragraphs, and the list of bulleted items. In Figure 6-2, you can see the HTML tags that mark up the text. By comparing these two figures, you can begin to understand how HTML controls the appearance of text on the Web. Notice that the HTML tags always appear `<inside>` brackets.

HTML Tag Formats

There are two HTML tag formats: paired tags and single tags. **Paired tags** come in pairs that consist of a **start tag** and a **stop tag**. Headings are an example of paired tags. For example, to make the words *Internet Technologies At Work* appear in the largest style of heading, you would mark them up as follows:

```
<h1>Internet Technologies At Work</h1>
```

<h1> is the start tag, and **</h1>** is the stop tag. The words between them will appear in heading style h1, which is the largest of the six heading styles. You can tell a start tag from a stop tag because the stop tag always has a slash, as in **</h1>**.

Single tags function on their own with no stop tag. For example, the tag **<hr>** makes a line known as a "horizontal rule" appear on your Web page; there is no stop tag for a horizontal rule.

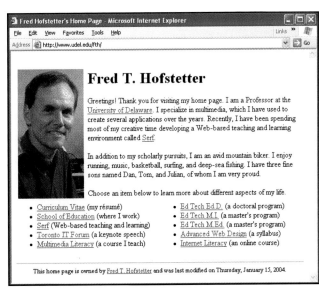

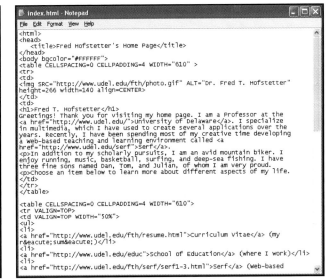

FIGURE 6-1 *This is how my home page appears on the Web. Notice the different-sized heading, the paragraphs, and the list of bulleted items.* ■

FIGURE 6-2 *This is the HTML source code that creates my home page. The codes in <brackets> are the HTML tags that mark up the text.* ■

Versions of HTML

HTML has progressed through several versions, each of which added new functionality to what you can do on a Web page. When HTML was invented, the Web was a text-only medium used to display simple text documents onscreen. To keep the markup simple enough for beginners to learn, HTML did not require all the structural elements defined by its parent language, which is the **standard generalizable markup language (SGML)**. According to SGML, for example, every begin tag needs some kind of logical ending. In early versions of HTML, however, several elements did not have end tags. The **list item tag** `<li>`, for example, did not have a corresponding end tag `</li>`. Moreover, SGML requires the order of the tags to adhere to the document's defined structure. If a bold italicized phrase begins, for example, with `<strong>` `<em>`, it must end with `</em>` `</strong>` and not `</strong>` `</em>`. Early versions of HTML permitted both kinds of endings, and to this day, the browsers permit them both.

Such loose encoding, however, does not lend itself to the kind of structure needed to transition the Web into an application model in which servers exchange data in a disciplined manner. Enter XML, which stands for eXtensible Markup Language. True to its name, XML enables you to extend a document's structure by defining new tags. This was not possible in HTML. Another difference between XML and HTML is that XML adheres to the structural rules of SGML. Every begin tag must have an ending, and the order in which the tags close must follow the structure of the document's definition.

More than a billion Web pages were created with HTML. The vast majority of these pages contain loose encodings that do not follow the strict rules of SGML. As a result, these pages will not validate in XML tools that require tags to follow the document's definition. To solve this problem, the W3C created a new language called XHTML. True to its name, **XHTML** includes most of the classic HTML codes, but they appear in the context of an XML schema (hence the X) that XML tools can understand.

Pages authored in XHTML will render not only on the Web but also on pagers, PDAs, cell phones, tablet PCs, and other devices that are following the new XML-based wireless protocols. XHTML pages can also be mined by XML tools as data that can be used in server-to-server and business-to-business applications. XHTML further enables you to use the extensible stylesheet language (XSL) to transform a document from one format into another, such as from an HTML Web page into a PDF document. Finally, XHTML makes it possible for you to use other XML languages on your Web page, such as the Synchronized Multimedia Integration Language (SMIL), which you will play with in the XML section of Chapter 8.

In this book, the HTML tags you will be learning follow the XHTML specification. To visit the official Web site where the HTML and XHTML specifications are found, go to www.w3.org/MarkUp.

Taxonomy of HTML Tags

There are more than a hundred HTML tags. Learning that many tags may seem like a foreboding task. You can simplify the process, however, if you think of the tags as families devoted to accomplishing similar tasks. The following taxonomy groups the HTML tags into 13 families:

- **Page structure tags** provide a framework for the document as a whole. They identify that the document is encoded in HTML and provide titling, framing, and header information that defines the structure of the file.

- **Block-style tags** control the flow of text into blocks on the screen. The most common block style is the paragraph.

- **Logical font-style tags** include styles for abbreviations, acronyms, citations, and quotations.

- **Physical font-style tags** let you create text that is blinking, bold, italic, subscripted, superscripted, or underlined.

- **Heading tags** let you create headings in six different levels or sizes of importance.

- **Lists and miscellaneous tags** let you create numbered lists, bulleted lists, menus, directories, horizontal dividing lines, and line breaks.

- **Form tags** let you create input fields, buttons, and selection boxes for gathering information from users.

- **Table tags** let you define tables that present data in neat rows and columns.

- **Character entities** provide a wide range of Greek characters and special symbols used in mathematical and scientific notation.

- **Anchor/link tags** let you create bookmarks, hypertext, and hyperpictures and link them to any resource or file on the World Wide Web.

- **Image tags** let you insert figures, center or align pictures with the left or right margin, flow text around images, or place little icons inline in the midst of your text.

- **Object tags** provide a means for defining a way to interact with plug-ins, media handlers, and Java applets, which are little applications that get downloaded to your computer along with a Web page.

Tags Used in the Web Page Creation Tutorial

Table 6-1 defines the HTML tags you will use in this chapter to create your Web page résumé. These tags are all a standard part of HTML and XHTML, and they work with almost any Web browser, including both Netscape Navigator and the Microsoft Internet Explorer.

HTML Tag Syntax	Use on Web Page
`<html>` and `</html>`	These tags define the beginning and end of an HTML document. Your Web pages will always begin with the `<html>` start tag and end with the `</html>` stop tag.
`<head>` and `</head>`	The headers of your HTML file will appear between these tags.
`<title>` and `</title>`	The title of your HTML file goes between these tags, which in turn go between the header tags.
`<body>` and `</body>`	The body of your HTML file goes between these tags.
`<h1>` and `</h1>`	You will use the h1 heading tags at the beginning of your résumé to make your name appear in the most important heading style.
`<p>` and `</p>`	The `<p>` tag marks the beginning of a new paragraph. The stop tag `</p>` is optional in HTML but required in strict XHTML. The `<p>` tag always begins a new paragraph, whether or not a `</p>` tag marks the end of the paragraph.
`<ul>` and `</ul>`	These unordered list tags will mark the beginning and end of the table of contents in your résumé.
`<li>` and `</li>`	The list item tag will mark each item in your table of contents.
`<hr>`	The horizontal rule tag makes the neat three-dimensional dividing lines on Web pages.
`<a name="name"> </a>`	A stands for *anchor*. An anchor tag with a `name` attribute creates names for the bookmarks in your résumé.
`<a href="url"> </a>`	*Href* stands for *hypertext reference*. An anchor tag with an `href` attribute creates hypertext links.
`<img src="filename">`	The image tag places pictures on your Web page.
`<body background="filename"> </body>`	The `background` attribute of the body tag tiles an image into the background of your Web page if you want to give your résumé a textured appearance.
`<table>` and `</table>`	Table cells go between these tags.
`<tr>` and `</tr>`	You use these to create a row in a table; *tr* stands for *table row*.
`<td>` and `</td>`	You use these to create a data cell inside a row of a table; *td* stands for *table data*.

TABLE 6-1   *HTML Tags Used in the Web Page Creation Tutorial* ∎

Creating Your Web Page Résumé

Now that you know how HTML works, you are ready to apply your new knowledge. The rest of this chapter takes you through all the steps needed to build your own online résumé with text, graphics, and links to other Web pages.

Starting the Page

To start a new Web page, follow these steps:

1. Get the Notepad running on your computer by double-clicking its Launch icon. If this icon is not visible, use the Windows Start | Programs | Accessories menu or the Macintosh Finder to locate the Notepad program. If you have decided to use another program instead of the Notepad to edit your HTML files, launch that other program and use it whenever these instructions tell you to use the Notepad.

2. Click to position your cursor in the Notepad window, and type the code illustrated in Figure 6-3. This is the minimal amount of HTML code needed to create a Web page. Notice that this code creates a head section and a body section. The body of your page will go between the `<body>` and `</body>` tags. The `<head>` will contain your page title, which you create in the next section of this chapter.

The tags `<html>` and `</html>` mark the beginning and end of an HTML document.

The document's head will go between the `<head>` and `</head>` tags.

The document's body will go between the `<body>` and `</body>` tags.

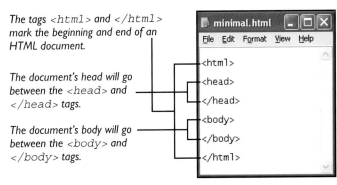

FIGURE 6-3 *This is the minimal amount of HTML code needed to create a Web page. The body of your page will go between the `<body>` and the `</body>` tags. The `<head>` will contain your page title, which you create in the next section of this chapter.* ∎

Creating the Page Title

The **page title** is the name that appears in the browser's title bar when people visit your Web page on the Internet. The title is also used by many Web search engines, so you want to make sure the title identifies the primary purpose of your Web page by including keywords you want search engines to find. To create the page title, follow these steps:

1. The page title goes in the **head** of the document, which is the section of the Notepad file that goes between the `<head>` and `</head>` tags. Therefore, click to position your cursor between the document's `<head>` and `</head>` tags.

2. Type the following code, replacing "Santa" with your own name:

```
<title>Santa's Resume</title>
```

Figure 6-4 shows how your HTML appears after you create the document's title. Notice that the title of the document gets typed between the `<title>` start tag and the `</title>` stop tag. At runtime out on the Web, this title will appear in your browser's title bar.

Insert the title tags between the `<head>` and `</head>` tags.

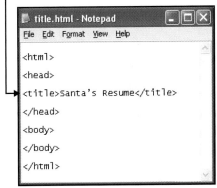

FIGURE 6-4 *You type the document's title tags between the `<head>` and `</head>` tags, which demarcate the head section of the Web page. When someone views the page out on the Web, this title will appear in the browser's title bar.* ∎

Writing the Heading

Because this Web page is your résumé, you want to start it with a heading that includes your name in big, bold letters at the top of the Web page. The largest heading style is the `<h1>` style. To create a heading, follow these steps:

1. Click to position your cursor in the **body** of the document, which is the section of the page that comes after the `<body>` start tag but before the `</body>` stop tag.

2. Type the following code, replacing "Santa Claus" with your own name:

```
<h1>Santa Claus's Resume</h1>
```

Figure 6-5 shows how your code will appear. In the next part of this tutorial, you save this page and then preview it by opening it with your browser. Read on.

Insert your résumé's content between the `<body>` and `</body>` tags.

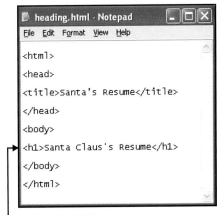

FIGURE 6-5 *You type the `<h1>` tag into the document's body, which is where you will type all of your résumé's content. The `<h1>` tag will cause the text between it and the `</h1>` stop tag to appear in heading style 1, which is a very large font. In the next part of this tutorial, you learn how to save and preview what this page will look like out on the Web.* ∎

Saving the Page

Whenever you make a change to a file you want to keep, you should save the file. Do so now by following these steps:

1. Pull down the File menu and choose Save. The first time you save a file, the Save As dialog appears, as illustrated in Figure 6-6.

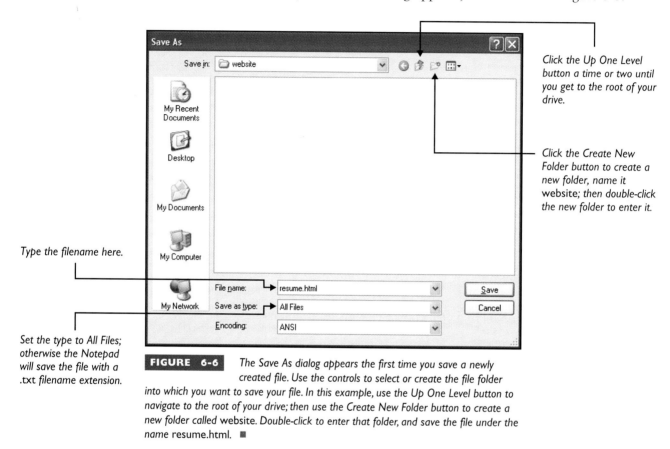

Click the Up One Level button a time or two until you get to the root of your drive.

Click the Create New Folder button to create a new folder, name it website; then double-click the new folder to enter it.

Type the filename here.

Set the type to All Files; otherwise the Notepad will save the file with a .txt filename extension.

FIGURE 6-6   *The Save As dialog appears the first time you save a newly created file. Use the controls to select or create the file folder into which you want to save your file. In this example, use the Up One Level button to navigate to the root of your drive; then use the Create New Folder button to create a new folder called website. Double-click to enter that folder, and save the file under the name resume.html.* ■

2. If the folder in which you want to save the file does not already exist, you can use the Save As dialog's icons to create a file folder. In this example, click the Up One Level icon to move up a level until you get to the root of your drive; then click the Create New Folder icon to create a new folder. Name the new folder *website* and then double-click that folder's icon to enter it.

3. In the File name field, type the name you want the file to have. In this example, type **resume.html**.

4. Pull down the Save As Type menu, and set it to All Files.

5. Click the Save button to save the file. From now on, to save this file after you make changes, all you need to do is pull down the File menu and click Save. If you ever want to save it under a different name, pull down the File menu and click Save As.

Viewing the Page with a Web Browser

While you are creating a new Web page, you will want to have a look at it with a Web browser from time to time so you can see how it is going to appear on the Web. To preview a Web page with a browser, follow these steps:

1. Pull down the browser's File menu and choose Open to make the Open dialog appear.

2. Click the Browse button and use the controls to select the file you want to view. In this example, assuming your hard drive is letter C, select your file named c:*website\resume.html*.

3. Click OK to open the file, which now appears in your browser, as illustrated in Figure 6-7.

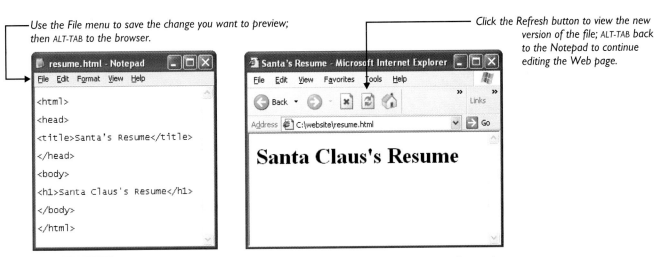

Use the File menu to save the change you want to preview; then ALT-TAB to the browser.

Click the Refresh button to view the new version of the file; ALT-TAB back to the Notepad to continue editing the Web page.

FIGURE 6-7 *You can save valuable time by keeping the Notepad and the browser open simultaneously when you are using them to edit and preview a Web page. Whenever you make a change in the Notepad that you want to view with the browser, save the file in the Notepad, and then ALT-TAB to the browser and click the browser's Refresh button to view the new version of the file. Then you can ALT-TAB back to the Notepad to continue editing the Web page. ∎*

4. When you finish viewing the file, you can save time by avoiding the temptation to close the browser window. Instead of closing the browser, hold down the ALT key and click TAB until you get back to your Notepad, where you can continue editing the file. Whenever you want to preview the file, use the Notepad to save it. Then ALT-TAB back to your browser and click the browser's Refresh button to read the new version of the file.

Writing Paragraphs

Now you are ready to type the first paragraph of your résumé. Move your cursor to the spot in the Notepad right after the heading's </h1> stop tag, and press ENTER. If you mistakenly press ENTER in the midst of the heading instead of at the end of it, you can pull down the Edit menu and choose Undo to fix the mistake.

To begin the new paragraph, type the <p> tag followed by a few sentences about yourself as an introduction to your résumé. Do not be bashful: a résumé should begin with a strongly stated summary of your professional qualifications and career goals. At the end of each paragraph, you should type the </p> stop tag, although the browsers may let you get away without it. Figure 6-8 shows how I began my résumé.

Each paragraph begins with a <p> start tag.

The character code é creates an é when displayed by a browser.

```
resume.html - Notepad

File  Edit  Format  View  Help

<h1>Fred Hofstetter's R&eacute;sum&eacute;</h1>
<p>
I am Professor of Instructional Technology at the University of
Delaware. My career goal is to help make multimedia easy enough
for everyone to become a creator, not just a consumer, of
multimedia. Recently, I've been developing a web-based educational
environment called Serf that makes it possible to create, deliver,
communicate, and assess multimedia course content over the web.
</p>
<p>
I have been developing multimedia tools and techniques since 1970.
This r&eacute;sum&eacute; summarizes my life's work according to
the following categories, which you can select to find out more:
</p>
```

Each paragraph ends with a </p> stop tag.

FIGURE 6-8 *How I typed the first two paragraphs of my résumé. Do not be bashful about promoting yourself. A résumé must impress upon potential employers that you are a desirable job candidate.* ∎

After you type your opening paragraphs, use the Notepad's File menu to save the page, and then use your browser to preview it. Remember that you can save time if you keep the Notepad and browser windows open and ALT-TAB between them while editing and previewing your page. Click the browser's Refresh button to view the new version of the page. Notice that the paragraphs you typed appear beneath the heading of your résumé.

Creating a List

You create lists with the **unordered list** <ul> start and </ul> stop tags for a bulleted list, or the **ordered list** <ol> start and </ol> stop tags for a numbered list. In between these tags, you type the list items, which must begin and end with the list item <li> start and </li> stop tags.

Now that you have created the two introductory paragraphs of your résumé, it is time to create the bulleted list that will serve as your table of contents. Follow these steps:

1. Position your cursor in the Notepad window just after the </p> stop tag at the end of your second paragraph, and press ENTER to move down to the next line.

2. Type the <ul> tag and press ENTER. The <ul> tag begins an unordered list.

3. Type the </ul> tag and press ENTER. The </ul> tag ends an unordered list. You may justifiably ask, why type the end-of-list tag before typing the list itself? The reason is to keep from forgetting to do so. Of course, the page will work regardless of whether you type the </ul> tag before or after typing the list.

4. Position your cursor between the `<ul>` and `</ul>` tags, which is where the list items will go.

5. For each item, type the `<li>` start tag to begin the list item, followed by the item itself, followed by the `</li>` stop tag to end the item. Figure 6-9 shows how I typed my list items into the Notepad, and Figure 6-10 shows the resulting Web page.

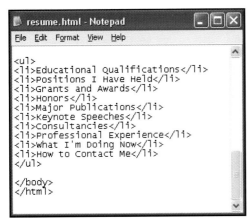

FIGURE 6-9 *My bulleted list consists of ten list items. Notice that the list is bounded by the <ul> start and </ul> stop tags. Similarly, each list item is demarcated by the <li> start and </li> stop tags.* ■

FIGURE 6-10 *This is a browser preview of the HTML in Figure 6-9. Notice that the browser displays the unordered list with bullets. If the list were ordered, on the other hand, the browser would have used numbers instead of bullets. Chapter 8 shows you how to use a style sheet to change the default appearance of bullets, numbers, and other elements onscreen.* ■

Horizontal Rules

A **horizontal rule** is a Web page element that creates a neat-looking dividing line between different parts of a Web page. To insert a horizontal rule after the bulleted table of contents in your résumé, follow these steps:

1. In the Notepad window, position your cursor after the `</ul>` stop tag at the end of the list. Press ENTER to move down to a new line.

2. Type the HTML tag for a horizontal rule, which is `<hr>`.

3. Save the file in the Notepad, and preview the new version of the file in the browser. Remember to click the browser's Refresh button to make sure you are viewing the newly saved version of the file.

Inserting horizontal rules in your documents is easy, and the dividing lines look nice. However, do not give in to the temptation to overuse them! Horizontal rules are best used to separate major sections of your document.

Remember to Save the File

Remember to save your HTML file periodically to prevent accidental data loss due to power failures or other accidents. To save the file, pull down the Notepad's File menu and choose Save. In addition to saving the file on your primary drive, it is also a good idea to make a copy of the file on another storage device from time to time. Such a spare copy is known as a *backup*. Having a backup will protect you from data loss in case of a power failure or a hard disk crash on your primary working drive. The backup also provides you with a way to retrieve your good work in case you make a mistake and really mess something up on your primary copy.

The importance of backing up your files cannot be overemphasized. Floppy disks, CD-R disks, and zip drives provide you with economical ways to back up your files. Keeping a copy of your backups in more than one physical location can help protect against data loss in case of a fire or some other kind of unforeseen calamity. I hope such a tragedy will never happen to you. According to Murphy's Law, if you faithfully keep a backup, you will never need it. In other words, always make a backup!

Inserting a New Heading

Every main section of your résumé should begin with a large-sized heading that identifies what that section is. It is common for Web pages to have a title displayed in the largest-sized heading, <h1>, and then to use the next smaller size, <h2>, for subheads. For example, when you enter the educational qualifications section of your résumé, follow these steps to give it a heading:

1. In the Notepad, position your cursor at the start of the education section of your résumé. This location will probably be right after the horizontal line you just inserted.

2. Press ENTER to move down to a new line.

3. Type the heading, which in this example will be **Educational Qualifications**. To make this have the heading 2 style, the tag to type is:

   ```
   <h2>Educational Qualifications</h2>
   ```

4. To begin a new paragraph after the heading, position your cursor at the end of the heading, press ENTER to move down to the next line, type the <p> tag to start a new paragraph, and type the content of the next section. Remember to end each paragraph with the </p> stop tag.

Creating Named Anchor Bookmarks

As you create the different sections in your résumé, it will grow too long for the browser to display it onscreen all at once. So users can easily find the parts of your résumé, you can insert bookmarks known as **named anchors** into your document. Then you can link each item in your résumé's bulleted list of topics to its corresponding bookmark to make it quick and easy for the user to find that section. To create a named anchor bookmark, follow these steps:

1. Click to position your cursor at the spot in the Notepad window where you want the bookmark to be. In this example, position your cursor at the start of the Education section, right before the `<h2>` tag that demarcates that section's heading.

2. You use the anchor tag to create a name for a bookmark. To make a bookmark named "education," type the following anchor tag:

```
<a name="education"></a>
```

Every `<a>` start tag must be followed by a `</a>` stop tag.

Figure 6-11 shows an example of how I completed this exercise. Now that the bookmark's name has been created, you must next create the link that will take users from the corresponding item in the table of contents to your education section. The next section of this tutorial shows you how to do this. Read on.

Creating Hypertext Links to Named Anchor Bookmarks

Think about the items in your bulleted table of contents. You want each item to serve as a hypertext link that, when clicked, will jump the page down to the bookmarked name of its corresponding anchor. The table of contents item "Educational Qualifications," for example, needs to become a link that, when clicked, takes users to the education bookmark in your résumé. To create such a link, follow these steps:

This is the horizontal rule at the end of the bulleted table of contents.

Name is an attribute of the anchor tag.

This is the heading that begins the education section.

```
resume.html - Notepad
File  Edit  Format  View  Help
<ul>
<li>Educational Qualifications</li>
<li>Positions I Have Held</li>
<li>Grants and Awards</li>
<li>Honors</li>
<li>Major Publications</li>
<li>Keynote Speeches</li>
<li>Consultancies</li>
<li>Professional Experience</li>
<li>What I'm Doing Now</li>
<li>How to Contact Me</li>
</ul>
<hr>

<a NAME="education"></a>
<h1>Educational Qualifications</h1>

<p>
```

FIGURE 6-11 *To create a name for a bookmark, you use the anchor tag. In this example, an anchor tag named "education" will serve as a bookmark enabling users to jump to the education section of your résumé. Thus, a named anchor is a bookmark to which you can create links that, when clicked, take users to that spot on the page. In the next section of this tutorial, you create the link that the users will click.* ∎

1. In the Notepad, click to position your cursor immediately before the word Educational in the unordered list that serves as your table of contents. Make sure the cursor is after the `<li>` tag and before the word Educational.

2. You create a hypertext link with an anchor tag. To begin such a tag, type the following code:

```
<a href="#education">
```

3. In this tag, `href` is an attribute that stands for **hypertext reference**. The word in quotes is the value of this attribute, which is set to `#education` to make the link point to the bookmark named education. The pound sign character # tells the browser that the target of the link is a named anchor bookmark on the same page.

4. Remember that every anchor tag must have a `</a>` stop tag. Therefore, click to position your cursor after the phrase Educational Qualifications and type the `</a>` tag. Figure 6-12 shows the completed Notepad file.

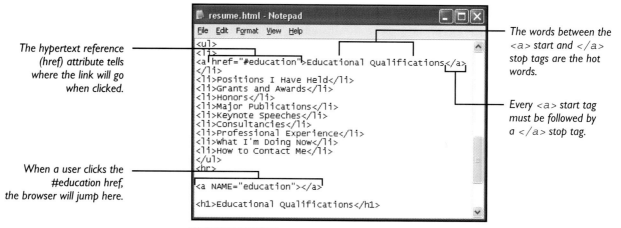

The hypertext reference (href) attribute tells where the link will go when clicked.

The words between the <a> start and </a> stop tags are the hot words.

Every <a> start tag must be followed by a </a> stop tag.

When a user clicks the #education href, the browser will jump here.

FIGURE 6-12   You create a hypertext link via the hypertext reference (href) attribute of an anchor tag. In this example, the href is #education, which links the text to the education bookmark further down on the page. After the hot words you are linking, remember that you must type the </a> close tag so the browser will know where the anchor ends. ∎

note *If your browser window is large enough to display the entire page, you may not see the browser jump when you click the link. Resize the window to make it small, and then you will see the browser jump when you click the link.*

5. Save the file and preview it with your Web browser. The words *Educational Qualifications* should appear in color in your résumé's bulleted table of contents. The coloration denotes hypertext; clicking the colored text will trigger the link.

6. Go ahead and click the link to see how it works. If your browser jumps to the Educational Qualifications section of your résumé, congratulate yourself! If not, repeat these steps, compare your HTML to the samples shown here, and keep trying until you get the bookmark link to work.

Returning to the Table of Contents

Web pages that use named anchor bookmarks should provide a way to return to the table of contents so the user can make another selection. Creating such a return-to-contents link is a two-step process. First, you create a named anchor bookmark at the start of the bulleted list to which you want users to return; then you create a return link to that bookmark at the end of each section in your document.

To create a return-to-contents link in the Education section of your résumé, follow these steps:

1. Click to position your cursor at the spot in the Notepad window where your table of contents begins. In this example, position your cursor in front of the `<ul>` tag that signals the beginning of your bulleted list.

2. Create a named anchor bookmark called *contents*—try to do this on your own, but if you need help, type the following command:

   `<a name="contents"></a>`

3. Position your cursor at the end of the Educational Qualifications section of your résumé. Insert a new paragraph that contains the

text *Table of Contents*, and link that text to the *contents* bookmark. Try to do this on your own, but if you need help, here is the code to type:

```
<a href="#contents">Return to Contents</a>
```

4. Save the file and preview it with your Web browser. Click your browser's Refresh button to make sure you are viewing the latest version of the page. Scroll down to the bottom of your educational qualifications, and click the link to return to contents. If your browser jumps back up to your résumé's table of contents, congratulate yourself! If not, keep trying until you get the bookmark link to work.

note *If you really get stuck, remember that you can go to my résumé at www.udel.edu/fth/ resume.html, pull down the View menu, and choose Source to see how I coded my return-to-contents link.*

Linking to URLs

There are more than a billion documents on the World Wide Web. You can link your résumé to any document for which you know the URL. For example, if the place where you work or go to school has a home page, you might want to provide a way for users to navigate there. Follow these steps:

1. In your Notepad window, position your cursor at the spot where you want the link to appear, and type the text that will trigger the link. For example, type the text:

```
University of Delaware
```

2. Surround the text you just typed by the anchor start and stop tags; the example now reads:

```
<a>University of Delaware</a>
```

3. Add to the start tag an `href` attribute that tells the browser where to go when users click the link. The completed example is:

```
<a href="http://www.udel.edu">University of Delaware</a>
```

4. Save the file and preview it with your Web browser. Click your browser's Refresh button to make sure you are viewing the latest version of the page. Click the link you created in the previous step. If it works, congratulate yourself. If the link does not work, troubleshoot the problem until you get it working. Make sure you are spelling your href correctly, and compare your code to the University of Delaware example in the previous step.

Identifying the Web Page Owner

Netiquette calls for Web pages to end with a few lines of text indicating who owns the page and how to contact the owner. To identify yourself as the owner of your Web page, follow these steps:

1. Click to position the cursor in your Notepad window at the bottom of the document.

2. Type the paragraph `<p>` start and `</p>` stop tags to create a new paragraph.

3. Between the paragraph start and stop tags, type the following words, replacing Santa's information with your own:

```
<p>
This Web page is owned by Santa Claus. My e-mail address is santa@northpole.com.
</p>
```

Mailto Links

warning *Beware that spammers can harvest e-mail addresses from Web pages that contain mailto links. You need to consider this risk in deciding whether to put a mailto link on your page.*

A **mailto** is a link that, when clicked, opens a new message window addressed to the person identified in the link. It is customary for Web page owners to include a mailto link to their e-mail address to make it easy for users to contact them. Consider the Web page owner statement, for example, that you put at the bottom of your home page. Your e-mail address appears there. To provide a mailto link to your e-mail address, you would modify the last sentence to read as follows:

```
My e-mail address is <a href="mailto:santa@northpole.com">santa@northpole.com</a>.
```

Creating White Space on Web Pages

By now you have probably noticed that white space does not work the same way in the browser as it does in the Notepad. If you press ENTER a few times to create some white space in your Notepad, for example, and then save the file and view it with your browser, you will notice that the browser ignores those line feeds. Similarly, if you type several spaces in a row to create a blank space in the Notepad, and then save the file and view it with your browser, you will observe that the browser prints only one of the spaces and ignores the others.

The browser ignores line feeds and multiple spaces because of the structural rules of HTML. When you want to create white space onscreen, you need to use the appropriate HTML code to do so. You have already mastered the most commonly used white space codes, which are the paragraph `<p>` start and `</p>` stop tags. Another handy white-space code is the **`<br>`** break tag, which makes the browser go down to the next line of the screen. There is also a code for a single white space character called a **nonbreaking space**. The code for this character is ** ** (including the semicolon, which signals the end of the special code). When the browser encounters the code   it prints a single white space onscreen. You could therefore type **   ** into the Notepad file to make the browser display five consecutive white spaces onscreen.

Character Attributes on Web Pages vs. Word Processors

Because word processors are habit-forming, no chapter on Web page creation would be complete without mentioning some caveats regarding things you commonly do with a word processor but should not do when you are editing a Web page.

Underlining

In a word-processed document, it is common to underline things for emphasis. On the Web, underlining normally means that the underlined text is linked as hypertext. If you want to emphasize something on the Web, therefore, use bolding or italics instead of underlining. To bold something you are editing with your Notepad, surround it by the **<strong>** start and **</strong>** stop tags. To italicize something, enclose it within the emphasis **<em>** start and **</em>** stop tags. You can further stylize the text with style sheets, which you study in Chapter 8.

Avoiding the Pagination Temptation

In a word processor, you can press ENTER repeatedly to add white space to arrange the text to fit the size of the printed page. A common mistake beginners make is to try to do the same thing on a Web page. It does not work, because there is no guarantee that the viewer's screen size or window size will fit the one for which you developed your page.

Resist the temptation to press the ENTER key repeatedly to add white space in an attempt to create pagination on a Web page. If you want a new page, create a new Web page and link to it from a hypertext link or a navigational icon. You learn how to link pages later, in the hypermedia design section of this chapter. If you want to control spacing on the screen, the best way to do that is with a table. You learn how to make tables in the layout section of this chapter.

HTML Graphics and Animated GIFs

It has often been said that a picture is worth a thousand words. The ease with which you can insert pictures into Web pages means you can illustrate documents and use images as design elements in the layout of a Web page. Before you can insert a picture into a Web page, however, you must get the picture into the proper format for display on a Web page. This chapter provides you with a utility that makes it easy to get images into the proper format. Then it shows you not only how to insert pictures into Web pages but also how to create special effects with techniques known as *tiling* and *watermarking*.

Obtaining Images to Use on a Web Page

Assume you have an image you want to insert into your Web page. Because you have created a Web page résumé, it would be natural to include your picture in the upper-left corner of the résumé so prospective employers can see what you look like. Many photo shops, such as Kodak, and mass-market retail stores, such as Eckerd Drugs, give you the option of having a floppy disk or a CD returned along with your prints when you have a roll of film developed. Eckerd Drugs, for example, charges $6 extra to get a Kodak Picture CD containing a JPEG digital image of each picture on the film. In partnership with Kodak, Eckerd also provides an online service called

n o t e *Previous versions of HTML used <b> and </b> tags to bold text, and <i> and </i> tags to italicize. The latest version of HTML deprecated these tags, replacing them by <strong> </strong> for bolding, and <em> </em> for italics. In strict XHTML, you create these kinds of effects with style sheets, which you study in Chapter 8.*

Kodak PhotoNet Online. When your film is developed, you can view your photos on the Web and order high-resolution copies of the images you want. For professional-quality imaging, you can order a Kodak Photo CD when you send in your film to be developed. The Photo CD contains five or six versions of each picture, sampled at resolutions ranging from a wallet-sized thumbnail to a poster version much larger than the size of your computer screen. For more information, follow this book's Web site links to Eckerd Drugs and Kodak Photo CD.

If you own a digital camera, you do not need to have your pictures developed: Digital cameras take pictures as bitmaps, which can be downloaded from the camera to your PC. Epson, Canon, Kodak, and Olympus are just a few of the companies that make digital cameras. To find out what digital cameras are available and how their features compare, follow this book's Web site links to Digital Cameras.

Scanners have dropped in price so much that they have become mass-market consumer items. Sometimes you get a scanner for free when you purchase a new multimedia PC. Scanners come with software that can digitize printed photographs you can put on Web pages.

On the other hand, if you prefer not to include your picture on your résumé, you may want to enhance the résumé's appearance by including some other graphics. There is a Web page full of general-purpose graphics at this book's Web site. You can download any image on this page by right-clicking the image to pop out the quick menu; then choose Save As to save the image file on your hard drive. To inspect these images, follow the links to general-purpose graphics at this book's Web site.

Preparing Images for a Web Page

Before you can insert an image into a Web page, you need to ask yourself the following questions:

- Is the image in the correct format for inserting onto a Web page? Images must be in either the GIF or JPEG file format. If the image is not in the correct format, you must convert it into the proper file format:

  - Use the GIF format if the image has 256 colors or fewer, or if you can live with reducing the color depth of a more fully colored image to 256 colors.

  - Use the JPEG file format if your image has more than 256 colors and you need true color.

  - Use the GIF format if you need one of the colors in the image to be transparent. On Web pages, for example, you will sometimes want the background of the image to be transparent so it can overlay or float on the page.

- Is the image the proper size for your Web page layout? Images that are too large need to be reduced in size with a graphics editor. Many people think they can skip this step and just resize the image with their Web editing software. This does not change the size of the file, however, and the quality will not be as good as when you resize an image with a graphics editor. That is because the browser is told to show the still-large file at a smaller size, but the browser is not as good at resizing images as the graphics editor. If you need to resize an image, therefore, you should do it with a graphics editor. As an added bonus, the smaller file size will save on bandwidth and make the page appear sooner.

■ What is the color format of the image? If the image is in 24-bit format (16 million colors), you may want to reduce it to an 8-bit color format (256 colors), which will greatly reduce its file size. Remember that the larger the file size of the image, the longer it will take to download from the Internet.

Happily, there are graphics programs that enable you to do all of these things. In the next section of this chapter, you learn how to use Paint Shop Pro for Windows to prepare images to put on your Web pages.

Configuring Paint Shop Pro

Paint Shop Pro is a Windows program for image capture, creation, viewing, and manipulation. Features include painting, photo retouching, image enhancement and editing, color enhancement, graphics format conversion, and color scanner support. More than 30 image file formats are supported, including GIF, JPEG, TIFF, Kodak Photo CD, BMP, and PNG. You can even browse images on your computer; Figure 6-13 shows how the images appear as thumbnails, which you can double-click to view full-screen.

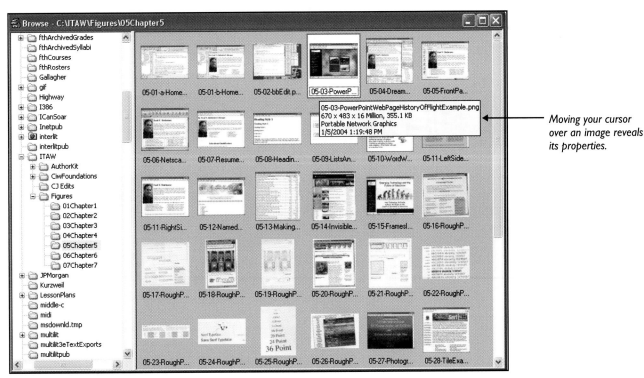

Moving your cursor over an image reveals its properties.

FIGURE 6-13 *Paint Shop Pro contains an image browser and many powerful graphics tools. Shown here is the browser, which comes in handy when you are looking for an image. You can double-click an image to bring it up in the Paint Shop Pro editor, or right-click it for a variety of image management functions.* ■

You can try an evaluation version of Paint Shop Pro before you buy. You can download it from the Web by following this book's Web site links to Paint Shop Pro. If you want to use the software after 60 days, you must pay the license fee, or the evaluation copy will expire.

The first time you run Paint Shop Pro, you must set up the hot key you will use to capture graphics. Follow these steps:

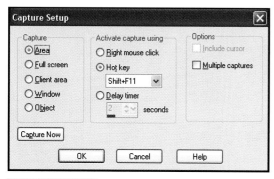

FIGURE 6-14 *The Paint Shop Pro Capture Setup dialog. This book recommends setting up the capture key to be* SHIFT-F11 *because it is my experience that* SHIFT-F11 *is most compatible with the mainstream of Windows programs. Other key combinations can conflict with hot keys predefined in these programs.* ■

1. Double-click the Paint Shop Pro icon to get Paint Shop Pro running.

2. Pull down the File menu and choose Import | Screen Capture | Setup. The Capture Setup dialog appears as shown in Figure 6-14.

3. Notice that the Capture group lets you set up to capture an area, the full screen, the client area of the current window, the entire current window, or an object. Set it to capture an area.

4. In the Activate Capture group, click the option to activate via Hot Key, and set the hot key to something you never use in any other application; I recommend you set the hot key to SHIFT-F11, which is the hot key this tutorial uses.

5. Click OK to close the dialog.

Capturing Images

A basic skill important to all Web page developers is the ability to capture an image, or part of an image, and save it on the hard drive. You have already learned that if the graphic is on a Web page, and if you are capturing the entire graphic, you can right-click the graphic and choose Save As to download it onto your hard drive. Sometimes, however, the right-click does not work. You may want to capture only part of the image, for example, or the image might be in an application that does not support the right-click method of copying. When the right-click method does not work or will not do what you want, follow these steps to capture the image:

1. Get the program running from which you want to capture a graphic. For example, suppose you want to capture my smiling face. Get your Web browser running, and go to http://www.udel.edu/fth where my photo appears on my Web page.

2. Get Paint Shop Pro running, if it is not running already.

3. Hold down the ALT key and keep pressing TAB until Paint Shop Pro appears. ALT-TAB is a special Windows key for switching among programs running simultaneously on your computer.

4. Click the Paint Shop Pro Start Capture button, or press SHIFT-C, or pull down Paint Shop Pro's File menu and select Import | Screen Capture | Start. Immediately, Paint Shop Pro disappears.

5. If the image you want to capture is not visible on your screen, hold down ALT and keep pressing TAB until the screen you want to capture appears.

6. Press the capture hot key (SHIFT-F11); the cursor turns into a crosshair.

7. Click the upper-left corner of the area of the screen you want to capture, and then click the lower-right corner to complete the capture. In this example, you first want to click the upper-left corner of my smiling face and then click the lower-right corner.

8. The captured image should now appear in the Paint Shop Pro window. To save the image, pull down the File menu and choose Save As.

9. In the Save As Type box, select the image format in which you want to save the image. In this example, select CompuServe Graphics Interchange (GIF).

10. In the File Name field, type the name you want the image to have. In this example, type **fred**. You do not need to type a filename extension, because Paint Shop Pro will supply one automatically, based on the file type you set in the Save As Type box.

11. Click the Save button to save the file; then pull down the File menu and choose Exit to leave Paint Shop Pro.

n o t e *To capture the full screen or the contents of a window, pull down the File menu, choose Import | Screen Capture | Setup, and set the Capture option accordingly.*

Converting Images

Converting images into the proper format for inserting onto Web pages is easy. As noted earlier, the best formats to use are GIF if the image has 256 colors or fewer or JPG if your image has up to 16 million colors. To convert an image from one file format into another, follow these steps:

1. Pull down the Paint Shop Pro File menu and choose Open; the Open dialog appears.

2. In the List Files of Type field, pull down the choices and select the file format of your original image.

3. Browse to the image and click OK to open it; the image appears onscreen.

4. To convert the image, pull down the File menu and choose Save As; the Save As dialog appears, as shown in Figure 6-15.

5. In the Save As Type field, pull down the choices and select either GIF or JPG.

6. Save the file in the folder of your choice (probably your *website* folder).

7. Make sure the name you give the image has the same filename extension as the file format you selected (GIF or JPG).

Set the file format here.

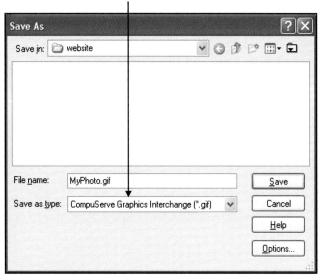

FIGURE 6-15 *The Paint Shop Pro Save As dialog. When you save the image, make sure the name you give it has the same filename extension as the file format you selected (GIF or JPG).* ■

When you save the file, it is important to save it in the same folder as the Web page for which it is intended. In this case, if you are making an image for your Web page résumé, save the converted image in your *website* folder. This will simplify the publication process when you transfer your files to the Web in Chapter 7.

Resizing Images

Images may be the wrong size for placement on your Web page. For example, the photo that appears on my Web page résumé was a 640 × 480 image. This would have covered way too much screen space, spoiling the layout of the résumé. Although you can make the image appear smaller by dragging its handles in a WYSIWYG Web page editor, this does not reduce the file size of the image and therefore consumes more bandwidth than a truly resized image. To truly resize an image, follow these steps:

Check this box if you want the resized image to have the same proportions as the original.

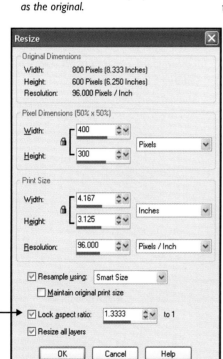

1. Pull down the Paint Shop Pro File menu and choose Open; the Open dialog appears.

2. In the List Files of Type field, pull down the choices and select the file format of your original image.

3. Browse to the image and click OK to open it. The image appears onscreen.

4. To resize the image, pull down the Image menu and choose Resize; the Resize dialog appears, as shown in Figure 6-16.

5. Use the controls to make the height and width settings larger or smaller, depending on whether you want the image to be larger or smaller. Check the Maintain Aspect Ratio box if you want the resized image to have the same proportions as the original.

6. Click OK; the resized image appears.

7. Pull down the File menu, and either choose Save to save this file under the same name as the original (this will replace the original file) or choose Save As to save it under another name.

FIGURE 6-16 *The Resize dialog in Paint Shop Pro. When you resize an image, you will normally want to maintain the same aspect ratio as the original to keep from distorting the image as you resize it.* ■

Make sure you save the resized file in the GIF or JPEG file format in the same folder as the Web page on which it will appear. If you are resizing an image for your Web page résumé, save the image in your *website* folder.

Color Adjustments

Unless you have a special reason for keeping your images encoded in 16 million colors (24-bit format), you should convert the images to 256 colors (8-bit format), which will make them appear three times faster on your Web page due to the smaller file size. To convert a 24-bit image into an 8-bit image, follow these steps:

1. Pull down the Paint Shop Pro File menu, choose Open, and open the image, which appears onscreen.

2. Pull down the Colors menu, choose Decrease Color Depth, and see if the 256-colors option is active. If it is not active, your image does not need to be reduced in color depth, so close the image and skip the rest of these instructions.

3. If the 256-colors option is active, select it; the Decrease Color Depth dialog appears, as shown in Figure 6-17.

4. If you choose one of the Optimized palette settings, click the option to Include Windows' Colors. If you are planning to publish this image to the Web, choose Standard/Web-safe.

5. Whether to choose Nearest Color or Error Diffusion is up to you. Click OK to close the dialog.

6. Pull down the File menu, and either choose Save to save this file under the same name as the original (this will replace the original file) or choose Save As to save it under another name.

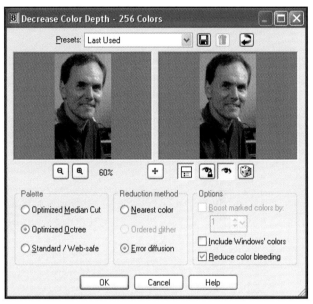

Make sure you save the color-converted file in the GIF or JPEG file format in the same folder as the Web page on which it will appear. If you are converting an image for your Web page résumé, save the image in your *website* folder.

FIGURE 6-17 *The Decrease Color Depth dialog in Paint Shop Pro. Decreasing the color depth can reduce the size of the file by a factor of two or three, thereby decreasing download times and improving bandwidth.* ■

Inserting an Image into Your Web Page Résumé

You will be happy to discover that inserting an image into a Web page is a lot easier than preparing the picture to fit the Web page's layout. To insert an image into a Web page, follow these steps:

1. Open the page with the Notepad, and click to position your cursor at the spot where you want the image to appear. In this example, position your cursor after the `</h1>` tag that concludes the heading of your résumé.

2. Type the following image tag, replacing the name of the image, *fred.gif*, with the name of your own image:

   ```
   <img src="fred.gif">
   ```

3. Save the file and preview it with your Web browser. Click your browser's Refresh button to make sure you are viewing the latest version of the page.

4. To make the text wrap around the image, you can use the *align* attribute. To position the image on the left side of the text, use the

align="left" setting; to position the image on the right side of the text, use the align="right" setting, as in:

```
<img src="fred.gif" align="right">
```

If you have trouble getting the image to position itself exactly where you want it on your Web page, do not worry. In the next part of this chapter, you learn how to use tables to control more precisely the layout and positioning of text and graphics on your Web pages.

Tiling an Image into the Background of a Web Page

As a final touch, you can consider adding some pizzazz to your résumé by setting a background image that the browser uses as a tile in creating the background. To **tile** an image means to draw it repeatedly across and down the screen until the entire window has been covered. If the image is designed in such a way as to hide the edges when tiled, you get a seamless appearance in the background.

If you plan to display printed text on the tiled background, be sure to choose a tile that will not interfere with the readability of your text. This book's Web site has a page that contains a few images designed for tiling on Web pages. These tiles have slight coloration and faint textures upon which you can place text that will be readable. The tiles at the Web site appear as follows:

| brick.gif | linoleum.gif | wooden.gif | woven.gif |

To download one of these tiles to your computer, right-click its image (Macintosh users use CONTROL-click), and choose Save As to download the tile. Make sure you save the tile in your *website* folder. Then follow these steps to make one of the tiles fill the background of your résumé:

1. Use your Notepad editor to open the page on which you want to tile the background, and locate the <body> tag that begins the body of the document.

2. Modify the <body> tag as follows, but replace *filename* by the name of the tile you want to use:

```
<body background="filename.gif">
```

3. Save the file and preview it with your Web browser. Click your browser's Refresh button to make sure you are viewing the latest version of the page.

note *If you did this correctly, you now see the tiled background behind the text of your Web page. As you can see, the* background *attribute of the body tag causes the image to tile across and down the screen. If you do not see the tiled background, however, repeat these steps more carefully until you get it working.*

Creating Transparent Images

Transparency is a special effect in which one of the colors in a bitmap becomes translucent. Instead of seeing that color, you see through it into the background color or image on the screen. Consider the example in

Figure 6-18, which shows two images overlaid on a background. In the first image, there is no transparency, and the image looks rectangular. In the second image, the red pixels are transparent, so you can see through them into the background.

To create a transparent GIF image, follow these steps:

▫ Use Paint Shop Pro to open the image.

▫ Use the eyedropper tool 🖉 to set the background color.

▫ Pull down the Colors menu and choose Set Palette Transparency. Paint Shop may prompt you to reduce the color depth if the image has more than 256 colors; click Yes to do so.

▫ When the Set Palette Transparency dialog appears, choose the option to set the transparency value to the current background color.

▫ Pull down the File menu and choose Save As to make the Save As dialog appear. In the Save As Type field, pull down the choices and select GIF. Save the file in the folder of your choice (probably your *website* folder).

▫ To insert the image into your Web page, insert into your Notepad file an image tag in the form of `<img src= "filename.gif">`. When you save the file and open it with your browser, you will notice that the transparent color in the GIF image becomes invisible.

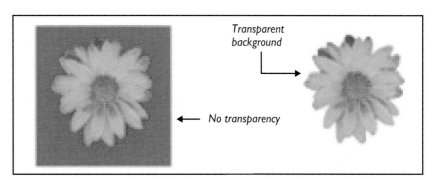

FIGURE 6-18 *Two images overlaid on a background: one with transparency (right), the other without (left). When the solid red color is defined as the transparent color, you see through it into the background onscreen.* ▪

Creating Animated Images

A special feature of the GIF graphics format is its capability to contain animated images. An **animated GIF** is a graphic that contains multiple images intended to be shown in a sequence at specific times and locations on the screen. A looping option causes your Web browser to keep showing the frames in the GIF file continually, and, as a result, you see an animation onscreen.

GIF Construction Set

There is a shareware application that Windows users can utilize to create animated GIFs. The name of the package is *GIF Construction Set*. To download it and take a tutorial on creating animated GIFs, follow this book's Web site link to the GIF Construction Set.

Animation Shop

You can also create animated GIFs with Animation Shop, which is part of the Paint Shop Pro software. To run Animation Shop, pull down the Paint Shop Pro File menu and choose Jasc Software Products | Launch Animation Shop.

Clip Art for Web Pages

Clip art is pre-drawn artwork organized into a catalog or library that you can browse in search of appropriate icons, buttons, banners, backgrounds, tiles, or animated GIFs for use on Web pages. Microsoft keeps an extensive clip art gallery, for example, that you can search by genre, topic, and keyword. Follow this book's Web site links to the Microsoft Clip Gallery and several other clip art libraries. Most of these libraries let you freely download and use the graphics on your personal Web pages. Make sure you check the clip art site's license or copyright policy, however, especially if you are planning to use the clip art in a product you will be offering for sale. Clip art vendors often require you to pay a special fee for a license that lets you use their clip art in a commercial product.

To download an item of clip art for use on a Web page, you can often simply right-click (Macintosh users use CONTROL-click) the object, and when the quick menu pops out, choose the option to save the graphic on your hard drive. Some clip art sites have special download buttons alongside the images, in which case you click the download button and follow the onscreen instructions. After you download the clip art, you can insert the graphic on your Web page by inserting into its Notepad file an image tag in the form of `<img src="filename.gif">` or `<img src="filename.jpg">`, depending on the filename extension.

HTML Tables and Web Page Layout

Compare the design of the Web pages illustrated in Figures 6-19 and 6-20. How are they alike? Both contain pictures, and both contain text. How do they differ? Figure 6-19 treats the screen as one large column of information, whereas Figure 6-20 divides the screen into rectangular regions that position the text and graphics in different sections of the Web page. Although both screens convey the same information, you probably will agree that the sectional layout of Figure 6-20 creates a more interesting Web page. This chapter shows how to use tables to arrange information into rows and columns on the screen. Then you will use tables to create a unique design for your home page on the Web.

note   *Tables became part of the HTML standard when version 3.2 was released in 1996. Web pages produced before then were limited to a single column of information.*

What Is a Table?

A **table** is a design element that divides the screen into a grid consisting of rectangular regions called *cells*. Into each cell you can enter text or graphics that align with the boundaries of the cell's rectangle. The grid that

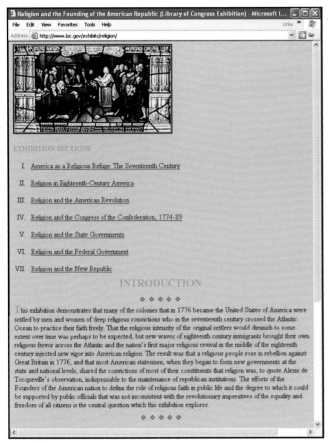

FIGURE 6-19 *How a Web page appears without the use of tables to create rectangular layout regions on the screen.* ■

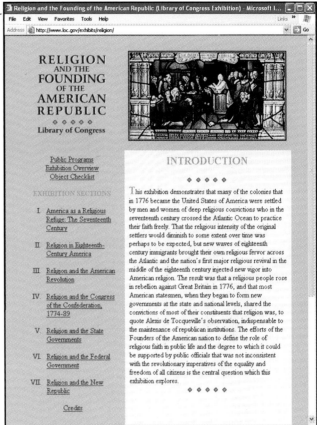

FIGURE 6-20 *Tables create rectangular regions used as design elements in advanced Web-page layout.* ■

forms the boundaries of the cells can be either visible or invisible. You normally make the grid visible when presenting a table full of technical information that would be hard to read without horizontal and vertical lines to help users follow the data across the table. HTML provides control over border thickness, and you can use thin or thick grid lines, depending on the situation.

Why Use Tables on Web Pages?

There are two reasons for using tables on Web pages. The first reason is rather obvious—to present data neatly in rows and columns that help users perceive the order or the relationships in the information. This book uses tables extensively to present complex information in an understandable manner. For example, consider the presentation of HTML tags that appeared earlier in this chapter in Table 6-1. Displaying the tags in column 1 followed by their description in column 2 provides an orderly presentation that enables readers to find a tag in column 1 and then read across to its definition in column 2. The grid is visible to help you read across the table to find the definitions of the different tags.

FIGURE 6-21 *An advanced Web page design employing multiple tables with varying cell heights and widths.* ∎

FIGURE 6-22 *Layout analysis of the tables used to create the Web page in Figure 6-21. Notice how tables are nested inside of other tables.* ∎

The second reason for using tables on a Web page is to create advanced layouts consisting of rectangular sections into which you can flow blocks of text or insert graphics. Tables consist of one or more rows of one or more cells. You can adjust the width and height of the cells to create a wide variety of Web page layouts. You can even have more than one table on the page at once, enabling you to create many interesting designs. For example, consider the layout of the Web page shown in Figure 6-21. The layout analysis in Figure 6-22 shows that this page consists of several tables with varying numbers of rows and columns and different cell heights and widths. Notice how the use of multiple tables adds interest to the design of this page. You can also vary the background colors or images in the table cells to create visible regions on the screen.

Creating a Table

You use three basic HTML tags to create tables. First, the `<table>` start and `</table>` stop tags begin and end the table. Inside the table, you use the `<tr>` start and `</tr>` stop tags to begin and end each row of the table. The code `<tr>` stands for *table row*. Inside each table row, you use the `<td>` start and `</td>` stop tags to begin and end each data cell. The code `<td>` stands for *table data*. Inside the table data cells, you put the textual and/or graphical content you want in that cell of the table. Because you can use a table to create any conceivable layout of cells onscreen, tables enable you to take control of the page and position your content exactly where you want it. On your

Web page résumé, for example, imagine you want your opening paragraph and your bulleted table of contents to appear alongside your photo. You can accomplish this by inserting a table after the heading that identifies your name at the top of your résumé. This table should have one row that contains two data cells. In the first data cell, you put your picture. In the second data cell, you put the paragraph and the bulleted table of contents you want alongside the picture. At runtime, because the picture appears in the table row's first cell, the picture appears on the left of the text you put in the second cell. If this sounds complicated, do not worry, because this is quite easily accomplished. To create this table in your résumé, follow these steps:

1. Use the Notepad to open your Web page résumé, and position your cursor after the `</h1>` tag that ends the heading that identifies your name at the top of the page.

2. Type the following HTML code, which creates the table, its first row, and its first data cell. For now, this code sets the table width to 100%, causing the table to stretch all the way across the page. Later in this tutorial, you learn how to change the `width` attribute to create other layout possibilities onscreen.

```
<table width="100%">
<tr align="left" valign="top">
<td>
```

3. Position your cursor at the spot where you want the first data cell to stop. In this example, click to position your cursor after the `<img>` tag that puts your picture onscreen. Then type the following code, which ends the first data cell and begins the second one:

```
</td>
<td>
```

4. Position your cursor at the spot where you want the table to stop. In this example, click to position your cursor after the `</li>` tag that ends your résumé's table of contents. Then type the following code, which ends the data cell, the table row, and the table:

```
</td>
</tr>
</table>
```

5. Save the file, and then open it with your browser to view how it will appear on the Web. Your picture should appear on the left, with your résumé's opening paragraph and table of contents alongside your image.

6. If you would like to see the table's edges onscreen, you can give the table a border. To do so, use the Notepad to modify the `<table>` tag as follows:

```
<table width="100%" border="1">
```

7. Save the file, and then view it with your browser to see the table's edges. Remember to click the browser's Refresh button to make sure you are viewing the current version of the file.

8. After you finish looking at the border, you will probably want to go back into the Notepad and remove the `border="1"` attribute, or set its value to zero to remove the table's border. Normally you turn on a table's borders only when you need the lines to show to help viewers follow straight across a row of data onscreen. When a table is used for layout purposes, on the other hand, you keep the borders turned off.

Adjusting the Attributes of a Table

The table you put in your Web page résumé has one row containing two cells. This is just one of the design patterns you can create with tables, which enable you to create any conceivable page layout onscreen. Consider the following table structure, which has three rows:

```
<table>
    <tr>
        <td> row one, cell one </td>
        <td> row one, cell two </td>
    </tr>
    <tr>
        <td> row two, cell one </td>
        <td> row two, cell two </td>
    </tr>
    <tr>
        <td> row three, cell one </td>
        <td> row three, cell two </td>
    </tr>
</table>
```

Tables with more cells in a row than this example have more `<td></td>` tags. Tables with more rows have more `<tr></tr>` tags. There is no limit to the number of design patterns you can create. In addition to creating different design patterns, you can use `formatting` and `alignment` attributes to change the appearance of the table's rows and cells onscreen.

Formatting Attributes

Attributes added to the table tag modify the table's formatting. You have already experienced how the *border* attribute causes the table to have a border; for example, if a table has a border thickness of 2, the tag is `<table border="2">`.

Alignment Attributes

The `align` attribute can modify the `<table>`, `<tr>`, and `<td>` tags to control horizontal alignment. Values of the `align` attribute can be *left, center*, *right*, or *justify*, which means to double-justify the text. For example, a table cell in which the data is right-justified has the tag `<td align="right">`. The default value is left.

The `valign` attribute controls vertical alignment. Its values can be *top*, *middle*, or *bottom*. For example, a table cell in which the data aligns with the bottom of the cell has the tag `<td valign="bottom">`. The default value is middle.

To control both horizontal and vertical alignment, you can specify both `align` and `valign` attributes. For example, a table cell in which the data is right-justified at the bottom of the cell has the tag `<td align="right" valign="bottom">`.

Cell Spacing and Padding

By default, the table cells fit fairly close against the data they contain. If you are displaying textual data, you will usually want to create a little more cell spacing or padding. **Cell spacing** is the amount of space the browser puts between the borders of the cells. **Cell padding** is the amount of white space the browser puts inside the borders of the cells. You set cell spacing and padding via the following attributes, which can be either integer values or percentages of the table's width:

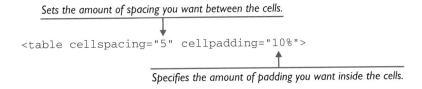

Sets the amount of spacing you want between the cells.

`<table cellspacing="5" cellpadding="10%">`

Specifies the amount of padding you want inside the cells.

Coloring Tables and Cells

Sometimes you may want a table, a row, or a cell to have a background color. You can create colored table backgrounds with the `bgcolor` attribute. For example, if you want the background to be silver, you can make the table tag say `<table bgcolor="silver">`. This is just one of 16 defined color names, which are listed in Table 6-2. You can also specify colors by hex codes, with which you can mix 16 million different hues. The format is #RRGGBB where RR is the red value, GG is the green value, and BB is the blue value. For example, `<table bgcolor="#000080">` creates a navy blue background because it has such a lot of blue (80) but no red or green in it. The highest color value is white, which is #FFFFFF. Note that in the hexadecimal notation used for these color values, there are 16 numbers that range from 0 through 9 followed by the letters A (which is 10) through F (which is 15). These letters are not case-sensitive in HTML. Hex values for the commonly used hues are linked to this book's Web site. You can also find out the hex value of any color by using Paint Shop Pro. Simply double-click the foreground or background color swatch to open the color picker dialog. Then click to select any color on the color wheel, and the hex value will be shown in the HTML field in the lower-right corner of the color picker.

Color	Name	RGB	Color	Name	RGB
	Black	#000000		Green	#008000
	Silver	#C0C0C0		Lime	#00FF00
	Gray	#808080		Olive	#808000
	White	#FFFFFF		Yellow	#FFFF00
	Maroon	#800000		Navy	#000080
	Red	#FF0000		Blue	#0000FF
	Purple	#800080		Teal	#008080
	Fuchsia	#FF00FF		Aqua	#00FFFF

TABLE 6-2 *Color Names of the Sixteen Predefined HTML Colors* ■

To color an individual table cell, you can edit the `<td>` tag that begins that cell. To color a cell, you once again use the `bgcolor` attribute. To make a cell's background color bright red, for example, you would type `<td bgcolor="#FF0000">` to turn on maximum red (FF) followed by no red or green (0000).

Remember that whenever you create a colored background for text, you must choose a color that does not detract from the readability of the text. Pastel colors such as pastel yellow (#FFFFCC) and pastel blue (#CCFFFF) work well behind dark text. The modern trend, however, is to make most of your text black on a white background, for maximum readability. Save the colors for special effects. Remember that a table can contain multiple colors. In cells that contain text, you can make the background "white" while using other colors in the `<table>` tag or in other nontext table cells.

note *In the latest version of HTML, color attributes are deprecated. Instead, developers are encouraged to use style sheets. Chapter 8 shows you how to do this. Billions of Web pages continue to use HTML color attributes, however.*

Make a Table of the World's Highest Mountains

An excellent way to reinforce your knowledge of HTML table commands is to create an actual table onscreen. After you code the table, you can experiment with different values to see how the table data looks centered, left-justified, or aligned to the right of the cells. By trying different vales for the border thickness and cell spacing, you learn how to adjust these attributes to achieve different table effects onscreen. This exercise steps you through the creation of a table that displays the world's six highest mountains. As illustrated in Figure 6-23, this table has four columns. The first column identifies the name of the mountain, the second column tells what country the mountain is in, and the third and fourth columns tell how high the mountain is in feet and meters, respectively. To create the HTML code for this table, follow these steps:

1. Pull down the Notepad's File menu and choose New to begin a new file. Type the following HTML to get the table started:

```
<html>
<head>
 <title>World's Highest Mountains</title>
</head>
<body>
<h1>Six Highest Mountains</h1>
```

```
<table border="1" cellpadding="5" cellspacing="1">
<tr align="center" valign="middle">
 <td><strong>Mountain</strong></td>
 <td><strong>Country</strong></td>
 <td><strong>Feet</strong></td>
 <td><strong>Meters</strong></td>
</tr>
</table>
</body>
</html>
```

2. Pull down the File menu, choose Save As, and save the file as *mountains.html* in your *website* folder. Then open the file with your browser and see if the first row of the table appears onscreen as illustrated in Figure 6-23, except for the color, which you add in step 6. If you do not see the first row of the table, go back to the previous step, proofread your code carefully, and troubleshoot any problems until you get the first row working.

3. Click to position your cursor in the Notepad file after the table row you typed in the previous step but prior to the </table> stop tag. Type the following code to create the second row of the table; then save the file and view it with your browser. Click the browser's Refresh button to make sure you are viewing the current version of the file.

```
<td>
<strong>Meters</strong>
</td>
</tr>

<tr align="center" valign="middle">
 <td>Everest</td>
 <td>Nepal/China</td>
 <td>29028</td>
 <td>8848</td>
</tr>

</table>
</body>
</html>
```

4. There are five more mountains to add to the table. For each of these mountains, repeat the process you followed in the previous step, substituting the specific mountain's data as provided in Figure 6-23. When you complete all the mountains, your table will appear as illustrated in Figure 6-23.

5. Experiment with different cellpadding and cellspacing values to get a feeling for what they do to the table. Set cellpadding="50" for example, and observe what effect that has on the table. Then set cellpadding back to 5, and set cellspacing="50" to compare how it works. Remember that each time you make a change, you must save the Notepad file and then click the browser's Refresh button to view the latest version of the file.

6. Use the bgcolor attribute to put different colors into the background of the table. Remember that you can apply the bgcolor attribute to the <table>, the <tr>, or the <td> tags, depending on

whether you want the color to apply to the entire table, the row, or a single data cell. You can pick color values from Table 6-2, but remember that if you want the text to be readable, lighter colors such as pastel yellow (bgcolor="#FFFFCC") and pastel blue (bgcolor="#CCFFFF") work better than the darker colors. Figure 6-23 shows how I striped the table with alternating rows of white and pastel yellow.

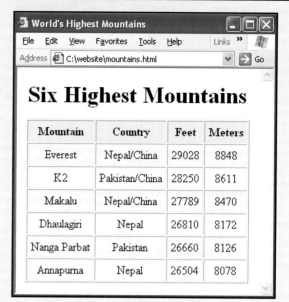

FIGURE 6-23 *The World's Highest Mountains. After you complete the Try This! exercise to get this table onscreen, experiment by making the borders thicker or thinner. Give some of the table rows pastel background colors, and experiment with centering, left-justifying, and right-aligning the table data onscreen. You will discover the power of tables for creating all kinds of layout possibilities onscreen. ■*

Indenting to Document the Structure of a Table

When you use tables to control the layout of a Web page, you should form the habit of indenting your table tags to show the document's structure. The browser ignores these indentations at runtime, so they will not affect your page's appearance. When you later need to edit or update something on your page, however, you can use the indentations to find more quickly the place in the document where you want to make your change. Consider how the indentations in the following example make this code easier to maintain than if you typed everything in a constant stream:

```
<table>
    <tr>
        <td>
This is the content of the first cell of the table. The indentations of the tags
make it easier to find the location of this cell than if the document were typed
in a continuous stream of characters.
        </td>
        <td>
This is the content of the second cell of the table. Because the browser ignores
the tabs and spacing between the tags, you can thus indent your HTML without
affecting the appearance of your page on the Web.
        </td>
    </tr>
    <tr>
        <td>
```

Notice how the indentations make the start of a new row especially easy to find.

```
        </td>
        <td>
```

I highly recommend this method of indenting your HTML table code. It takes hardly any time at all to press the indent key, but it can save you a lot of time later when you need to update your page or delete something.

```
        </td>
    </tr>
</table>
```

Subdividing Table Cells

You can subdivide any table cell by creating a table inside a cell. Putting a table inside a cell provides another layer of structure on the Web page. There is no limit to the number of cells you can subdivide. Because subdividing cells enables you to create any conceivable pattern of rectangular regions on the screen, it provides an unlimited array of possibilities for laying out Web pages. Figures 6-24 to 6-27 show layout analyses of Web pages that use subdivided table cells as design elements. To subdivide such a table cell, you simply create a new table inside it. Here is an example:

```
<table>
    <tr>
        <td>
Outer table, row one, cell one.
        </td>
        <td>
            <table>
                <tr>
                    <td>
Inner table, row one, cell one.
                    </td>
                    <td>
Inner table, row one, cell two.
                    </td>
                </tr>
            </table>
        </td>
    </tr>
</table>
```

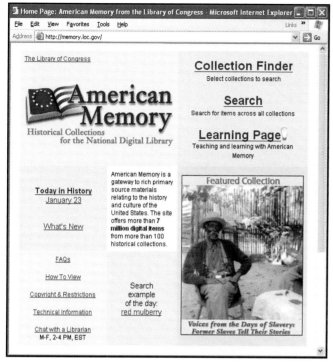

FIGURE 6-24 *This Web page has a table inside a table. This kind of design lets you create a design structure for one cell that functions independent of the cells in the outer table.* ■

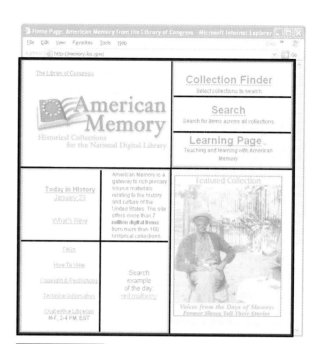

FIGURE 6-25 *Layout analysis of Figure 6-24. Study this analysis to visualize how the tables provide the structure for the page content in Figure 6-24.* ■

FIGURE 6-26 *This Web page is built by using one large outer table, a smaller table nested inside that one, and still smaller subtables inside that. Nesting tables in this manner enables you to create any conceivable page layout of content onscreen.* ■

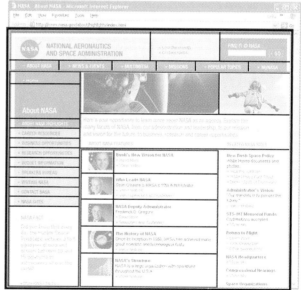

FIGURE 6-27 *Layout analysis of Figure 6-26. Study this analysis to visualize how the tables provide the structure for the page content in Figure 6-26.* ■

Making Cells That Span More Than One Row or Column

By default, each cell in a table is confined to just one row and column. To vary the layout of a table, you can expand a cell to make it span more than one row or column. To do so, you give the cell's `<td>` tag a *rowspan* or *colspan* attribute. For example, a cell that spans two rows and three columns has the tag:

```
<td rowspan="2" colspan="3">
```

HTML Hyperlinks and Web Design

In this chapter, you learned how to create HTML hyperlinks that either link to another Web page or provide users with a way to jump around to different places on a Web page via named anchor bookmarks. Any page on the Web can be the target of such a link. Now that you have this capability to link to other pages, it is appropriate to reflect on how links form Webs and how those Webs can have shapes that follow the five basic hypermedia design paradigms.

How Links Form Webs

Think about how a spider weaves a web. No matter how complicated the web turns out to be, each path gets created by the spider's creating a link from one spot to another. In technical networking jargon, these spots are called nodes. Out on the World Wide Web, your pages work like nodes. You can link any page to any other page, depending on the kind of navigational possibilities you want to provide. Just as the spider's web has a certain shape depending on how the spider connects its nodes, so also does your Web take on a shape, depending on the kinds of patterns you use in your linkages.

Try This!

Linking Your Home Page to Your Résumé Page

The simplest kind of hypermedia shape is formed by linking two pages together. If you have never done this before, you will understand the process better if you create such a link. Earlier in this chapter, you created a Web page called *resume.html*. In this exercise, you add to the résumé page a link to your home page. If you do not already have a home page, this is an excellent time to get one, and these instructions will coach you. To create a link to your home page, follow these steps:

1. Use the Notepad to open the *resume.html* page you created earlier in this chapter. Click to position your cursor at the spot where you would like to provide an option for users to go to your home page. A good place to put such a link is next to the return-to-contents links that you put at the end of each section of your résumé. If you do not have a home page yet, you still can create the link. Home page instructions come later in this exercise.

2. At the spot where you want to put the option to go to your home page, type the following code, which will create such a link. In the `href` attribute, if you already have a home page out on the Web, type the HTTP address of your home page. If you do not have a home page yet, simply type **index.html** as a placeholder for the home page you will create later in this exercise. To create the link to your home page, type this code:

```
<a href="http://www.northpole.com/santa/index.html">Go to my home page</a>.
```

3. Save the Notepad file and open it with your browser to see how your link appears onscreen. If it does not appear quite like you want, use the Notepad to fine-tune its appearance. Then save the file and click your browser's Refresh button to view the modified version of your page.

4. If you have a home page, click the link to go to your home page to see if the link works properly. Congratulate yourself heartily if the link works. If the link does not work, repeat the steps in this exercise more carefully, and keep trying until you get the link to work.

5. If you do not yet have a home page on the Web, you should start one. In this chapter, you have learned all the HTML codes you need to create a very attractive home page. To create a home page, you simply use the Notepad to create a new file. Into this new file, type the minimum HTML that is needed to create a Web page. For a home page, that HTML would read as follows:

```
<html>
<head>
  <title>Santa Claus's Home Page</title>
</head>
<body>
The text and graphics of your home page go here. The design is totally up to you.
Remember that home pages are normally short. The purpose of a home page is to
establish your identity and provide links that visitors can click to learn more
about you. See, for example, my home page at www.udel.edu/fth.
</body>
</html>
```

6. When you save your home page, put it in your *website* folder and give it the filename *index.html*. This is the default filename that comes up at a Web site if you go to the site's HTTP address without specifying a specific filename. You can go to my home page, for example, by going to www.udel.edu/fth, which automatically brings up the default file at www.udel.edu/fth/index.html.

7. If you save your home page as *index.html* in the *website* folder in which your *resume.html* file also resides, the link you type in step 2 of this exercise can simply read as follows:

```
<a href="index.html">Go to my home page</a>.
```

8. If you do not yet know how to publish pages on the World Wide Web, you are probably anxious to do so. Chapter 7 contains a complete Web page publishing tutorial that shows how to publish pages into your Web space. You will also find out how to get free Web space, in case you do not yet have a Web account for publishing your pages.

Hypermedia Design Paradigms

Whenever you link two or more Web pages, you create a hypermedia design that can be visualized. The extent to which you can visualize your webs determines how successful you will be in planning the navigational pathways users can traverse at your Web site. The goal is to provide your users with navigation options that are both appropriate and quick. Users get frustrated if they need to click more than three or four times to find the information they are looking for. If you can visualize your site's design, you can foresee pages that will take too long to click through. Then you can add links that create new pathways to these pages.

My *Multimedia Literacy* textbook, which is also published by McGraw-Hill, identifies five design paradigms you can use to create these kinds of links. This chapter concludes by presenting these five design paradigms. Your challenge is to reflect on these five paradigms and try to imagine if there might be some web design that they cannot describe. If you can think of a way of linking pages that cannot be described by these five paradigms, you may well have invented a new paradigm.

The five design paradigms are the linear list, the menu, the hierarchy, the network, and the hybrid.

Linear List

The simplest design is the **linear list paradigm** illustrated in Figure 6-28. The linear list is a hypermedia design paradigm that enables users to move back and forth through a serial sequence of pages, moving forward to new materials or backward to review. The linear list is most appropriate for situations in which you want to show a sequence of pages in a slideshow format.

FIGURE 6-28 *The linear list lets users move forward to see new pages or backward to review. This paradigm is appropriate for sequences of Web pages that you want users to view in a slideshow manner. If the sequence is long, however, you will also want to provide a link to the menu so users can jump out of the slideshow if they lose interest.* ■

Menu

The second way to design a navigational pathway is to create a menu like the one shown in Figure 6-29. A **menu paradigm** is a hypermedia design pattern that permits users to select one from a number of choices listed onscreen. When the user chooses an item on the menu, the item linked to it appears.

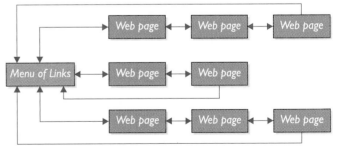

FIGURE 6-29 *The menu design presents users with a set of choices. In this example, the menu lets users begin one of three possible sequences of Web pages. Each sequence ends by going back to the menu, from which users can make another choice.* ■

Hierarchy

The third kind of design is the **hierarchy paradigm** shown in Figure 6-30. A hierarchy is a hypermedia design paradigm in which each object provides users with a menu of choices that trigger more menus with more choices. There is no limit to the size or number of menus and

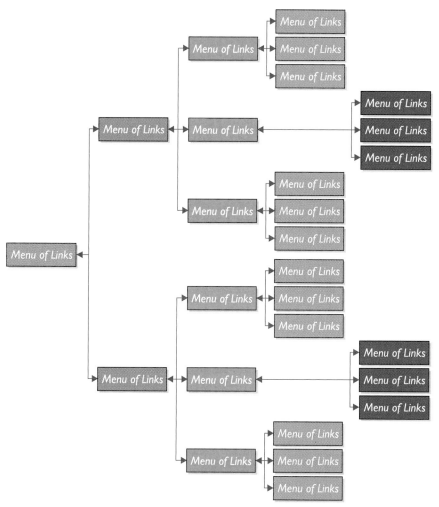

submenus you can have in such a hierarchy. Large Web sites typically use a hierarchy to provide a way for users to drill down to the information they want.

Network

The most complicated design is the network shown in Figure 6-31. The **network paradigm** is a hypermedia design pattern in which objects can be multiply linked in any direction to any object in your web. Especially when a web is large, the network design enables users to navigate to any page with a minimum of mouse clicks. A tight design enables users to get wherever they want within three clicks.

Hybrid

Web sites often use more than one design paradigm, employing lists, menus, hierarchies, and networks where appropriate. For example, a sophisticated network design may trigger a linear list with simple navigation that lets users move back and forth through the pages as in a slideshow. When a user gets to the end of the list, the network design returns to provide richer navigation options. Designs that combine paradigms are called hybrids. Figure 6-32 shows an example of a **hybrid paradigm**, which is a hypermedia design paradigm that provides multiple navigational pathways by employing linear lists, menus, hierarchies, and network designs as appropriate throughout a large Web site.

FIGURE 6-30 *The hierarchy presents users with a menu of menus. If you have a large Web site with dozens or hundreds of pages, the hierarchy enables you to design pathways through which users can drill down to the desired page.* ■

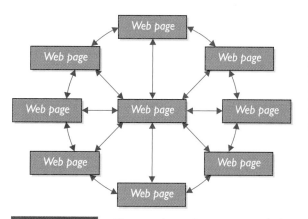

FIGURE 6-31 *The network paradigm contains multiply linked items that provide the richest kind of navigation. Users can find a way to get anywhere they want in this web within three clicks. You should use this design whenever you need to provide alternate pathways through a complex web.* ■

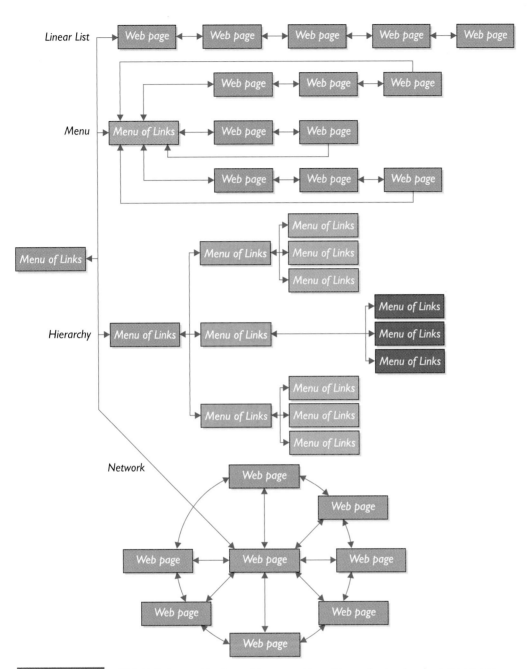

FIGURE 6-32   *Hybrid designs employ linear lists, menus, hierarchies, and networks where appropriate. If you think about the World Wide Web as a whole, its design represents the ultimate in hybrid hypermedia construction.* ■

Chapter 6 Review

▨ Chapter Summary

After reading this chapter and completing the step-by-step tutorials and Try This! exercises, you should understand the following facts about HTML coding:

How HTML Works

■ HTML is the markup language used to create hypertext documents for the World Wide Web. HTML stands for hypertext markup language. The key to understanding how HTML works is to know what it means to mark up a text.

■ To mark up a text means to insert special codes called tags into the text. The tags control how the text appears on a Web page.

■ There are two HTML tag formats: paired tags and single tags. Paired tags come in pairs that consist of a start tag and a stop tag. Single tags function on their own with no stop tag.

■ HTML has progressed through several versions, each of which added new functionality to what you can do on a Web page. However, HTML did not follow strictly the rules of its parent language, which is the standard generalizable markup language (SGML). To tighten up the HTML language and make it compatible with newly emerging XML tools, the W3C created a new language called XHTML.

■ Pages authored in XHTML will render not only on the Web but also on pagers, PDAs, cell phones, tablet PCs, and other devices that are following the new XML-based wireless protocols. XHTML pages can also be mined by XML tools as data that can be used in server-to-server and business-to-business applications.

Creating Your Web Page Résumé

■ An HTML document begins with the `<html>` start tag and ends with the `</html>` stop tag. Between those tags come the `<head>` start and `</head>` stop tags, followed by the `<body>` start and `</body>` stop tags.

■ You create the Web page title via the `<title>` start and `</title>` stop tags, which go between the document's `<head>` and `</head>` tags. The title you type between the `<title>` and `</title>` tags will appear in the browser's title bar when someone visits the page.

■ Heading styles cause the headings on a Web page to appear in progressively larger fonts, depending on the level of the heading. The smallest heading style is H6, and the largest is H1. In addition to making the text larger, heading styles create a structure that can be used to outline the document. You should use heading styles whenever a document has this kind of an outline structure. To create a heading 1 style, for example, you type the heading between the `<h1>` start and `</h1>` stop tags.

■ You create paragraphs on a Web page by typing the text between the paragraph `<p>` start and `</p>` stop tags. Although the browsers will forgive the omission of the `</p>` stop tag, the rules of XHTML, if strictly enforced, require every start tag to have a corresponding stop tag. Thus, you should form the habit of including the `</p>` stop tag at the end of each paragraph.

■ You create lists with the unordered list `<ul>` start and `</ul>` stop tags for a bulleted list or the ordered list `<ol>` start and `</ol>` stop tags for a numbered list. Between these tags, you type the list items, which must begin and end with the list item `<li>` start and `</li>` stop tags. Although the browsers will forgive the omission of the `</li>` stop tag, the rules of XHTML require its presence, so you should include it.

■ Horizontal rules create neat-looking dividing lines between different parts of a Web page. You create a horizontal rule by typing the `<hr>` tag at the spot on the page where you want the rule to appear. The `<hr>` tag is a single tag which, by definition, does not have a corresponding stop tag.

- You create bookmark names with the anchor tag, which has the format `<a name="`*`bookmarkname`*`"></a>`. In typing this command, you replace *bookmarkname* with the actual name you want the bookmark to have.

- You create links to a bookmark via the anchor tag by using the format `<a href="#`*`bookmarkname`*`>Click Me!</a>`. In typing this command, you replace *bookmarkname* with the actual name of the bookmark, and replace Click Me! with the hypertext that will appear onscreen.

- To link one Web page to another, you type an anchor tag by using the format `<a href="http://www.udel.edu">University of Delaware</a>`, and replace the Delaware information with your link's actual HTTP address and hypertext.

- Netiquette calls for Web pages to end with a few lines of text indicating who owns the page and how to contact the owner. A mailto is a link that, when clicked, opens a new message window addressed to the person identified in the link. It is customary for Web page owners to include a mailto link to their e-mail address to make it easy for you to contact them. The format is:

```
<a href="mailto:santa@northpole.com">
    santa@northpole.com</a>
```

- To create white space on a Web page, you use the `<p>` and `</p>` tags to begin and end a paragraph. To end the current line and move to a new line, you use the `<br>` break tag. To create a single white space onscreen, you use the ` ` space code, which can be used to display simultaneous white spaces onscreen, as in `     `.

- To make text appear bold on a Web page, you surround it with the `<strong>` start and `</strong>` stop tags. To italicize something, you surround it with the emphasis `<em>` start and `</em>` stop tags.

- Resist the temptation to press the ENTER key repeatedly to add white space in an attempt to create pagination on a Web page. If you want a new page, create a new Web page and link to it from a hypertext link or a navigational icon. Otherwise, just let your text flow onto the screen so users can scroll down to peruse it, uninterrupted by feigned white-space paging.

HTML Graphics and Animated GIFs

- Web page images should be in either the GIF or JPEG file format. You can also use the relatively newer PNG format discussed in Chapter 2. Paint Shop Pro is a Windows program you can use to convert images into the proper format. You can also use Paint Shop Pro for image capture, creation, viewing, and manipulation. A try-before-you-buy version lets you try Paint Shop Pro free for 60 days before deciding whether to purchase the software.

- To convert an image with Paint Shop Pro to a different file format, you use the File | Save As dialog, which has a Type field that lets you choose the format in which to save the converted file.

- Although you can make an image appear smaller by dragging its handles in a WYSIWYG Web page editor, this does not reduce the file size of the image and therefore consumes more bandwidth than a truly resized image. Paint Shop Pro has an Image | Resize option that enables you to reduce the actual size of the image, thereby saving valuable bandwidth. When you resize an image, you should choose the option to lock the aspect ratio so the image's dimensions do not distort and cause the picture to appear too thin or too short.

- Unless you have a special reason for keeping your images encoded in 16 million colors (24-bit format), you should convert the images to 256 colors (8-bit format), which will make them appear three times faster on your Web page due to the smaller file size.

- A background tile creates a special effect by drawing an image repeatedly across and down the screen until the entire window has been covered. If the image is designed in such a way as to hide the edges when tiled, you get a seamless appearance in the background. If you plan to display printed text on the tiled background, be sure to choose a tile that will not interfere with the readability of your text.

- Transparency is a special effect in which one of the colors in a bitmap becomes translucent. Instead of seeing that color, you see through it into the background color or image on the screen.

- An animated GIF is a graphic that contains multiple images intended to be shown in a sequence at specific times and locations on the screen. A looping option causes your Web browser to keep showing the frames in the GIF file continually, and, as a result, you see an animation onscreen.

- Clip art is pre-drawn artwork organized into a catalog or library that you can browse in search of appropriate icons, buttons, banners, backgrounds, tiles, or animated GIFs for use on Web pages.

HTML Tables and Web Page Layout

- A table is a Web page design element that divides the screen into a grid consisting of rectangular regions called cells. Into each cell you can enter text or graphics that align with the boundaries of the cell's rectangle. Because you can use a table to create any conceivable layout of cells onscreen, tables enable you to take control of the page and position your content exactly where you want it.

- You use three basic HTML tags to create tables. First, the `<table>` start and `</table>` stop tags begin and end the table. Inside the `<table>`, you use the `<tr>` start and `</tr>` stop tags to begin and end each row of the table. The code `<tr>` stands for table row. Inside each table row, you use the `<td>` start and `</td>` stop tags to begin and end each data cell. The code `<td>` stands for table data. Inside the table data cells, you put the textual and/or graphical content that you want in that cell of the table.

- Attributes added to the table tag modify the table's formatting. If you would like to see the table's edges onscreen, for example, you can give the table a border. The tag format is `<table border="2">` for a border that is two pixels thick.

- The `align` attribute can modify the `<table>`, `<tr>`, and `<td>` tags to control horizontal alignment. Values of the `align` attribute can be left, center, right, or justify, which means to double-justify the text. For example, a table cell in which the data is right-justified has the tag `<td align="right">`. The default value is left.

- The `valign` attribute controls vertical alignment. Its values can be top, middle, or bottom. For example, a table cell in which the data aligns with the bottom of the cell has the tag `<td valign="bottom">`. The default value is middle.

- To control both horizontal and vertical alignment, you can specify both `align` and `valign` attributes. For example, a table cell in which the data is right-justified at the bottom of the cell has the tag `<td align="right" valign="bottom">`.

- Sometimes you may want a table, a row, or a cell to have a background color. You can create colored backgrounds with the `bgcolor` attribute. For example, if you want the background of the entire table to be silver, you can make the table tag say `<table bgcolor="silver">`. If you want an individual cell to have a separate color, make the table data tag say `<td bgcolor="silver">`. This is just one of 16 defined color names, which are listed in Table 6-2.

- You can also specify colors by hex codes, with which you can mix 16 million different hues. The format is #RRGGBB, where RR is the red value, GG is the green value, and BB is the blue value. For example, `<table bgcolor="#000080">` creates a navy blue background because it has such a lot of blue (80) but no red or green in it. The highest color value is white, which is #FFFFFF.

■ Cell spacing is the amount of space the browser puts between the borders of the cells. Cell padding is the amount of white space the browser puts inside the borders of the cells. You set cell spacing and padding via the following table tag attributes, which can be either integer values or percentages

```
<table cellspacing="5" cellpadding="10%">
```

■ When you use tables to control the layout of a Web page, you should form the habit of indenting your table tags to show the document's structure. The browser ignores these indentations at runtime, so they will not affect your page's appearance. When you later need to edit or update something on your page, however, you can use the indentations to find more quickly the place in the document where you want to make your change.

■ You can subdivide any table cell by creating a table inside a cell. Putting a table inside a cell provides another layer of structure on the Web page. There is no limit to the number of cells you can subdivide. Because subdividing cells enables you to create any conceivable pattern of rectangular regions on the screen, it provides an unlimited array of possibilities for laying out Web pages.

■ By default, each cell in a table is confined to just one row and column. To vary the layout of a table, you can expand a cell to make it span more than one row or column. To do so, you give the cell's `<td>` tag a `rowspan` or `colspan` attribute. For example, a cell that spans two rows and three columns has the tag `<td rowspan="2" colspan="3">`.

HTML Hyperlinks and Web Design

■ Whenever you link two or more Web pages, you create a hypermedia design that can be visualized. The extent to which you can visualize your webs determines how successful you will be in planning the navigational pathways that users can traverse at your Web site. The goal is to provide your users with navigation options that are both appropriate and quick.

■ The linear list is a hypermedia design paradigm that enables users to move back and forth through a serial sequence of pages, moving forward to new materials or backward to review. This paradigm is appropriate for sequences of Web pages that you want users to view in a slideshow manner. If the sequence is long, however, you will also want to provide a link to the menu so users can jump out of the slideshow if they lose interest.

■ A menu is a hypermedia design paradigm that permits users to select one from a number of choices listed onscreen. When a user chooses an item on the menu, the item linked to it appears.

■ A hierarchy is a hypermedia design paradigm in which each object provides users with a menu of choices that trigger more menus with more choices. If you have a large Web site with dozens or hundreds of pages, the hierarchy enables you to design pathways through which users can drill down to the desired page.

■ The network is a hypermedia design pattern in which objects can be multiple linked in any direction to any object in your web. Especially when a web is large, the network design enables users to navigate to any page with a minimum of mouse clicks. A tight design enables users to get wherever they want within three clicks.

■ A hybrid is a hypermedia design paradigm that provides multiple navigational pathways by employing linear lists, menus, hierarchies, and network designs as appropriate throughout a large Web site. If you think about the World Wide Web as a whole, its design represents the ultimate in hybrid hypermedia construction.

■ Key Terms

animated GIF *(275)*	**linear list paradigm** *(289)*	**standard generalizable**
body *(257)*	**list item tag** *(254)*	**markup language**
cell padding *(281)*	**mailto** *(266)*	**(SGML)** *(254)*
cell spacing *(281)*	**mark up** *(253)*	**start tag** *(253)*
clip art *(276)*	**menu paradigm** *(289)*	**stop tag** *(253)*
head *(257)*	**named anchor** *(262)*	**table** *(276)*
hierarchy paradigm *(289)*	**network paradigm** *(290)*	**tag** *(253)*
horizontal rule *(261)*	**non-breaking space**	**tile** *(274)*
hybrid paradigm *(290)*	**( )** *(266)*	**transparency** *(274)*
hypertext markup language	**ordered list** *(260)*	**unordered list** *(260)*
(HTML) *(252)*	**page title** *(257)*	**XHTML** *(254)*
hypertext reference (href) *(263)*	**paired tag** *(253)*	

■ Key Terms Quiz

1. Loosely derived from SGML, _____ is the markup language used to create hypertext documents for the World Wide Web. A newer version called _____ brings the language into compliance with the stricter rules of SGML and makes it compatible with newly emerging XML tools.

2. To mark up a text means to insert special codes called _____ into the text.

3. To create a(n) _____, you type the `<hr>` tag at the spot in an HTML file where you want this Web page element to appear.

4. In HTML, bulleted lists are known as _____ lists, and numbered lists are called _____ lists.

5. A(n) _____ is a link that, when clicked, opens a new message window addressed to the person identified in the link.

6. To create a blank space on a Web page that will not cause a line break, you use the _____.

7. In an anchor tag, you specify the link via the _____ parameter.

8. In HTML, paired tags come in pairs that consist of a _____ and a stop tag.

9. A(n) _____ is a graphic that contains multiple images intended to be shown in a sequence at specific times and locations on the screen.

10. A(n) _____ is a Web page design element that divides the screen into a grid consisting of rectangular regions called cells.

■ Multiple-Choice Quiz

1. What tag marks the beginning of an HTML document?
   a. `<body>`
   b. `<head>`
   c. `<html>`
   d. `<start>`

2. What tags do you use to create the page title?
   a. `<body>` and `</body>`
   b. `<h1>` and `</h1>`
   c. `<label>` and `</label>`
   d. `<title>` and `</title>`

3. Which syntax do you use to create a named anchor bookmark?
   a. `<a name="bookmarkname"></a>`
   b. `<a href="#bookmarkname>Click Me!</a>`
   c. `<a href="http://www.udel.edu">University of Delaware</a>`
   d. `<a href="mailto:santa@northpole.com">santa@northpole.com</a>`

4. To make text appear bold on a Web page, you can surround it with what pair of tags?
   a. `<bold> </bold>`
   b. `<em> </em>`
   c. `<emphasize> </emphasize>`
   d. `<strong> </strong>`

5. An image encoded in 16 million colors (24-bit format) is about how many times larger than the same image encoded in 256 colors (8-bit format)?
   a. Three
   b. Five
   c. Six
   d. Twelve

6. In a table, the table data `<td>` start and `</td>` stop tags go between what pair of tags?
   a. `<td> </td>`
   b. `<tr> </tr>`
   c. `<td> <tr>`
   d. `<tr> <td>`

7. Which attribute controls horizontal alignment of a `<table>`, `<tr>`, or `<td>` table element?
   a. `Align`
   b. `Colspan`
   c. `Rowspan`
   d. `Valign`

8. Which hypermedia design pattern best describes the design of the World Wide Web when considered as a whole?
   a. Linear list
   b. Hierarchy
   c. Network
   d. Hybrid

9. What kind of a list is bulleted by default?
   a. Linear
   b. Linked
   c. Ordered
   d. Unordered

10. In HTML, how can you subdivide a table cell into several more cells?
    a. Create another table inside it.
    b. Press ENTER to move down to the next line.
    c. Press TAB to generate a new cell.
    d. Use a `<subdiv>` tag.

Essay Quiz

1. Go to www.w3.org/MarkUp and read how the World Wide Web consortium oversees the continued evolution of HTML. What mechanism is provided by the W3C for you to request new features to be added to HTML and XHTML?

2. This chapter got you started creating your Web page résumé. Now you should complete your résumé by adding all the sections you sketched when you designed your résumé at the start of this tutorial. If you have any trouble, refer to the step-by-step instructions in this chapter for creating new paragraphs, headings, list items, and horizontal rules.

3. Each item in your bulleted table of contents should be linked to its corresponding section in your résumé. Insert named anchor bookmarks at the beginning of each new section in your résumé. Then link each item in your table of contents to the corresponding bookmark in your résumé. Test the links to make sure they work. At the end of each section in your résumé, provide a way for users to return to your table of contents.

4. Take any image and use Paint Shop Pro to increase its color depth to 16 million colors (24-bit format). Inspect the file's size with the Windows Explorer and make a note of how large the file is. Now decrease the color depth to 256 colors (8-bit format). Inspect the file's size again. By what percentage has the size of the file decreased? Will this make the file appear more quickly when it gets downloaded from the Internet for display on a Web page?

5. This book's Web site contains several images designed for use as tiles on Web pages. Download several of these images, and try tiling them onto your Web page résumé. What is the filename of the tile that appears best on your Web page résumé? Why do you like that tile better than the others?

Lab Projects

• Lab Project 6-1: Graphic Design

The adage that a picture is worth a thousand words has never been more appropriate than on a Web page. One could argue that the hypermedia environment adds even more value to the picture because you can access it quickly when you need it. Being able to find the picture you want quickly may make the image worth a million words when it answers a question or solves a problem for which you need a solution quickly. Imagine that your employer has put you in this kind of a situation. Your school or small company is having budget problems, and your employer has asked you to develop a cost-effective strategy for creating Web site graphics. Get your word processor started, and follow these suggested ways of satisfying your employer's request for a graphic design strategy:

■ Several good banner- and button-making utilities are available on the Web. See if you can find a utility that creates banners and buttons in a style compatible with your school or company's look and feel. Follow this book's Web site links to banner and button makers. Using your word processor, take notes identifying the names of the sites you visited, and report whether you would recommend them for use in your workplace. At the site you like best, create a sample banner and copy it into your report as an example.

Note: To copy a graphic from the Web into your word processor, right-click (Macintosh users CONTROL-click) the image and choose Copy; then go into your word processor, pull down the Edit menu, and choose Paste.

■ Paint Shop Pro has a button-maker built in. Make a sample button with Paint Shop. Copy the button into the report in your word processor, and write a paragraph indicating that the button came from Paint Shop. State whether you would recommend using the Paint Shop button maker to make buttons at your school or company Web site.

■ FrontPage has a wide array of themes built in. If you are using FrontPage, you can audition these themes to see if there might be one suitable for use in your school or company. It is also possible to modify the FrontPage themes; if you find one that almost fits, you can fine-tune it. To audition the FrontPage themes, follow these steps:

1. In FrontPage, click the New Page button ⬜ to create a new page.

2. Pull down the Format menu and choose Theme; the Themes dialog appears.

3. In the list of themes on the left, click the theme you would like to see. The theme appears in the window on the right. Repeat this step and look at all the different themes.

4. If you see a theme you like, use your word processor to record its name in the report you are writing.

■ The Microsoft Clip Gallery is a rich source of graphics for illustrating Web pages. Follow this book's Web site link to the Microsoft Clip Gallery, and use the search tools to perform a keyword search for the kinds of graphics needed by your school or company. Use your word processor to add to your report any suitable graphics you may find. Type the graphic's filename, and paste a thumbnail of the graphic into your report.

If your instructor has asked you to hand in this assignment, make sure you put your name at the top; then save your graphic design recommendations on disk or follow the other instructions you may have been given for submitting this assignment.

• Lab Project 6-2: Page Layout

Page layout is a critical aspect of creating a Web site for any school or business. Because of the different screen sizes in common use today, you need to plan a design that will adjust to different window sizes. Every site on the Web faces this dilemma. Imagine that your employer has noticed that some Web sites seem to have better layout than others. Your employer has asked you to go out on the Web, analyze the designs of some of the better sites, and recommend a page layout strategy for your school or company Web site. To complete this assignment, follow these steps:

1. Visit some of the premier sites on the Web and observe how they lay out material on their Web pages. Sites with innovative screen layouts include:

   a. www.microsoft.com

   b. www.cnn.com

   c. www.amazon.com

   d. www.sony.com

   e. www.macromedia.com

   f. www.msn.com

2. At each of the sites you visited in step 1, resize your browser window and refresh the pages to see how they look at different screen resolutions.

3. All of these sites use tables to define their screen layout. As you learned in this chapter, tables permit you to design any conceivable layout pattern onscreen. One of the tricks you can use is to define certain columns of a table to be fixed to a predetermined pixel size, and set the others to a certain percentage of the window's width. When a user resizes the window, the columns that have percentage settings stretch or squeeze accordingly. Consider whether this kind of a design would be appropriate for your Web site.

4. At the microsoft.com site, notice especially how the menu bar at the top stretches or squeezes to fit the window when you resize your browser. Decide whether you want the menu bars at your site to work like this.

5. Use your word processor to write a three-part report, organized as follows:

   a. In the first part, describe the screen layout strategy you recommend for your workplace. If you found other Web sites by using this strategy, provide their Web addresses so your employer can go visit them to see what you mean.

   b. In part two, write a paragraph or two describing sites you found interesting but whose layouts you rejected. Give the Web addresses so your employer can visit them, and state why you decided not to follow their designs.

   c. In the third part, conclude your report with a brief paragraph stating why the solution you have recommended is better than the layouts you decided to reject.

If your instructor has asked you to hand in this assignment, make sure you put your name at the top; then save your page layout recommendation on disk or follow the other instructions you may have been given for submitting this assignment.

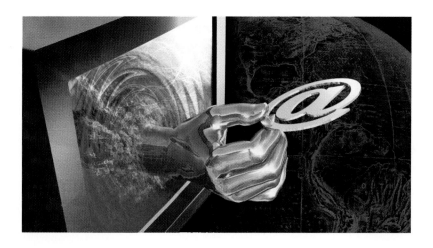

chapter

7

Interacting with Users

"Tell me and I will forget. Show me and I will remember. Involve me and I will understand."

—*Aristotle*

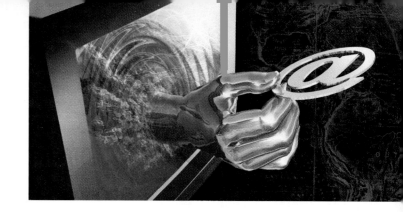

- Define the elements of an HTML form and create a Web form to collect information from site visitors.

- Create a PayPal button to enable someone to select a product advertised at your Web site and pay for it online.

- Define the elements of an HTML image map and create such a map to permit users to interact graphically with your Web site.

- Describe the concept of a frameset, define the HTML elements it comprises, and create a frameset that enables users to click items in a sidebar frame to display the corresponding content in the main content frame.

- List the steps involved in FTPing files to the Web and set file permissions that either make files publicly available or restrict access to authorized users.

T o unleash the true potential of the Web, you need to make your pages interactive. Why? Because it is through interacting with your users that you learn things about them, such as their preferences and needs. Then you can act on the basis of those needs to make your site responsive to what your users want. This just-in-time responsiveness is what differentiates interactive sites from static pages that have no way of obtaining knowledge about users.

This chapter teaches you how to create four kinds of interactions onscreen. First, you learn how to create an HTML form that can collect information from your users. This information can consist of a textual response that the user types in response to an onscreen prompt, or it can be a choice the user makes by selecting an item in a menu of possible choices. Second, you learn how to use a preprogrammed e-commerce button that people can click to buy things you offer for sale at your site. Later in this book, Chapter 12 will teach you how to program your own buttons by writing scripts that can save results and query a database to power your site.

Third, this chapter steps you through the process of creating a dashboard-style graphic known as an image map where users can click hotspots to make selections at your site. This kind of image mapping enables you to create graphical interactions that cannot be expressed in words. Finally, you learn how to use a frameset containing multiple windows called frames that interact with each other to minimize the time required for users to navigate your site. Because not all users like framesets, however, I will share with you a strategy for designing site content in such a way that you can give users their choice of either using the frameset or not. Then I show you how to publish your site to the Web by using an FTP client window.

Creating HTML Forms

A **form** is an HTML Web page element that prompts the user to fill in one or more blanks and/or select items from a menu of possible choices, after which the user clicks a button to submit the filled-out form. Many forms also contain a Reset button that the user can press to clear the form and start over. The blanks the user fills in can be short-answer fields or text areas capable of holding larger amounts of text. Forms can display specific choices in dropdown menus, check boxes, or radio buttons. All of these form controls have HTML tags explained in the following sections.

Getting Information from Users

As you might expect, the `<form>` start and `</form>` stop tags mark the beginning and ending of an HTML form. Between these tags go the controls that prompt the user for specific information, along with any onscreen instructions you may wish to provide. This tutorial teaches you these controls in the context of a real-world example in which you will create a form that prompts users to tell you their name, e-mail address, and the frequency with which they would like to receive news from your school or company. When a user clicks the Submit button, the form uses a mailto to send you a message telling you what the user filled in on the form. After you complete the coding of this mailto example, other methods of processing forms will be discussed, along with more advanced controls you can display onscreen as part of the form.

Designing the Prompts

A **prompt** is an onscreen instruction that asks the user to provide some information, either by typing a response into a text field or by choosing something from a selection of possible choices. The secret to creating a user-friendly form is to design the prompts in such a way that users can easily understand what you are asking them to provide. In this example, you prompt the users to type their name and e-mail address and then tell you whether they want to receive your news daily, weekly, or monthly. Think about how you might word these prompts. Then have a look at Figure 7-1, which shows how I decided to word them onscreen. If you prefer alternate wording, you can reword these instructions when you learn how to write the code for this example. Read on.

Coding the Form

To create the form that appears in Figure 7-1, you first use the Notepad to create a new HTML file into which you will type the tags that create the form's controls. Follow these steps:

1. Pull down the Notepad's File menu and choose New to start a new file. Into this new file, type the following code, which creates the overall structure of the page:

```
<html>
<head>
    <title>Newsletter Subscription Form</title>
</head>
<body>
<h1>Newsletter Subscription</h1>
</body>
</html>
```

2. Pull down the Notepad's File menu and choose Save As to save the file. When the Save dialog appears, use it to save the file in your *website* folder as **subscribe.html**. Use your browser to preview the file and see how it looks onscreen.

FIGURE 7-1 *When you create an HTML form, you should word the prompts clearly and arrange the controls logically so users can easily intuit how to fill out the form. In this example, the default value of the Submit button has been changed to Subscribe, because clicking the button will subscribe the user to the newsletter.* ■

3. In the Notepad file, click to position your cursor after the heading's `</h1>` stop tag, but before the `</body>` stop tag. This is where the form tag is going to go. Every `<form>` start tag has two attributes, namely, a `method` and an `action`. Because this form is going to post the results to a mailto that will e-mail you the form results, you type your form tags as follows, replacing Santa's e-mail address by your own. In this tutorial, the gray lines already exist in your Notepad file; you type the new black lines between the existing gray lines:

```
<h1>Newsletter Subscription</h1>
<form method="post" action="mailto:santa@northpole.com">
</form>
</body>
```

4. Save the file.

Now you are ready to code the input fields into which users will type their name and e-mail address.

Coding the Text Field Input Controls

In HTML, you use the **<input> tag** to create the form controls that receive input from the user. The `<input>` tag has a *type* attribute that specifies the kind of control you want. In this example, you are about to create the text fields into which the users will enter their name and e-mail address. To create a text field, you set the `<input>` tag's type to *text*. The `<input>` tag also has a **name attribute** that you use to specify the name of the control, and a **size attribute** that specifies how many characters wide the field will be onscreen. There is also a **maxlength attribute** that specifies the maximum number of characters the user can type. You will see all of these attributes in action as you follow these steps to create the text field input controls:

1. Click to position your cursor between the `<form>` start and `</form>` stop tags, and type the following code, which displays a prompt asking users to type their name, followed by the `<input>` tag that creates the corresponding text field:

```
<form method="post" action="mailto:santa@northpole.com">
<p>What is your name?
<br>
<input type="text" name="Name" size="50" maxlength="150">
</p>
</form>
```

2. Save the file and preview it with your browser. Click Refresh to make sure you are viewing the latest version of the file, which should now display the Name field. Troubleshoot any problems that may appear onscreen.

3. You follow a similar process to create the text field into which users will be asked to type their e-mail address. In the Notepad file, click to position your cursor immediately before the `</form>` tag, and type the following code to prompt users for their e-mail address:

```
</p>
<p>What is your e-mail address?
<br>
<input type="text" name="Email" size="50" maxlength="150">
</p>
</form>
```

4. Save the file and preview it with your browser.

After you troubleshoot any problems that may appear onscreen, you will be ready to code the radio buttons with which the user will choose whether to receive your news daily, weekly, or monthly.

Coding the Radio Button Input Controls

A **radio button** is a form control that displays a small round button with which the user can select one, but not more than one, item from a list of possible choices. Alongside each item, the browser displays a radio button that gets filled in when the user clicks it. If the user clicks a different item in the radio button group, the newly clicked button gets filled in and the previously selected button gets cleared. This is how the buttons work on a push-button radio; hence the term radio button.

In an HTML form, you create a radio button by setting an `<input>` tag's `type` attribute to `radio`. You use the `name` attribute to assign a name to the radio button group, which includes any other radio button of the same name within the form. You will see how this works as you code the radio buttons for the subscribe form you are creating in this tutorial. Follow these steps:

1. Use the Notepad to open the *subscribe.html* file you have been working on in this tutorial. Click to position your cursor after the e-mail paragraph's close tag, and type the following code to create the first radio button, which users will click if they want to receive your newsletter on a daily basis. Notice that the `<input>` tag includes the *checked* attribute, which will cause this item initially to be selected as the default choice on the form:

```
<input type="text" name="Email" size="50" maxlength="150">
</p>
<p>
How often do you want to get our news?
<br>
<input type="radio" name="Frequency" value="daily" checked>Daily
</form>
```

2. Save the file and view it with your browser to make sure the form looks good so far. After you troubleshoot any problems, type the following code, which adds the other two radio buttons to the form. Notice that these buttons have the same *name* attribute but different *value* attributes. Remember that the name attribute is the name of the radio button group, and the value attribute is the specific setting the user can choose from that group. Here is the code to type:

```
<input type="radio" name="Frequency" value="daily" checked>Daily
<br>
<input type="radio" name="Frequency" value="weekly">Weekly
<br>
<input type="radio" name="Frequency" value="monthly">Monthly
</p>
<p>
<input type="submit" value="Subscribe"> <input type="reset">
</p>
</form>
```

3. Save the file and preview it with your browser. Click Refresh to make sure you are viewing the latest version of the file. You should see three radio buttons onscreen. Troubleshoot any problems you may see onscreen.

Now you are ready to complete the form by coding the buttons that the user will click to submit or reset the data on the form.

Coding the Submit and Reset Buttons

The final step in creating a form is to create the **Submit button**, which is the onscreen control that users will click to submit the form. In an HTML form, you make a Submit button by creating an `<input>` tag that has a type attribute set to *submit*. By default, the value the browser prints inside the button is the same as its type. You can change this value via the value attribute. I like to make the buttons say what they are going to do. In the *subscribe.html* example you are creating in this tutorial, the button is going to subscribe the user to a newsletter. Therefore, we will make its value be "Subscribe" so the button will say Subscribe instead of Submit.

Many forms also have a **Reset button** users can click to return the controls to their default settings. In an HTML form, you make a Reset button by creating an `<input>` tag that has a type attribute set to reset. The *subscribe.html* example you are creating in this tutorial has both a Submit button and a Reset button. To code these buttons, follow these steps:

1. Click to position your cursor immediately before the `</form>` tag that ends the form, and type the following code:

```
<input type="submit" value="Subscribe"> <input type="reset">
</p>
<p>
<input type="submit" value="Subscribe"> <input type="reset">
</p>
</form>
```

2. Save the file and view it with your browser. Compare your screen to the model displayed previously in Figure 7-1 and see if everything looks okay. Troubleshoot any problems. Figure 7-2 shows the completed HTML source code for the model in Figure 7-1.

3. Now you are ready to fill in the form and click the buttons to see what they do. The first time you try this, click the Reset button. You will observe that it resets the form. Try clicking different radio buttons. Notice that clicking the Reset button always resets the form to the button you coded to be *checked* by default.

4. Fill in the form again, but this time, click the Subscribe button. Because the Subscribe button is of type submit, clicking the Subscribe button submits the form data. If this works properly, you have successfully coded the form.

```
subscribe.html - Notepad
File  Edit  Format  View  Help
<html>
<head><title>Newsletter Subscription Form</title></head>
<body>
<h1>Newsletter Subscription</h1>
<form method="post" action="mailto:santa@northpole.com">
<p>what is your name?
<br>
<input type="text" name="Name" size="50" maxlength="150">
</p>
<p>what is your e-mail address?
<br>
<input type="text" name="Email" size="50" maxlength="150">
</p>
<p>
How often do you want to get our news?
<br>
<input type="radio" name="Frequency" value="daily" checked>Daily
<br>
<input type="radio" name="Frequency" value="weekly">weekly
<br>
<input type="radio" name="Frequency" value="monthly">Monthly
</p>
<p>
<input type="submit" value="Subscribe"> <input type="reset">
</p>
</form>
</body>
</html>
```

FIGURE 7-2 *This is completed HTML source code that creates the form displayed in Figure 7-1. If you have any trouble getting the form to work, compare your HTML code closely to the commands displayed here. Correct any problems, save the file, and then view it with your browser. Remember to click the browser's Refresh button to make sure you are viewing the latest version of the form.* ■

Congratulations! Now we must discuss what happens in processing the response to a form.

Processing the Response

In the *submit.html* tutorial you just completed, you programmed the form tag to post its data to a mailto, which caused your browser to send a message to the e-mail address you provided in your mailto code. Depending on the brand of browser you are using, either the mail message contained the posted data in the body of the message or the data appeared in a file attachment. The IE browser, for example, attaches form data in a file named *Postdata.att*, which is a plain text file you can open with any text editor, such as the Notepad. Although this is a simple way to handle a form, mailto is very powerful because it provides you with a way to collect information from a site visitor without needing to do any fancy scripting or server-side programming. Thus, mailto is handy for beginners.

In developing more advanced Web applications such as e-commerce solutions, however, you must post the form data to a server that is programmed to read the information, save the form data in a database, decide how to act on it, and respond appropriately to the user . You use the form tag's method and action attributes to post data to a server-side program. One of the most popular server-side programming environments is Microsoft's active server page (ASP) technology. Imagine that Santa Claus has an ASP script named WishList.asp to which good little girls and boys can post information about the toys they want. Suppose the HTTP address of this script is http://toys.northpole.com/WishList.asp. To make a form post its data to this script, you would code the form tag as follows:

```
<form method="post" action="http://toys.northpole.com/WishList.asp">
```

The art of server-side programming is known as **common gateway interface (CGI)** scripting. There are many programming languages in which CGI scripts can be written. The CGI defines the protocol that these scripts use to send and receive data across the Internet. You learn more about CGI programming in Chapter 12.

Besides the **POST method** that sends the form data to a CGI script, there is also an HTTP **GET method** that appends the form data to the URL as a query string. You see forms with method="get" used especially at search engine sites, which use the query string to "get" what you are looking for. If you do a Google search, for example, take a look at the URL in the browser's Address field after you type your search terms and click the Search button to see how the form data gets appended to the URL. If you search Google for cars, for example, the form data gets appended to the URL as follows:

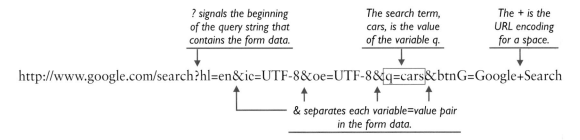

Table 7-1 summarizes the HTTP form submission methods. For more detailed information about these methods, go to www.w3.org/TR/html4 and follow the quick table of contents link to forms.

Creating Check Boxes

When you coded and tested the *subscribe.html* page earlier in this chapter, you observed that the radio button permits you to select only one of the items included in the control. For situations in which you want the user to be able to select more than one of the items contained in a form control, you use check boxes. A **check box** is a form control that presents the user

Attribute	What It Does
method="get"	The GET method puts the form data in a query string that gets appended to the URL specified in the form tag's action attribute.
method="post"	The POST method sends the form data to the process identified in the form tag's action attribute. This process is normally a server-side script that reads and processes the form data, saves appropriate information in a server-side database, and returns an HTML response to the user.

TABLE 7-1   *HTTP Form Submission Methods* ■

with a small box that the user can click to turn an option on or off. To create a check box, you make an <input> tag of type check box. The syntax is

Replace *VariableName* with the name of the variable in which you want the form to return the value.

Replace *VariableValue* with the value the variable will be assigned if the user checks this

```
<input type="checkbox" name="VariableName" value="VariableValue" checked>
```

Include the `checked` attribute only if you want the check box to be selected by default.

Imagine that you want to create check box controls that will enable users to tell what news topics they are interested in. You would code such controls with the HTML displayed in Figure 7-3. When viewed with a browser, the check boxes appear as illustrated in Figure 7-4. If you want to try these check boxes in a working example, type the HTML displayed in Figure 7-3 into your *subscribe.html* file right before the paragraph that contains the Submit button. Then save the file and view it with your browser.

Creating Single and Multiple Item Selection Menus

In user interface design, selection menus are a very popular and effective way of getting users to make choices. On a Web form, you can create selection menus that either drop down or display their contents in a scrolling menu onscreen. Furthermore, you can set up the menu for a single selection, or you can permit multiple selections.

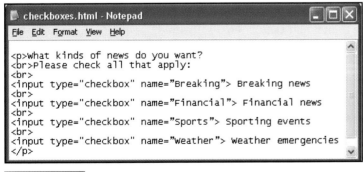

FIGURE 7-3 *You make an HTML check box control by creating an <input> tag of type check box. Compare this code to Figure 7-4, which shows this code being viewed by a browser.* ■

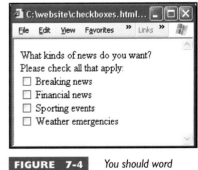

FIGURE 7-4 *You should word check box instructions in such a way that the user knows to check all that apply.* ■

You create a selection menu via the **\<select\> tag**, which has a corresponding \</select\> stop tag. Between the \<select\> start and \</select\> stop tags, you use the **\<option\> tag** to specify the menu options from which the user can make a selection. The command syntax is outlined as follows:

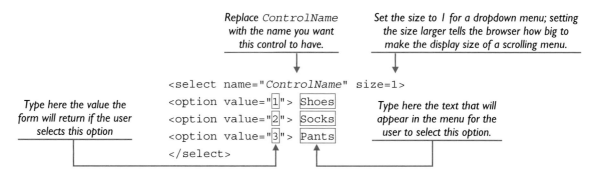

To permit multiple selections, you add the *multiple* attribute to the select tag. When you create a multiple selection menu, you normally set the size large enough to display all or many of the menu items at once. The following code, for example, creates a multiple selection menu that displays ten items at a time:

```
<select name="ControlName" size="10" multiple>
```

Be aware, however, that users must know how to CTRL-click to select multiple items from a menu. Naïve users will not know how to do this. Therefore, do not use the `multiple` attribute unless your site is for an experienced audience that will know how to make multiple selections from a menu.

Creating Text Areas

A text area is an HTML form control that displays a scrolling entry box into which the user can type a larger amount of text than will fit in a text field. Thus, you use a text area when you need to provide space for the user to type more than a text field could easily hold. To create a text area, you use the **\<textarea\>** start and **\</textarea\>** stop tags. Between these two tags, you type any initial text you want displayed in the text area. If you want a blank text area, do not enter any text between these tags. To set the width, you use the *cols* attribute, which tells the browser how many characters wide to make the text box. To set the height of the text area, you use the *rows* attribute, which tells how many rows high to make the text box. The syntax is as follows:

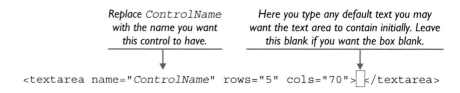

Creating Password Fields

A **password field** is a text box that works like a text field except that when the user types the entry, the browser displays asterisks instead of revealing the sensitive information onscreen. The purpose is to prevent someone looking over the user's shoulder from seeing the password in clear text onscreen. The syntax is as follows:

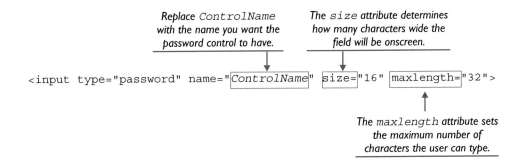

HTML Web Form Control Summary

Table 7-2 summarizes the HTML Web form controls you have studied in this chapter. For more detailed information about these controls, go to www.w3.org/TR/html4 and follow the quick table of contents link to forms.

HTML Form Control	Purpose and Examples
Text field	Text entry box into which users can type characters onscreen. `<input type="text" name="ControlName" size="50" maxlength="150">`
Password field	Works like a text field except whatever the user types is displayed as asterisks onscreen. `<input type="password" name="ControlName" size="25" maxlength="50">`
Radio button	Displays a small round button that enables the user to select one, but not more than one, item from a list of possible choices. `<input type="radio" name="ControlName" value="daily" checked>Daily`
Submit button	Displays a button that, when clicked, causes the form to submit its data. By default, the button displays the text "Submit," which you can change via the `value` attribute. `<input type="submit" value="Subscribe">`
Reset button	Displays a button that, when clicked, clears the form and displays any default values of the form's controls. `<input type="reset">`
Check box	Displays a small box that the user can check to select one or more items onscreen. `<input type="checkbox" name="VariableName" value="VariableValue" checked>`

Single item selection menu	Displays a menu that lets the user select one option from a list of possible selection items.
	`<select name="ControlName" size="1">`
	`<option value="1"> Shoes`
	`<option value="2"> Socks`
	`<option value="3"> Pants`
	`</select>`

TABLE 7-2   *HTML Web Form Control Summary* ■

HTML Form Control	Purpose and Examples

Multiple item selection menu	Displays a menu that lets the user select more than one option from a list of possible selection items. Normally you size a multiple item selection menu to display all or most of the options onscreen.
	`<select name="ControlName" size="3" multiple>`
	`<option value="1"> Shoes`
	`<option value="2"> Socks`
	`<option value="3"> Pants`
	`</select>`

Text area	Displays a scrolling entry box into which the user can type a larger amount of text than will fit in a text field. `<textarea name="ControlName" rows="5" cols="70"> default text </textarea>`

TABLE 7-2   *HTML Web Form Control Summary (continued)* ■

Making a PayPal Buy Now Button

In Chapter 4, you learned about PayPal, a person-to-person payment system individuals can use to sell products over the Web without needing to set up a complicated e-commerce solution. Instead, you simply create an HTML form containing a PayPal button that, when clicked, posts data to the PayPal server indicating what product the user wants to buy from you. The PayPal system handles all the rest.

PayPal uses two special form techniques to power its button. First, PayPal uses hidden fields to identify the business that is selling the product, the name of the product being sold, and the selling price. Second, PayPal substitutes the PayPal button's image for the Submit button that normally appears on an HTML form. After explaining these two special form techniques, this chapter steps you through the process of creating a PayPal Web form.

note *Everyone who is working through this book can create the PayPal form that this tutorial shows you how to construct. To make the PayPal Buy Now button actually sell something, however, you need to have a PayPal account. Do not worry about this. The tutorial does not require you to have a PayPal account. The purpose of this exercise is to show you how to create a form that uses hidden fields and an image button. The tutorial does not require you to buy or sell anything online.*

Hidden Fields

A **hidden field** is an HTML form control that creates a variable name and a corresponding value that are not displayed onscreen but are posted along with the rest of the form data when the user clicks the button to submit the form. You create a hidden field by setting an `<input>` tag's `type` attribute to hidden. In the `name` and `value` attributes, you type the variable name and its corresponding value. The command syntax is

Replace *VariableName* with the name of the variable. → ⬇ Replace *VariableValue* with the value of the variable. → ⬇

`<input type="hidden" name="VariableName" value="VariableValue">`

As you will see later in this tutorial, one of the hidden fields in a PayPal form identifies the business that is making the sale. In this particular field, the variable name is business, and the value is the business's e-mail address. The syntax is

Replace *me@mybusiness.com* with the e-mail address you registered at PayPal when you got your PayPal merchant account. → ⬇

`<input type="hidden" name="business" value="me@mybusiness.com">`

The advantage of using a hidden field is that the form can send information to PayPal without cluttering the screen. Thus, you can design your page to present your product any way you want. The PayPal form displays only the PayPal button, which the user clicks to buy the product. All the other product information resides in hidden fields that do not appear onscreen.

Image Buttons

Although the default Submit button looks pretty good on a Web page, most people would agree that the customized PayPal button looks better. One of its advantages is that users can clearly see that clicking this button will trigger a PayPal transaction. To make such an image substitute for the default Submit button in a Web form, you use an **image button**, an HTML form element you create with an <input> tag of type image. The syntax is

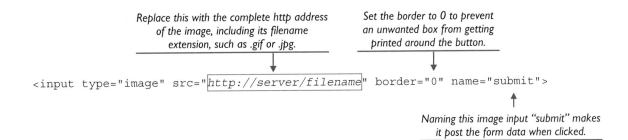

Coding a PayPal Buy Now Button

When clicked, the PayPal Buy Now button posts HTML form data to the PayPal e-commerce server. In addition to containing information about the product being purchased, the form data identifies the business that is making the sale. There are many options that can be present, plus a few that are always required. Table 7-3 lists the options that are always required and describes the form data that are typically used in a PayPal button.

Suppose you have a book for sale that is titled "Toymaking." The Web page on which you are advertising this book indicates that its sale price is $19.95. You have a PayPal merchant account registered under the e-mail address santa@northpole.com. To create a PayPal button to sell this product, you would follow these steps:

1. Click to position your cursor at the spot in the HTML code where you want the PayPal button to appear. Normally, you put it alongside or immediately under the product's description. Type the following tags to begin the form and identify your business. These tags must be present in every PayPal Buy Now form:

```
<form method="post" action="https://www.paypal.com/cgi-bin/webscr">
<input type="hidden" name="cmd" value="_xclick">
<input type="hidden" name="business" value="santa@northpole.com">
```

2. Having begun the form, you insert hidden fields to describe the product you have for sale. Type the following code, for example, to sell a book named "Toymaking" for $19.95:

```
<input type="hidden" name="item_name" value="Toymaking book">
<input type="hidden" name="amount" value="19.95">
```

To sell a different product, you change these value attributes. The rest of this code must always remain the same, including the names of these hidden fields.

3. Suppose you want to give the customer the option of getting an autographed copy of your book. When you ship the book, you will autograph it, if the user wants your autograph. To create such an option, type this code:

on0 and os0 are reserved names for the first of two possible options you can create. To create the other option, you use the names on1 and os1.

```
<table><tr><td>
<input type="hidden" name="on0" value="Autographed?">Autographed?
<select name="os0"> <option value="Yes">Yes <option value="No">No
</select></td></tr></table>
```

4. The final step is to display the PayPal button and conclude the form tag. To do so, type this code:

```
<input type="image" src="http://www.paypal.com/en_US/i/btn/x-click-but01.gif"
name="submit" alt="PayPal Buy Now Button">
</form>
```

The attribute alt, which stands for alternate, is an accessibility feature that specifies alternate text for this image. Chapter 9 is devoted to Web page accessibility.

Variable	Required?	Description
"post" action	Required	Must be set to "https://www.paypal.com/cgi-bin/webscr"
cmd	Required	Must be set to "_xclick"
business	Required	This is your PayPal ID or e-mail address where payments will be sent. This e-mail address must be confirmed and linked to your Verified Business or Premier PayPal account.
item_name	Optional	Description of item (maximum 127 characters). If omitted, the customer will see a field providing the option of entering an Item Name.
item_number	Optional	Pass-through variable for you to track payments. It will not be displayed to your customer but will be passed back to you at the completion of payment (maximum 127 characters). If omitted, no variable will be passed back.
amount	Optional	The price or amount of the purchase, not including shipping, handling, or tax. If omitted, the buyer will be able to adjust this value at the time of purchase.
return	Optional	An Internet URL where buyers will be returned after completing the payment, such as a Web page at your site thanking customers for their purchases. If the return is omitted, buyers will be taken to the PayPal site.
quantity	Optional	The quantity of items to be purchased. If omitted, this value will default to "1" and will not be shown in the payment flow.

TABLE 7-3 *Frequently Used PayPal Buy Now Button HTML and Hyperlink Variables* ■

Figure 7-5 shows the completed code from this exercise. Please remember that the PayPal site recommends that you always test each PayPal button you create to ensure that it works properly at your site. It is also possible that by the time you read this, some of the PayPal instructions may have changed. For the latest button-making instructions, follow this book's Web site link to PayPal's Buy Now Button Manual.

note *These are only a few of the possible form fields documented in PayPal's Buy Now Button Manual. To see the rest of the options that are available, follow this book's Web site link to PayPal's Buy Now Button Manual.*

Using the PayPal Button Factory

For users who are not programmatically inclined, PayPal has a button factory that generates automatically the HTML to paste onto your page to sell items at your Web site. To use the PayPal button factory, follow these steps:

1. Log on to your PayPal account at www.paypal.com and click the Merchant Tools tab. Under the Website Payments heading, follow the link to Buy Now Buttons to make the Button Factory appear.

2. The Button Factory prompts you to fill in some details about the product you want to sell. After you fill in these details, click the link labeled Create Button Now. In a text box titled "For Web pages," the button factory displays the HTML code to paste into your Web page.

3. Use your mouse to select all the HTML code in the text box, and then press CTRL-C to copy the code. Then click to position your cursor at the spot in your Notepad editor where you want the button, and press CTRL-V to paste the code. Normally, you paste this code alongside or immediately under the description of the product or service you are selling.

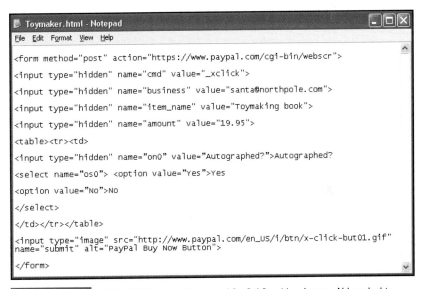

For more information about using the PayPal Buy Now Button on your Web site, follow this book's Web site link to PayPal's Buy Now Button Manual.

FIGURE 7-5 *The HTML code of a typical PayPal Buy Now button. Although this example is fully functional, it illustrates only a few of the PayPal fields you can put into an HTML form. To see the rest of the available form field options, follow this book's Web site link to PayPal's Buy Now Button Manual.* ■

Designing HTML Image Maps

An **image map** is an invisible layer of triggers placed over an image onscreen. The triggers can be rectangular, circular, or polygonal. When the user clicks inside one of the invisible triggers, the Web browser triggers the object of the link.

In earlier versions of HTML, using image maps required the use of a CGI call. When the user clicked a trigger in an image map, the browser sent the coordinates of the mouse click to a CGI program on a server, which told the browser what to do in response to the click. In the latest versions of HTML, it is possible to process image maps locally within the document instead of having to call on a CGI program for help in handling the mouse click.

Analyzing a Client-Side Image Map

One of the best ways of understanding image maps is to analyze a working example of an image map onscreen. Consider the example in Figure 7-6, which displays a piano keyboard on which the user is asked to click Middle C. If the user finds Middle C correctly, the user will be rewarded. If not, the user will be provided with an appropriate feedback message and given a chance to try again. To try this example yourself, go to this book's Web site and click the music keyboard icon.

Defining the Map and Area Tags

Figure 7-7 shows the HTML code that asks the question presented in Figure 7-6. The `<map>` and `</map>` tags demarcate the beginning and ending of the image map. Between them, you see the `<area>` tags that create the triggers. Inside each area tag is a *shape* attribute and a *coord* attribute that specifies the x,y coordinates of the links. These coordinates are pixel addresses inside the image. The top-left corner of an image is always pixel address 0,0 and is called the origin. The other addresses are all relative to the origin. The `coord` attribute has the syntax *coords= x1,y1,x2,y2*. The top-left corner of the area is x1,y1, and the bottom-right corner is x2,y2.

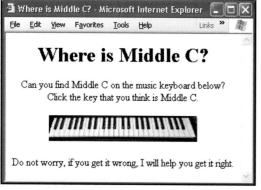

FIGURE 7-6 *This exercise asks the user to click Middle C on the music keyboard that is displayed onscreen. An invisible image map creates triggers for the correct answer and all the possible wrong answers. Depending on where the user clicks, these triggers bring up appropriate feedback screens, which are linked to the triggers in the image map. To try this example yourself, go to this book's Web site and click the music keyboard icon.* ∎

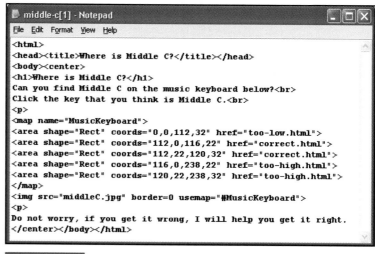

```
<html>
<head><title>Where is Middle C?</title></head>
<body><center>
<h1>Where is Middle C?</h1>
Can you find Middle C on the music keyboard below?<br>
Click the key that you think is Middle C.<br>
<p>
<map name="MusicKeyboard">
<area shape="Rect" coords="0,0,112,32" href="too-low.html">
<area shape="Rect" coords="112,0,116,22" href="correct.html">
<area shape="Rect" coords="112,22,120,32" href="correct.html">
<area shape="Rect" coords="116,0,238,22" href="too-high.html">
<area shape="Rect" coords="120,22,238,32" href="too-high.html">
</map>
<img src="middleC.jpg" border=0 usemap="#MusicKeyboard">
<p>
Do not worry, if you get it wrong, I will help you get it right.
</center></body></html>
```

FIGURE 7-7 *The HTML code that presents the Middle C question.* ∎

Visualizing the Coordinates

The Middle C image map contains five sets of coordinates. Figure 7-8 helps you visualize how these coordinates fit the too-low, too-high, and just-right regions of the music keyboard image.

The first set of coordinates has the HTML encoding of `coords=0,0,112,32`. The format of these coordinates is x1,y1,x2,y2. Therefore, they define an area that goes from 0,0 to 112,32, which is the portion of the keyboard below middle C. When the user clicks there, the too-low link gets triggered.

The second area has the coordinates 112,0,116,22, thereby specifying a rectangle from 112,0 to 116,22, which is where the top half of Middle C is in the image. The third area has the coordinates 112,22,120,32, which the bottom part of middle C comprises. The fourth and fifth areas define the "too high" regions to the right of Middle C.

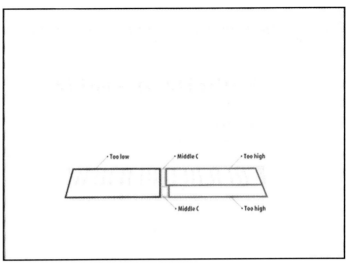

FIGURE 7-8 *Visualization of how the coordinates of the MusicKeyboard image map describe the too-low, just-right, and too-high regions of the music keyboard image.* ∎

Applying the Usemap Attribute

Once you have defined an image map with the `<map>` tag, you use the *usemap* attribute to apply it to any image on the page. The `usemap` attribute modifies the `<img>` tag that puts the image onscreen. Notice that the image tag in Figure 7-7 has a `usemap` attribute telling your browser to use the MusicKeyboard map on the middleC.jpg image:

```
<img src="middleC.jpg" border=0 usemap="#MusicKeyboard">
```

The syntax of the `usemap` attribute is usemap=#*area_name* where *area_name* is the name you gave the image map in the `<map>` tag's name attribute. When the mouse clicks on one of the areas in the image map, the user follows the corresponding link.

Creating Nonrectangular Areas

In the Middle C example, the regions in the image map are all rectangular. Image maps can also contain circle areas. If you wanted a volleyball to be a trigger, for example, you could make a circle area to do that. The HTML syntax for a circle area is as follows:

```
<area shape="circle" coords="center-x,center-y,radius" href="your_link.html">
```

Replace center-x, center-y, *and* radius *with integer values defining the center and size of your circle.*

You can even create polygonal areas with any conceivable shape. On a U.S. map, if you wanted to make the state of Florida trigger something, you could define a polygon the shape of Florida. There is no limit to the number of triggers or their shape. You can literally create any kind of triggering situation you can imagine. The HTML syntax for a polygonal area is

```
<area shape="poly" coords="x1,y1,x2,y2,x3,y3,x4,y4" href="your_link.html">
```

Replace *x1,y1,x2,y2,x3,y3,x4,y4* with integer values defining the coordinates of each successive endpoint along the polygon. Specify one coordinate for each endpoint. Keep going if there are more than the three sides in this example. The last pair of coordinates should be the same as the first, to close the polygon.

Many Web page creation tools have image map assistants built in that can help you create image maps. Or you can use a tool such as Paint Shop Pro to figure out pixel locations. To learn more about image maps and tools for creating them, follow this book's Web site link to the image map tutorial.

Try This!

Roll Your Own Image Map

Because client-side image maps execute in the browser, you can create an image map without needing access to a CGI server. With all of the processing done on your computer, you do not even need to be connected to the Internet. All you need is a browser and a text editor, such as the Notepad. To roll your own image map, follow these steps:

1. *Obtain an image.* In Chapter 6, you learned how to capture and convert images into a format suitable for displaying on a Web page. Following that process, obtain an image on which you would like to create two or three rectangular triggers. Save the image in your *website* folder. Remember that the image must have a *.gif*, *.jpg*, or *.png* filename extension.

2. *Plot the coordinates.* Using your graphics editor, figure out the x,y coordinates of the upper-left and lower-right corners of each trigger you want to make. Most graphics editors will tell you the x,y coordinates as you mouse over the image. Paint Shop Pro, for example, displays the coordinates in the lower-left corner of the status bar as you mouse over the image. Remember that the upper-left corner of the image is coordinate 0,0.

3. *Code the map.* Use the Notepad to start a new file, type the following HTML code, and save the file in your *website* folder. Give the file an *.html* filename extension, such as **MyFirstImageMap.html**. When you type this code, substitute your actual coordinates and links for the placeholder values that are italicized in this code sample, which links to your résumé and home page by default:

```
<html>
<head>
  <title>My First Image Map</title>
</head>
<body>
<map name="MyFirstMap">
<area shape="Rect" coords="0,0,50,50" href="resume.html">
<area shape="Rect" coords="0,51,99,99" href="index.html">
</map>
</body>
</html>
```

4. *Use the map.* After you create the HTML code for your image map, you can use it on any image on your Web page. In this example, you apply it to the image you selected in step 1. Click to position your cursor immediately prior to the </body> tag that ends the page you created in the previous step. Type the following code, replacing the italicized placeholder values with your actual image filename, width, and height attributes:

```
<img src="MyImage.jpg" border=0 usemap="#MyFirstMap" width="100" height="100">
```

5. *Test the map.* Save the file and open it with your browser. Mouse over the image and see if the cursor changes shape when you mouse over the hot spots. Click to try those links. If there are any problems, use the Notepad to make the necessary changes in your HTML, save the file again, and test it in your browser. Click your browser's Refresh button to make it read the new version of the file. Repeat this step until you get the image map working, and then congratulate yourself, because image maps enable you to create graphically rich user interfaces onscreen.

Creating HTML Frames

So far in this tutorial, you have created Web pages that appear individually when viewed with a browser onscreen. Because this is the simplest way to display a Web page, most Web sites present pages one at a time. In more complex designs, however, it is possible to divide the browser's display surface into multiple windows called *frames*. Each **frame** can display a different part of the same page or a totally different page. Through a technique called **frame targeting**, you can make clicks in one frame determine what gets displayed in another. Clicks on menu items in a left sidebar frame, for example, can make the chosen content appear in a main content frame.

This tutorial begins by having you create a simple frameset that will display different views of your Web page résumé. By trying out different layouts, you gain experience with the parameters you can use to split the screen into any frame design you can imagine. In practice, however, the most common use of frames is to create a narrow sidebar frame in which users can select menu items to display the desired document in a main content frame that appears alongside the menu. This tutorial concludes, therefore, by providing you with a step-by-step template you can use to set up this kind of sidebar frameset.

What Is a Frameset?

A **frameset** is an HTML Web page element that splits the browser window into two or more subdocuments called frames. You create a frameset with the **<frameset>** start and **</frameset>** stop tags. The start tag has `row` and `column` attributes that determine the layout. You specify the dimensions by pixels or percentages. Imagine that you want to create a frameset that splits the browser window into two equal frames. Follow these steps:

1. Pull down the Notepad's File menu and choose New to create a new file. Type the following code, which creates the frameset. In this code, you will notice that the `<body>` start and `</body>` stop tags are surrounded by the `<noframes>` start and `</noframes>` stop tags. That is because the bodies of the frames will be in the HTML source documents that flow into the frames. Only users who do not have frames will see this particular body, which tells the users to update their browser:

```
<html>
<head>
<title>Frameset Example</title>
</head>
<frameset rows="50%,50%">
  <frame src="resume.html">
  <frame src="resume.html">
<noframes>
<body>
<p>
This page uses frames. Either update your browser, or
<a href="resume.html">view this without frames</a>.
</p>
</body>
</noframes>
</frameset>
</html>
```

2. Save the file in your *website* folder under the name *frameset.html*. Then open this file with your browser to see how it appears onscreen. If you typed the frameset code correctly, you will see that the browser divides the screen into the two frames created by your `<frameset>` tag. If you do not see these frames, go back to the previous step and correct any typographical errors in your code. As you work to troubleshoot any problems, remember to click the browser's Refresh button to make sure you are viewing the latest version of the file.

Figure 7-9 shows that the browser obeys your frameset tag by dividing the window into two equal frames. In the next part of this tutorial, you learn how to create other frame layouts. Read on.

Creating Frameset Layouts

With framesets, you can create any number of frames with any onscreen layout you can imagine. Learning how to do this is fun. That is why the following examples are designed for you to learn by doing. In each example, the `<frameset>` code appears first, followed by an illustration that diagrams its effect onscreen. If you want to make these effects happen on your own screen, simply modify the *frameset.html* example you created earlier in this chapter. The only code you need to change is the `<frameset>` code. All the rest of the *frameset.html* file remains the same.

Vertical Frames

Vertical frames divide the browser window into side-by-side columns onscreen. You create vertical frames via the `cols` attribute. You can easily modify the *frameset.html* example to display the frames vertically by typing **cols="50%,50%"** in place of the *rows* setting. Figure 7-10 shows that this modification creates two vertical frames that divide the screen into two equal columns.

To reinforce this concept, you should actually try this example via your Notepad and browser instead of just looking at the figure. Use the Notepad to open your *frameset.html* file and modify the frameset code to read as follows:

```
<frameset cols="50%,50%">
 <frame src="resume.html">
 <frame src="resume.html">
</frameset>
```

Save the file and open it with your browser. Click the browser's Refresh button to make sure you are viewing the latest version of the file. Use the scrollbars to view different parts of your résumé simultaneously.

Horizontal Frames

Horizontal frames divide the browser window into rows that appear in order from top to bottom onscreen. You create horizontal frames via the `rows` attribute. You can create as many rows as you

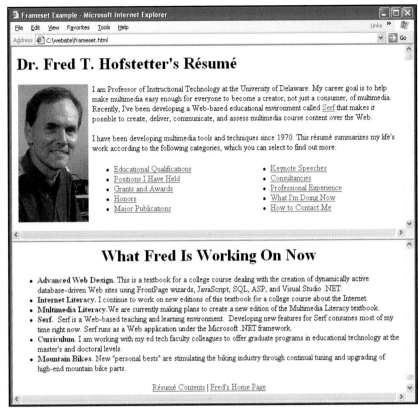

FIGURE 7-9 *The result of creating a frameset with rows="50%,50%", which divides the browser window into two equal horizontal frames. In this example, each frame is displaying the same document, which is a Web page résumé. Notice that each frame has a scrollbar you can use to scroll to different parts of the document.* ■

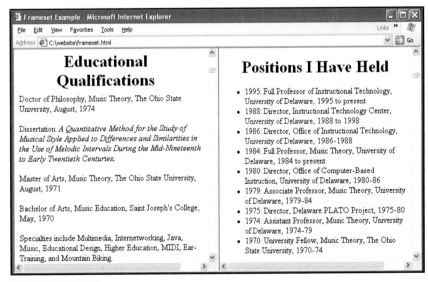

FIGURE 7-10 *You create vertical frames with the cols attribute. In this example, the attribute cols="50%,50%" is dividing the browser's window into two equal vertical frames.* ■

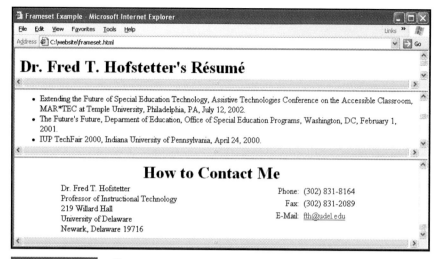

FIGURE 7-11 *You create horizontal frames with the rows attribute. In this example, the attribute rows="20%,30%,50%" creates three frames onscreen.* ■

want, but you should not go overboard. Imagine that you want three rows to be displayed onscreen. You want the top row to take up 20% of the screen, the middle row 30%, and the bottom row 50%. You can accomplish this with a `rows="20%,30%,50%"` attribute. Figure 7-11 shows the frames this creates in the browser window.

To reinforce this concept, you should actually try this example yourself by modifying the frameset section of your *frameset.html* file to read as follows:

```
<frameset rows="20%,30%,50%">
<frame src="resume.html">
<frame src="resume.html">
<frame src="resume.html">
</frameset>
```

Frameset Grids

A frameset grid is a layout in which there are both vertical and horizontal frames onscreen. You create a frameset grid by using both the `rows` and `cols` attributes in a frameset tag. Figure 7-12 shows an example that divides the screen into a grid of four frames. Here is the frameset code that created this example:

```
<frameset rows="50%,50%" cols="50%,50%">
<frame src="resume.html">
<frame src="resume.html">
<frame src="resume.html">
<frame src="resume.html">
</frameset>
```

Nested Framesets

As you just observed, creating a frameset that has both `rows` and `cols` attributes creates a grid of symmetrical frames onscreen. To divide one of the rows or columns, you must divide them all. In practice, you do not normally want all the frames to be divided. Instead, you would normally want to divide just one frame into subframes. To divide a single frame into subframes, you create a frameset inside that frame. A frameset that you create inside of another frame is called a **nested frameset**.

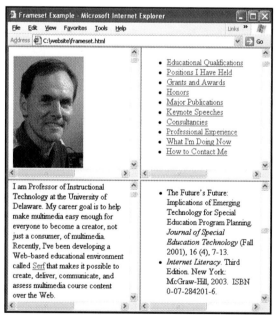

FIGURE 7-12 *You create a grid of both horizontal and vertical frames by using both the rows and cols attributes. In this example, the rows="50%,50%" and cols="50%,50%" attributes are creating a grid of four equal frames onscreen. You need to be careful, however, when creating frameset grids. Too many frames can make your page look like frames gone wild.* ■

The following code creates a nested frameset. As illustrated in Figure 7-13, this code begins by creating a frameset that uses rows="20%,80%" to divide the screen into two horizontal frames. Then a nested frameset uses cols="35%,65%" to divide the larger of these two frames into two vertical frames:

The outer frameset creates two horizontal frames that occupy 20% and 80% of the window.

```
<frameset rows="20%,80%">
<frame src="resume.html">
  <frameset cols="35%,65%">
    <frame src="resume.html">
    <frame src="resume.html">
  </frameset>
</frameset>
```

The inner frameset creates two vertical frames that occupy 35% and 65% of the window.

Borderless Frames

Now that you know how to create a frameset with any layout that you can imagine, you may be wondering how to turn off the frame borders for situations in which you would like a seamless transition between the frames. In Figure 7-13, for example, the narrow frame at the top may be intended to hold a constant page heading or graphical banner for which the scrollbars have no meaning and may interfere with the visual effect you are trying

Inside the second row of the outer frameset, a nested frameset created these two columns.

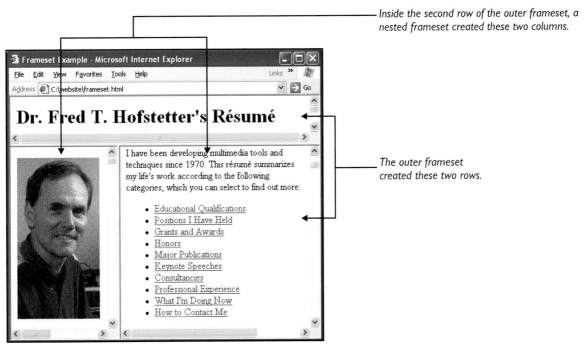

The outer frameset created these two rows.

FIGURE 7-13 *A nested frameset is one that you create inside of another frameset. In this example, an outer frameset creates two rows onscreen that occupy 20% and 80% of the browser's window, respectively. Inside the 80% row, a nested frameset creates two columns that occupy 35% and 65% of the frame. By nesting framesets, you can create any layout you can imagine. In the next part of this tutorial, you learn how to turn the borders invisible for situations in which you do not want the frame's outline to show.* ∎

to achieve onscreen. To remove the border around a frameset, you add the following attributes to the frameset tag:

```
frameborder="no" border="0" framespacing="0"
```

To remove the scrollbar from a frame, you add the following attribute to its frame tag:

```
scrolling="no"
```

To prevent users from being able to resize a frame, you add the *noresize* attribute to the frame tag. To see all of these settings in action, you can modify your *frameset.html* code to remove the border and the scrollbar from the top row as follows:

```
<frameset rows="20%,80%" frameborder="no" border="0" framespacing="0">
<frame src="resume.html" scrolling="no" noresize>
  <frameset cols="35%,65%">
   <frame src="resume.html">
   <frame src="resume.html">
  </frameset>
</frameset>
```

Fixed-Size Frames

As you have undoubtedly observed by now, when you use percentages to set the dimensions in the row and column attributes of a frame tag, the frame automatically adjusts in size to maintain those percentages as the user resizes the browser window. Sometimes you may want to fix the size of a frame to a certain pixel width or height instead of letting the frame resize. If you are creating a left sidebar, for example, you may want to set it to a fixed pixel size and let the main content frame fill the rest of the screen.

Suppose you want a sidebar frame that has 175 pixels and a main content frame that occupies the rest of the browser window. The following frameset would create such a layout. Notice that the wildcard character * tells the browser to create a frame consisting of all the window space that remains after creating the 175 pixel sidebar:

Replace 175 by the actual width you want the first column to have.   *The wildcard character * causes the other column to occupy the remaining screen space.*

```
<frameset cols="175,*">
        <frame src="leftSidebar.html">
        <frame src="mainContent.html">
</frameset>
```

Wildcard Sized Frames

You can get pretty creative with the * wildcard character. The following frameset, for example, would create a layout that has three columns. The first column has a fixed width of 175 pixels. The third column occupies

10% of the window. The * wildcard character makes the middle column occupy the rest of the window:

An integer creates a fixed pixel width. → A percentage creates a width relative to the window size. →

```
<frameset cols="175,*,10%">
        <frame src="leftSidebar.html">
        <frame src="mainContent.html">
        <frame src="rightSidebar.html">
</frameset>
```

You can use the * wildcard character to size frames proportionally. The following frameset, for example, creates a layout in which the second column is three times as wide as each of the first and third columns:

```
<frameset cols="*,3*,*">    ←——————  3* causes the middle frame
        <frame src="leftSidebar.html">       to be three times as wide as
        <frame src="mainContent.html">        the single * in the first and
        <frame src="rightSidebar.html">              third frames.
</frameset>
```

Frame Targeting

One of the most useful applications of a frameset is to establish a *targeting* relationship such that a mouse click in one frame can alter the display of a document in another frame. This is how you make hyperlinks in a left sidebar frame, for example, display their documents in the targeted main frame. Establishing such a targeting relationship is a two-step process. First, in the frameset, you use the `name` attribute to give the targeted frame a name. Second, in the document containing the hyperlinks, you use the `target` attribute to make the links come up in the targeted frame.

Naming the targeted frame in a frameset is the easy part. You do that simply by adding a `name` attribute to the targeted frame. Here is an example that names the targeted frame "mainContent" so items clicked in the left sidebar can target the main content frame:

```
<frameset cols="20%,80%">
 <frame src="sidebar.html">
 <frame src="resume.html" name="mainContent">
</frameset>
```

After you name the frame that the hyperlinks will target, you use the *target* tag to make the hyperlinks aim at the targeted frame. Here is an example, which you would put on the sidebar page:

```
<a href="resume.html#education" target="mainContent">
Educational Qualifications</a>
```

When clicked, such a hyperlink will bring up the educational qualifications section of your résumé in the mainContent frame, if it exists. If the mainContent frame does not exist, the browser will create a new window named "mainContent" to contain this content.

Using the Base Tag

You can avoid typing the `target` attribute in each hyperlink if you use the **`<base>`** tag to specify the default target of the sidebar links. The `<base>` tag goes into the `<head>` section of the document containing the hyperlinks. The format is:

```
<base target="your_target">
```

Replace *your_target* with the name of the targeted frame. By typing this single command into the `<head>` of the document, you make every hyperlink in the document inherit this target by default. To make every hyperlink in the document target by default the mainContent frame, for example, you would type the following tag:

```
<base target="mainContent">
```

You can override this default by hard-coding a different target on any hyperlink that you want pointing somewhere else.

The `<base>` tag also has a `URL` attribute in which you can specify the HTTP address of the targeted document. To make Santa Claus's résumé become the base document for the hyperlinks, for example, you could make the `<base>` tag read as follows:

```
<base url="http://www.northpole.com/santa/resume.html" target="mainContent">
```

In an anchor tag in that same document, this would make `href="#education"` point to http://www.northpole.com/santa/resume.html#education.

Try This!

Creating a Sidebar Frameset for Your Résumé

The best way to understand the concept of frame targeting is to work through an example. The *resume.html* file you created in the previous chapter provides an excellent subject, because your résumé contains a bulleted table of contents. Imagine using a frameset that divides your résumé into two vertical frames. On the left is a narrow sidebar consisting of your résumé's table of contents. On the right of the sidebar is a main content frame that displays the part of your résumé the user selects in the sidebar menu. The advantage of this two-sided approach is that the menu always remains onscreen in the sidebar. This enables users to select different parts of your résumé more quickly than when a sidebar is not present. To create a sidebar frameset for your résumé, follow these steps:

1. Pull down the Notepad's File menu and choose New to create a new file. Into this new file, type the code that is listed in Figure 7-14, and save it in your *website* folder as *sidebarframeset.html*. To save time, you can download this code by following this book's Web site link to Sidebar Frameset.

2. Pull down the Notepad's File menu and choose New to create a new file. Into this new file, type the code listed in Figure 7-15. The body of this file consists of the bulleted table of contents from my résumé. As instructed by the figure's callout, modify these items to fit your own résumé's contents. Then save the file in your *website* folder as *sidebar.html*.

Try This!
continued

This base tag makes the links in this file target the frame named mainContent.

The photo is optional. If you have a photo sized to fit inside the sidebar, use an `<img>` tag to display the image here.

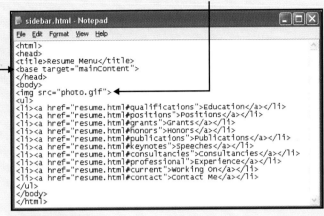

```
sidebarframeset.html - Notepad
File  Edit  Format  View  Help
<html>
<head>
<title>Sidebar Frameset</title>
</head>
<frameset cols="175,*">
  <frame src="sidebar.html" target="mainContent">
  <frame src="resume.html" name="mainContent">
<noframes>
  <body>
This page uses frames. Either update your browser, or
<a href="resume.html">view this without frames</a>.
  </body>
</noframes>
</frameset>
</html>
```

```
sidebar.html - Notepad
File  Edit  Format  View  Help
<html>
<head>
<title>Resume Menu</title>
<base target="mainContent">
</head>
<body>
<img src="photo.gif">
<ul>
<li><a href="resume.html#qualifications">Education</a></li>
<li><a href="resume.html#positions">Positions</a></li>
<li><a href="resume.html#grants">Grants</a></li>
<li><a href="resume.html#honors">Honors</a></li>
<li><a href="resume.html#publications">Publications</a></li>
<li><a href="resume.html#keynotes">Speeches</a></li>
<li><a href="resume.html#consultancies">Consultancies</a></li>
<li><a href="resume.html#professional">Experience</a></li>
<li><a href="resume.html#current">Working On</a></li>
<li><a href="resume.html#contact">Contact Me</a></li>
</ul>
</body>
</html>
```

FIGURE 7-14 *Type this code to create the sidebar frameset used in the Try This! exercise. The target= "mainContent" parameter makes the links clicked in the sidebar come up in the main content frame. Notice that the <noframes> section of this code provides users with an option to view the main content without frames. You can download this code by following this book's Web site link to Sidebar Frameset.* ■

FIGURE 7-15 *This is the sidebar.html file, into which you type the links your Web page résumé's Table of Contents comprises. The links in this example are from my résumé. You need to replace these with the links you decided to put into your own Web page résumé.* ■

3. Use your browser to open the *sidebarframeset.html* file. As illustrated in Figure 7-16, you should see a frameset in which your *sidebar.html* file appears in the left frame and your *resume.html* file appears to its right. If this is not what you see onscreen, go back to step 1 and follow these instructions more carefully to troubleshoot any problems.

4. To test the links in the sidebar, click each item in the left frame to see if it brings up the corresponding content in the main content frame on the right. If any of the links fail, use the Notepad to troubleshoot the problem by correcting the errant anchor tag in the *sidebar.html* file. If all of the links are failing, make sure you typed the `<base>` tag correctly in the `<head>` section of the *sidebar.html* file, as illustrated in Figure 7-15.

FIGURE 7-16 *When you open the sidebarframeset.html file with a browser, you get a frameset consisting of two frames. On the left, a sidebar displays a bulleted list of hyperlinks. When the user clicks a hyperlink, the requested information appears in the main content frame on the right. In this example, the user clicked the Working On link to display what I am working on now.* ■

5. When you get this working, congratulate yourself heartily, because you have created a working frameset you can use as a model whenever you need to create a sidebar frame.

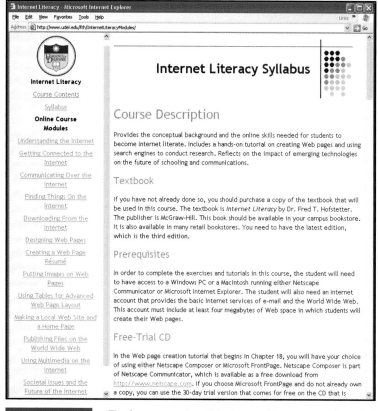

FIGURE 7-17 The frameset version of the Internet Literacy course has a left sidebar frame that lets users click to bring up modules in the main content frame. Compare this to the version without frames in Figure 7-18. To try the frameset online, go to www.udel.edu/fth/InternetLiteracyModules. ∎

When Should You Use or Not Use a Frameset?

I am not a huge fan of framesets. Although frames provide an easy way to create sidebars, multiple windows can be confusing, especially for users with special needs. For this reason, I use framesets only when required to do so. In such cases, I design the content in such a way that users who do not want frames can navigate without them. Consider, for example, the frameset illustrated in Figure 7-17. This is a frameset version of my online course on Internet Literacy. This online course is published by PBS, which wanted a frameset version that could snap in to frames-based instructional management systems. I made PBS happy by creating the frameset version. At the same time, I designed the content in such a way that users who do not want frames can navigate without them. Figure 7-18 shows how the non-frames version provides navigation options that enable the user to move forward or backward and drill down or up through the course content without the aid of frames.

Still, there are applications in which framesets are cool. I like the frameset that PowerPoint creates when you choose the option to save a PowerPoint show as a Web page. The HTML Translator section of Chapter 5, for example, illustrates the PowerPoint frameset in Figure 5-3. There is no quicker way to create a frameset so rich in hypermedia and navigational functions.

Publishing a Web Site via FTP

To publish a file on the World Wide Web means to transfer the file into a folder on a Web server so other people around the world can access the file with a Web browser. Unless your computer happens to be a Web server where you could save the files directly, you need a way to transfer your files to the Web. This tutorial provides you with the knowledge and the tools needed to transfer files from your computer to a World Wide Web file server.

As you work through this tutorial, you publish your home page and your résumé on the Web. Then you can provide access to your Web pages by telling people what URL to go to. For example, suppose your Web server is www.northpole.com and your Web site is located on that server in a Web account named santa. Assume further that the default filename on your server is *index.html*. After you complete the exercises in this chapter, the URL of your home page will be http://www.northpole.com/~santa/index.html.

Because *index.html* is the default filename, you will be able to shorten the URL and tell users to go to http://www.northpole.com/~santa to see your home page.

If *index.html* is not the default filename on your Web server, you use your Web server's default filename instead. If you do not know what the default filename is on your Web server, you should check the guidelines at your Web hosting site or contact your server administrator to find out. If your Web server does not have a default filename, you can give your home page an intuitive name such as *home.html*.

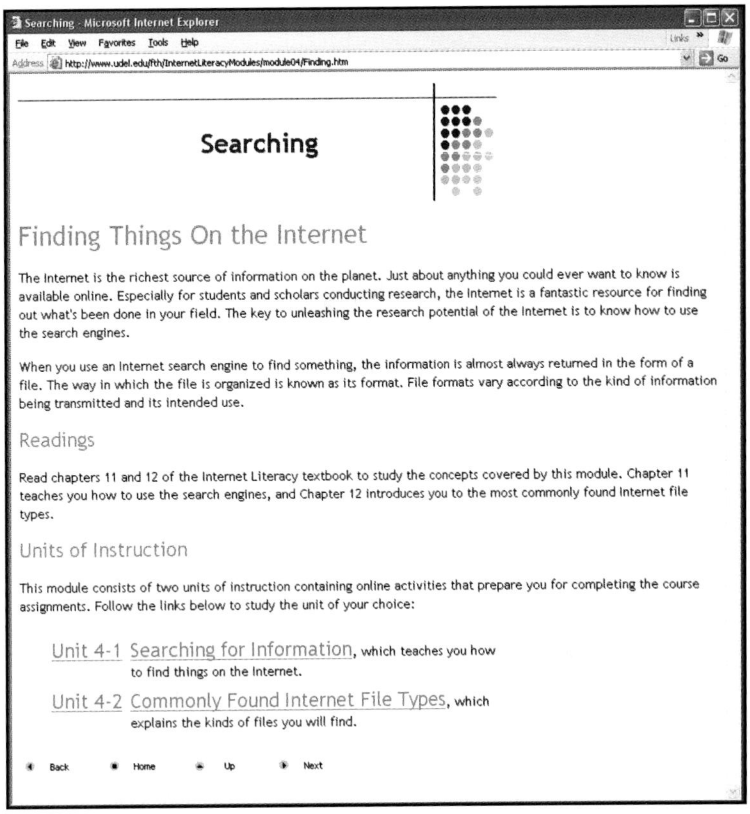

Getting Your Web Space

Before you can publish a file on the World Wide Web, you need to have some file space on the Web to hold your published files. There are three places where you can get file space on the Web. First, your ISP account probably includes a certain allotment of Web space. If you are not sure, check with your ISP. While you are checking, you might want to inquire as to what the limit is and how much it costs if you want to get more space. Second, your school or workplace may have a Web server on which you can obtain Web space. Check with your supervisor or IT staff to find out the policies for obtaining and using Web space at your school or workplace. Third, there are sites on the Web where you can get free Web space in return for registering your name at those sites. They give you the free space to keep you coming back to their sites, where you will see commercial advertising that pays for the free space. The free space may also cause ads to be placed on your Web pages, although some sites offer free Web space without putting ads on your Web pages.

Searching Google or Yahoo for the keywords "free FTP Web space" brings up many sites where you can get free FTP Web space.

Your Web Space Address

To transfer files to the Web, you need to know the name of your Web server and the path to your file space on that server. If you are using free Web space, you will be given the name of the server and the path to your file space when you register and get your free Web space. Make a note of this information, because it is very important. If you are using Web space from an ISP and you do not know the address of your Web space, contact your ISP and ask the question, "What is the FTP address of my Web space?" If Santa Claus had an AOL account named Santa, for example, and he asked AOL for the FTP address of his Web space, the answer would be something like **ftp://ftp.aol.com/santa**.

FIGURE 7-18 *The single-page version of the Internet Literacy course lets users navigate the main content minus the frameset illustrated in Figure 7-17. To surf the content without the frameset, go to www.udel.edu/fth/InternetLiteracyModules/mainContent.html.* ■

Choosing an FTP Client

Searching Google or Yahoo for the keywords "free ftp client" brings up many FTP clients that you can use to publish a Web. It is important for you to choose a client that has a good track record. This chapter's Web publishing tutorial teaches you the Core FTP Lite client that many students use because it is free for educational purposes and is easy to use. The Core FTP company also makes a professional edition called Core FTP Pro that is for commercial purposes. When this book went to press, a single-user Pro license cost $29.95. The following tutorial uses the free version called Core FTP Lite.

Installing the FTP Software

To download and install the free-trial version of the Core FTP Lite software, follow these steps:

1. Click the link at this book's Web site to download Core FTP Lite.

2. When the download page appears, click the link to download the free version of Core FTP Lite. When your browser asks what folder you want to download the file into, choose the folder you want to put it in. Normally, you use your *temp* folder.

3. When the file has finished downloading, click your computer's Start button, choose Run, and use the Run dialog's Browse control to locate the Core FTP Lite installation program. You will find this program in the folder where you saved the downloaded file in the previous step. Click the Run dialog's OK button to run the Core FTP Lite installation program.

4. The installation program guides you through the setup; follow the onscreen instructions.

How to Configure a New FTP Connection

The first time you use the Core FTP Lite program, you need to configure a new FTP connection. This is the connection through which the program will FTP the files that you want to publish to your Web site. To create a new FTP connection, follow these steps:

1. Double-click the Core FTP Lite icon on your Windows desktop to get Core FTP Lite running. You can also start Core FTP Lite by clicking the Windows Start button and choosing Programs | Core FTP | Core FTP.

2. The first time you run Core FTP Lite, it will ask if you want Core FTP to become your computer's default FTP program. I answered Yes to make Core FTP become the default FTP handler on my computer.

3. When the Core FTP window opens, it will display the Site Manager window, which you use to create a new FTP connection. Figure 7-19 shows the settings in the Site Manager window.

4. In the Site Name field, type the name of your site. When you make up this name, enter information that clearly identifies your site. Santa Claus, for example, could call his site Santa's North Pole Web Site.

5. In the Host/IP/URL field, type the address of your FTP server, such as ftp.northpole.com.

6. If the Anonymous box is checked, uncheck it.

7. In the User Name field, type the user ID by which you are known on your Web server; this will probably be the first part of your e-mail address, up to but not including the @ sign.

8. In the Password field, type your password. If you are the only person using this computer, you can let Core FTP remember your password. If other people use this computer, however, you should check the box titled *Don't save password*. When this box is checked, you have to type your password each time you log on to your FTP site.

9. Leave the rest of the settings in the Site Manager window alone for now. You learn about the advanced settings in Chapter 13, which covers Internet security.

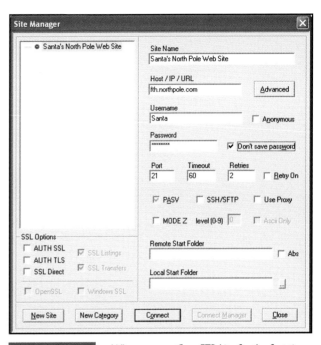

FIGURE 7-19 *When you run Core FTP Lite for the first time, you use the Site Manager to configure your FTP connection. Illustrated here are the settings Santa Claus entered to create his FTP connection.* ∎

How to FTP Files to the Web

Figure 7-20 shows that the Core FTP Lite program has graphical controls that make it easy to FTP a file to your Web site. For example, suppose you want to FTP your home page and your résumé from your computer to your World Wide Web account. Follow these steps:

1. If you do not already have Core FTP Lite running, click the Windows Start button and choose Programs | Core FTP | Core FTP. When the Site Manager window appears, select the site to which you want to connect. Santa Claus, for example, would choose Santa's North Pole Web Site.

During the transfer, status information displays here.

Click here to transfer a file from your PC to your Web site.

Click here to transfer a file from your Web site to your PC.

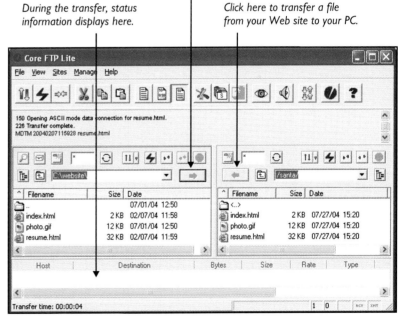

FIGURE 7-20 *The Core FTP Lite program displays folder listings for your local computer and the remote site.* ∎

2. At the bottom of the Site Manager window, click the Connect button. Wait a few seconds while Core FTP makes the connection.

3. The left side of the Core FTP window is the My Computer side, and the right side is the remote computer side. On the left side of the Core FTP window, browse to the folder in which the file you want to transfer resides; in this example, browse to the *website* folder on your hard drive. See Figure 7-20.

4. On the right side of the Core FTP window, browse to the folder in which you want to transfer the files; in this example, that will be the main folder of your World Wide Web account.

5. To transfer your résumé, click once on *resume.html* on the left side of the Core FTP window; then click the → button to transfer the file to the Web. After the transfer completes, you will see your *resume.html* file listed on the right side of the Core FTP window in your World Wide Web folder.

6. To transfer your home page, click once on *index.html* on the left side of the Core FTP window; then click the → button to transfer the file to the Web. After the transfer completes, you will see your *index.html* file listed on the right site side of the Core FTP window in your World Wide Web folder.

7. To transfer your images, click once on the name of an image on the left side of the Core FTP window; then click the → button to transfer the file to the Web. After the transfer completes, you will see your image file listed on the right side of the Core FTP window in your World Wide Web folder.

8. Repeat step 7 for each image you want to publish on the Web. If you click one file and then SHIFT-click another file, you can select multiple files to transfer all at once. To add a single file to a group of selected files, hold down the CTRL key and click the filename once. You can also transfer files by clicking and dragging them from the My Computer side to the remote-site side of the Core FTP window.

How to Delete and Rename Files at a Web Site

Your FTP software provides a way to delete files you no longer want on the Web. It also lets you rename files. To delete and rename files at a Web site, follow these steps:

1. If you do not already have Core FTP Lite running, click the Windows Start button and choose Programs | Core FTP | Core FTP. In the Site Manager window, select the site to which you want to connect and click the Connect button.

2. Click once on the name of the file you want to delete or rename on the remote-site side of the Core FTP window in your World Wide Web site.

3. To delete the file, click the Delete button. Core FTP will ask if you really want to delete it. Click the Yes button if you really want to.

4. To rename the file, click it once to select the name you want to change. Click the name a second time to enter text-editing mode. Type the new filename, or modify the existing name, and then press ENTER.

Coping with Case-Sensitive File Servers

Remember that many World Wide Web servers are case sensitive. If your Web server is case sensitive, you need to make sure that the filenames you FTP to the server match the case you gave them in your HTML source code. For example, the UNIX operating system is case sensitive. On a UNIX-based server, if an image is named *PORTRAIT.GIF* and your HTML file attempts to access it as *portrait.gif*, you will get a "File Not Found" error. Folder names are also case sensitive; make sure the case of your folders on the Web matches the case you gave them in your HTML source code.

To cope with case-sensitive file servers, always keep the names of your files and folders in all uppercase or all lowercase. Most people use all lowercase, which is what I recommend you do. You should also avoid typing spaces or special symbols in your filenames and folder names.

Correcting Problems and Updating Published Web Pages

Sometimes you will need to correct a problem or update information on a Web page that you have published to your Web site. A link might have gone out of date, for example, and you need to update it. Maybe you have received an award, and you want to put it on your résumé page. The way to correct a problem or update information on a published Web page is to open the page with your text editor, correct the problem, save the page, and republish it to your Web site.

After you republish the page, be sure to test it with your browser to make sure the changes work correctly. Because your browser will have cached the previous version of the file, you need to click your browser's Reload or Refresh button to make your browser read the new version of the file. To make your browser refresh everything, including the graphics as well as the text, hold down the SHIFT key while you click the browser's Reload or Refresh button.

Relative vs. Absolute Links

Links on the Web can be relative or absolute. A relative link means that a file has been specified without its complete URL. The browser will look for the file in folders related to the current Web page's folder; hence the term *relative*. An absolute link means that the complete URL has been specified.

Suppose Santa Claus has a folder at his Web site called *wishlist*. In the *wishlist* folder is a file called *danny.html* that contains the list of presents Danny wants for Christmas. On Santa's home page, Santa can link to Danny's wish list either as a relative link or as an absolute link. The relative link would be wishlist/danny.html. The absolute link would be http://www.northpole.com/~santa/wishlist/danny.html.

Because relative links make it easy to work with a Web site on your computer's hard drive, Web creation tools such as Netscape Composer, Microsoft FrontPage, and Dreamweaver use relative links when you create links to files relative to the page you are creating. In addition to making it easy to publish the site from your PC to the Web, relative links make it easier to move the site from one Web space to another, should you ever decide to move the site. For the relative links to work when you move or transfer the files to the Web, you must maintain a good directory structure on your PC and at your Web site.

Maintaining a Good Directory Structure

You need to be careful how you create folders and subfolders when you make a local web that you plan to mount on the World Wide Web. Because the links you make to local files are made relative to those files, the directory structure of the local web must be exactly the same as you intend to have out on the World Wide Web. Otherwise, the links will fail when you transfer your local web to the World Wide Web.

Suppose you have lots of HTML files, pictures, sounds, and movies that you plan to mount on the World Wide Web. You should keep them organized in a neat directory structure like the one illustrated in Figure 7-21.

If your files are scattered across multiple folders and multiple drives on your PC, it will be time consuming and tedious to re-create that same directory structure on your World Wide Web server. Troubleshooting problems that occur on Web sites that are not well organized is also difficult. One of the most common causes of links not working, for example, is when you move a file into a different folder after you have already created a Web page that links to it. You can avoid this kind of problem by adopting a good directory structure and adhering to it.

How to Create New Folders on the Web

As the number of files at your Web site increases, you may choose to create folders to help keep your site organized. For example, if you create a series of Web pages related to your work, you might create a folder called *work* to keep them in. The directory structure you create on the Web must mirror the structure of the *website* folder on your PC. If you create a *work* folder at your Web site, then you must also create a *work* subfolder in the *website* folder on your PC. To create a folder at your Web site, follow these steps:

1. If you do not already have Core FTP Lite running, click the Windows Start button and choose Programs | Core FTP | Core FTP. In the Site Manager window, select the site to which you want to connect and click the Connect button.

2. On the remote-site side of the Core FTP window, make sure your current directory is the one in which you want to create a new folder. If it's not, double-click on a directory name to select it, or click the Up Directory button to move back a level of directory structure.

FIGURE 7-21 *Maintaining a good directory structure is important in managing the files at a Web site. Because the links you make to local files are made relative to those files, the directory structure of the local web must be exactly the same as you intend to have out on the World Wide Web. If you keep the files in subfolders of the local web folder you plan to publish, relative links to those files will work fine out on the World Wide Web.* ■

3. Click the Make Directory button to open the Make Directory dialog.

4. Enter the name of the folder you want to create and click OK.

5. Wait for a second or two while the new folder gets created. When Core FTP refreshes the directory listing, the new folder will appear in it.

6. If you want to enter the new folder, double-click its icon.

n o t e *When you name the folder, avoid special characters and spaces. Instead of a space, you can type a dash or an underscore to represent the space.*

Setting the File Permission Attributes

After you FTP your files to the Web, if people are not able to access your files in the manner you want, you may need to set the **file permission attributes,** which are settings that determine who is allowed to read and execute your files. You will probably want to set these attributes to let anyone in the world read and execute your files but allow only you to modify or delete them. Core FTP makes it easy to change the permission attributes. To change the permission attributes of a file with Core FTP, follow these steps:

1. If you do not already have Core FTP Lite running, click the Windows Start button and choose Programs | Core FTP | Core FTP. In the Site Manager window, select the site to which you want to connect and click the Connect button.

2. Right-click the file or folder whose attributes you want to change.

3. When the menu pops up, choose Properties.

4. The File Properties dialog appears as illustrated in Figure 7-22.

5. Check the boxes to let Owner, Group, and Other read your files, but allow only the Owner to write them. (The owner is you!)

6. Click OK to close the dialog and make the changes take effect.

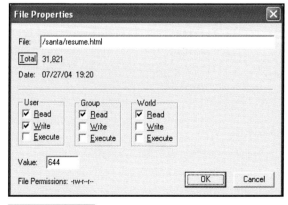

FIGURE 7-22 *The Core FTP Properties dialog lets you change the file permissions on UNIX hosts.* ■

Chapter 7 Review

Chapter Summary

After reading this chapter and completing the step-by-step tutorials and Try This! exercises, you should understand the following facts about the Internet:

Creating HTML Forms

- A form is an HTML Web page element that prompts the user to fill in one or more blanks and/or select items from a menu of possible choices, after which the user clicks a button to submit the filled-out form.

- The `<form>` start and `</form>` stop tags mark the beginning and ending of an HTML form. Between these tags go the controls that prompt the user for specific information, along with any onscreen instructions you may wish to provide.

- A prompt is an onscreen instruction that asks the user to provide some information, either by typing a response into a text field or by choosing something from a selection of possible choices.

- In HTML, you use the `<input>` tag to create the form controls that receive input from the user. The `<input>` tag has a `type` attribute that specifies the kind of control you want.

- To create a text field, you set the `<input>` tag's type to *text*. The `<input>` tag also has a `name` attribute that you use to specify the name of the control and a `size` attribute that specifies how many characters wide the field will be onscreen. There is also a `maxlength` attribute that specifies the maximum number of characters the user can type.

- A radio button is a form control that displays a small round button with which the user can select one, but not more than one, item from a list of possible choices. You create a radio button by setting an `<input>` tag's `type` attribute to `radio`. You use the `name` attribute to assign a name to the radio button group, which includes any other radio button of the same name within the form.

- To create a check box, you make an `<input>` tag of type check box.

- To create a selection menu, you use the `<select>` start and `</select>` stop tags. Between these tags, you use the `<option>` tag to specify the menu options from which the user can make a selection. To permit multiple selections, you add the `multiple` attribute to the select tag.

- To create a text area, you use the `<textarea>` start and `</textarea>` stop tags. To set the width, you use the `cols` attribute, which tells the browser how many characters wide to make the text box. To set the height of the text area, you use the `rows` attribute.

- A password field is a text box that works like a text field except that when the user types the entry, the browser displays asterisks instead of revealing the sensitive information onscreen. You create a password field by creating an `<input>` field that has its `type` attribute set to password.

- You make a Submit button by creating an `<input>` tag that has a `type` attribute set to submit. By default, the value the browser prints inside the button is the same as its type. You can change this value via the `value` attribute.

- You make a Reset button by creating an `<input>` tag that has a `type` attribute equal to `reset`.

- There are two HTTP methods that the `<form>` tag can use to submit the form's data when the user clicks the Submit button: method="get" and method="post". The GET method puts the form data in a query string that gets appended to the URL specified in the form tag's `action` attribute. The POST method sends the form data to the process identified in the form tag's `action` attribute. This process is normally a server-side script that reads and processes the form data, saves appropriate information in a server-side database, and returns an HTML response to the user.

Making a PayPal Buy Now Button

- PayPal uses two special form techniques to power its button. First, PayPal uses hidden fields to identify the business that is selling the product, the name of the product being sold, and the selling price. Second, PayPal substitutes the PayPal button image for the Submit button that normally appears on an HTML form.

- A hidden field is an HTML form control that creates a variable name and a corresponding value that are not displayed onscreen but are posted along with the rest of the form data when the user clicks the button to submit the form. You create a hidden field by setting an <input> tag's type attribute to hidden. In the name and value attributes, you type the variable name and its corresponding value.

- To make a different graphic substitute for the default Submit button in a Web form, you use an image button, an HTML form element you create with an <input> tag of type image. You set the tag's name attribute to submit, which makes the image button post the form data when clicked.

- When clicked, the PayPal Buy Now button posts HTML form data to the PayPal e-commerce server. In addition to containing information about the product being purchased, the form data identifies the business that is making the sale.

- For users who are not programmatically inclined, PayPal has a button factory that generates automatically the HTML to paste onto your page to sell items at your Web site.

Designing HTML Image Maps

- An image map is an invisible layer of triggers placed over an image on the screen. The triggers can be rectangular, circular, or polygonal. When the user clicks inside one of the invisible triggers, the Web browser triggers the object of the link.

- In earlier versions of HTML, using image maps required the use of a CGI call. When the user clicked a trigger in an image map, the browser sent the coordinates of the mouse click to a CGI program on a server, which told the browser what to do in response to the click. In the latest versions of HTML, it is possible to process image maps locally within the document instead of having to call on a CGI program for help in handling the mouse click.

- The <map> and </map> tags demarcate the beginning and ending of the image map. Between them, you see the <area> tags that create the triggers. Inside each area tag is a shape attribute and a coord attribute that specifies the x,y coordinates of the links. These coordinates are pixel addresses inside the image. The top-left corner of an image is always pixel address 0,0 and is called the origin. The other addresses are all relative to the origin. The coord attribute has the syntax *coords=x1,y1,x2,y2*. The top-left corner of the area is x1,y1, and the bottom-right corner is x2,y2.

- Once you have defined an image map with the <map> tag, you use the usemap attribute to apply it to any image on the page. The usemap attribute modifies the <img> tag that puts the image onscreen. The syntax of the usemap attribute is usemap=#*area_name* where *area_name* is the name you gave the image map in the <map> tag's name attribute. When the mouse clicks on one of the areas in the image map, the user follows the corresponding link.

- Many Web page creation tools have image map assistants built in that can help you create image maps. Or you can use a tool such as Paint Shop Pro to figure out pixel locations.

- Because client-side image maps execute in the browser, you can create an image map without needing access to a CGI server. With all of the processing done on your computer, you do not even need to be connected to the Internet. All you need is a browser and a text editor, such as the Notepad.

Creating HTML Frames

- A frameset is an HTML Web page element that splits the browser window into two or more subdocuments called frames. You create a frameset with the <frameset> start and </frameset> stop tags. The start tag has row and column attributes that determine the layout.

- Vertical frames divide the browser window into side-by-side columns onscreen. You create vertical frames via the cols attribute of the <frameset> tag.

- Horizontal frames divide the browser window into rows that appear in order from top to bottom onscreen. You create horizontal frames via the rows attribute of the <frameset> tag.

- A frameset grid is a layout in which there are both vertical and horizontal frames onscreen. You create a frameset grid by using both the `rows` and `cols` attributes in a frameset tag.

- To divide one of the rows or columns in a frameset grid, you must divide them all. In practice, you do not normally want all the frames to be divided. Instead, you would normally want to divide just one frame into subframes. To divide a single frame into subframes, you create a frameset inside that frame. A frameset that you create inside of another frame is called a nested frameset.

- To remove the border around a frameset, you add the following attributes to the frameset tag:

  `frameborder="no" border="0" framespacing="0"`

- To remove the scrollbar from a frame, you add the following attribute to its frame tag:

  `scrolling="no"`

- To prevent users from being able to resize a frame, you add the `noresize` attribute to the frame tag.

- You can use the * wildcard character to size frames proportionally. The following frameset, for example, creates a layout in which the second column is three times as wide as the first and third columns:

  `<frameset rows="*,3*,*">`

- One of the most useful applications of a frameset is to establish a targeting relationship such that a mouse click in one frame can alter the display of a document in another frame. This is how you make hyperlinks in a left sidebar frame, for example, display their documents in the targeted main frame. Establishing such a targeting relationship is a two-step process. First, in the frameset, you use the `name` attribute to give the targeted frame a name. Second, in the document containing the hyperlinks, you use the `target` attribute to make the links come up in the targeted frame.

- You can save a lot of time typing if you use the `<base>` tag to specify the target of the sidebar links. The `<base>` tag goes into the `<head>` section of the document containing the hyperlinks. The format is this:

  `<base target="your_target">`

Publishing a Web Site via FTP

- The first time you use your FTP software, you will need to configure a new connection for your Web site. The new connection configuration identifies the domain name of your Web server and your user ID on that server.

- In addition to enabling you to publish files to your Web site, the FTP software lets you delete files you no longer want on the Web. It also lets you rename files.

- Many World Wide Web servers are case sensitive. If your Web server is case sensitive, you need to make sure the filenames you FTP to the server match the case you gave them in your HTML source code.

- Links on the Web can be relative or absolute. A relative link means a file has been specified without its complete URL. The browser will look for the file in folders related to the current Web page's folder; hence the term *relative*. An absolute link means that the complete URL has been specified.

- You need to be careful how you create folders and subfolders when you make a local web that you plan to mount on the World Wide Web. Because the links you make to local files are made relative to those files, the directory structure of the local web must be exactly the same as you intend to have out on the World Wide Web. Otherwise, the links will fail when you transfer your local web to the World Wide Web.

- After you FTP your files to the Web, if people are not able to access your files in the manner you want, you may need to set the file permission attributes, which are settings that determine who is allowed to read and execute your files.

Key Terms

check box *(308)*	**hidden field** *(312)*	**POST** method *(308)*
common gateway interface (CGI) *(308)*	**image button** *(313)*	**prompt** *(303)*
	image map *(316)*	**radio button** *(305)*
file permission attributes *(335)*	**<input> tag** *(304)*	**Reset button** *(306)*
form *(302)*	**maxlength attribute** *(304)*	**<select> tag** *(310)*
frame *(319)*	**name attribute** *(304)*	**size attribute** *(304)*
frame targeting *(319)*	**nested frameset** *(322)*	**Submit button** *(306)*
frameset *(319)*	**<option> tag** *(310)*	
GET method *(308)*	**password field** *(311)*	

Key Terms Quiz

1. A(n) _____ is an HTML Web page element that prompts the user to fill in one or more blanks and/or select items from a menu of possible choices, after which the user clicks a button to submit the response.

2. A(n) _____ field is a text box that works like a text field except that when the user types the entry, the browser displays asterisks instead of revealing the sensitive information onscreen.

3. A(n) _____ button is a form control that displays a small round button that enables the user to select one, but not more than one, item from a list of possible choices.

4. A(n) _____ is a form control that displays a small box that the user can check to select one or more items onscreen.

5. The _____ causes an HTML form to put its data in a query string that gets appended to the URL specified in the form tag's `action` attribute.

6. The _____ causes an HTML form to send the form data to the process identified in the form tag's `action` attribute.

7. A(n) _____ field is an HTML form control that creates a variable name and a corresponding value that are not displayed onscreen but are posted along with the rest of the form data when the user clicks the button to submit the form.

8. To make a different graphic substitute for the default Submit button in a Web form, you use a(n) _____, which is an HTML form element you create with an `<input>` tag of type image.

9. A(n) _____ is an invisible layer of triggers placed over an image on the screen. The triggers can be rectangular, circular, or polygonal. When the user clicks inside one of the invisible triggers, the Web browser triggers the object of the link.

10. A(n) _____ is an HTML Web page element that splits the browser window into two or more subdocuments called _____.

Multiple-Choice Quiz

1. A form control that presents the user with a small box that the user can click to turn an option on or off is called a:
   a. Check box
   b. Radio button
   c. Multiple item selection menu
   d. Single item selection menu

2. To create a text field, you set the `<input>` tag's type to:
   a. Check box
   b. Password
   c. Radio
   d. Text

3. Which attribute sets the width of a text area?
   a. `cols`
   b. `height`
   c. `rows`
   d. `width`

4. Which attribute assigns a name to an `<input>` control?
   a. `label`
   b. `name`
   c. `size`
   d. `value`

5. In an `<input type="submit">` tag, which attribute changes the default word *submit* that the browser prints inside the form's Submit button?
   a. `label`
   b. `name`
   c. `size`
   d. `value`

6. Which tag creates a trigger that specifies the x,y coordinates of the links in an image map?
   a. `<area>`
   b. `<coord>`
   c. `<map>`
   d. `<usemap>`

7. Which tag specifies the code that will execute in a frames disabled browser?
   a. `<cancelframes></cancelframes>`
   b. `<framesdisabled></framesdisabled>`
   c. `<noframes></noframes>`
   d. `<noframeset></noframeset>`

8. Which frameset divides the window vertically into two equal halves with no other divisions or subdivisions?
   a. `<frameset rows="50%,50%">`
   b. `<frameset cols="50%,50%">`
   c. `<frameset rows="50%,50%" cols="50%,50%">`
   d. `<frameset rows="50%,*">`

9. Which tag creates a frameset grid?
   a. `<frameset rows="50%,50%">`
   b. `<frameset cols="50%,50%">`
   c. `<frameset rows="50%,50%" cols="50%,50%">`
   d. `<frameset rows="50%,*">`

10. Which frameset tag creates a layout in which the second row is three times as wide as each of the first and third rows?
   a. `<frameset cols="*,3*,*">`
   b. `<frameset rows="*,3*,*">`
   c. `<frameset cols="*,2*,*">`
   d. `<frameset rows="*,2*,*">`

■ Essay Quiz

1. The PayPal form uses an image button to replace an HTML form's default Submit button with PayPal's customized PayPal button, which contains the PayPal branding. Think of a situation in which you could create a custom button to use on forms in your school or workplace Web site. What graphical branding elements would you include in such a button, and what would you want to make happen when the user clicks it?

2. In this chapter, you learned how to make hidden fields containing form data that does not appear onscreen. Can hidden fields be used to contain confidential information that you wouldn't want the user to see? Before you answer this question, pull down your browser's View menu and choose Source to see how users can reveal the source code of any form onscreen.

3. Give an example of a situation in which you could use an image map on your current school or workplace Web site. Describe the graphic that the map would comprise, and explain what would happen when users click the map's hyperlink areas.

4. Figures 7-17 and 7-18 display frameset and frameless versions of an online course, respectively. Visit these live by going to www.udel.edu/fth/InternetLiteracyModules for the frameset and www.udel.edu/fth/InternetLiteracyModules/mainContent.htm for the frameless version. If you have any trouble getting them onscreen, be aware that www.udel.edu is a case-sensitive Web server, so you must type the lowercase and uppercase letters exactly where they appear in these folder names and filenames. After you get the course onscreen, try navigating via the sidebar in the frameset version, and also try clicking the navigational icons at the bottom of each screen in the frameless version. Compare the navigational impression that each version gives you. Then write a brief essay in which you express your personal position on framesets. In what kinds of situations would you want to use frames, and when would you recommend against them?

Lab Projects

• Lab Project 7-1: Person-to-Person Payment Processing

PayPal presents an interesting alternative for a small business that is considering how to power its e-commerce activities. In this chapter, for example, you have learned how to create Web forms that present users with onscreen controls for selecting things and making choices. By using a PayPal button to submit those choices to CGI scripts running on the PayPal server, it would seem as though small businesses could avoid the overhead of paying for more complex e-commerce hosting from an instant storefront provider such as Amazon, Yahoo, eBay, or bCentral. Imagine that your employer has asked you to evaluate these alternatives and recommend whether your small business should use PayPal Buy Now buttons to sell products directly from your Web site. Use your word processor to write a report in which you describe how PayPal works, compare it to the leading instant storefront alternatives, and recommend whether to use PayPal at your site. In creating this recommendation, address the following issues:

- **Functionality**   Earlier in this chapter, Table 7-3 listed the frequently used PayPal Buy Now Button HTML and hyperlink variables. Go to the PayPal site's Merchant Tools tab, and look over the complete list of hyperlink variables that the PayPal Buy Now button supports. Do these variables cover the kinds of options you will need on your company's e-commerce pages?

- **Cost**   Consider the costs involved in adding PayPal Buy Now buttons at your company Web site as compared to paying for an instant storefront solution. Be sure to include all costs in this comparison, such as fixed monthly fees and per-purchase percentages that you must pay for different kinds of payment processing.

- **Time**   Creating your own storefront may take more time than using an Instant Storefront solution. Consider whether you have that kind of time. Also consider whether the PayPal tools, such as the Buy Now Button Factory, can speed the process.

- **Opportunity**   Designing your own e-commerce pages may provide opportunities that you would not have at an instant storefront. Consider the options available at popular instant storefronts such as Amazon, Yahoo, eBay, or bCentral. Do you need features that are not supported by these instant storefronts?

If your instructor has asked you to hand in this assignment, make sure you put your name at the top of your essay; then copy it onto a disk or follow the other instructions you may have been given for submitting this assignment.

• Lab Project 7-2: Creating a Graphical Front End

If you think about what you actually see when you go to a Web site, what appears onscreen is either textual or graphical. Web sites that depend mainly on text, such as keyword search engines, typically have text-based user interfaces. Other sites get more creative and provide you with a visual image to click. You can see an example of a graphical user interface at the Library of Congress Web site at www.loc.gov. Imagine that your employer has asked you to look into the possibility of creating a graphical front end for your school or company Web site. In developing your recommendation, consider these alternatives:

- One way to create a graphical front end is to use an image map. This method is suitable if you have a picture or a graphic that illustrates or contains the objects you want users to click. I dream of creating a virtual tour of Fort McHenry, for example, which is located in Baltimore and chronicles the writing of the Star Spangled Banner. You could snap a wide-angled picture of the fort, put it on a Web page, and use an image map to create triggers on the doors and windows. To look into a window, the user would click it. To enter a room, the user would click its door.

- Another way of creating a graphical front end is to use tables to position individual graphics onscreen where you want them. To link the graphics to their intended targets, you surround each image by anchor tags that use the HREF attribute to specify the hyperlinks. In the previous chapter, Figure 6-22 analyzes the design of a Web page that uses tables to create this kind of layout.

- If your workplace has content that lends itself to the use of image maps, use your word processor to write a brief essay about that. Describe what the images would depict, tell where the triggers would be, and explain what will happen when the user clicks them.

If your instructor has asked you to hand in this assignment, make sure you put your name at the top of your essay; then copy it onto a disk or follow the other instructions you may have been given for submitting this assignment.

chapter

8

Creating Active Web Pages

"Their behavior, like the behavior of anything created by a computer program, is limited only by the programmer's imagination."

—Sherry Turkle,
author of
Second Self: Computers and the Human Spirit

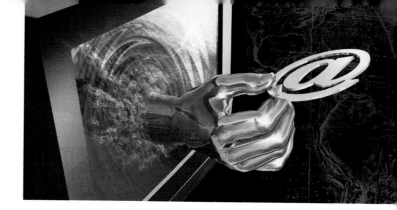

In this chapter, you will learn how to:

- List the primary scripting languages, understand the role of JavaScript, and write a script that uses variables to display dynamic messages onscreen.

- Understand the purpose of the document object model (DOM), describe the most popular JavaScript DOM objects, and use dot notation to access those objects in a script.

- Understand the concept of a cookie and write a script to maintain the user's state by setting and reading the values of cookies as the user interacts with your site.

- List the three kinds of cascading style sheets and explain when it is appropriate to use them on a Web page.

- Define how Dynamic HTML enables you to create animated Web pages by combining HTML with style sheets and scripts.

- Define and understand the purposes of and relationships among XML, XSL, XSLT, XHTML, and SMIL.

W E B developers make a distinction between static and active Web pages. A **static Web page** is a document in which the content is fixed in HTML codes that make the document always read the same when viewed in a browser. On the Internet are billions of static Web pages, which are appropriate for presenting documents whose contents do not change. The Declaration of Independence, for example, is a historical document whose content will never change. It is therefore appropriate for the National Archives to present this document in the static Web page at www.archives.gov/national_archives_experience/declaration_transcript.html.

Static Web pages, however, do not unleash the potential of the Web to provide users with custom screens generated just in time according to the specific needs of the user. Enter the **active Web page**, which uses the browser's window as a display surface through which the user can interact with dynamic objects onscreen. These objects can be powered by either client-side or server-side processes.

This chapter teaches client-side techniques you can use to create active Web pages that run in the browser window without requiring any server-side processing. First, you learn how to use the JavaScript language to write dynamic messages onscreen. Second, you study the document object model (DOM), which defines many kinds of objects you can manipulate onscreen. Third, you learn how cookies enable scripts to remember things from screen to screen. Fourth, you use cascading style sheets (CSS) to stylize the appearance of objects onscreen. Fifth, you use Dynamic HTML to bring these objects to life onscreen. Last, but certainly not least, you learn how to use an XML module called SMIL to caption a video and create other kinds of multimedia effects onscreen.

Everything you learn in this chapter executes on the client side, meaning that you do not need access to a Web server to do these things. Chapter 12 shows how server-side scripts use databases to enable users to interact with data-driven Web applications onscreen.

Introduction to Scripting

Scripting is the act of writing little computer programs that can enhance the appearance and functionality of a Web page. Browsers render Web pages by placing objects onscreen. Scripts let you grab hold of those objects to make them do things. You can grab hold of the browser's status bar, for example, and write a message into it. You can make text on your Web pages display active content, such as the current date and time. You can create rollover effects that highlight a graphic, make sounds, and pop out explanatory messages when the user mouses over an object onscreen. When the user clicks a button to submit something typed into a text field, you can grab hold of the text field and validate what the user entered. You can also write scripts that use cookies to remember things as the user navigates from screen to screen. Later in this book, Chapter 12 provides you with scripts that can store, query, and update information in server-side databases.

What Scripting Languages Are There?

There are many brands of scripting languages. Most well known is **JavaScript**, the language that runs client-side in the browser without requiring any server-side processing. That is why this chapter teaches you how to use JavaScript.

In Chapter 12, which teaches server-side scripting, you have your choice of programming in VBScript or JScript, Microsoft's Active Server Page (ASP) languages. All of these languages are similar in that they can store values in variables, manipulate values programmatically, use IF-THEN statements to make decisions, receive information from HTML forms, and print text or graphics to communicate with end users onscreen. JavaScript and JScript share much of the same syntax. You will find, therefore, that the JavaScript programming you learn in this chapter helps you learn JScript more quickly when you get to Chapter 12. Due to the popularity of Visual Basic (VB), Chapter 12 also provides VBScript versions of each tutorial example, thereby allowing you to choose to program in either JScript or VBScript.

Other popular server-side languages include C#, Java, and J#, Microsoft's version of Java. The C# and Java programming languages are for more advanced application development that is beyond the scope of this book. If you do well in the JavaScript and JScript sections of this book, however, you may well have the potential to become a successful application developer in one of the more advanced languages.

Where Do Scripts Go?

You can put JavaScript in the head or in the body section of a Web page. Scripts can also reside in a separate file called an **include file**, which gets included in the page at runtime. If you do a lot of scripting, an include file can save you time. If you need to revise a script, for example, you can make the change once in the include file instead of changing it on each page that uses the script.

If a script is brief and is not used a lot, you can simply type it into the body of the page. If you find yourself typing the same code often, however, it is better to put it inside a reusable function that goes into the head section of the Web page. A **function** is a named procedure you can call upon by name any time you need to execute the code in the function. When you call the function, you can pass to it one or more parameters that preset the values of variables the function manipulates. When the function finishes executing, it can return values to the script that called it.

Functions you find yourself using on many pages should be put into an include file. If you copy the code of a frequently used function into the heads of many Web pages, on the other hand, you will have many Web pages to modify if you need to update something in that code.

Where Do Scripts Run?

Scripts run either on the client (i.e., in the browser) or on the server that hosts the Web site. JavaScript is an example of a scripting language that runs on the client. When a browser encounters JavaScript on a Web page, the browser processes the script and renders the result onscreen. ASP scripts, on the other hand, run on the server. When a browser asks a server to display an ASP page, the server executes any JScript or VBScript on the page before sending the response to the browser.

When Should You Use JavaScript?

You should use JavaScript whenever the process you are handling can be accomplished by the browser without requiring any programming on the server side. Handling these processes on the client side reduces the number of round trips between the client and the server, thereby saving valuable bandwidth and speeding response time.

Certain effects can be accomplished only through the use of client-side scripting. Animated image effects, for example, happen on the client side. In the Dynamic HTML section of this chapter, therefore, you will use JavaScript to create animated effects onscreen.

Some situations use both client-side and server-side scripting. When a user enters information into a form, for example, you can use JavaScript to check whether the user has entered valid information before submitting the form data to the server. This eliminates the round-trip that would otherwise be required for the server to tell the user the form was incomplete.

JavaScript "Hello, World!" Project

The simplest script is the quintessential Hello, World! example that beginners typically create as their first programming project. The purpose of the Hello World! script is to print the words Hello, World! onscreen. Working through this example will teach you how to use the `<script>` start and `</script>` stop tags and the JavaScript `document.write()` method for printing information onscreen. Follow these steps:

1. Pull down the Notepad's File menu and choose New to create a new file. Into this new file, type the following code:

```
<html>
<head>
     <title>Hello, World! Project</title>
</head>
```

```
<body>
<script language="JavaScript">
document.write("Hello, World!");
</script>
</body>
</html>
```

2. Pull down the Notepad's File menu and choose Save As. When the Save dialog appears, save this file under the filename *Hello.html*. Then open the file with your browser. Figure 8-1 shows the completed Notepad file, and Figure 8-2 shows the browser displaying the Hello World! greeting onscreen. If you do not see this greeting onscreen, compare your code to the listing in Figure 8-1, correct any typographical errors, save the file, and click your browser's Refresh button to view the corrected code.

3. Reflect on the Hello, World! script you just created. Notice that the `<script>` tag uses the `language="JavaScript"` attribute to tell the browser you are programming in JavaScript. Observe that the `document.write()` command prints to the screen the string of characters between the quotation marks, which delimit the characters in a string.

4. Besides writing predetermined strings of characters onscreen, the `document.write()` command can also display dynamic content onscreen. The next part of this tutorial teaches you how to do that. Before proceeding, however, study the following code analysis to make sure you understand the concepts in the Hello, World! script.

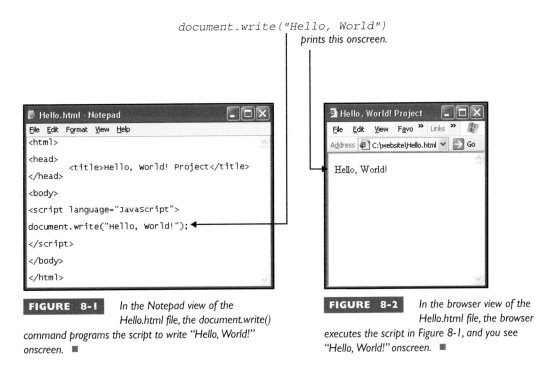

FIGURE 8-1 *In the Notepad view of the Hello.html file, the document.write() command programs the script to write "Hello, World!" onscreen.* ■

FIGURE 8-2 *In the browser view of the Hello.html file, the browser executes the script in Figure 8-1, and you see "Hello, World!" onscreen.* ■

Hello, World! Code Analysis

The Hello, World! script begins with the `<script>` start tag that you use to mark the beginning of a script on a Web page. The start tag identifies JavaScript as the scripting language via the *language* attribute: `<script language="JavaScript">`. You type the script between the start tag and the `</script>` stop tag. The script consists of one instruction, which writes Hello, world! onscreen. The script writes this message onscreen by invoking the *write* method of the *document* object:

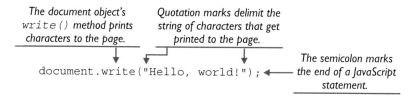

The document object's `write()` method prints characters to the page.

Quotation marks delimit the string of characters that get printed to the page.

The semicolon marks the end of a JavaScript statement.

```
document.write("Hello, world!");
```

The `write()` method causes a string of characters to be written onscreen. The string to be written onscreen appears inside the parentheses and must be delimited with quote signs, which demarcate the characters in a string. The command concludes with a semicolon, the termination character that ends a JavaScript statement.

The *document* object is one of dozens of JavaScript objects available for you to use in your scripts. Most objects contain methods that can do things for you and properties that expose the current settings of the object. You learn a lot more about objects, methods, and properties as this tutorial continues.

Variables and Assignments

We live in a world full of things that change. Variables enable scripts to process things that change. In a script that balances a checkbook, for example, the bottom line changes every time the user writes a check. Because the balance varies, it cannot be hard-coded into the script. Instead, the script must compute the balance and store the result somewhere. This tutorial teaches you how to store things in variables. After learning how to assign values to variables, you find out how to print their values onscreen. Through a process called concatenation, you learn how to combine variables into strings. By including style tags in the strings, you can display the values of your variables onscreen with style. To put variables and assignments to practical use, you learn how to display the current date and time onscreen by concatenating variables that contain the current year, month, day, hour, minute, and second.

What Is a Variable?

In computing, a **variable** is a place in the computer's RAM that remembers, or stores, the value of something changeable. It is called a variable because its value is subject to change.

What Is a String Variable?

A **string** is a sequence of one or more alphanumeric characters. A **string variable** is a place in computer memory that remembers, or stores, the alphanumeric characters in a string.

What Is a Numeric Variable?

A **numeric variable** is a place in computer memory that remembers, or stores, a number. In a script, the numbers can be integers or floating point. An **integer** is a whole number with no decimal point. A **floating point** number has a decimal point with one or more numbers after the decimal point.

What Is a Variable Name?

A **variable name** is the identifier used to refer to, or call upon, a place in computer memory that stores the value of a variable. When you write scripts that use variables, you make up your own names for the variables. When you name variables, I recommend that you follow a naming convention whereby integers begin with the letter *i*, strings begin with the letter *s*, and floating point numbers begin with the letter *f*. This book follows these naming conventions. Thus, a string that holds the user's first name might be named *sFirstName*, and an integer that holds the user's ID number might be named *iUserID*. A floating point number containing the user's account balance might be called *fAccountBalance*.

The reason you prefix the variable names with an *i*, *s*, or *f* is to help you keep track of which variables are integers, strings, or floating point numbers. If you mix them up, you can cause data-type conflict errors that make the browser display an error message when you run the script.

What Is an Operator?

An **operator** is a symbol that causes a script to perform some kind of action on a variable or a value. The most fundamental operator is the **assignment operator**, which assigns values to variables. The assignment operator uses the = symbol. You may be used to thinking of the = symbol as an equal sign. In scripts, however, the symbol = means to assign. To understand how this works, consider the following assignment statement:

```
sName = "Santa Claus";
```

This statement assigns the value "Santa Claus" to the variable called sName. Notice that the assignment goes from right to left. To understand this, think of the = operator as meaning *is assigned the value*. Thus, the statement sName = "Santa Claus" means:

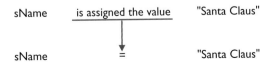

Assigning Values to String Variables

The following example teaches you how to use the = operator to assign values to string variables. In this example, you create variables that hold a person's first and last name. Follow these steps:

1. Pull down the Notepad's File menu and choose New to create a new file. Into this new file, type the following code:

```
<html>
<head>
        <title>Using Variables</title>
</head>
<body>
<script language="JavaScript">
//Assign values to string variables
sFirstName = "Santa";
sLastName = "Claus";
//Write values to the screen
document.write("First Name: ");
document.write(sFirstName);
document.write("<br>Last Name: ");
document.write(sLastName);
</script>
</body>
</html>
```

2. Pull down the Notepad's File menu, choose Save, and when the Save As dialog appears, save this file under the filename *variables.html*. Then open the file with your browser. Figure 8-3 shows the completed Notepad file, and Figure 8-4 shows how the browser displays the values of the variables onscreen. If you do not see these values, compare your code to the listing in Figure 8-3, correct any typographical errors, save the file, and click your browser's Refresh button to view the corrected code.

Using Variables Code Analysis

There are two assignment statements in the *variables.html* script. First, the statement sFirstName = "Santa" assigns the value "Santa" to a string variable called sFirstName. Second, the statement sLastName = "Claus" assigns the value "Claus" to a string called sLastName. Notice that the variable names begin with *s* to remind you that they will contain strings. Also notice that the names of the variables indicate what they will hold: sFirstName will hold the person's first name, and sLastName will hold the person's last name. The reason you create variable names that suggest what content the variables will hold is to make the code self-documenting. If you choose esoteric variable names such as sVariable1 and sVariable2, on the other hand, your code is harder to read and understand.

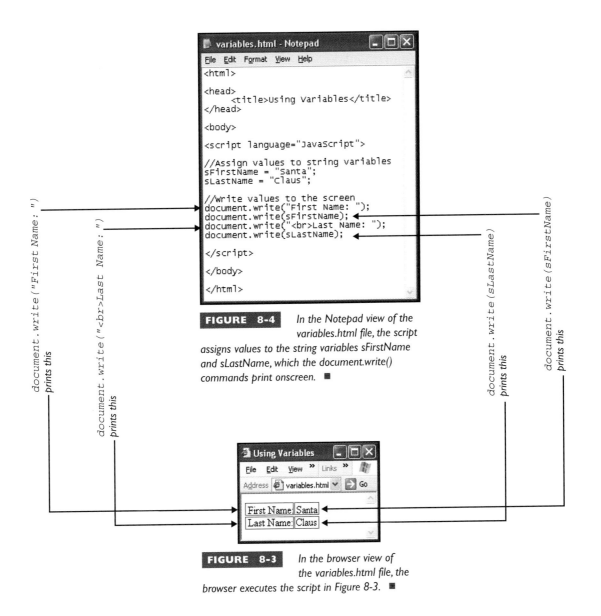

FIGURE 8-4 *In the Notepad view of the variables.html file, the script assigns values to the string variables sFirstName and sLastName, which the document.write() commands print onscreen.* ∎

FIGURE 8-3 *In the browser view of the variables.html file, the browser executes the script in Figure 8-3.* ∎

To make your code even easier to understand, you can include comment statements that document what your code does. Comment statements begin with the special symbol //. Two of the lines inside the *variables.html* script, for example, begin with the symbol //. Throughout this book, notice that the examples are full of comment statements. When you write scripts, you should form the habit of inserting your own comment statements to document what the code does. Later on, when you need to modify or troubleshoot problems in the code, the comment statements will save you time by making it easier for you to remember what the code is doing.

Concatenating String Variables

To **concatenate** means to join strings together via the concatenation operator. In JavaScript, the **concatenation operator** is the + sign. To learn how to use the concatenation operator, you add some code to the *variables* script you created earlier in this chapter. Follow these steps:

1. Use the Notepad to open the *variables.html* page you created in the previous exercise.

2. Position your cursor at the bottom of the script. Add the following lines of code to the end of the script by inserting them just above the `</script>` stop tag:

```
document.write(sLastName);
//Concatenation example
sFullName = sFirstName + " " + sLastName;
document.write("<br>Full Name: ");
document.write(sFullName);
</script>
```

3. Save the file and then open it with your browser. Figure 8-5 shows the completed Notepad file, and Figure 8-6 shows how the browser displays the concatenation onscreen. If you do not see these values, compare your code to the listing in Figure 8-5, correct any typographical errors, save the file, and click your browser's Refresh button to view the corrected code.

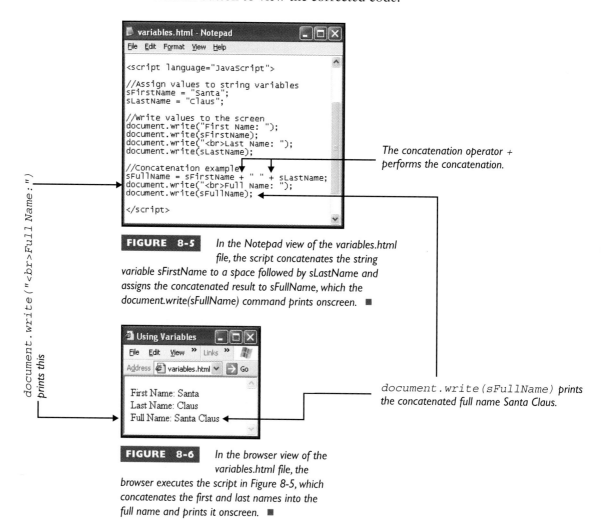

FIGURE 8-5 *In the Notepad view of the variables.html file, the script concatenates the string variable sFirstName to a space followed by sLastName and assigns the concatenated result to sFullName, which the document.write(sFullName) command prints onscreen.* ■

FIGURE 8-6 *In the browser view of the variables.html file, the browser executes the script in Figure 8-5, which concatenates the first and last names into the full name and prints it onscreen.* ■

The concatenation operator + performs the concatenation.

`document.write("<br>Full Name: ")` *prints this*

`document.write(sFullName)` *prints the concatenated full name Santa Claus.*

Concatenation Code Analysis

The string variable *sFullName* is so named because it will hold the person's full name. Notice that the concatenation inserts a space between the person's first and last names:

```
" " is a string consisting
of a single space.

sFullName = sFirstName + " " + sLastName;
```

Assigning Values to Numeric Variables

You use the = assignment operator to assign values to numeric variables. In this example, you create variables that hold a person's age and weight. Follow these steps:

1. Use the Notepad to open the *variables.html* page you created in the previous exercise.

2. Position your cursor at the bottom of the script. Add the following lines of code to the end of the script by inserting them just above the </script> stop tag:

```
document.write(sFullName);
//Assign values to numeric variables
iAge = 100;
iWeight = 350;
//Create the print string
sPrint = "<p>At age ";
sPrint += iAge;
sPrint += ", " + sFullName;
sPrint += " weighs ";
sPrint += iWeight;
sPrint += " pounds.</p>";
//Write the print string onscreen
document.write(sPrint);
</script>
```

3. Save the file and then open it with your browser. Figure 8-7 shows the completed Notepad file, and Figure 8-8 shows how the browser displays the age and weight onscreen. If you do not see these values, compare your code to the listing in Figure 8-7, correct any typographical errors, save the file, and click your browser's Refresh button to run the corrected code.

Numeric Variables Code Analysis

The age and weight are stored in variables named *iAge* and *iWeight*. You put an *i* at the beginning of these variables as a reminder that you are using them as integers. The letter *i* stands for integer.

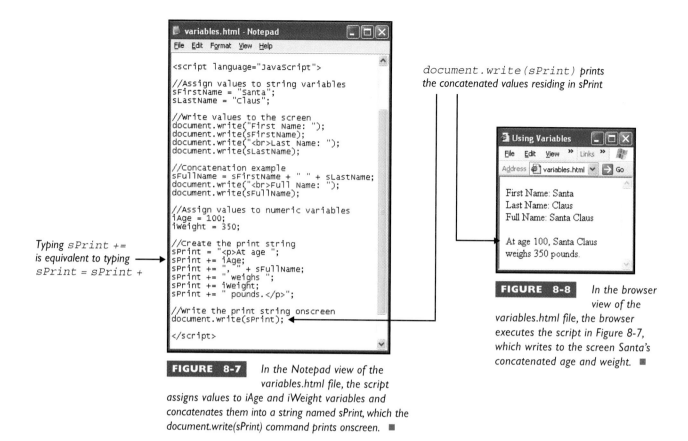

Typing sPrint +=
is equivalent to typing
sPrint = sPrint +

document.write(sPrint) prints
the concatenated values residing in sPrint

FIGURE   8-7   *In the Notepad view of the*
variables.html file, the script
assigns values to iAge and iWeight variables and
concatenates them into a string named sPrint, which the
document.write(sPrint) command prints onscreen. ■

FIGURE   8-8   *In the browser*
view of the
variables.html file, the browser
executes the script in Figure 8-7,
which writes to the screen Santa's
concatenated age and weight. ■

The string variable *sPrint* holds the string that will be printed onscreen. The print string gets created through a series of statements that keep adding more onto it through the process of concatenation.

Notice the use of the += operator in the concatenation statements. Typing sPrint += is equivalent to typing sPrint = sPrint +. Thus, += is a typing shortcut that can save you a lot of time.

Displaying Dynamic Messages Onscreen

Scripts can include tags that mark up the strings you display onscreen. For example, suppose you wanted the person's age and weight to appear bold. The <strong> and </strong> tags accomplish these boldings:

```
sPrint = "At age <strong>" + iAge + "</strong>, " + sFullName
+ " weighs <strong>" + iWeight + "</strong> pounds.";
```

Sooner or later, everyone who works with strings gets confronted with the challenge of including quotation marks inside a string. Suppose you need to create a string called *sQuotation*, for example, that contains the following characters:

```
Santa sang "Jingle Bells" as he drove the sleigh.
```

The dilemma is: How do you create a string like this when the quote sign delimits the string? To make it possible to do this, JavaScript uses the special symbol \" to denote a quote sign inside a string. Thus, the way to type this assignment statement is as follows:

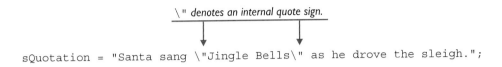

```
sQuotation = "Santa sang \"Jingle Bells\" as he drove the sleigh.";
```

Objects, Methods, and Properties

Think about what you see onscreen when you visit a Web page. There are menus, buttons, fields, paragraphs, tables, images, address fields, status bars, and links. Imagine being able to grab hold of these elements and manipulate them dynamically when a user visits the page. Think of how interactive such a Web page would be. If a user mouses over a link, for example, you could pop out a description of what will happen if the user clicks there. On a form that prompts the users to type their e-mail address, you could validate that address and make sure it has the proper format. In a product catalog where users can choose different colors, you could display a color palette and change the product's color dynamically as the user mouses over the color choices. On a Web page that contains a time-consuming process, you could write a message into the status bar informing the user of the progress of the operation.

Would you like to be able to do some of these things? Of course you would. Is doing so difficult? Not if you understand the two underlying principles that this tutorial is about to teach you. First, you need to know where to go to find out what the objects are that you can manipulate dynamically. Second, you need to know when and how you can grab hold of these objects and manipulate them dynamically.

What Is an Object?

In computing, an **object** is a self-contained entity consisting of properties and methods enabling you to do something programmatically. You already have experience using one of the objects that is built into the scripting languages. That is the document object you used to print to the screen in the JavaScript examples you completed earlier in this chapter. You were probably impressed by how easy it was to use the document object to write onscreen. Imagine being able to grab hold of different parts of a Web page and manipulate them just as easily. Soon you will know how to do so. Read on.

What Is a Method?

A **method** is a little computer program built into an object to enable the object to do something. In the Hello, World! script you wrote in the previous part of this chapter, for example, you learned how the `write()`

method enables the document object to print a message onscreen. In your script, you called upon this method with a statement in the form of:

```
document.write("Hello, World!")
```

What Is a Property?

A **property** is an attribute of an object that has a value. You can find out the value of the attribute by grabbing hold of the property and taking a look at its contents. Suppose someone has clicked the Submit button on a form that prompts users to type their e-mail address. Before submitting that address to the server, you would like to grab hold of the e-mail field and see what the user typed. You can easily do this by inspecting the text property of the e-mail field. When the user clicks the Submit button, you can run a script that inspects the text property of the e-mail field and checks to see if it contains the required elements. If the e-mail address does not include the @ sign, for example, you can pop out a box explaining the problem and ask the user to fix the error and try again.

Some objects have properties that you can manipulate to change the appearance of things onscreen. Colors, sizes, bolding, underlining, and positioning are just a few of the properties you can manipulate this way.

What Is an Event?

In computer programming, an **event** is an action that provides an opportunity to trigger a script that can use objects to inspect properties and execute methods that make things happen onscreen or keep records behind the scenes. The most commonly used events are (1) the mouseover, which fires when the user mouses over an object onscreen; (2) the click, which fires when the user clicks the mouse; (3) the double-click, which the user triggers by clicking twice quickly; and (4) the page load, which fires when the user visits a Web site and a page first comes onscreen. Whenever one of these events happens, you have the opportunity to run a script and party with the objects, methods, and properties in the DOM.

JavaScript Clock Project

The purpose of the JavaScript clock project is to give you some experience using the methods and properties of one of the objects in the JavaScript DOM. The clock project uses the JavaScript `Date()` object, which contains methods and properties that enable you to find out the current date and time in a wide range of formats. Combined with the numerical and string processing techniques you learned earlier in this chapter, the `Date()` object enables you to provide dynamic content onscreen in the form of a clock that tells the user what time it is. To create the JavaScript clock project, follow these steps:

1. Pull down the Notepad's File menu and choose New to create a new file. Into this new file, type the following code:

```
<html>
<head>
        <title>Clock Project</title>
</head>
<body>
<h1>The Clock Strikes!</h1>
<script language=javascript>
//What is the date and time now?
dateNow = new Date();
sPrint = "The time is ";
sPrint += dateNow.toString();
//display the print string
document.write(sPrint);
</script>
</body>
</html>
```

2. Pull down the Notepad's File menu and choose Save. When the Save dialog appears, save this file under the filename *clock.html*. Then open the file with your browser. Figure 8-9 shows the completed Notepad file, and Figure 8-10 shows how the script makes the browser display the current date and time onscreen. If you do not see the current date and time, compare your code to the listing in Figure 8-9, correct any typographical errors, save the file, and click your browser's Refresh button to view the corrected code.

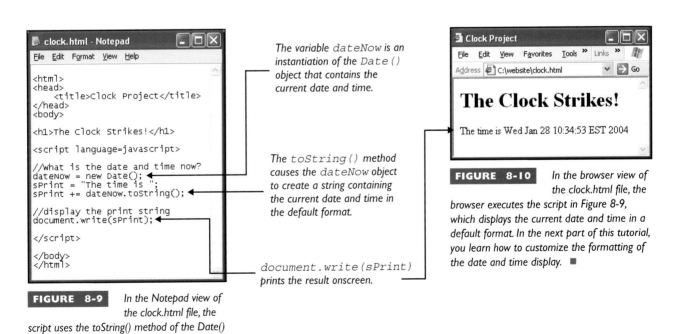

The variable `dateNow` is an instantiation of the `Date()` object that contains the current date and time.

The `toString()` method causes the `dateNow` object to create a string containing the current date and time in the default format.

`document.write(sPrint)` prints the result onscreen.

FIGURE 8-9 *In the Notepad view of the clock.html file, the script uses the toString() method of the Date() object to get the current date and time into the sPrint string, which the document.write() command displays onscreen.* ■

FIGURE 8-10 *In the browser view of the clock.html file, the browser executes the script in Figure 8-9, which displays the current date and time in a default format. In the next part of this tutorial, you learn how to customize the formatting of the date and time display.* ■

Clock Code Analysis

The clock script obtains the current date and time by creating a new instance of the Date() object. The keyword *new* creates this new instance, which is assigned to the variable named dateNow:

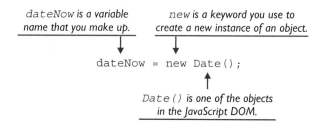

Then the clock script uses the toString() method to create the print string that displays the date and time onscreen. The method toString() can be used with many objects in the JavaScript DOM. When applied to the Date() object, the toString() method returns a string containing the date and time, as displayed in Figure 8-10.

Customizing the Date and Time Display

The manner in which the date and time appear onscreen in the clock project is just one of many ways you can format dates and times. Table 8-1 shows the Date() object methods and properties that let you grab hold of the individual date and time components and use them to customize the display of the current date and time. If you would like to try some of these customizations, add the following code to the script in your *clock.html* file. The place to put this code is right before the </script> end tag.

Method	What It Does
toString()	Returns the date and time in the default format
toUTCString()	Returns the date and time with Universal Time Code (UTC) formatting
toLocaleString()	Returns the date and time in the locale formatting defined on the user's computer
toDateString()	Returns the date only, in the default format
toTimeString()	Returns the time only, in the default format
toLocaleDateString()	Returns the date only, in the locale format
toLocaleTimeString()	Returns the time only, in the locale format

TABLE 8-1 *JavaScript Date() Methods for Customizing Date and Time Display Strings* ■

Then save the file and open it with your browser to see the customized print strings onscreen. Here is the code to type:

```
sPrint = "<br><br>The UTC time is ";
sPrint += dateNow.toUTCString();
document.write(sPrint);
sPrint = "<br><br>The locale time is ";
sPrint += dateNow.toLocaleString();
document.write(sPrint);
sPrint = "<br><br>The date is ";
sPrint += dateNow.toDateString();
document.write(sPrint);
sPrint = "<br><br>The time only is ";
sPrint += dateNow.toTimeString();
document.write(sPrint);
sPrint = "<br><br>The locale date is ";
sPrint += dateNow.toLocaleDateString();
document.write(sPrint);
sPrint = "<br><br>The locale time only is ";
sPrint += dateNow.toLocaleTimeString();
document.write(sPrint);
```

note *The* Date() *object contains many more methods for working with dates and times. In the next part of this chapter, you learn how to list all the methods and properties of the* Date() *object as well as all the other objects that are available to you when scripting.*

Document Object Model (DOM)

The **document object model (DOM)** is the official W3C structural definition of the objects, methods, and properties that comprise documents on the World Wide Web. Like many of the W3C standards, the DOM is evolving and taking on more exciting features. You need to be aware that if you use one of the newer features, it is possible that not all browsers support it. Therefore, you should always test your pages with the targeted browsers your users are likely to have. You can find the latest version of the DOM by going to www.w3.org/DOM, where you'll find a tremendous amount of information. Before wading in too deeply, you should work through this chapter's tutorial, which introduces you to things you can do with the DOM without getting overly technical.

Popular JavaScript DOM Objects

In JavaScript, the most commonly used DOM objects provide access to the HTML elements that comprise the document displayed inside the browser window. Of particular importance are the elements in the forms through which the user interacts by selecting things, entering textual information, and clicking to submit the form. Table 8-2 contains an outline of these methods and properties. Remember that this is just a small sampling of the vast array of objects defined in the DOM.

document In the current window.

body

alink Sets the color of active links (after mouse button down and before mouse button up).

background Tiles an image into the background.

bgColor Sets the background color of the page.

link Sets the color of links that are not active and not visited.

text Sets the document text color.

vlink Sets the color of visited links.

cookie Retrieves all cookies as a single string, with each name-value pair separated by a semicolon.

form

action Server-side form handler.

button

accesskey A single character access key to provide access to the form control.

form Returns the form element containing this button.

name Name of the button if named in the form.

type *Submit, reset,* or *button,* which creates a pushbutton.

value The current value of the button.

checkbox

checked *True* if checked or *false* if unchecked.

defaultChecked *True* if this box is checked by default.

form Returns the form element containing this check box.

name Name of the check box.

value The current value of the check box.

elements[] A collection of the controls in the form. *Note:* The brackets mean this is a collection of things.

length Number of elements in the collection.

length Number of controls in the form.

method Http method used to submit the form, which is either GET or POST.

name Name of the form.

password

form Returns the form element containing this password field.

name Name of the password field.

value The current value in the password field.

radio

checked *True* if checked or *false* if unchecked.

defaultChecked *True* if this radio button is checked by default.

form Returns the form element containing this radio button.

name Name of the radio button.

value The current value of the radio button.

TABLE 8-2 *Popular JavaScript DOM Objects* ■

TABLE 8-2 *Popular JavaScript DOM Objects* (continued) ■

Intrinsic Events

In addition to defining the objects that enable a script to manipulate elements on a Web page, the W3C has defined the intrinsic events that can trigger such a script. Table 8-3 lists and defines these intrinsic events. These definitions are based on the W3C specification at http://www.w3.org/TR/html401/interact/scripts.html#h-18.2.3. In the Dynamic HTML section of this chapter, you learn how to use these events to trigger scripts that access objects in the DOM to bring your Web pages to life and make the user interface more intelligent.

Accessing DOM Objects via Dot Notation

To access DOM objects in a script, you use dot notation to refer to the objects you want to manipulate. Following the document's hierarchical structure, dot notation places to the left of a period elements that are structurally higher than elements further down the tree. Let us work through a very simple example. Suppose you want to write a script that can alter dynamically the title of a Web page. As you saw in the list of popular JavaScript DOM objects presented in Table 8-2, the *document* object has a

Event	When It Occurs	May Be Used With
onclick	Occurs when the user clicks the pointing device button over an element	Most elements
ondblclick	Occurs when the user double-clicks the pointing device button over an element	Most elements
onmousedown	Occurs when the user presses the pointing device button over an element	Most elements
onmouseup	Occurs when the user releases the pointing device button over an element	Most elements
onmouseover	Occurs when the user moves the pointing device button onto an element	Most elements
onmousemove	Occurs when the user moves the pointing device button while it is over an element	Most elements
onmouseout	Occurs when the user moves the pointing device away from an element	Most elements
onfocus	Occurs when an element receives focus either via the pointing device or tabbing navigation	A, AREA, LABEL, INPUT, SELECT, TEXTAREA, and BUTTON
onblur	Occurs when an element loses focus either via the pointing device or tabbing navigation	A, AREA, LABEL, INPUT, SELECT, TEXTAREA, and BUTTON
onkeypress	Occurs when the user presses and releases a key over an element	Most elements
onkeydown	Occurs when the user presses down a key over an element	Most elements
onkeyup	Occurs when the user releases a key over an element	Most elements
onsubmit	Occurs upon the submission of a form	The FORM element
onreset	Occurs when a form is reset	The FORM element
onselect	Occurs when a user selects some text in a text field	INPUT and TEXTAREA
onchange	Occurs when a control loses the input focus and its value has been modified since gaining focus	INPUT, SELECT, and TEXTAREA
onload	Occurs when the browser finishes loading the window or all frames in a frameset	BODY and FRAMESET
onunload	Occurs when the browser removes a document from a window or frame	BODY and FRAMESET

TABLE 8-3   *Intrinsic Events that Can Trigger a Script* ■

title property that can be used to retrieve or set the title of the page. A script can grab hold of the title via the dot notation:

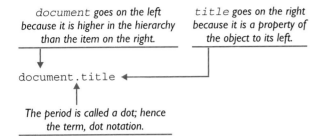

document goes on the left because it is higher in the hierarchy than the item on the right.

title goes on the right because it is a property of the object to its left.

```
document.title
```

The period is called a dot; hence the term, dot notation.

Try This!

Title Bar Clock Script

To experience how easy it is to manipulate an object defined by the DOM, you can write a little script that uses the dot notation *document.title* to set the title of a Web page. In this example, you make the title display the current time. Any time the user wants to know what time it is, the title bar will display it. Follow these steps:

1. Pull down the Notepad's File menu and choose New to start a new page. Type the following code to get the page started:

```
<html>
<head>
</head>
<body>
</body>
</html>
```

2. Pull down the Notepad's File menu and choose Save As; use the Save controls to save this file in your *website* folder under the filename *TitlebarClock.html*.

3. Click to position your cursor before the `</head>` tag that ends the head of the document. Type the following script into the head of the document, or download it from the book's Web site, where the script is called *titlebarclock.txt*:

```
<script language="JavaScript">
function clock()
{
        var dateNow = new Date();
        var hour = dateNow.getHours();
        var minute = dateNow.getMinutes();
        var second = dateNow.getSeconds();
        if (hour > 12)
                hour -= 12;
        if (minute < 10)
                minute = "0" + minute;
        if (second < 10)
                second = "0" + second;
        document.title = "The time is " + hour + ":" + minute + ":" + second;
        setTimeout("clock()", 1000);
}
</script>
```

Try This!
continued

4. Scroll down to the `<body>` tag and modify the `<body>` tag to make it read as follows:

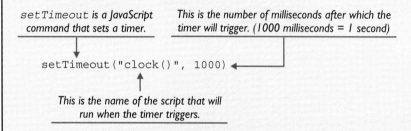

onLoad is an event that triggers when the browser loads the page.

```
<body onLoad="clock()">
```

clock() is the name of the function you typed in the previous step.

5. Save the page and open it with a browser. Notice that the browser's title bar displays the current time. See how the time updates every second. That update is triggered by the last command in the script, which has the format:

setTimeout is a JavaScript command that sets a timer.　*This is the number of milliseconds after which the timer will trigger. (1000 milliseconds = 1 second)*

```
setTimeout("clock()", 1000)
```

This is the name of the script that will run when the timer triggers.

Accessing DOM Objects by Arrays

An *array* is a named table of memory locations in which values can be stored. Like variables, arrays have names. You can define an array to have a fixed number of memory locations via the following JavaScript command, in which the number specifies the size of the array:

```
dayArray = new Array(6);
```

You use assignment statements to put values into the array, such as:

```
dayArray[0]="Sunday";
dayArray[1]="Monday";
dayArray[2]="Tuesday";
dayArray[3]="Wednesday";
dayArray[4]="Thursday";
dayArray[5]="Friday";
dayArray[6]="Saturday";
```

To access the value in one of the array's slots, you use a subscript. Arrays are zero-based, meaning that the numbering of the slots begins at zero. Thus, to access the value of the first slot in an array called *dayarray*, for example, you would refer to the value as dayArray[0]. To access the next slot, you would refer to the value as dayArray[1].

When a Web page loads, the browser creates arrays for the images, forms, links, anchors, and all the other elements onscreen. As the browser encounters objects on the page, it places them into these arrays. The arrays are indexed sequentially, beginning with zero. The first image on the page, therefore, goes into slot 0 of the images array. You could refer to it in a script as:

```
document.images[0]
```

In like manner, the fourth image on the page could be accessed as:

```
document.images[3]
```

The first form on the page goes into slot 0 of the forms array. You could refer to it in a script as:

```
document.forms[0]
```

Each entry in the forms array has another array inside it called elements, which contains the fields and buttons that comprise the form. If the first form on the screen begins with three radio buttons, for example, the third such button would be referred to as:

```
document.forms[0].elements[2]
```

Referring to the objects in this manner is not very intuitive, however. After you write code like this, if you later insert another radio button ahead of a button you already had onscreen, the insertion changes the indexing. What was formerly document.forms[0].elements[2] is now document.forms[0].elements[3], so all the code references to document.forms[0].elements[2] would need to be changed. Clearly, you would not want to code this way. You need to know about the arrays to understand how the browser stores the elements on a Web page, but you will not normally be referring to these elements via array indexes in your code.

Accessing DOM Objects by Name

Happily, there is a more direct way for you to access elements on a Web page: you simply name the elements when you put them on the page. At runtime, your scripts can refer to the elements by name. To name a Web page element, you use the *name* and *id* attributes to give the element a unique identifier. The attribute id stands for identifier. The reason you use both the name and id attributes is that older versions of HTML use the name attribute, but the latest version uses the id attribute. By using both name and id attributes, you can write code that is compatible with both old and new versions of HTML. Suppose you want to refer to the image on your Web page résumé by the name MyPhoto. To make such a name, you would code the image tag as follows:

```
<img src="photo.gif" name="MyPhoto" id="MyPhoto">
```

So named, the image can appear in a script that modifies the image attributes by referring to the image by name. Following this paragraph is an example that provides users with three buttons onscreen, followed by an image named MyPhoto. The buttons give users the choice of making the image larger or smaller or reloading the page. If the user clicks to make the image larger, the script multiplies MyPhoto.width and MyPhoto.height by 2, thereby doubling the size of the image. If the user clicks to make the image smaller, the script divides these attributes by 2, thereby reducing the image to half its former size. If the user clicks the Reset button, the script calls the `window.location.reload()` function to reload the page, thereby resetting the image to its original size. Here is the code that accomplishes this:

MyPhoto.height *= 2 is a shorthand way of writing MyPhoto.height = MyPhoto.height * 2.

```
<p>
Click the buttons to change the size of the picture.
<input type="submit" value="Bigger" onclick="MyPhoto.width *= 2; MyPhoto.height *= 2">
<input type="submit" value="Smaller" onclick="MyPhoto.width /= 2; MyPhoto.height /= 2">
<input type="reset" onclick="window.location.reload()">
</p>
<img src="photo.gif" name="MyPhoto" id="MyPhoto">
```

MyPhoto.height /= 2 is a shorthand way of writing MyPhoto.height = MyPhoto.height / 2.

Debugging JavaScript via the Alert Box

Writing scripts requires patience because you can run into some problems. When a script is not working, you need to take it from the top and work through it until you find what is causing the problem. Beginners can stumble by forgetting to click the browser's Reload button to refresh the page after modifying the script. Remember that the browser caches the file when the page loads. When you modify the script to fix a problem or add a feature, you must either click the browser's Reload button or pull down the View menu and click Refresh. Otherwise, the browser displays the previously cached version of the file, and you can become frustrated because it appears as though your fix is not working.

Sometimes the browser tells you the number of the offending line of code that is causing the problem. When this happens, pull down the Notepad's Edit menu and choose Go to. Programming glitches can happen in the line or two above the one the browser reports, so look there as well as in the line flagged by the browser.

The greatest aid to finding a problem in a script is to inspect the values of your variables while the script executes. To take a sneak peek at a variable, you can insert an alert box at the point in the script at which you want to inspect the value of the variable. An **alert box** is a window that a script creates by executing the `alert()` method of the JavaScript window object.

Try This!

Rollover Effects

A **rollover** is a special graphical effect you create by using the JavaScript onmouseover and onmouseout event handlers. When the user mouses over something, the onmouseover event fires, causing your script to do something onscreen. Similarly, when the user mouses out of something, the onmouseout event fires, providing another opportunity to run a script. In this exercise, you create the most common kind of rollover, in which a script changes the source of the image when the user mouses over it. To create this rollover, follow these steps:

1. Pull down the Notepad's File menu and choose New to create a new file. Into this new file, type the following code. When you type this, replace *photo.gif* and *photo2.gif* by the actual names of the images you want to see during the rollover:

```html
<html>
<head>
      <title>Rollover Effects</title>
</head>
<body>
<p>
Move your mouse on and off the picture.
</p>
<img src="photo.gif" name="MyPhoto" id="MyPhoto"
onmouseover="MyPhoto.src='photo2.gif'"
onmouseout="MyPhoto.src='photo.gif'">
</body>
</html>
```

Replace *photo.gif* and *photo2.gif* with the actual filenames of your images.

2. Pull down the Notepad's File menu and choose Save. When the Save dialog appears, save this file under the filename *rollover.html*. Then open the file with your browser. Move your mouse on and off the image. If the rollover works, congratulate yourself because you have just mastered one of the most popular special effects on the Web. If there are problems, go back to the previous step and troubleshoot the difficulties.

3. If you have the Internet Explorer Web browser, you can make a very nice rollover effect with a single image. Click to position your cursor in the notepad prior to the </body> tag that ends the document, and type the following code, replacing *photo.gif* by the name of your actual image:

```html
<img src="photo.gif" name="PalePhoto" id="PalePhoto"
style="filter:progid:DXImageTransform.Microsoft.Alpha(opacity=30)"
onmouseover="PalePhoto.style.filter='progid:DXImageTransform.Microsoft.Alpha(opacity=FF)'"
onmouseout="PalePhoto.style.filter='progid:DXImageTransform.Microsoft.Alpha(opacity=30)'">
```

4. Save the file and view it with your browser. At first, the image appears pale onscreen. Mouse over the pale image, and its full color appears. The image filter that creates this effect is a Dynamic HTML technique described later in the Dynamic HTML part of this chapter.

Inside the parentheses of the alert() method, you insert the string of characters and variables you want displayed in the alert box. At runtime, when the script encounters the alert, the script pauses while you study the contents of the alert box onscreen. When you click to dismiss the alert box, the script continues executing. By putting alert boxes in strategic places down through the path of execution in your code, you can step through the code and diagnose the point at which something is going wrong. To create an alert box, follow these steps:

1. Use the Notepad to open the page you want to debug. In this example, open the *clock.html* page you created earlier in this chapter.

2. Scroll to the point in the code at which you want to insert an alert box for debugging. In this example, imagine that you want to find out the value of the sPrint string. Position your cursor at the spot where you want the alert box and type the following code:

```
sDebug = "The value of sPrint is " + sPrint;
alert(sDebug);
```

3. Save the page and open it with your browser. See that the alert box comes onscreen. Reflect on what a simple yet powerful method this is for finding out what is going on behind the scenes when you are trying to solve a problem in your script.

4. After you finish debugging, you can either delete the debugging code you added to display the alert box, or you can comment it out without deleting it. Commenting out code that you think you might want to reactivate will save you the time needed to re-create the debugging code if you encounter another problem later on. To comment out this code, you type the comment character // in front of each line of debugging code, as follows:

The symbol // creates a comment that will not execute at runtime.

```
//sDebug = "The value of sPrint is " + sPrint;
//alert(sDebug);
```

5. To inspect the value of a variable at different points in a script, periodically insert into your code an alert box constructed in this manner:

Type the name of the variable here.

```
alert("The current value of the variable sVarName is: " + sVarName);
```

JavaScript Code Sources

Several Web sites provide free source code for creating a wide variety of JavaScript special effects. When you visit these sites, you will find thousands of scripts organized according to subject and topic. There is also a search feature you can use to locate scripts via keyword. Table 8-4 lists the JavaScript source code sites and tells what you will find there. Also remember to visit this book's Web site for links to new resources and updates that may have been made to the links in Table 8-4. Be sure to follow the link, for example, to the JavaScript clock at Spondoro.com. It is an amazing 3-D animated clock that will follow your mouse across the screen.

Site Name and Web Address	What You Will Find There
JavaScript Developer Central http://developer.netscape.com/tech/javascript	Netscape's JavaScript support site. Full of articles, documentation, and sample code. Includes a brief history of the DOM.
The JavaScript Source http://javascript.internet.com	Hundreds of cut-and-paste scripts to put on your Web page. See especially the generators that can create scripts according to your specifications.
Simply the Best Scripts http://www.simplythebest.net/info/dhtml_scripts.html	A collection of very good scripts. See especially the guitar chord machine at http://www.simplythebest.net/info/javascript38.html#.
Dynamic Drive http://www.dynamicdrive.com	Repository of DHTML scripts that use the latest JavaScript technology, with emphasis on practicality and backward compatibility.
JavaScript Kit http://www.javascriptkit.com	JavaScript tutorials, free JavaScripts, DHTML/CSS tutorials, Web building tutorials.
Builder.Com http://builder.com	To find the Builder.Com repository of JavaScripts, go to http://builder.com and search for JavaScript.
WebReference http://www.webreference.com/programming/javascript	JavaScript articles, tutorials, repositories, specifications, and documentation.
Webmonkey http://hotwired.lycos.com/webmonkey/reference/javascript_code_library/	The Webmonkey JavaScript code library, including free code samples and language extensions.

TABLE 8-4   *JavaScript Source Code Sites* ∎

Maintaining State in Cookies

Do you remember the PacMan game that was popular in video arcades in the 1980s? The game contained magic cookies that, when devoured, made you more powerful. On the Internet, cookies work a little differently but are much more powerful.

What Is a Cookie?

A **cookie** is a place in the computer's memory where browsers can store information about the user. If someone buys an audio CD by Britney Spears, for example, the site might create a cookie indicating that the user likes pop music. The next time the user visits the site, it might display ads for similar pop music titles. Or the cookie might keep track of screens visited and use that information to resume where the user left off.

There are two kinds of cookies, namely, *persistent cookies* that are stored in small text files on the user's hard disk, and *per-session cookies* that are stored in RAM. Because persistent cookies are stored on disk, they survive from session to session, even after the user closes the Web browser and turns off the computer. Per-session cookies, on the other hand, evaporate when the user closes the Web browser, which frees the RAM.

Why Does the Internet Need Cookies?

Without cookies, the Internet would be in deep trouble. Each time a user interacts with a Web site, the Internet closes the socket through which that interaction took place. In other words, the Internet hangs up on you after it finishes serving you the page. While you read what is onscreen, the Internet devotes its resources to serving other users. It does not pay you any attention until you click or select something that requires interaction with a server. Each time you interact, a socket opens and then closes again as soon as the Internet finishes serving you the page. The Internet does not keep track of which users get which sockets. For this reason, the Internet is said to be stateless. The Internet needs cookies so it can maintain state from screen to screen. When you interact with a secure Web site, it creates one or more session cookies that the browser stores temporarily in your computer's RAM. The next time you interact with that site, it inspects the cookies to find out who you are. Thus, the Internet uses cookies to maintain state from page to page.

The per-session cookies are very secure. Only the server that set the cookies is able to read them, and the cookies evaporate at the end of the session. Persistent cookies, on the other hand, reside on the user's hard disk drive. Knowledgeable users can find the cookie files and read their contents with any text editor. If these contents are unencrypted, the cookies can be read in plain text. It is appropriate to use persistent cookies to store information that would not cause a security problem if sniffed. The advantage of using persistent cookies is that a server can keep data on the user's PC, thereby avoiding the need to store that data in a server-side database. Cookies thereby provide a mechanism you can use to store nonsensitive data on every computer on the Internet from which someone visits your site—unless the user turns off the browser's cookie feature. The vast majority of users have their cookies turned on because virtually all sites that have you log on and off, including all of the Internet's e-commerce sites, use cookies to maintain state.

How to Read and Write the Value of a Cookie

Table 8-2 (earlier in this chapter) identifies the commonly used JavaScript DOM objects. One of the DOM objects is the cookie collection, which you access via the document.cookie property. As you might expect, setting the value of a cookie requires a little scripting. The following example uses a cookie to keep track of how many times the user clicks a button onscreen. Although the task is very simple, the cookie functions can be used to read or set the value of any cookie. To create the cookie cutter, follow these steps:

1. Pull down the Notepad's File menu and choose New to start a new file. Type the following code or download it from this book's Web site, where the filename is *cookiecutter.txt*:

```
<html>
<head>
<title>Cookie Cutting</title>
<script language="JavaScript">
function setCookie(sName,sValue,iMinutes)
{
    if (iMinutes == 0)
        document.cookie = sName + "=" + sValue;
    else
```

```
        {
            dateExpires = new Date();
            dateExpires.setMinutes(dateExpires.getMinutes()+iMinutes);
            document.cookie = sName + "=" + sValue
                            + ";expires="
                            + dateExpires.toGMTString();
        }
    }

    function readCookie(sName)
    {
        cookieChecker = document.cookie.split("; ");
        for (i=0; i<cookieChecker.length; i++)
        {
            if (sName == cookieChecker[i].split("=")[0])
                return cookieChecker[i].split("=")[1];
        }
        return ""; //returns nothing if cookie not found
    }

</script>
</head>

<body>
<h1>Hit Counter</h1>

<script language="JavaScript">
iClickCounter = readCookie("ClickCounter");
</script>

<form method="get" action="cookies.html">
<input type="submit" value="Click Me!"
onClick="setCookie('ClickCounter',++iClickCounter,0);">
</form>

<p>Number of clicks:
<script language="JavaScript">
document.write(iClickCounter);
</script>
</p>
</body>
</html>
```

2. Save the file in your *website* folder under the filename *cookies.html*. To see what it does, open the *cookies.html* file with your browser. If you get any error messages, the browser tells you the number of the line that is causing the problem. Troubleshoot the problem by proofreading your code more carefully until you get the page to open in the browser without reporting any errors.

3. Click the button and observe how the click counter increases. Each time you click the button, the script is adding 1 to the value of the click counter stored in the cookie named ClickCounter.

4. As printed in this exercise, the cookie is set to expire at the end of the session. Close all of your browser windows; then use your

browser to reopen the *cookies.html* file. Notice that the click counter starts over when you start clicking the button. That is because the cookie expired when you closed the browser windows.

5. To make the cookie persist, increase the value of the following variable, which tells the browser how many minutes to make the cookie last. In this example, set the value to 1, to make the cookie last one minute:

```
<form method="post" action="cookies.html">
<input type="submit" value="Click Me!"
onClick="setCookie('ClickCounter',++iClickCounter,0);">
</form>
```

Replace this 0 with the number of minutes you want the cookie to last.

6. Close all your browser windows. Then open the *cookies.html* page with your browser. Click the button a few times. Make a note of the value of the click counter. Then close all your browser windows. Immediately use your browser to reopen the *cookies.html* page. Notice that the value persists because you started the new session before the cookie expired.

7. Close all your browser windows again. This time, wait for a couple of minutes before you reopen the *cookies.html* file. This causes the one-minute cookie to expire. Open the page and notice that the click counter restarts because the cookie expired. In practice, you normally set a persistent cookie to last for several days or months, depending on the purpose. In this example, you set it to last just a minute so you can observe what happens when it expires, without having to wait so long.

Cookie Cutter Code Analysis

Figure 8-11 contains the completed code of the *cookies.html* page, and Figure 8-12 shows it running onscreen. The script stores the click counter in a cookie called ClickCounter. The page reads the value of this cookie into a variable named iClickCounter via the following script:

ClickCounter is the name of the cookie that keeps track of how many times the user clicks the button.

iClickCounter is a variable that will be used again later on this page.

```
<script language="JavaScript">
iClickCounter = readCookie("ClickCounter");
</script>
```

readCookie() is one of the functions defined in the <head> of the document.

Each time the user clicks the "Click Me!" button, the *onclick* event fires. The button's <input> tag takes this opportunity to increase the value of the variable iClickCounter and store the new value in the cookie called

ClickCounter. If this code seems a little complicated, worry not, because you do not need to know this to pass the CIW exam. By studying the following callouts, however, you can get an idea of how this code works:

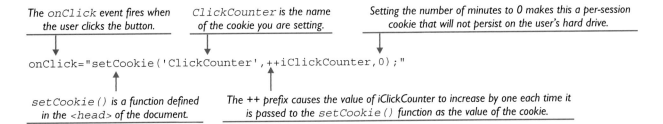

The onClick event fires when the user clicks the button. *ClickCounter is the name of the cookie you are setting.* *Setting the number of minutes to 0 makes this a per-session cookie that will not persist on the user's hard drive.*

```
onClick="setCookie('ClickCounter',++iClickCounter,0);"
```

setCookie() is a function defined in the <head> of the document. *The ++ prefix causes the value of iClickCounter to increase by one each time it is passed to the setCookie() function as the value of the cookie.*

Many Web developers criticize JavaScript for not having the `readCookie()` and `setCookie()` functions built in. Now that you have these functions working, you can use them on other pages any time you need to read or set the value of a cookie.

```
cookies.html - Notepad
File  Edit  Format  View  Help

<html>
<head>
<title>Cookie Cutting</title>
<script language="JavaScript">

function setCookie(sName,sValue,iMinutes)
{
    if (iMinutes == 0)
        document.cookie = sName + "=" + sValue;
    else
    {
        dateExpires = new Date();
        dateExpires.setMinutes(dateExpires.getMinutes()+iMinutes);
        document.cookie = sName + "=" + sValue
                        + ";expires="
                        + dateExpires.toGMTString();
    }
}

function readCookie(sName)
{
    cookieChecker = document.cookie.split("; ");
    for (i=0; i<cookieChecker.length; i++)
    {
        if (sName == cookieChecker[i].split("=")[0])
            return cookieChecker[i].split("=")[1];
    }
    return ""; //returns nothing if cookie not found
}

</script>
</head>

<body>
<h1>Hit Counter</h1>

<script language="JavaScript">
iClickCounter = readCookie("ClickCounter");
</script>

<form method="post" action="cookies.html">
<input type="submit" value="Click Me!"
onClick="setCookie('ClickCounter',++iClickCounter,0);">
</form>

<p>Number of clicks:
<script language="JavaScript">
document.write(iClickCounter);
</script>
</p>
</body>
</html>
```

FIGURE 8-12 *Powered by the code in Figure 8-11, the browser uses a cookie to keep track of how many times the user clicks the button.* ∎

FIGURE 8-11 *The head section of the cookies.html page contains JavaScript functions that you can use whenever you need to set or read the value of a cookie.* ∎

Inspecting Your Computer's Cookies

If you have never looked around your computer to see what cookies are stored there, you will be amazed by what this exercise will turn up. Remember that there are two kinds of cookies: (1) per-session cookies that are stored in RAM and evaporate when the user closes the browser windows and (2) persistent cookies that survive from session to session. Persistent cookies endure even when the user reboots or powers off the computer. The persistent cookies stick around because the browser stores them on the computer's hard drive. To inspect the cookies the browser is storing on your hard drive, follow these steps:

1. Click the Windows Start button and choose Search to make the Search window appear.
2. Click the option to search all files or folders. When the search criteria form appears, type the word *cookie* into the field titled *All or part of the file name.* Leave the other fields blank.
3. Click to reveal the more advanced options and set the options to search for hidden files and system files.
4. Click the Search button and wait while your computer looks for filenames containing the word *cookie.* One by one, your cookie files will begin to appear in the search window.
5. Look for a folder called *cookies.* Right-click it and choose the option to enter that folder. Here you will probably find many more cookie files.
6. To inspect a cookie file, right-click its filename to bring up the quick menu, choose Open, and choose the option to open the file with the Notepad. Many cookies are encrypted, so do not be disappointed if you cannot decipher the contents of these files.
7. Reflect on how servers all over the Internet, including commercial Web sites, are using your computer's hard drive as a storage medium.

Cascading Style Sheets

A **cascading style sheet (CSS)** is a set of rules that define styles to be applied to entire Web pages or individual Web page elements. Each rule consists of a selector followed by a set of curly braces containing the style properties and their values. The selector can be an HTML element, a user-defined style known as a class, or the ID of a specific element on a page. Here are some examples of style definitions that you might find on a CSS:

```
a:link{color: rgb(255,204,0) }
a:visited{color: rgb(153,204,204) }
a:active {color: rgb(102,255,0) }
body
{
        font-family: Garamond, Times New Roman, Times;
        background-color: rgb(51,102,204);
        color: rgb(255,255,153);
}
table
{
        table-border-color-light: rgb(153,255,204);
        table-border-color-dark: rgb(0,0,51);
}
```

```
h1, h2, h3, h4, h5, h6{font-family: Verdana, Arial, Helvetica}
h1 {color: rgb(255,204,0) }
h2 {color: rgb(153,255,51) }
h3 {color: rgb(0,255,204) }
h4 {color: rgb(255,204,0) }
h5 {color: rgb(153,255,51) }
h6 {color: rgb(0,255,204) }
.callout { font-size: small }
#trailer { font-family: serif }
```

User-defined style classes begin with a period.

ID selectors begin with a pound sign.

Three Kinds of Cascading Style Sheets

There are three ways of applying cascading style sheets to a Web page: external, embedded, and inline. An **external CSS** keeps all the style definitions in a separate CSS file that you include in a Web page at runtime by using the `<link>` tag to apply the style sheet to the page. An **embedded CSS** is a style sheet that gets copied physically into the head of the Web page and applies to the Web page as a whole. An **inline CSS** is a style sheet that applies to only one page element so it gets copied "inline" on the page with that element. The following exercises help you understand these definitions by walking you through some examples of the three ways of applying styles to a Web page.

Creating an Inline CSS

Sometimes, no matter how hard you try, you just aren't satisfied with the look of something on your page. You want part of the text to stand out more, for example, or you want to soften the appearance of something. Enter the inline CSS, which was invented to provide you with a way to change a single element on a page without affecting any others. Suppose you want to make the name and e-mail fields stand out a little more on the *subscribe.html* form you created in the previous chapter. You want to modify those two fields only, without changing the appearance of any other input controls onscreen. Follow these steps:

1. Use the Notepad to open the *subscribe.html* page you created in the previous chapter. You will find this file in your *website* folder.

2. Click to position your cursor inside the tag you want to stylize. In this example, click to position your cursor before the > that concludes the input tag that creates the Name field. Modify this tag to read as follows:

```
<input type="text" name="Name" size="50" maxlength="150"
style="border-style: inset; border-width: 4">
```

When an inline CSS has more than one style change, you separate the styles with a semicolon.

3. Save the file and open it with your browser to see how this inline style changes the style and width of the Name field's border.

4. Now that you have stylized the Name field, you should make a similar change to the Email field. Try to do this on your own, but if you need help, here is the modification to make to the Email field's input tag:

```
<input type="text" name="Email" size="50" maxlength="150"
style="border-style: inset; border-width: 4">
```

5. Save the file and click the browser's Refresh button to view the latest version of the page. Figure 8-13 shows that the text fields appear inset into the screen.

Creating an Embedded CSS

The purpose of an embedded CSS is to enable you to make style changes that apply to the Web page as a whole. The embedded CSS goes into the head section of the page, and the style rules defined there apply to the whole page. If any element on the page has a style whose attributes have been affected by the style sheet, those rules will take effect in displaying the element onscreen. The best way to understand this is to work through an example. Suppose you like the color blue and you want to make certain Web page elements appear in blue. To do this with an embedded CSS, follow these steps:

1. Use the Notepad to open the *subscribe.html* page you created in the previous chapter. You will find this file in your *website* folder.

2. Click to position your cursor in the head section of the document. Immediately prior to the `</head>` stop tag, type the following embedded style sheet. Notice that the `<style>` start and `</style>` stop tags demarcate the embedded style:

```
<head>
<title>Newsletter Subscription Form</title>
<style>
        h1 { font-family: Comic Sans MS; color: #0000DD }
</style>
</head>
```

3. Save the file and open it with your browser. The heading should appear blue in the comic font. If you do not see this on your screen, return to the previous step, proofread the code, and troubleshoot any problems.

4. Suppose you also want to make the paragraph text appear blue in the comic font. Use the Notepad to add the following line to the embedded style sheet in the head section of the *subscribe.html* page:

```
<style>
    h1 { color: #0000DD; font-family: Comic Sans MS }
    p { font-family: Comic Sans MS; color: #0000DD }
</style>
```

5. Save the file, view it with your browser, and click the browser's Refresh button. Figure 8-14 illustrates that this embedded style sheet makes the heading and paragraph text appear blue in the comic font.

Creating an External CSS

When you want a style to apply to multiple Web pages, you should create an external CSS and link the Web pages to it. This approach has two advantages. First, it saves you time when you create a new page. Instead of typing the styles into the page, you link the page to the style sheet, thereby saving the time you would otherwise spend keyboarding. Second, and more important, using an external style sheet makes your Web easier to maintain. If you want to make a style change that applies to the entire Web, you simply make that change to the external style sheet, thus saving

The inline style "border-style: inset; border-width: 4" causes the text input fields to appear inset into the screen.

h1 {color: #0000DD; font-family: Comic Sans MS} is the style rule that creates this shade of blue in the comic font.

FIGURE 8-13   *An inline style applies only to the particular element(s) in which you put it. In this example, the inline style "border-style: inset; border-width: 4" is in the Name and Email fields, causing them to appear inset into the screen.* ∎

FIGURE 8-14   *An embedded style sheet applies to every instance of a Web page element onscreen. In this example, the blue text and the comic font come from the style settings embedded in the <head> of the document.* ∎

the time you would otherwise need to spend changing the style on every page in the Web. To create an external cascading style sheet, follow these steps:

1. Pull down the Notepad's File menu and choose New to create a new file. Into this new file, type the following code. This code contains styling for some of the more popular font and color choices you see out on the Web. After you create this style sheet and gain experience using it, you can modify and add new settings to create your own style:

The color #003399 creates a dark shade of blue.

```
BODY    {background-color:"#FFFFFF"}
H1      {color:#003399; font-family:Arial}
A:link      {text-decoration:underline; color:#003399}
A:visited   {text-decoration:underline; color:#003399}
A:hover     {text-decoration:underline; color:red}
```

2. Pull down the Notepad's File menu and choose Save As. When the Save dialog appears, pull down the Save as Type menu and set it to All Files. Then use the controls to save this file in your *website* folder under the filename *MyStyles.css*.

3. You use the `<link>` tag to link the style sheet to any page in the Web. Suppose you want to link the style sheet, for example, to your Web page résumé. Use the Notepad to open the *resume.html* page and click to position your cursor in the `<head>` of the document. Immediately prior to the `</head>` tag, type the following `<link>` tag:

```
<link rel=stylesheet href="MyStyles.css" type="text/css">
```

Type the filename of your style sheet here.

4. Save the file and open it with your browser. Your *resume.html* page now appears with the styling in the cascading style sheet. The a:link styling makes the hyperlinks change color when the user mouses over them. To see this happen onscreen, move your cursor over one of the links in your bulleted table of contents, for example, and observe that the text changes color.

5. If you experiment with changing the style settings in your cascading style sheet, remember to save the file after you make the changes, and then click the browser's Refresh button. If the changes do not appear onscreen, click Ctrl-Refresh, which makes the browser reload everything associated with the page.

When to Use the <span> and <div> Tags

Sometimes you may want to stylize part, instead of all, of a Web page element. To provide a way for you to do that, the W3C invented the HTML inline `<span>` start and `</span>` stop tags. Suppose you wanted to colorize a few words in a paragraph. Instead of applying the color style to the <p> tag, which would colorize the entire paragraph, you can instead create a <span> around the words you want colorized, and apply the color to the <span> tag, as follows:

```
<p>Notice how <span style="color: yellow">yellow words</span> appear onscreen.</p>
```

Other situations may arise in which you want to apply a style to larger divisions of a document at the block level. You create block-level divisions with the <div> start and </div> stop tags, where <div> stands for division. The syntax for the <div> tag is exactly the same as for the <span> tag. Because <div> is a block-level tag, however, the browser begins a new line at the beginning of the division. If you do not want a new line, use the <span> tag, which enables you to stylize elements inline without starting a new block onscreen.

When to Create Style Classes and IDs

In cascading style sheets, a **class** is a named definition of one or more styles. You create the class by prefixing its name with a dot in the CSS file. Suppose you want a class you can use whenever you are displaying warning messages onscreen. In the style sheet, you could create such a class, as follows:

```
<style>
.warning { color: red; font-family: arial; font-weight: bold}
</style>
```

Whenever you want an HTML element to have that style, you use the *class* attribute, as in this example:

```
<p>Be careful when you try this, because <span class="warning">
the burner is hot!</span></p>
```

The "warning" class makes red and bold `the burner is hot!`

Style sheets also enable you to stylize elements via unique identifiers called IDs. In cascading style sheets, an ID is a unique style identifier intended to apply to one, and only one, Web page element onscreen. In the style sheet, you create an ID via the # character. Suppose there is a trailer that appears once, and only once, onscreen. In the style sheet, you could create a unique styling for the trailer, as follows:

```
<style>
#trailer { color: #808080; font-family: Century Schoolbook }
</style>
```

You can make the trailer have this style by referring to it in your HTML, as follows:

```
<span ID="trailer">
<p>Everything inside this span is the trailer.</p>
<p>It appears onscreen in the style of the ID named "trailer".</p>
</span>
```

What Is Absolute Positioning?

On the cutting edge of cascading style sheets is a feature called **absolute positioning**, which enables you to position page elements precisely on-screen based on x,y coordinates. The upper-left corner of the browser window is position 0,0. To position a page element 40 pixels down and 30 pixels across the screen, for example, the inline style would appear as follows:

```
style="position: absolute; top: 40; left: 30;"
```

Absolute positioning makes it possible to layer objects on top of each other. To provide control over the order in which the objects appear onscreen, you can use an attribute called the **z-index**. You can set the value of z-index to tell the browser the order in which to display objects that overlap. The lower the value, the sooner the layer displays onscreen. In other words, an item with a lower z-index will appear underneath overlapping items with higher z-index values.

warning   *You need to be aware that some browsers do not support absolute positioning. It is a hot feature that all browsers should support, but until they do, you may need to postpone creating pages with absolute positioning if any of your users have browsers that do not support it yet.*

Try This!

Pile Rocks with Absolute Positioning and z-index

With absolute positioning, you can be creative in placing graphics onscreen. In this example, you download the images of three rocks and view them individually onscreen. Then you use absolute positioning to create a rock pile in which the images appear in overlapping layers onscreen. Thus, you experience firsthand the concept of absolute positioning and layering. To create the rock pile, follow these steps:

1. The three rocks are located on this book's Web site. Right-click each rock and use the quick menu to save the rocks in your *website* folder. Do not change the filenames, which are *igneous.gif*, *metamorphic.gif*, and *sedimentary.gif*. If you have ever studied geology, you will recognize igneous, metamorphic, and sedimentary as the three basic kinds of rocks.

2. Pull down the Notepad's File menu and choose New to create a new file. Type the following code, which displays the three rocks onscreen:

```
<html>
<head>
<title>Rocks</title>
</head>
<body>
<img src="igneous.gif" width="320" height="240">
<img src="metamorphic.gif" width="320" height="240">
<img src="sedimentary.gif" width="320" height="240">
</body>
</html>
```

Try This!
continued

3. Pull down the Notepad's File menu and choose Save As. When the Save dialog appears, pull down the Save as Type menu and set it to All Files. Then use the controls to save this file in your *website* folder under the filename *rockpile.html* and open it with your browser. The three rocks appear onscreen, side by side, as illustrated in Figure 8-15.

4. Now comes the fun part. Use the Notepad to add the following <span> tags to the images displayed on the *rockpile.html* page. These <span> tags use inline styles to layer the rocks on top of each other:

```
<body>
<span style="position: absolute; left: 30; top: 150; z-index: 0">
<img src="igneous.gif" width="320" height="240">
</span>
<span style="position: absolute; left: 150; top: 35; z-index: 1">
<img src="metamorphic.gif" width="320" height="240">
</span>
<span style="position: absolute; left: 220; top: 140; z-index: 2">
<img src="sedimentary.gif" width="320" height="240">
</span>
</body>
```

5. Save the file and view it with your browser. Click Refresh to make sure you are viewing the current version of the file. Figure 8-16 shows how the rocks layer onscreen. You have made a rock pile!

6. Now reflect: Inside the <span> tags can go other html elements, such as headings and paragraphs and tables. In fact, any page element can be contained by the span and thereby positioned onscreen via absolute positioning. In the next chapter, you study how you can use CSS to lay out Web pages that may be more accessible than some kinds of table-driven layouts.

This is a dime. Geologists put coins atop rock samples to enable you to gauge the relative sizes of the rocks.

FIGURE 8-15 *Without layering, images appear individually onscreen. Compare this to Figure 8-16, which uses absolute positioning to layer the same images on top of each other.* ■

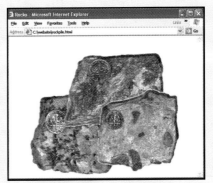

FIGURE 8-16 *A pile of three rocks created via absolute positioning. Compare this to Figure 8-15, in which the same images appear without the inline styles that layer the rocks into a pile.* ■

Dynamic HTML

Dynamic HTML is a term invented by Microsoft to refer to the animated Web pages you can create by using the DOM to combine HTML with style sheets and scripts that bring Web pages to life. Some people get confused by the term Dynamic HTML because they think it refers to some kind of a product. Dynamic HTML is not a product; rather, it is a concept. Whenever you create dynamic effects onscreen by manipulating objects in the DOM, you are doing what Microsoft refers to as Dynamic HTML. You will understand this more by working through the following examples.

Dynamic Animation Effects

In the style sheet section of this chapter, you learned how to use absolute positioning to place an image at any x,y location onscreen. JavaScript has a timer event you can use to manipulate the values of x and y dynamically, thereby creating an animation onscreen. To create such an animation, follow these steps:

1. Pull down the Notepad's File menu and choose New to create a new file. Into this new file, type the following code:

```
<html>
<head>
<title>Dynamic HTML Example</title>
<script language="JavaScript">
var id;
function BeginAnimation()
{
    id = window.setInterval("ContinueAnimation()",50);
}
function ContinueAnimation()
{
    MyPhoto.style.pixelLeft += 10;
    MyPhoto.style.pixelTop += 4;
    if (MyPhoto.style.pixelLeft>200)
    {
        window.clearInterval(id);
    }
}
</script>
</head>
<body onload="BeginAnimation()" marginheight="0" topmargin="0" leftmargin="0">
<img id="MyPhoto" style="position:absolute; top:0; left:0; z-index:-1" src="photo.gif">
</body>
</html>
```

Type the filename of the image you want this code to animate.

2. Pull down the Notepad's File menu and choose Save As. When the Save dialog appears, save this file under the filename *dynamic.html*. Then open the file with your browser. You should see the image move around the screen as the script alters the x,y values that position the image onscreen.

Dynamic HTML Code Analysis

To create an animation with Dynamic HTML, you need to latch onto an event that can get the animation started. The *dynamic.html* script does this in the <body> tag via the *onload* event, one of the intrinsic events identified earlier in this chapter in Table 8-3. Notice that the <body> start tag is programmed to fire the BeginAnimation() function when the page loads:

```
<body onload="BeginAnimation()">
```

The BeginAnimation() function is very brief. It calls upon the setInterval() method of the JavaScript window object to set a timer that will go off after 50 milliseconds and fire the ContinueAnimation() function:

Type the number of milliseconds after which you want the timer to fire.

```
function BeginAnimation()
{
    id = window.setInterval("ContinueAnimation()",50);
}
```

After you get an animation started, you need to keep it going. The ContinueAnimation() function does that by computing the image's next position and setting another timer. This process continues until the image moves past the point at which the IF statement stops the animation by calling upon the clearInterval() method to stop the timer from going off any more:

```
function ContinueAnimation()
{
    MyPhoto.style.pixelLeft += 10;          This controls how far over
                                            the picture will move.
    MyPhoto.style.pixelTop += 4;
    if (MyPhoto.style.pixelLeft>200)        This controls how far down
    {                                       the picture will move.

        window.clearInterval(id);           This determines when the
                                            animation will stop.
    }
}
```

The variable named id contains the identification number of the timer to be stopped.

The clearInterval() method stops the timer from firing.

There is no limit to the number of animation patterns you can create onscreen. This example moved the image along a straight line to keep the coding straightforward. If you know your math, however, there is no limit to the patterns of movement you can create onscreen.

Dynamic Gradient Effects

One of my favorite background effects is the **gradient**, a graphical effect created by colors fading gradually across or down the screen. Figure 8-17 shows examples of some of the gradients you can create with dynamic HTML. The code needed to do this is very straightforward, thanks to the built-in gradient method that creates these effects. To create a gradient background on any Web page, follow these steps:

1. Use the Notepad to open the page on which you want to create the gradient background. In this example, open the *resume.html* file you created in the previous chapter.

2. Modify the <body> tag to read as follows:

```
<body style="filter: progid:DXImageTransform.Microsoft.gradient
(startColorstr=#88BBF7F6, endColorstr=#FFFFFFC0)" >
```

3. Pull down the File menu and choose Save to save the page; then open it with your browser. If you typed everything correctly, you will see the gradient onscreen.

4. To experiment with different colors, you can alter the start and stop color strings, which are named *startColorstr* and *endColorstr*, respectively. Save the file and click the browser's Refresh button to view the revised gradient onscreen. The format of the color string is #AARRGGBB, where AA is the alpha value, RR is red, GG is green, and BB is blue. The alpha value controls opacity, with values ranging from 00 (transparent) to FF (full color).

Dynamic Page Transitions

A **page transition** is the style or manner in which the screen changes when the browser brings up a new document and displays it onscreen. You can use a wide variety of page transition effects for pizzazz. As with all special effects, you should not overuse page transitions or feel compelled to display a different effect each time you display a page. If there is an effect you like, however, you certainly may use it in good taste. To create a Dynamic HTML page transition, follow these steps:

1. Use the Notepad to open the page for which you want to create a transition effect. Click to position your cursor in the head of the document, prior to the </head> stop tag.

2. To set the transition effect that users will see when the page comes onscreen, type the following code:

```
<META http-equiv="Page-Enter"
CONTENT="progid:DXImageTransform.Microsoft.Blinds(Duration=2)" />
```

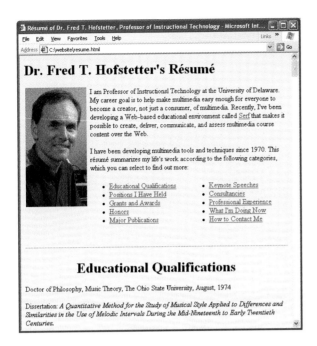

startColorstr=#88BBF7F6, endColorstr=#FFFFFFC0

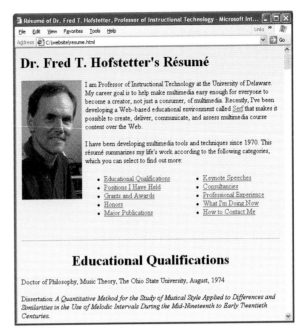

startColorstr=# F8D2EF, endColorstr=#C2C3FE

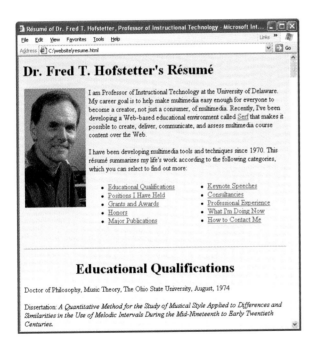

startColorstr=#88CCFBA3, endColorstr=#88EDFEDE

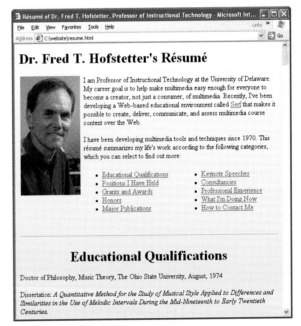

startColorstr=#44F8E4ED, endColorstr=#88F4C2DA

FIGURE 8-17 *These gradient backgrounds are some of the Dynamic HTML effects you can create via the gradient method of the DXImageTransform object. You can make millions of different gradients by manipulating the start and stop color strings.* ∎

3. To set the transition effect that users will see when the page leaves the screen, type the following code:

```
<META http-equiv="Page-Exit"
CONTENT="progid:DXImageTransform.Microsoft.Slide(Duration=2.500,slidestyle='HIDE')" />
```

note *There are many more transition effects besides the common examples listed in this table. For more, go to the DHTML workshop at msdn.microsoft.com/library/default.asp?url=/workshop/author/dhtml/dhtml.asp.*

4. Save the file and open it with your browser. Notice the effects you specified when the page goes on or off screen. Remember not to overuse these effects. They are cool, but users can grow tired of them, especially if you make the transitions last more than a second or two. Table 8-5 lists some of the other page transition effects. To audition them, go back to steps 2 and 3 and modify the settings according to the examples provided in Table 8-5.

Effect	Style Setting
Blinds Horizontal	DXImageTransform.Microsoft.Blinds(direction='down')
Blinds Vertical	DXImageTransform.Microsoft.Blinds(direction='right')
Box In	DXImageTransform.Microsoft.Iris(irisstyle='SQUARE', motion='in')
Box Out	DXImageTransform.Microsoft.Iris(irisstyle='SQUARE', motion='out')
Checkerboard Across	DXImageTransform.Microsoft.CheckerBoard(direction='right')
Checkerboard Down	DXImageTransform.Microsoft.CheckerBoard(direction='down')
Circle In	DXImageTransform.Microsoft.Iris(irisstyle='CIRCLE', motion='in')
Circle Out	DXImageTransform.Microsoft.Iris(irisstyle='CIRCLE', motion='out')
Random Bars Horizontal	DXImageTransform.Microsoft.RandomBars(orientation='horizontal')
Random Bars Vertical	DXImageTransform.Microsoft.RandomBars(orientation='vertical')
Random Dissolve	DXImageTransform.Microsoft.RandomDissolve
Split Horizontal In	DXImageTransform.Microsoft.Barn(orientation='horizontal', motion='in')
Split Horizontal Out	DXImageTransform.Microsoft.Barn(orientation='horizontal', motion='out')
Split Vertical In	DXImageTransform.Microsoft.Barn(orientation='vertical', motion='in')
Split Vertical Out	DXImageTransform.Microsoft.Barn(orientation='vertical', motion='out')
Strips Left Down	DXImageTransform.Microsoft.Strips(motion='leftdown')
Strips Left Up	DXImageTransform.Microsoft.Strips(motion='leftup')
Strips Right Down	DXImageTransform.Microsoft.Strips(motion='rightdown')
Strips Right Up	DXImageTransform.Microsoft.Strips(motion='rightup')
Wipe Up	DXImageTransform.Microsoft.Blinds(direction='up', bands=1)
Wipe Down	DXImageTransform.Microsoft.Blinds(direction='down', bands=1)
Wide Right	DXImageTransform.Microsoft.Blinds(direction='right', bands=1)
Wipe Left	DXImageTransform.Microsoft.Blinds(direction='left', bands=1)

TABLE 8-5   *Page Transition Effects* ■

Try This!

Dynamic HTML Code Generator

Microsoft's Dynamic HTML site has an HTML code generator called the Master Sample that lets you try out a wide range of special effects. For each kind of effect, there are controls that let you manipulate the values of the parameters that affect what you see onscreen. Figure 8-18 shows that you can audition the effects and fine-tune the settings until you get it just the way you want it. Then you can copy and paste the code to create the effect on pages of your own. To generate some Dynamic HTML code, follow these steps:

1. Go to msdn.microsoft.com/workshop/samples/author/dhtml/DXTidemo/DXTidemo.htm. If this does not bring up the HTML code generator, its address may have changed—follow this book's link to the Dynamic HTML Code Generator.

2. Choose the type of Dynamic HTML effect you would like to explore. The choices are Filters or Transitions. In this example, choose Transitions to bring up the Transition controls.

3. Pull down the menu to select the specific effect you want to explore. In this example, pull down the Select a Transition menu, choose GradientWipe, and click the Play button to see what the effect causes onscreen.

4. Use the controls beneath the Play button to explore the customization settings. Following your instincts, set the controls however you want, and click the Play button to see what happens. In this example, set the gradient size to 0.25, make the wipe style go from left to right, and set the motion to reverse. Then click Play to audition this effect.

5. When you have the effect ready to use on your page, click the Copy Code to Clipboard button. Then click in the Notepad to position your cursor at the spot in your page where you want to insert this effect. Press CTRL-V, or pull down the Edit menu and choose Paste, to insert the effect into your page. Save the page and open it with your browser to see the effect happen on your page.

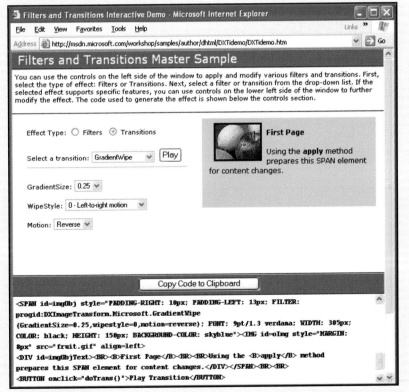

FIGURE 8-18 *Microsoft's Dynamic HTML online workshop includes this master sample that lets you select a transition and modify its parameters by manipulating the controls onscreen. To audition the effect, you click the Play button. When you have it working the way you want, click the Copy Code to Clipboard button. This enables you to paste the code onto your Web page.* ∎

XML and XHTML

The hottest three letters in advanced Web design are XML, which stands for eXtensible Markup Language. As the word extensible implies, XML enables you to create special tags for encoding different kinds of data. Virtually any kind of data can be represented in XML.

What Is XML?

XML is a simple, self-describing markup language that enables computers to read and understand the structure of different kinds of documents and to exchange data across different operating systems, software applications, and hardware configurations without requiring any human intervention. Like HTML, XML has tags, but there is an important difference in how the tags are used. In HTML, the tags mostly define the appearance of the content. In XML, on the other hand, the tags define the structure of the data.

Another important difference between HTML and XML is that in HTML, the tags are specified by the World Wide Web Consortium (W3C). If you want to create a new HTML tag, you cannot do so on your own; rather, you propose the new tag to the W3C and work through a lengthy standardization process. With XML, on the other hand, you can create your own customized tags.

Many disciplines are working to create XML encodings to enable the exchange of data and the creation of new document types beneficial to the industry. To peruse dozens of discipline-based XML projects, go to www.xml.org and follow the links to the various focus areas.

What Is an XML Schema?

An **XML schema** is the structural definition of the types of elements that can appear in a document, the attributes each element may have, and the relationships among the elements. The best way to understand this is to compare the structure of a familiar document to its schema. A document with which everyone is familiar is your checkbook. For each entry in a checkbook, you record the check number, the date, the payee, and the amount of money you are paying. Figure 8-19 shows the XML schema that defines this data structure. The name of the file that contains this schema is *checkbook.xsd*. The filename extension XSD stands for XML Schema Definition.

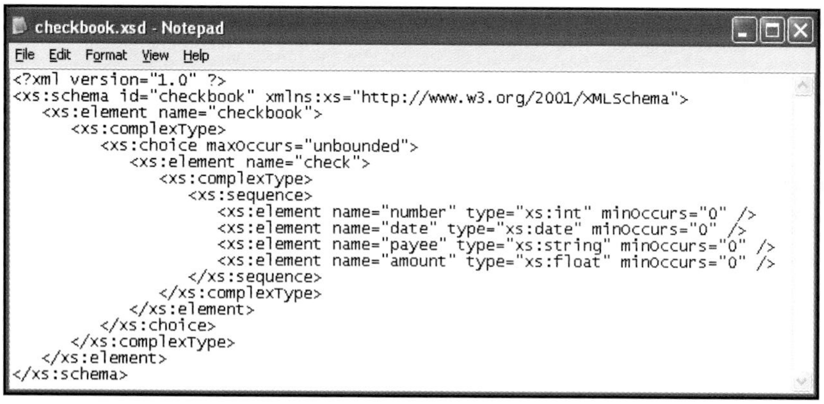

```
checkbook.xsd - Notepad
File  Edit  Format  View  Help
<?xml version="1.0" ?>
<xs:schema id="checkbook" xmlns:xs="http://www.w3.org/2001/XMLSchema">
    <xs:element name="checkbook">
        <xs:complexType>
            <xs:choice maxOccurs="unbounded">
                <xs:element name="check">
                    <xs:complexType>
                        <xs:sequence>
                            <xs:element name="number" type="xs:int" minOccurs="0" />
                            <xs:element name="date" type="xs:date" minOccurs="0" />
                            <xs:element name="payee" type="xs:string" minOccurs="0" />
                            <xs:element name="amount" type="xs:float" minOccurs="0" />
                        </xs:sequence>
                    </xs:complexType>
                </xs:element>
            </xs:choice>
        </xs:complexType>
    </xs:element>
</xs:schema>
```

FIGURE   8-19   *This is the XML schema in the file checkbook.xsd, which defines the elements and the structure of the checkbook document. I made up the names of the elements in this file. When you create a schema, you get to name the elements that are in it.* ■

Encoding Data in XML

Number	Date	Payee	Amount
1001	9/15/04	Columbia Gas	$248.29
1002	9/18/04	Sears	$327.99
1003	9/23/04	United Postal Service	$15.45

TABLE 8-6 *Three Hypothetical Checkbook Entries* ■

For the sake of this example, imagine that since opening your checking account, you have written the three checks illustrated in Table 8-6. To encode this data in XML, you must represent it inside the tags defined by the checkbook schema. Figure 8-20 shows such an encoding. Take special note of the second line of this file, which is a DOCTYPE declaration. For an XML document to be well formed, it must have a **DOCTYPE declaration**, which is a line of code that identifies the XML schema that defines the tag structure. In this example, the DOCTYPE is defining *checkbook.xsd* as the XML schema for this document. When all the tags in a document follow precisely the structural definitions in the schema, the document is said to *validate*. Documents that validate can be opened and processed with a variety of XML tools. Documents that do not validate are said to be *malformed* and will be rejected by XML tools that require strict adherence to the rules of XML. The XML document in Figure 8-20 validates against the *checkbook.xsd* schema and is well formed.

Editing the Data in an XML File

Because XML files are plain text, you can edit them with any text editor, such as the Notepad. If you have a lot of data to edit, or if the schema is complicated, however, you are better off using an XML editor to edit the data. When I edit an XML file, for example, I use the XML editing tools in Visual Studio .NET, Microsoft's premier suite of tools for creating Web applications. Figure 8-21 shows how Visual Studio reads the XML schema of a file and presents you with a visual tool for editing the data in a spreadsheet view. Any change or addition you make to this visual view of the data gets updated by Visual Studio in the XML view of the file. One of the advantages of editing an XML file with a tool such as Visual Studio is that you can be sure the XML will validate and be well formed. When you edit your XML with a text editor, on the other hand, you run the risk of making errors that may cause problems down the road.

What Is the Extensible Stylesheet Language (XSL)?

Much XML data never appears onscreen. In business-to-business applications, for example, there are many server-to-server communications that users never see. Data that never appears onscreen does not need stylistic layout. What do you do, however, when you need to display XML data onscreen? How do you transform that data into a representation that the browser can display with good style? That is where XSL comes in.

```
MyCheckbook.xml - Notepad
File  Edit  Format  View  Help
<?xml version="1.0" encoding="utf-8"?>
<!DOCTYPE checkbook SYSTEM "Checkbook.xsd">
<checkbook>
    <check>
        <number>1001</number>
        <date>9/15/04</date>
        <payee>Columbia Gas</payee>
        <amount>248.49</amount>
    </check>
    <check>
        <number>1002</number>
        <date>9/18/04</date>
        <payee>Sears</payee>
        <amount>327.99</amount>
    </check>
    <check>
        <number>1003</number>
        <date>9/23/04</date>
        <payee>United Postal Service</payee>
        <amount>15.45</amount>
    </check>
</checkbook>
```

FIGURE 8-20 *This is an XML file that encodes the three checkbook entries in Table 8-6. Notice that the DOCTYPE statement at the beginning of this file defines checkbook.xsd as the schema containing the structural rules to which this document must adhere. If you compare the contents of this file to the schema shown earlier in Figure 8-19, you will see that this file follows the rules of the schema and is well formed.* ■

Data for check				
	number	date	payee	amount
	1001	9/15/04	Columbia Gas	248.49
	1002	9/18/04	Sears	327.99
	1003	9/23/04	United Postal	15.45
▶	1004	9/28/04	AT&T	
*				

FIGURE 8-21 *Visual Studio .NET contains this visual tool for editing the contents of an XML file. Any change or addition you make to this visual view of the data gets updated by Visual Studio in the XML view of the file.* ■

The **extensible stylesheet language (XSL)** is an XML dialect that Web designers use to specify the styling, layout, and pagination of the structured content in an XML document for some targeted presentation medium, such as a Web browser, a printer, an eBook, a screen reader, or a hand-held device. The stylesheet language elements are defined by the XSL Working Group of the W3C Style Activity. The official W3C documentation is at www.w3.org/TR/xsl.

What Is the XSL Transformation Language?

The **XSL Transformation (XSLT) language** is an XML dialect that Web designers use to transform documents from one format into another. Although it is beyond the scope of this book to teach XSLT, the concept of document transformation is important for any IT professional to understand.

XSLT enables you to define a template into which you can flow part or all of the content of an XML document. The template combines the data from the XML file with device-specific formatting codes. If you want to format the document for display on a printer, for example, you would embed printer codes in the XSLT template. To display the document on a cell phone, you would use an XSLT template that creates codes according to the wireless application protocol (WAP). If a Web browser is the targeted display medium, you would use an XSLT template that formats the XML data in HTML for display onscreen. Figure 8-22 shows an XSLT template, for example, which formats the *checkbook.xml* file for display in a browser. Figure 8-23 shows how the browser displays the checkbook data via the HTML generated by the template in Figure 8-22.

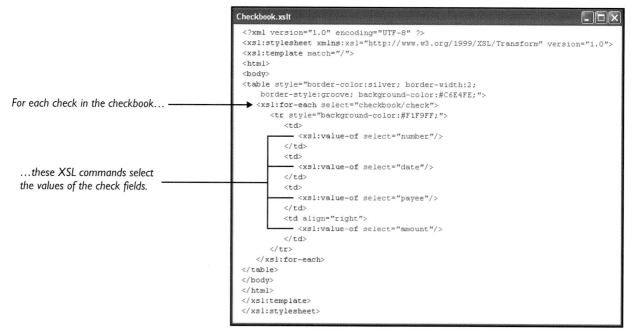

For each check in the checkbook...

...these XSL commands select the values of the check fields.

```
Checkbook.xslt
<?xml version="1.0" encoding="UTF-8" ?>
<xsl:stylesheet xmlns:xsl="http://www.w3.org/1999/XSL/Transform" version="1.0">
<xsl:template match="/">
<html>
<body>
<table style="border-color:silver; border-width:2;
    border-style:groove; background-color:#C6E4FE;">
    <xsl:for-each select="checkbook/check">
        <tr style="background-color:#F1F9FF;">
        <td>
            <xsl:value-of select="number"/>
        </td>
        <td>
            <xsl:value-of select="date"/>
        </td>
        <td>
            <xsl:value-of select="payee"/>
        </td>
        <td align="right">
            <xsl:value-of select="amount"/>
        </td>
        </tr>
    </xsl:for-each>
</table>
</body>
</html>
</xsl:template>
</xsl:stylesheet>
```

FIGURE 8-22 *This XSLT template reads the XML file checkbook.xml and formats the data in HTML for display by a Web browser. Compare this code to Figure 8-23, which shows how the browser displays the table. Just as this template formats the data for display in HTML, so also can you create XSLT templates for transforming XML files for different devices, including printers, PDAs, and cell phones. You can also use XSLT to transform documents into different file formats, such as PDF, DOC, XLS, and RTF.* ■

What Are the Flavors of XHTML?

Now that you have learned the basics of XML, it is time to revisit the definition of XHTML. In Chapter 6, you learned that **XHTML** is a re-formulation of HTML in XML. Now it is time to get more specific about the schema that differentiate the structure of HTML and XHTML files.

Most Web page editors begin a new page by declaring that the structural rules will use a loose, as opposed to strict, definition of HTML. This loose definition enables you to make use of presentation elements that still are in use today but will fade in the future when style sheets achieve widespread use. To declare that a Web page uses the loose definition, you insert the following declaration prior to the `<html>` tag at the top of the page:

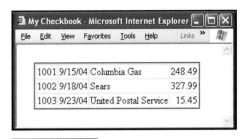

FIGURE 8-23 *This is how the browser displays the XML file checkbook.xml when it is transformed into HTML by the XSLT template in Figure 8-22. If you compare the XML data in Figure 8-20 to the template in Figure 8-22, you can begin to grasp the significance of being able to transform data in this manner.* ∎

```
<!DOCTYPE HTML PUBLIC "-//W3C//DTD HTML 4.01 Transitional//EN"
        "http://www.w3.org/TR/html4/loose.dtd">
```

If your page avoids the deprecated presentation tags and instead uses style sheets to define the presentation of HTML elements onscreen, you can use the strict version of HTML by making your declaration read as follows:

```
<!DOCTYPE HTML PUBLIC "-//W3C//DTD HTML 4.01 Strict//EN"
        "http://www.w3.org/TR/html4/strict.dtd">
```

XHTML also has loose and strict versions. The loose version is the same as HTML transitional except for changes due to the differences between XML and SGML. To use the loose version of XHTML, you make the DOCTYPE read as follows:

```
<!DOCTYPE html  PUBLIC "-//W3C//DTD XHTML 1.0 Transitional//EN"
        "http://www.w3.org/TR/xhtml1/DTD/xhtml1-transitional.dtd">
```

Similarly, the strict version of XHTML is the same as HTML strict except for changes due to the differences between XML and SGML. The DOCTYPE for strict XHTML is

```
<!DOCTYPE html PUBLIC "-//W3C//DTD XHTML 1.0 Strict//EN"
        "http://www.w3.org/TR/xhtml1/DTD/xhtml1-strict.dtd">
```

For an excellent discussion of the differences between strict and transitional XHTML, go to www.w3.org/TR/xhtml1.

What Is an XML Module?

An **XML module** is a collection of semantically related XML elements and attributes oriented toward accomplishing a certain task or function. An excellent example of modularization is the manner in which the W3C has organized into modules the various parts of the **Synchronized Multimedia Implementation Language (SMIL)**. SMIL is an XML-based language that was created by the W3C for the purpose of enabling developers to include multimedia events in Web documents.

When this book went to press, the SMIL modules were organized into ten functional areas: (1) timing, (2) time manipulations, (3) animation, (4) content control, (5) layout, (6) linking, (7) media objects, (8) metainformation, (9) structure, and (10) transitions.

What Is XHTML+SMIL?

A language profile is the combination of modules to create an XML language designed to meet certain objectives. The W3C has created a language profile you can use to add multimedia functionality to XHTML. The name of this profile is **XHTML+SMIL**. Its goal is to permit the Web designer to use SMIL animations, timings, and transitions within a conventional HTML or CSS page layout. Thus, XHTML+SMIL omits modules related to layout. As a result, the Web designer can create a layout via style sheets or HTML and include SMIL animations, timings, and transitions in traditional Web page elements.

Microsoft has created an implementation of XHTML+SMIL called **HTML+TIME** that works with Internet Explorer versions 5.5 and later. True to its name, the most important part of HTML+TIME is the timing module, because that is how you create synchronized multimedia events. An excellent example of a multimedia event that requires timing is the captioning of a video, which requires you to display onscreen subtitles at precise times in sync with the video. This chapter concludes with a Try This! exercise that lets you experience this for yourself onscreen.

Try This!

The Kennedy Moon Challenge Project

Because of its built-in support of HTML+TIME, the Internet Explorer Web browser gives you considerable multimedia authoring capability without requiring you to own any other tools. This exercise provides an example of how you can caption a video by displaying onscreen subtitles that appear at precise times in sync with the video. All you need to accomplish this is the Notepad text editor and the IE browser, version 5.5 or later. The video you will caption is a famous passage from President John F. Kennedy's famous moon challenge speech. To caption the video and play it onscreen, follow these steps:

1. Go to this chapter's section of this book's Web site. You will see a link to click to download a famous 30-second video clip from JFK's moon-challenge speech. Click the link and save the file in your *website* folder. Do not change the file's name, which is KennedyMoonChallenge.avi. The file size is 3.6 megabytes.

2. Pull down the Notepad's File menu and choose New to begin a new file. Type the following code to get the page started. Notice that the HTML tag has an XML namespace (`xmlns`) attribute that associates the prefix *t* with Microsoft's HTML+TIME schema:

```
<html xmlns:t="urn:schemas-microsoft-com:time">
<head>
<title>JFK SMIL Example</title>
</head>
<body>
</body>
</html>
```

3. Pull down the Notepad's File menu and choose Save As; use the Save controls to save this file in your *website* folder under the filename *Kennedy.html*.

4. In the head section of the document, type the following `<style>` tag to make the page use HTML+ TIME version 2:

```
<head>
<title>JFK SMIL Example</title>
<style>
    .time{ behavior: url(#default#time2);}
</style>
</head>
```

5. In the body of the document, position your cursor between the `<body>` start and `</body>` stop tag and type the following code. This creates a table with two rows. The top row shows the video, and the bottom row uses the sequence element seq to display the captions in time with the video. You can also download this code from this book's Web site, where the filename is *KennedyTable.txt*:

Try This!
continued

```html
<body>
<table cellspacing="0" style="background-color:White;font:bold;font-size:11pt;">
<tr>
    <td>
        <t:video class="time" ID="movie" src="KennedyMoonChallenge.avi" />
    </td>
</tr>
<tr>
    <td id="caption" align="center">
        <t:seq id="txSeq" class="time" begin="movie.begin+.5">
        <span id="1" class="time" dur="2">We choose to go to the moon in</span>
        <span id="2" class="time" dur="2.5">this decade and do the other things,</span>
        <span id="3" class="time" dur="2.15">not because they are easy,</span>
        <span id="4" class="time" dur="2.0">but because they are hard.</span>
        <span id="5" class="time" dur="1.8">Because that goal</span>
        <span id="6" class="time" dur="1.8">will serve to organize</span>
        <span id="7" class="time" dur="1.8">and measure the best</span>
        <span id="8" class="time" dur="2.2">of our energies and skills.</span>
        <span id="9" class="time" dur="2.1">Because that challenge is one</span>
        <span id="10" class="time" dur="1.9">that we're willing to accept,</span>
        <span id="11" class="time" dur="2.2">one we are unwilling to postpone,</span>
        <span id="12" class="time" dur="2.3">and one we intend to win,</span>
        <span id="13" class="time" dur="3">and the others too.</span>
        </t:seq>
    </td>
</tr>
</table>
</body>
```

6. Save the *Kennedy.html* file and open it with your browser. Notice how the captions appear onscreen in time with the video. You have successfully used XML to caption a video.

7. By modifying this file, you can make it display captions for any video. To change the video, replace *KennedyMoonChallenge.avi* by the movie you want to play instead. To change the captions, edit the <span> elements within which the caption attributes are set. The attribute *dur* creates the timing. In SMIL, *dur* stands for duration and specifies how many seconds the element will last. In this example, *dur* determines how many seconds the caption will remain onscreen.

8. This exercise demonstrates just one of the many multimedia capabilities of HTML+TIME. For more on the built-in multimedia capabilities of the IE Web browser, follow this book's Web site link to the HTML+TIME language reference.

Chapter 8 Review

▣ Chapter Summary

After reading this chapter and completing the step-by-step tutorials and Try This! exercises, you should understand the following facts about creating active Web pages:

Introduction to Scripting

- A static Web page is a document in which the content is fixed in HTML codes that make the document always read the same when viewed in a browser. An active Web page uses the browser's window as a display surface through which the user can interact with dynamic objects onscreen.

- Scripting is the act of writing little computer programs that can enhance the appearance and functionality of a Web page. Browsers render Web pages by placing objects onscreen. Scripts let you grab hold of those objects to make them do special things.

- There are many brands of scripting languages. Most well known is JavaScript, the language that runs client-side in the browser without requiring any server-side processing. On the server side, VBScript and JScript are Microsoft's Active Server Page (ASP) languages. Other popular server-side languages include C#, Java, and J#, Microsoft's version of Java.

- You can put JavaScript in the head or in the body section of a Web page. Scripts can also reside in a separate file called an include file, which gets included in the page at runtime.

- If a script is brief and is not used a lot, you can simply type it into the body of the page. If you find yourself typing the same code often, however, it is better to put it inside a reusable function that goes into the head section of the Web page.

- A function is a named procedure you can call upon by name any time you need to execute the code that function contains. When you call the function, you can pass to it one or more parameters that preset the values of variables that the function manipulates. When the function finishes executing, it can return values to the script that called it.

- A variable is a place in the computer's RAM that remembers, or stores, the value of something changeable. It is called a variable because its value is subject to change. A variable name is the identifier used to refer to, or call upon, a place in computer memory that stores the value of a variable.

- A string is a sequence of one or more alphanumeric characters. A string variable is a place in computer memory that remembers, or stores, the alphanumeric characters in a string.

- A numeric variable is a place in computer memory that remembers, or stores, a number. In a script, the numbers can be integers or floating point. An integer is a whole number with no decimal point. A floating point number has a decimal point with one or more numbers after the decimal point.

- An operator is a symbol that causes a script to perform some kind of action on a variable or a value. The most fundamental operator is the assignment operator, which assigns values to variables. The assignment operator uses the = symbol.

- To concatenate means to join strings together via the concatenation operator. In JavaScript, the concatenation operator is the + sign.

- In computing, an object is a self-contained entity consisting of properties and methods enabling you to do something programmatically. A method is a little computer program that has been built into an object to enable the object to do something. A property is an attribute of an object that has a value.

- In computer programming, an event is an action that provides an opportunity to trigger a script, which can use objects to inspect properties and execute methods that make things happen onscreen or keep records behind the scenes. The most commonly used events are (1) the mouseover, which fires when the user mouses over an object onscreen; (2) the click, which fires when the user clicks the mouse; (3) the double-click, which the user triggers by clicking twice quickly; and (4) the page load, which fires when the user visits a Web site and a page first comes onscreen.

Document Object Model (DOM)

■ The document object model (DOM) is the official W3C structural definition of the objects, methods, and properties that comprise documents on the World Wide Web. The latest version is at www.w3.org/DOM.

■ In JavaScript, the most commonly used DOM objects are the ones that provide access to the HTML elements that comprise the document displayed inside the browser window. Of particular importance are the elements in the forms through which the user interacts by selecting things, entering textual information, and clicking to submit the form.

■ In addition to defining the objects that enable a script to manipulate elements on a Web page, the W3C has defined the intrinsic events that can trigger such a script. Two popular events are onmouseover and onmouseout, which you use to create rollover effects onscreen. When the user mouses over something, the onmouseover event fires, causing your script to do something onscreen. Similarly, when the user mouses out of something, the onmouseout event fires, providing another opportunity to run a script.

■ To access DOM objects in a script, you use dot notation to refer to the objects you want to manipulate. Following the document's hierarchical structure, dot notation places to the left elements that are structurally higher than elements further down the tree. An example is document.title, which you use to retrieve or set the title of the page.

■ An array is a named table of memory locations in which values can be stored. When a Web page loads, the browser creates arrays for the images, forms, links, anchors, and all the other elements onscreen. As the browser encounters these objects on the page, it places them into these arrays. The arrays are indexed sequentially, beginning with zero. The first image on the page, therefore, goes into slot 0 of the images array. You could refer to it in a script as document.images[0].

■ An easier way to access elements on a Web page is to name the elements and then refer to them by name. An image named MyPhoto is easier to refer to, for example, as MyPhoto.width instead of document.images[0].width.

■ An alert box is a window that a script creates by executing the alert() method of the JavaScript window object. Inside the parentheses of the alert() method, you insert the string of characters and variables you want displayed in the alert box. At runtime, when the script encounters the alert, the script pauses while you study the contents of the alert box onscreen. When you click to dismiss the alert box, the script continues executing. By putting alert boxes in strategic places down through the path of execution in your code, you can step through the code and diagnose the point at which something is going wrong.

■ A rollover is a special graphical effect you create by using the JavaScript onmouseover and onmouseout event handlers. When the user mouses over something, the onmouseover event fires, causing your script to do something onscreen. Similarly, when the user mouses out of something, the onmouseout event fires, providing another opportunity to run a script. In the most common kind of rollover, a script changes the source of the image when the user mouses over it and reverts to the original image when the user mouses out of it.

Maintaining State in Cookies

■ A cookie is a place in the computer's memory where browsers can store information about the user. If someone buys an audio CD by Britney Spears, for example, the site might create a cookie indicating that the user likes pop music. The next time the user visits the site, it might display ads for similar pop music titles.

■ There are two kinds of cookies, namely, persistent cookies that are stored on the user's hard disk and per-session cookies that are stored in RAM. Because persistent cookies are stored on disk, they survive from session to session, even after the user closes the Web browser and turns off the computer. Per-session cookies, on the other hand, evaporate when the user closes the Web browser, which frees the RAM.

■ The Internet needs cookies to maintain state from screen to screen. Virtually all sites that have you log on and off, including all of the Internet's e-commerce sites, use per-session cookies to maintain state.

- Knowledgeable users can find the persistent cookie files and read their contents with any text editor. If these contents are unencrypted, the cookies can be read in plain text. It is appropriate to use persistent cookies to store information that would not cause a security problem if sniffed. The advantage of using persistent cookies is that a server can keep data on the user's PC, thereby avoiding the need to store that data in a server-side database.

Cascading Style Sheets

- A Cascading Style Sheet (CSS) is a set of rules that define styles to be applied to entire Web pages or individual Web page elements. Each rule consists of a selector followed by a set of curly braces containing the style properties and their values. The selector can be an HTML element, a user-defined style known as a class, or the ID of a specific element on a page. There are three ways of applying cascading style sheets to a Web page: external, embedded, and inline.

- An external CSS keeps all the style definitions in a separate CSS file that you include in a Web page at runtime by using the `<link>` tag to apply the style sheet to the page.

- An embedded CSS is a style sheet that gets copied physically into the head of the Web page and applies to the Web page as a whole.

- An inline CSS is a style sheet that applies to only one page element, so it gets copied "inline" on the page with that element.

- The W3C invented the HTML inline `<span>` start and `</span>` stop tags to provide you with a way to stylize part, instead of all, of a Web page element. An example is

```
Notice how <span style="color: yellow">
yellow words</span> appear onscreen.
```

- Other situations may arise in which you want to apply a style to larger divisions of a document at the block level. You create block-level divisions with the `<div>` start and `</div>` stop tags, where `<div>` stands for division. The syntax for the `<div>` tag is exactly the same as for the `<span>` tag. Because `<div>` is a block-level tag, however, the browser begins a new line at the beginning of the division.

- In cascading style sheets, a class is a named definition of one or more styles. You create the class by prefixing its name with a dot in the CSS file.

- On the cutting edge of cascading style sheets is a feature called absolute positioning, which enables you to position page elements onscreen based on x,y coordinates. The upper-left corner of the browser window is position 0,0.

- To provide control over the order in which the objects appear onscreen, absolute positioning has an attribute called the z-index, which tells the browser the order in which to display objects that overlap. The lower the z-index value, the sooner the layer displays onscreen. In other words, an item with a lower z-index will appear underneath overlapping items with higher z-index values.

Dynamic HTML

- Dynamic HTML is a term invented by Microsoft to refer to the animated Web pages you can create by using the DOM to combine HTML with style sheets and scripts that bring Web pages to life.

- JavaScript has a method called `setInterval()` that you can use to set a timer that fires periodic timer events. By manipulating the absolute positioning values of x and y dynamically during these timer events, you can create an animation onscreen. If you know your math, there is no limit to the patterns of movement you can create onscreen.

- A gradient is a graphical effect created by colors fading gradually across or down the screen. You can make millions of different gradients by manipulating the start and stop color strings in the `gradient()` method of the DXImageTransform object.

- A page transition is the style or manner in which the screen changes when the browser brings up a new document and displays it onscreen. You can create a wide range of page transitions via the `Barn()`, `Blinds()`, `Checkboard()`, `Iris()`, `RandomDissolve()`, `Slide()`, and `Strips()` methods of the DXImageTransform object.

- Microsoft's Dynamic HTML site has an HTML code generator called the Master Sample that lets you try out a wide range of special effects. For each kind of effect, there are controls that let you manipulate the values of the parameters that affect what you see onscreen. You can audition the effects and fine-tune the settings until you get it just the way you want it. Then you can copy and paste the code to create the effect on pages of your own.

XML and XHTML

- XML is a simple, self-describing markup language that enables computers to read and understand the structure of different kinds of documents and to exchange data across different operating systems, software applications, and hardware configurations without requiring any human intervention. Like HTML, XML has tags, but there is an important difference in how the tags are used. In HTML, the tags mostly define the appearance of the content. In XML, on the other hand, the tags define the structure of the data.

- Another important difference between HTML and XML is that in HTML, the tags are specified by the World Wide Web Consortium (W3C). If you want to create a new HTML tag, you cannot do so on your own; rather, you propose the new tag to the W3C and work through a lengthy standardization process. With XML, on the other hand, you can create your own customized tags. At www.xml.org, there are many focus areas in which various disciplines are creating XML tags for use within their industries.

- An XML schema is the structural definition of the types of elements that can appear in a document, the attributes each element may have, and the relationships among the elements.

- For an XML document to be well formed, it must have a DOCTYPE declaration, a line of code at the top of the file that identifies the XML schema that defines the tag structure. When all the tags in a document follow precisely the structural definitions in the schema, the document is said to validate. Documents that do not validate are said to be malformed and will be rejected by XML tools that require strict adherence to the rules of XML.

- The extensible stylesheet language (XSL) is an XML dialect that Web designers use to specify the styling, layout, and pagination of the structured content in an XML document for some targeted presentation medium, such as a Web browser, a printer, an eBook, a screen reader, or a hand-held device.

- The XSL Transformation (XSLT) language is an XML dialect that Web designers use to transform documents from one format into another, such as HTML, PDF, DOC, XLS, and RTF.

- XHTML is a reformulation of HTML in XML. The Web is a work in progress and is transitioning to rely more on XML than HTML. You use the DOCTYPE declaration to specify how strictly to adhere to the new rules.

- A so-called HTML Transitional document type definition (DTD) enables you to make use of presentation elements that are still in use today but will fade in the future when style sheets achieve widespread use. If your page avoids the deprecated presentation tags and instead uses style sheets to define the presentation of HTML elements onscreen, you can use the DTD called HTML Strict.

- XHTML also has loose and strict versions. The loose version is the same as HTML Transitional except for changes due to the differences between XML and SGML. Similarly, the strict version of XHTML is the same as HTML Strict except for the differences between XML and SGML. These differences are explained at www.w3.org/TR/xhtml1.

- An XML module is a collection of semantically related XML elements and attributes oriented toward accomplishing a certain task or function. An excellent example of modularization is the manner in which the W3C has organized into modules the various parts of the Synchronized Multimedia Implementation Language (SMIL), an XML-based language that enables you to include multimedia events in Web documents.

- The W3C has created a language profile called XHTML+SMIL that enables you to create a layout via style sheets or HTML and include SMIL animations, timings, and transitions in traditional Web page elements. Microsoft has created an implementation of XHTML+SMIL called HTML+TIME that works with Internet Explorer versions 5.5 and later. Due to its built-in support of HTML+TIME, the Internet Explorer Web browser gives you considerable multimedia authoring capability without requiring you to own any other tools.

Key Terms

absolute positioning *(380)*
active **Web** page *(344)*
alert box *(366)*
assignment operator *(349)*
cascading style sheet **(CSS)** *(374)*
class *(379)*
concatenate *(351)*
concatenation operator *(351)*
cookie *(369)*
DOCTYPE declaration *(389)*
document object model **(DOM)** *(359)*
dynamic **HTML** *(382)*
embedded **CSS** *(375)*
event *(356)*
extensible stylesheet language **(XSL)** *(390)*
external **CSS** *(375)*

floating point *(349)*
function *(345)*
gradient *(384)*
HTML+TIME *(392)*
include file *(345)*
inline **CSS** *(375)*
integer *(349)*
JavaScript *(345)*
method *(355)*
numeric variable *(349)*
object *(355)*
operator *(349)*
page transition *(384)*
property *(356)*
rollover *(367)*
scripting *(344)*

static **Web** page *(344)*
string *(349)*
string variable *(349)*
Synchronized Multimedia Implementation Language (SMIL) *(392)*
variable *(348)*
variable name *(349)*
XHTML *(391)*
XHTML+SMIL *(392)*
XML *(388)*
XML module *(392)*
XML schema *(388)*
XSL Transformation (XSLT) language *(390)*
z-index *(380)*

Key Terms Quiz

1. A(n) _____ uses the browser's window as a display surface through which users can interact with dynamic objects onscreen.

2. _____ is the act of writing little computer programs that can enhance the appearance and functionality of a Web page.

3. The most well-known scripting language is _____, which runs client-side in the browser without requiring any server-side processing.

4. A(n) _____ is a place in the computer's RAM that remembers, or stores, the value of something changeable.

5. A(n) _____ is a sequence of one or more alphanumeric characters.

6. The _____ is the official W3C structural definition of the objects, methods, and properties that comprise documents on the World Wide Web.

7. A(n) _____ is a set of rules that define styles to be applied to entire Web pages or individual Web page elements.

8. _____ enables you to position page elements onscreen based on x,y coordinates. The upper-left corner of the browser window is position 0,0.

9. _____ is a term invented by Microsoft to refer to the animated Web pages you can create by using the DOM to combine HTML with style sheets and scripts that bring Web pages to life.

10. _____ is a simple, self-describing markup language that enables computers to read and understand the structure of different kinds of documents and to exchange data across different operating systems, software applications, and hardware configurations without requiring any human intervention.

Multiple-Choice Quiz

1. If a script is brief and is not used a lot, you can simply type it into the body of the page. If you find yourself typing the same code often, however, it is better to put it inside a reusable:
   a. Cookie
   b. Function
   c. Method
   d. Property

2. In JavaScript, the concatenation operator uses the symbol:
   a. =
   b. *
   c. \
   d. +

3. Which event fires when the user visits a Web site and a page first comes onscreen?
   a. onclick
   b. ondblclick
   c. onmouseover
   d. onload

4. You can step through your script and diagnose the point at which something is going wrong by putting what diagnostic aid in strategic places down through the path of execution in your code?
   a. Alert box
   b. Documentation
   c. Help index
   d. Rollover

5. Which kind of cookie resides on the user's hard disk and survives even if the computer is rebooted?
   a. Incessant
   b. Insistent
   c. Persistent
   d. Per-session

6. The Internet needs per-session cookies to provide a way to:
   a. Count hits on a Web page
   b. Keep the socket open
   c. Maintain state from screen to screen
   d. Cut down on the amount of spam

7. Which kind of cascading style sheet keeps the style definitions in a separate CSS file?
   a. Embedded CSS
   b. External CSS
   c. Inline CSS
   d. Internal CSS

8. Which pair of tags would you use to stylize one small part of a Web page element without causing the browser to begin a new line onscreen?
   a. `<body> </body>`
   b. `<div> </div>`
   c. `<span> </span>`
   d. `<table> </table>`

9. In absolute positioning, what is the name of the attribute that enables you to control the order in which the Web page elements appear onscreen?
   a. x
   b. y
   c. z
   d. z-index

10. Which DTD enforces the structural rules of XML and demands that the Web page use style sheets in lieu of deprecated HTML positioning elements?
   a. HTML Transitional
   b. HTML Strict
   c. XHTML Transitional
   d. XHTML Strict

Essay Quiz

1. The *hello.html* script you created in this chapter wrote "Hello, world!" onscreen. Modify the script to say a little more. For example, edit the string "Hello, world!" to make it say something longer, such as, "Hello, world, from JavaScript!" Experiment with putting the break tag `<br>` somewhere in the midst of the string. What does the `<br>` cause onscreen when you view the page with a Web browser?

2. The *variables.html* example in this chapter used information for a person with the first name of Santa and the last name of Claus. Modify the *variables* script to make the names be your own first name and last name. Then run the script by opening the *variables* file with your Web browser. Does the script operate correctly when it computes your full name by concatenating your first and last names?

3. Between the first and last names of the *variables.html* example, add a variable to hold the person's middle initial, and modify the example to include this initial when the script concatenates the full name. When you make up a name for the variable that is going to hold the middle initial, make the variable name be something that indicates it is meant to hold a middle initial. Remember to prefix the name of the middle initial variable with an *s* to indicate its value will be a string. What name did you create for the variable that holds the value of the person's middle initial?

4. Suppose you want to change the look of an individual page element that appears many times on a Web page. You want to change just one occurrence of the element, without altering other renderings of this element onscreen. What kind of cascading style sheet would you use to accomplish this?

5. In the *rockpile.html* page, the rock pile you created with absolute positioning contained only three images. Increase the size of the rock pile by creating more instances of the three rocks. Vary the size and position of the rocks. Use the z-index to layer the rocks. See how creative you can be in creating a multi-layered rock pile. Make the rock pile contain at least a dozen rocks.

Lab Projects

• Lab Project 8-1: Dynamic Content

A static page that never changes does not project a very dynamic image out on the Web. Imagine that your school or workplace has hired you to transform its home page from static to dynamic. Your task is to create active Web page elements into which the site will flow dynamic content instead of displaying the same information every time someone visits the site. Before bringing these active elements online, your superior has asked you to submit a plan in which you (1) propose which parts of the page should become dynamic, (2) describe the manner in which they will become active, and (3) define the source of the content that will feed into the page. Use your word processor to create this plan. In developing your proposal, consider the following issues:

- **DOM Elements** The DOM defines the page elements you can manipulate dynamically. List the DOM elements you feel should be manipulated dynamically at your site. For each element you list, describe what the dynamism will be. The page title, for example, is a DOM element. Consider whether there is any active content you would want to put into the title of the page.

- **Rotating Banners** Many Web sites have banners that change depending on factors such as the season, the time of day, or user history stored in cookies that keep track of what the user has been doing at the site. Consider whether the banner on your page should be static or dynamic. If dynamic, describe how and when the banner will change.

- **RSS Feeds** In Chapter 2, you learned about RSS. Because the content of an RSS feed changes, it can be considered a dynamic element onscreen. Can you think of any ways in which an RSS feed, perhaps from other parts of your site or from related sites, would provide relevant dynamic content for your school or company home page?

- **Time and Date** Consider whether your site should display the current date or time. If so, recommend the strategy you will use to make sure your page displays the date or time in a format that is meaningful and unambiguous to the end user.

If your instructor has asked you to hand in this assignment, make sure you put your name at the top of your recommendation; then copy it onto a disk or follow the other instructions you may have been given for submitting this assignment.

• Lab Project 8-2: Using Cookies

Imagine that your superior has heard about cookies enabling certain Web sites to keep user information on the client side without requiring a server-side database. You have been asked to recommend whether your workplace could use this capability to reduce the load on your server. Use your word processor to write an essay in which you take a position on cookies and recommend how your site should use them. In developing your position, consider the following issues:

■ **Data**   What kinds of data will you store in the cookies, and how will that data be used by your site?

■ **Expiration**   How long should the cookies persist on the user's hard drive, if at all? In answering this question, consider the nature of the data, how it affects your site, and the amount of time after which the data would become irrelevant, if any.

■ **Security**   Knowledgeable users can inspect the contents of persistent cookies that are stored on their hard drives. Consider whether the persistent cookies your site creates will need to be encrypted to prevent their being read in clear text.

If your instructor has asked you to hand in this recommendation, make sure you put your name at the top of your essay; then copy it onto a disk or follow the other instructions you may have been given for submitting this assignment.

• Lab Project 8-3: Style Sheet Strategy

Style sheets provide a way to maintain a consistent look and feel for Web page elements across all the pages at your site, without requiring you to edit each page every time your school or company decides to change the style of an element onscreen. Imagine that your superior has put you in charge of creating a style-sheet strategy for your school or company Web site. Your task is to develop a set of guidelines defining which elements of your site's Web pages will be controlled by style sheets and specifying the techniques your team's Web authors should use in applying the styles to your site's content. Use your word processor to write an essay in which you present these guidelines, taking into account the following issues:

■ **Cascading**   It is possible to link more than one style sheet to a document. Styles defined by the first style sheet cascade onto the second style sheet, which can either redefine them or leave them alone. If there is a third style sheet, the cascade continues. There is no limit to the number of style sheets that can be on the cascade. If you have a large organization, consider whether there should be an institutional style sheet that defines elements that will be stylized site-wide, followed by departmental style sheets that define certain other styles for use within a department.

■ **Classes**   Style sheets enable you to create a named class of style rules that apply only to elements that have the `class` attribute set to that name. Consider whether your site should use style classes, and if so, define the class names and describe what each class will do.

■ **Conventions**   List the coding conventions you want your Web authors to follow in regard to style sheets. Specify the Web page elements that should never be modified so they will always inherit their styles from the cascade. Conversely, list the elements that should use the `class` attribute to identify the name of the style class to which they belong.

If your instructor has asked you to hand in these guidelines, make sure you put your name at the top of your essay; then copy it onto a disk or follow the other instructions you may have been given for submitting this assignment.

chapter

9

Making Web Pages Accessible

"The power of the Web is in its universality. Access by everyone regardless of disability is an essential aspect."

—*Tim Berners-Lee, director of the W3C and inventor of the World Wide Web*

- Define the concept of Web accessibility and list applicable guidelines and standards for making Web sites accessible.

- List the HTML coding practices you must follow to make a Web site meet the Section 508 accessibility standards.

- Identify resources other than HTML pages that must adhere to the accessibility guidelines in order for a Web site to be accessible.

- Define how style sheets can enhance a Web site's accessibility.

- List the tools you can use to assess the extent to which a site follows Web accessibility standards.

ACCESS to the Internet is vitally important for anyone who plans to participate in the twenty-first century information economy. So essential is the Web that to be denied access is to be disenfranchised. To help ensure that all U.S. citizens have access, the U.S. government has enacted laws mandating that certain accessibility features must be built into any Web site that receives public funding or serves constituents of federally funded programs. Because the need is worldwide, the W3C has initiated a Web Accessibility Initiative (WAI) that works with organizations around the world to coordinate efforts to enable all users to access the Web, regardless of disability or special needs.

Making the Web truly accessible to everyone is a great challenge, because users with special needs have many different kinds of disabilities. This chapter begins by making you aware of guidelines you can follow to make your Web pages accessible. Tutorial exercises will step you through the process of implementing HTML coding practices that bring a Web site into compliance with federally mandated accessibility standards. Because a Web site can include many kinds of multimedia documents, however, accessibility goes beyond HTML. In order for a site to be truly accessible, all of its printed, audio, and video formats must also comply with accessibility rules. This chapter will identify multimedia accessibility guidelines that are emerging for non-HTML resources typically found on the Web.

In the long run, however, creating alternate representations may not be the best approach. Rather, the key to achieving true accessibility may be for the computer industry to provide a way for end users to specify the kind of accessibility they need. Imagine how a style sheet, for example, could invoke an XML module to transform a certain class of Web content into a representation suited to the special needs of the viewer. After providing some examples of style sheets that provide new avenues for Web accessibility in the future, this chapter will conclude by providing tools you can use to evaluate the extent to which a Web page follows the guidelines currently in force.

Defining Web Accessibility

Web accessibility is the capability that makes it possible for users with special needs to receive, understand, and navigate content that people without handicaps can process without special assistance. Users with special needs have many different kinds of handicaps. As you will learn in this chapter, the Web accessibility guidelines currently in force address primarily the needs of seeing- or hearing-impaired users. The current guidelines fall short for other kinds of handicaps, such as physical motion impairments and mental cognitive differences. Making Web sites truly accessible to all users is an ongoing challenge, especially for people with multiple handicaps. After presenting the guidelines currently in force, this chapter will discuss efforts that are underway to build in accessibility to the Web from an architectural perspective known as universal design.

Accessibility Is a Right

In the United States, Web accessibility is a right that is guaranteed by law under **Section 508** of the Rehabilitation Act of 1973, as amended in 1998. According to the Section 508 law, a Web site is accessible when users with special needs can access it as well as people without disabilities. The law requires that all Web sites (as well as other forms of information technology) used, procured, developed, or maintained by government agencies and departments must be accessible. If your school or business receives any kind of federal funding, therefore, the law may require you to follow the Section 508 accessibility standards presented in this chapter. Whether or not the law applies to your particular situation, the Section 508 standards are not difficult to implement. This chapter's tutorial will provide you with step-by-step instructions for creating Web pages that are Section 508 compliant. On behalf of users with special needs, I encourage you to follow these guidelines, regardless of whether the law requires them in your workplace.

W3C Web Accessibility Initiative (WAI)

Before diving into the Section 508 accessibility standards, you need to learn a little historical background on the source of those standards. In 1997, the W3C launched the **Web Accessibility Initiative (WAI)**, which coordinates the Web's official efforts to achieve accessibility. WAI went right to work on HTML version 4.0, which introduced new mechanisms for making Web page elements accessible. To provide Web authors with guidance in using the new accessibility features, the WAI issued a set of guidelines called the WAI Web Content Accessibility Guidelines version 1.0. These guidelines influenced the formulation of the Section 508 guidelines that this chapter will present. The work of the WAI is documented at www.w3.org/WAI.

WAI Web Content Accessibility Guidelines

The **Web Content Accessibility Guidelines (WCAG)** consist of 65 checkpoints organized under 14 general guidelines. Each checkpoint is assigned to one of three priority levels, which define the degree to which the site is accessible. Priority 1 is defined as a checkpoint that must be met, otherwise many users with disabilities will find it impossible to access the material. Priority 2 is a checkpoint that should be met, otherwise users will find it

Logo	What the Logo Means
W3C WAI-A WCAG 1.0	Conformance Level A: this page satisfies all Priority 1 checkpoints.
W3C WAI-AA WCAG 1.0	Conformance Level Double-A: this page satisfies all Priority 1 and 2 checkpoints.
W3C WAI-AAA WCAG 1.0	Conformance Level Triple-A: this page satisfies all Priority 1, 2, and 3 checkpoints.

TABLE 9-1   *W3C Web Content Accessibility Guidelines 1.0 Conformance Logos* ■

difficult, but not impossible, to access the material. Priority 3 is a checkpoint that may be met, in order to further access to Web documents. The three levels of conformance are designated A, AA, and AAA, respectively. Conformance level A requires that a site pass all Priority 1 checkpoints. Conformance level AA (pronounced double-A) requires the passing of all Priority 1 and 2 checkpoints. Level AAA (triple-A) requires that a site pass all of the checkpoints at Priorities 1, 2, and 3. Depending on the level at which a Web site claims to conform, the site's pages can display one of three conformance logos described in Table 9-1.

Section 508 Accessibility Standards

The Section 508 accessibility standards do not include levels of conformance and as many checkpoints as the WCAG guidelines. Instead, Section 508 includes 16 Web accessibility requirements, all of which must be met in order for a Web site to be considered accessible. To see the standards, go to www.section508.gov and follow the link to the 508 law, which will give you the choice of viewing either a summary or a detailed presentation of the regulations. The next part of this chapter is a tutorial in making Web pages comply with the 16 Web accessibility standards in the Section 508 guidelines.

Coding to the Section 508 Web Accessibility Standards

Table 9-2 lists the 16 rules of the Section 508 Web accessibility standards. These rules are lettered from (a) through (p) in §1194.21 of the law. The following sections of this chapter are a brief guide to creating accessible Web pages that comply with these rules. The tutorial exercises cover the rules in the order in which they appear in the law. For more detailed examples, go to www.section508.gov and follow the link to 508 Training.

Textual Equivalents for Nontext Elements

Section 508 Web accessibility rule (a) requires that you must provide a textual equivalent for every nontext element onscreen. HTML has two attributes that you can use to create textual equivalents for nontext elements: the **alt attribute** and the **longdesc attribute**. The attribute `alt` stands for

Rule	Web Accessibility Requirement
(a)	A text equivalent for every non-text element shall be provided (e.g., via `alt`, `longdesc`, or in element content).
(b)	Equivalent alternatives for any multimedia presentation shall be synchronized with the presentation.
(c)	Web pages shall be designed so that all information conveyed with color is also available without color, for example from context or markup.
(d)	Documents shall be organized so they are readable without requiring an associated style sheet.
(e)	Redundant text links shall be provided for each active region of a server-side image map.
(f)	Client-side image maps shall be provided instead of server-side image maps except where the regions cannot be defined with an available geometric shape.
(g)	Row and column headers shall be identified for data tables.
(h)	Markup shall be used to associate data cells and header cells for data tables that have two or more logical levels of row or column headers.
(i)	Frames shall be titled with text that facilitates frame identification and navigation.
(j)	Pages shall be designed to avoid causing the screen to flicker with a frequency greater than 2 Hz and lower than 55 Hz.
(k)	A text-only page, with equivalent information or functionality, shall be provided to make a web site comply with the provisions of this part, when compliance cannot be accomplished in any other way. The content of the text-only page shall be updated whenever the primary page changes.
(l)	When pages utilize scripting languages to display content, or to create interface elements, the information provided by the script shall be identified with functional text that can be read by assistive technology.
(m)	When a web page requires that an applet, plug-in or other application be present on the client system to interpret page content, the page must provide a link to a plug-in or applet that complies with §1194.21(a) through (l).
(n)	When electronic forms are designed to be completed on-line, the form shall allow people using assistive technology to access the information, field elements, and functionality required for completion and submission of the form, including all directions and cues.
(o)	A method shall be provided that permits users to skip repetitive navigation links.
(p)	When a timed response is required, the user shall be alerted and given sufficient time to indicate more time is required.

TABLE 9-2   *The 16 Rules of the Section 508 Web Accessibility Standards* ■

alternate; true to its name, you use the `alt` attribute when you want to provide alternate text for a nontext element, such as an image. When a sighted user mouses over the element, the alternate text pops up in a tooltip window the user can see onscreen. When a seeing-impaired user accesses the page with a screen reader, it speaks the text aloud, thereby providing a way for users with vision impairments to know what is pictured in the image.

When you use the `alt` attribute, the alternate text should be brief. If the textual description is longer than 150 characters, you should use the attribute `longdesc`, which stands for long description.

Using the alt Attribute

Using the `alt` attribute is very straightforward. To provide alternate text for any image onscreen, follow these steps:

1. Use the Notepad to open the file containing the image. In this example, open the *resume.html* page you created in Chapter 6.

2. Click to position your cursor inside the `<img>` tag of the image for which you want to provide alternate text. In this example, position your cursor before the closing bracket of the `<img>` tag that displays your picture onscreen.

3. Using the `alt` attribute, type the alternate text you want the image to have. In this example, type an explanation that identifies who is pictured onscreen:

This is the filename of your image.   *Type the alternate text between the quote signs.*

```
<img src="santa.gif" alt="Santa Claus's picture">
```

4. Save the file, and then open it with your Web browser. Use your mouse to hover over the image until the tool-tip window appears. Notice how the alternate text appears in the tool-tip window.

Using the longdesc Attribute

If an image conveys more information than you can describe in 150 characters, you should use the `longdesc` attribute, which tells assistive devices the location of the HTML file that contains the long description. In conjunction with `longdesc`, you should also provide an `alt` attribute, which can identify the topic that the long description describes. The command syntax is as follows:

In this example, the image displays election results that require several paragraphs of text to describe.   *The `alt` attribute contains alternate text identifying the topic of the image.*

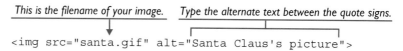

```
<img src="results.gif" alt="Election Results" longdesc="results.html">
```

The `longdesc` attribute specifies the URL of the file containing the full description of the election results.

Synchronized Alternatives for Multimedia Presentation

Section 508 Web accessibility rule (b) requires that "Equivalent alternatives for any multimedia presentation shall be synchronized with the presentation." In the previous chapter, you learned how to use the XHTML+ SMIL timing module to write synchronized text onscreen to caption a video clip from President John F. Kennedy's famous moon challenge speech. If you tried to caption another video following that same technique, you probably found that it can take quite some time to figure out the timing values. To save time, you can use captioning tools that can determine these timings more efficiently.

One of the most popular tools is called **MAGpie**, which you can download from the National Center for Accessible Media (NCAM) at ncam.wgbh.org/webaccess/magpie. The MAG in MAGpie stands for Media Access Generator. Figure 9-1 shows how MAGpie makes it easy to create closed captions for audio tracks and videos recorded for playback by Apple's QuickTime Player, Real Networks' Real Player, and Microsoft's Windows Media Player. MAGpie can also create captions for integration into SMIL presentations. In 2003, MAGpie won an honorable mention for best educational streaming program in *Streaming* magazine's reader's choice awards.

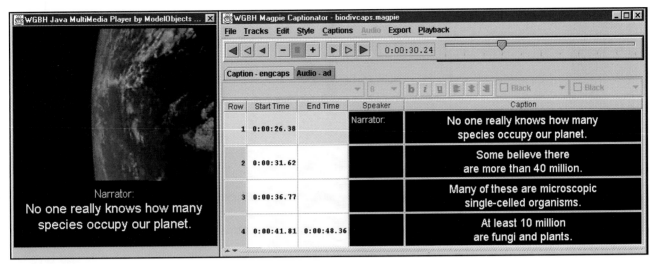

FIGURE 9-1 *MAGpie makes it easy to mark timings and type the captions that will appear onscreen when the clip reaches each time segment. MAGpie was created by the CPB/WGBH National Center for Accessible Media with funding from the Mitsubishi Electric America Foundation and the U.S. Department of Education's National Institute on Disability and Rehabilitation Research.* ∎

Conveying Color-Coded Information from Context or Markup

A significant number of users are color blind. About 10 percent of males, for example, are unable to perceive red or green. About half of a percent of females have similar difficulties distinguishing between red and green. That is why rule (c) forbids using color to convey information that cannot be understood in the absence of color. Whenever you are color-coding a chart or a graph, therefore, make sure you provide an alternate way in which someone who is color blind can understand the color-coded information. In the section "Table Row and Column Headers" later in this chapter, for example, you will learn how to create row and column headers in an HTML table. You can use these headers to explain any categorization conveyed by color-coded data cells.

You must also avoid navigational instructions that rely solely on color. Telling the user to press the red button, for example, violates rule (c). To bring such a statement into compliance, you could print the word stop inside the button and tell the user to press the red stop button. Thus, users who cannot see red can identify the button via the word stop.

When printing text on colored backgrounds, you must make sure that your color choices have enough contrast. On the left side of Figure 9-2, you see how people with different kinds of color blindness perceive a color combination which seems to have enough contrast but is lacking in blue hues. On the right side of the figure, you see the same image with more blue hues.

Making Web Pages Readable Without Requiring Style Sheets

The previous chapter touted the fanciful features of style sheets. Note however that Section 508 Web accessibility rule (d) requires that Web pages must be readable without requiring style sheets. Is this a contradiction? It depends on how you are using the style sheet. Rule (d) means that you must not use a style sheet so that it changes the meaning that the page would convey without the style sheet.

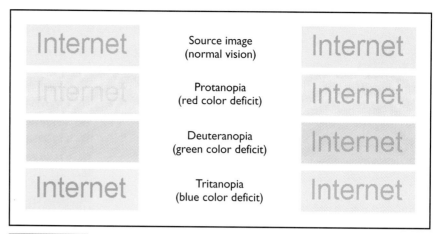

FIGURE 9-2 *Color combinations that seem to have enough contrast for normal vision may cause serious problems for users with certain kinds of color blindness. Notice how the green text in the source image on the left is indecipherable by someone with deuteranopia. The foreground text in the source image on the right contains more blue, thereby creating much better contrast.* ∎

Regardless of what style sheets the page may already call upon, the user can always add another style sheet by editing the browser's accessibility settings. Figure 9-3 shows how to do this via the IE browser's Accessibility dialog. Because the style sheet specified in the Accessibility dialog is always last on the cascade, the end user can redefine or override any style on the page. Thus, every user has the right to add a special style sheet to enhance the presentation of any Web page.

Text Links for Active Regions of Server-Side Image Maps

Because the image coordinates in a server-side image map are not processed by the server until the user clicks the mouse, the alternate text attribute does not work with server-side image maps. To provide a textual

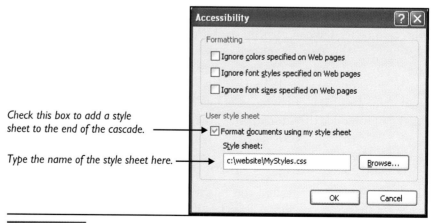

Check this box to add a style sheet to the end of the cascade.

Type the name of the style sheet here.

FIGURE 9-3 *In the IE Web browser, the Accessibility dialog enables the end user to add a style sheet to the end of the cascade. To bring up this Accessibility dialog, pull down the IE browser's Tools menu, choose Internet Options, and click the Accessibility button.* ∎

alternative to users with special needs, rule (e) of the Section 508 Web accessibility guidelines requires that you provide a text link for each active region of a server-side image map. Depending on the layout of the active regions in the map, printing text links onscreen may or may not work well with your page design. Before you fret about this requirement, read the next section of this chapter, "When to Use Client-Side vs. Server-Side Image Maps," where you will learn that server-side image maps are pretty much a thing of the past.

When to Use Client-Side vs. Server-Side Image Maps

Section 508 Web accessibility rule (f) requires that "Client-side image maps shall be provided instead of server-side image maps except where the regions cannot be defined with an available geometric shape." When you studied image maps in Chapter 7, you learned how to create round, rectangular, and polygonal shapes. Anyone who knows their math realizes that because a polygon can have any number of sides with any direction or length, you can define any conceivable shape with a polygon. One could argue, therefore, that there is no situation that requires a server-side image map. Whether or not this is always true, chances are that you will never encounter a situation in which a client-side image map cannot do the job. Rule (f) is saying that if a client-side image map can do it, you are not permitted to use a server-side map instead. In other words, use client-side instead of server-side image maps whenever possible.

To make a client-side image map accessible, you use the `alt` attribute to specify the alternate text for each area in the map. You can also use the `longdesc` attribute for any area that needs further explanation.

Imagine that you want to make accessible the music keyboard image map that you studied in Chapter 7. Figure 9-4 shows the modified code, and Figure 9-5 shows the effect of a user hovering over the first area defined by that code. Screen readers verbalize the alternate text when users with screen readers tab over the image map areas.

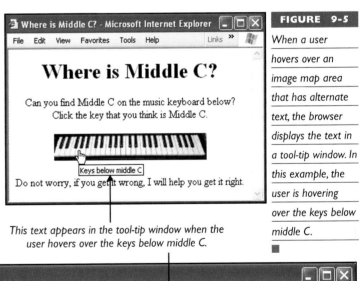

FIGURE 9-5

When a user hovers over an image map area that has alternate text, the browser displays the text in a tool-tip window. In this example, the user is hovering over the keys below middle C. ∎

This text appears in the tool-tip window when the user hovers over the keys below middle C.

```
middleCaccessible.html - Notepad
File  Edit  Format  View  Help
<map name="MusicKeyboard">
<area shape="Rect" coords="0,0,112,32" href="too-low.html" alt="Keys below middle C">
<area shape="Rect" coords="112,0,116,22" href="correct.html" alt="Top of Middle C">
<area shape="Rect" coords="112,22,120,32" href="correct.html" alt="Bottom of Middle C">
<area shape="Rect" coords="116,0,238,22" href="too-high.html" alt="Top of keys above middle C">
<area shape="Rect" coords="120,22,238,32" href="too-high.html" alt="Bottom of keys above middle C">
</map>
```

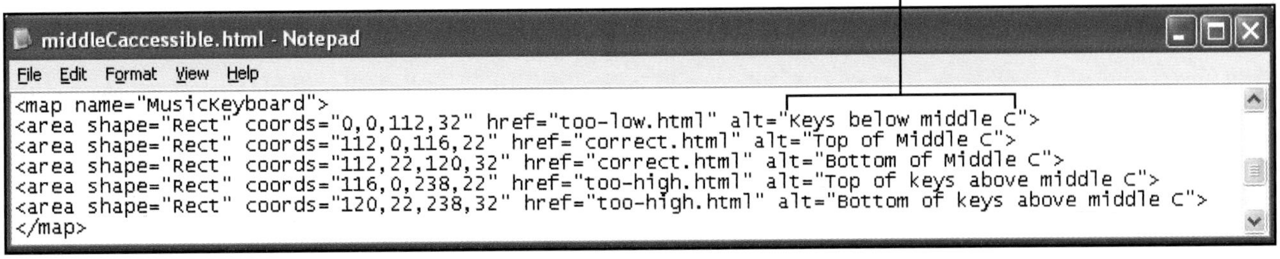

FIGURE 9-4 *You make an image map accessible by providing alternate text for each area in the map. Compare this code to Figure 9-5, which shows a user hovering over the part of the keyboard below middle C.* ∎

Table Row and Column Headers

Section 508 Web accessibility rule (g) requires that data tables must have clearly identified row and column headers. This requirement applies only to tables containing data that, in order to be understood, require that users know what specific row or column they are in. Out on the Web, most of the tables are used for page layout. When you learned how to design Web pages in Chapter 5, you saw an example of a table used purely for layout in Figure 5-14. Tables that are used purely for layout do not need row and column headers.

In Chapter 6, on the other hand, a step-by-step tutorial had you create a table of the world's highest mountains. In order to understand the information in this table, the user must be able to identify the category represented by the row and column of each data cell. Suppose you want to make this table accessible. To define the table headers, you use the HTML table header **<th>** start and **</th>** stop tags. To make the world's highest mountains table use these tags, you can modify the first row of the table. Instead of using the `<td>` and `</td>` tags to create the title cells in the first row, you use the `<th>` start and `</th>` stop tags. These table header tags both create a data cell and define it as a table header. The modified code appears as follows:

The `<th>` start and `</th>` stop tags create a data cell that functions as a table header. This is the table header for the first data column.

This is the table header for the third data column.

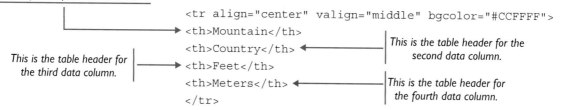

```
<tr align="center" valign="middle" bgcolor="#CCFFFF">
<th>Mountain</th>
<th>Country</th>
<th>Feet</th>
<th>Meters</th>
</tr>
```

This is the table header for the second data column.

This is the table header for the fourth data column.

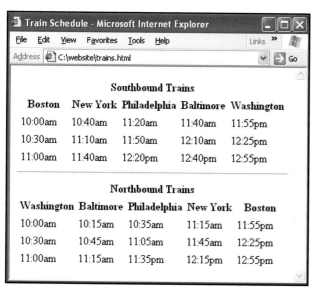

FIGURE   9-6   *In order for assistive devices to make sense of tables that require the user to understand the relationship between multiple headings, you use the id and headers attributes to associate each table cell with its corresponding headings. In this example, the user who is reading 12:20 pm should understand that it indicates the Philadelphia arrival time for a southbound train. See Figure 9-7 for the code that makes it possible for assistive devices to understand this relationship and communicate it to users with special needs.* ∎

Related Table Row and Column Headers

Situations can arise in which a data table contains groups of rows or columns that contain related data. The train schedule illustrated in Figure 9-6 has two main groupings: one for northbound and the other for southbound trains. A sighted person can clearly see these groupings onscreen, but imagine the difficulty someone using a screen reader would have trying to follow the information in such a table.

To provide assistive devices with a way to identify the structure of such a table, rule (h) requires that you use HTML markup to associate the data cells with their corresponding header cells. While this may sound complicated, it is easily achieved, thanks to the `id` and `headers` attributes. Whenever you have a table in which the association between the data cells and their corresponding headers is not straightforward, you use the **id attribute** to assign a unique identifier to each table

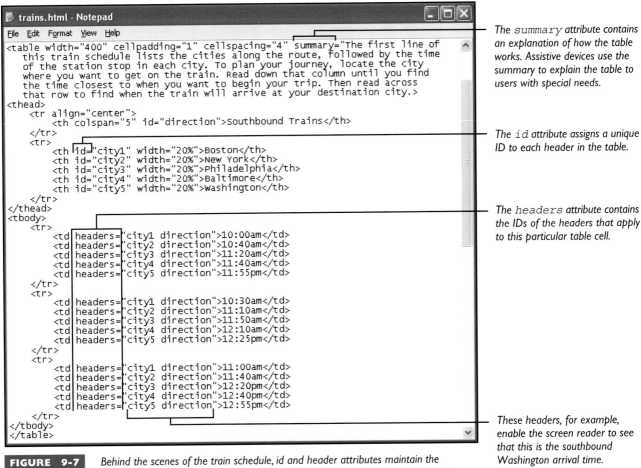

The *summary* attribute contains an explanation of how the table works. Assistive devices use the summary to explain the table to users with special needs.

The *id* attribute assigns a unique ID to each header in the table.

The *headers* attribute contains the IDs of the headers that apply to this particular table cell.

These headers, for example, enable the screen reader to see that this is the southbound Washington arrival time.

FIGURE 9-7 *Behind the scenes of the train schedule, id and header attributes maintain the association between the train direction and the city. Thus, users with screen readers can work their way down and across the columns, without losing track of these critical row and column relationships.* ■

header. Then you add to each `<td>` tag a **headers attribute** that identifies the header(s) associated with each data cell. To see how this works, study the callouts in Figure 9-7, which displays the code that creates the train schedule illustrated in Figure 9-6.

Frame Titling

Screen readers and other kinds of assistive devices use the text you type in a frame's **title attribute** to identify the frame to users with special needs. Section 508 Web accessibility rule (i) requires that when you create a frameset, you must give each frame a title that identifies the purpose and function of the frame. In addition to the `title` attribute, some assistive devices use the **name attribute** to identify the frames. You should therefore set both the `title` and `name` attributes. Imagine a frameset that has a top frame displaying a banner, a left sidebar containing navigation options, and a main content frame. The following HTML satisfies rule (h) by using the `title` and `name` attributes to give each frame a title that facilitates frame identification and navigation:

```
<frameset rows="64,*" title="Making Web Sites Accessible">
  <frame title="Top Banner" name="Top Banner" scrolling="no" noresize
target="Sidebar Navigation" src="Banner.html">
  <frameset cols="150,*">
    <frame title="Sidebar Navigation" name="Sidebar Navigation" target="Main Content" src="Navigation.html">
    <frame title="Main Content" name="Main Content" src="Main.html">
  </frameset>
  <noframes>
    <body>
This page uses frames. You can also <a href="noframes.html">use a version of
this page without frames</a>.
    </body>
  </noframes>
</frameset>
```

You should also make sure that each page displayed in a frameset has an appropriately descriptive `<title>` tag in the `<head>` section of the page. Even though these titles do not appear onscreen in the frameset, assistive devices may make use of them. Thus, the `<head>` sections of the three pages in the frameset just described should read as follows:

Main.html:	`<title>Main Content</title>`
Banner.html:	`<title>Top Banner</title>`
Navigation.html:	`<title>Sidebar Navigation</title>`

Avoiding Screen Flicker in the Range of 2 Hz to 55 Hz

Strobing, flashing, blinking, or flickering at a frequency of 2 to 55 times per second can induce seizures in users with certain genetic dispositions. To avoid the possibility of Web sites inducing seizures, Section 508 Web accessibility rule (j) forbids flicker in the range of 2 Hz to 55 Hz. The term Hz stands for **hertz**, which means vibrations per second.

Animations that blink are not particularly desirable at a Web site. Most users quickly tire of the repetition, and people who are easily distracted have a hard time concentrating on a text when something is moving in their field of vision onscreen. To learn more about the risk of inducing seizures from flicker at a Web site, go to usability.gov/web_508/tut-j.html.

Providing Text-Only Page Alternatives for Noncompliant Pages

Rule (k) requires that you must provide a text-only page to substitute for any Web page that you cannot make comply with all of the other rules in the Section 508 Web accessibility guidelines. Furthermore, rule (k) requires that you must update the text any time a change is made to the page for which it substitutes.

Please do not assume, however, that you can use rule (k) as an easy way out any time you cannot meet the rest of the guidelines. Rule (k) is a last resort. Whenever you find yourself resorting to rule (k), you should rethink the design of your page and make an honest effort to make the document accessible.

Describing Scripts with Functional Text

Section 508 Web accessibility rule (l) addresses the problem of making scripts accessible. Scripts can make things happen onscreen that assistive devices cannot interpret. Whenever you have a script doing something that displays content or provides interface elements onscreen, rule (l) requires that you identify this information with functional text that can be read by assistive technology. The HTML codes that you use to provide this text are the **<noscript>** start and **</noscript>** stop tags. You put these tags immediately after the `</script>` end tag of the script that you are describing. The syntax is

```
<script language="javascript">
      //The script goes here.
</script>
<noscript>
      <p>Describe what the script does here, or provide a link to an accessible
      document that provides the data generated by the script.</p>
</noscript>
```

The `<noscript>` *start tag must appear immediately after the* `</script>` *end tag of the script it is describing.*

When creating user interface elements with JavaScript, you need to make sure that users can operate them without a mouse, which is easy to test: Put your mouse aside, and make sure you can operate the controls via the computer keyboard.

Avoid using the `onDblClick` event handler, for which there is no keyboard equivalent. If you use the `onMouseDown` event handler, provide an `onKeyDown` handler so the mouse down event has a keyboard equivalent. In like manner, pair `onMouseUp` with `onKeyUp`.

Avoid using popup windows, which can cause users with assistive technology to lose track of where they are.

Applet and Plug-in Accessibility

In Chapter 2, you learned how applets and plug-ins can extend the multimedia capabilities of a Web page. In order for such a page to be accessible, the applets and plug-ins must follow the same accessibility guidelines as the other Web page elements onscreen. That is why Section 508 Web accessibility rule (m) requires that whenever an applet, a plug-in, or another application is called upon to interpret page content on the user's computer, the page must provide a link to a plug-in or an applet that complies with rules (a) through (l).

You should keep in mind three key points with regard to applet and plug-in accessibility. First, users with special needs must be able to navigate the page without a mouse. You can test this by putting your mouse aside and using the keyboard to operate the applet and navigate the page. Second, the user should be able to move from element to element onscreen. Once again, you can test this by putting your mouse aside and pressing the TAB key to make sure it lets the user move from item to item onscreen. Finally, you must remember that for every graphical element that conveys meaning or navigation in an applet or a plug-in, a textual equivalent that can be understood by assistive technologies must also be present.

Form Elements, Directions, and Cues

In Chapter 7, you learned how HTML forms enable the Web author to interact with and receive information from users at a Web site. Rule (n) requires that any time users complete a form, you must present the form in such a way that users with assistive technology can access the field elements, read all of the directions, understand the labeling, and follow the cues to complete and submit the form.

To clarify which instructions and labels go with which form elements onscreen, the W3C invented the **<label>** start and **</label>** stop tags. The <label> tag has a **for attribute** that you use to identify the ID of the <input> element with which the label is associated. Assistive devices use these attributes to determine which labels go with which form elements and cue the user accordingly. Consider, for example, the form in the *subscribe.html* page you created in Chapter 7. To make that form accessible, you can modify the code by using the <label> tag's for attribute to associate each label with the ID of its corresponding input. Study the callouts in the following example to see how the <label> tag's for attribute identifies which input has that label:

The for="Name" *attribute associates this label with the input field that has* id="Name".

```
<p><label for="Name">What is your name?</label><br>
<input id="Name" type="text" name="Name" size="50" maxlength="150"
       style="border-style: inset; border-width: 4">
</p>
<p><label for="Email">What is your e-mail address?</label><br>
<input id="Email" type="text" name="Email" size="50" maxlength="150"
       style="border-style: inset; border-width: 4">
</p>
```

The for="Email" *attribute associates this label with the input field that has* id="Email".

Many users who cannot use the mouse press the TAB key instead to move from field to field within a form. When you create a form, therefore, you should test it by pressing the TAB key repeatedly and observe whether the tab order is logical. If the focus moves illogically from field to field, you can clarify the tab order via the <input> field's tabindex attribute. To clarify the tab order on the *subscribe.html* page, for example, you would modify the input controls as follows:

The tabindex *attribute establishes the tab order. You do not need to use this attribute, however, unless the default tab order is illogical.*

```
<input tabindex="1" id="Name" type="text" name="Name" size="50" maxlength="150"
       style="border-style: inset; border-width: 4">
<input tabindex="2" id="Email" type="text" name="Email" size="50" maxlength="150"
       style="border-style: inset; border-width: 4">
<input tabindex="3" type="radio" name="Frequency" value="daily" checked>Daily
<input tabindex="4" type="radio" name="Frequency" value="weekly">Weekly
<input tabindex="5" type="radio" name="Frequency" value="monthly">Monthly
<input tabindex="6" type="submit" value="Subscribe">
<input tabindex="7" type="reset">
```

A final point about making forms accessible is that you need to avoid the temptation to use JavaScript event handlers to make the ENTER key submit form data without requiring the user to click a Submit button. Users who cannot use the mouse press the ENTER key to input or select information in a form field. That is why these users need a Submit button to press when they are done filling out the form. In order to make forms accessible, therefore, you must provide a Submit button for every form onscreen. Otherwise, many users with assistive devices have no way of submitting the information when they are finished filling out the form.

Skip Navigation

Many Web pages have navigational options across the top and down the left side of the page, with the main content occupying the rest of the page. When you create this kind of a layout with an HTML table, the top navigational options go into the first table row, and the sidebar navigation goes into the first column of the next row onscreen. Only after the sidebar gets populated does the main content flow onto the rest of the screen. Imagine someone accessing such a page with a screen reader. Without a way to skip these navigation options, the user has to tab through all of these navigation links before getting to the main content on the page.

To solve this problem, Section 508 Web accessibility rule (o) requires that you provide a way for the user to skip over these kinds of repetitive navigation links. Most sites do so by placing a **skip navigation link** at the start of such a page. A skip navigation link is a hyperlink that, when clicked, takes the user to a place on the page that is just past the navigation options that typically appear at the top or on the left of the screen. A user with a screen reader can follow the skip navigation link to jump to the main content of the page, just like a sighted user can glance past the navigation link to read the main content onscreen.

To create a skip navigation link, insert the following code at or near the top of the body of the page. Notice how you can make the link be invisible, if you do not want it appearing on the page of a sighted user:

```
<a href="#main content" style="display:none">Skip over navigation</a>
```

After you make the skip navigation link, you need to create the target of that link. The target of a skip navigation link is a named anchor that you type at the spot on the page where the main content begins. The HTML code for such a link appears as follows:

Setting the display style to "none" prevents this link from displaying onscreen. Assistive devices, such as screen readers, use this link to provide users with a way to skip the navigation.

```
<a name="main content" id="main content"></a>
```

In these examples, the name "main content" is arbitrary. You can make that name anything you want. I named the anchor "main content" because it marks the beginning of the main content on the page.

Timed Responses

Web designers generally frown upon timed responses because you normally want to give the user as much time as needed to respond. For security reasons, however, some sites may require users to interact every so often, otherwise the session times out and the user must log in again to start another session. Such a site should make it possible for a user with special needs to request a longer timeout interval. That is why Section 508 Web accessibility rule (p) requires that whenever a Web page requires the user to respond within a certain amount of time, the user must be informed and given an opportunity to request more time.

Making Applets, Helpers, and Plug-ins Accessible

In Chapter 2, you learned that whenever a browser encounters a multimedia resource that HTML cannot handle, the browser calls upon the appropriate plug-in or helper application to play or display the content onscreen. So much multimedia content is on the Web that almost every site includes resources that HTML cannot handle on its own. That is why this part of the book takes a closer look at how you go about making multimedia content accessible.

Flash Accessibility

Flash is the most popular multimedia plug-in on the Web. A large percentage of the Web's multimedia content, therefore, gets handled by the Flash player. Its parent company, Macromedia, has worked in partnership with Microsoft to make the latest version of the Flash player conform to **Microsoft Active Accessibility (MSAA)**, which is an application programming interface (API) that helps Windows applications interoperate with assistive technology. Flash authors who follow the guidelines can make accessible to screen readers text elements, buttons, input fields, and movie clips. Scalable graphics enable users to zoom in on Flash content, which enables visually impaired users to see small text or graphics. Content controls enable users to stop, fast-forward, rewind, and pause playback. Mouse-free navigation enables assistive technology to provide keyboard controls over all these functions. Synchronized audio tracks provide descriptive audio for users who need it. Customized color swatches enable developers to customize palettes for users who are color blind. Guidelines for making Flash movies comply with Section 508 are at www.macromedia.com/macromedia/accessibility.

Flash movies are inherently more complex than HTML documents. No matter how carefully you follow Macromedia's guidelines, you need to remember that some users will require simpler alternatives. Happily, the W3C kept this in mind when they invented the `<object>` start and `</object>` stop tags, which you use to put Flash movies (and other kinds of multimedia content) on a Web page. Consider the following `<object>` tag, which plays a Flash movie called *DNAsynthesis.swf*.

If the user has the Flash player installed, the movie appears onscreen, and the browser does not display the alternate text. If the user does not have Flash installed, however, the movie cannot play, so the browser continues on to display the alternate text onscreen:

```
<object title="Core DNA Synthesis"
classid="clsid:D27CDB6E-AE6D-11cf-96B8-444553540000"
codebase="http://download.macromedia.com/pub/shockwave/cabs/flash/swflash.cab
#version=6,0,0,0" width="100%" height="100%" align="">
    <param name=movie value="coreDNAsynthesis.swf">
    <param name=quality value=high>
    <param name=salign value=LT>
    <param name=bgcolor value=#FFFFFF>
This movie consists of an interactive demonstration of core DNA synthesis.
There is a <a href="coreDNAsynthesis.html">textual description</a> for users
who do not have Flash installed.
</object>
```

You put the alternate text before the `</object>` end tag. The browser displays this text if the user does not have Flash installed.

In their wisdom, the W3C further provided a mechanism whereby you can specify several alternative representations of an object. The browser works down the tree of these objects until it finds one it can play. Objects further down the tree get skipped. The following example shows how this works. Notice how (1) the content gets played by Flash, if the user has Flash installed. If not and the user has an MPEG movie player, (2) the content renders as an MPEG movie. If not, (3) the content appears in an animated GIF image. If all else fails, (4) alternate text appears onscreen.

```
                <!-- First, try the Flash movie -->
<object title="Core DNA Synthesis"
classid="clsid:D27CDB6E-AE6D-11cf-96B8-444553540000"
codebase="http://download.macromedia.com/pub/shockwave/cabs/flash/swflash.cab
#version=6,0,0,0" width="100%" height="100%" align="">
<param name=movie value="coreDNAsynthesis.swf"><param name=quality value=high>
<param name=salign value=LT><param name=bgcolor value=#FFFFFF>
                <!-- Else, try the MPEG video -->
  <object data=" coreDNAsynthesis.mpeg" type="application/mpeg">
                <!-- Else, try the GIF animation -->
    <object data=" coreDNAsynthesis.gif" type="image/gif">
                <!-- Else render the text -->
This movie consists of an interactive demonstration of core DNA synthesis.
There is a <a href="coreDNAsynthesis.html">textual description</a> for users
who do not have Flash installed.
    </object>
  </object>
</object>
```

PDF Accessibility

When objects are nested, the browser works its way down through them, executing the first object it can handle and skipping the rest.

Partly due to its televised mass-market ad campaign, Adobe's Portable Document Format (PDF) is the most popular file format for sharing non-

HTML documents over the Web. So flexible is this format that the product's family name Adobe Acrobat is very befitting this product. For every major word processor, for example, an Adobe Acrobat plug-in enables you to "print" to the Adobe distiller, which creates the PDF files. Thus, anyone who can use a word processor can create a PDF file. Therein lies the problem of accessibility: Can anyone who can word process make the file accessible?

The key to making PDF files accessible is to structure the document properly with your word processor prior to converting it into a PDF file. Type meaningful headings and subheadings at the beginning of each section and subsection of the document. Use the word processor's Style menu to give each heading or subheading the appropriate heading style. Microsoft Word, for example, has heading styles from Heading1 through Heading 6. These are equivalent to the HTML heading tags `<h1>` through `<h6>`. When you convert an MS Word document into a PDF file, Adobe Acrobat uses these headings to create structural tags in the PDF file. Screen readers and other assistive devices use the tagged PDF document to provide navigational options that make it easy for users with special needs to go to different sections in the document. If you do not use the heading styles, on the other hand, the PDF document will not contain these tags, and the document will not be accessible. Therefore, you should form the habit of always using heading styles to mark the sections and subsections of a word-processed document.

To be considered accessible, images in word-processed documents must have alternate text descriptions. To provide alternate text for an image in an MS Word document, you (1) right-click the image to pop out the quick menu, (2) choose Format Picture to display the Format Picture dialog, and (3) click the Web tab to display the Alternative text box. Figure 9-8 shows how you type the alternate text. Later, when you convert the document to a PDF file, Adobe Acrobat will make this alternate text available to users with screen readers and other kinds of assistive technology.

By default, the accessibility options in Adobe Acrobat are turned on. These include the options to embed tags in PDF and to create PDF bookmarks for the heading styles that mark the structure of your document. After you create the PDF file, it opens in Acrobat. To test the file for accessibility, run Acrobat's built-in Accessibility Checker, which checks the document for Section 508 compatibility and advises you of any problems. For more on creating accessible PDFs, go to www.adobe.com/products/acrobat/solutionsacc.html.

Multimedia Accessibility Showcase

The National Center for Accessible Media (NCAM) at the WGBH Boston public television station is an excellent source for learning about best practices of accessibility in all things media. By following the links to the rich media accessibility showcase at ncam.wgbh.org/richmedia, you can read about the latest innovations and best practices. The showcase contains examples of accessible media delivered in the following formats: Director, Flash, PDF, QuickTime, Real Media, Scalable Vector Graphics, SMIL, Windows Media, and XHTML+SMIL. Accessibility strategies include

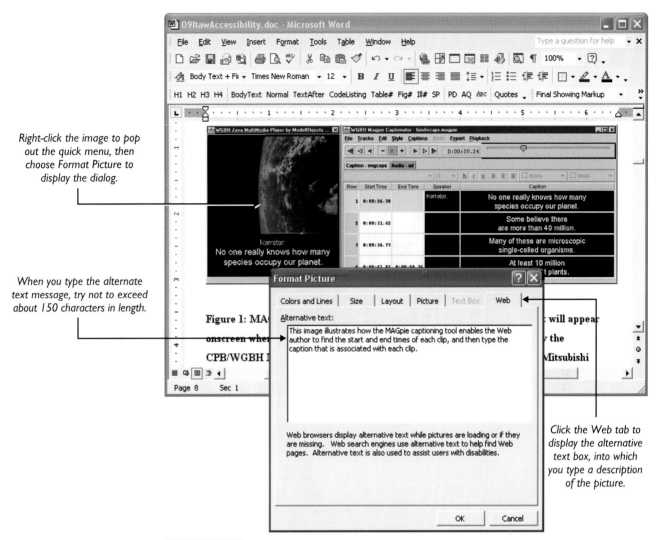

Right-click the image to pop out the quick menu, then choose Format Picture to display the dialog.

When you type the alternate text message, try not to exceed about 150 characters in length.

Click the Web tab to display the alternative text box, into which you type a description of the picture.

FIGURE 9-8 *Before you convert an MS Word document into a PDF file, you should provide alternative text for each image in the document. In this example, I am typing alternative text that explains the MAGpie illustration. The PDF version of this document makes this alternative text available to screen readers and other kinds of assistive devices.* ■

assistive devices, audio description, captions, extended audio description, keyboard access, self-voicing, and text transcript. You can search the showcase by format and strategy to see or hear examples of all these combinations.

Designing Style Sheets for Accessibility

In Chapter 8, you learned that instead of hard-coding presentation elements into the HTML of a Web page, it is better to separate content from style by assigning the HTML elements to style classes. At runtime, the browser looks to the style sheet for the rules that are associated with these classes. Thus, the style classes determine the look and feel of the HTML elements onscreen.

Separating content from style in this manner has an important advantage for users with special needs. If the style sheets you provide do not handle the content appropriate to the user's needs, the user can use the browser's accessibility controls to add another style sheet onto the cascade. By being last on the cascade, this style sheet can redefine any of the style classes that the user needs to have interpreted differently.

Although users with special needs have this ability to add a style sheet to the cascade, you should always try your best when authoring Web pages to create styles that are maximally accessible. The following sections recommend some best practices for creating accessible styles.

Font Selection and Spacing

Most browsers default to the Times Roman font. If you do not specify a different font, Times Roman is what you get. Studies have shown that the Times Roman font is one of the best choices if you are creating a document for printing on paper. The serifs, which are the angled decorations on the endpoints of the characters, enhance the flow of the text on the printed page. It is ironic that on the computer screen the serifs, which make Times Roman look cool on paper, can interfere with readability onscreen. Fonts without serifs, such as the Arial font, work better on the computer screen. This may be because the computer screen has far less resolution than the printed page. This book, for example, is printed at a resolution of 4,800 dots per inch (DPI). The typical computer screen, on the other hand, has a resolution of about 50 DPI. There is not enough resolution at 50 DPI to give the serifs the smooth flow they have on paper. Instead, serifs look jagged onscreen.

In an article published in the *International Journal of Human-Computer Studies*, Bernard et al. (2003) conducted a controlled experiment that compared Times New Roman and Arial typefaces in 10- and 12-point, dot-matrix and anti-aliased (i.e., edge-softened) versions. In terms of overall readability and legibility, the 12-point Arial dot matrix typeface was preferred to all of the other typefaces. The reason for this may be because Arial simply looks cleaner and neater onscreen. On paper, however, Times New Roman rules. In 2004, for example, the U.S. State Department issued an edict declaring Times New Roman as the font for all diplomatic notes (*ABC News Online*, January 30, 2004).

Besides choosing Arial to use on a Web page, you want the text onscreen to appear large enough for the user to read. Text that is large enough for one user, however, may be too small for another. Instead of hard-coding the fonts to a specific size, therefore, you should use relative sizing. The W3C has created two ways for you to do this. First, you can use the adjectives small, smaller, x-small, xx-small, medium, large, larger, x-large, and xx-large. Or you can specify the font size in a unit called an **em**, which is pronounced like the letter *m*. The setting 3em, for example, is three times the width of the letter *m*. Before printing such a font onscreen, the browser looks to the default text size that the user has specified in the browser's View menu. Thus, the font scales automatically to the visual needs of the user. Figure 9-9 provides examples of font size settings that scale in this manner, as well as examples that fail to scale. To create pages that are maximally acceptable, you should choose font settings that scale.

The font settings with fixed pixel sizes fail to scale.

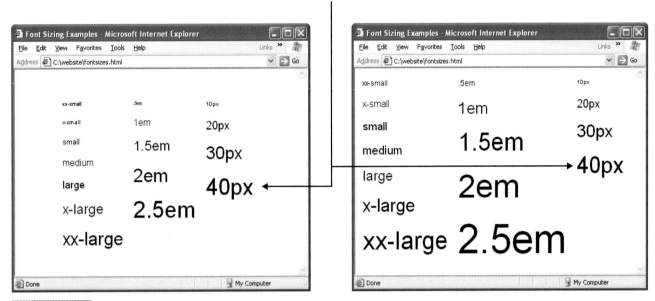

FIGURE 9-9   *On the left are font size examples displayed at the browser's default setting. On the right, the same examples appear with the browser's View | text-size setting configured to increase the font size. Notice how the font settings with relative values scale, while the settings that have fixed pixel sizes fail to scale, thereby defeating the browser's text-size feature.* ■

Color and Contrast

Without sufficient contrast between foreground text and background colors, users have trouble reading Web content, no matter how you style the font. That is why you must always use colors that are high in contrast. Figure 9-10 illustrates recommended style sheet settings that create good contrast onscreen. These examples adhere to the color contrast algorithm that the W3C recommends for determining whether there is enough contrast. According to this algorithm, you determine color brightness by the formula:

$$((\text{Red value} \times 299) + (\text{Green value} \times 587) + (\text{Blue value} \times 114)) / 1000$$

The difference between the brightness of the text and background colors must be greater than 125. If they are, you proceed to determine color difference by the formula:

(maximum (Red value 1, Red value 2) – minimum (Red value 1, Red value 2)) +
(maximum (Green value 1, Green value 2) – minimum (Green value 1, Green value 2)) +
(maximum (Blue value 1, Blue value 2) – minimum (Blue value 1, Blue value 2))

If the color difference is greater than 500, the colors are sufficiently high in contrast. A tool you can use to perform these calculations is at www.juicystudio.com/services/colourcontrast.asp. For more on the W3C color contrast algorithm, go to www.w3.org/TR/AERT#color-contrast.

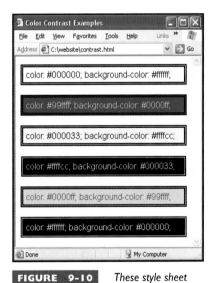

FIGURE 9-10   *These style sheet settings satisfy the W3C recommendation that the difference between the brightness of the text and background colors must be greater than 125 and the color difference must be more than 500.* ■

Web Page Color Blindness Simulator

Vischeck is a tool that simulates human vision. The simulation models three kinds of color blindness, namely, protonopia, a red color deficit; deuteranopia, a green color deficit; and tritanopia, a very rare blue color deficit. To run the Vischeck simulation and see how your Web page will appear to users with protonopia, deuteranopia, or tritanopia, follow these steps:

1. Go to www.vischeck.com, follow the link to Vischeck, and choose the option to Run Web pages.

2. Vischeck asks you to select the type of color vision you want to simulate. The choices are deuteranope, protanope, and tritanope. In this example, click deuteranope.

3. Vischeck will prompt you to type the URL of a Web page. In this example, type www.google.com.

4. Click the Run Vischeck button. You will get a message telling you to wait while Vischeck processes the page. Wait patiently while Vischeck prepares the results.

5. Vischeck will display links to the simulated page and its original version. In this example, follow the link to the Deuteranope simulation to see how the page appears to someone who has a green color deficit.

6. Repeat this process for the other two forms of color blindness, namely, protanope and tritanope. You will probably observe some striking differences. Figure 9-11, for example, shows how the Smithsonian home page appears through the eyes of a user with deuteranope. Notice the lack of greens as compared to Figure 9-12, which pictures the original page in full color.

FIGURE 9-11   *The way the Smithsonian home page appears through the eyes of a user with deuteranopia, which is a green color deficit. Compare this to Figure 9-12, which displays the original page in full color.* ■

FIGURE 9-12   *This is the unaltered, full-color version of the Smithsonian home page. Notice especially the green colors. Compare this full-color version to Figure 9-11, which pictures the same page viewed through the eyes of a user with deuteranopia.* ■

Layering and CSS Page Layout

Layout is one of the most important issues in making Web pages accessible. At the moment, most of the Web's pages use HTML tables to lay out content onscreen. This works fine for sighted users, who can quickly glance from place to place onscreen. Users with screen readers and other kinds of assistive devices, however, run into trouble because the order of the content in the HTML file is not necessarily the order in which the user wants to read the material.

Linearization is the process of thinking of a Web page in the order in which the elements occur in the HTML file. Earlier in this chapter, you learned how users with special needs have difficulty with the order in which Web page elements are presented in the most common kind of navigational layout, in which the navigation options appear at the top and down the left-hand column of the screen. Consider how such a design linearizes when created with tables: The navigational links come first in the file, followed by the page content that the user would most likely want to read first. Section 508 Web accessibility rule (o) addresses this problem by requiring that Web pages have a skip navigation link if the document begins with these kinds of navigational options. There is a more elegant way to linearize content on a Web page, however.

In the absolute positioning section of the previous chapter, you learned how the z-index style sheet property enables you to specify the order in which the browser prints layers onscreen. Imagine using the z-index property to tell the browser the order in which to print the main content layer, the left sidebar, and the top banner information onscreen. Because the z-index property determines the display order, you can put the most important layer first in the file, thereby enabling screen readers and other assistive devices to receive the main content first. To provide a way to divide the content of a page in this manner, the W3C invented the **<div>** start and **</div>** stop tags. <div> is an abbreviation for division. You use the <div> tag to create structural divisions onscreen.

Figure 9-13 shows a page that has three divisions onscreen: a top banner, a left sidebar, and a main content layer. When created with tables, this layout positions the content 190 lines below the start of the file. If you use <div> tags to lay out this page with absolute positioning, on the other hand, you can put the content at the very beginning of the document's

FIGURE 9-13   *HTML tables create the layout of this Web page. Because table-driven layout requires that the banner and sidebar precede the main content in this HTML file, screen readers must wade past more than 190 lines of code to get to the main content on this page.* ∎

body as shown in Figure 9-14. For sighted users, the page appears onscreen as illustrated in Figure 9-13. Users with special needs, on the other hand, get the main content first. The only problem is that some browsers do not yet properly support absolute positioning. Because of this uneven support for absolute positioning, you cannot rely on it for public use. That is why most sites continue to use tables to layout the pages. In future years, when CSS rolls out more broadly, absolute positioning may become the preferred way of laying out Web pages. If that happens, absolute positioning will obviate the need for rule (o), which requires that pages like this one must have a skip navigation link.

Tools for Assessing Web Site Accessibility

This chapter has presented many rules and suggestions for ways in which you can increase the accessibility of a Web site. You can spend many hours working to meet these guidelines. When do you know, however, that you have done enough for the site to be considered compliant?

Happily, you can use tools to determine the extent to which a Web site complies with the accessibility guidelines. These tools can analyze the code of any Web page, report specific rules and guidelines that the page may be violating, and suggest improvements you can make to bring the page into compliance.

Absolute positioning enables you to put the main content first in the document's body, even though the banner and the sidebar appear first onscreen.

These three style classes use absolute positioning to create the layout onscreen.

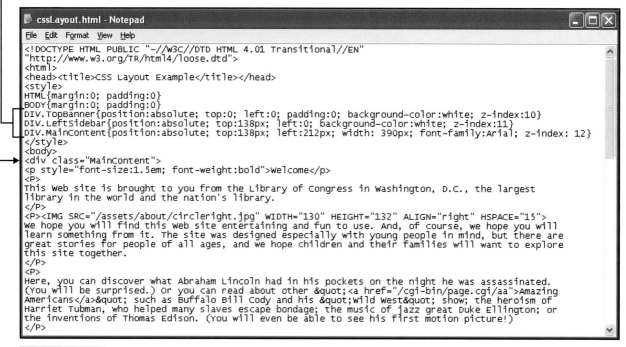

FIGURE 9-14 *This code uses absolute positioning to create the page layout illustrated in Figure 9-13. The cascading style sheet defines three classes of divisions entitled TopBanner, LeftSidebar, and MainContent, respectively. In the body of the page, <div> tags use the style classes to position the divisions onscreen. Because the style classes do the positioning, the file can contain the content in the optimal reading order for users with special needs. In the meantime, browsers continue to display the page as illustrated in Figure 9-13.* ■

Bobby

Created by the Center for Applied Special Technology (CAST), **Bobby** is a comprehensive Web accessibility tool that can analyze a single page or an entire Web site. Recently acquired by Watchfire Corporation, Bobby exposes barriers to accessibility, makes recommendations for necessary repairs, and encourages compliance with existing guidelines. For a demonstration of Bobby in action, go to bobby.watchfire.com and follow the onscreen instructions to enter the URL of a Web page you would like Bobby to analyze. The options onscreen let you choose whether to test for compliance with the U.S. Section 508 guidelines or the W3C's Web Content Accessibility Guidelines.

The free version of Bobby lets you evaluate only one page at a time, and it limits you to check no more than one Web page per minute. From Watchfire, you can purchase a copy of Bobby to run on your own server, where all of the Web developers at your site can evaluate pages as often as they want. Web pages that pass the Bobby test are entitled to display the appropriate Bobby conformance logo. Table 9-3 displays the Bobby conformance logos and explains what they signify.

LIFT

Produced by UsableNet and available at www.usablenet.com, **LIFT** is a suite of products that can test, monitor, report, and repair Web accessibility problems. Dreamweaver and FrontPage versions help authors create Web pages that are Section 508 or WCAG compliant. To try these tools before you buy, follow the links to request a demo at www.usablenet.com, where you can get a free accessibility test of the Web page of your choice.

WebKing

Produced by Parasoft, **WebKing** is a Web verification tool that integrates with IBM's WebSphere Studio Application Developer. WebKing performs (1) static analysis, (2) functional testing, and (3) load testing. As part of static analysis, WebKing checks to make sure your files do not contain any broken links or navigational problems. Along the way, WebKing checks

Logo	What the Logo Means
Bobby APPROVED	The Web page passes at least the WCAG Priority 1 checkpoints.
508 **Bobby** APPROVED	The Web page contains no Section 508 accessibility errors.
A **Bobby** APPROVED	Conformance Level A: This page satisfies all WCAG Priority 1 checkpoints.
AA **Bobby** APPROVED	Conformance Level Double-A: This page satisfies all WCAG Priority 1 and 2 checkpoints.
AAA **Bobby** APPROVED	Conformance Level Triple-A: This page satisfies all WCAG Priority 1, 2, and 3 checkpoints.

TABLE 9-3 *Bobby Conformance Logos* ■

your HTML and CSS code for Section 508 and WCAG accessibility. During the functional analysis phase, WebKing follows the user click paths to make sure they execute correctly. Under load testing, WebKing simulates virtual users and verifies the number of simultaneous users that the site can sustain under different kinds of usage patterns.

You can get a demonstration and download free evaluation software by following the link to WebKing at www.parasoft.com.

STEP508

Created for the federal government by the WGBH National Center for Accessible Media, STEP508 stands for **Simple Tool for Error Prioritization (STEP)** for Section 508 compliance. The STEP508 tool compares and analyzes the output of compliance tools, including Bobby, LIFT, and WebKing. Based on this analysis, STEP508 determines the severity of the errors and prioritizes the repairs needed to bring a Web site into compliance with Section 508. After computing a baseline compliance score, STEP508 provides a metric to track progress in improving the site's accessibility over time. Figure 9-15 shows how you can download STEP508 from the www.section508.gov Web site.

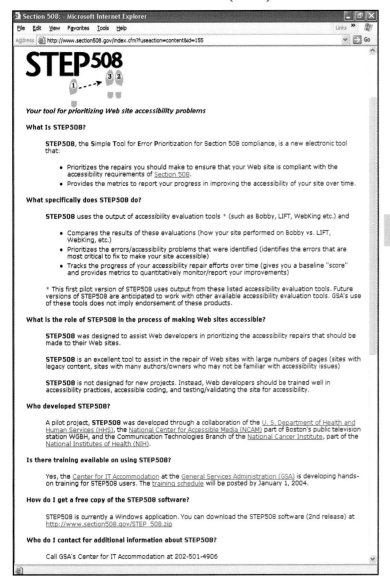

FIGURE 9-15 *STEP508 is a tool for prioritizing the repairs needed to bring a Web site into compliance with Section 508 Web accessibility guidelines. For the latest version, follow the link to STEP508 at www.section508.gov.* ∎

Learning More about Web Accessibility

If you would like to learn more about Web accessibility, I recommend an excellent book by Dr. John M. Slatin and Sharron Bush. Entitled *Maximum Accessibility*, this book presents, discusses, and demonstrates issues and techniques for making Web sites accessible. Published by Addison-Wesley, *Maximum Accessibility* does a very good job of explaining the relationship between the Section 508 rules and the W3C's Web Content Accessibility Guidelines.

An excellent online source of information regarding Web accessibility is the National Center for Accessible Media (NCAM) site at ncam.wgbh.org. Another good source is the Section 508 site at www.section508.gov. A Section 508 tutorial is at usability.gov/web_508/tutorial.html.

For the latest on Web accessibility, go to the W3C's Web Accessibility Initiative (WAI) at www.w3.org/WAI.

Chapter 9 Review

▉ Chapter Summary

After reading this chapter and completing the step-by-step tutorials and Try This! exercises, you should understand the following facts about creating accessible Web pages:

Defining Web Accessibility

- Web accessibility is the capability that results from the process of making it possible for users with special needs to receive, understand, and navigate content that people without handicaps can process in lieu of such special assistance.

- In the United States, Web accessibility is a right that is guaranteed by law under Section 508 of the Rehabilitation Act of 1973, as amended in 1998. Section 508 requires that all Web sites (as well as other forms of information technology) used, procured, developed, or maintained by government agencies and departments must be accessible.

- In 1997, the W3C launched the Web Accessibility Initiative (WAI), which coordinates the Web's official efforts to achieve accessibility. This initiative's Web Content Accessibility Guidelines (WCAG) consists of 65 checkpoints organized under 14 general guidelines. The three levels of conformance are called A, AA (pronounced double-A), and AAA (pronounced triple-A), respectively.

- The Section 508 accessibility standards do not contain as many checkpoints as the WCAG guidelines, and there are no levels of conformance. Instead, Section 508 includes 16 Web accessibility rules, all of which must be met in order for a Web site to be considered accessible. The Section 508 rules are online at www.section508.gov.

Coding to the Section 508 Web Accessibility Standards

- You must provide a textual equivalent for every nontext element onscreen. HTML has two attributes that you can use to create textual equivalents for nontext elements, namely, `alt` and `longdesc`.

- You may not use color to convey information that cannot be understood in the absence of color.

- You must not use a style sheet in such a way that it changes the meaning that the page would convey without the style sheet.

- To make an image map accessible, use the `alt` attribute to specify the alternate text for each area in the map. You can also use the `longdesc` attribute for any area in the map for which further explanation is required.

- Data tables must have clearly identified row and column headers, which you create via the `<th>` start and `</th>` stop tags. Tables that are used purely for layout, on the other hand, do not require header tags.

- In complex (i.e., nested) data tables, you must use the `headers` attribute to identify the header(s) that are associated with each data cell.

- When you create a frameset, you must give each frame a title that identifies the purpose and function of the frame. In addition to the `title` attribute, some assistive devices use the `name` attribute to identify the frames. You should therefore set both the `title` and `name` attributes for each frame.

- Scripts can make things happen onscreen that assistive devices cannot interpret. Whenever you have a script doing something that displays content or provides interface elements onscreen, you must use the `<noscript>` start and `</noscript>` stop tags to identify this information with functional text that can be read by assistive technology.

- To make forms accessible, you must use the `<label>` start and `</label>` stop tags to identify the ID of the `<input>` field with which the label is associated.

- When a Web page begins with repetitive navigation links, you must provide a way for the user to skip over them. You can accomplish this by creating skip navigation links.

Making Applets, Helpers, and Plug-ins Accessible

- Flash is the most popular multimedia plug-in on the Web. A large percentage of the Web's multimedia content, therefore, gets handled by the Flash player. Guidelines for making Flash movies comply with Section 508 are at www.macromedia.com/macromedia/accessibility.

- Adobe's Portable Document Format (PDF) is the most popular file format for sharing documents over the Web. Guidelines for creating accessible PDFs are at www.adobe.com/products/acrobat/solutionsacc.html.

- The rich media accessibility showcase at ncam.wgbh.org/richmedia contains examples of accessible media delivered in the following formats: Director, Flash, PDF, QuickTime, Real Media, Scalable Vector Graphics, SMIL, Windows Media, and XHTML+SMIL.

Designing Style Sheets for Accessibility

- Instead of hard-coding presentation elements into the HTML of a Web page, it is better to separate content from style by assigning the HTML elements to style classes. At runtime, the browser looks to the style sheet for the rules that are associated with these classes. Thus, the style classes determine the look and feel of the HTML elements onscreen.

- Separating content from style in this manner has an important advantage for users with special needs. If the style sheets you provide do not handle the content appropriate to the user's needs, the user can use the browser's accessibility controls to add another style sheet onto the cascade. By being last on the cascade, this style sheet can redefine any of the style classes that the user needs to have interpreted differently.

- Instead of hard-coding fonts to a specific size, you should use relative sizes. The W3C has created two ways for you to do this. First, you can use the adjectives small, smaller, x-small, xx-small, medium, large, larger, x-large, and xx-large. Or you can specify the font size in a unit called an em, which is pronounced like the letter *m*. The setting 3em, for example, is three times the width of the letter *m*.

- Layout is one of the largest issues in making Web pages accessible. At the moment, most of the Web's pages use HTML tables to lay out the content onscreen. This works fine for sighted users, who can quickly move their gaze from place to place onscreen. Users with screen readers and other kinds of assistive devices, however, can run into trouble because the order of the content in the HTML file is not necessarily the order in which the user would want to read the material. You can solve this problem by using CSS to create the layout through absolute positioning, which can place the document's structural divisions at the desired locations onscreen, regardless of the order in which the divisions appear in the file.

Tools for Assessing Web Site Accessibility

- Bobby is a comprehensive Web accessibility tool that can analyze a single page or an entire Web site. Bobby exposes barriers to accessibility, makes recommendations for necessary repairs, and encourages compliance with existing guidelines. For a demonstration of Bobby in action, go to bobby.watchfire.com.

- LIFT is a suite of products that can test, monitor, report, and repair Web accessibility problems. Dreamweaver and FrontPage versions help authors create Web pages that are Section 508 or WCAG compliant. To try the LIFT tools before you buy, follow the links at www.usablenet.com.

- WebKing is a Web verification tool that integrates with IBM's WebSphere Studio Application Developer. WebKing performs (1) static analysis, (2) functional testing, and (3) load testing. As part of static analysis, WebKing checks your HTML and CSS code for Section 508 and WCAG accessibility. You can get a demonstration and download free evaluation software by following the link to WebKing at www.parasoft.com.

- STEP508 stands for Simple Tool for Error Prioritization (STEP) for Section 508 compliance. The STEP508 tool compares and analyzes the output of compliance tools, including Bobby, LIFT, and WebKing. Based on this analysis, STEP508 (1) determines the severity of the errors, (2) prioritizes the repairs needed to bring a Web site into compliance with Section 508, and (3) provides a metric to track progress in improving the site's accessibility over time. You can download STEP508 from www.section508.gov.

Key Terms

alt attribute *(406)*
Bobby *(427)*
\<div> \</div> *(425)*
em *(422)*
for attribute *(416)*
headers attribute *(413)*
hertz (Hz.) *(414)*
id attribute *(412)*
\<label> \</label> *(416)*
LIFT *(427)*

linearization *(425)*
longdesc attribute *(406)*
MAGpie *(408)*
Microsoft Active Accessibility
  (MSAA) *(418)*
name attribute *(413)*
\<noscript> \</noscript> *(415)*
Section 508 *(405)*
Simple Tool for Error
  Prioritization (STEP) *(428)*

skip navigation link *(417)*
\<th> \</th> *(412)*
title attribute *(413)*
Web accessibility *(404)*
Web Accessibility Initiative
  (WAI) *(405)*
Web Content Accessibility
  Guidelines (WCAG) *(405)*
WebKing *(427)*

Key Terms Quiz

1. _____ is the capability that results from the process of making it possible for users with special needs to receive, understand, and navigate content that people without handicaps can process in lieu of such special assistance.

2. In the United States, Web accessibility is a right that is guaranteed by law under _____ of the Rehabilitation Act of 1973, as amended in 1998.

3. In 1997, the W3C launched the _____, which coordinates the Web's official efforts to achieve accessibility. This initiative's Web Content Accessibility Guidelines (WCAG) consists of 65 checkpoints organized under 14 general guidelines.

4. In HTML image tags, you create textual equivalents that are less than 150 characters via the _____. You should use the _____ for longer text descriptions.

5. Data tables must have clearly identified row and column headers, which you create via the <____> start and <____> stop tags.

6. In complex (i.e., nested) data tables, you must use the _____ to identify the header(s) that are associated with each data cell.

7. Whenever you have a script doing something that displays content or provides interface elements onscreen, you must use the <____> start and <____> stop tags to identify this information with functional text that can be read by assistive technology.

8. When a Web page begins with repetitive navigation links, you must provide a way for the user to skip over them. You can accomplish this by creating a(n) _____.

9. Available from watchfire.com, _____ is a Web accessibility tool that can analyze a single page or an entire Web site, expose barriers to accessibility, and make recommendations for necessary repairs in order to comply with accessibility guidelines.

10. In the STEP508 accessibility tool, STEP stands for _____.

Multiple-Choice Quiz

1. In the W3C's Web Content Accessibility Guidelines, what is a checkpoint that should be met, otherwise users will find it difficult, but not impossible, to access the material?
   a. Priority 1
   b. Priority 2
   c. Priority 3
   d. Priority 4

2. A Web site that passes all Priority 1, 2, and 3 checkpoints is entitled to display which W3C conformance logo?
   a.
   b.
   c.

3. How many rules are there in the Section 508 Web accessibility standards?
   a. 14
   b. 16
   c. 65
   d. 508

4. What does the MAG in MAGpie stand for?
   a. Maximum accessibility guidelines
   b. Media access generator
   c. Multimedia accessibility group
   d. Multiple accessibility guidelines

5. About how many people are color blind?
   a. 0.5 percent of males and females
   b. 10 percent of males and females
   c. 10 percent of females and 0.5 percent of males
   d. 10 percent of males and 0.5 percent of females

6. Regardless of which style sheets the page may already call upon, the user can always add another style sheet by editing the browser's accessibility settings. Such a style sheet is always:
   a. First on the cascade
   b. Second on the cascade
   c. Third on the cascade
   d. Last on the cascade

7. Which frequency range of screen flicker is forbidden by the Section 508 guidelines?
   a. 0 to 1.5 Hz
   b. 2 to 55 Hz
   c. 55 to 110 Hz
   d. 110 to 440 Hz

8. Which HTML code(s) do you use to describe functional text information displayed onscreen by a script?
   a. `alt`
   b. `longdesc`
   c. `title`
   d. `<noscript> </noscript>`

9. When should you take advantage of Section 508 rule (k) and provide a text-only page to substitute for a Web page that you cannot bring into compliance with all of the other Section 508 rules?
   a. As often as possible
   b. Only as a last resort
   c. When you are in a hurry
   d. When you want an easy way out

10. Which key do you press to move from element to element as an alternative to clicking the desired element with a mouse?
   a. CTRL
   b. ESC
   c. ENTER
   d. TAB

■ Essay Quiz

1. The Section 508 Web site explains the relationship between the 16 Section 508 Web accessibility rules and the W3C's Web Content Accessibility Guidelines (WCAG). In your own words, describe how the Section 508 rules compare to the WCAG. If you have trouble finding this information, go to section508.gov, set the search option to search the section 508 Web site, and search for the keyword **WCAG**.

2. In the Macintosh operating system, the buttons for closing, minimizing, or maximizing a window follow a traffic light metaphor according to which these options are color-coded red, yellow, and green:

   When the user moves the mouse over these options, icons appear inside the buttons:

   In your opinion, does this color coding violate Section 508 rule (c), which forbids using color to convey information that cannot be understood in the absence of color? Explain the reasons why you feel Apple complied with or violated Section 508 rule (c).

3. Many users who cannot use a mouse rely on the keyboard to navigate from element to element on a Web page. In an HTML form, why should a Web author not program the ENTER key to submit the form's data?

4. What cascading style sheet rule can you use to hide from sighted users hyperlinks that you want users with screen readers to receive? To help answer this question, review and reflect on the section entitled "Skip Navigation" earlier in this chapter.

5. In your own words, explain why it is important to use heading styles when you word process a document for which you plan to create a PDF file. To help answer this question, reflect on the kind of navigational element that will be available to users with special needs as a result of the heading styles.

Lab Projects

• Lab Project 9-1: Designing Accessible Web Sites

Imagine that the government notified your school or company that federal funding will be discontinued in six months if you do not bring your Web site into compliance with the Section 508 Web accessibility rules. In response to this warning, your institution went through the process of bringing the site into compliance. Your employer is concerned, however, that the site will fall back out of compliance if continued work does not comply with accessibility guidelines. To address this concern, your employer has assigned you the job of creating an accessibility checklist that Web developers must follow at your site whenever they create or update site content. Use your word processor to create this checklist. In deciding what to include on the checklist, consider the following issues:

■ **Textual Description for Nontext Elements** Section 508 requires that you must provide a textual description for every nontext element onscreen. Consider the kinds of nontext elements at your Web site, and create the appropriate checkpoints.

- **Forms**   You must code forms in such a manner that users who do not have a mouse can use the computer keyboard to navigate, fill in, and submit the form. Be sure to include checkpoints for the `<label>` tags, `for` attributes, and Submit button that every form must have.

- **PDF Accessibility**   Include a checkpoint that reminds your fellow employees to use heading styles when word processing documents that will be mounted at your site as PDF files. In the PDF file, these headings are tagged as bookmarks, which enable users with assistive devices to jump to different sections and subsections in the document.

- **Accessibility by Design**   As you learned in this chapter, good Web design principles can obviate the need for some of the Section 508 rules. By requiring your authors to use client-side image maps, for example, you can avoid needing to create a checkpoint requiring redundant text links for server-side maps.

If your instructor asked you to hand in the checklist, make sure you put your name at the top of the document, then copy it onto a disk or follow the other instructions you may have been given for submitting this assignment.

• Lab Project 9-2: Evaluating Web Site Accessibility

Imagine that your employer has heard about Web accessibility tools that can automatically scan all of the pages at a Web site and report violations of Section 508 or WCAG accessibility guidelines. Your employer wants to get one of these tools to help ensure that the pages at your school or company Web site are compliant. The stakes are high because of the federal funding that your organization stands to lose if the site violates the Section 508 rules. Your employer has asked you to recommend which tool your organization should adopt for periodically scanning the site for accessibility violations. Use your word processor to write an essay in which you discuss the alternatives and recommend how your organization should go about evaluating Web site accessibility. In developing this recommendation, consider the following issues:

- **Alternative Tools**   In this chapter, you learned about three tools for assessing the accessibility of a Web site—namely, Bobby, LIFT, and WebKing. There are about thirty other tools you can consider. The W3C keeps track of these tools at www.w3.org/WAI/ER/existingtools.html. Go there to read the summaries of what these tools do, and make a list of the tools you want to consider. In your essay, list the tools you considered, explain why you chose the tool you decided to recommend, and state the reasons why you rejected the others.

- **Authoring Environments**   Some of the accessibility tools plug into work with certain Web development tools. In this chapter, for example, you learned that versions of LIFT for Dreamweaver and FrontPage are available, while WebKing plugs into IBM's WebSphere Studio Application Developer. Read the tool summaries at www.w3.org/WAI/ER/existingtools.html to find out whether other accessibility tools exist that plug into specific Web development environments. If you find plug-ins for the Web-authoring tools used at your site, include them on your list of alternatives to be considered.

- **Trial Versions**   As you learned in this chapter, you can get trial versions of Bobby, LIFT, and WebKing. Find out whether trial versions exist for other alternatives you are considering. In your recommendation, consider proposing a trial period during which you test the tool before adopting it for production use at your Web site.

- **Prioritizing Errors**   Go to www.section508.gov and read about the STEP508 tool. Consider whether STEP508 would be useful at your Web site. In your recommendation, state the reasons why you decided to include or forego STEP508 at this time.

If your instructor asked you to hand in the recommendation, make sure you put your name at the top of the essay, then copy it onto a disk or follow the other instructions you may have been given for submitting this assignment.

part III

Networking Fundamentals

Back in the twentieth century, networking was a highly technical endeavor that most users happily let their network administrator perform for them. The rollout of digital television and the growing popularity of media center PCs are creating a new perspective on networking. Circuit City, Radio Shack, Best Buy, Sears, and Wal-Mart sell Ethernet hubs and wireless media center devices at mass market prices. Because of the mass market appeal of local area networking, end users want to network digital media devices throughout the home. This retail market makes all the more relevant this book's third and final part, which is devoted to networking. The hands-on exercises provide skills that you can use not only in the workplace, but also on digital devices throughout the home.

Students who are preparing for the CIW Foundations exam need not worry that this part of the book is all fun and games. To the contrary, all of the CIW objectives are covered, and the end-of-chapter materials contain practice tests that will help you prepare for the exam.

After covering general networking principles in Chapter 10 and Internetworking in Chapter 11, Chapter 12 contains a tutorial on providing database access over a network. Then Chapter 13 rounds things out by covering network security. The book concludes by stepping you through the process of publishing a Web site securely and providing access only to authorized users.

chapter

10

Introduction to Networking

"This is the power of the network.
Now."

—Cisco slogan from www.cisco.com

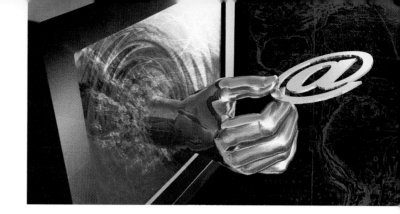

In this chapter, you will learn how to:

- Define the term *networking* and list the three critical components that must be present in a network.

- Define the five networking topologies used in describing the physical layout or shape of a network.

- Define the seven layers in the OSI Reference Model and identify the networking protocol suites that follow it.

- Describe the difference between a local area network (LAN), metropolitan area network (MAN), and a wide area network (WAN).

- Define the physical network components that LANs, MANs, and WANs comprise.

N E T W O R K I N G has a fascinating history that chronicles the invention of the technologies that power the Internet. Back in the 1950s, for example, people did not have personal computers. To use a computer, you had to go to the computing center and wait your turn at the card reader to feed in a deck of cards upon which you had typed your script using a keyboarding device called a *keypunch*. Compare this early technology to today's network, over which wireless devices enable people to work productively almost everywhere they go. During the transition from punched cards to ubiquity, the field of computing evolved through four functional stages of networking. This chapter introduces networking by defining these four networking models, all of which are in use today.

Another way of defining networks is to classify the geographical shapes that form when you connect computers in different physical arrangements. So far, the field of computer networking has evolved five distinct geographical network topologies. This chapter defines, diagrams, and explains them.

For computers to exchange data meaningfully, they must use a communications protocol that defines how the data flows. Most of the world has adopted an international standard for networking that is called the **OSI Reference Model (OSI/RM)**. After describing how data flows across the network in packets created according to the OSI/RM, this chapter concludes by presenting the physical hardware devices and transmission media that create the local and wide area networks over which these packets flow.

Understanding Networks

A **network** is the connection of two or more digital devices for the purpose of communicating, transferring, or obtaining data. In order to have a network, you must have three things that are characteristic of all networks. First, there must be a physical connection through which the data will flow. Second, there must be a set of communication rules called *protocols* that the networked devices use to communicate. Third, there must be one or more network services that will receive these communications and respond by providing the informational resources that are the reason why you want to create a network in the first place.

The act of communicating over a network is called **networking**. Advances in microelectronics enable networking to encompass a wide range of devices. Figure 10-1 illustrates how these devices can include network-ready home appliances as well as more traditional computing equipment.

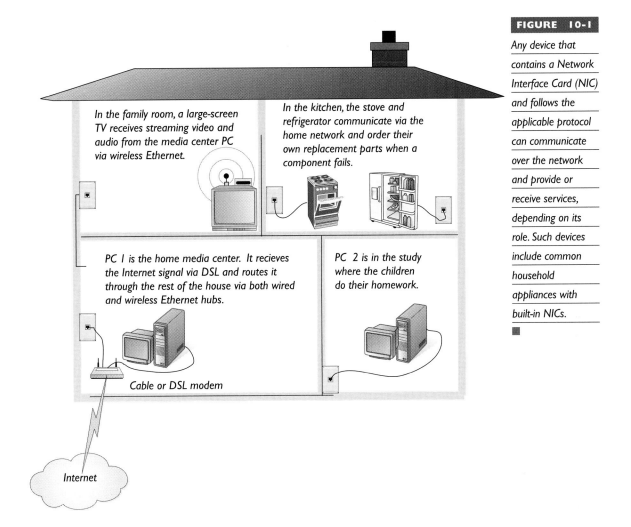

FIGURE 10-1

Any device that contains a Network Interface Card (NIC) and follows the applicable protocol can communicate over the network and provide or receive services, depending on its role. Such devices include common household appliances with built-in NICs.

In the family room, a large-screen TV receives streaming video and audio from the media center PC via wireless Ethernet.

In the kitchen, the stove and refrigerator communicate via the home network and order their own replacement parts when a component fails.

PC 1 is the home media center. It recieves the Internet signal via DSL and routes it through the rest of the house via both wired and wireless Ethernet hubs.

PC 2 is in the study where the children do their homework.

Cable or DSL modem

Internet

Mainframe/Terminal Model

When networking started, computers were large and expensive. They cost so much and required so much maintenance that you didn't even think about owning your own. Instead, you connected via the **mainframe/terminal model**, which Figure 10-2 illustrates. A **mainframe** is a centralized computer to which users connect in order to obtain network services. The **terminal** is a device with a keyboard upon which you type commands or enter data to communicate with the mainframe computer. The first terminals were typewriter-style devices that had no built-in intelligence, which is why they are often referred to as *dumb terminals*. Eventually, terminals got display screens and were called *graphics terminals*. The addition of computer chips created so-called *smart terminals*, which had some processing power but could not function on their own as stand-alone computers. Terminals that contain their own central processing unit (CPU) became known as *intelligent terminals*. Today, you can run terminal emu-

note *Since there is only one computer, this mainframe/terminal model can create bottlenecks. The single point of failure adversely affects every user if the mainframe goes down. Due to these vulnerabilities, the mainframe/terminal model is declining in popularity, although many large companies continue to operate legacy mainframe computers.*

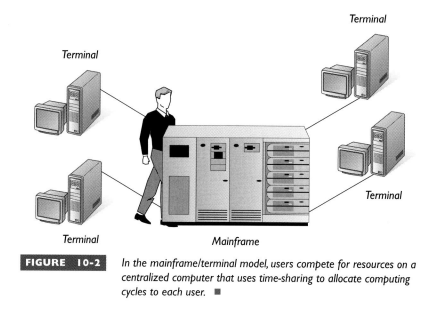

Terminal

Terminal

Terminal

Terminal

Terminal

Mainframe

FIGURE 10-2 In the mainframe/terminal model, users compete for resources on a centralized computer that uses time-sharing to allocate computing cycles to each user. ∎

lation software on personal computers whenever you need to connect to a legacy mainframe computer in terminal mode.

Client-Server Model

A more efficient way of distributing networked resources is the client-server model. As you learned in Chapter 1, the term *client-server* refers to the manner in which computers exchange information by sending it (as servers) and receiving it (as clients). Some computers are dedicated servers. A file server, for example, is dedicated to storing files that authorized users can upload or download via the network. A print server provides network access to one or more printers. A database server processes queries that retrieve or store information in a database. A network server manages network traffic.

Other computers serve multiple purposes. On a small network, for example, one computer can function as a file server, a print server, and a database server. Even workstations that are used primarily as clients can run network services. An end user who wants to permit other users to upload or download local files, for example, can run an FTP server that exposes certain folders to authorized users over the Internet. You will learn how to run an FTP server in Chapter 11, which is devoted to Internetworking.

The most strategic aspect of client-server computing is the manner in which computers can serve dual roles as both servers and clients. Figure 10-3 illustrates how this dual role enables the creation of multi-tier networks in which one server can become a client in order to request something from another server. This enables large organizations to subdivide complex applications into multiple stages called *tiers*. **Multi-tier** computing typically includes three tiers consisting of (1) the user interface tier, (2) the business tier, and (3) the database tier.

Figure 10-3 shows end users connecting to a Web application running on the business tier that serves the end users. When the Web application requires information from the corporate database, however, the business

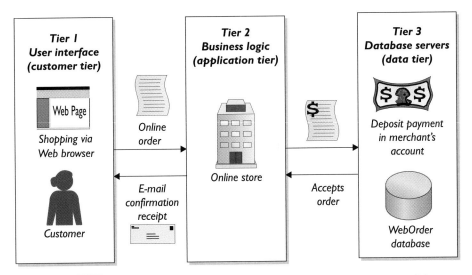

| Tier 1
User interface
(customer tier) | | Tier 2
Business logic
(application tier) | | Tier 3
Database servers
(data tier) |

FIGURE 10-3 *In multi-tier computing, mid-level computers perform the dual role of client and server. Pictured here is the classic e-commerce model in which end users connect to a Web application running on the business tier that serves the end users.* ■

tier becomes a client that issues a query against the database service running on the data tier. In large operations, more than one mid-level computer can share the responsibility for serving end users. Similarly, the data tier can distribute a large database over multiple computers known as a *server farm*.

Peer-to-Peer Model

In a LAN, **peer-to-peer (P2P)** is a network architecture in which each workstation has equal responsibilities. No dedicated server is in charge of managing a P2P network. In a home or small office environment, P2P is a simple way to set up a network that can share digital resources throughout the LAN. On larger networks under heavy loads, however, P2P does not perform as well as client-server networks, which do a better job of balancing and managing network traffic.

Out on the Internet, the term *P2P* refers to a form of peer-to-peer file sharing brought to public attention by the controversy over music file sharing. Figure 10-4 illustrates that no dedicated server is in charge of managing a P2P file-sharing environment. Because no one is in charge, the music industry finds it difficult to identify users who violate the law by using P2P file sharing to distribute copyrighted music over the Internet.

FIGURE 10-4 *In a peer-to-peer (P2P) network, workstations have equal responsibility for sharing files and accessing services on each other's computers. In the music industry, this absence of authority makes it difficult to identify and prosecute copyright infringers who share copyrighted music via P2P file sharing without permission.* ■

Enterprise Model

The term **enterprise model** refers to networking within large organizations that dedicate entire servers to handling important tasks in the most efficient manner. A large organization, for example, may need individual servers dedicated to the tasks of serving mail, hosting databases, managing security, and routing network traffic. Figure 10-5 shows that an enterprise network can include a large mainframe computer, which is front-ended by network servers that provide access to authenticated users. Within a large organization, individual departments may have minicomputers, which are smaller than mainframes but larger than individual workstations. As microelectronic technology continues to progress, the distinctions among mainframes, minicomputers, workstations, and personal computers begin to blur. The least expensive PC you can buy today, for example, dwarfs the early mainframes.

Push vs. Pull Technology

There are basically two ways to receive information from a network. Either you ask for it, and the information appears on demand each time you request it; or you subscribe to an information service, which provides you with the information automatically when the data becomes available. The computer industry uses the **push-pull metaphor** to distinguish between these two ways of receiving information.

When you browse the Web and click hyperlinks that bring requested resources onscreen, for example, you are pulling the information toward you. Thus, hyperlinks are an example of pull technology. If you install onto your computer a stock-monitoring client, on the other hand, financial news and stock prices scroll onscreen as the server pushes information onto your computer. Another application of push technology is automatic software and document updating, as exemplified by BackWeb's Polite Sync Server at www.backweb.com/products/html/psstech.html.

Push technology can also be used to broadcast important messages to network users. In a weather emergency, for example, a Windows network administrator can use the "net send" feature to push a warning message onto each logged-on worker's screen. Users who want to monitor the weather continuously can download the WeatherBug from www.weatherbug.com. The current temperature displays on the Windows status bar, and impending weather emergencies push warnings onto your screen.

Network Operating Systems

A **network operating system** is the software that adds to a computer the functions required for connecting computers together for the purpose of networking. The most popular network operating systems are Microsoft Windows, UNIX, Linux, the Mac OS, and Novel NetWare.

Microsoft Windows

The most widespread network operating system is Microsoft Windows. No matter what version of Windows you have, certain networking components are built right in. Every Windows user, for example, has the capability to use the NetBEUI, IPX/SPX, and TCP/IP protocols that are discussed later in this chapter. Not all versions of Windows, however, enable you to run certain

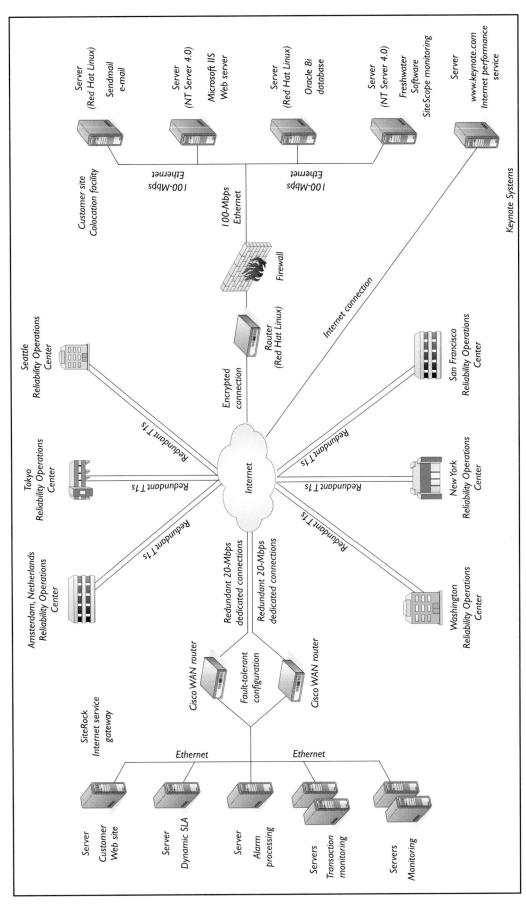

FIGURE 10-5 The enterprise model pulls out all the stops as large organizations combine different networking strategies to accomplish computing tasks efficiently. The network shown here has a legacy mainframe system front-ended by network servers that communicate with departmental minicomputers and local area networks that are primarily client-server based, although small groups use peer-to-peer networking to share files efficiently among team members. ■

networking services. Internet Information Services (IIS), which is the Windows Web application server, for example, does not come with every version of Windows. Windows XP Home Edition users, for example, cannot install IIS. Windows XP Pro, on the other hand, comes with IIS, as does the complete line of Windows Server products, including Windows NT, Windows 2000, and Windows 2003, which can host mail, news, directory, catalog, and transaction services. To find out which versions of Windows support which server products, go to the history of Windows Server products at www.microsoft.com/windows/winhistoryserver.mspx.

UNIX and Linux

The **UNIX** and **Linux** operating systems support the full range of networking services, including both client- and server-side components. Bell Labs invented UNIX in the early 1970s. Because UNIX was distributed in C source code, C programmers could modify the operating system, and many different versions of UNIX began circulating. In the 1980s, AT&T worked to create a standardized version of UNIX. Today, The Open Group holds the trademark and defines the official version of UNIX at www.unix-systems.org.

Developed by Linus Torvalds, Linux is an open source operating system that mimics the form and function of UNIX on an independently developed platform. The general public license permits anyone with the necessary technical skills to download and modify the Linux source code. As you have probably noticed in recent television commercials, IBM is touting Linux as an alternative to the Windows operating system for e-commerce solutions. To learn more about Linux, go to www.linux.org.

Mac OS

Another operating system that has networking built in is the **Macintosh OS X** operating system. According to Apple, OS X is the most widely distributed UNIX-based operating system. In other words, behind the Macintosh user interface, OS X is based on a UNIX environment. To learn more about the OS X implementation of UNIX, go to www.apple.com/macosx/features/unix.

Novell NetWare

Developed by Novell Corporation, **NetWare** is a PC-based local area networking product that was one of the most dominant network operating systems during the decade following its invention in 1983. Microsoft's release of Windows NT in 1993, however, created overwhelming competition. Nevertheless, Novell still markets NetWare and has added support for the Apache Web server, the database engine MySQL, the scripting languages Perl and PHP, and the Jakarta Tomcat container for Java servlets and Java Server Pages (JSP). For more information, go to www.novell.com/products/netware.

Classifying Network Topologies

A popular way of classifying networks is to describe the different kinds of geographical configurations that form when computers get connected for the purpose of networking. A network's geographical shape is referred to as the network's **topology**. The five kinds of network topology are (1) bus topology, (2) ring topology, (3) star topology, (4) hybrid topology, and (5) mesh topology.

Bus Topology

The **bus topology** has a single cable, called the **bus** or the **trunk**, to which every device on the network connects. Figure 10-6 shows that you can connect a wide range of devices to the bus or trunk, which is a coaxial cable. The fittings and connectors are similar to those used in cable TV. Like a cable TV signal, information on the bus travels in both directions along the entire length of the cable. To prevent the signal from feeding back when it reaches the end of the line, each end of the bus has a terminator that absorbs the signal.

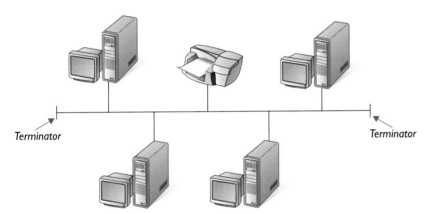

Terminator   *Terminator*

FIGURE   10-6   *The bus topology uses a single cable, called the bus or trunk, to connect every device on the network. The bus uses coaxial cable that is inexpensive and easy to install, although a break anywhere along the cable causes all network traffic to stop.* ∎

All of the messages on the bus pass by each device, or node, on the bus. Each device examines all of these messages, acts on the ones intended for that node, and ignores the others. The advantage of this design is its simplicity. The bus is inexpensive and easy to install. If a break occurs anywhere on the cable, however, all network traffic stops. Such a problem can be troublesome to correct because the break may be hard to find, especially if the bus is long and has many devices connected to it. Another disadvantage is that the speed of the bus declines as network traffic increases.

Ring Topology

Figure 10-7 shows how the **ring topology** takes its name from the loop that forms when you connect a network's nodes in a circle. Messages flow in a

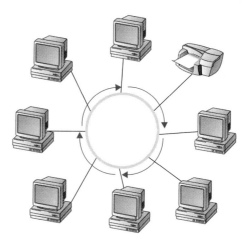

FIGURE   10-7   *The ring topology takes its name from the loop that forms when you connect the network's nodes in a circle. Messages flow in one direction around the ring, as does a token that provides each device its turn to communicate. Because the token enables the network to avoid data collisions, the ring topology is not as prone to slowdowns as networks that must cope with data collisions as traffic increases.* ∎

note   *Token ring networks can run extremely fast. My workplace at the University of Delaware (UD), for example, has a 10 gigabyte per second ring that runs from UD, to Philadelphia, to Wilmington, and back to UD. This network significantly increased UD's bandwidth at a lower cost than the university was paying previously.*

single direction around the ring. Each device acts on the messages addressed to it and passes the rest of the messages onto its neighbor. If a message comes all the way back around to the sender without being acted upon, the message is discarded.

Most rings use a small piece of data called a *token* to give every node an equal chance at obtaining bandwidth from the network. The token circles the ring continually as it passes from node to node. A device can communicate over the network only when it has the token. The advantage of this token ring design is that each node on the network gets an equal share of the bandwidth, and as traffic increases, the ring does a very good job of continuing to run fast by avoiding the data collisions that can slow down other types of networks. An obvious disadvantage of the ring topology is that the network stops working if one of the nodes fails and stops sending the data to its neighbor.

Star Topology

In a **star topology,** each device in the network connects to a central hub, which distributes messages from one node to another. As illustrated in Figure 10-8, one of the disadvantages of the star is that if the central hub fails, the central point of failure makes the network stop working. Stars also require more cabling than bus or ring topologies.

The advantages of a star topology are (1) centralized control, which makes the network easier to maintain and control; (2) easy expansion, which enables you to add a new device without affecting the rest of the network; and (3) fault tolerance, which enables the network to keep functioning if a node stops working, or if you disconnect a device to reconfigure it.

The central hub has jacks that each workstation's network cable plugs into.

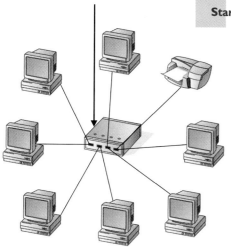

FIGURE   10-8   *The star topology arranges network devices as nodes that are each connected directly to a central hub. Network problems are solved more quickly because the hub makes it easy to trace the cable to the device that is failing.* ∎

Hybrid Topology

When you studied the hypermedia design paradigms in Chapter 6, you learned that a design is considered hybrid when it combines different paradigms to create a more complex web. In the field of networking, the term **hybrid topology** is used in a similar fashion to refer to a network that employs more than one topology to connect devices for the purpose of networking. Figure 10-9 shows an example of a star-ring hybrid topology that uses a ring to distribute packets rapidly among three star-shaped subnetworks. Figure 10-10 illustrates a bus-star hybrid that demonstrates a less expensive way of networking the three stars.

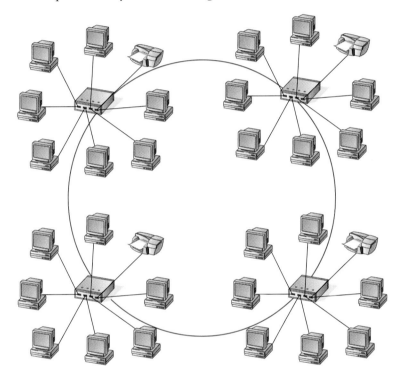

FIGURE 10-9

This hybrid topology uses a star-ring design to create a very fast and efficient network. Because the ring uses a token to synchronize the passing of messages from star to star, the network is not as prone to slowdowns as the star-bus design depicted in Figure 10-10. ■

The advantage of a hybrid topology is that you can easily add network nodes. Since there is no single point of failure, the network continues to function when one of the nodes stops working. The disadvantage is that if your part of the network is being served by the part of the trunk that has failed, your packets will not get through until that part of the trunk has been repaired. In the meantime, you can continue to communicate with local devices with which you still have connectivity.

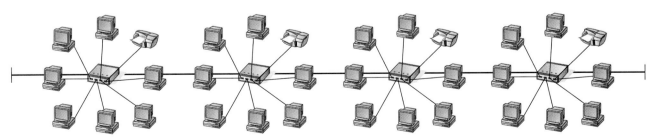

FIGURE 10-10   *A less expensive hybrid topology is the star-bus network pictured here. As traffic increases among the stars, however, this network is more prone to slowdowns than the star-ring network shown in Figure 10-9.* ■

Mesh Topology

In mission-critical operations, you want as much redundancy as possible so that if one part of the network goes down, the packets can find an alternate path to their destination. You achieve this kind of redundancy with the **mesh topology**, which has multiple paths between network hubs. As you will learn in the next chapter, the Internet uses mesh topology to help ensure that if one part of the network fails, packets find alternate routes to reach their destinations. Intelligent hubs called *routers* contain microprocessors that detect network outages, determine the most efficient alternate pathway, and reroute packets accordingly.

Figure 10-11 illustrates that a mesh provides alternate pathways between networks. The advantage of the mesh is that if one of the hubs fails, the packets will find an alternate path to their destination. The only disadvantage is that if you happen to be connected to the hub that has failed, your packets will not be able to get past your local network until the hub returns to service.

FIGURE 10-11

The mesh topology adds alternate pathways to the network to enable packets to find the most efficient routing to their destinations. The public Internet can be thought of as the ultimate in mesh technology, due to the multiple pathways that the telecomm carriers have provided to help prevent network failures. ∎

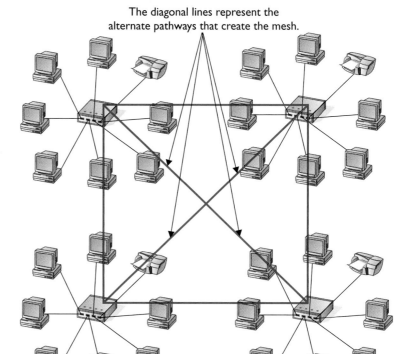

The diagonal lines represent the alternate pathways that create the mesh.

Adopting Network Protocols

In the field of computer networking, a protocol is a set of rules that define how computers communicate with each other. Without protocols, computers would not know how to exchange messages with each other, and the network would be a chaotic Tower of Babel.

Thanks to the work of the International Standards Organization (ISO), the world has agreed upon a networking specification called the Open System

Interconnection (OSI) Reference Model (OSI/RM). This model defines seven layers of communication that are involved in the networking process. At each layer, the OSI/RM defines the protocols that computers must follow to participate in these communications. The key to understanding the OSI/RM is to define what happens at each layer.

Defining the Seven Layers of the OSI Reference Model

Remember that the purpose of a network is to enable two computers to exchange messages. The seven OSI/RM layers account for what happens to the messages as they work their way down from the sending computer's Application Layer to the Physical Layer of the wire or transport medium that carries the messages across the network to the receiving computer, in which the messages work their way back up through the Application Layer to be processed. Imagine that you are using a Web browser on one computer, and you just clicked a link to view a Web page residing on a second computer. The following sections describe what happens to your request as it works its way down the seven OSI/RM layers:

Layer 7: The Application Layer

Through an Application Programming Interface (API), the browser informs the **Application Layer** of your request. The Application Layer begins to form the packet that will eventually travel across the network. This packet consists of the data that comprises the message, plus a header containing protocol information that is communicated down to the next layer. So far, the packet has the following structure:

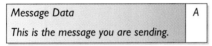

The A header contains protocol information from the Application Layer.

Layer 6: The Presentation Layer

The **Presentation Layer** translates the data into a standard network data format and may use data compression to streamline the packet so it does not consume unnecessary bandwidth on the network. The Presentation Layer may also encrypt the data for sensitive data transmissions, such as banking information. To the front of the packet, the Presentation Layer adds a header containing protocol information describing how it translated, compressed, or encrypted the data. So far, the packet has the following structure:

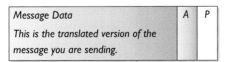

The P header contains protocol information from the Presentation Layer.

Layer 5: The Session Layer

The **Session Layer** negotiates the connection that will be made between the two computers exchanging data. If the amount of data being transmitted is large, the Session Layer inserts a **checkpoint**, which is a marker used to signal that a certain amount of the data has arrived all right. If errors occur in the sending of subsequent packets, the servers know not to resend data prior to the most recently acknowledged checkpoint. To the front of the packet, the Session Layer adds a header containing protocol information describing the connection to be negotiated. So far, the packet has the following structure:

Message Data		A	P	S
This is the connected version of the message you are sending.				

The S header contains protocol information from the Session Layer.

Layer 4: The Transport Layer

The **Transport Layer** works to ensure that the data arrives reliably at its destination. If the amount of data is large, the Transport Layer splits it into **fragments**, which are smaller data segments that the Transport Layer numbers sequentially. If any of the fragments do not arrive reliably, the sending computer retransmits them. To the front of the packet, the Transport Layer adds a header containing protocol information describing the reliability checks and any fragmentation. So far, the packet has the following structure:

Message Data		A	P	S	T
This is the segmented version of the message you are sending.					

The T header contains protocol information from the Transport Layer.

Layer 3: The Network Layer

The **Network Layer** organizes the data into **datagrams**, which combine the data from the Transport Layer with routing information that includes the source and destination addresses along with the recommended path depending on network conditions and the nature of the data. To the front of the packet, the Network Layer adds a header containing protocol information describing the addressing and routing. So far, the packet has the following structure:

Message Data		A	P	S	T	N
This is the datagram version of the message you are sending.						

The N header contains protocol information from the Network Layer.

Layer 2: The Data Link Layer

The **Data Link Layer** transforms the data into **data frames**, which use a raw bit format consisting of 0's and 1's to put the data into packets that can be passed down to the Physical Layer for transmission over the network. The Data Link Layer has two sublayers called **Logical Link Control (LLC)**, and **Media Access Control (MAC)**. The LLC performs error checking and regulates the flow of data to and from the Physical Layer. The MAC handles the actual placement of the packets onto the Physical Layer. To the front of the packet, the Data Link Layer adds a header containing framing information. To ensure that the data gets transmitted without error, the LLC performs a mathematical calculation called a **cyclic redundancy check (CRC)**. To the end of the packet, the LLC adds a trailer containing this CRC value. When the packet gets transmitted, the receiving computer performs its own cyclic redundancy check to determine whether the CRC values match. If not, the packet is discarded, and the sending computer re-sends it. The completed packet has the following structure:

CRC	Message Data This is the framed version of the message you are sending.	A	P	S	T	N	DL

The DL header contains protocol information from the Data Link Layer.

The trailer contains CRC information that is used to determine whether the packet arrives at its destination without error.

Layer 1: The Physical Layer

The **Physical Layer** transforms the 0's and 1's from the Data Link Layer into signals that flow over the transmission media. Depending on the type of transmission media, these signals may be electrical voltages, radio signals, air waves, or light pulses. At the receiving end, the Physical Layer converts these signals back into 0's and 1's and passes them up to the Data Link Layer. Figure 10-12 shows the receiving computer working its way back up in reverse order through the same seven layers through which the data passed on its way out from the sending computer. Because the receiving computer must understand the same protocols that the sending computer used to create the packets, both computers must be running the same networking protocols. The next part of this chapter describes the major networking protocol suites that follow the OSI/RM.

Remembering the Seven OSI/RM Layers

If you are studying for the CIW Foundations exam, you need to memorize the names and the order of the seven OSI/RM layers. Networking professionals use a seven-word slogan to help people remember the order of these layers. The slogan is "All people seem to need data processing."

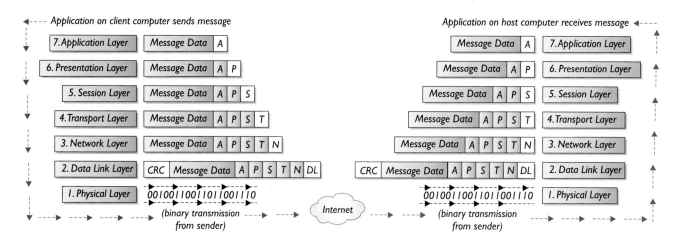

FIGURE 10-12 *When one computer communicates with another via the OSI/RM layers, the messages proceed down from the Application Layer on the sending computer to the Physical Layer, which transmits the message over the network's transmission medium. On the destination computer, the data travels back up the protocol stack. At each of the seven layers, both computers must be running the same protocols in order for this communication to be understood.* ■

Study the callouts below to see how this slogan can help you memorize the order of the seven OSI/RM layers:

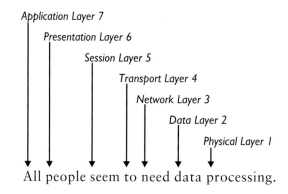

All people seem to need data processing.

OSI/RM Protocol Suite Examples

The term **protocol suite** refers to a collection of protocols that work together in order to conform to a multilayered protocol standard, such as the OSI/RM. Six major protocol suites follow the OSI/RM. These protocol suites include (1) TCP/IP, (2) NetBEUI, (3) IPX/SPX, (4) AppleTalk, (5) DLC, and (6) SNA.

TCP/IP

note *In the next chapter, you will learn how to configure the TCP/IP settings that enable a computer to communicate over the Internet and access the wide range of services that use the TCP/IP protocol suite.*

TCP/IP is the Internet's protocol suite. It has become so important in Internetworking that TCP/IP is built in to virtually every computer's operating system, including Microsoft Windows, the Mac OS, UNIX, and Linux. The TCP/IP protocol suite takes its name from the Transport Control Protocol (TCP) that manages the Transport Layer, and the Internet Protocol (IP) that handles the routing on the Network Layer.

NetBEUI

NetBEUI stands for NetBIOS Extended User Interface, and NetBIOS stands for Network Basic Input/Output System. On versions of the Windows operating system produced before 2001, NetBEUI was the native protocol suite for peer-to-peer networking on local networks. The advantage of NetBEUI is that it is very fast and efficient. Unlike TCP/IP, however, NetBEUI is not routable, which means you can use NetBEUI only to communicate with computers on the local network. To get beyond the local network, you need to use a routable protocol, such as TCP/IP.

IPX/SPX

Another routable protocol is **IPX/SPX**, which stands for Internetwork Packet Exchange (IPX) and Sequenced Packet Exchange (SPX). Developed by Novell for use with the NetWare network operating system, the proprietary IPX/SPX protocol suite has been declining in importance due to the popularity of TCP/IP, which is based on an open standard. The latest version of Novell NetWare, for example, defaults to TCP/IP instead of IPX/SPX.

AppleTalk

AppleTalk is to the Macintosh what NetBEUI is to Windows. In other words, AppleTalk is the legacy protocol suite for peer-to-peer networking on local networks of Macintosh computers, and TCP/IP has become the preferred protocol.

Data Link Control (DLC)

IBM invented **Data Link Control (DLC)** to enable microcomputers to connect as clients to legacy mainframes. Today, DLC lives on as the primary protocol used by Hewlett-Packard printers that have **Network Interface Cards (NICs)**.

Systems Network Architecture (SNA)

Invented by IBM in 1974, the **Systems Network Architecture (SNA)** is a protocol suite for connecting different kinds of networks. Still popular in the mainframe world, the SNA framework was an early model of the kind of layered network architecture that evolved into the OSI/RM.

Combining Protocols

Most computers run more than one networking protocol. In the next chapter, you will learn how to configure a computer's Network Interface Card (NIC) to use multiple protocols. The process of assigning a protocol to a NIC is called **protocol binding**.

When combining protocols, however, you should not overdo it. Each protocol adds overhead to your computer by creating processes that monitor the network for packets to handle. You can reduce this overhead

---

Try This!

Discover Your NIC's MAC Address

Every NIC has a unique Media Access Control (MAC) address. The Physical Layer of the OSI/RM uses MAC addresses to identify the nodes at the ends of each segment of a network. To find out your NIC's MAC address, follow these steps:

1. Click the Windows Start button, choose Control Panel, and double-click Network Connections. The Network Connections window appears onscreen.

2. Double-click the connection you are using to get on the network. If you are using a local area network connection, for example, double-click the Local Area Connection. The connection's Status window appears.

3. Click the Support tab, and then click the Details button. The Network Connection Details window appears.

4. Read the line that says Physical Address. It includes a value consisting of six hexadecimal numbers separated by hyphens. The first three hexadecimal numbers are your NIC vendor's unique manufacturer code, and the other three numbers are the serial number of your NIC. This NIC is the only one in the world containing that number.

---

by specifying the optimal binding order, which determines the order in which your computer tries protocols when attempting to communicate over the network.

Creating LANs, MANs, and WANs

A **local area network (LAN)** is the connection of two or more computer devices for the purpose of networking within a relatively small area, such as a home, school, or departmental office building. A **metropolitan area network (MAN)** connects local networks across a larger geographical region typically ranging in size up to 50 kilometers in diameter. The term *metropolitan* implies that MANs cover an area the size of a city, although they can also cover small groups of buildings within a corporation. Figure 10-13 shows that a MAN can provide access to other networks by connecting to a wide area network (WAN), which uses high-speed transmission lines to connect MANs and LANs over large geographical areas. The Internet is a network of WANs that use the Internet Protocol to route packets to their destinations through the MANs and LANs that the network comprises.

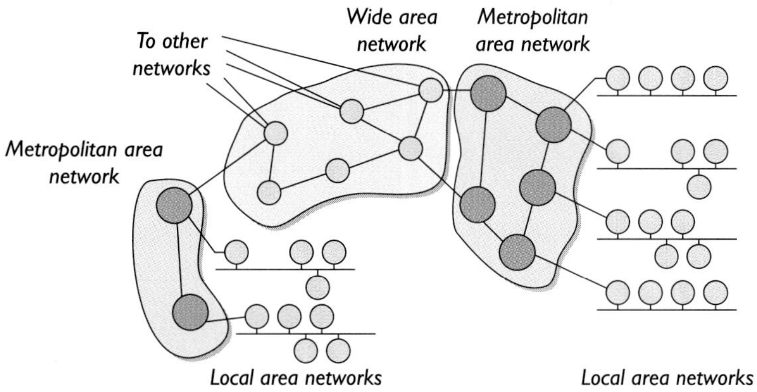

FIGURE 10-13 Metropolitan area networks (MANs) enable local area networks (LANs) to share the cost of connecting to wide area networks (WANs). The interconnection of LANs, MANs, and WANs that follow the TCP/IP protocol forms the Internet. ■

IEEE Project 802 Networking Standards

The Institute of Electrical and Electronic Engineers (IEEE, pronounced "I triple-E") is in charge of defining the networking standards that connect devices to form different kinds of local and metropolitan area networks. The IEEE's LAN/MAN Standards Committee (LMSC) performs this work under IEEE Project 802. Table 10-1 shows that this committee is organized according to working groups in charge of defining the networking standards. These groups are numbered from 802.0 through 802.20, as are their corresponding standards.

When a new standard gets created, it is available only to IEEE members for a period of six months. After this waiting period, the LMSC publishes the standards at www.ieee802.org, where anyone can download and study them.

Number	Purpose	Status
802.0	Sponsor Executive Committee	Coordinating, Active
802.1	High Level Interface (HILI) related to network management and Internetworking	Published, Active
802.2	Logical Link Control (LLC) sublayer of the OSI/RM Data Link Layer	Published, Hibernating
802.3	CSMA/CD (Ethernet)	Published, Active
802.4	Token Bus	Published, Hibernating
802.5	Token Ring	Published, Hibernating
802.6	Metropolitan area network (MAN)	Published, Hibernating
802.7	Broadband	Published, Hibernating
802.8	Fiber optics	Unpublished, Disbanded
802.9	Integrated Services LAN (ISLAN) for voice and data integration	Published, Hibernating
802.10	Standard for Interoperable LAN Security (SILS)	Published, Hibernating
802.11	Wireless LAN (WLAN)	Published, Active
802.12	Demand Priority Access LAN	Published, Hibernating
802.13	Not used for superstitious reasons	Avoided
802.14	Cable TV LAN	Unpublished, Disbanded
802.15	Wireless personal area network (WPAN)	Published, Active
802.16	Broadband Wireless Access (BBWA)	Published, Active
802.17	Resilient Packet Ring (RPR)	Published, Active
802.18	Radio Regulatory Technical Advisory Group	Published, Active
802.19	Coexistence Advisory Group	Published, Active
802.20	Mobile Wireless Access	Published, Active

TABLE 10-1   *Working Groups of the IEEE Project 802 LAN/MAN Standards Committee* ■

note   *IEEE Project 802 defines the LAN standards commonly used today, except for AppleTalk, which is Apple Computer's proprietary protocol suite for creating local networks of Macintosh computers.*

IEEE 802.2 Standard: Logical Link Control (LLC)

If you are studying for the CIW exam, you need to be able to identify IEEE standards 802.2, 802.3, 802.5, and 802.12. The **IEEE 802.2** standard is the Logical Link Control (LLC) sublayer of the OSI/RM Data Link Layer. The other 802 standards build upon the LLC, which performs error checking and regulates the flow of data to and from the Physical Layer.

The Data Link Layer's other sublayer is the Media Access Control (MAC), which handles the actual placement of the packets onto the Physical Layer. Most of the other 802 standards, including 802.3, 802.5, and 802.12, mainly define the MAC sublayer for different kinds of networks.

IEEE 802.3 CSMA/CD (Ethernet)

The **IEEE 802.3** standard defines Ethernet, which is the most popular method of local area networking. Bob Metcalfe invented Ethernet in his doctoral dissertation project at Harvard in 1973. To save you from having to read his dissertation, you can get a basic understanding of how Ethernet works by learning what **CSMA/CD** stands for, because the words in this acronym describe the essence of Metcalfe's invention. CSMA/CD stands for Carrier Sense Multiple Access with Collision Detection. In other words, Ethernet works by detecting the data collisions that can occur when two or more devices use a data channel simultaneously. According to the rules in Metcalfe's thesis, a device waits a random amount of time after detecting a collision and attempts to resend the message. If the data collides again, the device waits twice as long before resending the message.

Metcalfe's rules worked so well that the IEEE codified them as standard IEEE 802.3, which is the standard for ordinary Ethernet networks. The maximum speed of an ordinary 802.3 Ethernet is 10 Mbps. To run Ethernet networks at higher speeds, the IEEE CSMA/CD working group created standards for a so-called **Fast Ethernet** running at 100 Mbps, and an even faster **Gigabit Ethernet** running at 1000 Mpbs.

Table 10-2 defines and compares the ordinary, Fast, and Gigabit Ethernet standards. Notice that the Topology row of this table specifies that Fast and Gigabit Ethernet must have a star topology. In an Ethernet star topology, each device is connected to a central connecting point that is called an **Ethernet hub**. This hub functions as an Ethernet multiport repeater, which is also known as a *concentrator*.

	Ethernet	Fast Ethernet	Gigabit Ethernet
IEEE standard	802.3	802.3u (u stands for updated)	802.3z (specialty copper & fiber optic) 802.3ab (unshielded twisted pair)
Speed	10 Mbps	100 Mbps	1000 Mbps
Media Access Control (MAC) method	CSMA/CD	CSMA/CD	CSMA/CD
Topology	Bus or star	Star	Star
Wiring standards	10base2, 10base5, 10baseT, 10baseFL	100baseTX, 100baseT4, 100baseFX	1000baseT, 1000baseCX, 1000baseSX, 1000baseLX

TABLE 10-2   *Ordinary, Fast, and Gigabit Ethernet standards* ■

IEEE 802.5 Token Ring

The **IEEE 802.5** standard defines token ring, which derives from IBM's local area network design in which a token travels continually around the cable ring to which the network devices are attached. A device can send data only when it has the token. Thus, data collisions never occur on a token-ring network. Under heavy load, token-ring networks are not as likely to degrade as Ethernet networks, which can slow down when multiple data collisions are occurring.

Although IEEE 802.5 does not specify a wiring standard, token-ring networks run typically over twisted-pair wiring at either 4 Mbps or 16 Mbps. Each device attaches to a central connecting point called a **Multi-Station Access Unit (MAU)**. Although the MAU is analogous from a physical standpoint to the hub in an Ethernet network, the MAU contains the ring that passes the token, which prevents data collisions from slowing down the network.

IEEE 802.12 Demand Priority Access LAN (100VG-AnyLAN)

The **IEEE 802.12** standard defines a **Demand Priority Access LAN** that is known in the marketplace as 100VG-AnyLAN. 100VG means that the network is designed to transmit at a speed of 100 Mbps over voice grade (VG) telephone wiring. AnyLAN refers to the fact that this network can handle packets framed for transmission on either Ethernet or token-ring networks.

From a physical cabling standpoint, the 100VG-AnyLAN looks like a star-based Ethernet in that all of the devices are connected to hubs. If two nodes try to transmit data simultaneously, however, the 100VG-AnyLAN hub detects this and services first the device that has the higher priority. If the devices have equal priority, the hub randomly selects the node to service first. Moreover, the 100VG-AnyLAN hub sends the message only to its destination. Thus, the 100VG-AnyLAN hub is an intelligent hub with priority servicing and switching that prevents packets from going to every node on the network.

Fiber Distributed Data Interface (FDDI) Networks

As you can tell from its name, a **Fiber Distributed Data Interface (FDDI)** uses fiber optics to create a very fast network. Developed by American Standards Institute (ANSI) committee X3T9.5, FDDI uses two counter-rotating token rings operating at a speed of 100 Mbps. Each fiber optic ring can be up to 100 kilometers long, making FDDI popular for metropolitan area networks (MANs). Each cable can serve up to 500 nodes. Figure 10-14 shows that the two rings can run in parallel to provide redundancy for mission-critical operations in case one of the cables fails. Otherwise, the second ring can extend the network another 100 kilometers and serve up to 500 more nodes, for a total of 1,000 nodes over 200 kilometers. Due to its high reliability, FDDI is often used for **backbones**, which are network cables that act as the primary pathways for traffic that is most often destined for other networks.

FIGURE 10-14

To provide redundancy for mission-critical operations, FDDI can be configured to use counter-rotating primary and secondary rings. The concentrator is the building block of the FDDI network. Known as a dual-attachment concentrator (DAC), it attaches to both rings and enables the network to keep functioning whether or not the PCs connected on the network are powered on or off. ∎

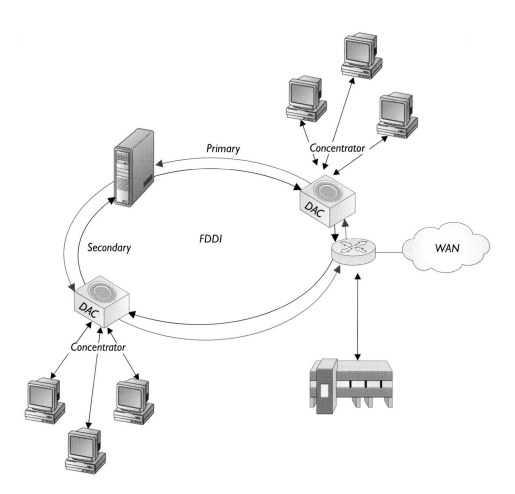

Wide Area Networks (WANs)

A **wide area network (WAN)** is the connection of two or more LANs that can be located in different buildings, cities, countries, or continents. Depending upon the distance and the bandwidth needed for communications among the LANs, you can use different telecommunication strategies for connecting the local networks, such as telephone lines, ISDN connections, broadband, and high-speed fiber optic devices employing frame relay and Asynchronous Transfer Mode (ATM) technologies. The world's largest WAN is the Internet.

X.25

Developed in the early 1970s, **X.25** is a WAN standard that enables data to be transmitted over the packet-switched networks (PSNs) of the telephone companies. In 1976, X.25 became an International Telecommunications Union (ITU) standard. Back then, telecommunication lines did not have the robust error checking of modern communications carriers. Therefore, the telephone companies built a lot of error checking into X.25, which double-checks the accuracy of the data many times along each packet's path. Today, X.25 is not fast enough for high-speed WAN connections, but it still is used by banks for automated tellers and card-swipe machines for credit-card verification.

Frame Relay

Frame Relay is a high-speed WAN standard that was originally developed for the Integrated Services Digital Network (ISDN) but is used today over many kinds of high-performance network interfaces. Sometimes referred to as a streamlined version of X.25, Frame Relay takes advantage of the higher reliability of modern telecommunication lines and does not have the overhead of the windowing and retransmission of last data features that are built into X.25. Frame Relay is an ITU standard, and in the United States, it is also an ANSI standard.

Frame Relay uses variable-length switching to route variable-length packets between various network segments until the final destination is reached. Through a technique called *statistical multiplexing*, packets headed for the same destination can travel different routes that may be available, therefore making more efficient use of available network resources.

Frame Relay connections can be either switched or permanent. A switched virtual circuit (SVC) gets created for each data transfer and is terminated when the data transfer is complete. A permanent virtual circuit (PVC), on the other hand, is a more expensive dedicated network connection that is constantly on. Because SVCs are less expensive, they are used in many of today's networks. Through a feature called **bandwidth on demand**, customers choose the connection speed of their Frame Relay port. The higher the speed, the more the cost.

Asynchronous Transfer Mode

Asynchronous Transfer Mode (ATM) is an ITU standard for cell relay that can transmit voice, video, or data in small, fixed-size 53-byte chunks called *cells*. The first 5 bytes contain the cell's header, and the other 48 bytes contain the transmission, which can be voice, video, or data. Because the cells have a fixed size, ATM switches and endpoints do not need to spend valuable processor time dealing with variable-length packets. Instead, the ATM switches can simply route the cells from their sources to their destinations, which are identified in each cell's header. Because the cells are small, clients do not experience the network delay that can occur while waiting for long packets to download. If multiple time slots are available, the addresses in the headers enable the ATM to go ahead and send them; hence the adjective *asynchronous*, which means that the cells do not have to line up and wait to be transmitted sequentially over a single connection.

ATM grew out of the ITU's Broadband Integrated Services Digital Network (B-ISDN) standard, which was originally conceived as a high-speed method for transferring voice, video, and data over public networks. Now available for use over private as well as public networks, ATM combines the flexibility of packet switching with the guaranteed capacity of circuit switching, with bandwidth scalable from a few megabits to many gigabits per second.

Figure 10-15 shows an ATM network comprising ATM switches and ATM endpoints. An ATM switch (1) receives the incoming cell from an ATM endpoint or another ATM switch, (2) reads and updates the cell

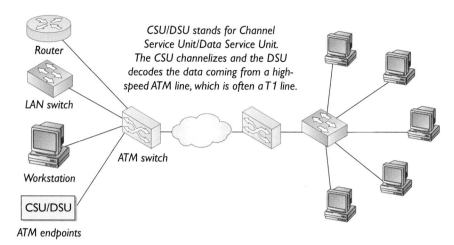

CSU/DSU stands for Channel Service Unit/Data Service Unit. The CSU channelizes and the DSU decodes the data coming from a high-speed ATM line, which is often a T1 line.

Router

LAN switch

Workstation

CSU/DSU

ATM endpoints

ATM switch

FIGURE 10-15 *An asynchronous transfer mode (ATM) network consists of an ATM switch that routes the traffic and ATM endpoints that send or receive the traffic. ATM sends the data in fixed-size units called cells. Because the switches do not need to deal with variable-length packets, they can process and route the data much faster than more traditional packet-switched technologies.* ■

header information, and (3) switches the cell toward its destination. An ATM endpoint is an end system that contains an ATM network interface adapter, which can reside in a workstation, router, digital service unit (DSU), LAN switch, or video coder-decoder (CODEC).

Network Access Points (NAPs)

A **network access point (NAP)** is a junction that provides direct access to the traffic on a network. To connect two or more LANs to form a WAN, for example, a network administrator connects them through a NAP. Internet service providers use NAPs to exchange traffic on the Internet's backbone. The three major NAPs used by the ISPs are located in New York City, Chicago, and San Francisco.

T-Carrier System

In North America, NAPs often use the T-carrier system to connect a LAN to a WAN. Table 10-3 shows the data rates of the different levels of T-carrier services. The telephone companies offer the public the T1 and T3 service levels, which you can lease for a monthly fee.

The **T1 service** consists of 24 channels running at 64 bps for a total bandwidth of 1.544 Mbps. Organizations that cannot afford the cost of a full T1 can lease a **fractional T1**, which is a subset of the T1's 24 channels.

The **T3 service** consists of 672 channels running at 64 bps for a total bandwidth of 44.736 Mpbs, which is equivalent to 28 T1 lines. As they can with T1, organizations can lease a fractional T3, which is a subset of the T3's 672 channels.

Service Level	Number of 64 Kbps Channels	Total Bandwidth
T1	24	1.544 Mbps
T2	96	6.312 Mbps
T3	672	44.736 Mbps
T4	4032	274.176 Mbps
T5	5760	400.352 Mbps

TABLE 10-3 *T-Carrier Service Levels Used in North America* ■

The T-carrier system uses the Time Division Multiplexing (TDM) transmission method, according to which information from multiple channels can be allocated bandwidth on a single wire based on preassigned time slots. Bandwidth is allocated to each channel regardless of whether the station has data to transmit. The advantage of TDM is that customers have guaranteed bandwidth available to them at all times. The disadvantage is that unused time slots do not carry any data. Therefore, the T-carrier is not as good as an ATM for time-sensitive information such as video transmissions.

E-Carrier System

In Europe, E-carrier services provide bandwidth equivalent to the T-carrier system, although the service levels are slightly different. Table 10-4 shows how each E-carrier service level increases bandwidth by a factor of four times higher than its predecessor.

Service Level	Number of 64 Kbps Channels	Total Bandwidth
E1	30	2.048 Mbps
E2	120	8.448 Mbps
E3	480	34.368 Mbps
E4	1920	139.268 Mbps
E5	7680	565.148 Mbps

TABLE 10-4 *E-Carrier Service Levels Used in Europe* ■

Wireless Access Points (WAPs)

The term **wireless access point (WAP)** refers to wireless network junctions that enable workstations to communicate without cables. Just as NAPs provide junctions for exchanging Internet traffic, so do WAPs provide access points for wireless devices to get on a network.

Network Address Translation (NAT)

NAPs and WAPs may use a technique called **network address translation (NAT)** to transform the IP addresses used for internal traffic into a second set of addresses for external traffic. There are three reasons why you may wish to consider using such a NAT. First, by hiding internal IP addresses, a NAT serves as a kind of firewall that helps protect the internal addresses from being attacked by worms and crackers. Second, a NAT enables a company to combine multiple ISDN connections into a single higher-speed Internet connection. Third, a NAT can translate multiple internal IP addresses into a smaller number of external IP addresses, or just one external IP address. Network administrators who use this third method, however, need to be aware that some NATs do not handle cookies properly.

tip *If you are planning to use a NAT for sharing one external IP address with multiple internal addresses, make sure you choose a NAT that brokers cookies properly so the users of this network can use applications that require cookies.*

Physical Network Components

Physical network components are the actual devices that you connect to create a network. In order to function as a node on the network, each workstation must have a Network Interface Card (NIC). Figure 10-16 shows the NIC containing the jack into which you plug the connector on the network cable. On FDDI equipment, the network interface is called a MIC, which stands for Media Interface Card. On wide area networking equipment, the network interface is called a WIC, for WAN interface card.

Seven kinds of physical devices are commonly found in computer networks: (1) client computers, (2) concentrators, (3) hubs, (4) repeaters,

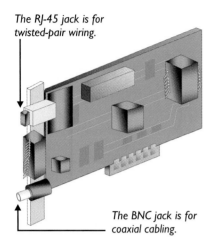

The RJ-45 jack is for twisted-pair wiring.

The BNC jack is for coaxial cabling.

FIGURE 10-16 *The Network Interface Card (NIC) contains the female network jack into which you plug the corresponding male connector that is at the end of the network cable. This particular NIC has both RJ-45 and BNC type connectors. Today, however, most NICs come with RJ-45 only.* ■

(5) switches, (6) bridges, (7) routers, (8) brouters, and (9) gateways. The following sections describe the functions that these devices serve.

Workstations

Also known as a client computer, the **workstation** is the node upon which end users perform their work. Most workstations that are sold today come with Ethernet jacks that are connected to the NIC that enables the workstation to function as a node on the network when you plug the network's Ethernet cable into that jack. In the next chapter, you learn how to configure a NIC for local as well as wide area networking.

Concentrators

In an IEEE 802.3 Ethernet network, a **concentrator** is an Ethernet multiport repeater. You use a concentrator when you want to connect multiple Ethernet devices to a single Ethernet cable. The term *concentrator* is synonymous with the term Ethernet hub.

Hubs

In general, the term **hub** refers to the device that serves as the center of a star network topology. In IEEE 802.3 Ethernet networks, a hub is an Ethernet multiport repeater, which is also known as a *concentrator*.

Repeaters

Operating at the Physical Layer of the OSI/RM, a **repeater** interconnects two network cables so they can be treated as a single cable. You use a repeater when you need to run a cable that is longer than the signal can travel without degrading. The number of repeaters you can use is limited by timing and other network issues, depending upon the protocol you are using.

Switches

Operating at the Data Link Layer of the OSI/RM, a **switch** is a network device that filters, forwards, and floods frames based on the destination MAC address of each frame. To **flood** is to pass traffic out all of the switch's connections except for the incoming interface through which the traffic was received.

Bridges

A **bridge** is a relay that operates at the Data Link Layer of the OSI/RM, connecting two network segments and passing packets between them based on the destination MAC address of each frame. The bridged segments must use the same communications protocol.

Routers

A **router** is a relay that operates at the Network Layer of the OSI/RM, forwarding network traffic along the optimal path based on information in the packet's Network Layer header.

Brouters

A bridge router (**brouter**) is a relay that functions as both a router and a bridge.

Gateways

A **gateway** is a computer that routes traffic from a workstation on an internal network to an external network such as the Internet. Thus, a gateway serves as both router and switch.

Physical Connection Media

Physical connection media are the cables, wires, radio signals, or air waves over which network signals travel. There are many categories of coaxial cable, twisted-pair wiring, fiber optic cables, and wireless transmission standards, depending on the distance the data needs to travel and the protocol that is being used to get it there. The following sections define the most commonly used categories.

Coaxial Cable

Coaxial cable, also known as coax (pronounced co-axe), consists of a cylindrically braided outer conductor that surrounds and shields a single solid inner copper wire conductor. Figure 10-17 shows these conductors separated by insulating layers. Two categories of coaxial cable are commonly used in LANs, namely, Thinnet and Thicknet.

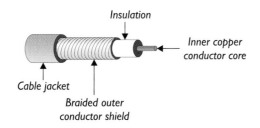

FIGURE 10-17 *From the inside out, coaxial cable consists of (1) a single solid inner copper wire, (2) a layer of nonconducting insulating material normally made of PVC or Teflon, (3) a cylindrically braided conductor that provides electromagnetic shielding, and (4) an outer layer of nonconducting material normally made of plastic or rubber.* ■

Thinnet Thin coaxial cable is called **Thinnet**, which is a very flexible cable about a quarter of an inch in diameter that is used in 10base2 Ethernet networks, in which the cable segments can run up to 185 meters long. Because the cables are so flexible, Thinnet has been a popular choice for connecting devices in small offices and computer labs with many twists and turns. In recent years, however, the use of coax has been declining in favor of the more popular 10baseT Ethernet wiring standard, which uses twisted-pair cabling.

Thicknet Thick coaxial cable is called **Thicknet**, which is a less flexible cable about half an inch thick that is used in 10base5 Ethernet networks, in which the cable segments can be up to 500 meters long. The thicker shielding and cable core enables Thicknet to transmit signals over more than twice the distance of Thinnet. Because of the thicker core, however, Thicknet is much less flexible and therefore considerably harder to work with.

BNC Connector In computer networking, coaxial cables use the **British Naval Connector (BNC)** to plug the cables into workstations, hubs, and other kinds of network devices. Figure 10-18 shows the male style of a BNC connector that is connected to the ends of the coaxial cables. The center pin of the male BNC connects to the copper core of the coax, and the metal tube connects to the braided shield. Outside the tube is a rotating ring that locks the cable to the female BNC connectors found on NICs, hubs, repeaters, and concentrators. You can see a female BNC connector on the NIC pictured previously in Figure 10-16.

This is the rotating ring on the outer tube of the male BNC connector.

This cutout shows the inner pin, which is connected to the copper core of the coax.

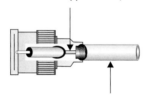

This is the coaxial network cable.

FIGURE 10-18 *The British Naval Connector (BNC) is also known as the Bayonet Nut Connector or the Bayonet Neill-Concelman connector, which is named for the bayonet mounting method and the BNC connector's coinventors, Paul Neill and Carl Concelman.* ■

Twisted Pair

Twisted pair is a transmission medium consisting of two insulated wires that are twisted together to create a double helix that reduces noise levels and eliminates crosstalk between the wires. There are two families of twisted-pair wiring: **unshielded twisted pair (UTP)** and **shielded twisted pair (STP)**, which has an extra layer of insulation that reduces electromagnetic interference. STP is used in gigabyte bandwidth applications. Figure 10-19 shows twisted-pair cabling containing four twisted pairs, and Table 10-5 defines the seven categories that are numbered 1 through 7. The higher the number, the faster the certified data rate.

Twisted-pair cabling is often referred to simply by its category. **CAT 5**, for example, means category five UTP wiring, which is commonly used for Ethernet LANs. In CAT 5, the wires in each pair are twisted four times per inch. The four twisted pairs terminate in an **RJ-45** connector, which has eight pin positions that hold the eight wires from the four twisted pairs.

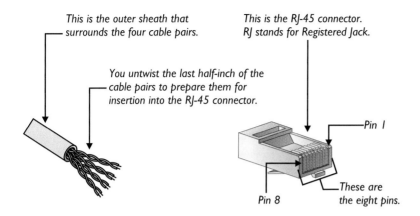

This is the outer sheath that surrounds the four cable pairs.

You untwist the last half-inch of the cable pairs to prepare them for insertion into the RJ-45 connector.

This is the RJ-45 connector. RJ stands for Registered Jack.

Pin 1

Pin 8

These are the eight pins.

FIGURE 10-19 *Twisted-pair cabling consists of four twisted pairs wrapped inside an outer sheath. The cabling is twisted to create a double helix that reduces noise levels and eliminates crosstalk between the wires. The four twisted pairs terminate in an RJ-45 connector, which has eight pin positions that hold the eight wires from the four twisted pairs. The Try This! exercise at the end of this section teaches you the order in which the wires of a 10/100baseT Ethernet cable must be connected to the pins in the RJ-45 connector.* ■

Fiber Optics

Fiber optics is a transmission method that transmits light-modulated video, voice, or data signals through hair-thin strands of glass called *fibers*. Because fiber-optic cables are not prone to the problems of electromagnetic interference that copper networks must cope with, fiber has much higher bandwidth potential than conventional copper wire. Fiber costs much more than copper, however, so fiber is normally reserved for applications that require very high bandwidth.

The light pulses that transmit signals through a fiber-optic cable move at the speed of light and can travel for miles without any degradation. At least two fiber strands are normally in each cable. These strands are encased by a layer of Kevlar-reinforced reflective material called *cladding*, which keeps the light inside the fiber.

Category	Type	Certified Speed	Commonly Used For
1	UTP	Not certified	Plain old telephone service (POTS)
2	UTP	4 Mbps	Token-ring networks
3	UTP	10 Mbps	Ethernet
4	UTP	16 Mbps	Token-ring networks
5	UTP	100 Mbps	Ethernet and Fast Ethernet
6	UTP	155 Mbps	Fast Ethernet
7	STP	1000 Mbps	Gigabit Ethernet

Legend: UTP = Unshielded twisted pair
STP = Shielded twisted pair

TABLE 10-5 *Categories of Twisted-Pair Wiring (all categories contain four twisted pairs)* ■

Due to the high cost and technical expertise required to make fiber-optic connections, the fiber normally terminates in a junction box from which coaxial or twisted-pair cables that are easier to work with carry the packets to their destination.

Wireless Media

Wireless transmission media include cellular, radio, microwave, satellite, and infrared signals. Network nodes that use wireless connections must have a wireless NIC, which connects to a transceiver known as a wireless access point (WAP). The convenience of being untethered by cables has made wireless devices a popular mass-market consumer item. Consumer electronic outlets such as Circuit City, CompUSA, and Best Buy sell many devices that follow the 802.11 wireless networking protocols. Wireless NICs are built in to many laptops, and home media centers use wireless LAN protocols to route digital video, audio, and computer signals to wireless devices throughout the home.

By the time you read this, for example, you will be able to buy a wireless Ethernet extender for the Media Center edition of Windows XP Pro. This extender can attach to any TV or monitor in your home, enabling you to view, control, record, or play up to five simultaneous media streams from the PC on five different display devices throughout your home. When you turn on one of these wireless Ethernet devices, it uses the Dynamic Host Configuration Protocol (DHCP) to establish an IP connection on your home network. You will learn about DHCP in the next chapter, which is devoted to TCP/IP. For the latest on the Windows Media Center Extender and related wireless Ethernet media devices, go to www.microsoft.com/windowsxp/mediacenter.

Try This!

Make a 10/100baseT Ethernet Cable

The two basic kinds of 10/100baseT Ethernet cables are straight through and crossover. You use straight through cables to connect PCs and workstations to an Ethernet hub. You use a crossover cable when you need to connect two hubs, or to connect one computer directly to a second computer, without going through a hub. If you have two computers that have Ethernet jacks, for example, a crossover cable can come in handy whenever you want to connect those computers directly to each other.

There is only one difference between straight-through and crossover cables. In a straight-through cable, the four pairs of wires go to the exact same pins in the RJ-45 connector that is on each end of the cable. In a crossover cable, on the other hand, the cable pairs that do the transmitting and receiving reverse their pin positions on each end of the cable.

This exercise enables you to create either a straight-through or a crossover 10/100baseT Ethernet cable. Follow these steps:

1. Go to your local electronic supply store, such as Radio Shack, and buy some category 5 wiring, a bag of RJ-45 connectors rated for use with 10/100baseT Ethernet, and an RJ-45 crimping tool. If you plan to do a lot of your own Ethernet wiring around the home or office, you can buy CAT 5 wiring in bulk. The author, for example, bought from Home Depot a thousand feet of CAT 5 wiring for about $35.

Try This!
continued

2. Cut a length of CAT 5 cable that is a few feet longer than you need. You want to leave some slack so you can easily maneuver and reposition equipment if you need to reconfigure it. Ethernet does not work well with a lot of extra cable coiled up, however, so you should not make the cable excessively longer than you need. The maximum length you can make a 10/100baseT cable is 100 meters (328 feet).

3. Remove about an inch from each end of the CAT 5 cable's outer sheath or jacket. As you do this, be careful not to harm or nick any of the insulation on the twisted pairs inside the jacket.

4. Inspect the twisted pairs carefully. If you see any nicks, cut off the end of the CAT 5 cable and return to step 3.

5. Untwist the protruding inch of the four twisted pairs. To avoid crosstalk, do not untwist more of the wiring than necessary. You will notice that the wires are color coded.

6. Arrange the wires in the proper order according to their color. The two wiring standards are called T-568A and T-568B. If you are making a straight-through cable, you must use either T-568A or T-568B on both ends of the cable. If you are making a crossover cable, you make one end follow T-568A and the other T-568B. Arrange the wires in the order needed for the kind of cable you are creating:

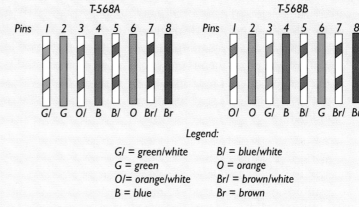

Legend:
G/ = green/white   B/ = blue/white
G = green   O = orange
O/ = orange/white   Br/ = brown/white
B = blue   Br = brown

7. Use the cable-cutting part of the crimping tool to trim the eight wires to make them even with each other. When you do this trim, you must let only slightly less than half of an inch of the wires protrude from end of the CAT 5 cable's jacket. If you let more than half an inch protrude, the cable is prone to crosstalk.

8. Hold the RJ-45 connector in one hand with the clip facing down or away from you, and insert the cable slowly yet firmly. Make sure it goes all the way in.

9. Double-check to make sure each pin has the proper color wire. As you look down through the connector from the top, it must appear as follows, depending on whether you followed T-568A or T-568B:

10. After you are sure the pins have the proper color wires, insert the cable into the RJ-45 socket of your crimping tool. Hold the wires in place, and squeeze the crimper handles quite firmly. After you do this to both ends of the cable, you can test it by plugging it in to your network.

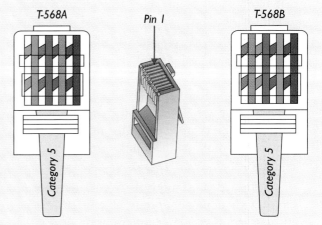

11. Reflection: If you compare the T-568A and T-568B wiring standards presented in step 6, you can see that they reverse the transmit (pins 1 and 2) and receive (pins 3 and 6) wiring pairs.

Chapter 10 Review

Chapter Summary

After reading this chapter and completing the step-by-step tutorials and Try This! exercises, you should understand the following facts about the Internet:

Understanding Networks

- A network is the connection of two or more digital devices for the purpose of communicating, transferring, or obtaining data.

- In order to have a network, you must have three things characteristic of all networks: (1) a physical connection through which the data flows; (2) a set of communication rules called *protocols* that the networked devices use to communicate; and (3) one or more network services that receive these communications and respond appropriately.

- Networking is the act of communicating over a network. In the mainframe/terminal model of networking, users compete for resources on a centralized computer that uses time sharing to allocate computing cycles to each user.

- A more efficient way of distributing networked resources is the client-server model, in which computers exchange information by sending it (as servers) and receiving it (as clients). The most strategic aspect of client-server computing is the manner in which computers can serve dual roles as both servers and clients.

- In a peer-to-peer (P2P) network, workstations have equal responsibility for sharing files and accessing services on each other's computers. In the music industry, this absence of authority makes it difficult to identify and prosecute copyright infringers who share copyrighted music over P2P networks without permission.

- The term *enterprise model* refers to networking within large organizations that dedicate entire servers to handling important tasks in the most efficient manner. A large organization, for example, may need individual servers dedicated to the tasks of serving mail, hosting databases, managing security, and routing network traffic.

- A network operating system is the software that adds to a computer the functions required for connecting computers for the purpose of networking. The most popular network operating systems are Microsoft Windows, UNIX, Linux, the Mac OS, and Novel NetWare.

Classifying Network Topologies

- The geographical shape of a network is referred to as the network's *topology*. The five kinds of network topology are (1) bus topology, (2) ring topology, (3) star topology, (4) hybrid topology, and (5) mesh topology.

- The bus topology has a single cable, called the *bus* or the *trunk*, to which every device on the network connects.

- The ring topology takes its name from the loop that forms when you connect the network's nodes in a circle. Messages flow in one direction around the ring, as does a token that provides each device its turn to communicate.

- In a star topology, each device in the network connects to a central hub, which distributes messages from one node to another.

- The term *hybrid topology* refers to a network that employs more than one topology to connect devices for the purpose of networking. An example is a star-ring hybrid that uses a token to synchronize the passing of messages from star to star.

- Mesh topology creates redundancy by creating multiple paths between network hubs. If part of the network goes down, the packets can find another path to their destination. The public Internet can be thought of as the ultimate in mesh technology, due to the multiple pathways that the telecomm carriers have provided to help prevent network failures.

Adopting Network Protocols

- Layer 7 of the OSI/RM is the Application Layer. Through an API, Layer 7 receives the message from the client computer and begins to form the packet that will eventually travel across the network.

■ Layer 6, the Presentation Layer, translates the data into a standard network data format and may use data compression to streamline the packet so it does not consume unnecessary bandwidth on the network. The Presentation Layer may also encrypt the data for sensitive data transmissions, such as banking information.

■ Layer 5 is the Session Layer, which negotiates the connection that will be made between the two computers that are exchanging data. If the amount of data being transmitted is large, the Session Layer inserts a checkpoint, which is a marker used to signal that a certain amount of the data has successfully arrived.

■ Layer 4 is the Transport Layer, which works to ensure that the data arrives reliably at its destination. If the amount of data is large, the Transport Layer splits it into fragments, which are smaller data segments that the Transport Layer numbers sequentially.

■ Layer 3, the Network Layer, organizes the data into datagrams, which combine the data from the Transport Layer with routing information that includes the source and destination addresses along with the recommended path depending on network conditions and the nature of the data.

■ Layer 2, the Data Link Layer, transforms the data into data frames, which use a raw bit format consisting of 0's and 1's to put the data into packets that can be passed down to the Physical Layer for transmission over the network.

■ Layer 1 is the Physical Layer, which transforms the 0's and 1's from the Data Link Layer into signals that flow over the transmission media. Depending on the type of transmission media, these signals may be electrical voltages, radio signals, air waves, or light pulses.

■ The six major protocol suites that follow the OSI/RM networking standard are (1) TCP/IP, which powers the Internet; (2) NetBEUI, which was Microsoft's native protocol suite for peer-to-peer networking on local networks of Windows computers prior to 2001; (3) IPX/SPX, which was developed by Novell for use with the NetWare network operating system; (4) AppleTalk, which is the legacy protocol suite for peer-to-peer networking on local networks of Macintosh computers; (5) DLC, which IBM invented to connect microcomputers as clients to legacy mainframe computers, and HP still uses in printers that have NICs; and (6) SNA, which IBM invented for connecting different kinds of networks.

Creating LANs, MANs, and WANs

■ A local area network (LAN) is the connection of two or more computer devices for the purpose of networking within a relatively small area, such as a home, school, or departmental office building. A metropolitan area network (MAN) connects local networks across a larger geographical region typically ranging in size up to 50 kilometers in diameter.

■ A wide area network (WAN) uses high-speed transmission lines to connect MANs and LANs over large geographical areas. The Internet is a network of WANs that use the Internet Protocol to route packets to their destinations through the MANs and LANs that the network comprises.

■ The Institute of Electrical and Electronic Engineers (IEEE, pronounced I triple-E) is in charge of defining the networking standards that connect devices to form different kinds of local and metropolitan area networks. The IEEE's LAN/MAN Standards Committee (LMSC) performs this work under IEEE Project 802, which has issued a series of 802 networking standards numbered from 802.0 to 802.20.

■ If you are studying for the CIW exam, you must be able to identify IEEE standards 802.2, 802.3, 802.5, and 802.12. The 802.2 standard is the Logical Link Control (LLC) sublayer of the OSI/RM Data Link Layer. The other sublayer is the Media Access Control (MAC). Most of the other 802 standards, including 802.3, 802.5, and 802.12, mainly define the MAC sublayer for different kinds of networks. IEEE standard 802.3 defines CSMA/CD (Ethernet), 802.5 defines token ring, and 802.12 defines Demand Priority Access LAN (100VG-AnyLAN).

- Fiber Distributed Data Interface (FDDI) is a fiber-optics networking standard developed by the American Standards Institute (ANSI). FDDI uses two counter-rotating token rings operating at a speed of 100 Mbps. Due to its high reliability, FDDI is often used for backbones, which are network cables that act as the primary pathways for traffic most often destined for other networks.

- X.25 is a WAN standard that enables data to be transmitted over the packet-switched networks (PSNs) of the telephone companies. By modern standards, however, X.25 is relatively slow.

- Frame Relay is a high-speed WAN standard originally developed for the Integrated Services Digital Network (ISDN) but is used today over many kinds of high-performance network interfaces. Sometimes referred to as a streamlined version of X.25, Frame Relay takes advantage of the higher reliability of modern telecommunication lines and does not have the overhead of the windowing and retransmission of last data features that are built into X.25.

- Asynchronous Transfer Mode (ATM) is another high-speed WAN standard that sends the data in fixed-size units called *cells*. Because the switches do not have to deal with variable-length packets, they can process and route the data much faster than more traditional packet-switched technologies.

- A network access point (NAP) is a junction that provides direct access to the traffic on a network. To connect two or more LANs to a WAN, for example, a network administrator connects them through a NAP. Internet service providers use NAPs to exchange each other's traffic on the Internet's backbone. The three major NAPs used by the ISPs are located in New York City, Chicago, and San Francisco.

- Physical network components are the actual devices that you connect together to create a network. In order to function as a node on the network, each workstation must have a Network Interface Card (NIC), which contains the jack into which you plug the connector on the network cable. On FDDI equipment, the network interface is called a MIC, which stands for media interface card. On wide area networking equipment, the network interface is called a WIC, for WAN interface card.

- Other physical components commonly found in computer networks include concentrators, hubs, repeaters, switches, bridges, and routers. A concentrator is an Ethernet multiport repeater, which connects multiple Ethernet devices to a single Ethernet cable. A hub is the device that serves as the center of a star network topology.

- A repeater interconnects two network cables so they can be treated as a single cable. A switch is a network device that filters, forwards, and floods frames based on their destination MAC address.

- A bridge is a relay that operates at the Data Link Layer of the OSI/RM, connecting two network segments and passing packets between them based on the destination MAC address of each frame.

- A router is a relay that operates at the Network Layer of the OSI/RM, forwarding network traffic along the optimal path based on information in the packet's Network Layer header.

- A bridge router (brouter) is a relay that functions as both a router and a bridge.

- A gateway is a computer that routes traffic from a workstation on an internal network to an external network such as the Internet. Thus, a gateway serves as both router and switch.

- To connect PCs and workstations to an Ethernet hub, you use a straight-through 10/100baseT Ethernet cable, which can be up to 100 meters (328 feet) long. To connect a PC directly to a PC, or to connect a hub to a hub, you use a crossover cable, which reverses the location of transmit and receive wires in the RJ-45 connector at one end of the cable.

Key Terms

AppleTalk *(453)*

Application Layer *(449)*

Asynchronous Transfer Mode (ATM) *(459)*

backbone *(457)*

bandwidth on demand *(459)*

British Naval Connector (BNC) *(464)*

bridge *(462)*

brouter *(463)*

bus *(445)*

bus topology *(445)*

CAT 5 *(464)*

checkpoint *(450)*

concentrator *(462)*

CSMA/CD *(456)*

cyclic redundancy check (CRC) *(451)*

data frames *(451)*

Data Link Control (DLC) *(453)*

Data Link Layer *(451)*

datagrams *(450)*

Demand Priority Access LAN (100VG-AnyLAN) *(457)*

enterprise model *(441)*

Ethernet hub *(456)*

Fast Ethernet *(456)*

Fiber Distributed Data Interface (FDDI) *(457)*

fiber optics *(465)*

flood *(462)*

fractional T1 *(460)*

fragments *(450)*

Frame Relay *(459)*

gateway *(463)*

Gigabit Ethernet *(456)*

hub *(462)*

hybrid topology *(447)*

IEEE 802.12 *(457)*

IEEE 802.2 *(456)*

IEEE 802.3 *(456)*

IEEE 802.5 *(457)*

IPX/SPX *(453)*

Linux *(444)*

local area network (LAN) *(454)*

Logical Link Control (LLC) *(451)*

Macintosh OS X *(444)*

mainframe *(439)*

mainframe/terminal model *(439)*

Media Access Control (MAC) *(451)*

mesh topology *(448)*

metropolitan area network (MAN) *(454)*

Multi-Station Access Unit (MAU) *(457)*

multi-tier *(440)*

NetBEUI *(453)*

NetWare *(444)*

network *(438)*

network access point (NAP) *(460)*

network address translation (NAT) *(461)*

Network Interface Card (NIC) *(453)*

Network Layer *(450)*

network operating system *(442)*

networking *(438)*

OSI Reference Model (OSI/RM) *(438)*

peer-to-peer (P2P) *(441)*

Physical Layer *(451)*

Presentation Layer *(449)*

protocol binding *(453)*

protocol suite *(452)*

push-pull metaphor *(442)*

repeater *(462)*

ring topology *(445)*

RJ-45 *(464)*

router *(463)*

Session Layer *(450)*

shielded twisted pair (STP) *(464)*

star topology *(446)*

switch *(462)*

Systems Network Architecture (SNA) *(453)*

T1 service *(460)*

T3 service *(460)*

TCP/IP *(452)*

terminal *(439)*

Thicknet *(464)*

Thinnet *(464)*

topology *(445)*

Transport Layer *(450)*

trunk *(445)*

twisted pair *(464)*

UNIX *(444)*

unshielded twisted pair (UTP) *(464)*

wide area network (WAN) *(458)*

wireless access point (WAP) *(461)*

workstation *(462)*

X.25 *(458)*

▓ Key Terms Quiz

1. In a(n) _____ network, workstations have equal responsibility for sharing files and accessing services on each other's computers.

2. The networking topology called _____ has a single cable to which every device on the network connects.

3. In the networking topology called _____, each device in the network connects to a central hub, which distributes messages from one node to another.

4. The networking topology called _____ creates redundancy by creating multiple paths between network hubs.

5. In the OSI/RM, the _____ negotiates the connection made between the two computers that are exchanging data.

6. In the OSI/RM, the _____ transforms the data into data frames, which use a raw bit format consisting of 0's and 1's to put the data into packets that can be passed down to the Physical Layer for transmission over the network.

7. The IEEE 802.2 standard is the Logical Link Control (LLC) sublayer of the OSI/RM _____.

8. CSMA/CD (Ethernet) is defined by the _____ standard.

9. _____ is a high-speed WAN standard that sends the data in fixed-size units called cells. Because the switches do not need to deal with variable-length packets, they can process and route the data much faster than more traditional packet-switched technologies.

10. In order to function as a node on the network, each workstation must have a(n) _____, which contains the jack into which you plug the connector on the network cable.

▓ Multiple-Choice Quiz

1. Which of the following networking models is historically the oldest?
   a. Client-server
   b. Enterprise
   c. Mainframe/terminal
   d. Peer-to-peer

2. What kind of topology is formed when a network uses a token ring to distribute data to the Ethernet hubs of each of four star networks?
   a. Bus
   b. Hybrid
   c. Mesh
   d. Superstar

3. Which of the following OSI/RM layers is responsible for performing the data encryption that is used by banks, for example, to keep financial information secret as it winds its way across the Internet?
   a. Application Layer
   b. Presentation Layer
   c. Session Layer
   d. Transport Layer

4. Of the following protocol suites that follow the OSI reference model, which one powers the Internet?
   a. AppleTalk
   b. IPX/SPX
   c. NetBEUI
   d. TCP/IP

5. Which one of the following IEEE 802 standards defines token-ring networking?
   a. 802.2
   b. 802.3
   c. 802.5
   d. 802.12

6. Which one of the following IEEE 802 standards defines Ethernet networking?
   a. 802.2
   b. 802.3
   c. 802.5
   d. 802.12

7. Sometimes referred to as a streamlined version of X.25, which high-speed WAN standard originally developed for the Integrated Services Digital Network (ISDN) is used today over

many kinds of high-performance network interfaces?
a. 100VG-AnyLAN
b. ATM
c. FDDI
d. Frame Relay

8. Which junction provides direct access to the traffic on a network?
a. LAP
b. NAP
c. SAP
d. TAP

9. On wide area networking equipment, the network interface is called a:
a. LIC
b. MIC
c. NIC
d. WIC

10. Which device operates at the Network Layer of the OSI/RM, forwarding network traffic along the optimal path based on information in the packet's Network Layer header?
a. Bridge
b. Hub
c. Router
d. Switch

Essay Quiz

1. The legacy mainframe/terminal networking model that arose in the mid-twentieth century has been superseded by the more efficient client-server model. Many large corporations, however, still have mainframe computers. Describe the kind of software that can enable a client computer to obtain access to the corporate mainframe.

2. Discuss the fundamental design differences between the collision detection of the IEEE 802.3 Ethernet standard as compared to the token passing method of the 802.5 token ring. Under what kind of situation would token ring be better than Ethernet?

3. Why do fiber-optic cables work better than copper as the physical transmission media for network backbones?

4. During the early 1970s, the X.25 standard played an important role in the creation of the Internet. What did the X.25 standard enable that was so critically important in the creation of a public Internet?

5. In creating a network cable that can be used either on a regular 10 Mbps Ethernet or on a 100 Mbps Fast Ethernet, what category of UTP wiring should you use?

Lab Projects

• Lab Project 10-1: Network Needs Analysis

Imagine that you work for a mid-sized company or school district that is looking to revamp its networking strategy. Several buildings must be interconnected, each of which contains a couple dozen workstations that have to function as nodes on the network. Your employer has assigned you the task of analyzing their needs and recommending alternative networking strategies. As part of this analysis, your employer wants to know the relative advantages and disadvantages of each alternative in order to make an informed decision regarding the networking strategy your organization should adopt. Use your word processor to write an essay in which you assess the needs and discuss the relative pluses and minuses of possible networking alternatives. In developing this needs assessment, consider the following issues:

■ **Bandwidth requirements** What are the bandwidth requirements of the workers who use the network? Do some of the buildings have higher bandwidth requirements than others?

- **Comparative analysis** Compare alternative methods for providing this bandwidth. Search Google or Yahoo for networking companies, and peruse the LAN and MAN solutions provided by the major manufacturers, such as Cisco, 3Com, and Nortel. Which appear to be the best alternatives for providing the required bandwidth?

- **Architecture and topology** Discuss the relative advantages and disadvantages of the different networking topologies that appear to be relevant in the context of this analysis.

- **Network operating system** What network operating system(s) do the workstations need to run in order to access the network? Are the recommended operating systems already running on these workstations, or will new software have to be obtained?

- **Scope of work** Consider the amount of work that will be required to implement the various alternatives you are putting forward, and include an estimate of the amount of time it will take to accomplish them.

If your instructor asked you to hand in the needs analysis, make sure you put your name at the top of the essay, then copy it onto a disk or follow the other instructions you may have been given for submitting this assignment.

• Lab Project 10-2: Network Design

Your mid-sized company or school district has asked you to design a hybrid network in which you will use an appropriate mix of networking topologies to provide efficient and reliable connections among the local area networks operating in five different buildings that are within a ten-mile radius. At the moment, these LANs are using a bus topology that is prone to slow down under heavy traffic and is time consuming to repair when a node goes down and renders the LAN unusable. Connections between the LANs are slow due to the use of legacy X.25 lines leased from the local telephone company. Use your word processor to write an essay in which you present an improved network design for solving these problems. In developing this design, consider the following issues:

- **LAN topology** You clearly need to replace the bus networks with a better LAN topology. Which topology do you recommend for the LANs within each building?

- **MAN topology** The physical distance between buildings is within the geographical radius of metropolitan area network technology. Which MAN topology is most appropriate for your network design?

- **WAN connection** Which WAN protocol or method will you use to connect the MAN to the Internet?

- **Integration** How can your design better integrate the organization's programs and services? If there are databases that serve information through different business processes that interact with end users, for example, could a multi-tier approach make the development, production, and maintenance of these processes more efficient?

- **Wiring plan** What kind of wiring does your plan require? Specify the wiring categories, and state whether any of the existing wiring can continue to be used.

- **Wireless facilities** If users will be accessing the network via wireless devices, specify the WAPs needed to connect them.

- **Draw the network diagram** Depending on your artistic ability, you may find it helpful to use a networking clip art library or design tool. To find these tools, search Google or Yahoo for network design, network symbols, or network clip art. See also the public domain Cisco icon library at www.cisco.com/warp/public/503/2.html, where you will find full color and black-and-white icons as well as stencils for drawing network diagrams with Microsoft Visio.

If your instructor asked you to hand in the network design, make sure you put your name at the top of the essay, then copy it onto a disk or follow the other instructions you may have been given for submitting this assignment.

chapter

11

Architecting
the Internet

"... barring total disaster, all elements
are eventually acknowledged, even if
they require retransmission."

—*TCP inventor Vint Cerf, 1973*

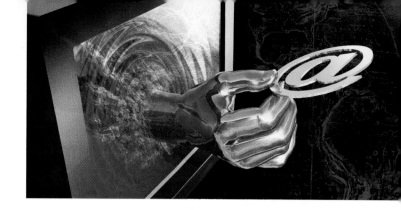

In this chapter, you will learn how to:

▪ Define how the four layers of the Internet Architecture map to the seven layers of the OSI Reference Model.

▪ Explain the Internet addressing rules and configure TCP/IP on a personal computer.

▪ List the network utilities used to analyze, troubleshoot, and optimize Web sites for maximum performance.

▪ Explain how domain names map to IP addresses and define the roles that different kinds of Internetworking servers play in transmitting information to these addresses.

▪ List the content and delivery services that the most popular server products provide to end users via the Internet.

N the previous chapter, you studied the theory behind the seven layers of the OSI Reference Model (OSI/RM). This chapter puts theory into practice by showing you how the Internet implements the OSI/RM through a suite of protocols called TCP/IP. Because it powers the Internet, TCP/IP is the most famous protocol suite in the world.

This chapter begins by explaining the process through which TCP/IP implements the OSI/RM protocols for packet creation, addressing, and routing. Then you learn how to configure TCP/IP on PCs and workstations and optimize them for maximum network performance.

Every network must have one or more servers to respond to requests and provide the services that are the reason why you created the network in the first place. The Internet has many kinds of servers. Web servers, for example, respond to requests from browsers. Mail servers, news servers, FTP servers, and streaming media servers provide communication, entertainment, and information resources that are very popular among end users.

Behind the scenes are servers that are not so well known. Some enhance network performance, while others provide catalog, directory, and back-end database services. This chapter concludes by taking you behind the scenes to the Internetworking servers that provide the infrastructure for the more well-known services that end users crave.

Understanding TCP/IP

Emerging from the pioneering efforts of Vint Cerf and others in the 1970s, TCP/IP became the U.S. military's preferred networking protocol in 1980. When the major networks adopted it in 1983, TCP/IP officially became the Internet's protocol suite. Understanding TCP/IP begins with a comparison of the Internet's Architecture to the OSI Reference Model.

Internet Architecture

As you learned in the previous chapter, the OSI/RM has seven layers. The **Internet Architecture** model, on the other hand, has four layers. Figure 11-1 compares the seven OSI/RM layers to the four Internet Architecture layers. Each Internet Architecture Layer corresponds to one or two of the OSI/RM layers.

Internet Engineering Task Force (IETF)

The **Internet Engineering Task Force (IETF)** is the standards body in charge of defining Internet protocols. Any interested person or organization can join the IETF by following the link to membership at www.ietf.org.

The IETF defines protocols through a **Request for Comments (RFC)** process. Most of the RFCs are generated by working committees of the IETF, but any individual or organization can submit an RFC for the IETF to consider. Once an RFC has been accepted for consideration, the IETF assigns it an **RFC number** and an **RFC maturity state**. An RFC moves through three maturity states on its way to becoming a standard:

Internet Architecture Layers	OSI/RM Layers
Application	7. Application 6. Presentation
Transport	5. Session 4. Transport
Internet	3. Network
Network Access	2. Data link 1. Physical

FIGURE 11-1 *The Internet Architecture model implements in four layers the seven separate layers of the OSI Reference Model. The color-coding in this figure illustrates that each layer of Internet Architecture corresponds to one or two of the OSI/RM layers.* ■

- **Proposed** The protocol has been accepted for consideration and may possibly advance through the rest of the stages to become an Internet standard. The IETF invites interested parties and researchers to test the proposed protocol and to identify any issues or problems that may need to be solved prior to standardization.

- **Draft** The protocol passed its preliminary testing at the proposal stage. The IETF is now seriously considering adopting the protocol as an Internet standard. The IETF invites large-scale testing and requires that at least two independent trials prove the interoperability of the proposed protocol. If major problems arise, the protocol's maturity level may be downgraded to the proposed state.

- **Internet standard** The protocol passed the testing and proved its merit on the Internet. The RFC is considered to be an established Internet standard.

In special circumstances, the IETF may assign three other maturity states to an RFC. These other three states are

- **Experimental** The protocol is not ready for testing outside carefully controlled laboratory situations. Testing on the public Internet could cause protocol conflicts.

- **Historic** The standard has become obsolete or unnecessary, or it has been superseded by a newer standard.

- **Informational** The standard is from a non-IETF vendor or standards body. The IETF provides access to the standard for the benefit of site visitors, but it is not being proposed as an Internet standard.

You can bring any RFC onscreen by typing its number into the search engine at www.ietf.org/rfc.html. The complete list of RFCs is at www.ietf.org/iesg/1rfc_index.txt, which indexes the protocols in numerical order. If you take a moment to scroll down through this list, it provides an interesting historical perspective on the evolutionary nature of the Internet.

At the top of the Internet Architecture's protocol stack is the **Application Layer,** which encompasses OSI/RM Layers 7 and 6. Some of the Internet's most well-known protocols reside at the Application Layer. The Application Layer protocols and their corresponding RFC standard numbers are listed as follows:

- **Hypertext Transfer Protocol (HTTP)** True to its name, HTTP is the protocol that transfers hypertext Web pages across the Internet. There are two versions known as HTTP 1.0 and HTTP 1.1. Version 1.0 opens a separate connection for each downloaded file. HTTP 1.1 avoids the overhead of creating separate sessions for each file by keeping the connection open so multiple files associated with a page can be downloaded all at once. Both the client and the server must be running HTTP 1.1 for the multiple download feature to work. Otherwise, the files get downloaded separately via HTTP 1.0. The IETF standards are RFC 1945 for HTTP 1.0, and RFC 2616 for HTTP 1.1.

- **File Transfer Protocol (FTP)** RFC 959 specifies the File Transfer Protocol, which you use when you log on to an FTP server to transfer files over the Internet from one computer to another. Chapter 13 teaches you how to use an FTP client that encrypts the transfers to keep them secure as your documents wind their way across the Internet.

- **Trivial File Transfer Protocol (TFTP)** RFC 1350 defines a simpler form of FTP called Trivial File Transfer Protocol, which diskless workstations and some routers use to get their configuration files during startup. Unlike FTP, TFTP uses the connectionless UDP protocol that does not have a logon process for user authentication.

- **Telnet** RFC 854 defines telnet, which is the terminal emulation protocol that enables users to log on to remote host computers over the Internet.

- **Gopher** RFC 1436 specifies the Gopher protocol for distributed document search and retrieval. As you learned in Chapter 2, Gopher was the rage prior to the invention of the World Wide Web.

- **Simple Mail Transfer Protocol (SMTP)** RFC 821 defines the Simple Mail Transfer Protocol, which specifies the rules for transferring e-mail over the Internet. A related standard that is not part of TCP/IP is RFC 1939, which specifies how version 3 of the Post Office Protocol (POP3) stores mail on a server until users log on and download it.

- **Network News Transfer Protocol (NNTP)** RFC 977 specifies the NNTP protocol that powers USENET newsgroups. The newsgroup servers to which you connected to read news in Chapter 2, for example, are NNTP servers.

■ **Domain Name System (DNS)** RFCs 1034 and 1035 define the DNS protocol that translates a fully qualified domain name (e.g., www.loc.gov) into a numeric IP address (e.g., 140.147.249.7) needed to route information across the Internet.

■ **Simple Network Management Protocol (SNMP)** RFC 1157 specifies SNMP, which network administrators use to remotely manage TCP/IP network devices that are SNMP compliant. An administrator who needs to reconfigure or get statistics from a router, for example, can use an SNMP utility to contact the router. Network administrators like how SNMP enables them to administer all of their SNMP network devices from a central location.

■ **Bootstrap Protocol (BOOTP)** RFC 951 defines BOOTP, which is a startup protocol that enables a workstation to discover configuration information including its IP address, router address, and DNS server address.

■ **Dynamic Host Configuration Protocol (DHCP)** RFC 2131 defines DHCP, which works in conjunction with BOOTP to assign during workstation initialization an IP address, router address, and other configuration parameters. During startup, the client computer sends a DHCP message to which a DHCP server, if present, responds. This automatic IP configuration process is very popular among network administrators, because it saves the time they would otherwise need to spend manually configuring each workstation.

Transport Layer Protocols

The Internet Architecture's **Transport Layer** encompasses OSI/RM Layers 5 and 4. It is the responsibility of the Transport Layer to divide into packets the data received from the Application Layer. Depending on the kind of session being serviced, the Transport Layer uses one of the following two protocols:

■ **Transmission Control Protocol (TCP)** The vitally important role of the Transmission Control Protocol (TCP) is evident from the inclusion of its acronym in the name of the TCP/IP protocol suite. As defined by RFC 793, TCP establishes and manages the connection between the computers that are exchanging data, numbers the packets on the sending computer, reassembles the packets on the receiving computer, and ensures that all of the data is intact with no omissions or duplications.

■ **User Datagram Protocol (UDP)** As defined by RFC 768, UDP is a connectionless protocol that does not require the negotiation and establishment of a session between the sending and receiving computers. Instead, the sending computer simply puts each output from the Application Layer into a packet. Because there is no provision for the resending of lost packets, UDP is considered to be an unreliable transport protocol that should be used only by applications that transmit relatively small amounts of data without establishing a session between the sending and receiving computers.

Internet Layer Protocols

In the Internet Architecture, the **Internet Layer** corresponds to layer 3, which is the Network Layer, of the OSI/RM. It is the responsibility of the Internet Layer to take the packet from the Transport Layer, determine the best way to route it across the Internet, and transform it into an IP packet containing an IP header and trailer. To accomplish this, the Internet Layer uses the following protocols:

- **Internet Protocol (IP)** As defined by RFC 791, the Internet Protocol (1) determines the best path for routing the packet to its destination address, (2) addresses the packet accordingly, and (3) fragments the packet if it is too long for the network segment. The critical importance of these tasks earned IP its place in the name of the TCP/IP protocol suite.

- **Address Resolution Protocol (ARP)** In order to transmit a packet from one node to another, the Physical Layer must know the nodes' physical MAC addresses. RFC 826 defines how ARP translates IP addresses into physical MAC addresses.

- **Reverse Address Resolution Protocol (RARP)** Given the MAC address of a network device, RARP determines its IP address. RFC 903 defines this process as Reverse ARP (RARP), because it reverses the translation performed by ARP.

- **Internet Group Management Protocol (IGMP)** RFC 1112 defines the IGMP group management protocol used for **multicasting**, which is the sending of a message from one computer to a group of IP addresses belonging to users who subscribe to the group. Videoconferencing is an example of multicasting.

- **Internet Control Message Protocol (ICMP)** RFC 792 defines the ICMP messaging protocol that TCP/IP uses for troubleshooting. Routers and servers normally send error messages in ICMP packets when things fail on a TCP/IP network.

Network Access Layer Protocols

In the Internet Architecture, the **Network Access Layer** corresponds to OSI/RM Layers 2 and 1, which transform the packets into a binary encoded stream of 0's and 1's for transmission over the physical network. Then the NIC transforms the 0's and 1's into the signals that get transmitted physically over the network. The specific protocols are determined by the device drivers and the physical connections from the workstation to the network cable or wireless transmission medium.

Figure 11-2 summarizes the Internet Architecture by showing the protocols that come into play as the messages work their way down from the Application Layer to the Network Access Layer.

Demultiplexing

This chapter presented the four layers of the Internet Architecture in the order in which a message on the sending computer would pass down through the Application, Transport, Internet, and Network Access Layers to the physical transmission medium that carries the packet across the Internet. When the packets reach their destination on the receiving computer, the message must ascend back up through the same four layers, which decode, unpack, and reassemble the message and make sure it arrives without error. The process of unpacking the message by processing and removing the headers added to the packets at each layer is called **demultiplexing**. There are four stages in the demultiplexing process:

Application Layer—OSI/RM Layers 7 (Application) and 6 (Presentation)				
HTTP	SMTP	NNTP	SNMP	TFTP
FTP	telnet	DNS	DHCP	BOOTP
Transport Layer—OSI/RM Layers 5 (Session) and 4 (Transport)				
TCP			UDP	
Internet Layer—OSI/RM Layer 3 (Network)				
ICMP		IP		ARP
IGMP				RARP
Network Access Layer—OSI/RM Layers 2 (Data Link) and 1 (Physical)				
...000101110011010110100000110101011010101101011010101010101...				

FIGURE 11-2 *Protocols that come into play as messages work their way through the four layers of the TCP/IP protocol suite.* ∎

1. On the receiving computer, the Network Access Layer takes a look at the packet and uses the MAC address to determine whether it should be processed here. Packets that do not get processed here are ignored and are passed on to other network nodes.

2. Packets that belong here pass up to the Internet Layer, which takes a look at the IP addressing in the packet to determine whether any further routing is required.

3. The Transport Layer takes a look at the TCP or UDP port number to determine which service needs to receive the message.

4. The Application Layer passes the message to the service or application that will act on the message. If the message contains an HTTP request for a Web page, for example, the server answers by sending the page.

Routing

Routing is the process of determining the network path over which packets are sent. It is the responsibility of the Internet Protocol to determine this optimal path. The two main kinds of routing are direct and indirect.

Direct routing occurs when two computers on the same network communicate with each other. Direct routing happens on an Ethernet, for example, when the Address Resolution Protocol (ARP) converts an IP address into a MAC address to transmit packets between sending and receiving computers on the same local network.

Indirect routing happens when the sending and receiving computers are not on the same local network. The packets get sent to the MAC address of a router, which analyzes the destination address and forwards the packet on toward the appropriate network. The router to which the packets first get sent is called the **default gateway,** which is one of the IP addresses you set when you manually configure a PC for network operation. If the PC is configured for dynamic host addressing, the DHCP server determines the IP address of the default gateway.

The router uses the **routing information table** to keep track of the routes over which it will send packets to different networks to which the router is connected. When a packet arrives, the router examines the packet's destination IP address, consults the routing table to determine the optimum route, and sends the packet to the corresponding router. Each trip between routers is called a **hop.** The number of trips between the packet's origin and destination addresses is called a **hop count.** Figure 11-3 illustrates that routers typically send packets along the path with the lowest hop count, unless network traffic conditions dictate otherwise.

Static vs. Dynamic Routers

Network administrators consider a router to be static or dynamic, depending on the nature of the router's information tables. If the tables are fixed and can be updated only by manual changes made by the network administrator, the router is said to be a **statically configured router.** Routers in stable networks that connect to a relatively small number of other networks can use static routing tables effectively. If a new route is added to the network, however, the network administrator has to add the new path to all of the static routing tables to enable them to route traffic along that path.

A dynamic router, on the other hand, communicates with other routers to exchange information about new routes that have been added, or old routes that are no longer available. As this information changes, the router information table updates automatically; hence the term **dynamically configured router.**

Routing Protocols

When routers share information, they follow routing protocols that define how to communicate changes in the routing tables. There are two basic kinds of routing protocols, namely, exterior and interior. As you might expect, exterior routing protocols are

Router Table #1		
Network	Router	Hops
A	1	1
B	1	1
C	2	2
D	2	3
E	2	2

Router Table #3		
Network	Router	Hops
A	2	3
B	2	2
C	3	2
D	3	1
E	3	1

Router Table #2		
Network	Router	Hops
A	1	2
B	2	1
C	2	1
D	3	2
E	2	1

FIGURE 11-3 *Routers consult routing information tables to determine the best path for sending the packet on toward its destination. In this example, the routing follows the paths with the lowest hop counts.* ■

for communicating with routers that are outside of an organization's network. If you are studying for the CIW exam, you should learn the names of the following two exterior routing protocols:

- **External Gateway Protocol (EGP)**   Defined by RFC 904, the EGP defines the protocol used to exchange net-reachability information between Internet gateways belonging to autonomous systems. An **autonomous system (AS)** is a set of routers under a single technical administration, such as an ISP or a backbone such as the NSFNET.

- **Border Gateway Protocol (BGP)**   Defined by RFCs 1267 and 1268, the BGP builds on experience gained with EGP on the NSFNET backbone. A border router keeps track of the status of neighboring AS's and uses a pruning process to select optimum routes.

Interior routing protocols are for communicating with routers inside of an organization's network. You should know the following two interior routing protocols:

- **Routing Information Protocol (RIP)**   Defined by RFCs 1058 and 2453, RIP is a protocol whereby routers periodically send their information tables every thirty seconds across their network connections to their neighboring routers. Based on this information, dynamic routers update their tables to reflect any changes on the neighboring routers and route packets over the path with the lowest hop count.

- **Open Shortest Path First (OSPF)**   Defined by RFC 2328, OSPF is a routing information protocol that improves upon RIP in three ways. First, changes in router tables get exchanged as soon as they happen, instead of having to wait thirty seconds. Second, only the changes get sent, instead of the whole table, thereby saving bandwidth. Third, and most importantly, OSPF exchanges statistics on the transmission speed of multiple possible routings, enabling the router to take advantage of faster routes that would otherwise be unused under the hop count rule. Hence the name, Open Shortest Path First (OSPF), which can use routes that have faster transmission times even though they may have higher hop counts.

Port Numbers

Servers on the Internet typically run many services at once. It is common, for example, to have HTTP Web serving, SMTP mail transfer, DNS name resolving, telnet remote logon, FTP file transfer, and POP3 mail delivery services running on a single server. To provide the Transport Layer with a fast way of determining which application should receive an incoming request, each packet contains a destination **port number**, which is a 16-bit number indicating the service that the packet is using. The range of a 16-bit

Port Number	Protocol
21	FTP
23	Telnet
25	SMTP
53	DNS
80	HTTP
110	POP3
194	IRC

TABLE 11-1 *Well Known Port Numbers for Selected Internet Services* ■

number is from 0 to 65535. Of these, the ports numbered from 0 to 1023 are known as **Well Known Ports**. The Internet Corporation for Assigned Names and Numbers (ICANN) is in charge of assigning these well-known, or reserved, port numbers. Table 11-1 lists the port numbers for some of the Internet's most popular services.

Ports numbered from 1024 to 49151 are called **registered ports**. Many well-known applications use these registered ports. Microsoft SQL Server, for example, uses port 1433, Macromedia Shockwave uses 1626, and Cisco License Management uses 1986.

The rest of the port numbers from 49152 to 65535 are called **Dynamic and/or Private Ports**. ICANN does not control these port numbers, and any process can use them. Because they are intended for short-lived processes, they are also known as ephemeral or temporary ports. The complete list of assigned ports is at www.iana.org/assignments/port-numbers.

Internet Addressing

To participate as a node on the Internet, every computer or network device must have a unique IP address. As you learned in Chapter 1, an IP address consists of four bytes separated by periods. Each byte is an eight-bit number that ranges in value from 0 to 255. The smallest address is 0.0.0.0 and the largest is 255.255.255.255. The number of IP addresses this scheme allows is 256^4, which is 4,294,967,296.

The Internet Corporation for Assigned Names and Numbers (ICANN) is in charge of assigning IP addresses. Every IP address consists of two basic parts: the Network ID and the host ID. The Network ID always comes first, followed by the host ID. Depending on the size of the network, the Network ID occupies the first one, two, or three bytes in the IP address. The remainder of the address is the host ID.

Internet Address Classes

When an organization applies for a range of IP addresses to serve the computers in its network, ICANN considers the size of the organization and determines the size of an address space to allocate. Five **Internet address classes** can be assigned. These classes are named A, B, C, D, and E.

- **Class A** Extremely large organizations that have more than 16 million hosts receive Class A Internet addresses. In a Class A address, the first byte in the dotted quad IP address is the Network ID, and the other three bytes are the host ID.

- **Class B** Medium to large organizations with up to 65,534 hosts get Class B addresses, in which the first two bytes are the Network ID, and the other two bytes are the host ID.

- **Class C** Small organizations with up to 254 hosts get Class C addresses, in which the first three bytes are the Network ID, and the last byte is the host ID.

- **Class D** Multicast groups receive Class D addresses, which are set aside for multicasting. In a Class D address, all four bytes are the Network ID. There is no host ID because everyone in the group receives the multicast.

- **Class E** The Internet has reserved some addresses for future use. These are the Class E addresses.

Figure 11-4 shows the range of IP addresses set aside for each of the five Internet address classes. Studying this figure will enable you to recognize the class of a network from the first byte of its IP address.

IP Addressing Rules

If you do the math, you may wonder why some of the network numbers in the last two columns of Figure 11-4 do not seem to encompass all of the possible network addresses. The reason is because of special rules whereby the Internet reserves certain addresses for special purposes. The special cases are loopback, broadcast, network source, and private IP addresses. These four cases are described in the sections that follow.

IP Loopback Address

The Internet reserves the Network ID 127 as the **loopback address,** which is a diagnostic IP address reserved for testing purposes that redirects packets to the same computer that sent them. When a developer wants to test a Web server running on the local host (i.e., the same computer that the developer is using), the developer typically uses the address 127.0.0.1. You can find out whether a Web server is running on your computer, for example, by using your browser to go to http://127.0.0.1. If you get no response, there is no Web server on your local host.

Address Class	IP Address Range	IP Structure (Network ID versus Host ID)	Potential Number of Networks	Potential Number of Hosts per Network
A	0.0.0.0 to 127.255.255.255	24.131.47.114	126	16,777,214
B	128.0.0.0 to 191.255.255.255	134.123.174.201	16,384	65,534
C	192.0.0.0 to 223.255.255.255	201.113.241.196	2,097,152	254
D	224.0.0.0 to 239.255.255.255	230.148.32.157	1,048,560 multicast goups (no networks or hosts)	
E	240.0.0.0 to 255.255.255.255	Class E is reserved for future use.		

FIGURE 11-4 *The five Internet address classes are named A, B, C, D, and E. In a Class A Internet address, the first byte can be 0 to 127. In Class B addresses, the first byte ranges from 128 to 191. The first byte in Class C ranges from 192 to 223. Multicast addresses in Class D have first bytes ranging from 224 to 239. Class E comprises IP addresses that have first bytes ranging from 240 to 255, which are reserved for future use.* ■

IP Broadcast Addresses

A broadcast is a message that gets sent to all of the hosts on a network. The **IP broadcast address byte** is 255, which sets all eight bits in the address byte to 1. There are four kinds of broadcast addresses:

- **Limited broadcast**   The **limited broadcast** address is 255.255.255.255. Routers block this address, keeping it inside the local network—hence the name, *limited broadcast*. Computers that do not have IP addresses typically send a 255.255.255.255 broadcast on startup to find a DHCP or BOOTP server that can respond with an IP address assignment.

- **Net-directed broadcast**   On a Class A network, the **Net-directed broadcast** address is *netid.255.255.255*, where *netid* is the Network ID. This broadcasts a message to all the hosts on that network. On a Class B network, the Net-directed broadcast address is *netid.netid.255.255*, where *netid.netid* is the Network ID. On a Class C network, the Net-directed broadcast address is *netid.netid.netid.255*.

- **Subnet-directed broadcast**   When a large network is divided into subnets, you send a **subnet-directed broadcast** to a subnet by giving as much of the Network ID as needed to identify the subnet, followed by 255 or 255.255, depending on how many bytes were needed to identify the subnet. You learn how to create subnets later in this chapter.

- **All-subnets-directed broadcast**   The all-subnets-directed broadcast sends a message to all hosts on a network. It is now considered obsolete, because multicasting using Class D addresses has replaced it.

Special Case IP Addresses Containing Zeros

IP addresses in which the Network ID or the host ID are all zeros are special network addresses that cannot be assigned as a host's IP address. Any zeros used in IP addresses must observe the following rules:

- In a Class A network address, the first byte cannot be zero, and the last three bytes cannot all be zeros.

- In a Class B address, the first two bytes cannot both be zeros, and the last two bytes cannot both be zeros.

- In a Class C address, the first three bytes cannot all be zeros, and the last byte cannot be zero.

- A special case is the IP address 0.0.0.0, which is the source address that dynamically configured hosts use when broadcasting a request for an IP address. You may never assign a host a permanent IP address of 0.0.0.0.

Reserved or Private IP Addresses

In the previous chapter, you learned that an organization can use a NAT to enable many private internal IP addresses to access the Internet through one or more ICANN-assigned external IP addresses. Whenever an organization creates private, internal IP addresses, they must fall within the following ranges:

- **Class A**   10.0.0.0 to 10.255.255.255
- **Class B**   172.16.0.0 to 172.31.255.255
- **Class C**   192.168.0.0 to 192.168.255.255

Routers on the public Internet reject packets that use these private addresses. When users dial up to the Internet, their ISP usually assigns them one of these private addresses. Out on the public Internet, the ISP uses one of its public IP addresses on behalf of the user. The switch happens behind the scenes, so to speak, and the vast majority of end users are happy to be totally unaware of it.

Subnet Masks

A **subnet mask** is a dotted quad number that enables the local network to determine whether any given IP address is internal or external to the local network. If a network node makes a request from an IP address that is internal, the local network knows to handle it without routing the request over the Internet. If the request is an external address, on the other hand, the routers send the request on its way over the Internet.

Most subnet masks have one of the following forms:

- **Class A: 255.0.0.0**   The 255, which is a byte with all bits on, signifies that the first byte of this host's IP address is its local Network ID. The zeros in the other three bytes indicate that all of the addresses within that Network ID are internal to that network.

- **Class B: 255.255.0.0**   The two leading 255s mean that the first two bytes of this host's IP address are its local Network ID. The zeros in the other two bytes indicate that all of the addresses within that Network ID are part of the local network.

- **Class C: 255.255.255.0**   The three leading 255s mean that the first three bytes of this host's IP address are its local Network ID. The zero in the fourth byte indicates that all of the addresses within that Network ID are part of the local network.

True to its name, the subnet mask can also be used to mask out parts of the local Network ID that are not on the local host's network segment. At my home, for example, the subnet mask is 255.255.255.240. That mask means that sixteen local addresses are on the subnet in my home (240–255). All other addresses are external to my subnet, making my router handle requests directed to those other addresses.

The subnet mask is a critically important part of a network host's configuration. If the subnet mask is incorrect, the errant host's packets can be misdirected and lost. Therefore, you want your organization's subnet masks to be set by network administrators who know what they are doing.

Configuring TCP/IP on a Personal Computer

In order for a personal computer to communicate on a TCP/IP network, you must first configure the computer's TCP/IP settings. At a minimum, the computer must have an IP address and a subnet mask, which enable communications with hosts on the local network. To communicate with computers on a WAN, such as the Internet, the computer must also have a default gateway.

The Internet uses the Domain Name System (DNS) to enable end users to access resources by name, such as www.loc.gov, instead of requiring users to type the site's numeric IP address. In addition to DNS, the Windows operating system has a naming system called **Windows Internet Naming Service (WINS)**. You must configure PCs to use either DNS or WINS. Because DNS is so important on the Internet, you should configure DNS if the computer has access to the Internet. WINS enables a Windows computer to be known by its NetBIOS name, which is the "computer name" on the Computer Name tab of the Windows Control Panel's System settings.

TCP/IP settings can be configured in two ways, namely, statically or dynamically. True to its name, a static configuration consists of predetermined settings that you type by hand into the computer's TCP/IP window. Dynamic configuration uses DHCP to configure the network settings automatically during the computer's booting process on startup. Happily, the settings for static and dynamic PC configuration are in the same place. Follow these steps:

1. Click the Windows Start button and choose Control Panel. When the Control Panel window appears, double-click Network Connections.

2. When the Network Connections window appears, double-click Local Area Connection to bring up the Local Area Connection Properties window, which displays in a listbox the protocols that have been assigned to your computer's NIC. **Protocol binding** is the act of assigning a protocol to a network interface card.

3. Scroll the listbox down to reveal the Internet Protocol (TCP/IP), as illustrated in Figure 11-5.

4. Click once on Internet Protocol (TCP/IP) to select it, and then click the Properties button to bring up the TCP/IP Properties window.

5. If you are dynamically configuring the PC, click to select the options entitled Obtain an IP address automatically and Obtain DNS server address automatically. Click OK to close the windows, and you are finished.

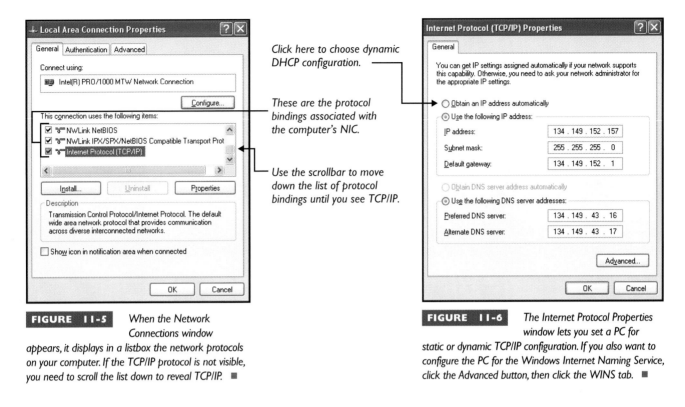

FIGURE 11-5 *When the Network Connections window appears, it displays in a listbox the network protocols on your computer. If the TCP/IP protocol is not visible, you need to scroll the list down to reveal TCP/IP.* ■

FIGURE 11-6 *The Internet Protocol Properties window lets you set a PC for static or dynamic TCP/IP configuration. If you also want to configure the PC for the Windows Internet Naming Service, click the Advanced button, then click the WINS tab.* ■

6. If you are statically configuring the PC, click to select the options entitled Use the following IP address, and Use the following DNS server addresses. Clicking these options activates the fields illustrated in Figure 11-6.

7. Fill out the fields by typing the IP address, subnet mask, default gateway (i.e., router), and DNS server addresses.

8. If you want to configure the PC for WINS, click the Advanced button, select the WINS tab, and use the Add button to add the network's WINS server address.

9. Click OK to close the windows.

Configuring Networks for Optimum Performance

Network technicians and troubleshooters use diagnostic tools that help solve problems and tune networks for optimum performance. This part of the book introduces seven such tools and provides hands-on experience monitoring network performance. The seven tools are (1) ping, (2) traceroute, (3) netstat, (4) ipconfig, (5) winipcfg, (6) arp, and (7) network analyzers.

ping

The most basic network troubleshooting utility is the Packet Internet Groper (**ping**), which sends ICMP echo request packets to a destination IP address. When the destination returns the echo, the ping utility measures the response time and displays a message indicating the duration of the round trip. You use the ping utility when you want a quick test of whether a PC has connectivity with the network, or whether a certain server is responding. To try the ping utility, follow these steps:

1. Get a command prompt onscreen. If you need help doing this, click the Windows Start button and choose Programs | Accessories | Command Prompt.

2. At the command prompt, type: **ping 127.0.0.1**

3. Press ENTER, and see how your computer responds. Remember that 127.0.0.1 is the special IP address that lets you run tests in which your local computer issues commands to itself. By executing the command ping 127.0.0.1, you are testing whether your computer can ping itself. If this test fails, your computer's NIC is not configured properly or has failed. The response you get should look something like this:

```
Pinging 127.0.0.1 with 32 bytes of data:
Reply from 127.0.0.1: bytes=32 time<1ms TTL=128
Reply from 127.0.0.1: bytes=32 time<1ms TTL=128
Reply from 127.0.0.1: bytes=32 time<1ms TTL=128
Reply from 127.0.0.1: bytes=32 time<1ms TTL=128

Ping statistics for 127.0.0.1:
    Packets: Sent = 4, Received = 4, Lost = 0 (0% loss),
Approximate round trip times in milli-seconds:
    Minimum = 0ms, Maximum = 0ms, Average = 0ms
```

4. Now try pinging the Library of Congress. When I tried this, I got an average response time of 48 milliseconds. To ping the LOC, type one of the following commands, press ENTER, and watch what happens:

```
ping  140.147.249.7
```

or

```
ping www.loc.gov
```

A few hosts on the Internet have disabled ping. If you try to ping www.microsoft.com, for example, you will get no reply because Microsoft has disabled ping on that server.

traceroute

The **traceroute** networking utility reports the path data follow as a packet winds its way over the network from the source to the destination computer. You use the traceroute utility when you need to isolate the source of a network connectivity problem. The best way to see how traceroute works is to try it. On UNIX and Linux systems, the command is **traceroute**. Under Windows, however, the command is **tracert**. Assuming you have Windows, these instructions use tracert:

1. Get a command prompt onscreen and type:

```
tracert www.mcgraw-hill.com
```

2. Press ENTER to execute the command. When I tried this,
I got the following report of 15 hops the packet took on its
way from the University of Delaware to McGraw-Hill.
For each hop, tracert reports three timings as it tries each
hop three times:

```
Tracing  ^1route to www.elb.mcgraw-hill.com [198.45.19.151]
over a maximum of 30 hops:

   1     5 ms    10 ms     5 ms   128.175.__.__ [the author's machine]
   2    37 ms    38 ms    38 ms   host-214-65.nss.udel.edu [128.175.214.65]
   3    70 ms    39 ms    38 ms   chp-rt2-v-7.nss.udel.edu [128.175.13.254]
   4    37 ms    39 ms    37 ms   spare-7206-g0-3-9.nss.udel.edu [128.175.111.11]
   5    40 ms    39 ms    39 ms   g1.ba21.b003003-1.phl01.atlas.cogentco.com [38.112.7.61]
   6    39 ms    39 ms    39 ms   g9-0.core01.phl01.atlas.cogentco.com [38.112.34.141]
   7    43 ms    46 ms    43 ms   p5-0.core02.jfk02.atlas.cogentco.com [66.28.4.1]
   8    42 ms    41 ms    41 ms   p6-0.pr01.jfk05.atlas.psi.net [154.54.1.166]
   9    41 ms    42 ms    42 ms   204.255.169.13
  10    41 ms    42 ms    42 ms   0.so-6-0-0.XL2.NYC4.ALTER.NET [152.63.21.82]
  11    42 ms    41 ms    42 ms   0.so-3-1-0.XL2.NYC9.ALTER.NET [152.63.21.14]
  12    41 ms    41 ms    42 ms   POS7-0.GW6.NYC9.ALTER.NET [152.63.24.69]
  13    42 ms    43 ms    42 ms   mgh-t3-gw.customer.ALTER.NET [157.130.18.70]
  14    45 ms    44 ms    45 ms   gw2.mcgraw-hill.com [198.45.19.20]
  15    43 ms    44 ms    43 ms   198.45.19.151
Trace complete.
```

netstat

The **netstat** utility displays information about the connections that are
open and the protocol processes that are currently running on a network
host. The name netstat stands for network statistics. To run the netstat
utility, follow these steps:

1. Get a command prompt onscreen and type: **netstat**

2. Press ENTER to execute the command. You will get a list of the
connections currently open on your machine.

3. The netstat utility can do much more, however. To see a list of the
netstat options, type the following command and press ENTER:
netstat ?

4. Try the netstat options that interest you. When you type an
option, you must precede it with a hyphen. To see the router table,
for example, you type: **netstat -r**

ipconfig

As you can tell from its name, **ipconfig** is a TCP/IP configuration utility that runs on computers with Windows NT/2000/XP/2003 or later operating systems. You use ipconfig whenever you want to inspect the current IP configuration. Furthermore, if the computer's IP settings are dynamically configured, you can use ipconfig to release, renew, or refresh the DHCP leases. To use ipconfig, follow these steps:

1. At a command prompt, type **ipconfig** and press ENTER. You will see a report revealing the computer's IP address, subnet mask, and default gateway.

2. If you want a more detailed report that includes the computer's name and physical MAC address, execute the command followed by the /all switch, as follows: **ipconfig /all**

3. To release the leases on IP addresses obtained from a DHCP server, type the following command: **ipconfig /release**

4. To renew the leases, type the following command: **ipconfig /renew**

5. To learn about other options, type the command: **ipconfig ?**

winipcfg

winipcfg is an older version of ipconfig for Windows 95/98/Me. If you want to run winipcfg on one of these older Windows versions, follow these steps:

1. Click the Windows Start button and choose Run to make the Run dialog appear.

2. In the Run dialog, type **winipcfg** and press ENTER.

3. When the IP Configuration window appears, use the onscreen controls to inspect the IP addresses. If the computer is dynamically configured, you can release and renew the DHCP leases.

If you want a more detailed report, click the More info button.

arp

Earlier in this chapter, you learned how the Address Resolution Protocol (ARP) translates IP addresses into physical MAC addresses. You can use a command-line utility called **arp** to inspect the current contents of your computer's ARP table, which contains the MAC addresses of computers with which you have communicated recently. The arp utility can also delete entries or add permanent entries into the ARP table. To use the arp utility, follow these steps:

1. Get a command prompt onscreen and type: **arp -a**

2. Press ENTER to execute the command, which will list the current contents of your computer's ARP table.

3. The arp command can also query the ARP table of a specific IP address. You can use this feature, for example, to see the ARP table in your default gateway. Execute the following command, replacing *xxx.xxx.xxx.xxx* by your router's IP address:

   ```
   arp  -a   xxx.xxx.xxx.xxx
   ```

4. To delete an entry from the ARP table, you run the following command, replacing *xxx.xxx.xxx.xxx* with the IP address of the entry you want removed:

   ```
   arp  -d   xxx.xxx.xxx.xxx
   ```

5. To find out about other arp command options, execute the arp command by itself, without typing any parameters. The arp utility will reply with a help screen describing all the options.

Network Analyzers

A **network analyzer** is a tool that enables a network administrator to capture and analyze packets crossing a network. Network analyzers come in handy when you need to:

- **Test connections** By sending test packets, a network analyzer enables you to troubleshoot network connections and identify faulty cables or malfunctioning network devices.

- **Send alerts** A network analyzer can be configured to send an alert to an operator when something fails on the network.

- **Sniff packets for analysis** Network analyzers are sometimes called *packet sniffers*, because they can grab packets and save them for later analysis. Chapter 13 teaches techniques you can use to keep sniffers from deciphering sensitive information, such as passwords or credit card information, that may be crossing the Internet.

- **Generate reports** Network analyzers can keep statistics and generate reports that can help identify peak usage patterns or bottlenecks on different segments of the network.

Some of the leading network analyzer products include Microsoft's Network Monitor, Network Associates' Sniffer product line, and Agilent's family of network analyzers. For more on network analyzers, search Google or Yahoo for *network analyzer*.

Create the World's Smallest Network

You can learn a lot about networking by cabling two PCs together and exploring how the TCI/IP protocols and diagnostic tools function on those PCs. Because two nodes are the minimum number needed to create a network, you will by definition create the world's smallest network. To complete this exercise, you need two PCs with Ethernet jacks. To cable them together, you need a crossover cable. You can either buy a crossover cable from an electronics store such as Radio Shack, or you can make your own cable following the Try This! instructions for creating 10/100baseT cables in the previous chapter. Once you have the two PCs and the crossover cable, you can create and test the world's smallest network by following these steps:

1. On each of the two PCs, click the Windows Start button and choose Control Panel. When the Control Panel window appears, double-click Network Connections.

2. When the Network Connections window appears, double-click Local Area Connection to bring up the Status window, then click the Properties button to bring up the Local Area Connection Properties window, which displays in a listbox the protocol bindings on each computer's NIC.

3. Scroll the listbox down to reveal the Internet Protocol (TCP/IP), click it once to select it, then click the Properties button to bring up the TCP/IP Properties window.

4. On a piece of paper, write down the current settings that you see in the TCP/IP Properties window. You make note of the current settings so you can reset them when you are finished with this exercise.

5. Click to select the option entitled Use the following IP address. Fill out the IP addresses on the two computers as follows, which assigns each computer an IP address within the ICANN address range reserved for private networks:

   Computer A: IP address 192.168.0.1, subnet mask 255.255.255.0
   Computer B: IP address 192.168.0.2, subnet mask 255.255.255.0

6. Click OK to close the windows.

7. Use the crossover cable to connect the two PCs. Now you have the world's smallest network. In the rest of these instructions, you run tests to make sure you have the network configured properly.

8. On each computer, click the Windows Start button and choose Programs | Accessories | Command Prompt. At the command prompt, type the following command:

   Computer A: ping 192.168.0.1
   Computer B: ping 192.168.0.2

9. Press ENTER, and see how the computers respond. If each ping succeeds in obtaining an echo from the other computer, you have succeeded in creating the world's smallest network. Congratulations!

10. To return the computers to their previous configurations, repeat steps 1, 2, and 3. Then repeat step 5 using the settings you wrote down in step 4.

Internetworking Servers

Now that you know how to configure a PC to get on a network as a TCP/IP client, it is time to learn how Internetworking servers run utility services that provide basic infrastructure and enhance the network by making it more efficient. We begin by considering the critical role that DNS servers play in the infrastructure of the Internet.

DNS Servers

The Domain Name System (DNS) was invented because people prefer to go to Internet sites by domain names, such as www.loc.gov, instead of numeric IP addresses, such as 140.147.249.7. Before a client workstation can send a request that is addressed to a site's domain name, the Application Layer must convert the domain name to its corresponding IP address. The servers that perform this conversion are DNS Servers. The process they perform is known as *domain name resolution*. To resolve a Domain Name is to convert it into the corresponding IP address.

Because DNS name resolution is such an integral part of the Internet Architecture, it is important that a client be configured to use a DNS server that runs fast. Large organizations, for example, may dedicate one or more servers to performing the task of domain name resolution. As you noticed previously in this chapter in Figure 11-6, the TCP/IP configuration settings let you specify an alternate DNS server that can resolve the names if the primary DNS server goes down or is not responding.

DNS Name Space Hierarchy

Figure 11-7 shows how the DNS system is powered by a hierarchically distributed database called the *name space*, which is organized according to three levels: (1) the root level, (2) the top level, and (3) the second level. Each level contains DNS servers that are in charge of keeping track of the domains in the next lower level.

At the highest level of the hierarchy are the **root servers**, which keep track of the top-level domains, such as .com, .net, .edu, .gov, .org, and .us. The top-level DNS servers keep track of the second-level domains, such as mcgraw-hill.com, loc.gov, w3.org, and ny.us. The second-level DNS servers keep track of the names assigned by the organizations that own the domains. Examples of host names assigned in second-level domains are www.mcgraw-hill.com and mail.mcgraw-hill.com. Large organizations can further subdivide second-level domains into subdomains, such as investor.mcgraw-hill.com.

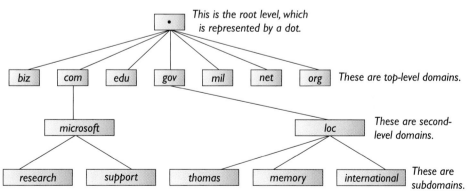

FIGURE   11-7   *The DNS name space has three levels: (1) the root level, (2) the top level, and (3) the second level. At each level, DNS servers keep track of the names assigned in that level. Root level servers, for example, keep track of the top-level domains. In this illustration, notice how the root level domain has a dot (.) for its designation. In a fully qualified domain name, you can include this dot, although in practice it is seldom used. Try going to thomas.loc.gov., however, to see how the Internet accepts the root dot as part of the name.* ■

DNS Name Servers and Resolvers

The DNS service has two components that work together to streamline the process of resolving names. These components are the (1) name server and (2) name resolver.

- **Name server** When a client workstation requests to resolve a domain name, the request first goes to a **name server,** which is in charge of responding with the IP address that corresponds to the domain name in the request. To speed the process of looking up these addresses, the name server maintains a cache containing the IP addresses for domain names that the server has already looked up. When a request comes in, the name server looks first in the cache and responds instantly if the requested address is there.

- **Name resolver** If the name server does not already know the IP address of the domain name in the request, the name server calls upon a **name resolver,** which goes out on the Internet and consults the necessary name servers in the DNS hierarchy. If those name servers do not know, they consult name resolvers further up the hierarchy. The cache that is kept on the name servers, however, minimizes the amount of actual name resolving. As a result, most names on the Internet can be resolved within a second or two.

Three Types of DNS Servers

Something all DNS servers have in common is that if they do not already know the IP address for a requested domain name, they become a client and request the address from the nearest name resolver. Thus, the DNS system follows the client-server model. Included in this model are the following DNS server types:

- **Root server** At the top of the DNS hierarchy, root servers can resolve all of the top-level domains on the Internet. If none of the name servers closer to the requesting workstation can resolve the name, one of the DNS root servers assumes responsibility for finding the name within the requested domain's name space.

- **Primary server** The first DNS server in a domain is called its **primary server.** As the domain's naming authority, the primary server maintains the master copy of the database containing the assigned names and IP addresses that are in the primary server's domain.

- **Secondary server** A domain can have one or more **secondary servers,** which help share the name-serving load and provide backup in case the primary server goes down. The secondary server contains a copy of the database from the primary server. In large networks, the primary server can delegate authority for different parts of the database to multiple secondary servers that resolve names in the network's subdomains.

Common DNS Record Types

Many types of resource records are in the DNS database. If you are studying for the CIW Foundations exam, you should learn to recognize the most common resource record types, which Table 11-2 describes. Only DNS programmers and troubleshooters need to know the other types.

Host Tables and Files

Back in the good old days before 1983 when DNS began evolving into an Internet standard, there was no hierarchically distributed database of domain names and IP addresses. Instead, one huge file called the **hosts table** contained the name and IP address of every named host on the Internet. The Stanford Research Institute's Network Information Center (SRI-NIC) managed and updated this file. Server administrators downloaded this file periodically to keep their local systems updated. As the Internet grew, however, the hosts table became too large for server administrators to download regularly.

Why, then, am I telling you this story? Because to this day, personal computers still have a hosts table, which you can use in the following situations:

1. You would like to refer to a computer on another network by a nickname instead of having to type its complete domain name.

2. You want to enhance performance on your local network, so you copy onto each PC on the network a hosts table identifying each node's name and IP address.

3. You have an isolated internal network with no DNS server, and you want each computer to have a fully qualified domain name.

To see the hosts table on your computer, follow these steps:

1. Get the Notepad running, pull down the Notepad's Files of Type menu, and set it to look for files of all types.

2. Use the Look in menu to navigate to the system32\drivers\etc subfolder of your Windows system folder. The complete path probably will be one of the following:

    c:\windows\system32\drivers\etc

    or

    c:\winnt\system32\drivers\etc

DNS Record Type	Purpose
Address (A)	Identifies the IP address of a domain name. This record occurs most often in the DNS database.
Canonical Name (CNAME)	An alias that lets a host with one name be accessed also by another name. A computer fulfilling the dual role of Web and news server, for example, could answer to requests addressed to both www.mydomain.com and news.mydomain.com.
Mail Exchanger (MX)	Identifies the IP address of a mail exchanger on a domain.
Name Server (NS)	Identifies the IP addresses of the primary and secondary name servers for a domain.
Start of Authority (SOA)	Identifies the IP address of the DNS server that is the primary authority for a domain.

TABLE 11-2   *Important DNS Resource Record Types* ∎

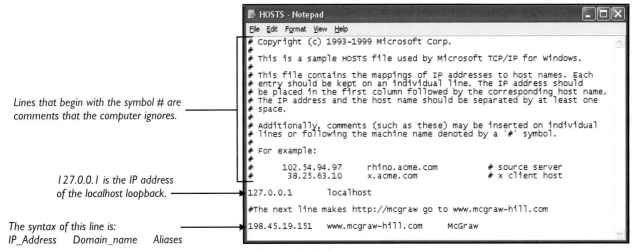

Lines that begin with the symbol # are comments that the computer ignores.

127.0.0.1 is the IP address of the localhost loopback.

The syntax of this line is:
IP_Address   Domain_name   Aliases

FIGURE 11-8 *The HOSTS file associates IP addresses with domain names. An important duty of the HOSTS file is to define the IP address of the computer's localhost loopback address. You can also use the HOSTS file to set up aliases. In this example, I created the alias McGraw and directed it to 198.45.19.151, thereby saving the time required to type www.mcgraw-hill.com.* ∎

3. One of the files in this folder is named HOSTS. Use the Notepad to open the HOSTS file.

4. Figure 11-8 shows my HOSTS file. Notice that I created an alias that enables me to browse to www.mcgraw-hill.com simply by typing mcgraw.

Proxy Servers

In everyday life, people send a proxy when they cannot go somewhere themselves. On the Internet, proxy servers work somewhat like that. In computer networking, a **proxy server** is a computer that serves as an intermediary between client workstations and the external network.

At the University of Delaware, for example, students who live off campus configure their browsers to use a proxy server that enables them to access the same network privileges as on-campus students. The proxy server receives the off-campus requests and reissues them to the campus network. The campus network sees the request as coming from the proxy, to which the campus servers respond. Anyone from off campus who does not come in through the proxy is denied access to secured student resources.

Just as the Delaware students must configure their browsers to use the proxy, so must the clients on private networks that run behind a proxy. To configure Internet Explorer to use a proxy, you pull down the Tools menu, choose Internet Options, click the Connections tab, and click the LAN Settings button to reveal the proxy server settings. Other kinds of client applications, including FTP programs, mail readers, and telnet clients can similarly be configured to access the Internet through a proxy server. Here are some reasons why you may choose to use a proxy server:

- **Private IP address hiding** When the proxy server accesses the public Internet, it uses a different IP address than the private addresses assigned to the workstations running behind the proxy. Thus, the proxy hides the internal addresses on the private network from the public Internet.

- **Public IP address pooling** The proxy server can conserve resources by accessing the Internet from a smaller number of public IP addresses than the number of client workstations running behind the proxy.

- **Enhanced network security** The proxy server can block users on the public Internet from accessing network hosts running on the private network behind the proxy. Thus, the proxy serves as a kind of firewall.

- **Web content caching** The proxy server caches documents that it requests on behalf of users running behind the proxy. If other users running behind the proxy request the same documents, the proxy can serve the content instantly from the cache instead of having to retrieve it from the Internet.

- **Transaction filtering** You may want to block access on a private network to certain kinds of Internet resources. A proxy server can monitor the requests coming from the private network and block access to forbidden resources. This kind of monitoring and blocking is called **transaction filtering**. You can deny access, for example, to certain IP addresses, Web pages, URLs, host names, or computer names. You can even block individual users from accessing specific resources.

- **Transaction logging** A proxy server can record and timestamp the URLs, IP addresses, and external services accessed by clients running behind the proxy. By tracking the number of bytes received along with transmission times, the proxy server can keep vital statistics that network administrators use to monitor network performance.

Caching Servers

A **caching server** speeds access to resources by making a local copy of resources requested from the network so Web content and other kinds of documents and files can be served more quickly to subsequent users who request the same resources. Only if the date on the original document changes will the caching server download a fresh copy of the requested resource.

Caching servers can run either on a standalone computer that is dedicated to caching or as server components alongside other services on the same computer. Proxy servers, for example, normally include a caching server component. Computers that come preconfigured as caching servers are sometimes called *cache-in-a-box* because the server is ready to run as soon as you take it out of the box.

Mirrored Servers

A **mirrored server** is a computer whose data reads and writes are simultaneously executed on another computer that keeps an updated faithful copy of everything on the system from which the data are copied. The purpose of a mirrored server is to provide redundancy and fault tolerance in mission-critical operations in which server failure could cause serious problems.

Another use of mirroring is on a single server that has a redundant array of independent drives (RAID) controller. One of the RAID configurations known as *RAID level one* mirrors the data on multiple disk drives within a single computer. I use RAID level one, for example, to mirror the drive containing the operating system. If the operating system drive fails, the mirror drive automatically takes over, and the RAID controller sends an e-mail message alerting me that the failed drive needs maintenance. End users never notice the problem, because the server keeps operating.

Certificate Servers

There are two main categories of security concerns on the Internet. First, because packet sniffers can inspect the contents of data packets as they wind their way over the Internet, companies need a way to ensure that only intended recipients can read the data. Second, recipients need a way to determine the authenticity of the information to make sure it is coming from a trusted source and has not been modified along the way. A cracker, for example, could be masquerading as a legitimate vendor while sending you malicious code in disguise.

To shore up these security issues, the Internet uses **certificate servers** to issue digital certificates that network hosts use to digitally sign and encrypt messages using public-private key pairs. When you download a new version of the Flash player, for example, you get a message telling you that Macromedia digitally signed the software. The message includes a link to the certificate authority where you can verify that Macromedia is the source of the software. Then you can decide whether you want to proceed with installing the software.

Because of the threat of malicious code, you need to be wary of downloading software that is not digitally signed. Chapter 13 provides detailed coverage of Internet security best practices including certificates, digital signatures, and public-private key encryption.

Directory Servers

A **directory server** is a standalone computer or server component in charge of managing a database that keeps track of all the users, passwords, resources, printers, servers, e-mail addresses, phone numbers, and departmental contacts throughout an organization's network. When a user logs on to the network, the directory server provides access to those resources that the user has permission to use.

To make it possible for directory servers to communicate with each other and distribute the directory database over multiple networks, the International Standards Organization (ISO) in 1984 began work on creating a **Directory Access Protocol (DAP)** called **X.500**. The X.500 database has a hierarchical design that allows different parts of the database to reside on different directory servers. A large multinational company, for example, can have a directory server on each continent keeping track of employee information and resources for the local country networks. Through DAP, these directory servers can exchange information, thereby creating a worldwide directory of the company's employees and resources. An advantage of this exchange is that each employee's information need be entered and maintained on just one server, thereby avoiding the problems that can be caused by storing employee data in multiple places that all must be updated if the information changes.

In practice, however, X.500 was overly complex. To streamline the process, the University of Michigan invented in 1993 a lighter version called the **Lightweight Directory Access Protocol (LDAP)** that can run over TCP/IP. The streamlined LDAP protocol became an instant success. Netscape adopted LDAP in 1997 to power the Netscape directory server. Bigfoot used LDAP to create its directory of people at www.bigfoot.com, and Yahoo used LDAP to power the people search at people.yahoo.com. Most significantly, Microsoft used LDAP to create Active Directory, which is a core server component that provides directory services on Windows servers.

RFC 1487 defines the LDAP standard. If you are studying for the CIW exam, you should understand three advantages of the X.500 and LDAP directory strategies:

- **Synchronization** The directory on one server can synchronize with the directory on another, thereby keeping the data current.

- **Replication** Part or all of the directory database on one server can copy itself onto another server. This advantage provides backup and fault tolerance in case one of the servers fails, and it speeds access to resources by reducing the number of hops needed to look up a given resource.

- **Scalability** Because network administrators can distribute the database over multiple servers, there is no limit to the size to which the directory can grow.

Catalog Servers

A **catalog server** uses robots called *spiders* that comb through a network's files and create an index of everything they find. When users need to find something on the network, they search this catalog. Because the search looks up the keywords in the prebuilt index, users quickly find what they seek.

Catalog servers can index all kinds of information, including Web pages, newsgroups, word-processed documents, PDF files, mail messages, images, movies, audio, and software applications. In addition to indexing the full text of written documents, the catalog indexes all of the file's properties. Thus, you can search for all of the documents written by a certain author or modified after a specific date. When users conduct a search, they are shown only resources to which they have access.

Transaction Servers

Transaction servers work behind the scenes in the business tier of the multi-tier e-commerce model to ensure that when a financial transaction occurs, all of the necessary databases get updated and related services receive the proper notifications. A transaction is a set of events that must be performed or rolled back simultaneously. For example, when someone transfers money from a savings account to a checking account, a transaction server makes sure that the savings account gets debited when the checking account is credited. A more complex transaction occurs when someone uses a credit card to purchase a product online; the online storefront's transaction server (1) finances the purchase by debiting the customer's account in the mercantile database at the bank that issued the card, (2) updates the inventory database, (3) arranges for shipping and updates the shipping database, and (4) may notify the manufacturing database if product inventory dips too low.

One of the most well-known transaction systems is IBM's Customer Information Control System (CICS). Originally designed as a legacy mainframe application, CICS now is available in a client-server version. Another popular example is Microsoft Transaction Server (MTS), which debuted in Windows NT Server. In Windows 2003 and later Microsoft server products, MTS is an integral part of component services.

Serving Internet Resources

After studying the Internetworking servers that power the network's infrastructure behind the scenes, now it is time to look more deeply into the well-known services that are the reason for the Internet's mass-market popularity. We begin with the Internet's most popular servers, which are Web servers.

Web Servers

Web servers are standalone computers or server components that respond to HTTP requests from browsers and other kinds of Internet clients, including media players and handheld devices. Because Web servers use the HTTP protocol, they are also called HTTP servers.

Home Page Default Filenames

When you visit a site without specifying a filename, the Web server responds by sending you the site's default page. Thus, the end user does not have to know the filename of the default page. Behind the scenes, however, the filename is important, because competing brands of Web servers have different default filename conventions. The default page's author needs to know the name to give the page to make it appear when a user visits the site without specifying a filename. Table 11-3 identifies the default filenames that may be used by various brands of Web servers. Consult your server administrator to find out your Web site's default filename convention.

Web Server Hit Logs

Every time a request hits a Web site, the site's Web server may log certain information about the hit. Depending on the brand of Web server, the specific information logged may vary, but all brands are capable of recording three general categories of information:

Default Filename	Web Server Brand
default.asp default.htm default.html	Internet Information Server (IIS) on Microsoft Windows servers
index.htm index.html	Apache on UNIX and Linux servers
home.htm home.html	Vendor neutral
main.htm main.html	Vendor neutral
welcome.htm welcome.html	Vendor neutral

TABLE 11-3   *Filenames Typically Used for a Web Site's Default Page* ■

- **Client access data**   For each hit, the log identifies the IP address of the client that issued the request. Remember that this address can be the one used by a proxy server making the request on behalf of a client. Therefore, this address does not necessarily identify the specific client that made the request.

- **Referrer data**   The referrer data reveals the URL that the user typed or clicked to reach the site, the filename or command that may have been appended to this URL, and the HTTP method of the request (i.e., GET or POST).

- **Error data**   If errors occur, they appear in status codes that the server administrator can study to improve site operations. Dropped connections, security access violations, and malformed URLs are some of the errors that can occur.

The Windows IIS Web server keeps logs by default, meaning that logging is on unless the server administrator turns it off. Information recorded in IIS logs includes (1) the date and timestamp, (2) the destination IP address, (3) the request method (i.e., GET or POST), (4) the URL requested, (5) the port (normally 80, which is the Web's default port), (6) the IP address of the requestor, (7) the name and version of the browser or other client issuing the request, and (8) status codes related to the success or failure of the server's handling of the request.

Web Root Folders

On a Web server, the **Web root** is the physical folder that represents the beginning of the server's Web space. On Windows IIS servers, the Web root is typically located at c:\inetpub\wwwroot. When someone browses to an IIS server's Web address without specifying a filename, the server responds by sending the file c:\inetpub\wwwroot\default.htm, default.html, or default.asp. Sites hosted on that server typically reside in subfolders off the root. If Santa Claus has a site on this server, for example, it could be located in the folder c:\inetpub\wwwroot\santa.

Depending on the nature of the site, however, it may not be possible to store all of the site's files on a single drive. Even if all the files could fit on one drive, it may be more efficient to put some of the site's folders on other drives. To accomplish this, the server administrator can create virtual directories and aliases.

Virtual Directories and Aliases

A virtual directory is the name of a path to a Web folder that may reside anywhere in the host computer's file space, even in a physical location outside the scope of the server's root Web space. A virtual directory's physical location is often on a different drive from that of the server's root Web space. Locating a virtual folder on a different drive enables the server to distribute the file-serving workload among multiple drives. Situations arise, however, in which it helps to create virtual directories within the Web root's directory tree. Imagine a situation in which a site's Web address contains many folder and subfolder names, such as:

http://many.sites.com/external/northern/nonprofit/toymakers/santa

Creating a virtual directory named santa for the path c:\inetpub\ wwwroot\external\northern\nonprofit\toymakers\santa enables users to access the same site via the simpler Web address:

http://many.sites.com/santa

File Permissions and Access Control

Many public Web sites allow anonymous access to all of the Web pages at the site. Other sites restrict access to authorized users. A restricted site can decide whether a user should be permitted to access it in two ways. The first way is via file permissions, and the second way is through authenticated access control.

- **File permissions**   Most Web servers, including the most popular Windows, UNIX, and Linux Web servers, observe the operating system's file permission settings that the server administrator can configure for any individual file or folder at the site. Typical permissions include the ability to read a file, write (create or delete a file), execute (run a program), modify (edit a file), or deny access. Figure 11-9 shows that the Windows operating system enables you to set different file permissions depending on the role of the person who is accessing the site. Using this role-based model, for example, you can permit network managers to read, write, execute, and modify, while granting ordinary employees permission only to read and execute.

- **Authenticated user access control**   To authenticate means to have a user log on by entering a user name and password, which the site looks up in a database to find out whether or not the user should be granted access. The database of users can be application specific, or the site can use the operating system's database of assigned user names and passwords. You have no doubt visited Web portals that invite you to register by choosing your own user name and password. Web applications that power such portals maintain a separate database of user names and passwords. You learn how to create this kind of user database in the next chapter.

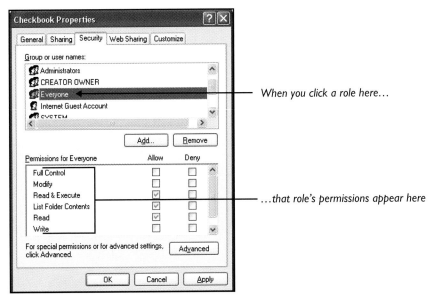

Checkbook Properties

General | Sharing | Security | Web Sharing | Customize

Group or user names:

- Administrators
- CREATOR OWNER
- Everyone
- Internet Guest Account
- SYSTEM

When you click a role here...

Add... | Remove

Permissions for Everyone | Allow | Deny

	Allow	Deny
Full Control	☐	☐
Modify	☐	☐
Read & Execute	☑	☐
List Folder Contents	☑	☐
Read	☑	☐
Write	☐	☐

...that role's permissions appear here

For special permissions or for advanced settings, click Advanced. | Advanced

OK | Cancel | Apply

FIGURE 11-9 *In the Windows operating system, the Security tab of a file or folder's Properties window enables the server administrator to assign role-based permissions that provide different levels of access depending on the category of users visiting the site. Clicking a role in the top window displays that role's permissions in the bottom window.* ■

Web Gateways

When lay people think of a Web site, they conjure a collection of Web pages that the user can bring onscreen by browsing to the desired page. Certain sites called *gateways*, however, consist of no pages whatsoever. Instead of serving traditional HTML pages, a Web gateway runs a computer application consisting of one or more programs, or scripts, which generate the HTML response that the end user sees onscreen. Because the browser displays this HTML as though it were an ordinary Web page, many users are unaware that they are communicating with a Web application as opposed to viewing a traditional Web page.

To provide a standard way for Web gateways to communicate with browsers and other kinds of clients, the National Center for Supercomputing Applications (NCSA) created the **Common Gateway Interface (CGI)** protocol. The CGI protocol defines the manner in which forms data, cookies, and other kinds of information in a Web request get submitted to the program or script that processes and responds to the request. The programs that respond to CGI requests are often referred to as **CGI scripts**. CGI is language neutral, meaning that CGI scripts can be authored in any computer language. Perl and Python are different brands of CGI-scripting languages. I write my CGI programs in C# and Java.

CGI is an open protocol. Any application that can open an Internet socket can implement the CGI interface. The latest version of Flash, for example, supports CGI. This enables the Flash author to create shows that can display Web forms and interact with users in a browser-like manner. Thus, the Flash author can use CGI to create a custom Web client that can replace the browser in situations requiring a custom user interface.

Mail Servers

True to its name, the Simple Mail Transfer Protocol (SMTP) defines the manner in which e-mail gets sent over the Internet. As you learned in Chapter 3, either clients can use POP3 to deliver the mail post-office style by downloading the messages to the user's PC, or you can use IMAP to leave the mail on the server, which enables you to read the mail from different client workstations. I keep an IMAP folder, for example, for each of my student advisees. Whenever I need to look up something about a student, such as during an office meeting, over coffee in a café, or while traveling, I can easily consult the IMAP folder from my desktop computer or wireless PDA. Thus, I am a huge fan of IMAP.

It is now time for you to learn about some of the more subtle distinctions related to the manner in which mail gets formatted for transmission over the Internet. We begin with MIME.

MIME

RFCs 2045 through 2049 define **Multipurpose Internet Mail Extensions (MIME)**, which are a set of standards that specify the formatting of Internet message bodies, the media types of Internet files and message bodies, and the method for attaching files that do not consist of plain ASCII text. Although the "ME" in "MIME" stands for Mail Extensions, MIME is used for a lot more than mail. Each file that gets transmitted over the Web, for example, has a MIME header that identifies the file's media type. Browsers, e-mail programs, and other kinds of Internet clients rely on MIME headers when deciding how to handle files. Table 11-4 identifies the most common MIME types.

Uuencoding

Prior to the invention of MIME and its adoption by modern mail clients, users had to go through a manual encoding process to send binary files in a mail message. This process was UNIX to UNIX encoding (**uuencoding**). It worked so well that uuencoding became popular under Windows as well as the UNIX operating system.

Uuencoding works by translating the 8-bit character stream of a binary (i.e., non-ASCII) file attachment into a stream of 7-bit characters. Because the resulting 7-bit file stream is all ASCII characters, you can simply paste a uuencoded file into the mail message's text body. When an end user receives a message containing a uuencoded file, the user must copy the uuencoded portion into a separate file and run the uudecode program to decode it. The result of the uudecode process is an exact copy of the binary file as it existed prior to being uuencoded.

For most practical purposes, MIME happily obsoletes manual uuencoding, although you could encounter some uuencoded files in legacy situations.

BinHex Encoding

BinHex encoding is to the Macintosh what uuencoding is to UNIX. To decode a BinHex file received from a Macintosh, you need to use the appropriate decoder. There are different versions of BinHex encoding, so you need to make sure you use the proper decoder. The first line of a BinHex file identifies its version.

Mailing List Servers

Chapter 3 provided a detailed tutorial on joining and using a listserv. Behind the scenes, mailing list servers are powered by SMTP. When a member of the list e-mails a message to the list, the mailing list server e-mails the message via SMTP to everyone on the list.

The listserv instructions in Chapter 3 are based on a specific brand of mailing list server that is called *listserv*, which is distributed by L-Soft at www.lsoft.com. On the Windows platform, Microsoft Exchange supports the creation and management of mailing lists. Another popular brand of mailing list manager is the freely distributed UNIX-based Majordomo list server at www.greatcircle.com. GreatCircle hosts Majordomo listservs for the purpose of supporting and developing Majordomo.

Filename Extension	MIME Type	Media Type
.css	text/css	Cascading style sheet
.doc	application/msword	Microsoft Word document
.exe	application/octet-stream	Executable file
.gif	image/gif	GIF image
.html	text/html	Web page
.jpg	image/jpeg	JPEG image
.midi	audio/x-midi	MIDI music file
.mp3	audio/mpeg	MP3 music file
.mpeg	video/mpeg	MPEG movie
.pdf	application/pdf	Adobe PDF
.png	image/png	PNG image
.ppt	application/vnd.ms-powerpoint	PowerPoint presentation
.qt	video/quicktime	QuickTime video
.rtf	application/rtf	Rich text document
.sit	application/x-stuffit	Stuffit archive
.swf	application/x-shockwave-flash	Flash animation
.txt	text/plain	ASCII text
.wav	audio/wav, audio/x-wav	Waveform audio
.xls	application/vnd.ms-excel	Spreadsheet
.xml	application/xml	XML file
.zip	application/zip application/x-compressed-zip	Zipped archive

TABLE 11-4 *The Most Common MIME Types* ∎

Streaming Media Servers

Microsoft, Apple, and Real Networks are the primary vendors of the streaming media services you studied in Chapter 3. Behind the scenes, the streaming media servers use UDP, as opposed to TCP, to transfer their packets. UDP transmits more continuously by putting each output from the Application Layer directly into a packet, thereby avoiding the overhead of TCP session management. The fact that no provision has been made for the resending of lost packets does not cause as much of a problem for video as it would for a mission-critical financial transaction. In the case of a lost video packet, the retransmission arrives out of sequence, making it too late to view anyway. To paraphrase the old Broadway saying, "the stream must go on."

note *If you are watching a stream and the video appears choppy due to lost packets, use your media player's settings to configure the stream to play at a lower bit rate. Figure 11-10 shows the typical bit rate settings.*

Microsoft recommends that you let the media player auto detect the connection speed.

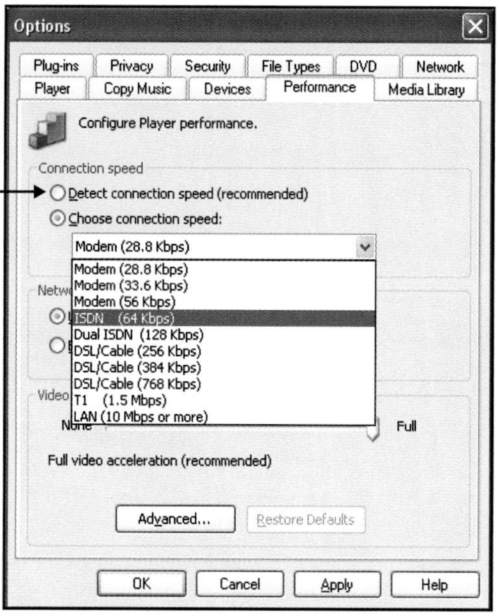

FIGURE 11-10 *If a media stream plays choppily due to dropped packets, use your media player's options to select a slower connection speed. Shown here are the Windows Media Player connection speeds.* ■

FTP Servers

Chapter 2 touted the many advantages of the File Transfer Protocol (FTP). You need to be careful setting up an FTP server on your network for two reasons. First, many brands of FTP servers transmit user names and passwords in clear text, making them prone to detection by packet sniffing. One way to avoid this problem is to let users log on anonymously, but this solution is not always practical. Chapter 13 teaches you how to set up an FTP server that encrypts user names, passwords, and file transfers.

Second, you may unknowingly expose files that you would not want the public to access. When you install an FTP server on your computer, you must carefully configure it so as to expose only the files and folders to which you want to provide remote access.

If FTP is prone to all these problems, you may justifiably ask, why should you install an FTP server when you could just e-mail the files instead? There are three reasons. First, most mail servers impose a file attachment limit of 2 or 3 megabytes per message. If a file is larger than the e-mail server's limit, you cannot e-mail it. Second, FTP servers let users download a file at their convenience, instead of having to ask you to e-mail it. Third, FTP is faster than e-mail and makes more efficient use of Internet bandwidth. These are the reasons why Chapter 13 teaches you how to use FTP securely.

News Servers

Chapter 3 taught you how to participate in USENET newsgroups. Behind the scenes, USENET newsgroup servers run on port 119, following the Network News Transport Protocol (NNTP) as defined by RFC 1036.

As an alternative to reading news with NNTP newsgroup clients, Web interfaces let you read USENET newsgroups via HTTP. For example, the newsgroup gateways at groups.google.com and www.mailgate.org enable you to participate in USENET newsgroups via your browser using the Web's HTTP protocol.

Popular Server Products

Two leading brands of server products are UNIX/Linux and Microsoft Windows Server. Both of these product families can host all of the Internet services and run all of the Internetworking servers covered in this chapter, either on stand-alone computers dedicated to running one type of service on a large network, or as server components on computers that serve multiple functions on smaller networks.

UNIX and Linux

UNIX and Linux listen for Internet requests through a program called **inetd**, which stands for **Internet daemon**. In Greek mythology, daemons are supernatural guardian spirits that serve as intermediaries between gods and humans. On UNIX and Linux systems, the term *daemon* refers to any process that runs in the background, waiting to respond to certain kinds of requests. The role of the Internet daemon is to dispatch requests coming from the Internet to the server components that will handle them. The network administrator uses a configuration file named *inetd.conf* to define the different kinds of Internet requests to which the server will respond, and the name of the service daemon that will handle them. If a mail message comes in, for example, inetd routes it to smtpd, which is the SMTP mail daemon. Similarly, inetd routes telnet requests to telnetd, which is the telnet daemon. FTP requests go to ftpd, the FTP daemon.

To permit a UNIX/Linux system to appear in the Windows Network Neighborhood, a UNIX/Linux file server called Samba enables drag-and-drop file transfers between Windows and UNIX/Linux systems. Samba further enables UNIX/Linux users to send printed output to printers attached to a Windows system. When the Internet daemon sees a NetBIOS packet, inetd routes it to smbd, which stands for Samba daemon. There is also a NetBIOS name server daemon called nmbd. Figure 11-11 shows a sample *inetd.conf* file configured to participate in a NetBIOS network as well as respond to mail, telnet, FTP, and HTTP requests.

The Internet daemon runs with root privileges, which are the UNIX/Linux equivalent to Administrator status on a Windows server. Because inetd has root privileges, it is important to restrict access to the *inetd.conf* file so that only the network or system administrators can modify it. If a cracker should gain access to the *inetd.conf* file, system security is seriously compromised.

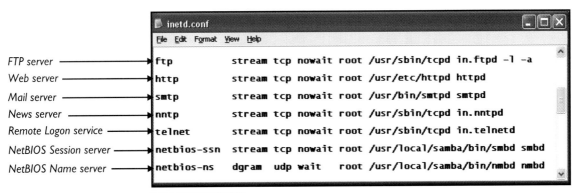

FIGURE 11-11 *The network administrator uses the inetd.conf file to identify the kinds of requests to which the Internet daemon responds, and the process handler to which the daemon passes those requests. In addition to the popular Internet services of FTP, HTTP, SMTP, NNTP, and telnet, this example includes the Samba support for NetBIOS, which enables the UNIX/Linux server to appear in the Network Neighborhood on a Windows client workstation.* ∎

Microsoft Windows Server

When a Microsoft Windows server boots up, the computer goes through a startup process that starts the Internet services. This preloading makes the services ready to respond to various kinds of Internet requests as soon as they come in.

Depending on the size and complexity of the network, the system administrator decides which Internet services to run on each server. Figure 11-12 shows the Windows Components Wizard, with which the system adminis-

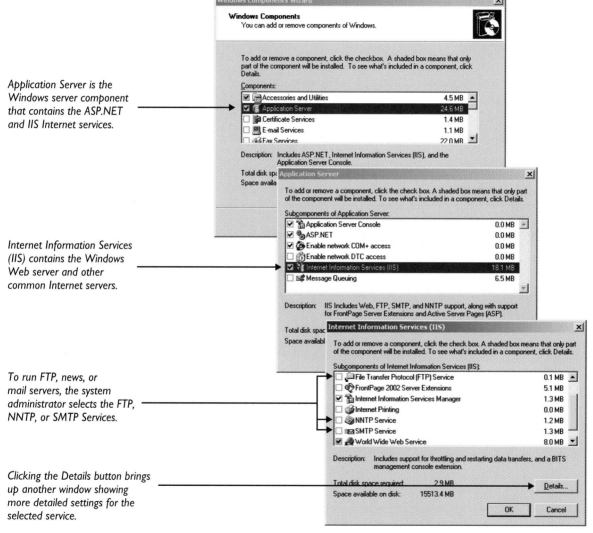

Application Server is the Windows server component that contains the ASP.NET and IIS Internet services.

Internet Information Services (IIS) contains the Windows Web server and other common Internet servers.

To run FTP, news, or mail servers, the system administrator selects the FTP, NNTP, or SMTP Services.

Clicking the Details button brings up another window showing more detailed settings for the selected service.

FIGURE 11-12 *The system administrator uses the Windows Components Wizard to select the Internet components that the server will run. The configuration shown here is dedicated to serving Web pages and running ASP.NET Web applications.* ∎

trator selects the services to run. Most versions of Windows have this wizard, although the Windows Server version has more options than the typical client computer. If you want to launch the Windows Components Wizard to see how it appears on your computer, click the Windows Start button, choose Control Panel, double-click Add or Remove Programs, and click Add/Remove Windows Components.

After selecting the Windows components that will run on a given server, the system administrator uses the Microsoft Management Console (MMC) to configure them. In Figure 11-13, the MMC displays the IIS Manager, with which the system administrator configures Internet services. Thus, the Windows operating system provides graphical property windows for settings that UNIX and Linux administrators configure manually in the *inetd.conf* file.

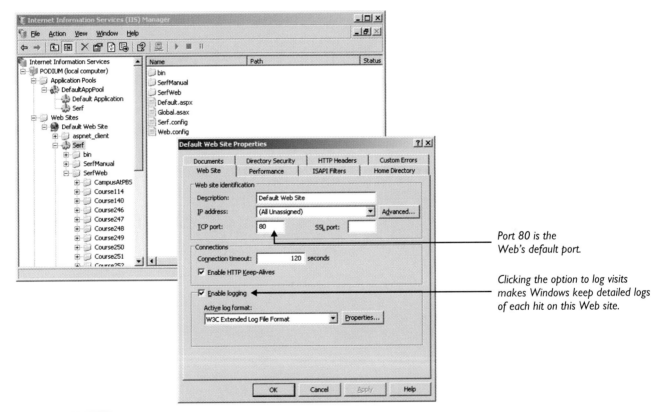

Port 80 is the Web's default port.

Clicking the option to log visits makes Windows keep detailed logs of each hit on this Web site.

FIGURE 11-13 *On a Windows server, the system administrator uses the Microsoft Management Console (MMC) to configure Windows components. You right-click any component to pop out its quick menu, and then choose Properties to bring up the settings. In this example, the system administrator is reviewing the settings for the server's default Web site.* ∎

Inspect Your Computer's Services

Try This!

The Windows operating system runs many services that listen for requests to be received on various Internet ports. Not all computers run all services. To find out what services are running on your computer, follow these steps:

1. Click the Windows Start button and choose Control Panel. When the Control Panel opens, double-click Administrative Tools.

2. When the Administrative Tools window appears, double-click Services. When the Services window appears, click the Extended tab near the bottom of the window.

3. Scroll the window up or down to see all the services running on your computer.

4. To find out what a service does, click to select it and read the service description at the left of the window. Another way to read the service description is to double-click the name of the service and see its service description in the properties window.

5. You should not make any changes to the services unless you know what you are doing. Many services depend on each other to perform interrelated tasks. If you stop one service, other services that depend on it will also stop working.

6. If you notice any suspicious processes running on your computer, particularly unsigned services that do not have names, it is possible that your computer may have been hacked. Chapter 13 discusses methods crackers use to install rogue services.

Chapter 11 Review

Chapter Summary

After reading this chapter and completing the step-by-step tutorials and Try This! exercises, you should understand the following facts about the Internet:

Understanding TCP/IP

- The Internet Architecture implements in four layers the seven separate layers of the OSI Reference Model.

- At the top of the Internet Architecture's protocol stack is the Application Layer, which encompasses OSI/RM Layers 7 and 6. It is at the Application Layer that some of the Internet's most well-known protocols reside, such as HTTP, FTP, TFTP, telnet, Gopher, SMTP, NNTP, DNS, SNMP, BOOTP, and DHCP.

- The Internet Architecture's Transport Layer encompasses OSI/RM Layers 5 and 4. It is the responsibility of the Transport Layer to divide into packets the data received from the Application Layer. Depending on the kind of session being serviced, the Transport Layer uses either TCP or UDP.

- The Internet Architecture's Internet Layer corresponds to OSI/RM Layer 3. It is the responsibility of the Internet Layer to take the packet from the Transport Layer, determine the best way to route it across the Internet, and transform it into an IP packet containing an IP header and trailer.

- The Internet Architecture's Network Access Layer corresponds to OSI/RM Layers 2 and 1, which transform the packets into a binary encoded stream of 0's and 1's for transmission over the physical network. Then the NIC transforms the 0's and 1's into the signals that get transmitted physically over the network.

- Routing is the process of determining the network path over which the packets will be sent. It is the responsibility of the Internet Protocol to determine this optimal path. Associated routing protocols include EGP, BGP, RIP, and OSPF.

- At the destination computer on the receiving end, the process of unpacking the message by processing and removing the headers added to the packets at each layer is called *demultiplexing*.

- To provide the Transport Layer with a fast way of determining which application should receive an incoming request, each packet contains a destination port number, which is a 16-bit number indicating the service that the packet is using.

- The Internet Engineering Task Force (IETF) defines the Internet Architecture protocols through a Request for Comments (RFC) process. The maturity states that an RFC moves through on its way to becoming a standard are called (1) Proposed, (2) Draft, and (3) Internet standard.

Internet Addressing

- The Internet Corporation for Assigned Names and Numbers (ICANN) is in charge of assigning IP addresses. Every IP address consists of two basic parts: the Network ID and the host ID. The Network ID always comes first, followed by the host ID. Depending on the size of the network, the Network ID occupies the first one, two, or three numbers in the IP address. The remainder of the address is the host ID.

- The five classes of Internet addresses are named A, B, C, D, and E.

- Extremely large organizations that have more than 16 million hosts receive class A Internet addresses. In a class A address, the first byte in the dotted quad IP address is the Network ID, and the other three bytes are the host ID.

- Medium to large organizations with up to 65,534 hosts get class B addresses, in which the first two bytes are the Network ID and the other two bytes are the host ID.

- Small organizations with up to 254 hosts get class C addresses, in which the first three bytes are the Network ID and the last byte is the host ID.

- Multicast groups receive class D addresses, which are set aside for multicasting. In a class D address, all four bytes are the Network ID. There is no host ID because everyone in the group receives the multicast.

- The Internet has reserved some addresses for future use. These are the class E addresses.

- The Network ID 127 is the loopback address, which is a diagnostic IP address reserved for testing purposes that redirects packets to the same computer that sent them.

- A broadcast is a message that gets sent to all of the hosts on a network. The IP broadcast address byte is 255, which sets all eight bits in the address byte to 1. Computers that do not have IP addresses typically send a 255.255.255.255 broadcast on startup to find a DHCP or BOOTP server that can respond with an IP address assignment.

- A subnet mask is a dotted quad number that enables the local network to determine whether any given IP address is internal or external to the local network.

- In order for a personal computer to communicate on a TCP/IP network, you must first configure the computer's TCP/IP settings. At a minimum, the computer must have an IP address and a subnet mask, which enable communications with hosts on the local network. To communicate with computers on a WAN, such as the Internet, the computer must also have a default gateway.

Configuring Networks for Optimum Performance

- The most basic network troubleshooting utility is the Packet Internet Groper (ping), which sends ICMP echo request packets to a destination IP address. When the destination returns the echo, the ping utility measures the response time and displays a message telling the duration of the round trip.

- The traceroute program is a networking utility that reports the path data followed as a packet winds its way over the network from the source to the destination computer. You use the traceroute utility when you need to isolate the source of a network connectivity problem.

- The netstat program, which stands for network statistics, is a utility that displays information about the connections that are open and the protocol processes that are currently running on a network host.

- The ipconfig program is a TCP/IP configuration utility that runs on computers with Windows NT/ 2000/XP/2003 or later operating systems. You use ipconfig whenever you want to inspect the current IP configuration. Furthermore, if the computer's IP settings are dynamically configured, you can use ipconfig to release, renew, or refresh the DHCP leases. winipcfg is an older version of ipconfig for Windows 95/98/Me.

- The arp program is a command-line utility that you can use to inspect the current contents of your computer's Address Resolution Protocol (ARP) table, which contains the MAC addresses of computers with which you have communicated recently. The arp utility can also delete entries or add permanent entries into the ARP table.

- A network analyzer is a tool that enables a network administrator to capture and analyze packets crossing a network. Network analyzers are sometimes called *packet sniffers*, because they can grab packets and save them for later analysis.

Internetworking Servers

- The DNS system is powered by a hierarchically distributed database called the *name space*, which is organized according to three levels: (1) the root level, (2) the top level, and (3) the second level. Each level contains DNS servers that are in charge of keeping track of the domains in the next lower level.

- When a client workstation requests to resolve a domain name, the request first goes to a name server, which is in charge of responding with the IP address that corresponds to the domain name in the request. If the name server does not already know the IP address of the domain name in the request, the name server calls upon a name resolver that goes out on the Internet and consults the necessary name servers in the DNS hierarchy.

- A proxy server is a computer that serves as an intermediary between client workstations and the external network.

- A caching server speeds access to resources by making a local copy of resources requested from the network so Web content and other kinds of documents and files can be served more quickly to subsequent users who request the same resources. Only if the date on the original document changes will the caching server download a fresh copy of the requested resource.

- A mirrored server is a computer whose data reads and writes are simultaneously executed on another computer that keeps an updated faithful copy of everything on the system from which the data are copied.

- Certificate servers issue digital certificates that network hosts use to digitally sign and encrypt messages using public-private key pairs.

- A directory server is a stand-alone computer or server component in charge of managing a database that keeps track of all the users, passwords, resources, printers, servers, e-mail addresses, phone numbers, and departmental contacts throughout an organization's network. When a user logs on to the network, the directory server provides access to those resources that the user has permission to use.

- A catalog server uses robots called *spiders* that comb through a network's files and create an index of everything that they find. When users want to find something on the network, they search this catalog. Because the search looks up the keywords in the prebuilt index, users quickly find what they seek.

- Transaction servers work behind the scenes in the business tier of the multi-tier e-commerce model to ensure that when a financial transaction occurs, all of the necessary databases get updated and related services receive the proper notifications.

Serving Internet Resources

- Web servers are the stand-alone computers or server components that respond to HTTP requests from browsers and other kinds of Internet clients, including media players and handheld devices. Because Web servers use the HTTP protocol, they are also called HTTP servers.

- The Common Gateway Interface (CGI) protocol defines the manner in which forms data, cookies, and other kinds of information in a Web request get submitted to the program or script that will process and respond to the request. The programs that respond to CGI requests are often referred to as CGI scripts.

- The Simple Mail Transfer Protocol (SMTP) defines the manner in which e-mail gets sent over the Internet.

- The Multipurpose Internet Mail Extensions (MIME) are a set of standards that specify the formatting of Internet message bodies, the media types of Internet files and message bodies, and the method for attaching files that do not consist of plain ASCII text.

- Streaming media servers use UDP, as opposed to TCP, to transfer their packets. UDP transmits more continuously by putting each output from the Application Layer directly into a packet, thereby avoiding the overhead of TCP session management.

- USENET newsgroup servers run on port 119, following the Network News Transport Protocol (NNTP).

- UNIX and Linux listen for Internet requests through a program called *inetd*, which stands for Internet daemon. The UNIX/Linux system administrator uses the *inetd.conf* file to identify the kinds of requests to which the Internet daemon will respond, and the process handler to which the daemon will pass those requests.

- Windows system administrators use the Microsoft Management Console (MMC) to configure via graphical property windows the settings that UNIX/Linux system administrators configure manually in the *inetd.conf* file.

■ Key Terms

Address Resolution Protocol (ARP) *(480)*

Application Layer *(478)*

arp *(492)*

autonomous system (AS) *(483)*

BinHex *(507)*

Bootstrap Protocol (BOOTP) *(479)*

Border Gateway Protocol (BGP) *(483)*

caching server *(499)*

catalog server *(501)*

certificate server *(500)*

CGI script *(505)*

Common Gateway Interface (CGI) *(505)*

default gateway *(482)*

demultiplexing *(481)*

direct routing *(481)*

Directory Access Protocol (DAP) *(501)*

directory server *(500)*

Domain Name System (DNS) *(479)*

Dynamic and/or Private Ports *(484)*

Dynamic Host Configuration Protocol (DHCP) *(479)*

dynamically configured router *(482)*

External Gateway Protocol (EGP) *(483)*

File Transfer Protocol (FTP) *(478)*

Gopher *(478)*

hop *(482)*

hop count *(482)*

hosts table *(497)*

Hypertext Transfer Protocol (HTTP) *(478)*

indirect routing *(481)*

inetd *(509)*

Internet address classes *(484)*

Internet Architecture *(476)*

Internet Control Message Protocol (ICMP) *(480)*

Internet daemon *(509)*

Internet Engineering Task Force (IETF) *(477)*

Internet Group Management Protocol (IGMP) *(480)*

Internet Layer *(480)*

Internet Protocol (IP) *(480)*

IP broadcast address byte *(486)*

ipconfig *(492)*

Lightweight Directory Access Protocol (LDAP) *(501)*

limited broadcast *(486)*

loopback address *(485)*

mirrored server *(500)*

multicasting *(480)*

Multipurpose Internet Mail Extensions (MIME) *(506)*

name resolver *(496)*

name server *(496)*

Net-directed broadcast *(486)*

netstat *(491)*

Network Access Layer *(480)*

network analyzer *(493)*

Network News Transfer Protocol (NNTP) *(478)*

Open Shortest Path First (OSPF) *(483)*

ping *(489)*

port number *(483)*

primary server *(496)*

protocol binding *(488)*

proxy server *(498)*

registered ports *(484)*

Request for Comments (RFC) *(477)*

Reverse Address Resolution Protocol (RARP) *(480)*

RFC maturity state *(477)*

RFC number *(477)*

root servers *(495)*

routing *(481)*

Routing Information Protocol (RIP) *(483)*

routing information table *(482)*

secondary server *(496)*

Simple Mail Transfer Protocol (SMTP) *(478)*

Simple Network Management Protocol (SNMP) *(479)*

statically configured router *(482)*

subnet-directed broadcast *(486)*

subnet mask *(487)*

telnet *(478)*

traceroute *(490)*

transaction filtering *(499)*

transaction server *(502)*

Transmission Control Protocol (TCP) *(479)*

Transport Layer *(479)*

Trivial File Transfer Protocol (TFTP) *(478)*

User Datagram Protocol (UDP) *(479)*

uuencoding *(506)*

Web root *(503)*

Web server *(502)*

Well Known Ports *(484)*

Windows Internet Naming Service (WINS) *(488)*

winipcfg *(492)*

X.500 *(501)*

Key Terms Quiz

1. The _____ implements in four layers the seven separate layers of the OSI Reference Model.

2. _____ is the process of determining the network path over which the packets will be sent.

3. At the destination computer on the receiving end, the process of unpacking the message by processing and removing the headers added to the packets at each layer is called _____.

4. The Internet Engineering Task Force (IETF) defines the Internet Architecture protocols through a(n) _____ process.

5. The Network ID 127 is the _____, which is a diagnostic IP address reserved for testing purposes that redirects packets to the same computer that sent them.

6. A(n) _____ is a dotted quad number that enables the local network to determine whether any given IP address is internal or external to the local network.

7. I am the most basic network troubleshooting utility that sends ICMP echo request packets to a destination IP address. When the destination returns the echo, I measure the response time and display a message indicating the duration of the round trip. My name is _____.

8. A(n) _____ is a computer that serves as an intermediary between client workstations and the external network.

9. The _____ protocol defines the manner in which forms data, cookies, and other kinds of information in a Web request get submitted to the program or script that will process and respond to the request.

10. The _____ are a set of standards that specify the formatting of Internet message bodies, the media types of Internet files and message bodies, and the method for attaching files that do not consist of plain ASCII text.

Multiple-Choice Quiz

1. Which layer of the Internet Architecture has the responsibility to take the packet from the Transport Layer, figure out the best way to route it across the Internet, and transform it into an IP packet containing an IP header and trailer?
   a. Application Layer
   b. Transport Layer
   c. Internet Layer
   d. Network Access Layer

2. Which part of an IP address always comes first?
   a. Host ID
   b. Loopback address
   c. Network ID
   d. Subnet mask

3. Medium to large organizations with up to 65,534 hosts get what kind of IP addresses?
   a. Class A
   b. Class B
   c. Class C
   d. Class D
   e. Class E

4. Which kind of IP address does a multicasting group receive?
   a. Class A
   b. Class B
   c. Class C
   d. Class D
   e. Class E

5. The IP broadcast address byte is:
   a. 0
   b. 127
   c. 128
   d. 255

6. Which network utility reports the path data followed as a packet winds its way over the network from the source to the destination computer?
   a. ipconfig
   b. netstat
   c. traceroute
   d. winipcfg

7. Which kind of Internetworking server speeds access to resources by making a local copy of resources requested from the network so Web content and other kinds of documents and files can be served more quickly to subsequent users who request the same resources?
   a. Caching
   b. Directory
   c. Mirrored
   d. Transaction

8. Which protocol defines the messaging rules that newsgroup servers follow on port 119?
   a. NNTP
   b. SMTP
   c. TCP
   d. UDP

9. Which protocol do streaming media servers use to avoid the overhead of transmission control session management?
   a. NNTP
   b. SMTP
   c. TCP
   d. UDP

10. What is the name of the configuration file in which UNIX and Linux system administrators manually edit the settings that identify the kinds of requests to which the Internet daemon will respond?
   a. autoexec.bat
   b. config.sys
   c. inetd.conf
   d. web.config

Essay Quiz

1. What role does the port number play in determining which service will handle an incoming message from the Internet?

2. Imagine that on port 80, a packet is coming in to its destination server. In chronological order, describe what happens at each of the four layers through which this incoming packet ascends during the demultiplexing process of the Internet Architecture. At the end of this ascent, identify the service that will ultimately handle this packet.

3. Explain the differences among class A, class B, and class C Internet addresses. Of the four bytes in the dotted quad IP addresses, which bytes in each class belong to the Network ID, and which bytes are the host ID? For what size organization is each class intended?

4. Compare the roles that name servers and name resolvers play in translating domain names into IP addresses in the Internet's DNS system.

5. Explain the role that the Internet daemon plays on UNIX and Linux operating systems.

Lab Projects

• Lab Project 11-1: Creating an Internet Address Allocation Plan

Imagine that a lot of turnover occurred in the IT division at your school or workplace, and there are shoddy records of which computers were assigned to different IP addresses. Your superior has asked you to review the situation and create a revised IP address allocation plan for your school or workplace. Use your word processor to write an essay in which you assess the current situation and present your plan for revamping the IP address allocation. In developing this plan, consider the following issues:

■ **Domain name space**   Does your organization have a class A, B, or C Internet address space? Does this class have a sufficient number of addresses to cover the number of hosts that need external IP addresses?

- **Private IP address range**   What is the specified range of private IP addresses for your organization's Internet address class? If your organization has workstations with private IP addresses, are these addresses within the specified range for your address class?

- **Proxy servers**   Consider whether your organization could use proxy servers to save costs and bolster security by hiding workstations on the internal network from hackers and crackers on the public Internet. If proxies are already in place, make sure they are configured to assign IP addresses within the correct range.

- **Static versus dynamic configuration**   How many of the network hosts need to be statically configured? Could you save time and cost by letting the others use DHCP?

- **Current IP address outline**   Create an outline that lists the current names and IP addresses of each network host within your organization. Use indentations to group the hosts under the subdomain or subnet to which they belong. For workstations that obtain temporary IP addresses via dynamic configuration, write DHCP in place of the IP address.

- **Planned IP address outline**   Create an outline that shows how you propose to revise the current IP addressing scheme. Depending on how closely this revision follows the current addressing scheme, you may be able to add a "proposed" column to the outline you created in the previous step; otherwise, you will need to create a separate outline of your planned IP addressing scheme.

If your instructor asked you to hand in the IP address allocation plan, make sure you put your name at the top of the essay, then copy it onto a disk or follow the other instructions you may have been given for submitting this assignment.

• Lab Project 11-2: Preparing a Network Troubleshooting Guide

Networking problems can cause a lot of lost time and productivity when workers are unable to perform their jobs in a transaction-oriented workplace. Imagine that out of concern over these kinds of delays, your employer has asked you to prepare a network troubleshooting guide. The purpose of this guide is twofold. First, it will consist of a section intended for end users to diagnose and report network problems that nontechnical users cannot repair on their own. Second, the guide will contain a troubleshooting procedure for IT staff and more technically inclined users, who may be able to ease the burden on the IT staff by learning how to solve simple problems on their own. Use your word processor to write an essay in which you present your network troubleshooting guide. In formulating this guide, consider the following issues:

- **Configuration problems**   Many network failures, especially with newly acquired workstations, result from incorrect PC network configuration. Include instructions for checking the PC configuration to ensure that the IP address, subnet mask, DNS server address, and gateway settings are correct.

- **Ping**   The ping utility enables users to check for basic connectivity with other network devices. Include instructions for using ping to reach strategic network addresses, such as the nearest router and DNS server. If users can reach these devices, their network segment has connectivity.

- **Problem reporting**   Provide users with a format for reporting problems they cannot solve on their own. Ask users to report whether the problem consistently occurs or is intermittent. If it is intermittent, ask whether the user can make the problem recur, and if so, ask what the user does to make the problem occur. Ask whether the problem occurs on just a single workstation or if other workstations have the same issue. If so, ask which specific workstations have the problem. Ask users to differentiate between total outages versus slow response times, and specify whether the slow periods are related to the time of day. Ask the user to describe any hardware or software changes that may have been made recently to the problematic workstation or local network segment.

- **Equipment for testing**   To troubleshoot connectivity problems, you need spare network cables with connectors of the type used on your network. Swapping a questionable cable with one you know works is an effective way to determine whether you have a failed cable. Similarly, swapping a hub with a spare that you know works is a good way to determine whether a local hub has failed. More sophisticated problems can be diagnosed by plugging in a laptop running network troubleshooting software that can identify specific problems on the local network segment.

- **Other troubleshooting guides**   Several network troubleshooting guides are available on the Internet. Use Google or Yahoo to search for the keywords "network troubleshooting guide." Perusing guidelines from the major networking vendors such as 3Com, Cabletron, and Cisco can provide ideas for techniques and strategies to include in your local troubleshooting guide.

If your instructor asked you to hand in the network troubleshooting guide, make sure you put your name at the top of the essay, then copy it onto a disk or follow the other instructions you may have been given for submitting this assignment.

chapter

12

Database Connectivity and Server-Side Scripting

"High definition is the state of being well filled with data."

—*Marshall McLuhan,*
Understanding Media

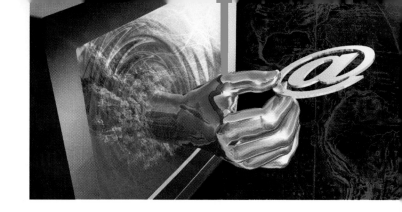

In this chapter, you will learn how to:

- Define the technologies through which Web servers provide client access to server-side databases.
- Describe the three basic kinds of databases and list the steps involved in designing a relational database.
- Define the purpose of a database connection object and an SQL statement.
- Describe how server-side scripts use loops and logical expressions to make decisions based on dynamic database content.

T HE three-tier Web application model consists of the user interface in tier 1, the business object in tier 2, and the back office databases in tier 3. The first two parts of this book concentrated on what happens in the first two tiers. Now it is time to go behind the scenes and understand what happens in the data tier. Accordingly, this chapter defines the technologies through which Web servers provide client access to server-side databases.

Databases can be flat, relational, or object-oriented. After explaining the pluses and minuses of these three kinds of databases, this chapter steps through the process of creating a relational database. You will understand how the business tier queries the database to determine the dynamic content that the user sees onscreen. One of the greatest strengths of a data-driven Web site is its extensibility; you will understand how a properly designed relational database enables you to key new data structures to preexisting data, thereby enabling the business tier to handle new processes as the site expands its service offerings.

The business tier uses server-side programs or scripts to interact with the data tier. This chapter describes how these programs connect to the database, issue commands to query or update the data, and use computer logic to make decisions based on the contents of the database. Through interactions with end users in the user interface tier, the business tier conducts transactions that update databases in the data tier. Because the database content is dynamic, so are the screens that the business tier presents to the users based on the status of their data records. By the end of this chapter, you will understand how databases power the Internet's data-driven Web sites.

Providing Web Access to Server-Side Databases

Because the Web uses the HTTP protocol, Web sites that provide access to server-side databases are sometimes called HTTP gateways. These gateways enable the business object or script to process forms data received from the user interface tier. While processing this data, the business object opens connections to the appropriate back-end databases in the data tier. Through these connections, the business object can retrieve, update, delete, or insert information in the database.

Common Gateway Interface (CGI)

As you learned in the previous chapter, the first HTTP gateway protocol was the **common gateway interface (CGI)**, which defines the manner in which forms data, cookies, and other kinds of information in a Web request get submitted to the program or script that processes and responds to the request. Any programming language that runs on the server can process the data and respond to the request. The form tag's action parameter tells the server which program to run by providing the HTTP address of the CGI script.

The National Center for Supercomputing Applications (NCSA) invented CGI back in 1993 for use on a UNIX-based Web server, HTTPd, which stands for HTTP daemon. On the server, CGI scripts typically reside in the *cgi-bin* directory, so named because the scripts were binary files. When HTTPd received a request addressed to a CGI script, it stored the forms data in UNIX shell environment variables and launched the CGI program as a separate process. After the script processed the request, HTTPd returned the CGI program's response to the user.

In the beginning, many developers wrote CGI programs in **Perl**, which is a scripting language invented by Larry Wall for people who need to write relatively short programs. More technically inclined programmers write CGI scripts in C, which is the programming language used to develop many popular applications, including Perl. Because CGI is language neutral, however, you can write CGI scripts in any programming language. You can even write CGI scripts in the **Bourne shell language**, which is the original scripting language of the UNIX shell.

The NCSA stopped work on the HTTPd server in 1998, but the code lives on in Apache, which is the most popular Web server on UNIX and Linux systems. For more information about Apache projects, go to www.apache.org.

Server Application Programming Interfaces (SAPIs)

A **Server Application Programming Interface (SAPI)** is a collection of software components used by the business tier to obtain, process, and respond to forms data submitted when end users interact with the site and make requests through the user interface tier. Instead of running separate CGI scripts to process the forms data, SAPI has integrated libraries of precompiled code containing the software components out of which the Web developer creates the business object. SAPI uses multithreading to enable these components to load once and process multiple user requests, as opposed to CGI scripts, which run out of process, meaning that each incoming request launches a separate code instance. By running in process, SAPI enables the server to handle a higher number of simultaneous users.

Microsoft's brand of SAPI is called **Internet SAPI (ISAPI)**, and Netscape's is called **Netscape SAPI (NSAPI)**. Both brands use dynamic link libraries (DLLs) to contain the precompiled software components that SAPI comprises. Microsoft continues to develop ISAPI, which is a key component of its Web server architecture. Netscape has discontinued work on NSAPI.

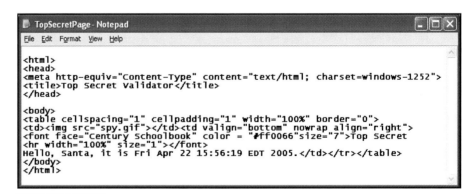

```
TopSecretPage.asp - Notepad
File  Edit  Format  View  Help
<% @language=jscript %>
<html>

<head>
<meta http-equiv="Content-Type" content="text/html; charset=windows-1252">
<title>Top Secret Validator</title>
</head>

<body>
<%
//Get the name and password submitted by the login form
sUsername = Request.Form("username");
sPassword = Request.Form("password");
//Create the database connection object
connection = Server.CreateObject("ADODB.Connection");
connection.mode = 1; //read only mode
sConnectionString = "Provider=Microsoft.Jet.OLEDB.4.0;"
    + "Data Source=" + Server.MapPath("/website/_private/TopSecret.mdb");
connection.open(sConnectionString);
//create the sql query
sQuery = "SELECT * FROM Users WHERE UserName = '" + sUsername
    + "' AND Password = '" + sPassword + "'";
//execute the query and get its results into a resultset
rsResults = connection.Execute(sQuery);
if (rsResults.EOF)
{
    //destroy any validation cookie
    Response.Cookies("Validation") = "-1";
    //send the user back to the login screen
    Response.Redirect("Login.html");
}
else
{
    sFirstName = rsResults("FirstName");
    sLastName = rsResults("LastName");
    sUserID = rsResults("UserID");
    //Set the validation cookie
    Response.Cookies("Validation") = sUserID;
    //Say hello to the newly logged on user inside a table
    //that displays the top secret logo and page heading
    sPrint = "<table cellspacing=\"1\" cellpadding=\"1\""
        + " width=\"100%\" border=\"0\">";
    Response.Write(sPrint);
    sPrint = "<td><img src=\"spy.gif\"></td>";
    Response.Write(sPrint);
    sPrint = "<td valign=\"bottom\" nowrap align=\"right\">"
        + "<font face=\"Century Schoolbook\" color = \"#ff0066\""
        + " size=\"7\">Top Secret<hr width=\"100%\" size=\"1\"></font>";
    Response.Write(sPrint);
    sPrint = "Hello, " + sFirstName + ", it is ";
    dateNow = new Date();
    sPrint += dateNow.toString() + ".</td></tr></table>";
    Response.Write(sPrint);
}
connection.close();
%>
</body>
</html>
```

< % is the script start tag.

% > is the script stop tag.

FIGURE 12-1 *This source code of an ASP page contains a script that will greet an authenticated user by name. The script is the code between the <% script start and %> script stop tags. Compare this code to Figures 12-2 and 12-3.* ■

Active Server Pages (ASP)

Active Server Pages (ASP) is a Microsoft ISAPI technology that enables Web developers to embed on a Web page server-side scripts written in either the JScript or VBScript programming languages. End users never see the scripts, which the server executes when the user accesses the page. Instead of seeing an embedded script, end users view the results of the script's execution. You can understand this by comparing Figures 12-1, 12-2, and 12-3. Figure 12-1 shows the code of an ASP page programmed to greet users when they log in or deny access to unauthorized users. Figure 12-2 shows the HTML source code that the ASP code generates when an authenticated user logs on, and Figure 12-3 shows what the user sees onscreen. If the user tries to see the script via the browser's View | Source option, the user sees only the HTML source code shown in Figure 12-2, which is the result of running the script. Thus, ASP pages provide a way for developers to include scripts on a Web page without the user seeing their code.

```
TopSecretPage - Notepad
File  Edit  Format  View  Help
<html>
<head>
<meta http-equiv="Content-Type" content="text/html; charset=windows-1252">
<title>Top Secret Validator</title>
</head>

<body>
<table cellspacing="1" cellpadding="1" width="100%" border="0">
<td><img src="spy.gif"></td><td valign="bottom" nowrap align="right">
<font face="Century Schoolbook" color = "#ff0066"size="7">Top Secret
<hr width="100%" size="1"></font>
Hello, Santa, it is Fri Apr 22 15:56:19 EDT 2005.</td></tr></table>
</body>
</html>
```

FIGURE 12-2 *This is the HTML code that the server returns when an authenticated user visits the page illustrated in Figure 12-1. Notice how the result of running the script appears in place of the script's source code. Thus, end users never see the server-side code on an Active Server Page.* ■

FIGURE 12-3 *The browser displays this screen when an authenticated user logs on and the Active Server Page illustrated in Figure 12-1 responds. Notice how the script displays the user's name onscreen. If the user pulls down the browser's View menu and chooses Source, the browser displays the HTML code shown in Figure 12-2. Thus, end users never see the server-side code of the ASP page in Figure 12-1.* ■

Java Servlets and Java Server Pages (JSP)

Sun's Java is a hot technology in spite of the legal battles waged between Sun and Microsoft regarding whether Microsoft has the right to create its own version of Java, and whether Microsoft must include the Java Virtual Machine (JVM) as part of Windows. As this book goes to press, the understanding is that yes, Microsoft can create its own version of Java, and yes, Microsoft will include Sun's Java Virtual Machine (JVM) in future versions of Windows. As a developer, I believe this agreement is beneficial for both sides.

Java is an object-oriented programming language that developers can use to create almost any kind of software. Java code compiles into an intermediary language that executes on any platform running the JVM. Versions of the JVM exist for practically every operating system, including UNIX, Linux, Macintosh, and Windows. Thus, Java code is machine independent.

Earlier in this book, you learned how Java applets can download as part of a Web page and execute on the client in the browser window. On the server side, the most well-known uses of Java are for creating Java servlets and Java Server Pages. A **servlet** is a Java applet that runs on the server instead of in the browser; hence the name, *servlet*. The servlet runs in the JVM under a multithreaded environment that can listen for Internet requests to come in and serve multiple users from the same instance of the code.

Java Server Pages (JSP) is an active Web page technology that is Sun's equivalent to Microsoft's ASP. In the midst of the page, the Web developer can write Java code to be run when a user accesses the page. At runtime, when a user hits the JSP, the server executes the code and sends the user the resulting page. JSP is therefore similar to ASP, although JSP runs in the JVM, while ASP runs in Microsoft's ISAPI.

PHP Hypertext Preprocessor (PHP)

The **PHP Hypertext Preprocessor (PHP)** is another active page technology that enables the Web developer to include code on the page that will run on the server, which executes the code before sending the completed page to the user. The command syntax is like that of C and Perl. As an open source Apache project, PHP runs primarily with Apache on UNIX and Linux servers, although versions of PHP are also available for Windows. For more on PHP, go to us3.php.net.

ColdFusion

A product of Macromedia, **ColdFusion** is an active scripting technology that uses its own proprietary scripting language, the ColdFusion Markup Language. Web developers can include in their HTML pages ColdFusion tags, which begin with the letters *CF* for ColdFusion. ColdFusion pages have the filename extension *.cfm*, which stands for ColdFusion markup. When a Web server that is running ColdFusion encounters a *.cfm* page, the server executes the Cold Fusion tags and replaces them with the output generated by the server in executing that code. Thus, end users never see the CF tags, just as PHP, JSP, and ASP pages strip the server-side script before presenting the page to the user. Macromedia markets ColdFusion components for Web servers running on Windows, UNIX, Linux, Macintosh, HP, and IBM operating systems. For more on ColdFusion, go to www.macromedia.com/software/coldfusion.

ASP.NET

Microsoft's **ASP.NET** is much more than a new version of ASP. Besides letting you include code on a Web page, ASP.NET lets you create code behind the Web page, on so-called *code-behind pages*. These code-behind pages can be part of complete applications with which the user interacts from the browser window, which becomes the Web application's display surface. From my personal experience developing the Serf instructional management system in ASP.NET, I can attest to the .NET framework's elegance and power. Serf consists of several dozen code-behind pages and C# classes that the Serf name space comprises. More information about Serf is at www.serfsoft.com.

ASP continues to be a popular choice for developers who are not quite ready to dive into ASP.NET. My *Advanced Web Design* textbook (ISBN 0-07-256594-2) contains tutorials in both ASP and ASP.NET, offering students a choice of where to jump in. When compared to the other SAPI technologies described in this chapter, however, ASP is more like JSP, PHP, and ColdFusion. The ASP.NET environment is a totally new platform, written from the ground up and offering a choice of programming languages including VBScript, JScript, C++, C#, and J#, which is Microsoft's version of Java. The source code compiles into the Microsoft Intermediate Language (MSIL) that executes in the common language runtime (CLR), which is the execution layer of the .NET framework. For more on the .NET framework, go to www.microsoft.com/net.

Understanding Databases

The three basic kinds of databases are called (1) flat file, (2) relational, and (3) object-oriented. A **flat file database** keeps all of the records in a single file, in which the data elements are separated by a break character such as a comma or a tab. The terms **comma-delimited data** or **tab-delimited data** refer to data stored in this manner. Flat file databases typically contain just one **data table**, which is a database structure that organizes the data into rows and columns. Each row contains one record, and the columns contain the data fields that the record comprises. An example of a flat file database appears in Figure 12-4, which contains the data table illustrated in Figure 12-5. By comparing these two figures, you can see how the commas in the file delimit the fields in the data table.

A **relational database** is a data structure that comprises multiple tables containing primary key columns through which the records in one table can relate (i.e., key) to the data in another table. A data table's **primary key** is a column in which every entry is unique—for example, the UserID column that appears in Figure 12-5. Notice how every user has a unique UserID. In a relational database, other tables can refer to those users by their unique ID. Figure 12-6 shows how a log table, for example, can keep track of the history of each user's visits to the site. In the log table, the UserID column is called a **foreign key**, which is a data field that relates the record to the table in which that same column occurs as a primary key. The color-coding in Figure 12-6 helps you see this relationship, from which the term

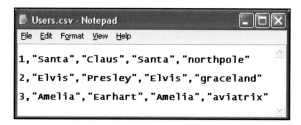

FIGURE 12-4 *A flat file database contains data records typically delimited by commas or tab characters. The database illustrated here consists of comma-delimited data. Compare this database to Figure 12-5, which shows the data table in a columnar format, which is how a script interprets it.* ■

Users : Table

UserID	FirstName	LastName	UserName	Password
1	Santa	Claus	Santa	northpole
2	Elvis	Presley	Elvis	graceland
3	Amelia	Earhart	Amelia	aviatrix

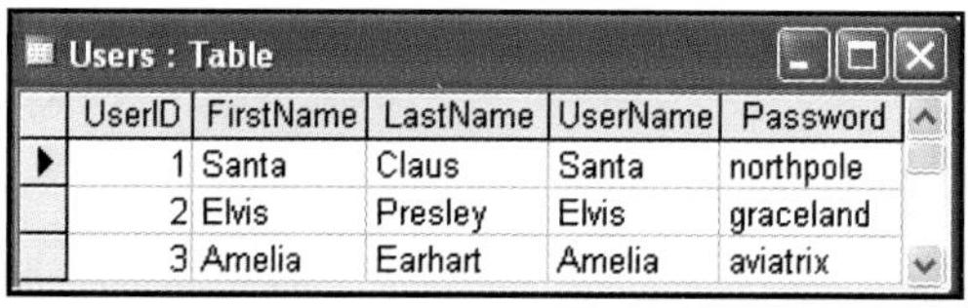

FIGURE 12-5 *In a data table, each row is called a record, and each column contains one of the data fields in that record. In this example, the table contains the UserIDs, names, and passwords of the people who are permitted to visit a Web site. Compare this table to Figure 12-4, which shows this table in a flat file database.* ■

Users : Table

UserID	FirstName	LastName	UserName	Password
1	Santa	Claus	Santa	northpole
2	Elvis	Presley	Elvis	graceland
3	Amelia	Earhart	Amelia	aviatrix

Log : Table

VisitID	Timestamp	UserID
1	4/1/2005 10:10:07 AM	2
2	4/1/2005 10:11:57 AM	1
3	4/1/2005 10:12:30 AM	3
4	4/1/2005 10:12:45 AM	2
5	4/1/2005 10:13:11 AM	3
6	4/1/2005 10:14:05 AM	3
7	4/1/2005 10:14:33 AM	1
8	4/1/2005 10:15:47 AM	1
9	4/1/2005 10:16:12 AM	3
10	4/1/2005 10:16:28 AM	2

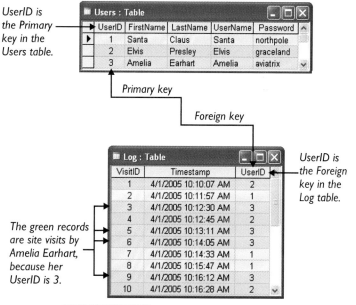

FIGURE 12-6 *In a relational database, the primary key of one table relates its data to the records in another table containing a foreign key column consisting of values from the first table's primary key column. In this example, study the color-coding to see how the log table keeps track of the dates and times when people in the Users table visited the site.* ■

relational database arises. The technical term for the kind of software that powers this kind of database is RDBMS, which stands for **relational database management system (RDBMS)**.

The third and final kind of database is an **object-oriented database**, in which programmers writing code in object-oriented languages can create complex data structures in which one data type can build upon, or inherit, properties from another. The technical term for this kind of database is **object-oriented database management system (ODBMS)**. It is beyond the scope of this book to teach object-oriented programming. This chapter teaches you how to design a relational database, which is the most popular kind of database. By studying this process, you will understand that the simple concept of a key enables the creation of data structures that are infinitely expandable and thereby capable of powering new features as your enterprise grows and offers new services to your users.

Designing a Relational Database

I use an eight-step process to design a relational database. You begin by defining the purpose of the database and creating the data tables. Then you specify the data columns that will contain the data. After defining the relationships among the primary and foreign key columns, you take an imaginary walk through your database. You think about how a typical user will navigate through your application. Then you write a little essay, called a *walkthrough*, describing what will happen in the database as the user walks through the Web site. Writing such an essay helps ensure you have not omitted any essential tables or fields in the design of the database. Considering how you will retrieve the data, make decisions about it, and report results helps ensure that you have included all of the necessary keys that relate the data tables to each other. If a table contains data that cannot be retrieved in the context you need, you can supply the missing foreign key. If a table of items purchased, for example, does not identify the buyer who purchased them, you can add a buyerID column as a foreign key that you can use to indicate who made the purchase. The steps you follow in creating a database in this manner are as follows:

1. Write a paragraph describing the purpose of the database.

2. Make a list of the tables that the database will comprise.

3. List the fields (i.e., data columns) each table will comprise.

4. Indicate the kind of data (i.e., data type) that each column will hold.

5. Indicate which data columns are primary keys. Remember that a primary key field cannot contain any duplicate values; each value in a primary key column must be unique.

6. Indicate which data columns are foreign keys and state the name of the table and data column in which each foreign key is a primary key.

7. Write a walkthrough to make sure you haven't missed something important. Describe how the typical user will enter your site and

navigate its pages. State what will happen in the database as the user submits information. Explain how the data will be used onscreen to create pages whose contents vary depending on the contents of the database. If anything is absent from your database design, writing a complete walkthrough helps you identify the missing elements.

8. If you have any data tables with no keys, ask yourself whether the data really stands alone. If not, add the necessary foreign key column to key the data to the primary key column of the data table to which it relates.

Normalizing a Database

Some database designs are more efficient than others. If a design is inefficient, the database requires more computing resources to process. This slows down the Web site, and the delays frustrate users.

In an efficient design, each table plays one role in the database. In an inefficient design, on the other hand, a table takes on too many roles. **Normalization** is the process of separating a large table fulfilling multiple roles into smaller tables that increase efficiency by serving smaller roles that relate through keys to other tables in the database. A database that has not been normalized has wide tables (i.e., more columns) that require more time to query, sort, and retrieve records. A normalized database contains data tables that are narrower (i.e., fewer columns) and serve efficiently a single purpose that, when related through keys to other tables, enable the database to accomplish its goal more quickly.

Indexing a Database

If a lot of users begin interacting with a database-driven Web site, the data tables can grow quite large. The larger your tables get, the more time it takes the server to search them and return the results of your queries. As the data tables grow in size, queries take longer because the computer has more data to search.

To increase database performance, you can create indexes. An **index** is a database column or collection of columns that the database engine uses to keep the data presorted in the order in which you plan to query it. In the Users table, for example, if you plan to use queries that look up users alphabetically, you create a two-column index based on last name, first name. I can attest from first-hand experience that the performance boost gained from indexing is phenomenal.

Database Design Principles

When designing a database, keep the following principles in mind:

1. Each table should have a column containing a unique row ID number. This enables the column to serve as the table's primary key.

2. A table should store data for a single type of entity. Attempting to store too many different kinds of information in a single table can slow down the database and make it inefficient.

3. A table should avoid columns that are allowed to contain null values. Although you may use null values in isolated cases, they require special handling in the database and should be avoided if possible. If you must have empty values, consider using an empty string, for example, instead of a null value. If you must have null values in a data column, put that column in a separate table so the design of the main table can be simple.

4. A table should not have repeating values. If you need to keep a list of values for one of the items in a table, create another table to hold the list and link it to the item's primary key.

5. A field should have the same meaning in each row of a table. If the meaning of the data column is not consistent, you should create another table to encode the data with a different meaning.

6. Multiple instances of an entity should not be represented as multiple columns. In the Log table, for example, it would be a mistake to limit the number of visits by creating data columns to hold each hit. Suppose you created five columns called Visit1, Visit2, Visit3, Visit4, and Visit5. What if someone wanted to visit the site a sixth time? Such a design accounts for only five visits.

Try This!

Creating a TopSecret Database

In this exercise, you will use Microsoft Access to create a database named TopSecret, which will consist of the user names and passwords of users permitted to access the secret pages at your Web site. Because everyone else will be denied access, the pages will be top secret—hence the name of the database. To create the TopSecret database, follow these steps:

1. When you create a database for use at a Web site, you put it in a separate folder that is not in Web space to prevent unauthorized users from downloading the database. Use the Windows Explorer or My Computer to create a folder named *TopSecret* that is not in Web space. In this example, create the *TopSecret* folder on the root of your hard drive so that its location will be *c:\TopSecret*.

2. Start Microsoft Access, pull down its File menu, and choose the option to create a new blank database. When the File New Database dialog appears, name the database *TopSecret.mdb*, and save it in your *TopSecret* folder. Thus, the complete path/filename of your database is *c:\TopSecret\TopSecret.mdb*.

3. Double-click the option to create a table in Design view. When the Table window opens, create the following four fields. After you type each Field Name, press the Tab key, and a pull-down menu appears in the Data Type column. Pull down that menu and make the field's data type match the ones illustrated here. Also type the following descriptions into each field's description field:

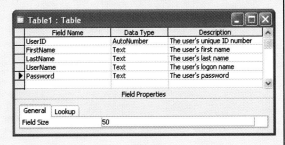

Try This!
continued

4. Pull down the File menu and choose Save; when the Save dialog appears, name the table Users. When Access asks if you want a primary key, say yes. Access will make UserID the primary key, because the autonumber data type makes each user have a unique UserID.

5. Close the table by clicking its close icon ☒. Then double-click the name of the table to open it in data entry mode. Type the following records into the table. You may substitute names of your own for the fictitious entries shown here. At any time, you can repeat this step to modify, add, or delete users from the table. Begin by typing the first name of the first user; Access will populate the UserID column automatically, since it is an autonumber:

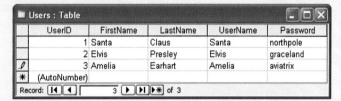

	UserID	FirstName	LastName	UserName	Password
	1	Santa	Claus	Santa	northpole
	2	Elvis	Presley	Elvis	graceland
	3	Amelia	Earhart	Amelia	aviatrix
	(AutoNumber)				

6. This completes the creation of the Users table. Click its close icon to close it, and say yes when Access asks if you want to save the data you entered in the previous step. You will use this table again in the next Try This! exercise later in this chapter.

Note: Whenever you name a database, data table, or data field, you should avoid typing spaces or special characters. Out on the Web, situations can arise in which spaces and special characters cause problems in data names and filenames. It is best to avoid these problems by forming the habit of avoiding spaces and special characters when naming databases, data tables, and data fields.

Accessing Server-Side Databases

Figure 12-7 shows the three-tier Web application model, in which the middle tier business object accesses databases in the data tier through server-

The business tier establishes connections with databases in the data tier.

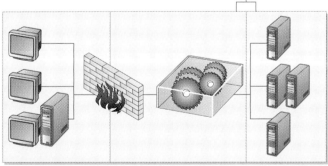

Tier 1: User interface   Tier 2: Business logic   Tier 3: Back office
databases

FIGURE 12-7 *The business tier communicates with the data tier by establishing database connections. Depending upon the brand of database and server architecture, these connections may follow OCBC, JDBC, OLE DB, or XML Web Service protocols.* ▪

side programs or scripts that open connections to the databases and issue commands to retrieve or manipulate the data. As you might expect, standard protocols exist for making database connections and issuing commands that can retrieve or manipulate the data.

Connectivity Options

The major brands of databases include Microsoft SQL Server, Oracle 9i, Borland Interbase, IBM DB2, and iPlanet Application Server. To make these database products work across a broad range of application development environments and scripting languages, the computer industry has developed standards defining alternate means for connecting with databases. When creating a data-driven application, the Web developer chooses the connection method that is most appropriate for the task at hand. The two primary connection options are:

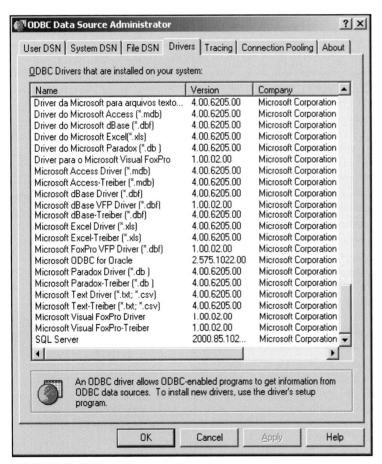

FIGURE 12-8 *Due to the popularity and industry-wide acceptance of the open database connectivity (ODBC) standard, an ODBC driver exists for almost every brand of database. Pictured here are the ODBC drivers that come preinstalled for use with Windows 2003 Server. Notice how Microsoft provides a driver for Oracle, which is the largest competitor to Microsoft's SQL Server enterprise database product.* ■

- **ODBC** **Open database connectivity (ODBC)** is a standard database access method created by Microsoft based on the Call-Level Interface (CLI) specifications from the X/Open and ISO/IEC database APIs. The goal is to make it possible for any application to access any database, regardless of its vendor. ODBC accomplishes this goal through database drivers that translate queries and commands issued by the application into a format that the database can process. An ODBC driver exists for almost every brand of relational database. Figure 12-8 shows the ODBC Data Source Administrator controls that a Windows server administrator uses to configure a company's ODBC driver for use with a data source name (DSN), through which an application will access the data.

- **JDBC** Developed by JavaSoft for Sun Microsystems, **Java database connectivity (JDBC)** enables Java programs to communicate with SQL-based database systems. A JDBC-ODBC bridge can translate JCBC calls into ODBC calls, but Java developers are encouraged to use native JDBC drivers that communicate directly with the database, thereby avoiding the overhead introduced by the bridge.

OLE DB Data Sources

A vast amount of information exists outside the traditional DBMS data sources accessed through ODBC and JDBC connections. Microsoft invented a data source technology called **object linking and embedding database (OLE DB)** to enable Windows applications to open a wide variety of connections to data stored not only in ODBC data sources, but also in file systems, media catalogs, e-mail, spreadsheets, active directories, project management tools, and XML files. Figure 12-9 shows the wide range of data source connections that OLE DB enables. Through these connections, the application can issue queries as if the data source were a database. Hence the name, OLE DB.

ActiveX Data Objects (ADO)

On the Windows operating system, **ActiveX Data Objects (ADO)** is an API that enables business objects to make connections and issue commands against many different kinds of data sources. Because Windows is a prevalent operating system, I am going to show you examples of ADO programming to give you an idea of what it is like to create a server-side script.

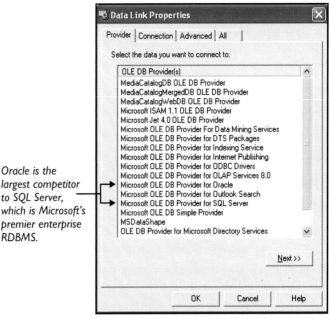

Oracle is the largest competitor to SQL Server, which is Microsoft's premier enterprise RDBMS.

FIGURE 12-9 *The business tier communicates with the data tier by establishing database connections. Depending upon the brand of database and server architecture, these connections may follow OCBC, JDBC, OLE DB, or XML Web Service protocols. ∎*

Creating an ADO Connection Object

True to its name, the **connection object** is the ADO component that connects you to the database. Once you have the connection open, you can execute queries that insert, update, retrieve, or delete records from the database. The following code opens the connection in the two popular ASP programming languages, namely, JScript and VBScript.

JScript version

```
connection = Server.CreateObject("ADODB.Connection");
connection.mode = 3;  //read-write mode
sConnectionString = "Provider=Microsoft.Jet.OLEDB.4.0;"
    + "Data Source=YourDrive:/YourFolder/YourDatabase.mdb";
connection.Open(sConnectionString);
```

The name of your folder and your database file go here.

VBScript version

```
connection = Server.CreateObject("ADODB.Connection")
connection.mode = 3  //read-write mode
sConnectionString = "Provider=Microsoft.Jet.OLEDB.4.0;"_
    & "Data Source=YourDrive:/YourFolder/YourDatabase.mdb"
connection.Open(sConnectionString)
```

As you can see, the JScript and VBScript coding is very similar because both languages use the same ADO components, which many other Microsoft programming languages can also use. The connection object is very powerful, because you can write connection strings to open almost any kind of data source from any database vendor. Here are some examples of different kinds of connection strings:

Open an Access database on a local drive:

```
Provider=Microsoft.Jet.OLEDB.4.0;Data Source=C:/YourFolder/YourDatabase.mdb
```

Open an SQL Server database:

```
server=YourServerName;database=YourDatabaseName;uid=userid;pwd=password
```

Open an Oracle database:

```
Provider=msdaora;Data Source=YourOracleServer;USER ID=userid;PASSWORD=password
```

Open an Excel spreadsheet on a local drive:

```
Provider=Microsoft.Jet.OLEDB.4.0;Data Source=C:/YourFolder/YourExcel.xls
```

Access plaintext files in a local folder:

```
Provider=Microsoft.Jet.OLEDB.4.0;Data Source=c:/YourFolder/;Extended
Properties="text;HDR=Yes;FMT=Delimited"
```

Open a data store from a data source name (DSN):

```
DSN=yourDSN;uid=userid;pwd=password
```

Using the Structured Query Language (SQL)

Once you have the ADO connection established, you can issue SQL commands against the database. The **Structured Query Language (SQL)** is an international standard that defines the syntax for issuing commands that can query, update, insert, or delete records in a database. SQL is a rich language that contains dozens of commands. While it is beyond the purpose of this book to teach SQL commands, you can get a feeling for how SQL works by studying the functions of the SELECT command, which you use to retrieve records from a data table. The simplest form of the SELECT statement is

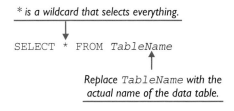

Instead of using * to select everything, you can specify the names of the columns you want to retrieve. To select a single column, the command syntax is

```
SELECT ColumnName FROM TableName
```

Replace *ColumnName* with the name of the column you want to retrieve.

Replace *TableName* with the name of the data table containing that column.

To select more than one specific column, you type a comma-separated list of the names of the columns you want to retrieve, as in:

There is no limit to the number of columns you can specify; to add another column, type a comma here followed by the name of the column.

```
SELECT ColumnName1, ColumnName2, ColumnName3 FROM TableName
```

Replace *ColumnName1, ColumnName2, and ColumnName3* with the names of the columns you want to retrieve.

Unless you specify otherwise, SQL commands return results in the order in which they were stored in the database. To change the order in which the results are returned, you can add an ORDER BY clause to the SELECT command. The syntax is

```
SELECT * FROM TableName ORDER BY ColumnName
```

You can replace the * with a comma-separated list of specific column names.

Replace *ColumnName* with the name of the column that will control the ordering.

If more than one column is involved in the ordering, you can specify a comma-separated list of columns to order by. The sorting will be based on the columns you specify, with the leftmost column sorted first. The syntax is

Replace *ColumnName1* with the name of the column you want sorted first.

Replace *ColumnName3* by the name of the column you want sorted third.

```
SELECT * FROM TableName ORDER BY ColumnName1, ColumnName2, ColumnName3
```

ColumnName2 is the name of the column that will be sorted.

There is no limit to the number of columns you can specify; to add another column, type a comma here followed by the name of the column.

One of the most important features of a database is its ability to find information. In the SQL language, this kind of searching is provided by the WHERE clause. By filtering out unwanted information, the WHERE clause lets you focus on the data you are looking for. It is easy to add a WHERE clause to the SELECT statement. The syntax is

```
SELECT * FROM TableName WHERE ColumnName = DataValue
```

The WHERE clause acts like a filter that lets you focus on the data you are looking for.

You can replace the = with other operators including < for less than, > for greater than, and <> for not equal.

In the Try This! exercise that follows, you encounter a situation where you need to make a WHERE clause to handle more than one condition. You can accomplish that with an AND, which you use to specify another condition for the search. The syntax is

```
SELECT * FROM TableName WHERE ColumnName = DataValue AND ColumnName2 = DataValue2
```

Besides AND, you can use OR and AND NOT and OR NOT.

Try This!

Selecting TopSecret Users

In the first Try This! exercise earlier in this chapter, you created the TopSecret database consisting of the names of users who will be permitted to access your top secret pages. The TopSecret database is a good place to practice creating SQL queries. Follow these steps:

1. Start Microsoft Access. Pull down the File menu and open the TopSecret database containing the data you entered in the Try This! exercise earlier in this chapter.

2. Under Objects, click Queries, or pull down the View menu and choose Database Objects | Queries.

3. Double-click the option to Create query in Design view. The Show Table window opens.

4. You do not need to use the Show Table window because you will be typing the SQL command manually. Close the Show Table window.

5. Pull down the View menu and choose SQL view; the SQL view appears with a query partially started.

6. Replace the partially started query with the command you want to practice. In this example, type the query:

```
SELECT * FROM Users ORDER BY LastName, FirstName
```

7. Click the run icon to execute the query; the results of issuing the query appear onscreen.

8. Pull down the View menu and choose SQL view again. Modify the query to read as follows:

```
SELECT * FROM Users where UserName = 'Santa' AND Password = 'northpole'
```

9. Click the run icon to execute the query; the results of issuing the modified query appear onscreen. If a user in your table is named Santa and has the password northpole, that user's data appears onscreen. If no user was listed under that name and password, no data would be returned. You will use that strategy later in this chapter's final Try This! exercise, in which you will create a script that will deny access to users who do not appear in this table.

10. Repeat the last two steps to practice this process of typing an SQL command and viewing the results. Here are some additional queries you can try:

```
SELECT LastName, FirstName FROM Users where UserID < 3
SELECT * from Users where UserName = 'anybody' and password = 'anything'
```

Creating Data-Driven Web Pages

A **data-driven Web page** is an HTML document in which part or all of the content derives from or depends on records or relationships in one or more databases. In the typical ASP page, the Web developer includes a server-side script in the HTML body of a page. At runtime, the server executes the script, which uses the ADO connection object to open a database connection. Through this connection, the script executes SQL statements that query the database.

The queries return data in a set of records called a **recordset**. The script reads the data in the recordset. Through computer logic known as IF-THEN statements, the script makes decisions based on the content of the data. If a user's bank account contains a negative balance, for example, the script can deny a pending sale and respond to the user with a message explaining the account is overdrawn. At runtime, when the user accesses the ASP page, the server replaces the script with the result of the script's execution. If the user inspects the source code of the page via the browser's View | Source menu, the user will see the HTML code of the insufficient funds message in place of the JScript or VBScript code that created the message.

Without getting overly technical, the last few pages of this chapter walk you through some ASP code that reads data from a recordset and makes decisions based on the status of this data. In the concluding Try This! exercise, you have the opportunity to try this code yourself.

Reading Data from a Recordset

The ADO recordset object contains methods that enable a script to move through its contents, record by record, and obtain information to display directly onscreen or to use in making decisions that result in deciding what to display onscreen. The following script, for example, reads the names of registered users from a Users table and prints the names onscreen. The script contains documentation explaining how it works. In an ASP script, each line of documentation begins with the symbol //. Reading this documentation gives you a sense of the underlying concepts that programmers use in creating these kinds of scripts. If you want to learn more about ASP scripting, my textbook *Advanced Web Design* teaches JScript and VBScript in more detail.

JScript version

```
//Create and open the database connection
connection = Server.CreateObject("ADODB.Connection");
connection.mode = 1; //read only mode
sConnectionString = "Provider=Microsoft.Jet.OLEDB.4.0;"
    + "Data Source=c:/TopSecret/TopSecret.mdb";
connection.Open(sConnectionString);
//Create and execute the SQL query
sQuery = "SELECT * FROM Users ORDER BY LastName, FirstName";
rsResults = connection.Execute(sQuery);
//While the recordset is not (!) at the end of file (EOF)
while (! rsResults.EOF)
```

```
{
    sFirstName = rsResults("FirstName");
    sLastName = rsResults("LastName");
    Response.Write(sLastName + ", " + sFirstName + "<br>");
    //Move to the next record in the recordset
    rsResults.MoveNext;
}
connection.Close();
%>
```

VBScript version

```
//Create and open the database connection
Set connection = Server.CreateObject("ADODB.Connection")
connection.mode = 1 //read only mode
sConnectionString = "Provider=Microsoft.Jet.OLEDB.4.0;" _
    & "Data Source=c:/TopSecret/TopSecret.mdb"
connection.Open(sConnectionString)
//Create and execute the SQL query
sQuery = "SELECT * FROM Users ORDER BY LastName, FirstName"
Set rsResults = connection.Execute(sQuery)
//While the recordset is not at the end of file (EOF)
Do Until rsResults.EOF
    sFirstName = rsResults("FirstName")
    sLastName = rsResults("LastName")
    Response.Write(sLastName & ", " & sFirstName & "<br>")
    //Move to the next record in the recordset
    rsResults.MoveNext
Loop
//Close the connection
connection.Close()
```

Using Logic to Make Decisions

The true power of data-driven Web pages comes from the script's ability to make decisions based on the current contents of the database. One of the most important decisions is to decide whether to permit or deny access to a page. Imagine a situation in which a Login form posts to a script the user name and password of someone attempting to access your site. You want only members of the Users table in the TopSecret database to have access to the page. Think about the steps a script must take to decide whether a user should be allowed in. Consider it for a moment, and then study the following steps, which describe what the script would do:

1. Retrieve the user name and password from the incoming form data.

2. Open a connection to the TopSecret database.

3. Issue an SQL command to query the database. This query asks the database to retrieve the record containing the user name and password that the user entered on the Login form.

4. Use an IF-THEN statement to make the following decision based on the contents of the recordset that the query in step 3 returns:

 a. If the recordset is empty, this user is not valid, so you deny access.

 b. If the recordset contains the requested record, the user is allowed in. Set the authentication cookie and send the user to the welcome screen.

A script that accomplishes these four steps follows. Study the documentation (i.e., the green lines beginning with the // symbol) to get a sense of how the script works. If the user is allowed in, the script sets an authentication cookie that subsequent pages can check to decide whether the user should be permitted access. In the Try This! exercise that concludes this section, you learn how to put a one-line script on any page that you want to make top secret by denying access to users who do not belong to the TopSecret database. This exercise does not require you to write any database scripts. Rather, you follow the step-by-step instructions to download the scripts from the book's Web site and use them to make selected pages top secret.

JScript version

```
//Get the data coming in from the Login form
sUsername = Request.Form("Username");
sPassword = Request.Form("password");
//Create the database connection object
connection = Server.CreateObject("ADODB.Connection");
connection.mode = 1; //read only mode
sConnectionString = "Provider=Microsoft.Jet.OLEDB.4.0;"
    + "Data Source=c:/TopSecret/TopSecret.mdb";
connection.Open(sConnectionString);
//Create the SQL query
sQuery = "SELECT * FROM Users WHERE UserName = '" + sUsername
    + "' AND Password = '" + sPassword + "'";
//Execute the query and get its results into a recordset
rsResults = connection.Execute(sQuery);
//Decide whether the user is allowed in
if (rsResults.EOF)
{
    Response.Write("<br>You are not a top secret user.");
    //Negate any validation cookie
    Response.Cookies("Validation") = "-1";
}
else
{
    sUserID = rsResults("UserID");
    //Set the validation cookie
    Response.Cookies("Validation") = sUserID;
    //Send the user to the Welcome page
    Response.Redirect("Welcome.html");
}
connection.Close();
```

VBScript version

```
//Get the data coming in from the Login form
sUsername = Request.Form("Username")
sPassword = Request.Form("password")
//Create the database connection object
Set connection = Server.CreateObject("ADODB.Connection")
connection.mode = 1 //read only mode
sConnectionString = "Provider=Microsoft.Jet.OLEDB.4.0;" _
    & "Data Source="c:/TopSecret/TopSecret.mdb"
connection.Open(sConnectionString)
//Create the SQL query
sQuery = "SELECT * FROM Users WHERE UserName = '" & sUsername _
    & "' AND Password = '" & sPassword & "'"
//Execute the query and get its results into a recordset
Set rsResults = connection.Execute(sQuery)
//Decide whether the user is allowed in
if (rsResults.EOF) then
Response.Write("<br>You are not a top secret user.")
    //Negate any validation cookie
    Response.Cookies("Validation") = "-1"
else
    sUserID = rsResults("UserID")
    //Set the validation cookie
    Response.Cookies("Validation") = sUserID
    //Send the user to the Welcome page
    Response.Redirect("Welcome.html")
end if
connection.Close()
```

Try This!

Creating Top Secret Web Pages

This exercise teaches you to use ASP to make Web pages deny access to users who are not in the TopSecret database you created in an earlier Try This! exercise. To run these pages, however, you must have the IIS Web server running on your computer. If you do not have IIS, you can read through this exercise to see how it works, but you will not be able to run it on your computer. If you have Windows NT Workstation, Windows 2000 Pro, Windows 2003, Windows XP Pro, or Windows XP Media Edition, you can install IIS from the Add/Remove Windows Components option under Add or Remove Programs in the Windows Control Panel. Once you have IIS running on your computer, you can create the ASP page by following these steps:

1. Use My Computer or the Windows Explorer to move the *website* folder into your computer's Web root folder, which is probably located at c:\inetpub\wwwroot.

2. Into your *website* folder, download from this book's Web site the files *login.html*, *TopSecret.asp*, and *TopSecretValidator.js*. Follow the onscreen instructions explaining how to download instead of run the executable files.

3. Use Notepad to open the HTML of any page you want to protect. In this example, open the file *hello.html*, *mountains.html*, or *resume.html*. Immediately after the <body> tag, paste the following code:

```
<script src="TopSecretValidator.js" language=javascript></script>
```

4. After saving the file you modified in the previous step, use your browser to open it. Because you have not yet logged on, the script will redirect you to the login page, which prompts you to type your user name and password. If you respond with the user name and password of a user in your TopSecret database, you will get in. If you respond otherwise, the script will deny access until you log on as a TopSecret user.

5. Some pretty nifty code runs behind the scenes of this exercise. First, the *TopSecretValidator.js* script checks whether the user has a validated authentication cookie. If not, it redirects the user to the *Login.html* page, which prompts the user for a user name and password. When the user clicks the Login button, the form submits its data to the *TopSecret.asp* page.

6. The *TopSecret.asp* page uses a script that creates an ADO connection object, through which it queries the TopSecret database. The code on the *TopSecret.asp* page is self-documenting. To study how the code works, use Notepad to open the *TopSecret.asp* file, and read the documentation contained in the script.

Chapter 12 Review

Chapter Summary

After reading this chapter and completing the step-by-step tutorials and Try This! exercises, you should understand the following facts about the Internet:

Providing Web Access to Server-Side Databases

- The first HTTP gateway protocol was the Common Gateway Interface (CGI), which defines the manner in which forms data, cookies, and other kinds of information in a Web request get submitted to the program or script that will process and respond to the request. Perl, C, and the UNIX shell were the programming languages of the first generation of CGI scripts.

- A Server Application Programming Interface (SAPI) is a collection of software components used by the business tier to obtain, process, and respond to forms data submitted when end users interact with the site and make requests through the user interface tier. Microsoft's brand of SAPI is Internet SAPI (ISAPI), and Netscape's is Netscape SAPI (NSAPI).

- Active Server Pages (ASP) is a Microsoft ISAPI technology that enables Web developers to embed on a Web page server-side scripts written in either the JScript or VBScript programming languages. End users never see the scripts, which the server executes when the user accesses the page. Instead of seeing an embedded script, end users view the results of the script's execution.

- Java is an object-oriented programming language that developers can use to create almost any kind of software. Java code compiles into an intermediary language that executes on any platform running the JVM. Versions of the JVM exist for practically every operating system, including UNIX, Linux, Macintosh, and Windows. Thus, Java code is machine independent.

- A Java Server Page (JSP) is an active Web page technology that is Sun's equivalent to Microsoft's ASP. In the midst of the page, the Web developer can write Java code to be run when a user accesses the page. At runtime, when a user hits the JSP, the server executes the code and sends the user the resulting page. JSP is therefore similar to ASP, although JSP runs in the JVM, while ASP runs in Microsoft's ISAPI.

- The PHP Hypertext Preprocessor (PHP) is another active page technology. The command syntax is like that of C and Perl. As an open source Apache project, PHP runs primarily with Apache on UNIX and Linux servers, although versions of PHP for Windows are also available.

- ColdFusion is an active scripting technology that uses its own proprietary scripting language called the ColdFusion Markup Language.

- Microsoft's ASP.NET lets you create code behind the Web page, on so-called *code-behind pages*. These code-behind pages can be part of complete applications with which the user interacts from the browser window, which becomes the Web application's display surface.

Understanding Databases

- Three basic kinds of databases are (1) flat file, (2) relational, and (3) object-oriented. A flat file database keeps all of the records in a single file, in which the data elements are separated by a break character such as a comma or a tab.

- A relational database management system (RDBMS) is a data structure that contains multiple tables containing primary key columns through which the records in one table can relate (i.e., key) to the data in another table, in which the related column is called a *foreign key*.

- In an object-oriented database management system (ODBMS), programmers writing code in object-oriented languages can create complex data structures in which one data type can build upon, or inherit, properties from another.

- To design a relational database, you (1) describe its purpose, (2) list its tables, (3) list the fields (i.e., data columns) in each table, (4) define the data types of each column, (5) define the primary keys, (6) identify the foreign key columns, (7) write a walkthrough, and (8) ask yourself if any relations are missing. This design process is not a standard protocol that is asked on the CIW exam; rather, this process is how I design my databases.

- Normalization is the process of separating a large table fulfilling multiple roles into smaller tables that increase efficiency by serving smaller roles that relate through keys to other tables in the database. A database that has not been normalized has wide tables (i.e., more columns) that require more time to query, sort, and retrieve records. A normalized database has data tables that are narrower (i.e., fewer columns) and serve efficiently a single purpose which, when related through keys to other tables, enables the database to accomplish its goal more quickly.

- An index is a database column or collection of columns that the database engine uses to keep the data presorted in the order in which you plan to query it. Creating an index can lead to a significant boost in database performance.

Accessing Server-Side Databases

- Open database connectivity (ODBC) is a standard database access method created by Microsoft and based on the Call-Level Interface (CLI) specifications from the X/Open and ISO/IEC database APIs. An ODBC driver is available for almost every brand of relational database.

- Developed by JavaSoft for Sun Microsystems, Java database connectivity (JDBC) enables Java programs to communicate with SQL-based database systems.

- Object linking and embedding database (OLE DB) connections enable Windows applications to open a wide variety of connections to data stored not only in ODBC data sources, but also in file systems, media catalogs, e-mail, spreadsheets, active directories, project management tools, and XML files.

- On the Windows operating system, ActiveX Data Objects (ADO) is an API that enables business objects to make connections and issue commands against many different kinds of data sources.

- The connection object is the ADO component that connects you to the database. Once you have the connection open, you can execute SQL commands.

- SQL stands for Structured Query Language, which is an international standard that defines the syntax for issuing commands that can query, update, insert, or delete records in a database.

Creating Data-Driven Web Pages

- SQL queries return data in sets of records called a *recordset*. The script of a data-driven Web page reads the data in the recordset.

- The ADO recordset object contains methods that enable a script to move through its contents, record by record, and obtain information to display directly onscreen or to use in making decisions that will result in deciding what to display onscreen.

- Through computer logic known as IF-THEN statements, the script makes decisions based on the content of the data.

- At runtime, when the user accesses the data-driven Web page, the server replaces the script with the result of the script's execution. If the user inspects the source code of the page via the browser's View | Source menu, the user views the HTML output of the script instead of the server-side code that generated this content.

Key Terms

Active Server Pages (ASP) *(524)*

ActiveX Data Objects (ADO) *(533)*

ASP.NET *(526)*

Bourne shell language *(523)*

ColdFusion *(526)*

comma-delimited data *(527)*

common gateway interface (CGI) *(523)*

connection object *(533)*

data table *(527)*

data-driven Web page *(537)*

flat file database *(527)*

foreign key *(527)*

index *(529)*

Internet SAPI (ISAPI) *(523)*

Java *(525)*

Java database connectivity (JDBC) *(532)*

Java Server Pages (JSP) *(525)*

Netscape SAPI (NSAPI) *(523)*

normalization *(529)*

object-oriented database *(528)*

object-oriented database management system (ODBMS) *(528)*

object linking and embedding database (OLE DB) *(533)*

**open database connectivity
(ODBC)** *(532)*
Perl *(523)*
**PHP Hypertext Preprocessor
(PHP)** *(526)*
primary key *(527)*

recordset *(537)*
relational database *(527)*
**relational database management
system (RDBMS)** *(528)*
**Server Application Programming
Interface (SAPI)** *(523)*

servlet *(525)*
**Structured Query Language
(SQL)** *(534)*
tab-delimited data *(527)*

■ Key Terms Quiz

1. The first HTTP gateway protocol was the
_____, which defines the
manner in which forms data, cookies, and other
kinds of information in a Web request get
submitted to the program or script that will
process and respond to the request.

2. Microsoft's brand of SAPI is called _____.

3. _____ is a Microsoft SAPI
technology that enables Web developers to
embed on a Web page server-side scripts written
in either the JScript or VBScript programming
languages.

4. _____ code compiles into an
intermediary language that executes on any
platform running the JVM.

5. _____ is an active Web page
technology that is Sun's equivalent to
Microsoft's ASP.

6. _____ is a CGI scripting
language invented by Larry Wall for people
who need to write relatively short programs.

7. A(n) _____ keeps all of the
records in a single file, in which the data
elements are separated by a break character
such as a comma or a tab.

8. A(n) _____ is a data structure
that contains multiple tables containing primary
key columns through which the records in one
table can relate (i.e., key) to the data in another
table.

9. A data table's _____ is a column
in which every entry is unique; it keys to the
_____ column in the related table.

10. In a(n) _____, programmers
writing code in object-oriented languages can
create complex data structures in which one
data type can build upon, or inherit, properties
from another.

■ Multiple-Choice Quiz

1. What runs in the JVM under a multithreaded
environment that can listen for Internet requests
to come in and serve multiple users from the
same instance of the code?
   a. Applet
   b. inetd
   c. ISAPI
   d. Servlet

2. What is the open source Apache project's active
page technology that enables the Web developer
to include code on the page that will run on the
server, which executes the code before sending
the completed page to the user?

   a. ASP
   b. ColdFusion
   c. JSP
   d. PHP

3. Which active scripting technology uses
proprietary tags that begin with the letters CF?
   a. ASP
   b. ColdFusion
   c. JSP
   d. PHP

4. Which programming environment enables you
to create code behind the Web page, on so-
called code-behind pages, which can be part

of complete applications with which the user interacts via the browser window?
a. ASP.NET
b. ColdFusion
c. Perl
d. PHP

5. What kind of database typically stores its data in comma-delimited or tab-delimited records?
a. Flat file
b. Object-oriented
c. OLE DB
d. Relational

6. The process of separating a large table fulfilling multiple roles into smaller tables that increase efficiency by serving smaller roles that relate through keys to other database tables is called:
a. Datamation
b. Economization
c. Normalization
d. Standardization

7. What is a database column or collection of columns that the database engine uses to keep the data presorted?
a. Catalog
b. Directory
c. Index
d. Query

8. What is a standard database access method created by Microsoft based on the Call-Level Interface (CLI) specifications to make it possible for any application to access any database, regardless of its vendor?
a. JDBC
b. ODBC
c. OLE DB
d. RDBMS

9. What is the international standard that defines the syntax for issuing commands that can query, update, insert, or delete records in a database?
a. CFML
b. PHP
c. SQL
d. XML

10. Which clause enables an SQL statement to filter out unwanted information?
a. FROM
b. ORDER BY
c. SELECT
d. WHERE

Essay Quiz

1. In terms of efficient use of operating system resources, what is the primary advantage of a SAPI over the original CGI?

2. In your own words, explain the fundamental difference between a Java applet and a Java servlet.

3. Explain what ASP, JSP, and PHP have in common in terms of where the scripts reside, where they execute, and what happens at runtime to prevent the end user from seeing the scripts via the browser's View | Source option.

4. Refer to the summary of database design principles presented in this chapter. Which rule does the following data table's design violate?

Data Table: Children

ParentID	Child1	Child2	Child3	Child4	Child5
1	Fred	Mary Ann	Linda	Bobby	Thomas
2	John	Michael	Susan	Chrystal	Amber
3	Samuel	Jacob	Julian	Alexis	Tommy

5. Suppose you wanted to write a script to judge whether a user answered a test question right or wrong, and you need to decide whether to write the judging code in JavaScript, JScript, or VBScript. Which would be the more secure scripting language(s) in which to write such code? Explain why this language is more secure.

Lab Projects

• Lab Project 12-1: Database Analysis and Design

Imagine that you work for a school or company that needs to create a Web-based discussion forum that will contain confidential discussions by different working groups within your organization. Your employer has assigned you the task of analyzing the needs, specifying the features, and designing the relational database that will contain these discussions. Based on your design, a programming team will write the scripts that power the discussions. Use your word processor to write an essay in which you present your database analysis and design. In formulating this design, consider the following issues:

■ **Needs analysis** Before you can design the data tables that the discussion database will comprise, you need to make an outline of the discussion features your coworkers require. Make a preliminary list and consult with your coworkers to make sure the list includes all the discussion features they think are needed.

■ **Data table design** Make a list of the tables that the database will comprise. In each table, indicate which column is the primary key, and state which columns in other tables, if any, have a foreign key relationship. In designing these tables, remember that you will need columns to identify the author of each message.

■ **Data type definition** Specify the type of data that will reside in each column, such as integer, text, or date/timestamp. Most databases can handle text fields up to 5,000 characters long, which is plenty long for storing discussion messages. If your design permits users to upload file attachments, however, you should plan to store the uploaded files in the server's file system instead of in the database. It is more efficient to store in the database the path/filename of the uploaded file, rather than the file itself.

■ **Normalization** Beginners tend to create one or two data tables that are very wide—that is, contain many columns. Relational database engines normally work better when you store data in smaller tables that use primary and foreign key relationships. Tables that are too wide tend to store redundant data. Especially when you find a table repeating data, such as storing the user's first and last name in each discussion record, you should create a secondary table that stores the redundant information more efficiently.

■ **Indexing** For optimal database performance, you should specify the sort order for each table and have the database programmers create indexes based on the sort order. Make the sort order be the order in which the discussions will most often retrieve the data. An example of a sort order is DiscussionID, MessageID, ResponseID.

■ **Walkthrough** Write a walkthrough to make sure you haven't missed something important. Describe how the typical user will enter the discussion forum and use its options. Explain what will happen in the database as the user posts and responds to messages. If your design permits users to upload file attachments, describe how the database will store them. If the walkthrough uncovers anything missing from your database design, correct the design by supplying the missing elements.

■ **Search engines** To ensure you have not missed something important, use Google or Yahoo to search for the following keywords: discussion forum database design. Perusing other database designs can provide ideas for features you may wish to include, and help guard against omitting something important.

If your instructor asked you to hand in the database analysis and design, make sure you put your name at the top of the essay, then copy it onto a disk or follow the other instructions you may have been given for submitting this assignment.

• Lab Project 12-2: Database Backup and Recovery Planning

Without proper database backup and recovery planning, all the hard work and effort you put into creating a data-driven Web site can go down the drain in the event of a hard disk crash, destructive virus attack, or other catastrophic data loss. Imagine that your employer has tasked you with developing a database backup and recovery plan. Use your word processor to write an essay in which you present this plan. In formulating the backup and recovery strategy, consider the following issues:

- **Backup schedule**   In the event of catastrophic data loss, you restore the database from the most recent backup. Every transaction recorded since the timestamp of the backup is lost. In deciding how often to back up the database (e.g., hourly, daily, weekly), take into account how frequently the data tends to change and the financial or operational impact of data loss.

- **Off-site backups**   Planning where to keep the backup is just as important as deciding how often to make it. A catastrophic fire or explosion, for example, could destroy all of the data in your building, including all of the backups residing there. It is very important, therefore, to keep extra copies of the backup in secure places off site. Large companies, for example, can keep backups in different buildings, cities, states, or countries. Small businesses can keep backups at home as well as in the office.

- **Recovery methods**   Create a written procedure explaining how your organization will go about recovering data from the backups in the event of different kinds of failures. Include a range of scenarios from a hard disk crash on the server to total destruction of the site housing the server. Thinking about disasters can be depressing. Remember Murphy's Law: if you have a disaster recovery plan, you will never need it.

- **Emergency hosting**   In the event of a catastrophic disaster that destroys the machine room, you will need a plan for hosting the site at a different location on an emergency basis. Regardless of how you feel about Murphy's Law, you must include recovery from catastrophic disaster in your plans.

- **Recovery testing**   Unless the recovery procedure works, the backup is of no use. You should recommend that your organization conduct a test in which you format the drives on a spare server, and then rebuild that machine to perform the same function as your production system. Perform tests to make sure the rebuilt system is functioning properly with all the data intact.

- **Best practices**   Consider best practice advice you can discover via Google or Yahoo by searching for the following keywords: database backup recovery planning.

If your instructor asked you to hand in the database backup and recovery plan, make sure you put your name at the top of the essay, then copy it onto a disk or follow the other instructions you may have been given for submitting this assignment.

chapter

13

Securing the Internet

"Billions of dollars fly through the air . . .
Watch your head."

—*IBM E-commerce commercial*

In this chapter, you will learn how to:

- Define the security threats and attacks that hackers use to gain unauthorized access to network services and resources.
- List the Internet security safeguards that protect networks by detecting intrusions and defeating attacks.
- Define the methods for digitally signing and encrypting network transmissions to thwart masquerading and deciphering by unauthorized parties.
- Describe how to publish a Web securely with the SFTP protocol.

MAGINE what would happen if the Net stopped working. The world got a warning when Slammer attacked on January 25, 2003. For several hours that Saturday morning, while network administrators scurried to patch hundreds of thousands of database servers infected by the attack, bank networks were out of service. People could not withdraw money or buy anything online. Luckily, Slammer attacked on a weekend, when the stock markets were closed. Imagine the pandemonium of bringing down the markets.

This chapter is about securing the Internet. By defining the security threats that can bring down a network, you will know the techniques crackers use to attack the Internet. You will learn best-practice methods of detecting intrusions and defeating attacks. The vulnerability Slammer exploited, for example, was a known issue. Server administrators who follow best practices had already installed the patch. Slammer succeeded because too many networks had neglected to install the patch. The extent of the outage demonstrated how important it is for all server administrators to follow the best security practices this chapter presents.

The Internet exists because of the wonderfully creative minds of its inventors. Hackers also have creative minds. Malicious hackers, who are more correctly called crackers, continue to scheme and dream of new ways to attack the Internet. To fool you into installing malicious code, crackers masquerading as legitimate vendors try to trick you by sending messages disguised as security update bulletins. On first glance, the messages appear legitimate, because the crackers emulate the look and feel of the vendor's official update mechanism. This chapter teaches you the digital signing technology that legitimate vendors use to foil the masquerade. Learning how to use the Internet's public-key infrastructure will enable you to encrypt messages and prevent deciphering by unauthorized users. The chapter concludes by teaching you how to publish a Web site securely and set permissions that determine which users have different kinds of access to your site.

Identifying Internet Security Issues

Internet security risks fall into three general categories: (1) unauthorized access, (2) data manipulation, and (3) service interruption. Unauthorized access happens when someone who is not permitted manages to obtain information from the site. Prime targets of unauthorized intruders include financial records, credit card numbers, and mailing lists.

Data manipulation happens when an intruder modifies records in the database. This kind of attack occurs less frequently because modifying data leaves tracks that can lead to identifying the intruder.

Service interruption happens when malicious code floods a server with bogus requests. Legitimate users experience long delays or cannot log on at all because the server is busy processing the bogus requests or the server crashed under the onslaught.

User-level Issues

It is generally believed that about two-thirds of all security breaches come from inside an organization's network architecture. Known as **inside attacks**, these breaches happen when employees hack in to obtain unauthorized access to network services or data. Malicious employees can cause a lot of harm, especially if they happen to be IT staff members or system administrators. Because of this threat, companies typically remove an employee's computer access before terminating employment. Even so, knowledgeable employees may still have ways to hack into the network, such as through a back door, which is a loophole a programmer creates to bypass the application security mechanisms.

Physical Access Security

To help guard against inside attacks, you should locate equipment behind locked doors and limit access to authorized personnel. Require employees to log off before walking away from their workstations to prevent someone unauthorized from sitting down and continuing the session. Keep employees from writing down their passwords on slips of paper that an eavesdropper could see. Encourage employees to report suspicious activity, such as equipment being moved or worked on by someone who is not a member of the IT staff.

Network Security Threats

Some security threats are more sophisticated than others. Network security threats that rely on technical measures may take the following forms:

- **Data interception** Packet sniffers and network analyzers can intercept data that moves across the network. If the data transmissions are in clear text, unauthorized personnel can capture and access sensitive data. Later in this chapter, you learn how to encrypt network transmissions to prevent sensitive information from crossing the Internet in clear text.

- **Identity interception** Most sites rely on user names and passwords as the first level of security. If the logon form sends user names and passwords across the network in clear text, intruders with packet sniffers can intercept identities. Hackers also intercept identities by guessing passwords. Because password hacking tools use dictionaries of common words in many languages, you should require employees to have passwords consisting of a combination of characters and numbers. Hackers can also use search engines to find out information about you; avoid passwords consisting of information that can be searched or guessed, such as family member names, birth dates, hobbies, phone numbers, or license plate numbers.

- **Masquerading** When unauthorized users assume the privileges of an authorized user, they are **masquerading**. This can happen through identity interception and is especially dangerous if a hacker discovers a system administrator's username and password. A more subtle form of masquerading is **IP address spoofing**, which happens when an intruder uses the IP address of a trusted system to gain access rights granted to that system.

- **Replay attacks** If a hacker uses a packet sniffer to record a logon sequence, the hacker can playback the sequence at a later time in an attempt to gain access. In this kind of **replay attack**, the intruder does not need to know the username or password. Even if the logon information is encrypted, the replay attack will succeed if the logon server accepts the same codes.

The technical measures employed in these kinds of attacks are sophisticated, and the hackers who can pull them off are impressive. Nevertheless, you must also be on guard for less technically sophisticated means of compromising network security. The following methods exploit human weaknesses that are no less dangerous than the more technical security threats:

- **Social engineering attack** A **social engineering attack** exploits human weaknesses to gain access to the organization's network. The attacker may pretend to be from the IT department, call new employees on the phone, and ask them to verify their passwords. An attacker may call the IT help desk in the guise of a user who needs help logging on. To thwart this kind of attack, the organization should communicate clearly outlined IT procedures to all staff, especially newcomers, to clarify the manner in which passwords and other kinds of sensitive information will be communicated.

- **Misuse of privileges** A network administrator with a high level of system privileges could use them to poke into different parts of the system and look up information about fellow employees or alter financial information such as the payroll. You must therefore give system privileges only to trusted employees of the highest integrity.

Identifying Assets

Depending on the nature of the organization, some security threats will be more of an issue than others. Because it is impossible to prepare for all possible attacks, identifying assets helps prioritize the need for different kinds of defenses.

At a public service Web site that has the goal of making information freely available, for example, the greatest threat is denial of service. In a bank, on the other hand, security administrators must guard against fraud, which insiders as well as outsiders can commit. Critical assets may reside on one of the following resource groups:

- **Data tier information resources** Any organization that conducts transactions has a back office database that you do not want hacked. Customer information, payroll, student grades, credit card numbers, and mailing lists are prime targets of crackers.

- **Server resources** All of the servers covered in Chapter 11, including Web servers, mail servers, FTP servers, and directory servers, may contain assets that you wouldn't want hacked.

- **Network resources** You need to protect network resources from tapping and spoofing to prevent crackers from gaining unauthorized access to the network.

- **Local workstations** End-user workstations are especially prone to viruses that can cause significant productivity losses, destroy data, and spread to other computers on the network. Every organization must guard against virus attacks.

Viruses and the Hacker Process

Hackers are constantly trying to devise new ways of breaking through network security mechanisms. Some hackers obtain satisfaction from the act of breaking in. For them, cracking security is a kind of game that proves their prowess in hacking. Malicious hackers, on the other hand, can disrupt business, resulting in financial losses that can be considerable.

Defending a network is a two-stage process that requires (1) a proactive pre-attack strategy and (2) a reactive post-attack strategy. In formulating a pre-attack strategy, you list the threats and identify the IT staff that will be responsible for the defenses. The IT staff must be proactive, meaning that they keep up with the latest intelligence on the hacking process, anticipate things that could go wrong, and implement defensive measures in advance of an attack.

Attackers will sometimes succeed, however, especially if your network gets hit by a new virus before security patches become available. You must therefore have a post-attack strategy for mobilizing the appropriate staff to take corrective actions. When my organization got hit by the Slammer worm, for example, dozens of servers were affected. Fast-acting IT staff minimized damage by blocking traffic on port 1434, which runs the Microsoft SQL resolution service over which Slammer waged its attack. This bought precious time for server administrators to apply the security patch before reopening port 1434 to network traffic.

Viruses top the list of attacker's tools. Viruses propagate by attaching themselves to software programs or other kinds of files. When a user executes or opens a file thus infected, the user's computer catches the virus. Types of viruses include the following:

- **Boot record virus** When a computer boots, it runs code from the boot record of the startup device. **Boot record viruses** spread through malicious code that runs when the computer boots. You need to warn all employees to be leery of removable media such as USB drives and floppy disks, which can transmit a boot record virus on startup if left in the drive.

- **File infector virus** Malicious code can attach to individual files, which propagate primarily via e-mail attachments. When the user opens the attachment, the **file infector virus** executes. Every workstation should have a virus scanner configured to scan all incoming files for these kinds of viruses.

- **Macro virus** A macro is a command that executes a set of instructions in a computer application such as a word processor or a spreadsheet to save time users would otherwise spend typing the instructions individually. Macros can carry viruses. One of the most common transmission methods is attaching to an e-mail message a document or spreadsheet containing the **macro virus**. You must therefore institute policies and take protective measures to prevent employees from opening documents from non-trusted sources.

- **Trojan horse** A **Trojan horse** is malicious code that masquerades as a desirable program. Users fooled into running the program execute the malicious code. Hackers have succeeded in delivering Trojans in the guise of security updates attached to e-mail messages made to look as though they are coming from legitimate sources. You need to make sure everyone in your organization knows that no legitimate vendor would ever send a security patch as an attachment to an unsolicited e-mail message.

- **Embedded code** Crackers can embed malicious executable code in Web pages via Java applets or ActiveX controls. You must warn users about the danger of following links to non-trusted sites.

Another kind of malicious code is the **worm**, which can propagate across the Internet and infect other computers without attaching itself to other programs. Worms can wreak havoc by replicating themselves on an infected system to tie up all its resources and then following that system's network connections to attack other computers.

Try This!

Detecting Unauthorized Services

Many users are unaware that a clever attacker can install services that run on the end user's computer. An attacker who gains access to your computer can install an FTP service, for example, and use your computer to distribute files to other computers, including files propagating the virus that installed the unauthorized process on your workstation. To discover whether any unknown services are running on your computer, you can download and install a freeware program called Process Explorer. Follow these steps:

Try This!
continued

1. The free download version of Process Explorer is a zip file. If you do not have a zip file extractor on your computer, go to www.pkware.com and install PKZip for Windows. There is an evaluation version in the free download section at www.pkware.com/products/free_eval.html.

2. Go to www.sysinternals.com and look for a link to Process Explorer. When this book went to press, the link was www.sysinternals.com/ntw2k/freeware/procexp.shtml. Click the Process Explorer link.

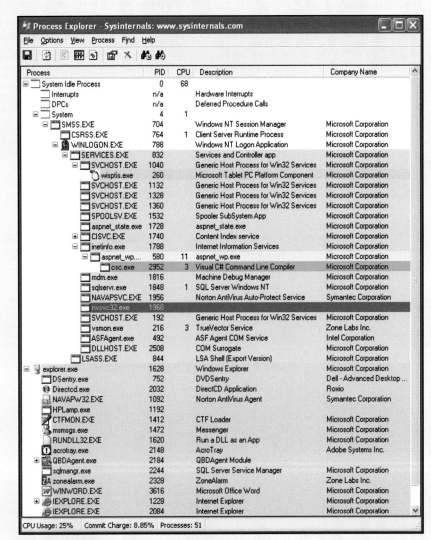

3. On the Process Explorer page, scroll down to find the download link for the version of Process Explorer appropriate for your operating system. You will see links to download versions of Process Explorer for Win9x/Me, WinNT/2K/XP, and 64-bit versions of Windows.

4. Click the download link appropriate for your operating system. When prompted, choose the option to open the file.

5. After the zip file downloads and opens, double-click the file named *procexp.exe*, which runs the Process Explorer.

6. If you get a warning that symbols are not configured, click OK to dismiss the warning. You will not need symbols for this exercise.

7. Figure 13-1 shows how the Process Explorer displays the processes running on your computer. Peruse this display to determine whether any unauthorized services are running on your computer.

FIGURE 13-1 *The freeware program Process Explorer displays the processes running on your computer. Be leery of processes that have no descriptions or company names. In this example, I suspected nvsvc32.exe because it has neither a description nor a company name. Upon closer inspection, however, this turned out to be the computer's graphics driver.* ■

Applying Internet Security Safeguards

Due to the global importance of Internet security, the computer industry has evolved best practices you can follow to safeguard your network's client workstations and servers. These best practices include (1) subscribing to a security newsletter that keeps you apprised of the latest security issues and threats, (2) using an automatic update service to install the latest security patches, (3) identifying the kinds of attacks to which your network is prone, (4) auditing the network for traces of these attacks, (5) installing software that can automatically detect intrusions, (6) planning how to recover from network disasters, and (7) using firewalls to block non-trusted traffic or processes.

Microsoft Security Newsletters

For millions of end users and server administrators that have the Windows operating system, subscribing to one or more of the Microsoft Security Newsletters is an excellent way to keep up with Microsoft's security strategies and guidance. To subscribe, follow these steps:

1. Go to www.microsoft.com/technet/security/secnews/newsletter.htm and follow the link to subscribe to a newsletter.

2. When the Passport screen appears, log on via your Passport credentials. If you do not have a Passport, follow the onscreen instructions to get one.

note *Passport is Microsoft's online authentication service.*

3. The Microsoft subscription center appears, as illustrated in Figure 13-2. Follow the link to Newsletter Subscriptions.

4. Figure 13-3 shows how you can subscribe to a wide range of newsletters. Server administrators and IT staff should subscribe

FIGURE 13-2 *The Microsoft Subscription Center lets you set your Newsletter Preferences. Follow the link to Newsletter Subscriptions to bring up the newsletter choices in Figure 13-3.* ■

FIGURE 13-3 *Check the boxes alongside the newsletters to which you want to subscribe, and then click the Update button. To find out more about a newsletter, click its plus sign.* ■

to the Microsoft Security Notification Service, which provides detailed technical information on security issues. Other employees should subscribe to the Microsoft Security Newsletter.

5. Check the boxes alongside the newsletters to which you want to subscribe and click the Update button.

6. If you later decide to unsubscribe, repeat these steps but uncheck the boxes alongside the newsletters you want to stop and click the Update button.

Microsoft Windows Update Service

Microsoft runs a **Windows Update Service** that can automatically download the latest security patches to your computer. You can configure the service to install the patches right away or to notify you when the patches are ready to install. To configure the Microsoft Windows Update Service, follow these steps:

1. Log on to your computer as the administrator. Only the administrator can configure the Windows Update Service.

2. Click the Windows Start button, go to the Control Panel and double-click System to bring up your computer's System Properties window.

3. Click the Automatic Updates tab. Figure 13-4 shows how the configuration settings appear onscreen. To enable automatic updating, check the box alongside the option to *Keep my computer up to date*.

4. The settings let you choose one of three service levels. The first level notifies you before downloading any updates. The second level downloads the updates automatically but notifies you before installing them. The third level downloads and installs the updates automatically.

5. Click OK when you finish configuring the settings.

Besides configuring Windows Update to run automatically, you can also force it to run manually at any time. To run Windows Update manually, follow these steps:

1. Click the Windows Start button and choose Help and Support to bring the help center onscreen.

2. Follow the link to Windows Update. When the Windows Update screen appears, follow the link to scan for updates.

3. After scanning for updates, the Windows Update service will display a list of (1) critical updates that are very important for you to install, (2) operating system updates, and (3) driver updates. Follow the

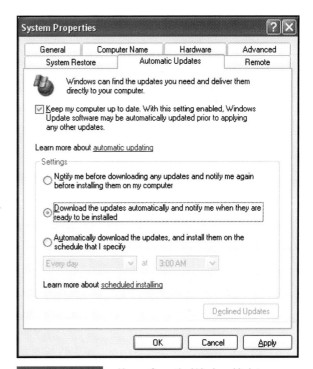

FIGURE 13-4 *You configure the Windows Update settings on the Automatic Updates tab of the System Properties window that you bring onscreen by choosing System from the Windows Control Panel. Shown here are the settings on my home computer, which downloads the updates automatically and notifies me when they are ready to be installed.* ∎

onscreen instructions to review the updates and choose the ones you want installed on your computer. By definition, you should always install the critical updates because they patch serious bugs and security holes that make your computer vulnerable to attack.

Defeating Attacks

No matter how careful you are about protecting your network, it will inevitably come under attack. The more you understand about the methods employed by different kinds of attacks, the better your instincts will work in guiding you to take appropriate actions.

The most frequent kind of attack is **Denial of Service (DoS)**, in which the attacker seeks to consume so much of a server's resources that the host cannot respond to legitimate requests. A DoS attacker may send a flood of requests, such as ping commands, in an attempt to overflow the server's input buffer. Due to the overflow, legitimate requests cannot get in. The worm named Slammer, for example, waged its attack by flooding port 1434 with SQL ping requests. When hundreds of thousands of SQL servers began echoing each other's ping requests, large portions of the Internet went out of service for several hours until server administrators applied the patch.

Another mode of DoS attack is the SYN flood, in which an attacker floods a server with the synchronize (SYN) command that is the first part of the TCP handshake. To thwart these kinds of floods, routers can block traffic from an IP address that is obviously sending too many packets. Crackers will continue to find other ways to launch a DoS attack, however. They may send you a flood of megabyte e-mail messages to use up all of your server's memory. To keep you from blocking the attack, crackers may use multiple servers and e-mail addresses from which to launch the attack. It is important for you to subscribe to the security newsletters and apply patches promptly to thwart newly emerging attacks. Most of the recent DoS attacks succeeded because server administrators and end users were slow to apply the patches.

You need to guard against ways in which computers can be programmed to guess usernames and passwords. In a so-called **brute force attack** or **front door attack**, for example, a cracker programs a computer to look up words in a dictionary and generate variants with which the computer keeps trying to log on until it discovers a password that gets in. You can minimize the risk of a front-door attack by limiting the number of logon attempts permitted from an IP address that keeps getting the password wrong.

Do not forget that human beings can create security gaps that require less sophistication to exploit. Dumpster diving is a term used to describe the practice of looking through trash for discarded records that may display in clear text important information such as account numbers, passwords, and social security numbers. Your security policy needs to require that sensitive printed information be shredded before being discarded.

Another security risk created by well-intentioned IT staff is the trapdoor attack, in which crackers find a way into your computer by running diagnostic tools that your IT staff left on the system after troubleshooting some kind of problem. It is important for the IT staff to remove diagnostic tools and restore security settings to their original state after debugging a problem.

Security Auditing and Intrusion Detection

Security needs to be proactive as well as reactive. **Security auditing** is a proactive process that considers the risks associated with security assets, predicts the methods crackers may use to exploit each risk, and takes protective steps to thwart them. Just as crackers may write computer code to attack your network, so also can you use software to detect attempts to compromise your assets. Microsoft Windows servers, for example, have intrusion detection software for keeping an audit trail that tracks logon attempts and logs changes made to vital assets. The audit trail enables the server administrator to determine whether an attacker is trying to guess passwords. By keeping track of who changes what, the audit trail can identify insiders who may use legitimate logons to make inappropriate use of network assets.

To activate intrusion detection on a Windows server, you set an audit policy on the asset you wish to track. You can specify whether to audit successes, failures, or both. Figure 13-5 shows how audit policies can apply to logons, account management, directory services, objects, policy changes, privileges, processes, and system events. To determine whether an insider may have changed a security setting that opened a trapdoor, you can audit policy changes.

You need to be aware of some pitfalls related to security auditing. In a denial of service attack that sends a flood of requests against the process you are auditing, the attacker may succeed in filling up the log. One of the audit policy settings calls for shutting down the server if security audits cannot be logged. If you have the shut-down setting configured for an asset targeted by a denial of service attack that manages to fill the log, the shut-down will enable the attacker to succeed in denying service to other users.

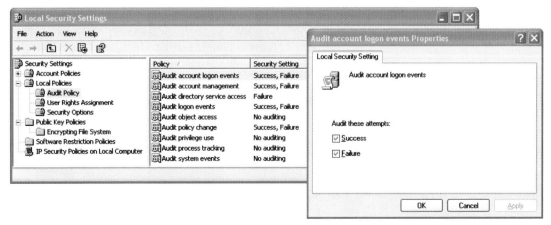

FIGURE   13-5   *To set an audit policy, use Windows control panel | Administrative tools to open the Local Security Policy Settings window shown here. Click to expand the Local Policies tree, and click Audit Policy to display the audit policies. Double-click the policy you want to change. Check the boxes to set whether you want to audit successes, failures, or both.* ∎

It is not good practice to log more than you would ever have time to look at. Before you begin setting audit policies, decide what assets are vital, and let this decision be your guide.

Remember that security logs are computer files that crackers could destroy to cover their tracks in a successful attack. Because the logs prior to the attack may track the attacker's attempts to hack your server, studying these logs could be invaluable in identifying the source of the attack. You should back up the security logs regularly and keep them on secondary storage devices, such as optical media that would not get erased in an attack.

Firewall Strategies

The typical end user does not have the degree of sophistication required to guard against many of the different kinds of attacks described in this chapter. Happily, firewall technology enables an organization to take some of the burden off end users. A **firewall** is a combination of hardware, software, and security policies that block certain kinds of traffic from entering or leaving a network, subnet, or individual host computer. There are many ways of configuring firewalls. Depending on the security risks and the importance of the assets being protected, firewalls may make use of one or more of the following strategies:

- **Packet Filtering** In a firewall, a packet filter works at OSI/RM Layers 2 and 3 to inspect the headers of all incoming and outgoing packets and can block transmissions based on source or destination ports or IP addresses. Thus, packet filters can stop attacks waged on specific ports and block access to malicious or forbidden sites. Blocking access to ports that a network does not use protects the network from attackers that may launch attacks on those ports.

- **Proxy Servers and Network Address Translation** In the previous chapter, you learned how a proxy server can apply a technique known as Network Address Translation (NAT) to use different IP addressing for external traffic than the addresses on an internal network. Keeping the internal IP addresses private helps hide them from crackers.

- **Circuit Level Gateway** Figure 13-6 illustrates how a **circuit level gateway** prevents the establishment of end-to-end TCP connections. Instead, the gateway establishes a connection on behalf of an inside host with an outside host, which views the gateway as its destination address. Thus, the circuit level gateway serves as a proxy at the Transport Layer of the Internet.

- **Application Level Gateway** Neither packet filters nor circuit level gateways inspect the packets' contents at the Internet's Application Layer, which can transmit viruses attached to e-mail messages or Trojans embedded in Web

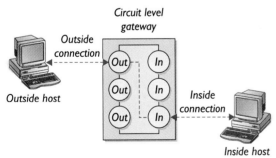

FIGURE 13-6 *When an inside host requests a connection with an outside host, a circuit level gateway sets up two TCP connections, one with the outside network and the other with the inside. Thus, the circuit level gateway works as a proxy that does not permit end-to-end TCP connections.* ■

pages. To protect an internal network from these kinds of attacks, Figure 13-7 shows how you can install an **application level gateway,** a type of firewall that can scan packets for malicious content spread through SMTP (mail), HTTP (Web pages), FTP (file transfers), DNS (attacks on name servers), or Telnet (remote logon). Depending on the network's security policy, an application level gateway can detect and block viruses, perform lexical analysis on message content, block access to offensive content, and report suspicious activity. This kind of analysis can be time-consuming, however; network administrators need to consider the impact of this degree of screening on overall network performance.

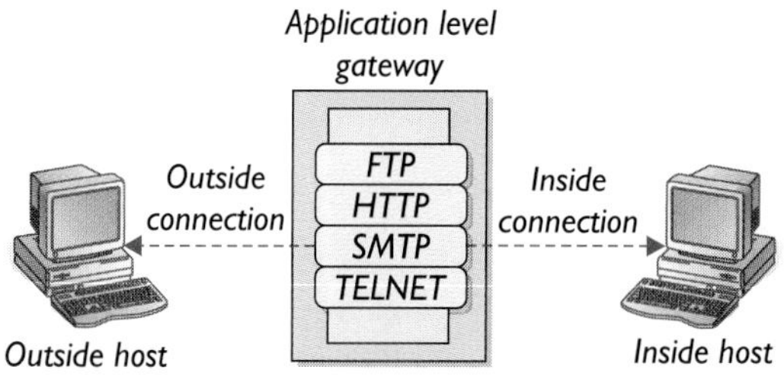

FIGURE 13-7 *An application level gateway acts as a relay that has full packet awareness. It can scan incoming mail messages for viruses, and it can perform lexical analysis to block access to offensive content and report suspicious activity. This kind of application-level screening adds overhead, however, so you should use it only when you really need it.* ∎

- **Stateful Inspection** Many applications open temporary ports at addresses above the Internet's Well Known Ports from 0 through 1023. To thwart attacks on temporary ports, a firewall technique known as **stateful inspection** can keep track of when a port opens, what session is using it, and how long the port stays open. If an attacker tries to hijack a session, the firewall can detect the attack and drop the session.

Firewall Topologies

After considering the risks against the security assets, the network administrator implements the appropriate strategies by configuring the hardware, software, and security policies that the firewall comprises. Depending on the configuration, the resulting firewall has one of four topologies, which the following sections define and illustrate the following:

- Packet filtering firewall
- Single-homed bastion host firewall
- Dual-homed bastion host firewall
- Screened subnet firewall with DMZ

Packet Filtering Firewall

The simplest kind of firewall uses a **packet filter,** which monitors the headers of all incoming or outgoing packets and can block transmissions based on source or destination ports or IP addresses. Figure 13-8 illustrates how a packet filtering router can protect an entire network. Because the packet filter operates at Layers 2 and 3 of the OSI reference model, it can quickly inspect the TCP/UDP ports and IP addresses in each packet. Network administrators configure the filter to block certain kinds of traffic that the organization's security policies forbid.

Locating the packet filter at the entrance to the network provides a systemic way for a network administrator to act quickly in thwarting an attack on a specific incoming port. Packet filters enabled network

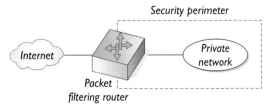

FIGURE 13-8 Packet filtering firewalls work at OSI/RM Layers 2 and 3 by monitoring the TCP/UDP port numbers and IP addresses in each packet. Routers with packet filtering are relatively inexpensive and easy to install. Locating the packet filter at the entrance to the network provides a systemic way for a network administrator to act quickly in thwarting an attack on a specific incoming port, such as the Slammer attack that exploited the SQL ping vulnerability on port 1434. ▪

administrators to stop the Slammer attack, for example, by blocking traffic on port 1434, which Slammer used to wage its attack. Unprotected networks without packet filtering firewalls were not so lucky.

Single-Homed Bastion Firewall

Although packet filtering firewalls perform an important and essential function by monitoring headers at OSI/RM Layers 2 and 3, certain kinds of attacks happen higher up the protocol stack. Viruses that come in via e-mail, for example, attack at the application level. To detect e-mail viruses, you need to scan the mail messages and attachments. To accomplish this kind of application scanning, Figure 13-9 shows how you can install a bastion host to screen traffic inside the perimeter of your network. A **bastion host** is a computer that sits on the perimeter of a local network and serves as an application-level gateway between the external network and the internal client workstations.

Because the bastion host shown in Figure 13-9 has a single Network Interface Card (NIC), this kind of firewall configuration is called a **single-homed bastion**, which can monitor all of the network's incoming and outgoing traffic at the Application Layer. A single-homed bastion firewall could scan all mail messages for viruses, for example, and quarantine infected messages instead of passing the viruses on to the network. The bastion host could also prevent downloading from the Internet, block access to certain Web sites, or alert administrators when messages contain certain keywords, such as obscenities or sexually explicit content. Before installing a bastion host, however, you need to weigh the potential benefits against the overhead of the added processing time. The more monitoring you do at the application level, the longer end users need to wait because of increased network delay. When used in combination with a packet filter, on the other hand, the bastion introduces a second layer of security that makes it harder for a cracker to break in.

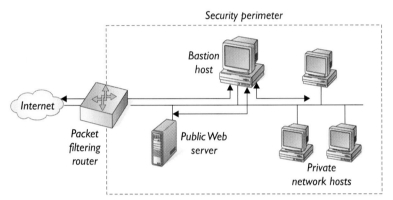

FIGURE 13-9 The single-homed bastion firewall topology uses a packet filter to establish the security perimeter, inside of which a gateway computer containing a single NIC (hence the term single-homed) serves as a bastion host through which all local network traffic passes. The bastion host can inspect messages at the Application Layer and, depending on the organization's security policies, block transmissions containing viruses or offensive content. ▪

Dual-Homed Bastion Firewall

Figure 13-10 illustrates how the **dual-homed bastion** firewall uses two NICs (hence the term dual-homed) on which IP forwarding is disabled, thereby creating a complete physical break between the internal and external networks. This adds a second layer of defense by making it impossible for a cracker to sneak packets past the perimeter without being screened

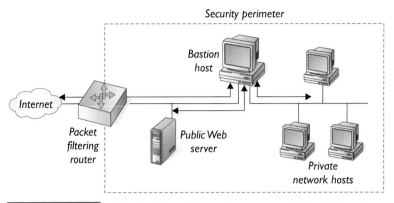

FIGURE	**13-10**

The dual-homed bastion host uses two NICs with IP packet forwarding disabled, thereby completely isolating the internal network from the external Internet. This topology makes it impossible for a packet to sneak past the bastion, which can monitor, filter, block, quarantine, and log any kind of information passing through the network. ■

n o t e *At first glance, you may not notice the subtle difference between the single-homed bastion host in Figure 13-9 and the dual-homed host in Figure 13-10. The only difference is the number of NICs in the bastion host. In Figure 13-9, the network traffic flows in and out of the bastion via the single NIC. In Figure 13-10, on the other hand, there are two NICs with IP packet forwarding disabled, which completely isolates the internal network from the external Internet.*

by the bastion. Because the dual-homed bastion firewall screens each incoming and outgoing packet, it is also known as a screened host firewall.

DMZ Screened-Subnet Firewall

Figure 13-11 shows how the **screened-subnet firewall** establishes a **demilitarized zone** (DMZ) by placing packet filtering routers on both the Internet side and the private network side of the bastion host. This makes it impossible for insiders to communicate directly over the Internet, because the inside router's address does not appear in the Internet's routing tables, which see only the DMZ's outside router. Thus, insiders cannot bypass the private network's security measures. External crackers must now fool three devices, namely, the bastion host and the two packet filtering routers. Furthermore, the DMZ provides a secure location for the network's modem pool and the organization's public Web and FTP servers.

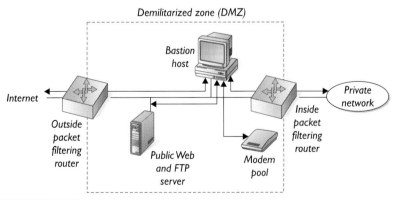

FIGURE	**13-11**

A screened subnet firewall uses two packet filtering routers to create a demilitarized zone (DMZ), in which you locate the bastion host, the public Web and FTP servers, and the organization's modem pool. Because the Internet's routing tables do not know the address of the inside router, the DMZ blocks direct traffic across the screened subnet. This makes the internal network invisible to the public Internet. ■

For more on firewalls, go to Microsoft's firewall page at www.microsoft.com/technet/security/guidance/secmod155.mspx, which explains the security policies you can configure with different kinds of firewalls.

Try This!

Installing ZoneAlarm

ZoneAlarm is a popular firewall product. There is a freeware version you can download and install at no cost on any Windows computer. Millions of users run the free version as their personal firewall. In this exercise, you install the freeware version and explore its abilities to block traffic from computers that are not trusted, restrict specific programs on your computer from accessing or serving other computers, view security alerts and logs, and quarantine VBScript files in e-mail attachments. To download and install the free version of ZoneAlarm, follow these steps:

1. Go to www.zonelabs.com and follow the link to ZoneAlarm (free). When the download screen appears, click the ZoneAlarm download button. Then click the link to download free ZoneAlarm.

2. The free ZoneAlarm download is a self-extracting archive that has the *.exe* filename extension. When prompted, save this file on your computer in the folder of your choice.

3. When the download completes, click the Open button to run the self-extracting archive, and follow the onscreen instructions to install ZoneAlarm. When asked whether you want to take the tutorial to learn how to use ZoneAlarm, say Yes to study the instructions.

4. Figure 13-12 shows that ZoneAlarm presents the settings in five categories named Overview, Firewall, Program Control, Alerts & Logs, and E-mail Protection. You should set up ZoneAlarm to load automatically on startup. To check that setting, click the Preferences tab in the Overview category.

5. Figure 13-13 shows that the ZoneAlarm Firewall category has two zones. The Internet zone contains unknown computers, and the trusted zone is where you define the computers you choose to trust. To put a computer into the trusted zone, click the Firewall category's Zones tab and then click the Add button. A menu prompts you to enter a host by name or IP address. Make your choice and follow the onscreen instructions.

6. When programs on your computer attempt to access the Internet, ZoneAlarm will prompt you to permit, deny, or allow access just this once. Figure 13-14 shows the Program Control setting that makes this happen. You need to be careful, however, in granting programs permission to access the Internet. To review the programs to which you have permitted or denied access, click the Programs tab, which brings up the screen illustrated in Figure 13-15.

7. To see the logs kept by ZoneAlarm, click the Alerts & Logs category and then click the Log Viewer tab. For help on this or any other ZoneAlarm feature, click the Help button that is in the upper-right corner of every ZoneAlarm screen.

8. If you like the free version of ZoneAlarm, you may wish to consider the added security features of ZoneAlarm Pro, which quarantines many kinds of harmful e-mail attachments, protects against spoofing, identifies the physical location of attackers, blocks ads and popups, manages the cache, and controls cookies. Go to www.zonelabs.com and follow the link to learn more about ZoneAlarm Pro.

Try This!
continued

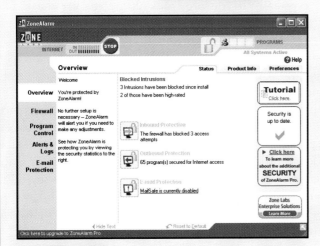

FIGURE 13-12 To configure ZoneAlarm, you click one of the five general categories in the menu on the left, and then click the tab containing the settings you want. Shown here is the status tab of the Overview category. ■

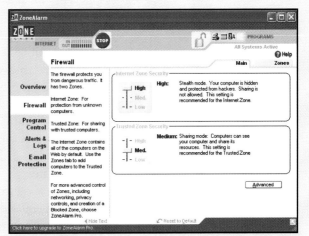

FIGURE 13-13 ZoneAlerm's Firewall category has two zones: the Internet zone and the trusted zone. The Internet zone contains unknown computers, and the trusted zone is where you define the computers you choose to trust. You should set the Internet zone's security to the high setting, which hides your computer from workstations that are not in your trusted zone. ■

FIGURE 13-14 Setting the program control to Medium causes ZoneAlarm to prompt you before permitting programs to access the Internet and respond to external requests. When a program asks for permission, think carefully before permitting it. The biggest problem with ZoneAlarm is that many users click Yes without thinking. If you open an e-mail message, for example, and ZoneAlarm asks whether you want to permit a new program to have Internet access, it could be malicious code coming in via the e-mail. ■

FIGURE 13-15 The Programs tab of ZoneAlarm's Program Control category reveals the programs to which you have allowed or denied access. The question mark means that the program needs to ask for permission. A green check mark means the program does not need to ask, and a red X means the program is denied. To change a setting, click it to open a popout menu from which you can choose a green check mark, a red X, or a question mark. ■

Transmitting Network Data Securely

Whenever you transfer data that needs to remain confidential, you should encrypt the data, especially if you are transmitting it over the public Internet. To **encrypt** means to encode the data stream by manipulating the symbols with a set of rules called an algorithm that makes the message appear scrambled and unintelligible. To decipher the data, the person who receives the message must have the **encryption key**, the secret algorithm comprising the rules used to encode the message.

Consider a simple example of an encryption key "123" that shifts each successive character in the message by 1, 2, or 3 characters in the alphabet. So encrypted, the plaintext message *Hello world* appears in cyphertext as *Igomq zptoe*. To decrypt the cyphertext, the person receiving the message needs to have the encryption key. Because "123" is a very simple key, however, a cracker could easily figure it out. In practice, encryption keys are much longer, and the encoding process is so complex that you would need a supercomputer to crack the encryption key.

Symmetric Cryptography and Secret-Key Encryption

Encryption systems are either symmetric or asymmetric. **Symmetric cryptography**, also called secret-key cryptography, uses the same secret key for both encryption and decryption. The most popular symmetric encryption standard is the Data Encryption Standard (DES). Figure 13-16 illustrates the DES algorithm. Even with a supercomputer and a staff of talented cryptologists, cracking such encryption can take many days or weeks. Due to advances in supercomputer technology that crackers may use to discover a DES key, the U.S. government uses triple DES (3DES) encryption, in which a message undergoes the DES process three times. Other symmetric encryption algorithms include RC2, RC4, RC5, and RC6, which Ronald Rivest developed for RSA Security. RC stands for Ron's Code. To learn more about the RC algorithms, go to www.rsasecurity.com/rsalabs/faq. Another popular secret-key algorithm is the International Data Encryption Algorithm (IDEA), a 64-bit iterative block cipher with a 128-bit key. More information about IDEA is at en.wikipedia.org/wiki/International_Data_Encryption_Algorithm.

The obvious weakness of secret-key cryptography is that the privacy of the information is only as good as the secrecy of the key. If a cracker learns the key by sniffing it in an Internet transmission, for example, or by fooling an insider into divulging it, the mathematical elegance of the encryption algorithm offers little protection.

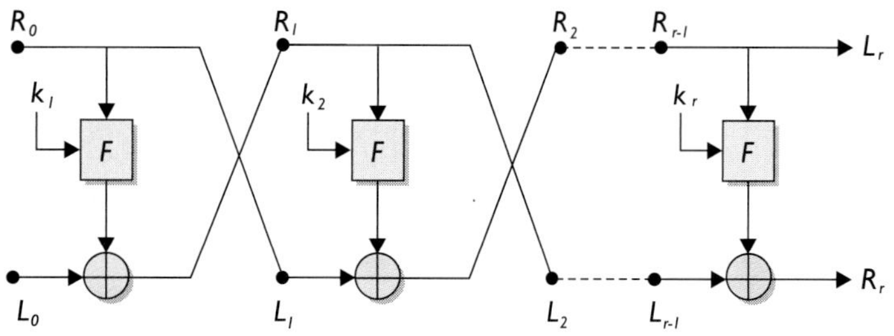

FIGURE 13-16 *DES uses a 16-round Feistel cipher based on a 56-bit encryption key. The block of plaintext being encrypted goes through an iterative process that calculates the ciphertext by repeated application of the Feistel transformation.* ■

Advanced Encryption Standard

Inside Info

By the time you read this, the U.S. government will be transitioning to a newer encryption scheme called the Advanced Encryption Standard (AES), which supports key sizes of 128 bits, 192 bits, and 256 bits.

Asymmetric Cryptography and Public Key Infrastructure (PKI)

To avoid the security risk posed by having users share secret keys, you can use a **public key infrastructure (PKI),** a certificate authority system that assigns to each user a digital certificate containing a key pair consisting of a public key and a private key. The person sending a message uses the public key to encrypt the message, and the person receiving the message uses the private key to decrypt it. Because the key that encrypts the message is different from the key that decrypts it, this process is called **asymmetric cryptography.**

In a PKI, many users within an organization can share the public key. The security comes from the private key, which the user never transmits or shares. Thus, the PKI eliminates the weakness of symmetric cryptography's reliance on a shared secret, because the sender and receiver never transmit a secret key that crackers can sniff. Most PKI implementations use X.509 certificates, following standards issued by the Internet Engineering Task Force's Public Key Infrastructure X.509 (PKIX) working group, whose charter is at www.ietf.org/html.charters/pkix-charter.html.

The most popular form of public-key cryptography is the RSA public-key cryptosystem. RSA stands for Rivest, Shamir, and Adleman, the cryptographers who invented the system. The RSA algorithm works as follows:

> Take two large primes, p and q, and compute their product $n = pq$; n is called the modulus. Choose a number, e, less than n and relatively prime to $(p-1)(q-1)$, which means e and $(p-1)(q-1)$ have no common factors except 1. Find another number d such that $(ed - 1)$ is divisible by $(p-1)(q-1)$. The values e and d are called the public and private exponents, respectively. The public key is the pair (n, e); the private key is (n, d). The factors p and q may be destroyed or kept with the private key.
>
> *Source:* www.rsasecurity.com/rsalabs/node.asp?id=2214

Using mathematical methods known today, obtaining the private key d from the public key (n, e) is extremely difficult. A cracker who could factor n into p and q, however, could obtain the private key d. To prove how hard this is to do, an ongoing contest called the RSA Factoring Challenge offers prize money to anyone who can factor the kinds of large numbers that RSA uses to design its secure cryptosystems. When this book went to press, the prize money ranged from $10,000 for the 576-bit challenge to $200,000 for factoring a number consisting of 2048 bits. For more information, go to www.rsasecurity.com/rsalabs, click Challenges, and follow the link to the new RSA factoring challenge.

Digital Signatures and Hash Encryption

Besides keeping confidential data private, you also need a way to tell whether the message is authentic. In other words, did the message truly come from the person who appears to have sent it, and has the message been altered along the way? Digital signatures provide a way for you to know.

A **digital signature** is an identification method that binds a document to the possessor of a particular key by creating a message digest and encrypting the digest with the sender's key. When you receive a message that contains a digital signature, Figure 13-17 shows how you can inspect the signature to see where the message came from, who owns the key that signed the message, what certificate authority issued the key, and what algorithms created the signature and the message digest.

A one-way encryption method called **hash encryption** creates the message digest. Hash encryption performs mathematical calculations on the message as a whole and computes a fixed-length number called a **message digest**, which is the message's digital fingerprint. When a digitally signed message arrives at its destination, the receiver's computer employs the same hash algorithm to see if the resulting calculation matches the message digest. The formula is $md = H(m)$, where md is the message digest, H is the hash function, and m is the message. The message can be of any length, but the message digest has a fixed length. It is computationally infeasible to reconstruct the message from its digest. Thus, hash values can verify the in-

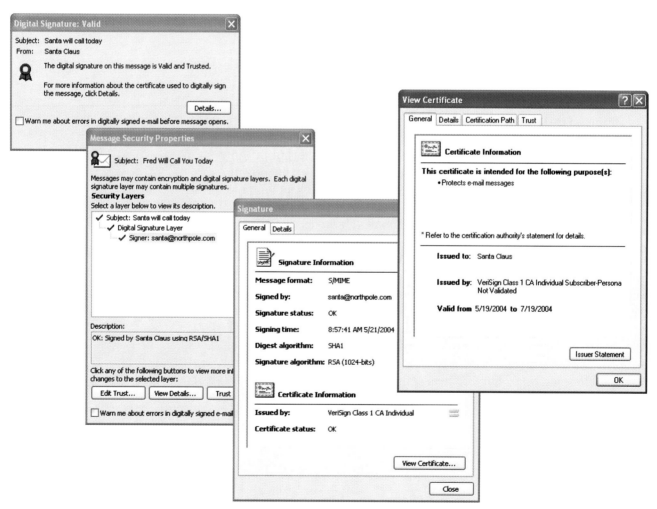

FIGURE   13-17 *When you receive a digitally signed e-mail message and click the digital signature to inspect it, you can see who sent the message and click the Details buttons to reveal the certificate authority that issued the Digital ID, the algorithms used in the signing, and the signing time.* ■

tegrity of a message without transmitting the message itself. The two most commonly used hash encryption algorithms include:

- **SHA-1** Invented by the National Institute of Standards and Technology (NIST), SHA-1 is a corrected version of the Secure Hash Algorithm (SHA), which takes a message up to 2^{64} bits in length and produces a 160-bit message digest.

- **MD5** Rivest, who is the R in RSA, invented the MD2, MD4, and MD5 message digest (MD) algorithms. The latest and greatest version is MD5, which creates a 128-bit message digest using an improved version of the MD4 algorithm. Details and source code for MD2, MD4, and MD5 are in RFC 1319, 1320, and 1321, respectively.

Using a Digital ID with Microsoft Outlook

Microsoft follows the X.509 digital certificate standard throughout its client and server products. If you have Microsoft Outlook, for example, you can get an X.509 certificate consisting of a key pair that enables you to digitally sign your mail and/or send mail encrypted. The certificate authority (CA) recommended by Microsoft is VeriSign, which offers a 60-day free trial, after which the cost of keeping the certificate is $14.95 per year. To get a VeriSign certificate for use with Microsoft Outlook, follow these steps:

1. Pull down the Microsoft Outlook Tools menu and choose Options to bring up the Options dialog.

2. When the Options dialog appears, click the Security tab. Near the bottom of the Security settings, click the button titled Get a Digital ID to bring up a Web page listing the digital ID services recommended by Microsoft. Figure 13-18 shows that these services include VeriSign, which provides digital IDs for secure e-mail.

3. Follow the link to VeriSign, one of the Internet's primary certificate authorities. Figure 13-19 shows that VeriSign offers a 60-day free trial. Click the link to the free trial, and follow the onscreen instructions to get a digital ID. These instructions take you through a four-step process that includes (1) filling out the enrollment form, (2) checking your e-mail for instructions, (3) picking up your digital ID, and (4) installing your digital ID.

4. After you fill out the enrollment form and follow the onscreen instructions to submit it, VeriSign will send you an e-mail message within the hour. Figure 13-20 shows that this message has a Continue button. Click the Continue button to proceed.

5. The final step of the installation process appears as illustrated in Figure 13-21. Click the Install button. A dialog comes onscreen warning you that installing certificates from untrusted Web sites is a security risk. When asked whether you really want to install the certificate, click OK.

note *The term digital ID refers to an X.509 certificate containing a key pair that consists of a public key and a private key.*

note *The purpose of this e-mail verification step is to ensure that you are the person who applied for this digital ID.*

6. To activate your Digital ID for use in sending e-mail, pull down the Outlook Tools menu, choose Options, click the Security tab, check the option to *Add digital signature to outgoing message*, and click the Settings button. When the Change Security Settings dialog appears, use the Choose buttons to select the certificate you want used for signing and encrypting messages. If you have no other certificates, the only choice will be the one you received

Click here to find out about obtaining a digital ID from the VeriSign certificate authority.

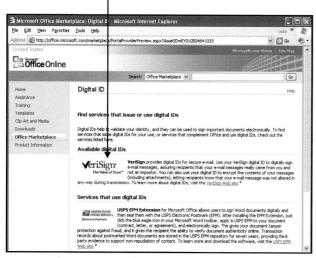

FIGURE 13-18 *Microsoft recommends VeriSign as the certificate authority from which you can obtain a Digital ID consisting of an X.509 certificate comprising a key pair that contains a public key and a private key. You can use this key pair to send encrypted e-mail. You can also sign and seal MS Word documents to prove you are the author and verify that the contents have not been tampered with.* ∎

FIGURE 13-19 *The certificate authority VeriSign has a 60-day free trial whereby you can get a Digital ID that you can use to send encrypted e-mail messages.* ∎

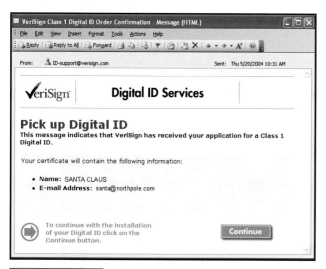

FIGURE 13-20 *Within an hour of submitting the Digital ID application form, VeriSign sends you an e-mail message. When you receive this message, click the Continue button, which brings up the installation screen illustrated in Figure 13-21.* ∎

FIGURE 13-21 *The final step in the VeriSign Digital ID procurement process is to click the Install button and follow the onscreen instructions.* ∎

when you worked through this exercise. After you finish reviewing the settings, click OK to close the dialogs.

7. Use Outlook to send yourself an e-mail message. When you click the Send button, Outlook informs you that the message is being signed. When you receive the message, you should see a new header named *Signed by* telling you who signed the message.

8. Alongside that header, note the Digital Signature button on the right edge of the message. Click that button to see validation information regarding the signature.

9. When someone who has a key sends you a digitally signed message and you want to add their key to your contact list, right-click their name in the From box and choose Add to Contacts. If the person already has a contact entry, select *Update new information from this contact to the existing one.*

10. To send mail that is encrypted, pull down the Outlook Tools menu, choose Options, click the Security tab, and check the option to Encrypt contents and attachments for outgoing messages. If you then send a message to someone who does not have a key pair, a dialog will warn you that the person does not have a key pair and ask if you want to send the message unencrypted.

11. In the future, if you ever need to change your Digital ID settings or learn more about the things you can do with your Digital ID, go to www.verisign.com/client/guide.

Secure Sockets Layer (SSL) Handshake Protocol

So far, this chapter has presented encryption methods that operate on blocks of information in e-mail messages, for example, or in word-processed documents. Algorithms designed to encrypt blocks of text are called **block ciphers**. There is another important class of algorithms called **stream ciphers**, which operate at the byte (*i.e.*, character) level to encrypt real-time communications. When you use a browser to conduct financial transactions at an online store, for example, the e-commerce site uses a stream cipher to encrypt the session. The most popular stream cipher is RC4, which Ronald Rivest designed for RSA Security.

One of the protocols that use RC4 is the **secure sockets layer (SSL)**, a handshake protocol that defines how a server establishes a secure session in response to an end user's request to transact. During this first part of the handshake, the server sends its certificate and cipher preferences, which the client uses to create a master key. After encrypting the master key with the server's public key, the client sends the encrypted master key to the server, which authenticates itself to the client via the master key. For the remainder of the session, the client and the server encrypt subsequent communications with keys derived from the master key. Periodically, the server may send a challenge to the client, which authenticates by sending its digital signature and public key certificate in response to the challenge.

SSL supports many encryption algorithms that may be used after the handshake, including RC2, RC4, IDEA, DES, and triple-DES.

Transport Layer Security (TLS) Handshake Protocol

The IETF is working on a successor to SSL called **transport layer security (TLS)**. SSL and TLS have a lot in common. Both run on port 443, the Internet port reserved for secure HTTP sessions. Like SSL, TLS supports RC2, RC4, IDEA, DES, and triple DES. In addition, the IETF is building into TLS support for AES, which will eventually replace DES.

When you visit a Web site running secure over SSL or TLS, the URL in the Web address field begins with *https* instead of http. The letter *s* in https stands for secure. During the secure session, the browser displays the Security icon in the browser's status bar. This icon signals to the user, for example, that confidential forms data and credit card information are being encrypted instead of passing over the Internet in clear text.

The transport layer security working group of the IETF is responsible for creating the https protocols. For the latest on SSL and TLS, visit the IETF working group at www.ietf.org/html.charters/tls-charter.html.

IPSec and Virtual Private Networks (VPN)

The IETF's **Internet Protocol Security (IPSec)** working group is defining a framework of open standards that use cryptography services to ensure private, secure communications over IP networks. Intended to be the future standard for secure Internet communications, IPSec is already the de facto standard. Microsoft, for example, has integrated IPSec into the Active Directory service. Windows 2000, Windows 2003, and Windows XP support the use of IPSec for network-level peer authentication, data origin authentication, data integrity, encryption, and replay protection.

An important application of IPSec is the creation of a **virtual private network (VPN)**, a private data network that makes use of the public Internet's telecommunication infrastructure, maintaining privacy through the use of session keys and an HTTP tunneling protocol over which encrypted data passes. There are two basic types of VPNs. First, you can use a VPN to connect two private networks across the Internet. Second, you can use a VPN to create an extranet in which authorized users who have the necessary keys can access a private network from a remote Internet location that is outside the private net. Figure 13-22 illustrates how the IPSec driver operates at the datagram layer of the Internet by translating IP packets from the Transport Layer into secure IP packets for transmission over the Internet Layer. IPSec's Internet Key Exchange (IKE) framework governs the establishment and management of session keys. For more on IPSec and the RFCs it comprises, go to the Virtual Private Network Consortium (VPNC) at www.vpnc.org.

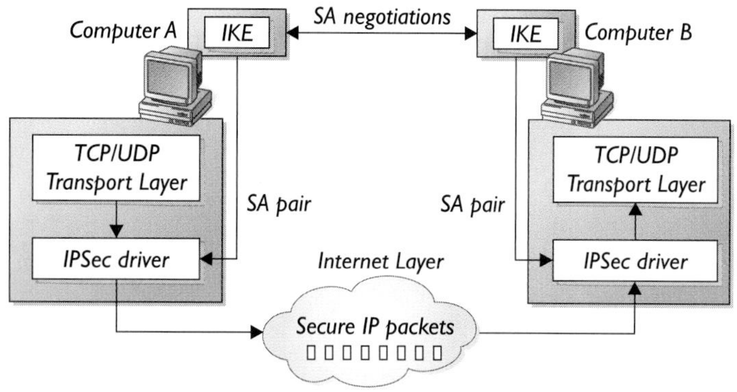

FIGURE   13-22   *The IPSec process consists of an Internet key exchange (IKE) through which two computers negotiate the keys that will encrypt the session, and an IPSec driver that translates IP packets from the Transport Layer into secure IP packets for transmission over the Internet Layer.* ■

Pretty Good Privacy (PGP)

Invented by Phil Zimmerman in 1991, **Pretty Good Privacy (PGP)** is a data integrity system that uses encryption, data compression, and digital signatures to provide for the secure transmission of e-mail messages and other kinds of store-and-forward file systems. PGP can work with many different algorithms, including Elgamal or RSA for key transport, IDEA or CAST5 for block data encryption, DSA or RSA for signing, and SHA-1 or MD5 for computing message digests. The shareware program ZIP compresses the messages to conserve bandwidth in data transmission and to save space in file storage. The PGP corporate Web site at www.pgp.com sells commercial versions of PGP in corporate, workgroup, and personal desktop versions. The IETF has an OpenPGP working group that is creating an open specification for Pretty Good Privacy at http://www.ietf.org/html.charters/openpgp-charter.html.

Pretty Good Privacy is actually very good. Perhaps the best testimonial is Microsoft's use of PGP signatures to verify the authenticity of messages that come from the Microsoft Security Notification Service. You can download Microsoft's public PGP key from www.microsoft.com/technet/security/bulletin/notify.mspx.

Publishing a Web Securely

As you learned in Chapter 1, FTP is the protocol for transferring files over the Internet. One of the most common uses of FTP is to publish files to the Web. You learned how to do this in the Web publishing tutorial at the end of Chapter 7. Many people do not realize, however, that when you log on to a Web site by using an ordinary FTP client, your user name and password traverse the Internet in plain text. This is not very secure, because a cracker can use a packet sniffer to see your password in clear text. To prevent this from happening, you should have a secure FTP (SFTP) program that uses the secure shell (SSH) protocol to prevent your password and data from passing over the Internet in plain text.

Using a Secure Shell (SSH) Protocol

The **secure shell (SSH)** protocol enables two computers to negotiate and establish a secure connection that uses encryption to thwart crackers who may try to sniff passwords and data that would otherwise traverse the Internet in clear text. Through a process called **tunneling**, other kinds of TCP/IP connections can funnel through the SSH connection, which provides a secure communication channel for doing mail, accessing the Web, logging on securely to remote sites, and publishing files via SFTP.

The IETF's secure shell working group is in charge of standardizing the SSH protocols. You can read the charter at www.ietf.org/html.charters/secsh-charter.html.

Making a Secure FTP (SFTP) File Transfer

Searching Google or Yahoo for the keywords *sftp client* brings up many SFTP clients you can use to publish a Web securely. You will be happy to discover that the Core FTP client you learned in Chapter 7 supports SSH. If the Web server to which you transfer your files also supports SSH, you can use Core FTP to make an SFTP transfer. To make Core FTP use SSH, follow these steps:

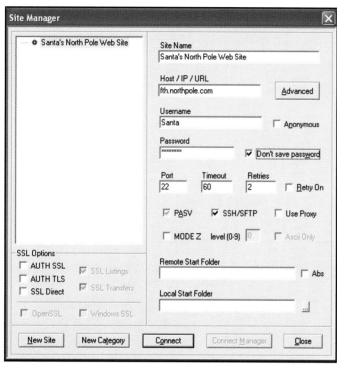

1. Click the Windows Start button and choose Programs | Core FTP | Core FTP. In the Site Manager window, select the site to which you want to connect.

2. Near the middle of the Site Manager window, check the box titled SSH/SFTP. Figure 13-23 shows that when you do this, the port number will change from 21 to 22, which is the SFTP port number.

3. Click the Connect button to connect to the FTP site. If the site supports SFTP, you will get a message asking if you trust the host and want to add its key to your SSH cache. Click Yes to store the key and continue. By storing this key you will get a warning if the remote key ever changes, which may clue you to a cracker trying a **man in the middle (MITM) attack** in which a cracker tries to hijack your session.

4. From now on, your Core FTP sessions at this site will use the SFTP protocol.

FIGURE 13-23 *To make the Core FTP program use the SSH protocol, check the box titled SSH/SFTP. When you check this box, the port automatically changes from 21 to 22, which is the SFTP port number.* ■

Having learned how to make a secure FTP (SFTP) transfer, you may now conclude this book with a clear conscience.

Chapter 13 Review

Chapter Summary

After reading this chapter and completing the step-by-step tutorials and Try This! exercises, you should understand the following facts about Internet security:

Identifying Internet Security Issues

- Internet security risks fall into three general categories: (1) unauthorized access, (2) data manipulation, and (3) service interruption.

- About two-thirds of all security breaches come from inside an organization's network architecture. To help guard against inside attacks, you should locate equipment behind locked doors and limit access to authorized personnel.

- A social engineering attack exploits human weaknesses to gain access to the organization's network.

- Depending on the nature of the organization, some security threats will be more of an issue than others. Because it is impossible to prepare for all possible attacks, identifying assets helps prioritize the need for different kinds of defenses.

- Viruses top the list of attacker's tools. Viruses propagate by attaching themselves to software programs or other kinds of files. When a user executes or opens a file thus infected, the user's computer catches the virus.

- Another kind of malicious code is the worm, which can propagate across the Internet and infect other computers without attaching itself to other programs. Worms can wreak havoc by replicating themselves on an infected system to tie up all its resources and then following that system's network connections to attack other computers.

Applying Internet Security Safeguards

- For millions of end users and server administrators who have the Windows operating system, subscribing to one or more of the Microsoft Security Newsletters is an excellent way to keep up with Microsoft's security strategies and guidance.

- Microsoft runs a service called Windows Update that can automatically download the latest security patches to your computer. You can configure the service to install the patches right away or to notify you when the patches are ready to install.

- The most frequent kind of attack is Denial of Service (DoS), in which the attacker seeks to consume so much of a server's resources that the host cannot respond to legitimate requests.

- In a so-called brute force or front door attack, a cracker programs a computer to look up words in a dictionary and generate variants with which the computer keeps trying to log on until it discovers a password that gets in.

- Another security risk created by well-intentioned IT staff is the trapdoor attack, in which crackers find a way into your computer by running diagnostic tools that your IT staff left on the system after troubleshooting some kind of problem.

- Security auditing is a proactive process that considers the risks associated with security assets, predicts the methods crackers may use to exploit each risk, and takes protective steps to thwart them.

- A firewall is a combination of hardware, software, and security policies that block certain kinds of traffic from entering or leaving an entire network, subnet, or individual host computer. Depending on the configuration, the firewall has one of four topologies: (1) packet filtering firewall, (2) single-homed bastion host firewall, (3) dual-homed bastion host firewall, or (4) screened subnet firewall with DMZ.

Transmitting Network Data Securely

- To encrypt means to encode the data stream by manipulating the symbols with a set of rules called an algorithm that makes the message appear scrambled and unintelligible. To decipher the data, the person who receives the message must have the encryption key, the secret algorithm comprising the rules used to encode the message.

- Symmetric cryptography, also called secret-key cryptography, uses the same secret key for both encryption and decryption.

- To avoid the security risk posed by having users share secret keys, you can use a public key infrastructure (PKI), a certificate authority system that assigns to each user a digital certificate containing a key pair consisting of a public key and a private key. The person sending a message uses the public key to encrypt the message, and the person receiving the message uses the private key to decrypt it. Because the key that encrypts the message is different from the key that decrypts it, this process is called asymmetric cryptography.

- A digital signature is an identification method that binds a document to the possessor of a particular key by creating a message digest and encrypting the digest with the sender's key. A one-way encryption method called hash encryption creates the message digest.

- Microsoft follows the X.509 digital certificate standard throughout its client and server products. The certificate authority (CA) recommended by Microsoft is VeriSign, which refers to digital certificates via the term Digital ID.

- The Secure Sockets Layer (SSL) is a handshake protocol that defines how a server establishes a secure session in response to an end user's request to transact. SSL supports many encryption algorithms that may be used after the handshake, including RC2, RC4, IDEA, DES, and triple-DES. The IETF is working on a successor to SSL called transport layer security (TLS).

- The IETF's Internet Protocol Security (IPSec) working group is defining a framework of open standards that use cryptography services to ensure private, secure communications over IP networks. An important application of IPSec is the creation of a virtual private network (VPN), a private data network that makes use of the public Internet's telecommunication infrastructure, maintaining privacy through the use of session keys and an HTTP tunneling protocol over which encrypted data passes.

- Invented by Phil Zimmerman in 1991, Pretty Good Privacy (PGP) is a data integrity system that uses encryption, data compression, and digital signatures to provide for the secure transmission of e-mail messages and other kinds of store-and-forward file systems. Microsoft uses PGP signatures to verify the authenticity of messages that come from the Microsoft Security Notification Service.

Publishing a Web Securely

- Many people do not realize that when you log on to a Web site by using an ordinary FTP client, your password traverses the Internet in plain text. To keep this from happening, you should have an FTP program that uses the secure shell (SSH) protocol to prevent your password and data from passing over the Internet in plaintext.

- The Core FTP client supports the SFTP protocol. To make Core FTP use the SFTP protocol, check the SSH/SFTP box in the Site Manager.

Key Terms

application level gateway *(561)*

asymmetric cryptography *(567)*

bastion host *(562)*

block cipher *(571)*

boot record virus *(553)*

brute force attack *(558)*

circuit level gateway *(560)*

demilitarized zone (DMZ) *(563)*

Denial of Service (DoS) *(558)*

digital signature *(567)*

dual-homed bastion *(562)*

encrypt *(566)*

encryption key *(566)*

file infector virus *(554)*

firewall *(560)*

front door attack *(558)*

hash encryption *(568)*

inside attack *(551)*

IP address spoofing *(552)*

Internet Protocol Security (IPSec) *(572)*

macro virus *(554)*

man in the middle (MITM) attack *(574)*

masquerading *(552)*

message digest *(568)*

packet filter *(561)*

Pretty Good Privacy (PGP) *(573)*

public key infrastructure (PKI) *(567)*

replay attack *(552)*

screened-subnet firewall *(563)*

secure shell (SSH) *(573)*

secure sockets layer (SSL) *(571)*
security auditing *(559)*
single-homed bastion *(562)*
social engineering attack *(552)*
stateful inspection *(561)*

stream cipher *(571)*
symmetric cryptography *(566)*
transport layer security (TLS) *(572)*
Trojan horse *(554)*

tunneling *(573)*
virtual private network (VPN) *(572)*
Windows Update Service *(557)*
worm *(554)*

Key Terms Quiz

1. _____ is a masquerade that happens when an intruder uses the IP address of a trusted system to gain access rights granted to that system.

2. A(n) _____ is malicious code that can propagate across the Internet and infect other computers without attaching itself to other programs.

3. In a brute force attack or _____, a cracker programs a computer to look up words in a dictionary and generate variants with which the computer keeps trying to log on until it discovers a password that gets in.

4. _____ is a proactive process that considers the risks associated with security assets, predicts the methods crackers may use to exploit each risk, and takes protective steps to thwart them.

5. The simplest kind of firewall uses a(n) _____, which monitors the headers of all incoming or outgoing packets and can block transmissions based on source or destination ports or IP addresses.

6. A(n) _____ is a computer that sits on the perimeter of a local network and serves as an application level gateway between the external network and the internal client workstations.

7. The _____ topology establishes a demilitarized zone (DMZ) by placing packet filtering routers on both the Internet side and the private network side of the application gateway.

8. _____, also called secret-key cryptography, uses the same secret key for both encryption and decryption.

9. To avoid the security risk posed by having users share secret keys, you can use a(n) _____, a certificate authority system that assigns to each user a digital certificate containing a key pair consisting of a public key and a private key.

10. The _____ is a protocol that enables two computers to negotiate and establish a secure connection that uses encryption to thwart crackers who may try to sniff usernames, passwords, and data that would otherwise traverse the Internet in clear text. Through a process called tunneling, other kinds of TCP/IP connections can funnel through this connection, which provides a secure communication channel for doing mail, accessing the Web, logging on securely to telnet sites, and publishing files via FTP.

Multiple-Choice Quiz

1. When a cracker uses a packet sniffer to record a logon sequence to play back at a later time in an attempt to gain access, what kind of an attack is it?
   a. Brute force
   b. Inside
   c. Masquerade
   d. Replay

2. What kind of virus runs code from the startup device when you turn the power on?

   a. Boot record
   b. File infector
   c. Macro
   d. Trojan horse

3. Which safeguard can download and install security patches automatically?
   a. Microsoft Security Notification Service
   b. Passport
   c. Process Explorer
   d. Windows Update Service

4. Which firewall strategy can detect a hijack by keeping track of when a port opens, what session is using it, and how long it stays open?
   a. Application level gateway
   b. Circuit level gateway
   c. Network address translation
   d. Stateful inspection

5. Which firewall topology uses two NICs on which IP forwarding is disabled, thereby creating a complete physical break between the internal and external networks?
   a. Dual-homed bastion
   b. Packet filtering
   c. Screened subnet
   d. Single-homed bastion

6. Which one of the following applications is popular as a personal firewall product?
   a. IPSec
   b. Process Explorer
   c. SSH secure shell
   d. ZoneAlarm

7. Which of the following is a hash algorithm used for one-way encryption?
   a. AES
   b. DES

c. MD5
d. RC4

8. What protocol does X.509 define?
   a. Digital certificates
   b. SSL
   c. SFTP
   d. SSH

9. What kind of network can you create by using the IPSec protocol to create an Extranet in which authorized users who have the necessary keys can access a private network from a remote Internet location that is outside the private net?
   a. IKE
   b. SSH
   c. STP
   d. VPN

10. Which of the following products is a data integrity system that uses encryption, data compression, and digital signatures to provide for the secure transmission of e-mail messages and other kinds of store-and-forward file systems?
    a. DES
    b. PKI
    c. PGP
    d. SSL

▪ Essay Quiz

1. Explain how a network administrator could have used a packet filtering firewall to stop Slammer, which attacked through the Microsoft SQL resolution service that runs on port 1434.

2. Describe the architectural difference between single-homed and dual-homed bastion firewall topologies. In particular, describe the nature of the second layer of defense you can achieve by using two NICs instead of one inside the bastion host.

3. Explain why you must warn users about the danger of following links to non-trusted sites. In particular, explain the Web page technology through which a cracker can run malicious code on the user's computer.

4. How does a public key infrastructure (PKI) avoid the security risk posed by having users share secret keys? If the key is public, what prevents a cracker from using the public key to decrypt the message?

5. What does it mean when a Web address begins with https instead of http? Tell what the *s* in https stands for, and explain the handshaking that goes on behind the scenes.

Lab Projects

• Lab Project 13-1: Choosing a Virus Scanner

Schools and companies can lose a lot of time and money when viruses strike. It is critically important for both the servers and the client computers in your workplace to be protected from viruses. Imagine that you work for a school or company that has recently undergone a bad virus attack. Your employer wants to prevent such an attack from happening again. Your employer has asked you to recommend the brand of virus scanner that should be installed on all the machines at your workplace. You have also been asked to look into protecting the computers your fellow employees have at home, to minimize the risk that employees might inadvertently transmit to the workplace a virus from their home computer. In adopting a virus scanner for use in your school or company, consider these issues:

- Dangerous viruses can spread quickly across the Internet. The virus scanner you recommend should have an update service that automatically updates the virus definitions when new viruses come on the Net.

- Home computers need to be protected as well as machines in the workplace. If school children are using an employee's computer at home, for example, viruses from school can be transmitted to the employee's home computer, from which the infection could propagate to the workplace.

- If there is a mix of Windows and Macintosh machines in the workplace and in coworker homes, you need to consider virus protection for both brands of operating systems. Also consider other operating systems that may be used on your workplace network.

- Viruses can be caught both coming and going. Consider whether the virus scanner you are considering can scan outgoing as well as incoming messages.

- Consider all the ways information can come and go, including E-mail, IM, FTP, and peer-to-peer file sharing. Check to see whether the virus scanner you are proposing scans all these ways of transmitting viruses.

- New ways of transmitting viruses may have been discovered or invented since this book went to press. Check the virus alert centers at www.sarc.com and www.mcafee.com to see if any new transmission modes have arisen.

Use a word processor to write up your virus scanner recommendation in the form of a brief essay. Report the brand names of the virus scanners you considered, identify the one you recommend for adoption in your workplace, and explain why you selected it instead of the others. If your instructor has asked you to hand in the report, make sure you put your name at the top; then save it on disk or follow the other instructions you may have been given for submitting this assignment.

• Lab Project 13-2: Determining Network Vulnerabilities

In a series of Microsoft white papers titled "Best Practices for Enterprise Security," Benson published a framework for determining network vulnerabilities. The framework consists of a series of questions organized according to the three categories of (1) physical security, (2) data security, and (3) network security. Imagine that your employer has asked you to use the Benson framework in determining the vulnerabilities of your school or workplace network. Use your word processor to write an essay in which you answer the questions in the Benson framework and make recommendations for shoring up vulnerabilities you uncover. The questions to answer are as follows:

Category I: Physical Security

1. Are there locks and entry procedures to gain access to servers?
2. Is there sufficient air conditioning and are air filters being cleaned out regularly? Are air conditioning ducts safeguarded against break-ins?
3. Are there uninterruptible power supplies and generators, and are they being checked through maintenance procedures?
4. Is there fire suppression and pumping equipment and proper maintenance procedures for the equipment?
5. Is there protection against hardware and software theft? Are software packages and licenses and backups kept in safes?
6. Are there procedures for storing data, backups, and licensed software off-site and onsite?

Category II: Data Security

7. What access controls, integrity controls, and backup procedures are in place to limit attacks?
8. Are there privacy policies and procedures to which users must comply?
9. What data access controls (authorization, authentication, and implementation) are there?
10. What user responsibilities exist for management of data and applications?
11. Have direct access storage device management techniques been defined? What is their impact on user file integrity?
12. Are there procedures for handling sensitive data?

Category III: Network Security

13. What kinds of access controls (Internet, wide area network connections, etc.) are in place?
14. Are there authentication procedures? What authentication protocols are used for local area networks, wide area networks, and dialup servers? Who has the responsibility for security administration?
15. What types of network media (e.g., cables, switches, and routers) are used? What type of security do they have?
16. Is security implemented on file and print servers?
17. Does your organization make use of encryption and cryptography for use over the Internet, Virtual Private Networks (VPNs), e-mail systems, and remote access?
18. Does the organization conform to networking standards?

If your instructor asked you to hand in your answers to these questions, make sure you put your name at the top of the essay; then copy it onto a disk or follow the other instructions you may have been given for submitting this assignment.

Note: The full text of the Benson white paper that contains these questions is at www.microsoft.com/technet/security/bestprac/bpent/sec1/secstrat.mspx. More security resources are at www.microsoft.com/technet/security.

Glossary

10BaseT   Ethernet baseband wiring standard that uses category 5 twisted-pair telephone wiring to deliver networking speeds up to 10 Mbps. *See* CAT 5.

10/100BaseT   Ethernet wiring standard that can run at 10 or 100 megabits per second over category 5 twisted-pair telephone wiring. *See* 10BaseT.

10GbE   Ethernet wiring standard that uses fiber optics to push Ethernet into speeds ranging up to 10 gigabits per second (Gbps). The prefix giga means billion; 10 Gbps is therefore 10 billion bits per second.

absolute positioning   A Cascading Style Sheet feature that enables you to position page elements precisely onscreen based on x,y coordinates.

account   The file space on a server where your e-mail queues up waiting for you to read it and a login procedure that enables you to type your account name and password to log on and access your files.

Active Server Page (ASP)   A Microsoft ISAPI technology that enables Web developers to embed on a Web page server-side scripts written in either the JScript or VBScript programming language. *See* Internet SAPI (ISAPI).

active Web page   A document that uses the browser's window as a display surface through which the user can interact with dynamic objects onscreen.

ActiveX   Microsoft standard for creating controls that enable a wide variety of applications and content to be embedded in Web pages and other kinds of documents that support the ActiveX technology.

ActiveX Data Objects (ADO)   In the Windows operating system, an application programming interface (API) that enables business objects to make connections and issue commands against many different kinds of data sources.

address book   An index of the e-mail addresses you want to keep for future use, thereby avoiding the need to look up a person's e-mail address every time you want to send e-mail.

Address Resolution Protocol (ARP)   Defined by RFC 826, the method whereby the network's physical layer learns the nodes' physical MAC addresses in order to transmit a packet from one node to another. *See* MAC address; Media Access Control (MAC).

alert box   A window that a script creates by executing the alert() method of the JavaScript window object.

alt attribute   In Web accessibility, an attribute that provides alternate text for a non-text element such as an image.

analysis, design, development, implementation, and evaluation (ADDIE)   A project development cycle typically followed by software development projects.

animated GIF   A graphic that contains multiple images intended to be shown in a sequence at specific times and locations on the screen.

applet   Written in Java, a little application that can be transmitted over the Internet as part of a Web page. *See* Java.

AppleTalk   The legacy protocol suite for peer-to-peer networking on local networks of Macintosh computers.

Application Layer   In the OSI/RM, Layer 7, which receives the message from the client computer and begins to form the packet that will eventually travel across the network. In the Internet Architecture, the highest layer, encompassing OSI/RM Layers 7 and 6, where some of the Internet's most well-known protocols reside, such as HTTP, FTP, TFTP, Telnet, Gopher, SMTP, NNTP, DNS, SNMP, BOOTP, and DHCP. *See* OSI/RM.

application level gateway   A type of firewall that can scan packets for malicious content spread through SMTP (mail), HTTP (Web pages), FTP (file transfers), DNS (attacks on name servers), or Telnet (remote logon).

Archie   A search tool for finding files on FTP servers; a play on the word archive.

archive   A container into which one or more files has been compressed to save space and packed into a single file that can be transmitted easily over a network.

arp   *See* Address Resolution Protocol (ARP).

ARPANET   A packet-switched network invented in 1969 by the Advanced Research Projects Agency (ARPA) of the United States Department of Defense. Its goal was to support military research about how to build a network that could continue to function in the midst of partial outages that could be caused by bomb attacks.

ASP.NET   A powerful version of ASP that lets you create code behind the Web page on so-called code-behind pages that can be part of complete applications. Users interact with these pages from the browser window, which becomes the Web application's display surface. *See* Active Server Page (ASP).

assignment operator   In computer programming, the most fundamental operator, which uses the = symbol to assign values to variables.

asymmetric cryptography   A type of cryptography in which the key that encrypts the message is different from the key that decrypts it. *See public key infrastructure (PKI).*

Asynchronous Transfer Mode (ATM)   A high-speed WAN standard that sends the data in fixed-size units called cells, freeing the switches from the need to deal with variable-length packets. The switches can therefore process and route the data much faster than more traditional packet-switched technologies.

autonomous system (AS)   A set of routers under a single technical administration, such as an ISP or a backbone such as the NSFNet.

backbone   A network cable that acts as the primary pathway for traffic that is most often destined for other networks.

bandwidth on demand   A feature of the frame relay WAN standard that lets customers choose the connection speed of their frame relay port.

bastion host   A computer that sits on the perimeter of a local network and serves as an application-level gateway between the external network and the internal client workstations. *See application level gateway.*

BinHex   The Macintosh equivalent of uuencoding under UNIX. *See uuencoding.*

bits per second (bps)   The unit of measurement in which modem speed is often expressed. *See Kbps.*

block cipher   An algorithm designed to encrypt blocks of text, such as the text in the body of an e-mail message. *See encrypt; stream cipher.*

blog   A Web-accessible log written by an individual who wants to chronicle activity related to a given topic that is often personal.

Bluetooth   An emerging standard for high-speed wireless communications that enables the synchronization and exchange of information between mobile computers, telephones, portable handheld devices, and the Internet. Bluetooth transmits a short-range radio signal intended to replace the cables connecting electronic devices. It offers wireless connections to LANs, the public switched telephone network, and the Internet.

Bobby   A comprehensive Web accessibility tool that can analyze a single page or an entire Web site, expose barriers to accessibility, make recommendations for necessary repairs, and encourage compliance with existing guidelines. *See Web accessibility.*

body   The section of the Web page that comes after the `<body>` start tag but before the `</body>` stop tag.

bookmark   In a browser, a pointer to a favorite Web page that enables you to jump directly to that page without having to navigate the Web to get there. In an HTML file, a named anchor to which a hypertext reference can link.

Boolean   Named after the nineteenth-century mathematician George Boole, a form of algebra in which all values reduce to either TRUE or FALSE. The Boolean operators AND, OR, and NOT are widely used in computer programming and in search engines to construct queries that narrow a search to find precisely what you are looking for.

boot record virus   A type of virus that spreads through malicious code that runs from the boot record of the startup device when the computer boots.

Bootstrap Protocol (BOOTP)   Defined by RFC 951, a startup protocol that enables a workstation to discover configuration information, including its IP address, router address, and DNS server address.

Border Gateway Protocol (BGP)   Defined by RFCs 1267 and 1268, a routing protocol that keeps track of the status of neighboring ASs and uses a pruning process to select optimum routes. *See autonomous system (AS).*

bot   Short for robot, a software application programmed to act as an intelligent agent that goes out on the network to find or do things for you. You tell a bot what you want, and it worms its way through the Internet, finding all the relevant information, digesting it, and reporting it to you succinctly.

Bourne shell language   The original scripting language of the UNIX shell. *See UNIX.*

bridge   A relay that operates at the Data Link Layer of the OSI/RM, connecting two network segments and passing packets between them based on the destination MAC address of each frame.

British Naval Connector (BNC)   Also known as the Bayonet Nut Connector, a coaxial cable connector that has a male center pin connecting to the copper core of the coax, inside a metal tube connecting to the braided shield. Outside the tube is a rotating ring that locks the cable to the female BNC connectors found on NICs, hubs, repeaters, and concentrators.

broadband   A connection that carries multiple channels of information over a single cable.

brouter   A bridge router; a relay that functions as both a router and a bridge. *See bridge; router.*

browser   A computer application that enables you to surf the Web and go from site to site in search of information that interests you.

browsing   Progressively clicking through the Web by triggering the links that interest you. Synonymous with surfing. *See browser.*

brute force attack   A type of attack in which a cracker programs a computer to look up words in a dictionary and generate variants with which the computer keeps trying to log on until it discovers a password that gets in. Also called a front door attack.

bus   The single cable, also called a trunk, to which every device connects in a bus topology network.

bus topology   A network architecture in which every device on the network connects to a single cable called a bus or a trunk, which is a coaxial cable.

business-to-business (B2B)   An e-commerce model describing transactions that occur when companies conduct business electronically between themselves.

business-to-consumer (B2C)   An e-commerce model that occurs when an end user buys something from a company's online storefront.

cable modem   A network adapter used to connect PCs to TV cables in neighborhoods where cable TV companies offer Internet services over TV cables. The term broadband is used to refer to this type of connection that carries multiple channels of information over a single cable. *See broadband.*

cache   The location on your hard disk where the browser keeps copies of the most recently visited Web sites when you surf the Web.

caching server   A server that speeds access to resources by making a local copy of resources requested from the network so Web content and other kinds of documents and files can be served more quickly to subsequent users who request the same resources. Only if the date on the original document changed will the caching server download a fresh copy of the requested resource.

Canonical Name (CNAME)   An alias that lets a host with one name be accessed also by another name.

Carnivore   An FBI surveillance system that can scan the Internet's e-mail traffic looking for key words and phrases related to terrorist plots and criminal investigations.

cascading style sheet (CSS)   A set of rules that define styles to be applied to entire Web pages or individual Web page elements.

CAT 5   Category 5 unshielded twisted pair (UTP) wiring commonly used for Ethernet LANs. The outer sheath contains four twisted pairs in which the wires in each pair are twisted four times per inch.

catalog server   A server that uses robots called spiders to comb through a network's files and create an index of everything that is found. When users need to find something on the network, they search this catalog to find quickly what they seek.

cell padding   The amount of white space the browser puts inside the borders of the cells in a table.

cell spacing   The amount of space the browser puts between the borders of the cells in a table.

certificate server   A server that issues digital certificates that network hosts use to digitally sign and encrypt messages using public-private key pairs. *See digital certificate.*

CGI script   A computer program that responds to a CGI request. *See common gateway interface (CGI).*

chat   A popular form of real-time communication that enables people to converse with one another over the Internet.

check box   An HTML form control that displays a small box the user can check to select one or more items onscreen.

checkpoint   In the OSI/RM Session Layer, a marker used to signal that a certain amount of the data has arrived okay. *See Session Layer.*

checkout   At an online store, the process of paying for merchandise and any related shipping costs.

circuit level gateway   Operating at the Internet's Transport Layer, a type of gateway that prevents the establishment of end-to-end TCP connections by establishing instead a proxy connection on behalf of an inside host with an outside host, which views the gateway as its destination address.

class   In Cascading Style Sheets, a named definition of one or more styles.

client-server computing   A network architecture in which computers exchange information by sending it (as servers) and receiving it (as clients).

clip art   Pre-drawn artwork organized into a catalog or library that you can browse in search of appropriate icons, buttons, banners, backgrounds, tiles, or animated GIFs for use on Web pages.

ColdFusion   From Macromedia, an active scripting technology that uses its own proprietary scripting language called the ColdFusion Markup Language (CFML). *See active Web page.*

comma-delimited data   A flat-file method of storing all of a data table's records in a single file in which the data elements are separated by commas that serve as break characters. *See tab-delimited data.*

common gateway interface (CGI)   The protocol that browsers use to communicate with server-side scripts to send and receive data across the Internet. The CGI protocol defines the manner in which forms data, cookies, and other kinds of information in a Web request get submitted to the program or script that will process and respond to the request. *See CGI script.*

concatenate   To join strings together via the concatenation operator.

concatenation operator   In Java, JScript, and JavaScript, the + sign; in VBScript, the & sign. *See concatenate.*

concentrator   In an IEEE 802.3 Ethernet network, a multiport repeater that connects multiple Ethernet devices to a single Ethernet cable. Also called Ethernet hub.

connection object   The ADO component that connects you to the database and enables you to execute queries that insert, update, retrieve, or delete records from the database. *See ActiveX Data Objects (ADO).*

convergence   The process of unification that digitalization causes by enabling all the world's traditional ways of communicating to work over a common communications medium on the Internet.

cookie   A place in the computer's memory where browsers can store information about the user. Persistent cookies are stored on the user's hard disk; per-session cookies are stored in RAM.

CSMA/CD (Ethernet) The Carrier Sense Multiple Access with Collision Detection scheme employed by Ethernet networks to detect the data collisions that can occur when two or more devices use a data channel simultaneously and wait a random amount of time before resending the message after detecting a collision.

customer-to-customer (C2C) An e-commerce model that enables online users to bypass the storefronts and pay each other directly for goods or services that people want to sell to each other.

cyclic redundancy check (CRC) A mathematical calculation that the OSI/RM Data Link Layer places in the trailer of a packet so the destination computer can check the value to make sure the data was transmitted without error.

data frame The packets encoded in a raw bit format consisting of 0's and 1's that the OSI/RM Data Link Layer passes down to the Physical Layer for transmission over the network.

Data Link Control (DLC) A networking protocol invented by IBM to enable microcomputers to connect as clients to legacy mainframes.

Data Link Layer OSI/RM Layer 2, which transforms the data into data frames. *See data frame.*

data table A database structure that organizes the data into rows and columns; each row contains one record, and the columns contain the data fields that the record comprises.

data-driven Web page An HTML document in which part or all of the content derives from or depends on records or relationships in one or more databases.

datagram The format into which the OSI/RM Network layer combines the data with routing information that includes the source and destination addresses along with the recommended path, depending on network conditions and the nature of the data.

default gateway The router to which the packets first are sent when the sending and receiving computers are not on the same local network.

default page The Web page that appears onscreen when you visit a Web site without requesting a specific document. The default page is often the home page of the company or person who owns the site. *See home page.*

Demand Priority Access LAN (100VG-AnyLAN) The IEEE 802.12 local area networking standard designed to transmit at a speed of 100 Mbps over voice-grade (VG) telephone wiring.

demilitarized zone (DMZ) The security zone created when a screened-subnet firewall places packet filtering routers both on the Internet side and the private network side of the bastion host. *See bastion host; firewall.*

demultiplexing At the destination computer on the receiving end, the process of unpacking the message by processing and removing the headers added to the packets at each layer of the networking protocol stack.

Denial of Service (DoS) The most frequent kind of attack on the Internet, in which the attacker seeks to consume so much of a server's resources that the host cannot respond to legitimate requests.

digital cash Tokens with which the user pays for goods and services purchased online.

digital certificate In a public key infrastructure, a key pair consisting of a public key and a private key. The person sending a message uses the public key to encrypt the message, while the person receiving the message uses the private key to decrypt it. *See public key infrastructure (PKI).*

digital check A token that gets transmitted from your digital checkbook. As with a printed check, the merchant does not get paid until the digital check clears your bank.

digital divide A term used to refer to the barriers faced by people who are not connected to the Internet.

digital hub A multimedia computer that can distribute audio/ video streams to Ethernet receivers located in different parts of the house.

Digital Millennium Copyright Act (DMCA) Legislation enacted into law in the United States in 1998 to bring the United States into conformance with the World Intellectual Property Organization (WIPO) treaties. *See World Intellectual Property Organization (WIPO).*

digital signature An identification method that binds a document to the possessor of a particular key by creating a message digest and encrypting the digest with the sender's key. *See hash encryption; public key infrastructure (PKI).*

Digital Subscriber Line (DSL) A broadband method of connecting to the Internet over existing telephone lines. *See broadband.*

digital wallet The container for the digital cash or tokens with which the user pays for goods and services purchased online.

direct connection An Internet connection that is always on, such as Ethernet, ISDN, cable modem, DSL, and satellite connections.

direct routing The kind of routing that occurs when two computers on the same network communicate with each other. *See indirect routing.*

Directory Access Protocol (DAP) The X.500 directory standard created by the International Standards Organization (ISO) to make it possible for directory servers to communicate with each other and distribute the directory database over multiple networks.

directory server A standalone computer or server component in charge of managing a database that keeps track of all the users, passwords, resources, printers, servers, e-mail addresses, phone numbers, and departmental contacts throughout an organization's network.

div tag   In HTML, the `<div>` start and `</div>` stop tags create structural divisions onscreen. `<div>` is an abbreviation for division.

DOCTYPE declaration   A line of code at the top of a file that identifies the XML schema that defines the tag structure of the document.

document object model (DOM)   The official W3C structural definition of the objects, methods, and properties that comprise documents on the World Wide Web.

domain   Everything after the host name in a fully qualified domain name. *See* fully qualified domain name (FQDN).

Domain Name System (DNS)   As defined by RFCs 1034 and 1035, the protocol that translates a fully qualified domain name (e.g., www.loc.gov) into the numeric IP address (e.g., 140.147.249.7) needed to route information across the Internet.

dotted quad notation   The format of an IP address that has four 8-bit bytes separated by periods. *See* Domain Name System (DNS).

dual-homed bastion   A type of firewall that uses two NICs (hence the term, dual-homed) on which IP forwarding is disabled; creates a complete physical break between the internal and external networks.

Dynamic and/or Private Ports   Internet port numbers from 49152 to 65535, which are also known as ephemeral or temporary ports because they are intended for short-lived processes.

Dynamic Host Configuration Protocol (DHCP)   Defined by RFC 2131, a protocol that works in conjunction with BOOTP to assign during workstation initialization an IP address, router address, and other configuration parameters.

dynamic HTML   A term invented by Microsoft to refer to the animated Web pages you can create by using the DOM to combine HTML with style sheets and scripts that bring Web pages to life.

dynamically configured router   A type of router that updates its router information table automatically as it communicates with other routers about new routes that have been added or old routes that are no longer available.

e-commerce   The integration of digital communications, data management, and security capabilities that allow organizations to exchange information related to the sale of goods and services.

electronic data interchange (EDI)   The computerized exchange of business information between trading partners over computer networks.

em   A font size unit pronounced like the letter M. The setting 3em, for example, is three times the width of the letter *m*.

e-mail   The most often used Internet service; electronic mail messages queue up in your "in box," and you read and respond to the messages at your convenience. Many users read their electronic mail several times a day.

e-mail client   The software program you use to read your e-mail.

e-mail signature   A block of text that automatically gets appended to the e-mail messages you send.

embedded CSS   A style sheet that gets copied physically into the head of the Web page and applies to the Web page as a whole.

emoticon   A character combination that, when turned sideways, conjures a facial expression. The most common form of emoticon is the smiley. Turn your book clockwise to see that the characters `:)` convey a happy face.

encrypt   To run a message through an encoder that uses an encryption key to alter the characters in the message. Unless the person wanting to read the message has the encryption key needed to decode it, the message appears garbled. *See* asymmetric cryptography; encryption key; symmetric cryptography.

encryption key   The secret algorithm comprising the rules used to encode a message. *See* encrypt; public key infrastructure (PKI).

enterprise model   Networking architecture used in large organizations that dedicate entire servers to handling important tasks such as transferring mail, hosting databases, managing security, and routing network traffic.

Ethernet   Baseband networking standard that works by detecting the data collisions that can occur when two or more devices use a data channel simultaneously. A device waits a random amount of time after detecting a collision and attempts to resend the message. If the data collides again, the device waits twice as long before resending the message.

Ethernet hub   An Ethernet multiport repeater, also known as a concentrator. *See* concentrator.

event   In computer programming, an action that provides an opportunity to trigger a script that can use objects to inspect properties and execute methods that make things happen onscreen or keep records behind the scenes.

extensible stylesheet language (XSL)   An XML dialect that Web designers use to specify the styling, layout, and pagination of the structured content in an XML document for some targeted presentation medium, such as a Web browser, a printer, an eBook, a screen reader, or a handheld device.

external CSS   A kind of style sheet that keeps all style definitions in a separate CSS file that you include in a Web page at runtime by using the `<link>` tag to apply the style sheet to the page.

External Gateway Protocol (EGP)   Defined by RFC 904, the protocol used to exchange net-reachability information between Internet gateways belonging to autonomous systems. *See* autonomous system (AS).

extranet   Network resources, such as Web sites, that are beyond the public's reach and require authorized users to do something extra, such as type a logon name and password, to obtain access. An extranet enables authorized users to access an intranet from outside its normal boundaries. *See* intranet.

e-zine An electronic magazine periodically distributed to users who subscribe to it.

fair use A section of the U.S. Copyright Law that allows the use of copyrighted works in reporting news, conducting research, and teaching.

Fast Ethernet A standard created by the IEEE CSMA/CD working group to run Ethernet networks at speeds up to 100 Mbps. *See* Gigabit Ethernet.

Fiber Distributed Data Interface (FDDI) Developed by American Standards Institute (ANSI) committee X3T9.5 for use in metropolitan are networks, FDDI uses two counter-rotating Token Rings operating at a speed of 100 Mbps.

fiber optics A high-speed transmission method that transmits light-modulated video, voice, or data signals through hair-thin strands of glass called fibers.

file infector virus Malicious code that attaches to individual files, which propagate primarily via e-mail attachments. *See* virus.

file permission attributes Settings that determine who is allowed to read, write, and execute your files.

File Transfer Protocol (FTP) As defined by RFC 959, the standard method for transferring files over the Internet from one computer to another. FTP can be used as a verb or a noun.

firefighter A peacemaker who works to diminish flames on the Internet. *See* flame.

firewall A combination of hardware, software, and security policies that block certain kinds of traffic from entering or leaving a network, subnet, or individual host computer. *See* application level gateway; circuit level gateway; network address translation (NAT); packet filter; stateful inspection.

flame On the Internet, a message written in anger.

Flash Freely distributed by Macromedia, a multimedia plug-in that is installed on more than 97% of the Internet's computers. *See* plug-in.

flat-file database A database that keeps all of the records in a single file, in which the data elements are separated by a break character such as a comma or a tab. *See* comma-delimited data; tab-delimited data.

floating point A number containing a decimal point with one or more numbers after the decimal point.

flood To pass traffic out of every network switch connection except the incoming interface through which the traffic was received.

for attribute In Web accessibility, an attribute that identifies the ID of the `<input>` element with which a label is associated. Assistive devices use these attributes to determine which labels go with which form elements and cue the user accordingly.

foreign key In a database, a data field that relates a record to the table in which that same column occurs as a primary key. *See* primary key.

form An HTML Web page element that prompts the user to fill in one or more blanks and/or select items from a menu of possible choices. These are followed by a button that the user clicks to submit the response after filling in the form.

fractional T1 A subset of a T1 line's 24 data channels.

fragments Sequentially numbered small data segments into which the OSI/RM Transport Layer splits the data if the amount of data is large.

frame One of the subdocuments in a frameset. *See* frameset.

Frame Relay A high-speed WAN standard that was originally developed for the Integrated Services Digital Network (ISDN) but is used today over many kinds of high-performance network interfaces.

frame targeting The process of making clicks on links in one frame determine what gets displayed in another frame. *See* frameset.

frameset An HTML Web page element that splits the browser window into two or more subdocuments called frames.

front door attack *See* brute force attack.

fully qualified domain name (FQDN) A complete DNS address that has the format hostname.registered-domain-name.top-level-domain. *See* Domain Name System (DNS).

function In computer programming, a named procedure you can call on by name any time you need to execute the code in the function.

gateway A computer that routes traffic from a workstation on an internal network to an external network such as the Internet, thereby serving as both router and switch. *See* router; switch.

Gbps Gigabits per second. *See* gigabit.

GET method An HTTP form method that puts the form data in a query string that gets appended to the URL specified in the form tag's action attribute.

gigabit A billion bits; giga means billion.

Gigabit Ethernet A networking standard developed by the IEEE CSMA/CD working group to run an Ethernet network at 1000 Mpbs.

gigapop A high-speed connection point strategically placed throughout the Internet2 network to guarantee high-speed bandwidth between universities, schools, and companies that are implementing the Internet2 standards. *See* Internet2.

Gopher As defined by RFC 1436, the legacy protocol for organizing information hierarchically on the Internet. Invented in 1991 at the University of Minnesota, home of the Golden Gophers. Its function on the Internet is to help you "go fer" things; thus, the term Gopher is a play on words.

gradient   A graphical effect created by colors fading gradually across or down the screen.

Graphics Interchange Format (GIF)   Invented by Compu-Serve for use on computer networks, GIF is the most prevalent graphics format for images on the Web.

hash encryption   A one-way encryption method that performs mathematical calculations on the message as a whole to create a message digest. See message digest.

head   The section of a Web page that goes between the <head> and </head> tags.

headers attribute   In Web accessibility, an attribute that iden-tifies the header(s) associated with each data cell in a table.

heading   The title of a section or subsection of a document. In HTML, there are six heading styles, numbered from H1 to H6.

helper app   An application the browser launches to help it han-dle something for which a player is not built in.

hertz (Hz.)   Vibrations or cycles per second.

hidden field   An HTML form control that creates a variable name and a corresponding value. These are not displayed onscreen but are posted along with the rest of the form data when the user clicks the button to submit the form.

hierarchy paradigm   A hypermedia design paradigm in which each object provides the user with a menu of choices that trig-ger more menus with more choices.

high-definition television (HDTV)   A digital television signal intended to replace NTSC as the television standard for the United States. HDTV is based on four technologies: (1) MPEG digital video compression; (2) transmission in packets that will permit any combination of video, audio, and data; (3) progres-sive scanning for computer interoperability up to 60 frames per second (fps) at 1920 x 1080 pixels; and (4) CD-quality digital surround sound using Dolby AC-3 audio technology.

home page   On the Web, the page you define as your browser's take-off point or start page.

hop   Each trip between routers taken by a packet as it works its way across a network to its destination address.

hop count   The number of trips between routers taken by a packet on its way from its origin to its destination address.

horizontal rule   A Web page element that creates a neat-look-ing dividing line between different parts of a Web page.

host computer   A computer that has an IP address on a TCP/IP network, such as the Internet.

hosts table   Prior to the 1983 invention of the hierarchically dis-tributed database of domain names and IP addresses, a huge file containing the name and IP address of every named host on the Internet. *See Domain Name System (DNS).*

hot word   *See hypertext link.*

hover   To use the mouse to position the pointer over a link and then hold the mouse stationary, thereby keeping the pointer over the link.

HTML   *See hypertext markup language (HTML).*

HTML editor   An editor that lets you create Web pages by working directly with the HTML tags.

HTML translator   A tool that can convert an existing docu-ment into the HTML format. Microsoft Word, Excel, Access, and PowerPoint have HTML translators built in.

HTML+TIME   In the Internet Explorer Web browser, Microsoft's implementation of XHTML+SMIL. See XHTML+SMIL.

hub   The device that serves as the center of a star network to-pology. In IEEE 802.3 Ethernet networks, a hub is an Ethernet multiport repeater, also known as a concentrator. *See concen-trator.*

hybrid paradigm   A hypermedia design paradigm that provides multiple navigational pathways by employing linear lists, menus, hierarchies, and network designs as appropriate throughout a large Web site.

hybrid topology   A network that employs more than one to-pology to connect devices for the purpose of networking, such as a star-ring hybrid that uses a token to synchronize the passing of messages from star to star.

hypergraphic trigger   A pictorial hot spot you click to trigger events linked to images on the screen.

hypertext   A term coined by Ted Nelson in 1965 to describe text that has been linked. When you view a hypertext and click a word that has been linked, your computer launches the object of that link. The links give the text an added dimension, which is why it is called hyper.

hypertext link   One or more words you click to trigger the events linked to the text. Synonymous with hot word. *See hypertext.*

hypertext markup language (HTML)   The standard format used for hypertext documents on the Web.

hypertext reference (href)   An HTML attribute that indicates where the link will go when clicked.

Hypertext Transfer Protocol (HTTP)   The protocol that transfers hypertext Web pages across the Internet. RFC 1945 defines HTTP 1.0, which opens a separate connection for each downloaded file. RFC 2616 defines HTTP 1.1, which avoids the overhead of creating separate sessions for each file by keeping the connection open so multiple files associated with a page can be downloaded all at once.

ICANN   The Internet Corporation for Assigned Names and Numbers that is in charge of the assignment of domain names, IP address numbers, and protocol parameter and port numbers.

id attribute   Assigns a unique ID to a specific HTML element, such as a header in a table.

IEEE 802.12   The demand priority access LAN standard. *See* Demand Priority Access LAN (100VG-AnyLAN).

IEEE 802.2   The Logical Link Control (LLC) sublayer of the OSI/RM Data Link Layer. *See* Data Link Layer.

IEEE 802.3   The standardization of Ethernet, which Bob Metcalfe invented in his doctoral dissertation project at Harvard in 1973. *See* Ethernet.

IEEE 802.5   The Token Ring standard. *See* Token Ring.

image button   An HTML form element you create with an `<input>` tag of type image to make the graphic substitute for the default submit button in a Web form.

image map   An invisible layer of triggers placed over an image on the screen. The triggers can be rectangular, circular, or polygonal. When the user clicks inside one of the invisible triggers, the Web browser triggers the object of the link.

include file   In computer programming, a separate file containing code that gets included in the page at runtime.

index   In database performance optimization, a database column or collection of columns that the database engine uses to keep the data presorted in the order in which you plan to query it.

indirect routing   The kind of routing that happens when the sending and receiving computers are not on the same local network, so the packets are sent to the MAC address of a router, which analyzes the destination address and forwards the packet on toward the appropriate network. *See* direct routing.

inetd   The UNIX and Linux utility that listens for incoming Internet requests and dispatches them to the appropriate server components that will process and respond to the requests. Short for Internet daemon. *See* Internet daemon.

information warfare   Electronic invasion of a nation's computer networks.

inline CSS   A style sheet that applies to only one page element, so it is copied "inline" on the page with that element.

input tag   An HTML form control in which the type attribute specifies the kind of control that will appear onscreen.

inside attack   A security breach that happens when employees from inside an organization's network architecture hack in to obtain unauthorized access to network services or data.

instant messaging (IM)   A real-time communication protocol that lets you send and receive instant messages over the Internet. IM can be used as a verb or a noun. You put onto a buddy list the names of the users who are permitted to contact you. Only the people on your buddy list can IM you.

instant storefront   A pre-programmed e-commerce system into which you enter your catalog of products and begin conducting business online.

integer   A whole number with no decimal point.

Integrated Services Digital Network (ISDN)   The digital telephone system that the regional Bell companies are installing in most of the United States. The Basic Rate Interface (BRI) service of ISDN is 144 Kbps, made up of two 64 Kbps data channels and one 16 Kbps control channel. The Primary Rate Interface (PRI) service uses 23 data channels and a 64 Kbps control channel to boost the data rate to 1,544 Kbps (1.544 Mbps).

Internet   The worldwide connection of more than 171 million computers that use the TCI/IP protocol suite to communicate.

Internet2   A high-speed version of the Internet that revolves around high-speed connection points called gigapops, which connect members of a consortium of research universities working in partnership with industry and government to create the faster network.

Internet address classes   Five classifications that may be assigned to an organization applying to ICANN for a range of IP addresses. Class A is for extremely large organizations that have more than 16 million hosts. Class B is for medium to large organizations with up to 65,534 hosts. Class C is for small organizations with up to 254 hosts. Class D is for multicast groups. Class E contains addresses reserved for future use.

Internet Architecture   Created by the IETF, an Internetworking model that implements in four layers the seven separate layers of the OSI/RM. The Internet Architecture layers are named Network Access (OSI/RM Layers 1 and 2), Internet (OSI/RM layer 3), Transport (OSI/RM Layers 4 and 5), and Application (OSI/RM Layers 6 and 7). *See* IETF; OSI/RM.

Internet Control Message Protocol (ICMP)   Defined by RFC 792, the messaging protocol that TCP/IP uses for troubleshooting. Routers and servers normally send error messages in ICMP packets when things fail on a TCP/IP network.

Internet daemon   In Greek mythology, daemons are supernatural guardian spirits that serve as intermediaries between gods and humans. On UNIX and Linux systems, the term daemon refers to any process that runs in the background, waiting to respond to certain kinds of requests. The role of the Internet daemon is to dispatch requests coming in from the Internet to the server components that will handle them. *See* inetd.

Internet Engineering Task Force (IETF)   The organization that defines the Internet Architecture protocols through a Request for Comments (RFC) process. An RFC moves through the following maturity states on its way to becoming a standard: (1) Proposed, (2) Draft, and (3) Internet Standard.

Internet Explorer (IE)   The Microsoft Web browser that ships as part of the Windows operating system.

Internet Group Management Protocol (IGMP)   Defined by RFC 1112, the protocol used for multicasting. *See* multicasting.

Internet Layer   Corresponding to OSI/RM Layer 3, the Internet Architecture Layer that takes the packet from the Transport

Layer, figures out the best way to route it across the Internet, and transforms it into an IP packet containing an IP header and trailer.

Internet Message Access Protocol (IMAP) An e-mail protocol designed for situations in which you want the mail to remain on the server instead of being delivered physically to your PC. This enables you to read your mail from different computers.

Internet Protocol (IP) The addressing system TCP uses to transmit packets over the Internet. As defined by RFC 791, the Internet Protocol (1) determines the best path for routing the packet on to its destination address, (2) addresses the packet accordingly, and (3) fragments the packet if it is too long for the network segment. The critical importance of these tasks earned IP its place in the name of the TCP/IP protocol suite. *See* IP address; TCP/IP.

Internet Protocol Security (IPSec) A framework of open standards that use cryptography services to ensure private, secure communications over IP networks. *See* virtual private network (VPN).

Internet SAPI (ISAPI) Microsoft's brand of SAPI. *See* Server Application Programming Interface (SAPI).

Internet Service Provider (ISP) A networking company that connects you to the Internet and provides you with Internet services, including access to the World Wide Web, e-mail, listserv, chat, and newsgroups.

intranet A network that uses the TCP/IP protocols to provide private services within an organization whose computers are not publicly accessible on the Internet. Intra is a Latin word that means within.

IP address Four numbers separated by periods. The numbers are 8-bit bytes that range in value from 0 to 255. The smallest address is 0.0.0.0 and the largest is 255.255.255.255. The number of IP addresses this scheme allows is 256^4, which is 4,294,967,296.

IP address spoofing A form of masquerading that happens when an intruder uses the IP address of a trusted system to gain access rights granted to that system. *See* masquerading.

IP broadcast address byte An 8-bit byte in which all bits are turned on, as in 11111111, which has the decimal value of 255. On the Internet, a message sent to an IP address ending with one or more 255s gets broadcast to all the hosts on the corresponding network. The address 255.255.255.255 broadcasts to all the hosts on a local area network but is not transmitted past the LAN's router. *See* limited broadcast; Net-directed broadcast; subnet-directed broadcast.

ipconfig On computers with Windows NT/2000/XP/2003 or later operating systems, a TCP/IP configuration utility that inspects the current IP configuration and can release, renew, or refresh DHCP leases if the computer's IP settings are dynamically configured. *See* Dynamic Host Configuration Protocol (DHCP).

IPv6 A new version of IP addressing that has eight numbers instead of four. Each number is a 16-bit value ranging from 0 to 65,535. The number of IP addresses this scheme allows is 65536^8, a huge number that provides thousands of addresses per square meter of the earth's surface.

IPX/SPX The Internetwork Packet Exchange (IPX) and Sequenced Packet Exchange (SPX) networking protocol suite developed by Novell for use with the NetWare network operating system.

Java A machine-independent, object-oriented programming language invented by Sun Microsystems.

Java database connectivity (JDBC) Developed by JavaSoft for Sun Microsystems, a Java API that enables Java programs to communicate with SQL-based database systems.

JavaScript A client-side, object-based programming language that enables you to create dynamic Web pages without having to become a full-fledged Java programmer. JavaScript runs client-side in the browser without requiring any server-side processing.

Java Server Page (JSP) An active Web page technology that is Sun's equivalent to Microsoft's ASP, allowing the Web developer to embed on a Web page Java code that will run on the server when a user accesses the page. *See* active Web page; Active Server Page (ASP); Java.

Joint Photographic Experts Group (JPEG) An image format named after the standards committee that formed it. Intended to become a platform-independent graphics format, JPEG is arguably the best choice for publishing full-color photographs on the Web.

Kbps Kilobits per second. *See* kilobit.

kilobit A thousand bits. Kilo means thousand.

label tag Web accessibility element invented by the W3C to clarify which instructions and labels go with which form elements onscreen.

layout The relationship among the design elements that appear onscreen, including headings, paragraphs, horizontal rules, lists, images, backgrounds, bookmarks, links, special characters, tables, and frames.

legacy browser An old version of a Web browser possibly used by people who have not upgraded to the latest version.

license Permission to use a good or a service provided by a third party who owns the good or provides the service.

LIFT A suite of products from UsableNet that can test, monitor, report, and repair Web accessibility problems.

Lightweight Directory Access Protocol (LDAP) A lighter version of X.500 invented by the University of Michigan to streamline the process of maintaining directories on the Internet. *See* Directory Access Protocol (DAP).

limited broadcast   The IP address 255.255.255.255. Routers block this address, keeping it inside the local network—hence the name, limited broadcast. Computers that do not have IP addresses typically send a 255.255.255.255 broadcast on startup to find a DHCP or BOOTP server that can respond with an IP address assignment. *See* Dynamic Host Configuration Protocol (DHCP); IP broadcast address byte.

linear list paradigm   A hypermedia design paradigm that enables the user to move back and forth through a serial sequence of pages, moving forward to new materials or backward to review.

linearization   The process of thinking of a Web page in the order in which the elements occur in the HTML file and will therefore be read in that order by assistive devices.

link   A hot spot that, when selected, triggers the object of the link. You select the link by clicking on the word or picture that triggers it.

Linux   Developed by Linus Torvalds, an open-source operating system that mimics the form and function of UNIX on an independently developed platform. *See* UNIX.

listserv   A mailing list service that enables users to send a message to a particular mailing list, which e-mails a copy of the message to each member of the list. Listserv stands for list server.

list item tag   The `<li>` start and `</li>` stop tags that mark an item in an ordered or unordered list.

local area network (LAN)   The connection of two or more computer devices for the purpose of networking within a relatively small area, such as a home, school, or departmental office building.

Logical Link Control (LLC)   The OSI/RM data link layer's sublayer that performs error checking and regulates the flow of data to and from the Physical Layer.

longdesc attribute   In Web accessibility, an attribute that enables the Web author to provide a longer description than the alt attribute can hold. *See* alt attribute.

loopback address   The network ID 127, which is a diagnostic IP address reserved for testing purposes that redirects packets to the same computer that sent them. Thus, the IP address 127.0.0.1 is the local host address.

lossless   A kind of graphical file compression in which none of the original information in the image gets lost in the compression/decompression process.

lossy   A kind of graphical file compression in which some of the image data can become lost, depending on how much compression is used when the image gets saved.

lurk   To participate in a conversation on the Internet without responding to any of the messages.

MAC address   The media access control (MAC) address used by the Physical Layer of the Internet. Every network interface card (NIC) has a unique MAC address.

Macintosh OS X   The UNIX-based operating system on Macintosh computers. *See* UNIX.

macro virus   Malicious code that propagates through a macro command that executes a set of instructions in a computer application such as a word processor or a spreadsheet.

MAGpie   Developed by the National Center for Accessible Media (NCAM), a Media Access Generator (MAG) for close-captioning audio tracks and videos recorded for playback by Apple's QuickTime Player, Real Networks' Real Player, and Microsoft's Windows Media Player.

mailto   A link that, when clicked, opens a new message window addressed to the person identified in the link.

mainframe   A centralized computer to which users connect to obtain network services. *See* terminal.

mainframe/terminal model   A networking architecture in which users compete for resources on a centralized computer that uses time-sharing to allocate computing cycles to each user.

man in the middle (MITM) attack   A type of Internet attack in which a cracker tries to hijack your session. *See* IP address spoofing; masquerading.

mark up   To insert into a document special codes called tags that control how the text appears on a Web page.

masquerading   A type of Internet attack in which a cracker intercepts the identity of an authorized user to assume the user's network privileges. *See* IP address spoofing; man in the middle (MITM) attack.

maxlength attribute   In an input tag, an attribute that specifies the maximum number of characters the user can type.

Mbps   A million bits per second. *See* megabit.

Media Access Control (MAC)   The Data Link Layer's sublayer that handles the actual placement of the packets onto the Physical Layer.

megabit   A million bits; mega means million.

menu paradigm   A hypermedia paradigm that permits the user to select one from a number of choices listed onscreen. When the user chooses an item on the menu, the item linked to it appears.

mesh topology   A network architecture that creates redundancy by creating multiple paths between network hubs, thereby enabling packets to find another path to their destination if part of the network goes down.

message digest   A message's digital fingerprint, which is created through hash encryption. *See* hash encryption; public key infrastructure (PKI).

metasearching   The searching of searching, which you perform with a metasearch engine that invokes other search engines automatically, synthesizes the results, and reports back with a single integrated list of hits.

method   A little computer program built into an object to enable the object to do something. *See* object.

metropolitan area network (MAN)   A network design that connects local networks together across a geographical region typically ranging in size up to 50 kilometers in diameter. *See* local area network (LAN); wide area network (WAN).

Microsoft Active Accessibility (MSAA)   An application programming interface (API) that helps Windows applications interoperate with assistive technology.

Microsoft Media Player   The name of Microsoft's free player for playing back streaming audio and video distributed over the Web by Microsoft's product line of streaming media servers.

MILNET   The military network that formed when the military segment separated from the Internet in 1983.

mirrored server   A computer whose data reads and writes are simultaneously executed on another computer that keeps an updated faithful copy of everything on the system from which the data are copied, thereby providing redundancy and fault tolerance in mission-critical operations in which server failure could cause serious problems.

modem   A combination of the terms modulate and demodulate, which describe how your computer sends and receives digital information over analog phone lines. The device that performs this modulation and demodulation is called a modem.

Mosaic   The world's first graphical Web browser, which was released by the National Center for Supercomputer Applications (NCSA) in 1993.

Motion Picture Experts Group (MPEG)   The digital video standard for compact discs, DVD, cable TV, direct satellite broadcast, and high-definition television. Compresses video by using a discrete cosine transform algorithm to eliminate redundant data in blocks of pixels on the screen and then compresses the video further by recording only changes from frame to frame through a process known as delta-frame encoding.

Mozilla   The open-source version of the Netscape Navigator Web browser. *See* open source.

MP3   MPEG audio layer 3, an audio file format that uses an MPEG audio codec to encode (compress) and decode (decompress) recorded music. MP3 can compress a CD audio track into a substantially smaller-sized file requiring significantly less bandwidth (about 10%) to transmit over the Internet without degrading the original sound track's quality.

Multicast Backbone (MBONE)   A network of computers on the Internet specially designed for the transmission of simultaneous live video and audio broadcasts. Instead of sending multiple copies of these transmissions, multicasting sends only one copy of the message and replicates the information only at branch points in the network.

multicasting   The sending of a message from one computer to a group of IP addresses belonging to users who subscribe to the group, such as a videoconferencing group. *See* IP broadcast address byte.

multimedia   The use of a computer to present and combine text, graphics, audio, and video with links and tools that let the user navigate, interact, create, and communicate.

Multipurpose Internet Mail Extensions (MIME)   As defined by RFCs 2045 through 2049, a set of standards that specify the formatting of Internet message bodies, the media types of Internet files and message bodies, and the method for attaching files that do not consist of plain ASCII text.

Multi-Station Access Unit (MAU)   The connecting point to which devices typically attach in a Token Ring network. The MAU contains the ring that passes the token. *See* Token Ring.

multi-tier   A division of complex applications into multiple stages typically consisting of (1) the user interface tier, (2) the business tier, and (3) the database tier.

Musical Instrument Digital Interface (MIDI)   A low-bandwidth music synthesizer file format that consists of a stream of codes telling your computer when to turn notes on and off, how loud to make them, what instrument should make the sound (such as trumpet, flute, or drum), and whether to bend the notes or add other special effects.

name attribute   Enables you to name HTML elements onscreen so you can refer to those elements by name in a script.

name resolver   On a name server, a software utility that goes out on the Internet and consults the necessary name servers in the DNS hierarchy if the name server does not already know the IP address of the domain name in the request. *See* domain name system (DNS).

name server   The computer in charge of resolving a domain name by responding with the corresponding IP address when a client workstation requests to resolve a domain name. If the name server does not know the name, it forwards the request to a name resolver. *See* name resolver.

named anchor   An anchor tag with a name to which a hypertext reference can link, thereby creating a bookmark in the midst of a Web page.

nested frameset   A frameset you create inside of another frame. *See* frameset.

Net   Synonym for Internet. *See* Internet.

NetBEUI   The NetBIOS Extended User Interface that was the native protocol suite for peer-to-peer networking on local networks in early versions of the Windows operating system produced before 2001.

Net-directed broadcast   On a Class A network, the address *netid*.255.255.255, where *netid* is the network ID. This broadcasts a message to all the hosts on that network. On a Class B network, the net-directed broadcast address is *netid.netid*.255.255, where *netid.netid* is the network ID. On a Class C network, the net-directed broadcast address is *netid.netid.netid*.255. *See* multicasting.

Netiquette   Internet etiquette, which is the observance of certain rules and conventions that have evolved to keep the Internet from becoming a free-for-all in which tons of unwanted messages and junk mail would clog your inbox and make the Net an unfriendly place to be.

Netscape   Corporation formed in 1994 by some of Mosaic's developers. *See* Mosaic.

Netscape Navigator   The Web browser in the Netscape software suite. *See* Netscape.

Netscape SAPI (NSAPI)   Netscape's brand of SAPI. *See* Server Application Programming Interface (SAPI).

netstat   The network statistics utility that displays information about the connections that are open and the protocol processes that are currently running on a network host.

NetWare   A PC-based local area networking product that was one of the most dominant network operating systems during the decade following its invention in 1983 by Novell Corporation.

network   The connection of two or more digital devices for the purpose of communicating, transferring, or obtaining data.

Network Access Layer   The Internet architecture layer that corresponds to OSI/RM Layers 2 and 1, which convert the packets into a binary encoded stream of 0's and 1's that the NIC transforms into the signals that get transmitted physically over the network.

network access point (NAP)   A junction that provides direct access to the traffic on a network.

network address translation (NAT)   A technique used by NAPs and WAPs to transform the IP addresses used for internal traffic into a second set of addresses for external traffic.

network analyzer   A tool that enables a network administrator to capture and analyze packets crossing a network in order to test connections, send alerts, sniff packets for analysis, and generate reports.

Network Interface Card (NIC)   The physical network component that contains the jack into which you plug the connector on a network cable.

Network Layer   OSI/RM Layer 3, which organizes the data into datagrams that combine the data from the Transport Layer with routing information containing the source and destination addresses along with the recommended path, depending on network conditions and the nature of the data.

Network News Transfer Protocol (NNTP)   As defined by RFC 977, the protocol that powers USENET newsgroups. *See* USENET.

network operating system   The software that adds to a computer the functions required for connecting computers for the purpose of networking.

network paradigm   A hypermedia design pattern in which objects can be multiply linked in any direction to any object in a web.

networking   The act of communicating over a network. *See* network.

newsgroup   *See* USENET.

non-breaking space ( )   The HTML code for a single white space character that does not cause a line feed onscreen.

normalization   In a relational database, the process of separating a large table fulfilling multiple roles into smaller tables that increase efficiency by serving smaller roles that relate through keys to other tables in the database. *See* foreign key; primary key.

noscript tag   For Web accessibility, an HTML tag pair consisting of `<noscript>` start and `</noscript>` stop tags that enable the Web author to describe with functional text the actions or content rendered by active scripts onscreen.

Notepad   The plain text editor that is built into every Windows computer.

NSFNET   Created by the National Science Foundation (NSF) in 1986, a backbone that connected the nation's five supercomputer centers at high speed.

numeric variable   A place in computer memory that remembers, or stores, a number. In a script, the numbers can be integers or floating point. *See* floating point; integer.

object   In computer programming, a self-contained entity consisting of properties and methods enabling you to do something programmatically.

object linking and embedding database (OLE DB)   A type of database access method that enables Windows applications to open a wide variety of connections to data stored not only in ODBC data sources but also in file systems, media catalogs, e-mail, spreadsheets, active directories, project management tools, and XML files.

object-oriented database management system (ODBMS)   A database management system in which programmers writing code in object-oriented languages can create complex data structures in which one data type can build upon, or inherit, properties from another.

open database connectivity (ODBC)   Based on the Call-Level Interface (CLI) specifications from the X/Open and ISO/IEC database APIs, a standard database access method created by Microsoft with the goal of making it possible for any application to access any database, regardless of its vendor.

Open Shortest Path First (OSPF)   As defined by RFC 2328, a routing information protocol that improves on RIP by (1) exchanging updates in router tables as soon as they happen, (2) sending only the changes instead of the whole table, and (3) exchanging statistics on the transmission speed of multiple possible routings, enabling the router to take advantage of faster routes that would otherwise be unused under the hop count rule. *See* hop count; Routing Information Protocol (RIP).

open source   Software for which the source code is available to the general public free of charge. Anyone can download the source code, use it freely, and make enhancements.

operator A symbol that causes a script to perform some kind of action on a variable or a value. *See assignment operator; concatenation operator.*

option tag Specifies one of the choices from which the user can select in an input tag of type select. *See input tag.*

ordered list A web page element in which the items in a list are numbered automatically.

OSI Reference Model (OSI/RM) The International Standards Organization's Open System Interconnection Reference Model (OSI/RM) that defines the seven layers of communication involved in the networking process.

packet Also known as a datagram, a container for a segment of the data that comprises a message, plus a header containing protocol information and addressing. *See datagram.*

packet filter In a firewall, a filter that works at OSI/RM layers 2 and 3 to inspect the headers of all incoming and outgoing packets and block transmissions based on certain source or destination ports or IP addresses, thereby enabling the firewall to stop attacks waged on specific ports and block access to malicious or forbidden sites. *See firewall.*

page title Created by the `<title>` tag in the head section of the document, the name that appears in the browser's title bar when people visit your Web page on the Internet.

page transition The style or manner in which the screen changes when the browser brings up a new document and displays it onscreen.

paired tag An HTML tag format that consists of a start tag and a stop tag.

password field A text box that works like a text field except that when the user types the entry, the browser displays asterisks instead of revealing the sensitive information onscreen. You create a password field by creating an `<input>` field that has its type attribute set to password.

patent The granting to an inventor of a property right for an invention to exclude others from making, using, offering for sale, or selling the invention in the United States or "importing" the invention into the United States for a reasonable period of time (20 years) before the patent expires.

peer-to-peer (P2P) A network architecture in which each workstation has equal responsibilities.

Perl A scripting language invented by Larry Wall for people who need to write relatively short CGI programs; more technically inclined programmers write CGI scripts in C, which is the programming language used to develop many popular applications, including Perl. *See common gateway interface (CGI).*

Personal Digital Assistant (PDA) A portable, handheld computer you can take with you to work, school, or anyplace where a PC might come in handy. You can easily synchronize a PDA with your personal computer and take almost any information with you, such as your address book, calendar, and key Web sites.

PHP Hypertext Preprocessor (PHP) An open source active Web page technology that enables the developer to include code on the page that will run on the server, which executes the code before sending the completed page to the user. *See Active Server Page (ASP); active Web page; Java Server Page (JSP).*

Physical Layer OSI/RM Layer 1, which transforms the 0's and 1's from the Data Link Layer into signals that flow over the transmission media.

ping An acronym for Packet Internet Groper, the most basic network troubleshooting utility, which (1) sends ICMP echo request packets to a destination IP address, (2) waits for the destination to return the echo, (3) measures the response time, and (4) displays a message telling how long the round-trip took. *See Internet Control Message Protocol (ICMP).*

plug-in A software component that adds functionality when installed into an existing computer application. The advantage of plug-ins over helper apps is that the plug-in usually gives you better integration of the media than the helper app. Plug-ins normally make multimedia play in the browser's window, whereas helper apps often launch a separate window to play the file. *See helper app.*

PocketPC The trade name for palm-sized PDAs based on the Windows CE operating system. *See Personal Digital Assistant.*

point size A unit of measure that indicates how high the text is. In print media, a point is one-seventy-second (1/72) of an inch. On a typical computer screen, a point is about the height of a single pixel. Due to different sized monitors, the actual size of the text will vary somewhat, depending on the physical height of the screen.

Point to Point Protocol (PPP) The telephone modem protocol that supports not only TCP/IP but also NetBEUI and IPX/SPX.

port number A 16-bit number (ranging from 0 to 65535) indicating the service that an Internet packet is using. *See Dynamic and/or Private Ports; registered ports; Well Known Ports.*

Portable Document Format (PDF) Created by Adobe, a platform-independent mechanism for sharing documents across the Internet.

Portable Network Graphics (PNG) An image format created by the World Wide Web consortium to replace the patented GIF format. *See Graphics Interchange Format (GIF).*

POST method An HTTP method that sends the form data to the process identified in the form tag's action attribute. This process is normally a server-side script that reads and processes the form data, saves appropriate information in a server-side database, and returns an HTML response to the user.

Post Office Protocol (POP) An e-mail protocol invented for the purpose of delivering mail post-office style from the server to your PC.

Presentation Layer OSI/RM Layer 6, which translates the data into a standard network data format. It may use data compression to streamline the packet so it does not consume unnecessary bandwidth on the network and use encryption to protect the privacy of the data for sensitive data transmissions such as banking information.

Pretty Good Privacy (PGP) Invented by Phil Zimmerman in 1991, a data integrity system that uses encryption, data compression, and digital signatures to provide for the secure transmission of e-mail messages and other kinds of store-and-forward file systems. *See* digital signature; encrypt.

primary key In a data table, a column in which every entry is unique, through which the records in that table can relate (i.e., key) to the data in another table. *See* foreign key; relational database.

primary server In a domain, the first DNS server that has the responsibility to maintain the master copy of the database containing the assigned names and IP addresses in that domain. *See* Domain Name System (DNS); secondary server.

project management The application of knowledge, skills, tools, and techniques to project activities to meet proper requirements.

prompt An onscreen instruction that asks the user to provide some information, either by typing a response into a text field or by choosing something from a selection of possible choices.

property An attribute of an object that has a value. *See* object.

proportional font A font in which the fat letters such as *m* and *w* take up more space than thin letters such as *l* and *i*.

protocol binding The act of assigning a protocol to a network interface card. *See* Network Interface Card (NIC).

protocol suite A collection of protocols that work together to conform to a multilayered protocol standard, such as the OSI/RM. *See* OSI Reference Model (OSI/RM).

proxy server A computer that serves as an intermediary between client workstations and the external network.

public key infrastructure (PKI) A certificate authority system that assigns to each user a digital certificate containing a key pair consisting of a public key and a private key. The person sending a message uses the public key to encrypt the message, while the person receiving the message uses the private key to decrypt it. *See* asymmetric cryptography.

push-pull metaphor A metaphor used by the computer industry to distinguish between receiving information by (1) browsing the Web and clicking hyperlinks that bring requested resources onscreen, thereby pulling the information toward you or (2) having information pushed onto your screen automatically by software that monitors real-time information services to which you may have subscribed.

QuickTime Apple's brand of multimedia. Originally for the Macintosh only, QuickTime is now one of the finest cross-platform tools available for multimedia creation and delivery. The free QuickTime player plugs in seamlessly to Microsoft Internet Explorer, and it works on Windows as well as Macintosh computers.

radio button A form control that displays a small round button that enables the user to select one, but not more than one, item from a list of possible choices.

RealOne The RealNetworks multimedia brand in which the two main families of products are RealOne Music and RealOne Player.

recordset In the ADO, the set of records in which the database returns the result of a query. *See* ActiveX Data Objects (ADO); Structured Query Language (SQL).

registered ports Internet ports numbered from 1024 to 49151 and reserved for use by many well-known applications, such as Microsoft SQL Server on port 1433, Macromedia Shockwave on port 1626, and Cisco License Management on port 1986. *See* port number.

relational database A data structure that comprises multiple tables containing primary key columns through which the records in one table can relate (i.e., key) to the data in another table. *See* foreign key; primary key.

relational database management system (RDBMS) A database management system in which programmers can create relational databases. *See* relational database.

repeater A device that functions at the Physical Layer of the OSI/RM by interconnecting two network cables so they can be treated as a single cable.

replay attack A type of Internet attack in which a hacker uses a packet sniffer to record a logon sequence, which the hacker later plays back in an attempt to gain access.

Request for Comments (RFC) The process through which the IETF defines the Internet's protocols. *See* Internet Engineering Task Force (IETF); RFC maturity state; RFC number.

Reset button A button the user can click to return a form's controls to their default settings.

Reverse Address Resolution Protocol (RARP) As defined in RFC 903, the protocol that determines an IP address from a network device's physical MAC address. *See* Address Resolution Protocol (ARP); MAC address; Media Access Control (MAC).

RFC maturity state One of the states an RFC moves through on its way to becoming a standard; the states are called (1) Proposed, (2) Draft, and (3) Internet Standard. *See* Request for Comments (RFC).

RFC number The numerical ID assigned to a request for comments (RFC) proposal after it has been submitted to the IETF. *See* Internet Engineering Task Force (IETF); Request for Comments (RFC).

Rich Site Summary (RSS) An XML format for syndicating the content of a Web site in a form that can be registered with an RSS publisher to which other sites can subscribe to access the RSS feed and display its content onscreen.

ring topology   A network architecture in which you connect a network's nodes in a circle and messages flow in a single direction around the loop. This provides each device with an opportunity to act on the messages addressed to it and pass the rest of the messages on to its neighbor.

RJ-45   A type of connector with eight pin positions that hold the eight wires from the four twisted pairs in CAT 5 Ethernet cabling. *See CAT 5; Ethernet.*

rollover   A special graphical effect created by using the JavaScript `onmouseover` and `onmouseout` event handlers. In the most common kind of rollover, a script changes the source of the image when the user mouses over it and reverts to the original image when the user mouses out.

root servers   At the highest level of the DNS hierarchy, the servers that keep track of the top-level domains, such as .com, .net, .edu, .gov, .org, and .us. *See Domain Name System (DNS); primary server; secondary server.*

router   A relay that operates at the Network Layer of the OSI/RM, forwarding network traffic along the optimal path based on information in the packet's Network Layer header.

routing   The process conducted by the Internet Protocol in determining the optimal network path over which the packets will be sent. *See Border Gateway Protocol (BGP); External Gateway Protocol (EGP); Open Shortest Path First (OSPF); Routing Information Protocol (RIP).*

Routing Information Protocol (RIP)   As defined by RFCs 1058 and 2453, the protocol whereby routers send their information tables every 30 seconds across their network connections to their neighboring routers. Based on this information, dynamic routers update their tables to reflect any changes on the neighboring routers and route packets over the path with the lowest hop count. *See dynamically configured router; routing; routing information table.*

routing information table   The table in which a router keeps track of the routes over which it will send packets to different networks to which the router is connected. *See dynamically configured router; hop count; routing.*

Safari   The default Web browser that ships with every new Macintosh.

screened-subnet firewall   A type of firewall that establishes a demilitarized zone (DMZ) by placing packet filtering routers both on the Internet side and the private network side of the bastion host. *See demilitarized zone (DMZ).*

scripting   The act of writing little computer programs that can enhance the appearance and functionality of a Web page.

seamless   The appearance of a background tile when its bitmap replicates itself up and down the screen in such a way that you cannot perceive the edges of the bitmap or detect a regular interruption in the pattern caused by the edges of the bitmap not fitting against each other smoothly.

secondary server   In the DNS, a computer that helps share the name serving load and provides backup in case the primary server goes down. *See Domain Name System (DNS); primary server.*

Section 508   A law that is part of the Rehabilitation Act of 1973, as amended in 1998, requiring that all Web sites (as well as other forms of information technology) used, procured, developed, or maintained by government agencies and departments must be accessible.

secure electronic transactions (SET)   An open standard for conducting secure payment card transactions over the Internet. Digital certificates create a trust chain that verifies cardholder and merchant validity throughout the transaction. In order to display the SET Mark on their products, e-commerce vendors must pass SET Compliance Testing, which ensures that the software is following the required security best practices. *See digital certificate.*

secure shell (SSH)   As used in secure FTP (SFTP), a protocol that enables two computers to negotiate and establish a secure connection that uses encryption to thwart crackers who may try to sniff passwords and data that would otherwise traverse the Internet in clear text. *See tunneling.*

secure sockets layer (SSL)   As used on the Internet to encrypt forms data and protect private information such as passwords and credit card numbers, a handshake protocol that defines how a server establishes a secure session in response to an end user's request to transact. *See transport layer security (TLS).*

security auditing   A proactive process that considers the risks associated with security assets, predicts the methods crackers may use to exploit each risk, and takes protective steps to thwart them.

select tag   An HTML form control that creates a selection menu. *See option tag.*

self-extracting archive   An executable file that, when executed, automatically extracts the files that are contained in the archive.

Serial Line Internet Protocol (SLIP)   A telephone modem protocol that handles the Internet Protocol only. *See Point to Point Protocol (PPP).*

server   A computer that is devoted primarily to sending information in response to requests from client computers. *See client-server computing.*

Server Application Programming Interface (SAPI)
A collection of software components used by the business tier to obtain, process, and respond to forms data submitted when end users interact with the site and make requests through the user interface tier. *See Internet SAPI (ISAPI); multi-tier; Netscape SAPI (NSAPI).*

servlet   A Java applet that runs on the server (instead of in the browser) in a multithreaded environment, listening for Internet requests to come in and serving multiple users from the same instance of the code. *See Java.*

Session Layer OSI/RM Layer 5, which negotiates the connection that will be made between two computers that are exchanging data and inserts a checkpoint if the amount of data being transmitted is large. *See* checkpoint.

shareware Software you can download for free, try out for a limited time period (usually 30 to 60 days), and then, if you decide to keep using it, pay a reasonable fee (usually $29 to $39) to the vendor to purchase the software.

shielded twisted pair (STP) Typically used in gigabyte bandwidth applications, a type of twisted pair wiring with an extra layer of insulation that reduces electromagnetic interference.

shopping cart In an online store, the virtual basket into which the customer places each item selected for purchase.

shout To write a message IN ALL CAPITAL LETTERS on the Internet. Shouting is almost always regarded in poor taste.

Simple Mail Transfer Protocol (SMTP) As defined by RFC 821, the protocol that specifies the manner in which e-mail gets sent over the Internet. *See* e-mail; Multipurpose Internet Mail Extensions (MIME).

Simple Network Management Protocol (SNMP) As defined by RFC 1157, the manner in which network administrators manage remotely TCP/IP network devices such as routers that are SNMP-compliant.

Simple Object Access Protocol (SOAP) An XML language for exposing the methods and properties of a Web Service to a consumer, which is any Web client authorized to interact with the Web Service. The consumer can be, and often is, another Web Service.

Simple Tool for Error Prioritization (STEP) *See* STEP508.

single-homed bastion In a firewall, a bastion host that uses a single network interface card (NIC) to monitor all of the network's incoming and outgoing traffic at the Application Layer. *See* bastion host; dual-homed bastion; firewall.

site license A license that permits software to be used on multiple computers located in the workplace. *See* license.

size attribute A setting that determines how many characters wide a form field will be onscreen.

skip navigation link A hyperlink that, when clicked, takes the user to a place on the page that is just past the navigation options that typically appear at the top or on the left of the screen.

smart card A credit-card sized plastic card with an embedded computer chip and memory that can store more than a hundred times as much digital information as the magnetic strip on a credit card. Because the chip can handle digitally signed and encrypted transactions, the smart card enables the cardholder to take advantage of the Internet's best-practice security measures.

social engineering attack A type of Internet attack in which the cracker exploits human weaknesses, such as writing down passwords or divulging private information over the phone, to gain access to the organization's network.

spam Unwanted messages posted to newsgroups or sent to a list of users through e-mail. The term can be used either as a verb or a noun. To spam means to send unwanted messages to a list of users on the Internet. Likewise, unwanted messages that you receive are called spam.

spider A robot that searches the Web continually, organizing what is found into a hierarchical directory of topics. When you conduct a subject-oriented search, the search engine searches this directory and provides you with a list of items related to your topic.

standard generalizable markup language (SGML) The parent markup language from which HTML was derived.

star topology A network architecture in which each device in the network connects to a central hub that distributes messages from one node to another.

start tag The first of the two tags in a paired tag. *See* paired tag.

stateful inspection A firewall technique that keeps track of when a port opens, what session is using it, and how long the port stays open in order to detect and thwart attempts by attackers to hijack a session. *See* firewall; Dynamic and/or Private Ports.

static Web page A document in which the content is fixed in HTML codes that make the document always read the same when viewed in a browser. *See* active Web page.

statically configured router A router in which the router information tables are fixed and can be updated only by manual changes made by the network administrator. *See* dynamically configured router.

STEP508 Created for the federal government by the National Center for Accessible Media, a software program that compares and analyzes the output of Section 508 compliance tools, including Bobby, LIFT, and WebKing. Based on this analysis, STEP508 determines the severity of the errors and prioritizes the repairs needed to bring a Web site into compliance with Section 508. *See* Section 508.

stock-keeping unit (SKU) A unique alphanumeric code assigned to each product in a catalog or inventory.

stop tag The last of the two tags in a paired tag. *See* paired tag.

storyboard A series of sketches that depict what will appear on each screen of a presentation or application.

stream A real-time feed from an audio or video source, encoded in such a way that the media can begin playing steadily without making users wait for the entire file to download.

stream cipher An encryption algorithm that operates at the byte (i.e., character) level to encrypt real-time communications, such as when you use a browser to conduct financial transactions at an online store and the e-commerce site uses a stream cipher to encrypt the session. *See* secure sockets layer (SSL).

streaming The digital transmission of a real-time feed from an audio or video source, encoded in such a way that the media can begin playing steadily without making users wait for the entire file to download.

string   A sequence of one or more alphanumeric characters.

string variable   A place in computer memory that remembers, or stores, the alphanumeric characters in a string.

Structured Query Language (SQL)   An international standard that defines the syntax for issuing commands that can query, update, insert, or delete records in a database.

subdomain   In the Domain Name System, a division of a domain. *See Domain Name System (DNS).*

Submit button   An HTML form control that, when clicked, causes the form to submit its data.

subnet-directed broadcast   When a large network is divided into subnets, a broadcast that is addressed to as much of the network ID as needed to identify the subnet, followed by 255 or 255.255, depending on how many bytes were needed to identify the subnet. *See IP broadcast address byte; multicasting.*

subnet mask   A dotted quad number that enables the local network to determine whether any given IP address is internal or external to the local network. On a Class A network, the subnet mask is typically 255.0.0.0; on Class B, 255.255.0.0; and on Class C, 255.255.255.0. *See Internet address classes.*

surf   To use a program called a browser to go from site to site in search of information that interests you.

switch   At the Data Link Layer, a network device that filters, forwards, and floods frames based on the destination MAC address of each frame. *See flood; frame; MAC address.*

symmetric cryptography   A type of encryption, also called secret-key cryptography, that uses the same secret key for both encryption and decryption. *See asymmetric cryptography; encrypt.*

Synchronized Multimedia Implementation Language (SMIL)   An XML-based language that enables authors to include multimedia events in Web documents.

Systems Network Architecture (SNA)   Invented by IBM in 1974, a protocol suite for connecting different kinds of networks together, serving an early model of the kind of layered network architecture that evolved into the OSI/RM.

T1 service   A North American T-carrier system service consisting of 24 channels running at 64 bps for a total bandwidth of 1.544 Mbps.

T3 service   A North American T-carrier system service consisting of 672 channels running at 64 bps for a total bandwidth of 44.736 Mpbs. This is equivalent to 28 T1 lines. *See T1 service.*

tab-delimited data   A flat file method of storing all of a data table's records in a single file in which the data elements are separated by tabs that function as break characters. *See comma-delimited data.*

table   A design element that provides a way of dividing the screen into rectangular regions into which you can lay out text and graphics on a Web page.

tags   Markup codes that determine how the text will flow onto the screen, whether it will contain pictures and where they will appear, and what will happen when the user triggers items linked to the document.

task analysis   The process of organizing a project into goals and sub-goals.

TCP/IP   The Internet's protocol suite, which takes its name from the Transport Control Protocol (TCP) that manages the Transport Layer and the Internet Protocol (IP) that handles the routing on the Network Layer. *See Internet Protocol (IP); Transmission Control Protocol (TCP).*

telecommuting   The act of working from home, using computers, dialup modems or broadband network connections and fax machines to perform work that formerly required a person to travel physically to work.

teleworker   Someone who works by telecommuting. *See telecommuting.*

telnet   As defined by RFC 854, the terminal emulation protocol that enables users to log on to remote host computers over the Internet.

terminal   A device typically equipped with a keyboard on which you type commands or enter data to communicate with a mainframe computer. *See mainframe.*

th tag   Table header `<th>` start and `</th>` stop tags that define table column titles used by assistive technology to help users with special needs associate table data with its corresponding column headings.

Thicknet   A stiff coaxial cable about half an inch thick that is used in 10base5 Ethernet networks; the cable segments can be up to 500 meters long. *See Thinnet.*

Thinnet   A very flexible coaxial cable about a quarter of an inch in diameter that is used in 10base2 Ethernet networks; the cable segments can run up to 185 meters long. *See Thicknet.*

three-letter acronym (TLA)   Shorthand method of reducing the amount of keyboarding required to write a message.

tile   To draw an image repeatedly across and down the screen until the entire window has been covered. *See seamless.*

tiled background   A graphical effect created by tiling. *See tile.*

title attribute   An HTML assistive technology attribute that screen readers and other kinds of assistive devices use to identify an element such as a frame to users with special needs.

Token Ring   As defined by IEEE standard 802.5, a local area network design in which a token travels continually around the cable ring to which the network devices are attached. A device can send data only when it has the token. Thus, data collisions never occur on a token-ring network. Under a heavy load, token-ring networks are not as likely to degrade as Ethernet networks, which can slow down when multiple data collisions are occurring. *See Ethernet.*

top-level domain (TLD) The highest level of the Domain Name System, including the well-known domains of .com, .gov, .org, and .net, as well as the country codes typically used for domains outside the United States.

topology The classification of a network according to geographical shape. *See* bus topology; hybrid topology; mesh topology; ring topology; star topology.

traceroute A network troubleshooting utility that reports the path followed by data as a packet winds its way over the network from the source to the destination computer.

trademark A word, phrase, symbol, or design, or a combination of words, phrases, symbols, or designs, that identifies and distinguishes the source of the goods of one party from those of others.

transaction filtering The blocking or monitoring of certain kinds of Internet resources or messages from sites or users to which you want to block access on a private network.

transaction server A computer that works behind the scenes in the business tier of the multi-tier e-commerce model to ensure that when a financial transaction occurs, all of the necessary databases get updated and related services receive the proper notifications. *See* multi-tier.

Transmission Control Protocol (TCP) As defined by RFC 793, the protocol that establishes and manages the connection between computers that are exchanging data, numbers the packets on the sending computer, reassembles the packets on the receiving computer, and ensures that all the data is intact, with no omissions or duplications. *See* TCP/IP.

transparency A special effect in which one of the colors in a bitmap becomes translucent. Instead of seeing that color, you see through it into the background color or image on the screen.

Transport Layer The Internet Architecture Layer that encompasses OSI/RM Layers 5 and 4 by dividing into packets the data received from the Application Layer. Depending on the kind of session being serviced, the Transport Layer uses either TCP or UDP. *See* Transmission Control Protocol (TCP); User Datagram Protocol (UDP).

transport layer security (TLS) A successor to SSL that the IETF is working on. *See* Internet Engineering Task Force (IETF); secure sockets layer (SSL).

Trivial File Transfer Protocol (TFTP) As defined by RFC 1350, a simpler form of FTP that diskless workstations and some routers use to get their configuration files during startup. Unlike FTP, TFTP uses the connectionless UDP protocol that does not have a logon process for user authentication. *See* User Datagram Protocol (UDP).

Trojan A malicious application that masquerades as a desired object that you download knowingly to your computer.

Trojan horse *See* Trojan.

trunk In a bus topology, the single cable, also called the bus, to which every device on the network connects. *See* bus topology.

tunneling The process of funneling different kinds of TCP/IP connections through an SSH connection, which provides a secure communication channel for doing mail, accessing the Web, logging on securely to remote sites, and publishing files via SFTP. *See* secure shell (SSH).

twisted pair A transmission medium consisting of two insulated wires that are twisted together to create a double helix that reduces noise levels and eliminates crosstalk between the wires. *See* shielded twisted pair (STP); unshielded twisted pair (UTP).

Uniform Resource Locator (URL) A global address that uniquely identifies the location of resources on the World Wide Web, including hypertext documents, pictures, sounds, movies, animations, and application software.

Universal Description, Discovery, and Integration (UDDI) An online yellow pages directory of Web Services that business computers can use to discover and learn how to use the B2B services offered by various companies over the Internet. *See* Web Service.

UNIX Invented by Bell Labs in the early 1970s, an operating system that supports the full range of networking services, including both client-side and server-side components. *See* Linux; Macintosh OS X.

unordered list A list in which the items are bulleted instead of numbered.

unshielded twisted pair (UTP) Twisted pair cabling that is not shielded and therefore cannot transmit data as fast as shielded twisted pair (STP) cabling. *See* shielded twisted pair; twisted pair.

USA Patriot Act Signed into law in October 2001 in the aftermath of the 9/11 attacks on America, legislation that gives the U.S. government wide latitude in using Internet surveillance systems, including Carnivore and its successors.

USENET A distributed bulletin board system hosting more than 10,000 newsgroups.

User Datagram Protocol (UDP) As defined by RFC 768, a connectionless protocol that does not require the negotiation and establishment of a session between the sending and receiving computers. Instead, the sending computer simply puts each output from the Application Layer into a packet. Because there is no provision for the resending of lost packets, UDP is considered to be an unreliable transport protocol that should be used only by applications that transmit relatively small amounts of data without establishing a session between the sending and receiving computers. *See* Transmission Control Protocol (TCP).

uuencoding UNIX to UNIX encoding, which translates the 8-bit character stream of a binary (i.e., non-ASCII) file attachment into a stream of 7-bit ASCII characters that can be pasted into a mail message's text body. In all but legacy situations, uuencoding has happily been replaced by MIME. *See* Multipurpose Internet Mail Extensions (MIME).

variable   A place in the computer's RAM that remembers, or stores, the value of something changeable. It is called a variable because its value is subject to change.

variable name   The identifier used to refer to, or call upon, a place in computer memory that stores the value of a variable. See variable.

videoconferencing   The use of real-time video and audio streaming to enable people conversing over the Internet to be able to see and hear each other. See streaming.

virtual private network (VPN)   A private data network that makes use of the public Internet's telecommunication infrastructure, maintaining privacy through the use of session keys and an HTTP tunneling protocol over which encrypted data passes. See Internet Protocol Security (IPSec).

virus   Malicious or unwanted code that installs itself on your computer without your knowledge by hiding inside other programmed objects. Viruses are dangerous because they can consume all of the memory on your computer, destroy data, and spread across the network to other computers that are connected to yours.

Voice over IP (VoIP)   A real-time telecommunication technology that is converging the public switched telephone network (PSTN) with IP telephony.

Web accessibility   The capability that results from the process of making it possible for users with special needs to receive, understand, and navigate content that people without handicaps can process without such special assistance.

Web Accessibility Initiative (WAI)   Begun in 1997, the Web's official efforts to achieve accessibility. See Web accessibility.

Web Content Accessibility Guidelines (WCAG) Web accessibility standards consisting of 65 checkpoints organized under 14 general guidelines created as part of the Web Accessibility Initiative. See Web Accessibility Initiative (WAI).

Web page   An HTML file stored at a Web site where users can view the page with a browser. See browser.

Web root   On a Web server, the physical folder that represents the beginning of the server's Web space; on Windows IIS servers, the Web root is typically located at c:\inetpub\wwwroot.

Web server   The standalone computer or server component that responds to HTTP requests from browsers and other kinds of Internet clients, including media players and handheld devices. Because Web servers use the HTTP protocol, they are also called HTTP servers. See Hypertext Transfer Protocol (HTTP).

Web Service   A software system that uses an XML protocol to support interoperable machine-to-machine interaction over a network.

Web Service Description Language (WSDL)   An XML language used to identify the methods in a Web Service, define how those methods behave, and instruct clients how to interact with the service. The filename extension for documents written in the Web Service Description Language is *.wsdl*. Every published

Web Service has a WSDL file describing what the service does and how to interact with it.

Web site   The place where an Internet resource such as a hypertext document is stored on the World Wide Web.

Webcasting   The simultaneous broadcast of a live event over the Web.

WebKing   Web verification tool that integrates with IBM's WebSphere Studio Application Developer to check your HTML and CSS code for Section 508 and WCAG accessibility. See Section 508; Web Content Accessibility Guidelines (WCAG).

Well Known Ports   Also called reserved ports, the Internet ports numbered from 0 to 1023 that are assigned by the Internet Corporation for Assigned Names and Numbers (ICANN). See Dynamic and/or Private Ports; ICANN; registered ports.

what you see is what you get (WYSIWYG)   A kind of editor that lets you create Web pages by typing your text directly onscreen, where it appears exactly as it will look on the Web. To change a font, size, color, or other text attribute, you select the text you want to change and then click a button or icon that makes the change. You do not need to know the HTML codes, which the WYSIWYG editor inserts automatically as you click the controls.

whiteboard   A kind of computer program that enables remote users to share a common screen across the network.

Wi-Fi   The industry trade name for products based on the IEEE 802.11 specification for wireless Local Area Networking.

wide area network (WAN)   A network that uses high-speed transmission lines to connect MANs and LANs over large geographical areas. See local area network (LAN); metropolitan area network (MAN).

Windows CE   A compact modular version of the Microsoft Windows operating system designed for use on consumer electronic devices. See PocketPC.

Windows Update Service   An online Microsoft security service that can automatically download the latest security patches to your computer and, depending on the configuration settings, install the patches right away or notify the user when the patches are ready to install.

Windows Internet Naming Service (WINS)   The naming system built into the Windows operating system that enables a Windows computer to be known by its NetBIOS Name, which is the "computer name" on the Computer Name tab of the Windows Control Panel's system settings. See Domain Name System (DNS).

winipcfg   An older version of ipconfig for Windows 95/98/Me. See ipconfig.

wireless access point (WAP)   A wireless network junction that enables workstations to communicate without cables by providing access points for wireless devices to get on a network.

Wireless Application Protocol (WAP)   A protocol for translating Web pages into a format appropriate for display on mobile phones, thereby making it possible for mobile telephone users to access the Internet.

Wireless Markup Language (WML) The syntax followed by the Wireless Application Protocol in formatting Web pages for display on mobile telephones. *See Wireless Application Protocol (WAP).*

workstation Also known as a client computer, the network node on which end users perform their work.

worm A special kind of virus that can propagate across the Internet and infect other computers without hiding inside other objects or attaching itself to other programs. *See virus.*

World Intellectual Property Organization (WIPO) An international organization in charge of administering 23 treaties comprising an international Intellectual Property (IP) system.

World Wide Web (WWW) A networked hypertext system that allows multimedia documents to be shared over the Internet without requiring people to travel anywhere physically to obtain the information. *See hypertext.*

World Wide Web Consortium (W3C) Located online at www.w3.org, the organization that coordinates the research and development of new standards and features for the Web.

X.25 Considered slow in terms of modern networking, a wide area networking standard that enables data to be transmitted over the packet-switched networks (PSNs) of the telephone companies.

X.500 *See Directory Access Protocol (DAP).*

XHTML The Extensible Hypertext Markup Language, which is a reformulation of HTML in XML. *See XML.*

XHTML+SMIL A language profile that permits the Web designer to use SMIL animations, timings, and transitions within a conventional HTML or CSS page layout. *See Synchronized Multimedia Implementation Language (SMIL).*

XML A simple, self-describing markup language that enables computers to read and understand the structure of different kinds of documents and to exchange data across different operating systems, software applications, and hardware configurations without requiring any human intervention.

XML module A collection of semantically related XML elements and attributes oriented toward accomplishing a certain task or function.

XML schema Structural definition of the types of elements that can appear in a document, the attributes each element may have, and the relationships among the elements.

XSL Transformation (XSLT) language An XML dialect that Web designers use to transform documents from one format into another. *See extensible stylesheet language (XSL).*

z-index In absolute positioning, an attribute that tells the browser the order in which to display objects that overlap. *See absolute positioning.*

zone A predefined range or selection of Web sites or addresses. Browsers enable you to configure special security settings in different zones.

Bibliography

Most of the resources used in this book are online references linked to this book's Web site. Listed here are the scholarly citations and some print-only resources you will not find at the Web site. For the hundreds of online references, follow the links at the book's Web site.

American Electronics Association. "U.S. High-Tech Workforce Surges to 5 Million," *AEA News Release*, May 17, 2000. http://www.aeanet.org/aeanet/aeacommon/displaystartlink.asp?file=/aeanet/pressroom/pradet0000_nationalcyberstates051700.htm (accessed August 8, 2000).

Amrich, Denise. "The Internet, Legality, and You," *Windows CE Power Magazine*, August 1999. http://www.cepower.com/issuesprint/issue199908/ceeditorial0899.html (accessed August 29, 2000).

Bane, P. William, Stephen P. Bradley, and David J. Collis. "Colliding Worlds," Harvard Business School Colloquium, October 5–7, 1994. Revised March 1995.

Bane, P. William, and Debra B. McMahon. "Learning to Grow: The New Marketing Challenge in Telecommunications." *Mercer Management Journal*, 2 (1994), 83–92.

Bergman, Michael K. "The Deep Web: Surfacing Hidden Value," *Journal of Electronic Publishing,* 7(1), August 2001. http://www.press.umich.edu/jep/07-01/bergman.html (accessed June 9, 2004).

Bernard, Michael L., Barbara S. Chaparro, Melissa M. Mills, and Charles G. Halcomb. "Comparing the effects of text size and format on the readability of computer-displayed Times New Roman and Arial text." *International Journal of Human-Computer Studies*, 59, no. 6 (December 2003), 823–835.

Berners-Lee, Tim. "Information Management: A Proposal." CERN, March 1989. http://www.w3.org/History/1989/proposal.html (accessed February 3, 2002).

BizReport. "Nortel: eBusiness to Grow by 86 Percent Annually." *BizReport*, January 31, 2000. http://www.bizreport.com/news/2000/01/20000131-4.htm (accessed July 27, 2000).

Bloomberg News. "EarthLink, MindSpring Complete Merger." *Bloomberg News*, February 4, 2000, http://news.cnet.com/news/0-1004-200-1543009.html?tag=st (accessed August 8, 2000).

CAUCE. "CAUCE Does the Math—Why Can't the Marketing Industry?" *CAUCE*, May 15, 2001. http://www.cauce.org/pressreleases/math.shtml (accessed January 4, 2002).

Cheskin Research. *Trust in the Wired Americas.* Redwood Shores, CA: Cheskin Research, 2000. http://www.cheskin.com/think/studies/trust2.html.

Cyber Dialogue. "Telecommuting Boosted in 1998 by Internet and Economy," *Cyberdialogue*, October 28, 1999. http://www.cyberdialogue.com/resource/press/releases/1998/10-28-sb-telecommuting.html (accessed July 29, 2000).

eMarketer. "Online Advertising," *eMarket eReports*, August 1, 2001. http://www.emarketer.com/ereports/advert_onl/ (accessed December 8, 2001).

Godwin, Mike. "Sex and the Single Sysadmin: The Risks of Carrying Graphic Sexual Materials." *Internet World*, 5, no. 2 (March/April 1994), 11–13.

Hofstetter, Fred T. *Multimedia Literacy, 3ʳᵈ ed.* New York: McGraw-Hill, 2001.

Horton, Frank. *The Computer and the Invasion of Privacy: Hearings before the Special Subcommittee on Invasion of Privacy of the House Committee on Government Operations.* 89th Cong., 2d Sess. 6 (1966).

Kathman, David. "The Merger Express of 1999." *Morningstar*, January 1, 2000. http://news.morningstar.com/news/ms/specialreports/99endmergers.html (accessed July 29, 2000).

Kulik, James A, Chen-Lin C. Kulik, and Peter A. Cohen. "Effectiveness of Computer-based College Teaching: A Meta-analysis of Findings." *Review of Educational Research*, 50, no. 4 (1998), 525–544.

Kulik, James A. "School Mathematics and Science Programs Benefit from Instructional Technology." NSF InfoBrief 03-301, NSF Division of Science Resources Statistics, Arlington, VA, 2000. Also available from ERIC document ED472100, 2000.

Lee, Lydia. "RealAudio Goes Mainstream: SDK in Beta." *NewMedia*, October 7, 1996, 30.

Liu, Wenhai, Ernest Chuang, and Demetri Psaltis. "Holographic Memory Design for Petaflop Computing." Proceedings of HTMT Meeting, Princeton, NJ, July 1998. http://optics.caltech.edu/wliu/htmt/tech.pdf.

Murphy, Dave. "Hackers Get Bill Gates' Credit Card." *ITinfo,* March 26, 2000. http://trainonline.org/itinfo/2000/it000326.html (accessed August 28, 2000).

Nelson, Theodore H. "The Hypertext." *Proceedings of the World Documentation Federation,* 1965.

Perine, Keith. "ToysMart Settles with FTC." *The Standard*, July 21, 2000. http://biz.yahoo.com/st/000721/17051.html (accessed July 27, 2000).

Rohde, Laura. "European Online Sales Doubled in 1999." *The Standard*, November 24, 1999. http://www.thestandard.com/article/display/0,1151,7873,00.html (accessed July 27, 2000).

Saunders, Christopher. "Study: Pop-Under Ads Can Backfire." *NewMedia*, August 2, 2001. http://www.newmedia.com/nm-ie.asp?articleID=2900 (accessed December 16, 2001).

UCLA Center for Communication Policy. "The UCLA Internet Report: Year Two—Surveying the Digital Future." UCLA Center for Communication Policy, Los Angeles, CA, November 29, 2001. http://www.ccp.ucla.edu/pages/internet-report.asp (accessed January 27, 2002).

TeleWork America. "Research Results." *ITAC*, 2001. http://www.telecommute.org/twa/twa2000/research_results_summary.shtml (accessed December 16, 2001).

TNS Research. *Global eCommerce Report 2001.* TNS Research. http://www.tnsofres.com/ger2001/.

Verton, Dan. "DOD Pushing Forward on Internet Disconnect." *Federal Computer Week*, April 26, 2000. http://www.fcw.com/fcw/articles/2000/0424/web-dod-04-26-00.asp (accessed August 8, 2000).

Wimpsett, Kim. "Who says you can't get something for nothing?" *CNET Review*, July 11, 2000. http://home-internal.cnet.com/internet/0-3765-7-2198531.html?tag=st.cn.sr1.ssr.cn_isp (accessed November 16, 2000).

Index

Numbers

3DES (triple DES), description of, 566
3.5 floppy drives, introduction of, 9
8-bit images, converting 24-bit images to, 272–273
10/100BaseT Ethernet, significance of, 56, 466–467
10BaseT Ethernet, significance of, 56
10GBE Ethernet standard, significance of, 56
24-bit images, converting to 8-bit images, 272–273
32-bit microprocessor, introduction of, 11
100VG-AnyLAN standard, overview of, 457
386 processor, release of, 10
486 chip, introduction of, 11
802.* networking standards, purpose and status of, 455–457
68040 microprocessor, introduction of, 11
80386 processor, release of, 10
80486 chip, introduction of, 11

Symbols

(pound sign)
    appearance in browsers, 263–264
    using with IDs, 379
* (asterisk) wildcard character, using with HTML frames, 325
// (comment statements), using, 351
// (double slash) in ASP scripts, meaning of, 537, 539
\ (backslash), denoting quote signs with, 355
+ (concatenating operator), using in JavaScript, 351–353
= (assignment operator), example of, 349–350, 353
" (quotation marks), including inside strings, 354–355

A

</a> stop tags, importance of, 263–264
<a href; "url"></a> tags, using in Web page résumés, 256, 265, 266
<a name; "name"></a> tags, using in Web page résumés, 256
About.com, searching with, 91

absolute positioning
    example of, 380–381
    overview of, 380
absolute versus relative links, 333–334
access control, relationship to Web servers, 504
Access HTML translator, using, 226
Accessibility dialog box, displaying in IE, 410
active Web pages, definition of, 344. See also data-driven Web pages; static Web pages; top secret Web pages; Web pages
ActiveX language, overview of, 83
ADDIE software development cycle
    as model for continuous improvement, 197–198
    stages of, 196–198
address books, using for e-mail, 135–136
Address DNS record type, purpose of, 497
ADO (ActiveX Data Objects), relationship to server-side databases, 533
ADO connection objects, creating, 533–534
ADO recordset object, methods in, 537
ADSL (Asynchronous DSL), explanation of, 57
advertising, impact of Internet on, 25
A-E Internet classes
    explanations of, 484–485
    ranges for private IP addresses, 487
    and subnet masks, 487
    zeros in, 486
.aero top-level domain, meaning of, 20
AES (Advanced Encryption Standard), description of, 566
AI (artificial intelligence)
    bots, 40
    foreign language translation, 39
    image recognition, 39
    overview of, 38
    text-to-speech conversion, 38–39
    voice recognition, 38
AIFF (Audio Interchange File Format), overview of, 105
AIM (AOL Instant Messenger), features of, 156

alert boxes, debugging JavaScript with, 366–368
alerts, sending with network analyzers, 493
aliases, relationship to Web servers, 504
align attribute, effect of, 281
alignment attributes, adjusting in Web-page tables, 280–281
all-subnets-directed broadcasts, explanation of, 486
alt attribute, using to comply with Section 508, 407
AltaVista
    adding Web sites to, 97
    performing keyword searches with, 87
AltaVista Multimedia, searching with, 93
Amazon.com's Web Services, overview of, 184
analysis stage of ADDIE, explanation of, 196
anchor/link HTML tags, description of, 255
anchors
    explanation of, 63
    linking in Web pages, 234
AND Boolean operator, example of, 88
AND NOT, using with SELECT statement and WHERE clause, 536
AND, using with SELECT statement and WHERE clause, 536
animated images, creating for Web pages, 275, 293–294. See also images; transparent images
Animation Shop, using with Web pages, 276
animations, creating with Dynamic HTML, 382–383
AOL (America Online)
    availability of, 12
    overview of, 53
Apple Computer, founding of, 7
Apple QuickTime, features of, 77
AppleTalk, overview of, 453
applets
    features of, 81
    making accessible, 415, 430
Application Layer of OSI/RM
    overview of, 449
    protocols associated with, 478–479

application level gateways, using with firewalls, 560–561

aqua, RGB code for, 282

Archie, searching with, 94

archives, downloading from Internet, 108–109

<area> tags, defining in HTML image maps, 316

Arial versus Times font, 239, 422

ARP (Address Resolution Protocol), relationship to TCP/IP, 480

ARPANET, (Advanced Research Projects Agency), goal of, 30

arrays, accessing DOM objects by, 364–365

art command-line utility, using, 492–493

AS2 (Applicability Statement), editing EDI Internet standards with, 181

ASCII files, overview of, 99

ascii legacy-system FTP command, description of, 167

Ask An Expert searches, performing, 90–91

ASP (Active Server Pages). *See also* ISAPI (Internet SAPI) features of, 524–525 using to deny access to Web pages, 540–541

ASP.NET, features of, 526

asset identification, security risks associated with, 552–553

assignment operator (=), example of, 349–350, 353

assignment statements, example of, 350

assignment variables, using with DOM objects and arrays, 364

asterisk (*) wildcard character, using with HTML frames, 325

asymmetric cryptography, overview of, 567

AT&T WorldNet, overview of, 53

Athlon CPU, release of, 13

ATM (Asynchronous Transfer Mode) standard, overview of, 459–460

attachments, sending, 134

attacks, defeating, 558–559

.au code, country associated with, 21

AU file format, overview of, 104

auctions, overview of, 189

audio controls, using in Windows Media Player, 74

audio, downloading from Internet, 103

audioconferencing features of, 159 overview of, 170

audiovisual file formats AIF, AIFF, and AIFC, 105 AU and SND, 104 MIDI (Musical Instrument Digital Interface), 105–106 MP3 (MPEG audio layer 3), 105 overview of, 104

RA (RealAudio) and RAM (RealAudio metafile), 104–105 WAV (wafeform), 104

audit policies, setting, 559

authenticated user access control, overview of, 504

Auto Completion feature in IE, using, 70

AVI (audio/video interleave) format, overview of, 106

B

B2B (business-to-business) e-commerce explanation of, 178 impact on Internet on, 31 overview of, 179–180

B2C (business-to-consumer) e-commerce explanation of, 178 overview of, 179

backbones, using FDDI for, 457

background colors, using in Web pages, 239

backgrounds, using in Web pages, 233, 239–240

backslash (\), denoting quote signs with, 355

<base> tags, using with HTML frames, 326

BASIC language, development of, 7

BBEdit HTML editor, creating Web pages with, 225

bCentral Commerce Manager. *See also* FrontPage E-Commerce Wizard adding Web sites to, 98 choosing marketplace for, 191, 193 creating product for, 189–191 payment settings in, 194–195 setting up e-commerce account for, 190

BeginAnimation() function, using with Dynamic HTML, 383

Berners-Lee, Tim and WWW, 14

BGP (Border Gateway Protocol), overview of, 483

Bigfoot search engine, finding people with, 95

binary legacy-system FTP command, description of, 167

BinHex encoding, overview of, 507

.biz top-level domain, meaning of, 20

black, RGB code for, 282

block ciphers, description of, 571

block-style HTML tags, description of, 255

blogging overview of, 17–18, 169–170 popularity of, 152

blue, RGB code for, 282

Bluetooth, overview of, 35

.bmp graphics format, description of, 101

BNC (British Naval Connector), relationship to coaxial cable, 464

Bobby Web accessibility tool, features of, 427

<body background="*filename*"></body> tags, using in Web page résumés, 256

<body></body> tags, using in Web page résumés, 256–257

bold text, including on Web pages, 267, 354

bookmarked Favorites, importing and exporting, 70

bookmarking Favorites, 69

bookmarks organizing in folders, 69–70 using in Web pages, 233, 262–263

Boolean searches, performing, 87–88

boot record virus, description of, 553–554

BOOTP (Bootstrap Protocol), relationship to TCP/IP, 479

borderless frames, creating, 323–324

borders, using in Web pages, 235

bots, overview of, 40

bps (bits per second), measuring modem speed by, 55

BRI (Basic Rate Interface), relationship to ISDN, 56–57

bridges, description of, 462

Britannica.com, searching with, 92

brouters, description of, 463

browser security, configuring, 84–85, 113–114

browsers. *See also* legacy browsers description of, 60 fonts supported by, 238 interrupting with Stop button, 68 managing cache for, 71–72 selecting, 60–61 support for plug-ins, 79–80 using, 112–113 viewing Web page résumés in, 259

brute force attacks, effect of, 558

BSD UNIX, development of, 8

buddies in IM, communicating with, 12

budgeting, role in project management, 198

Builder.Com, Web address for, 369

bulleted lists, including in Web page résumés, 261

bus topology, overview of, 445

business, impact of Internet on, 25

business tier, establishing connections with, 531

buttons, including in HTML forms, 313

C

C# language, overview of, 82

C2C (customer-to-customer) e-commerce, explanation of, 187

CA (certificate authority),
VeriSign as, 569
.ca code, country associated with, 21
cable modems, features of, 57
cache, managing for browsers, 71–72
caching servers, overview of, 499
captions, providing for videos,
393–394
car purchases, impact of Internet on, 25
Carnivore system, purpose of, 28
case sensitivity, managing on files
servers, 333
Case Study of Microsoft bCentral
Commerce Manager, 189–195
cash model, applying to processing
payments online, 185
CAT 5 cabling, features of, 464–465
CataList Catalog, Web address for, 140
catalog servers, overview of, 501
CAUCE (Coalition Against
Unsolicited Commercial Email),
significance of, 122
cd legacy-system FTP commands,
descriptions of, 167
cell padding, including in Web-page
tables, 281
cell spacing, including in Web-page
tables, 281
cells and tables, coloring, 281–282.
See also table cells
cells, relationship to ATM, 459
certificate servers, overview of, 500
CGI (common gateway interface)
overview of, 523
purpose of, 308, 505
.ch code, country associated with, 21
chain letters, example of, 123
character attributes, using on
Web pages, 266–267
character-entity HTML tags,
description of, 255
chat rooms, overview of, 153–154, 170
chats, overview of, 10–12
check boxes, creating in HTML forms,
308–309, 311
check model, applying to processing
payments online, 185–186
checkbook.xsd file,
XML schema in, 388
checkout, relationship to
e-commerce, 177
circle areas, HTML syntax for, 317
circuit level gateways, using with
firewalls, 560
Cisco Systems, founding of, 9
Class A-E Internet classes
explanations of, 484–485
ranges for private IP addresses, 487
and subnet masks, 487
zeros in, 486
client software, features of, 52
clients versus servers, 19

client-server computing
explanation of, 18
networking model for, 440–441
overview of, 19
client-side image maps, analyzing, 316
clip art, using with Web pages, 276
clock project
clock code analysis of, 358
creating, 356–357
customizing date and time display
in, 358–359
close legacy-system FTP command,
description of, 167
.cn code, country associated with, 21
CNAME (Canonical Name) DNS
record type, purpose of, 497
CNET Search.com, metasearching
with, 90
coaxial cable
and BNC connectors, 464
diagram of, 463
Thicknet, 464
Thinnet, 464
ColdFusion scripting, features of, 526
color adjustments, applying to
Web pages, 272–273
color blindness simulator, 423
coloring tables and cells, 281–282
cols attribute, creating vertical frames
with, 321
columns, spanning in tables, 287
.com top-level domain
meaning of, 20
registering, 22
comma-delimited data,
explanation of, 527
comment statements (//), using, 351
Commerce Manager. *See* bCentral
Commerce Manager
communications, relationship
to e-commerce, 180
compressed archives, downloading
from Internet, 108–109
Compton's Multimedia Search patent,
significance of, 205–206
CompuServe Internet access,
availability of, 12
computer conferencing, relationship
to Usenet newsgroups, 146
computer ethics, relationship to
Netiquette, 121–122
computer services, inspecting, 512
concatenating operator (+), using in
JavaScript, 351–353
concatenating string variables, 351–352
concentrators, description of, 462
concept searches, performing, 89
connection media
coaxial cable, 463–464
fiber optics, 465–466
twisted pair cabling, 464–465

connections, testing with network
analyzers, 493. *See also* Internet
connections
consistency, considering in Web page
design, 242
contingency planning, role in project
management, 198
ContinueAnimation() function, using
with Dynamic HTML, 383
cookie cutter code analysis, 372–373
cookies
definition of, 369
as hit counters, 373
inspecting, 374
maintaining state in, 369–373,
396–397
necessity to Internet, 369–370
persisting, 372
reading and writing value of,
370–372
.coop top-level domain, meaning of, 20
copyrights
overview of, 200–201
regulating, 211–212
Core FTP Lite program
configuring connection for,
330–331
setting file permission attributes
with, 335
corporate mergers and alliances,
relevance of, 23–24
costs, saving with EDI, 181
Courier New font, including in
Web pages, 239
crackers, definition of, 550
CRC (cyclic redundancy check),
relationship to Data Link Layer, 451
credit model, applying to processing
payments online, 186
Cross Checks
Comparing the Ways to Connect, 59
Downloading a Picture from the
Internet, 103
Inter! Intra! Extra!, 23
Internet History Timeline, 31
Matching Internet Services, 17
MIDI vs. Wave, 106
CSMA/CD (Ethernet) networking
standard, overview of, 456
CSS (cascading style sheets)
designing for accessibility, 430
overview of, 374–375, 397
types of, 375
CSS design for accessibility.
See also Section 508 of Rehabilitation
Act of 1973; Web accessibility
color and contrast, 423
font selection and spacing, 422–423
layering and CSS page layout,
425–426
overview of, 421–422

.css filename extension, MIME and media types for, 507

CTRL-R keys, replying to e-mail senders with, 133

currencies, relationship to trading internationally, 208

CUseeMe videoconferencing, features of, 160–161

CUworld service, Web address for, 161

cyberfinder.com, finding Usenet newsgroups at, 151

.cz code, country associated with, 21

D

DAP (Directory Access Protocol), development of, 500–501

data, downloading from Internet, 108–111

data interception, significance of, 551

Data Link Layer of OSI/RM
overview of, 451
relationship to switches and bridges, 462

data management, relationship to e-commerce, 180–181

data manipulation, occurrence of, 551

data tables, rows and records in, 527

database design principles, overview of, 529–530

databases
example of, 530–531
indexing, 529
normalizing, 529
overview of, 527–528, 542–543
types of, 522

data-driven Web pages, creating, 537–540, 543. *See also* active Web pages; static Web pages; top secret Web pages; Web pages

datagrams, organization of data into, 450

date and time display, customizing in JavaScript clock project, 358–359

Date() object, using in JavaScript clock project, 356–359

.de code, country associated with, 21

decisions, using logic in, 538–540

Decrease Color Depth dialog box, displaying in Paint Shop Pro, 273

default gateway, role in routing, 482

default pages, viewing for Web sites, 65

delta-frame encoding
description of, 106
relationship to MPEG digital video, 41

Demand Priority Access LAN standard, overview of, 457. *See also* LANs (local area networks)

demultiplexing, stages of, 481

DES (Data Encryption Standard), diagram of, 566

design stage of ADDIE, explanation of, 196

deuteranopia, simulating, 423

development stage of ADDIE, explanation of, 197

DHCP (Dynamic Host Configuration Protocol), relationship to TCP/IP, 479

digest mode, receiving listserv messages in, 144

digital cash, relationship to e-commerce, 177

digital checkbook model, applying to processing payments online, 177, 185–186

digital divide, significance of, 23

digital hubs, home PCs as, 42–43

digital IDs, using with Microsoft Outlook, 569–571

digital signatures, overview of, 567–569

digital television and video, overview of, 40–41

digital wallets, relationship to e-commerce, 177

dir legacy-system FTP command, description of, 167

direct connections, using, 59

direct routing, explanation of, 481

directories, searching by subject, 86–87

directory servers, overview of, 500–501

directory structure, maintaining for local Webs, 334

discussion forums
overview of, 169
participating in, 151–152

 tags
using, 378–379
and Web accessibility, 425

DLC (Data Link Control), overview of, 453

DMCA (Digital Millennium Copyright Act), overview of, 202

DMZ screened-subnet firewalls, features of, 563–564

DNS (Domain Name System)
creation of, 9
explanation of, 18
overview of, 20–21
relationship to TCP/IP, 479
transfer of management of, 13

DNS name space hierarchy, overview of, 495

DNS record types, examples of, 497

DNS servers
and DNS name servers, 496
and DNS name space hierarchy, 495
and DNS resolvers, 496

and files, 497–498
and host tables, 497–498
overview of, 495
types of, 496

.doc filename extension, MIME and media types for, 507

DOC text file format, overview of, 100

documents, downloading from Internet, 108

document.write() command, effect of, 347

Dogpile, metasearching with, 90

DOM (document object model), overview of, 359

DOM objects in JavaScript
accessing by arrays, 364–365
accessing by name, 365–366
accessing via dot notation, 362–363
examples of, 359–361
manipulating, 363–364
overview of, 396

domain name resolution, explanation of, 495

domain names, registering, 22

domains and subdomains, overview of, 20–21

DoS (Denial of Service) attacks
early occurrence of, 13
effect of, 558

dot notation, accessing DOM objects with, 362–363

dotted quad notation, relationship to IP addresses, 20

double slash (//) in ASP scripts, meaning of, 537, 539

Download.com, searching with, 95

Dreamweaver WYSIWYG editor, creating Web pages with, 228–229

DSL (Digital Subscriber Line), overview of, 57

dual-homed bastion firewalls, features of, 562–563

dumb terminals, explanation of, 439

DVD (digital video/versatile disk) technology, introduction of, 13

dynamic animation effects, example of, 382–383

Dynamic Drive, Web address for, 369

dynamic gradient effects, example of, 384–385

Dynamic HTML
code generator example of, 387
overview of, 382, 397–398

dynamic messages, displaying onscreen, 354–355

dynamic page transitions, example of, 384, 386

Dynamic ports, explanation of, 484

dynamic versus static routers, 482

E

EarthLink, overview of, 54
E-carrier systems, relationship to
  T-carrier systems, 461
e-commerce
  B2B (business-to-business)
    model of, 178
  B2C (business-to-consumer)
    model of, 178
  C2C (customer-to-customer)
    model of, 187
  defining, 210
  overview of, 177–178
  types of, 178
  users of, 178
e-commerce solutions
  auctions, 189
  choosing, 211
  instant storefronts, 188–189
  overview of, 188
e-commerce technologies. *See also*
  in-house e-commerce systems
  EDI (electronic data interchange),
    181–182
  enabling, 210
  overview of, 180–181
  SET (Secure Electronic
    Transactions), 182
  XML Web Services, 182–185
E-Commerce Wizard
  installing, 193
  running, 193–194
EDI (electronic data interchange),
  overview of, 181–182
.edu top-level domain, meaning of, 20
EGP (External Gateway Protocol),
  overview of, 483
electronic publishing, impact of
  Internet on, 28–29
<em></em> tags, using on
  Web pages, 267
e-mail. *See also* unwanted e-mail
  accessing advanced configuration
    settings for, 130–131
  addressing to groups, 136
  answering and forwarding, 133
  applying priority settings to, 138
  deciding on POP versus IMAP and
    HTTP, 128–129
  encrypting, 137–138
  filing and retrieving messages,
    133–134
  filing from listservs, 143
  overview of, 127, 168–169
  reading on Web, 138–139
  requesting return receipts for, 138
  searching, 136
  sending and reading, 131–132
  sending as HTML, 139
  sending to listservs, 143
  spell checking, 138

e-mail accounts, getting, 127–128
e-mail address books, using, 135–136
e-mail attachments, sending, 134
e-mail clients
  configuring, 129–130
  selecting, 128
e-mail filters, using, 137
e-mail folders, creating and using, 133
e-mail IDs, verifying validity of, 137
e-mail, overview of, 7–8
e-mail signatures, creating, 134
embedded code virus, description of, 554
embedded CSS
  creating, 376–377
  example of, 377
  explanation of, 375
emoticons, relationship to
  Netiquette, 126
encrypting e-mail, 137–138
enterprise networking model,
  overview of, 441–443
entertainment, impact of Internet on, 29
Eolas '096 patent, significance of,
  206–207
ERIC (Educational Resources
  Information Center), searching
  with, 91
errors, reducing with EDI, 181
Essay Quizzes
  for Architecting the Internet, 518
  for Commercializing the Internet, 214
  for Communicating Over the
    Internet, 173
  for Creating Active Web Pages,
    400–401
  for Creating Web Pages, 247–248
  for Database Connectivity and
    Server-Side Scripting, 545
  for HTML Coding, 297–298
  for Interacting with Users, 340–341
  for Introduction to Networking, 473
  for Making Web Pages
    Accessible, 433
  for Securing the Internet, 578
  for Surfing and Searching the
    Internet, 117
  for Understanding the Internet,
    48–49
Ethernet CSMA/CD networking
  standard, overview of, 456
Ethernet hubs, definition of, 456
Ethernet, overview of, 56
Ethernet standards, overview of, 456
evaluation stage of ADDIE,
  explanation of, 197
events, definition of, 356
Excel HTML translator, using, 226
Excite, performing concept searches
  with, 89
.exe filename extension
  meaning of, 109–110
  MIME and media types for, 507

external CSS
  creating, 377–379
  explanation of, 375
extranetworking
  explanation of, 29
  overview of, 23

F

fair use, overview of, 201–202
fake e-mail IDs, detecting, 137
Fast Ethernet, speed of, 456
Favorites, bookmarking, 69
FBI (Federal Bureau of Investigation),
  Web address for, 137
FDDI (Fiber Distributed Data
  Interface)networks, overview of,
  457–458
fiber optics, overview of, 465–466
file formats. *See* audiovisual file
  formats; graphics file formats;
  text file formats
file infector virus, description of, 554
file permissions
  relationship to Web servers,
    504–505
  setting with Core FTP, 335
file searches, performing, 94
file servers, case sensitivity of, 333
filename associations for IE, inspecting
  and changing, 75–76
filenames in URLs, explanation of, 63
files, transferring via legacy FTP
  commands, 165–167
filters, using with e-mail, 137:46
firefighters, relationship to flaming and
  Netiquette, 126
firewall strategies, overview of,
  560–561
firewall topologies.
  See also ZoneAlarm firewall
  DMZ screened-subnet firewalls,
    563–564
  dual-homed bastion firewalls,
    562–563
  overview of, 561
  packet filtering firewalls, 561–562
  single-homed bastion firewalls, 562
fixed-size frames, creating, 324
flames, relationship to Netiquette,
  125–126
Flash plug-in
  features of, 78–79
  making accessible, 418–419
flat file databases, definition of, 527
folders
  creating on Web, 334–335
  organizing bookmarks in, 69–70
fonts, selecting for Web pages,
  238–239
font-style HTML tags,
  description of, 255

for attribute, relationship to
Web accessibility, 416
foreground colors, using in
Web pages, 239
foreign keys, role in databases, 527
foreign language translation,
overview of, 39
form HTML tags, description of, 255
<form></form> tags, using in HTML
forms, 303–305
formatting attributes, adjusting in
Web-page tables, 280
forms. *See* HTML forms
forums
overview of, 169
participating in, 151–152
FQDN (fully qualified domain name),
relationship to DNS, 20–21
.fr code, country associated with, 21
fractional T1 service, explanation of, 460
fragments, splitting data into, 450
Frame Relay WAN standard,
overview of, 459
frame targeting, overview of, 325–326
frames
creating, 337–338
overview of, 319
preventing resizing of, 324
using in Web pages, 234–235
frameset layouts
borderless frames, 323–324
frameset grids, 322
horizontal frames, 321–322
nested framesets, 322–323
overview of, 320–321
vertical frames, 321
framesets
creating, 320
definition of, 235–236
fixed-size frames, 324
guidelines for use of, 328
overview of, 319–320
removing borders from, 324
wildcard sized frames, 324–325
FrontPage E-Commerce Wizard.
See also bCentral Commerce Manager
installing, 193
running, 193–194
FrontPage WYSIWYG editor, creating
Web pages with, 228–229
FTP clients
choosing, 330
types of, 165
FTP commands, transferring files by
means of, 165–167, 171
FTP connections, configuring, 330–331
FTP (File Transfer Protocol). *See also*
SFTP (Secure FTP) file transfers
overview of, 13

publishing Web sites by
means of, 338
relationship to TCP/IP (Transport
Control Protocol/Internet
Protocol), 478
uses for, 573
FTP searches, current status of, 94
FTP servers, overview of, 508
FTP software, installing, 330
FTP Web space and address, getting, 329
FTPing files to Web, 331–332
fuchsia, RGB code for, 282
functions, relationship to scripts,
345–346

G

gateways, description of, 463, 505
get legacy-system FTP command,
description of, 167
GET method, role in CGI scripts, 308
GIF (Graphics Interchange Format),
overview of, 102
GIF Construction Set, creating
animated images with, 275, 293–294
.gif filename extension
description of, 101
MIME and media types for, 507
GIF images, creating for
Web pages, 275
Gigabit Ethernet, speed of, 456
gigapops, explanation of, 34
Google, performing concept searches
with, 89
Google.com, growth of, 14
Gopher
relationship to TCP/IP, 478
searching with, 94–95
.gov top-level domain, meaning of, 20
government, impact of Internet on, 26
Gpbs (gigabits per second), relationship
to Ethernet networks, 56
gradient effects, example of, 384–385
graphical screen design, example of, 237
graphics. *See* images
graphics file formats
GIF (Graphics Interchange
Format), 102
JPEG (Joint Photographic Experts
Group), 102
overview of, 100
PNG (Portable Network Graphics),
102–103
graphics terminals, explanation of, 439
gray, RGB code for, 282
green, RGB code for, 282
GUI clients, relationship to FTP, 165

H

H.323 multimedia communication
standard, explanation of, 162
<h1></h1> tags
meaning of, 253
using in Web page résumés, 256,
259, 262
hacker process, relationship to viruses,
553–554
hackers, definition of, 550–551
hash encryption, overview of, 567–569
HDTV (high-definition television),
features of, 40–41
<head></head> tags, using in
Web page résumés, 255–257
headings
using in Web pages, 231–232
writing for Web page résumés, 257
"Hello, World!" project in JavaScript
code analysis of, 348
example of, 346–348
help legacy-system FTP command,
description of, 167
helper app, relationship to
multimedia, 74
helpers, making accessible, 430
hex codes, specifying color by,
281–282
hidden fields, including in HTML
forms, 312–313
hierarchy hypermedia paradigm,
example of, 289–290
History folder, accessing in IE, 70
hit counters, using cookies as, 373
hit logs, using with Web servers, 503
hoaxes, relationship to Netiquette,
123–124
Hobbes' Internet Timeline,
significance of, 7
home pages
changing in IE (Internet
Explorer), 68
default filenames for, 502
linking to résumé pages, 287–288
purpose of, 64–65
Homeland Security, impact of
Internet on, 28
HomeSite HTML editor, creating
Web pages with, 224
horizontal frames, creating, 321–322
horizontal rules, 256, 261
HTML tag for, 253
using in Web pages, 231–232, 261
HOSTS files, relationship to DNS
servers, 498
hosts tables, relationship to
DNS servers, 497
hot words, explanation of, 65

<hr> tags
  effect of, 253
  using in Web page résumés,
    256, 261
href attribute, using in Web pages,
  263–264
HTML (hypertext markup language)
  development of, 11
  dynamics of, 292
  overview of, 99
  versions of, 254
HTML colors, color names of, 281
HTML components
  markup, 253
  tag formats, 253
HTML editors
  BBEdit, 225
  creating Web pages with, 223–225
  HomeSite, 224
.html filename extension, MIME and
  media types for, 507
HTML format, sending e-mail in, 139
HTML forms
  coding radio button input controls
    for, 305–306
  coding Submit and Reset buttons
    for, 306–307
  coding text field input controls for,
    304–305
  creating, 336
  creating check boxes in, 308–309
  creating menus in, 309–310
  creating password fields in, 311
  creating text areas in, 310
  defining prompts for, 303
  including hidden fields in, 312–313
  including image buttons in, 313
  making accessible, 416
  overview of, 302
  processing response for, 307–308
  using to get information from
    users, 303
HTML frames
  creating, 337–338
  overview of, 319
  preventing resizing of, 324
  using in Web pages, 234–235
HTML image maps
  applying usemap attribute to, 317
  creating nonretangular areas in,
    317–318
  defining <map> and <area>
    tags in, 316
  designing, 337
  explanation of, 67, 316
  making accessible, 411
  rolling your own, 318–319
  visualizing coordinates for, 317

HTML tables, using in Web page
  layout, 276–278, 294–295.
  See also tables
HTML tags
  for creating tables, 278
  taxonomy of, 255
  for Web page résumés, 255–256
HTML translators
  creating Web pages with, 225–227
  Microsoft Access, 226
  Microsoft Excel, 226
  Microsoft PowerPoint, 226
  Microsoft Word, 226
HTML Web form controls, overview
  of, 311–312
HTML+TIME implementation
  example of, 393–394
  overview of, 392
<html></html> tags, using in Web page
  résumés, 256
HTTP forms, submission methods
  for, 308
HTTP gateways, definition of, 522
HTTP (Hypertext Transfer Protocol)
  explanation of, 129
  relationship to TCP/IP, 478
hubs, description of, 462
human-based searches, performing,
  90–91
hybrid hypermedia paradigm,
  example of, 290–291
hypergraphic triggers,
  explanation of, 66
hyperlinks
  creating for named anchor
    bookmarks, 262–264
  dynamics of, 287–288
  overview of, 65–66
  and Web design, 295
hypermedia designs
  hierarchy paradigm, 289–290
  hybrid paradigm, 290–291
  linear list paradigm, 289
  menu paradigm, 289
  network paradigm, 290
  overview of, 289
hypertext, coining of, 14, 65

I

IBM PC AT, introduction of, 9
IBM Token Ring, development of, 10
ICANN (Internet Corporation for
  Assigned Names and Numbers),
  significance of, 21, 31
ICMP (Internet Control Message
  Protocol), relationship to TCP/IP, 480
ICQ instant messaging, features of, 155
identity interception, significance of,
  551–552

IDs and style classes, guidelines for
  creation of, 379–380
IE (Internet Explorer)
  Auto Completion feature of, 70
  changing default home page for, 68
  configuring security settings in,
    84–85
  displaying Accessibility dialog box
    in, 410
  displaying New Message window
    in, 131–132
  features of, 60
  manipulating cache in, 71–72
  resetting browser settings in, 73
  updating, 61
  using advanced browser
    settings in, 72
  using History folder in, 70
  Windows filename associations for,
    75–76
IEEE Project 802 networking
  standards, overview of, 455–457
IETF (Internet Engineering Task
  Force), relationship to TCP/IP, 477
IF-THEN statement, example of, 539
IGMP (Internet Group Management
  Protocol), relationship to TCP/IP, 480
IIS logs, information recorded in, 503
IKE (Internet key exchange),
  relationship to IPSec, 572
IM (instant messaging)
  AIM (AOL Instant Messenger), 156
  ICQ, 155
  MSN Messenger Service, 156–158
  overview of, 12, 154–155, 170
  Yahoo! Messenger, 157–158
iMac, release of, 13
image buttons, including in HTML
  forms, 313
image HTML tags, description of, 255
image maps. *See* HTML image maps
image recognition, overview of, 39
images. *See also* animated images;
  transparent images
  capturing for Web pages, 270–271
  converting for Web pages, 271–272
  downloading from Internet,
    101–102
  including in Web pages, 293–294
  inserting into Web page résumés,
    273–274
  obtaining for Web pages, 267–268
  preparing for Web pages, 268–269
  resizing for Web pages, 272
  revealing properties of, 269
  tiling into backgrounds of
    Web pages, 274
  using in Web pages, 233
IMAP (Internet Message Access
  Protocol), explanation of, 129

<img src="*filename*"> tags, using in
   Web page résumés, 256
implementation stage of ADDIE,
   explanation of, 197
include files, placing scripts in, 345
indirect routing, explanation of,
   481–482
inetd (Internet daemon), relationship to
   UNIX and Linux, 509
.info top-level domain, meaning of, 20
information warfare, impact of
   Internet on, 28
in-house e-commerce systems.
   See also e-commerce technologies
   and ADDIE software development
      cycle, 196–197
   developing, 211
   overview of, 195–196
inline CSS
   creating, 375–376
   example of, 377
   explanation of, 375
<input> tags, using in HTML forms,
   304–305
Inside Info
   Car Buying and the Internet, 25
   H.323 Multimedia Communication
      Standard, 162
   Microsoft Technical Support
      Newsgroups, 151
   Newsgroups Are Searchable, 150
   The Story of the Trojan Horse, 84
   Using the Stop Button to Interrupt
      Your Browser, 68
instant storefronts
   benefits of, 196
   setting up, 189–195
   types of, 188–189
.int top-level domain, meaning of, 20
intelligent terminals, explanation of, 439
interactive TV, explanation of, 29
Internet
   coining of, 8
   connecting to, 112
   defining, 4–5, 44
   dependence on cookies, 369–370
   downloading audio and video
      from, 103
   downloading from, 98, 114–115
   downloading images from, 101–102
   downloading pictures from, 103
   downloading software and data
      from, 108–111
   future of, 32, 46
   growth of, 5–6
   history of, 30–31, 45–46
   improving infrastructure for, 32–36
   infrastructure of, 18–23, 45
   size of, 7
   traffic on, 5
   users of, 5

Internet addresses
   classes of, 484–485
   overview of, 484, 513–514
Internet Architecture model,
   relationship to TCP/IP, 476–477, 481
Internet calling cards, prepaying,
   58–59
Internet components, selecting with
   Components Wizard, 510
Internet Connection Wizard
   configuring e-mail clients with,
      129–130
   configuring newsgroup clients in, 147
Internet connections.
   See also connections
   comparing methods of, 58
   requirements for, 52–53
Internet Layer protocols
   ARP (Address Resolution
      Protocol), 480
   ICMP (Internet Control
      Message Protocol), 480
   IGMP (Internet Group
      Management Protocol), 480
   RARP (Reverse Address
      Resolution Protocol), 480
   and TCP/IP, 480
Internet services
   blogging, 17
   chats, 10–12
   e-mail, 7–8
   FTP (File Transfer Protocol), 13
   identifying, 44–45
   IM (instant messaging), 12–13
   listservs, 9
   multimedia streaming, 13–14
   newsgroups, 9
   overview of, 6
   RSS (Rich Site Summary), 16–17
   videoconferencing, 12–13
   WWW (World Wide Web), 14–15
Internet2, overview of, 34
Internetworking servers
   caching servers, 499
   catalog servers, 501
   certificate servers, 500
   directory servers, 500–501
   DNS servers, 495–498
   mirrored servers, 500
   overview of, 494, 514–515
   proxy servers, 498–499
   transaction servers, 502
intranetworking
   explanation of, 18–19
   overview of, 22
intrinsic events, triggering scripts
   with, 362
IP addresses, components of, 19–20
IP addressing rules
   for IP broadcast addresses, 486
   for IP loopback addresses, 485

overview of, 485
   for reserved or private
      IP addresses, 487
   for special case IP addresses
      containing zeros, 486
IP (Internet Protocol)
   invention of, 4
   purpose of, 6
   relationship to TCP/IP, 480
   and TCP/IP, 8, 19
IP telephony, overview of, 35–36
ipconfig utility, using, 492
IPSec (Internet Protocol Security),
   significance of, 572
IPv6
   relationship to Internet2, 34
   significance of, 20
IPX/SPX (Internetwork Packet
   Exchange/Sequenced Packet
   Exchange), overview of, 453
IRC (Internet Relay Chat), overview of,
   153–154, 170
IRS (Internal Revenue Service) Web site,
   downloading tax forms from, 27
ISAPI (Internet SAPI), explanation
   of, 523. *See also* ASP (Active
   Server Pages)
ISDN (Integrated Services Digital
   Network), overview of, 56–57
ISO 9000 family, relationship to
   project management, 199
ISPs (Internet Service Providers)
   America Online, 53
   AT&T WorldNet, 53
   EarthLink, 54
   MSN (Microsoft Network), 53
   rating by user satisfaction, 54
   regional and local networks, 54
   school and college networks, 54
italics, including on Web pages, 267

J

J# language, overview of, 82
Jargon File, obtaining, 126
Java applets, features of, 81
Java language
   description of, 525
   development of, 12
   overview of, 80–81
Java servlets, purpose of, 525
JavaScript
   code sources for, 368–369
   debugging with alert boxes,
      366–368
   guidelines for use of, 346
   "Hello, World!" project written in,
      346–348
JavaScript clock project
   clock code analysis of, 358
   creating, 356–357

customizing date and time display in, 358–359
JavaScript DOM objects, examples of, 359–361
JavaScript language, overview of, 81–82
JDBC (Java database connectivity), relationship to server-side databases, 532
JPEG (Joint Photographic Experts Group) format, overview of, 102
.jpg filename extension, MIME and media types for, 507
.jpg or .jpeg graphics format, description of, 101
JScript language
    creating ADO connection objects with, 533
    overview of, 82–83
    reading data from recordsets with, 537–538
    using to make decisions with logic, 539
JSP (Java Server Pages), features of, 525
Jughead, searching with, 94
junk mail, managing, 136

K

K20 project, significance of, 34
Kbps (kilobits per second), measuring modem speed by, 55
Key Terms
    for Architecting the Internet, 516
    for Commercializing the Internet, 212
    for Communicating Over the Internet, 171
    for Creating Active Web Pages, 399
    for Creating Web Pages, 246
    for Database Connectivity and Server-Side Scripting, 543–544
    for HTML Coding, 296
    for Interacting with Users, 339
    for Introduction to Networking, 471
    for Making Web Pages Accessible, 431
    for Securing the Internet, 576–577
    for Surfing and Searching the Internet, 115–116
    for Understanding the Internet, 47
Key Terms Quizzes
    for Architecting the Internet, 517
    for Commercializing the Internet, 213
    for Communicating Over the Internet, 171–172
    for Creating Active Web Pages, 399
    for Creating Web Pages, 246
    for Database Connectivity and Server-Side Scripting, 544
    for HTML Coding, 296

for Interacting with Users, 339
for Introduction to Networking, 472
for Making Web Pages Accessible, 431
for Securing the Internet, 577
for Surfing and Searching the Internet, 116
for Understanding the Internet, 47
keyboard shortcuts, replying to e-mail senders with, 133
keyword searches, performing with AltaVista, 87
Kleinrock, Leonard and packet switching theory, 6
Kulik, James and computer-based learning, 30

L

Lab Projects
    for Architecting the Internet, 518–520
    for Commercializing the Internet, 214–217
    for Communicating Over the Internet, 173–174
    for Creating Active Web Pages, 401–402
    for Creating Web Pages, 248–250
    for Database Connectivity and Server-Side Scripting, 546–547
    for HTML Coding, 298–299
    for Interacting with Users, 341–342
    for Introduction to Networking, 473–474
    for Making Web Pages Accessible, 433–434
    for Securing the Internet, 579–580
    for Surfing and Searching the Internet, 118
    for Understanding the Internet, 49–50
<label></label> tags, relationship to Web accessibility, 416
language issues, relationship to trading internationally, 209
LANs (local area networks).
    See also Demand Priority Access LAN standard
    creating, 470
    definition of, 454
Laserjet printers, introduction of, 10
Law.com, searching with, 96
layout
    considering in designing Web pages, 236–238
    for subdivided table cells, 286
    and Web accessibility, 425–426
LDAP (Lightweight Directory Access Protocol), development of, 501
learning, impact of Internet on, 30
legacy browsers, overview of, 61–62

legacy FTP commands, transferring files by means of, 165–167
legacy systems, using telnet to log onto, 163–165, 171
legal information, searching for, 96–97
LexisONE legal search engine, using, 97
<li></li> tags, using in Web page résumés, 256, 260–261
licensing
    open source licenses, 204
    overview of, 203
    regulating, 211–212
    single-user licenses, 203
    site licenses, 203
LIFT Web accessibility tool, features of, 427
lime, RGB code for, 282
limited broadcasts, explanation of, 486
linear list hypermedia paradigm, example of, 289
linearization, relationship to Web accessibility, 425
linked anchors, using in Web pages, 234
links
    activating, 65
    using in Web pages, 234
Linux operating system
    and inetd, 509
    overview of, 444
Lisa computer, development of, 9
list and miscellaneous HTML tags, description of, 255
lists
    creating in Web page résumés, 260–261
    using in Web pages, 231
listserv archives, examining, 144
listserv commands, list of, 145
listserv messages
    filing, 143
    receiving, 141–142
    receiving in digest mode, 144
    responding to, 142–143
    sending, 143
LISTSERV REFCARD command, effect of, 145
listservs
    finding out who belongs to, 143–144
    overview of, 9, 139–140, 169
    pausing, 143
    setting up, 145
    subscribing to, 140–141
    unsubscribing from, 144
Liszt Directory, Web address for, 140
LiveMeeting videoconferencing, features of, 162
LLC (Logical Link Control) networking standard
    overview of, 456
    relationship to Data Link Layer, 451

local echo option, setting in telnet, 164

local Webs, maintaining good directory structure for, 334. *See also* Web sites

LockerGnome listserv, subscribing to, 140

logic, using to make decisions, 538–540

logical font-style HTML tags, description of, 255

longdesc attribute, using to comply with Section 508, 408

Lotus 1-2-3, development of, 9

Love Bug virus, explanation of, 124

lurking, relationship to Netiquette, 125

Lycos, adding Web sites to, 97

Lycos Multimedia, searching with, 92–93

M

MAC address, discovering for NICs, 454

MAC (Media Access Control), relationship to Data Link Layer, 451

Mac OS, overview of, 444

Mac OS X Jaguar, release of, 14

Macintosh OS X, release of, 14

Macintosh System 7.0, release of, 11

Macintoshes
  release of, 9
  running self-extracting archives in, 110
  triggering menus on, 67

macro virus, description of, 554

MAGPie, using to comply with Section 508, 408–409

mail. *See* e-mail

mail servers
  and BinHex encoding, 507
  and MIME (Multipurpose Internet Mail Extensions), 506
  overview of, 506
  and Uuencoding, 506

mailing list servers, overview of, 507

mailto links, including in Web pages, 266

mainframe/terminal networking model, overview of, 439–440

malformed XML documents, explanation of, 389

malicious code, guarding against, 136

MANs (metropolitan networks)
  creating, 470
  definition of, 454

<map> tags, defining in HTML image maps, 316

MapQuest search engine, finding places with, 96

mark up of text, explanation of, 253

marketplace, choosing for bCentral Commerce Manager, 193

maroon, RGB code for, 282

masquerading, significance of, 552

MAU (Multi-Station Access Unit), relationship to token ring, 457

maxlength attributes, using with <input> tags, 304

MBONE (Multicast Backbone), overview of, 32–33

Mbps (megabits per second), relationship to Ethernet networks, 56

md = H(m) formula, meaning of, 568

MD5 encryption algorithm, description of, 569

media accessibility showcase, accessing, 420–422

Media Player, features of, 78

menu hypermedia paradigm, example of, 289

menus, creating in HTML forms, 309–312

mesh topology, overview of, 448

message digests, relationship to hash encryption, 568

MetaCrawler, metasearching with, 90

metasearching, performing, 89–90

methods, definition of, 355–356

mget legacy-system FTP command, description of, 167

Microsoft Security Newsletters, subscribing to, 556–557

Microsoft software, 8
  Access HTML translator, using, 226
  bCentral Commerce Manager. *See* bCentral Commerce Manager
  Excel HTML translator, 226
  Internet Explorer. *See* IE (Internet Explorer)
  Media Player, 78
  Office (audiovisual conference calls), 162–163
  Outlook (digital IDs), 569–571
  PowerPoint HTML translator, 226–227
  Virtual Server 2005, 14
  Windows, 10, 442, 444
  Windows 3.0, 11
  Windows 3.1, 11
  Windows 98, 13
  Windows 2000, 13
  Windows for Workgroups 3.1, 11
  Windows NT 3.1, release of, 12
  Windows NT Workstation 4.0, release of, 12
  Windows Server 2003 family, release of, 14
  Windows XP, release of, 14
  Windows XP Media Center, release of, 14
  Word (HTML translator), 226–227

Microsoft Windows servers, overview of, 510–511

Microsoft Windows XP Tablet PC, release of, 14

Microsoft's newsgroup server, Web address for, 151

Middle C image map, 316
  creating nonretangular areas in, 317–318
  visualizing coordinates in, 317

MIDI (Musical Instrument Digital Interface) format, overview of, 105–106

.midi filename extension, MIME and media types for, 507

.mil top-level domain, meaning of, 20

MILNET, emergence of, 9, 31

MIME (Multipurpose Internet Mail Extensions), overview of, 506–507

The Mining Company. *See* About.com

mirrored servers, overview of, 500

misuse of privileges, significance of, 552

MMC (Microsoft Management Console), configuring Windows components with, 511

mobile Internet technologies, Web resource for, 73

modems, overview of, 55

Mosaic Web browser, development of, 12, 14

Motley Fool, Web address for, 152

MOV and QT video formats, overview of, 106–107

Mozilla browser, current state of, 61

MP3 (MPEG audio layer 3) format, overview of, 105

.mp3 filename extension, MIME and media types for, 507

MPEG digital video, overview of, 41

MPEG (Motion Picture Experts Group) format, overview of, 107

.mpeg filename extension, MIME and media types for, 507

mput legacy-system FTP command, description of, 167

MS BASIC, introduction of, 8

MSAA (Microsoft Active Accessibility), significance of, 418

MS-DOS
  version 5.0, 11
  version 6.0, release of, 12
  version 6.22, release of, 12

MSN (Microsoft Network), overview of, 53

MSN Messenger Service, features of, 156–158

MSN TV receivers, availability of, 29, 41–42

multilink PPP, relationship to ISDN, 56–57

multimedia
  audio controls, 74
  built-in browser support for, 74
  definition of, 73
  overview of, 113

plug-ins, 77–80
   streaming media, 76–77
   video controls, 75
multimedia chats, dynamics of,
   154–155
multimedia searches, performing,
   92–93
multimedia streaming, overview of,
   13–14
Multiple-Choice Quizzes
   for Architecting the Internet,
      517–518
   for Commercializing the Internet,
      213–214
   for Communicating Over the
      Internet, 172
   for Creating Active Web Pages, 400
   for Creating Web Pages, 246–247
   for Database Connectivity and
      Server-Side Scripting, 544–545
   for HTML Coding, 296–297
   for Interacting with Users, 339–340
   for Introduction to Networking,
      472–473
   for Making Web Pages
      Accessible, 432
   for Securing the Internet, 577–578
   for Surfing and Searching the
      Internet, 116–117
   for Understanding the Internet, 48
multitier computing, tiers involved in,
   440–441
.museum top-level domain,
   meaning of, 20
.mx code, country associated with, 21
MX (Mail Exchanger) DNS record
   type, purpose of, 497

N

name attributes, using with <input>
   tags, 304
name servers and resolvers,
   relationship to DNS servers, 496
name space, relationship to DNS, 495
.name top-level domain, meaning of, 20
named anchor bookmarks
   creating hypertext links to, 262–264
   including in Web page résumés,
      262–263
NAPs (network access points)
   and E-carrier systems, 461
   overview of, 460
   and T-carrier systems, 460–461
Napster file-sharing program,
   creation of, 13
NAT (network address translation)
   overview of, 461
   using with firewalls, 560
navigation buttons, using, 67–68
navigation, making accessible, 417

navigational icons, using in
   Web pages, 240
navy, RGB code for, 282
  (non-breaking space),
   including on Web pages, 266
NCP (Network Control Protocol),
   creation of, 6
Nelson, Ted and hypertext, 14
nested framesets, creating, 322–323
Net. *See* Internet
.net domains, registering, 22
.net top-level domain, meaning of, 20
NetBEUI (NetBIOS Extended User
   Interface), overview of, 453
Net-directed broadcasts,
   explanation of, 486
netid.255.255.255, explanation of, 486
Netiquette
   and computer ethics, 121–122
   definition of, 120
   and emoticons, 126
   and firefighters, 126
   and flames, 125–126
   guidelines for, 120–121
   and hoaxes, 123–124
   identifying owners of Web pages,
      265–266
   and lurking, 125
   for newsgroups, 149
   overview of, 168
   and smileys, 126
   and spam, 122–123
   and TLAs (three-letter
      acronyms), 126
   and viruses, 124–125
NetMeeting videoconferencing,
   features of, 162
Netscape Composer WYSIWYG editor,
   creating Web pages with, 230
Netscape Navigator
   current state of, 61
   release of, 12, 14–15
   updating, 61
Netscape-AOL giveaway hoax,
   explanation of, 123
netstat utility, using, 491
NetWare operating system
   demonstration of, 9
   introduction of, 10
   overview of, 444
   version 4.0 of, 12
Network Access Layer protocols,
   overview of, 480
network analyzers, using, 493
network components
   bridges, 462
   brouters, 463
   concentrators, 462
   gateways, 463
   hubs, 462
   NICs (Network Interface Cards), 461
   repeaters, 462

routers, 463
   switches, 462
   workstations, 462
network data, transmitting securely,
   566–573, 575–576
network hypermedia paradigm,
   example of, 290
Network Layer of OSI/RM,
   overview of, 450
network operating systems
   definition of, 442
   Mac OS, 444
   Microsoft Windows, 442, 444
   Novell NetWare, 444
   UNIX and Linux, 444
network protocols
   adopting, 469–470
   combining, 453–454
   and OSI/RM (Open System
      Interconnection/Reference
      Model), 449–452
network security, enhancing with
   proxy servers, 499
network security threats
   data interception, 551
   identifying assets, 552–553
   identity interception, 551–552
   masquerading, 552
   miuse of privileges, 552
   replay attacks, 552
   social engineering attacks, 552
   viruses and hacker process,
      553–554
network topologies
   bus topology, 445
   classifying, 468
   hybrid topology, 446
   mesh topology, 448
   ring topology, 445–446
   star topology, 446
networking, history of, 438
networking models
   client-server model, 440–441
   enterprise model, 441–443
   mainframe/terminal model,
      439–440
   P2P (peer-to-peer) model, 441
networks
   configuring for optimum
      performance, 489–493, 514
   defending, 553
   example of, 494
   overview of, 438–439, 468
   receiving information from, 442
New Message window, displaying in
   Internet Explorer, 131–132
news servers, overview of, 508
newsgroup clients, configuring, 147
newsgroup searches, performing,
   93–94
newsgroup server by Microsoft,
   Web address for, 151

newsgroups. *See also* USENET
    newsgroups
        choosing, 147–149
        creating new topics in, 151
        finding in particular professions, 151
        overview of, 9, 169
        reading, 149
        responding to, 149–150
        searching, 150
        subscribing to, 149
NewsScan listserv, subscribing to,
    140–141
NeXt, purchase of, 12
NICs (Network Interface Cards)
    diagram of, 462
    relationship to DLC, 453–454
NNTP (Network News Transfer
    Protocol), relationship to TCP/IP, 478
non-breaking space ( ),
    including on Web pages, 266
normalizing databases, 529
NOT Boolean operator, example of, 88
NOT, using with SELECT statement
    and WHERE clause, 536
Notepad text editor, 256–257
        creating HTML forms with,
            303–304
        creating Web pages with, 223–225
        navigating, 259
        using with Web page résumés,
            256–257
Novell NetWare operating system
    demonstration of, 9
    introduction of, 10
    overview of, 444
    version 4.0 of, 12
NS (Name Server) DNS record type,
    purpose of, 497
NSAPI (Netscape SAPI), explanation
    of, 523
NSFNET backbone, beginning of,
    10, 31
numeric variables
    assigning values to, 353–354
    definition of, 349

O

object HTML tags, description of, 255
objects
    definition of, 80
    security issues related to, 83–84
ODBC (open database connectivity),
    relationship to server-side
    databases, 532
ODBMS (object-oriented database
    management system), explanation
    of, 528
Office, making audiovisual conference
    calls with, 162–163
offline instant storefronts,
    explanation of, 188

<ol></ol> tags, using in Web page
    résumés, 260–261
OLE DB data sources, relationship to
    server-side databases, 533
olive, RGB code for, 282
on* events, triggering scripts with, 362
online banking and investing,
    significance of, 26
online instant storefronts,
    explanation of, 188
online shopping
    significance of, 25–26
    statistics related to, 178
open legacy-system FTP command,
    description of, 167
open source
    licensing, 204
    meaning of, 61
operating systems
    definition of, 442
    Linux, 444, 509
    Mac OS, 444
    Microsoft Windows, 442, 444
    Novell NetWare, 444
    UNIX and Linux, 444
operators, definition of, 349
<option> tag, using with selection
    menus in HTML forms, 310
OR Boolean operator, example of, 88
OR, using with SELECT statement and
    WHERE clause, 536
ordered lists, using in Web page
    résumés, 260–261
.org top-level domain, meaning of, 20
OS X Jaguar, release of, 14
OS X, release of, 14
OS/2, introduction of, 10
OS/2 2.0, release of, 11
OS/2 Warp 4 and Warp Server,
    release of, 12
Osborne I, introduction of, 8
OSI/RM layers, remembering, 451–452
OSI/RM (Open System
    Interconnection/Reference Model)
        Application Layer of, 449
        Data Link Layer of, 451
        versus Internet Architecture model,
            476–477
        layers in, 468–469
        Network Layer of, 450
        overview of, 449
        Physical Layer of, 451
        Presentation Layer of, 449
        Session Layer of, 450
        Transport Layer of, 450
OSI/RM protocol suite examples
        AppleTalk, 453
        DLC (Data Link Control), 453
        IPX/SPX (Internetwork Packet
            Exchange/Sequenced Packet
            Exchange), 453

NetBEUI (NetBIOS Extended User
    Interface), 453
        SNA (Systems Network
            Architecture), 453
        TCP/IP (Transport Control
            Protocol/Internet Protocol), 452
OSPF (Open Shortest Path First),
    overview of, 483
Outlook, using digital IDs with,
    569–571
Outlook Express
    applying priority settings in, 138
    choosing newsgroups in, 147–149
    creating e-mail folders in, 133
    creating mailing lists in, 136
    filing mail into e-mail folders in, 133
    retrieving filed e-mail messages in,
        133–134
    searching e-mail in, 136
    setting e-mail filters in, 137
    sorting newsgroup messages in, 150
    using e-mail address books in,
        135–136
Outlook Express Inbox, displaying
    incoming messages in, 132

P

<p></p> tags, using in Web page
    résumés, 256, 260, 265
P2P (peer-to-peer) networking model,
    overview of, 441
packet filtering firewalls, features of,
    560–562
packet sniffers, purpose of, 493
packets
    port numbers assigned to, 483–484
    relationship to TCP/IP, 19
page structure HTML tags,
    description of, 255
page title, creating for Web page
    résumés, 257
page transition effects
    definition of, 384
    style settings for, 386
Paint Shop Pro
    configuring for Web pages,
        269–270
    creating transparent images with, 275
    making color adjustments in,
        272–273
    resizing images in, 271
    setting file formats in, 271
paired HTML tags, explanation of, 253
Palm OS, overview of, 37–38
PalmPilot, release of, 12
paragraphs
    using in Web pages, 231
    writing in Web page résumés,
        259–260, 265
password fields, creating in
    HTML forms, 311

passwords, using with e-mail accounts, 127
patents
Compton's Multimedia Search patent, 205–206
Eolas '096 patent, 206–207
overview of, 204–205
regulating, 211–212
Unisys GIF patent, 206
paths in URLs, explanation of, 63
Patriot Act, purpose of, 28
payment processing online
cash model for, 185
check model for, 185–186
credit model for, 186
overview of, 185, 210–211
person-to-person model for, 187–188
smart card model for, 187
PayPal Button factory
making, 337
using, 314–315
PayPal Buy Now button, coding, 313–315
PayPal model, applying to processing payments online, 187–188
PC Convertible computer, introduction of, 10
.pcd graphics format, description of, 101
PCs (personal computers)
configuring TCP/IP on, 488–489
using as digital hubs, 42–43
PDAs (personal digital assistants)
overview of, 36
and Palm OS, 37–38
and Windows CE, 36–37
PDF (Portable Document Format)
accessibility of, 419–421
overview of, 100
.pdf filename extension, MIME and media types for, 507
peer-to-peer networking model, overview of, 441
Pentium 4 HT processor, release of, 14
Pentium II chip, release of, 13
Pentium III processor, release of, 13
Pentium Pro processor, release of, 12
Pentium processor, release of, 12
people, finding with search engines, 95
People.yahoo.com search engine, finding people with, 95
permissions
relationship to Web servers, 504–505
setting with Core FTP, 335
person-to-person model, applying to processing payments online, 187
PGP (Pretty Good Privacy), overview of, 573
photographic backgrounds, using in Web pages, 239–240

PHP (PHP Hypertext Preprocessor), features of, 526
physical access security issues, overview of, 551
physical font-style HTML tags, description of, 255
Physical Layer of OSI/RM
overview of, 451
relationship to repeaters, 462
.pict graphics format, description of, 101
pictures, downloading from Internet, 103
piloting, role in project management, 199
ping code, creation of, 9
ping troubleshooting utility, using, 489–490
PKI (public key infrastructure), overview of, 567
PKZIP for Windows, compressing and decompressing files with, 108–109
places, finding with search engines, 96
plug-ins
Apple QuickTime, 77
browser support for, 79–80
definition of, 77
Flash plug-in, 78–79
making accessible, 430
Microsoft Media Player, 78
RealNetworks, 78
security risks associated with, 80
PNG (Portable Network Graphics) format, overview of, 102–103
.png filename extension
description of, 101
MIME and media types for, 507
PocketPCs, features of, 36–37
point sizes, considering for Web pages, 239
politics, impact of Internet on, 26
polygonal areas, HTML syntax for, 318
POP (Post Office Protocol), explanation of, 128
pop-up versus pop-under ads, 25
port 1434, relationship to Slammer attack, 553
port numbers
explanation of, 62
overview of, 483–484
POST method, role in CGI scripts, 308
postmaster, sending e-mail to, 137
POTS (plain old telephone service), significance of, 55
pound sign (#)
appearance in browsers, 263–264
using with IDs, 379
PowerPC chip, release of, 12
PowerPoint HTML translator, using, 226–227
PPP (Point to Point Protocol) versus SLIP (Serial Line Internet Protocol), 56–57

.ppt filename extension, MIME and media types for, 507
prepaid Internet calling cards, using, 58–59
Presentation Layer of OSI/RM, overview of, 449
PRI (Primary Rate Interface), relationship to ISDN, 57
primary DNS servers, purpose of, 496
primary keys in data tables, purpose of, 527
priority settings, applying to e-mail, 138
private IP addresses, hiding with proxy servers, 499
Private ports, explanation of, 484
.pro top-level domain, meaning of, 20
Process Explorer, downloading, 555
Prodigy Internet access, availability of, 12
products, creating for bCentral Commerce Manager, 190–192
project management, fundamentals of, 198–199
prompts, defining for HTML forms, 303
properties, definition of, 356
proportional fonts and spacing, definitions of, 238–239
protocols
port numbers associated with, 484
in URLs, 62
protonopia, simulating, 424
proxy servers
overview of, 498–499
using with firewalls, 560
public IP addresses, pooling with proxy servers, 499
published Web pages, correcting and updating, 333
purple, RGB code for, 282
push versus pull technology, 442
put legacy-system FTP command, description of, 167
PVCs (permanent virtual circuits), relationship to Frame Relay, 459

Q

.qt filename extension, MIME and media types for, 507
QUERY listserv command, effect of, 145
QuickTime, audio controls in, 74
QuickTime for Windows video player, using, 75
quotation marks ("), including inside strings, 354–355

R

RA (RealAudio) file format, overview of, 104–105

radio button input controls, coding for HTML forms, 305–306, 311

RAM (RealAudio metafile) file format, overview of, 104–105

RARP (Reverse Address Resolution Protocol), relationship to TCP/IP, 480

RC4 stream cipher, relationship to SSL, 571

RDBMS (relational database management system), explanation of, 528

RealNetworks plug-in, features of, 78

recordsets
definition of, 537
reading data from, 537–538

red, RGB code for, 282

registered ports, explanation of, 484

relational databases
definition of, 527–528
designing, 528–529

relative versus absolute links, 333–334

RELEASE listserv command, effect of, 145

repeaters, description of, 462

replay attacks, significance of, 552

reporting, role in project management, 199

reports, generating with network analyzers, 493

Reset buttons, coding for HTML forms, 306–307, 311

Resize dialog box, displaying in Paint Shop Pro, 272

résumés. *See* Web page résumés

return receipts, requesting for e-mail, 138

REVIEW command, using with listservs, 143, 145

RFC 1855, relationship to Netiquette, 121

RFC process, maturity states assigned to, 477

RFCs (Request for Comments)
768 (UDP), 479
791 (IP), 480
792 (ICMP), 480
793 (TCP), 479
821 (SMTP), 478
826 (ARP), 480
854 (telnet), 478
903 (RARP), 480
904 (EGP), 483
951 (BOOTP), 479
959 (FTP), 478
977 (NNTP), 478
1034 and 1035 (DNS), 479
1058 (RIP), 483
1112 (IGMP), 480
1157 (SNMP), 479
1267 (BGP), 483
1350 (TFTP), 478
1436 (Gopher), 478

1487 (LDAP), 501
1945 (HTTP), 478
2045-2049 (MIME), 506
2131 (DHCP), 479
2328 (OSPF), 483
accessing, 477

ring topology, overview of, 445–446

RIP (Routing Information Protocol), overview of, 483

risk evaluation, role in project management, 198

RJ-5 connectors, using with twisted pair cabling, 464–465

RM (Real metafile) video format, overview of, 107

rock pile, creating in absolute positioning example, 380–381

role definition, relationship to project management, 199

rollover effect, example of, 82, 367

root DNS servers, purpose of, 496

root servers, relationship to DNS, 495

routers, description of, 463

routing, overview of, 481–482

routing protocols
BGP (Border Gateway Protocol), 483
EGP (External Gateway Protocol), 483
OSPF (Open Shortest Path First), 483
overview of, 482–483
RIP (Routing Information Protocol), 483

rows, spanning in tables, 287

#RRGGBB format for colors, explanation of, 281

RSS (Rich Site Summary), overview of, 16–17

RSS channels and feeds, reading, 152–153, 170

RSVP (Resource Reservation Protocol), relationship to Internet2, 34

.rtf filename extension, MIME and media types for, 507

RTSP (real-time streaming protocol), resource for, 107

run-length encoding, description of, 106

S

Safari browser, updating and downloading, 61

sans serif typeface, example of, 239

SAPI (Server Application Programming Interface), features of, 523

satellite Internet service, using, 58

scheduling, role in project management, 198

scholarly searches, performing, 91–92

scope-creep prevention, role in project management, 198–199

screen space, increasing, 71

<script></script> tags, using, 346–348

scripting languages, examples of, 345

scripting, overview of, 344–345, 395

scripts
making accessible, 415
placement of, 345–346
running, 346
triggering with intrinsic events, 362
troubleshooting with alert boxes, 366–368

scrollbars, removing from HTML frames, 324

scrolling, considering in Web page design, 241

SDSL (Synchronous DSL), explanation of, 57

search engines
adding Web sites to, 97–98
and advanced Boolean searching, 87–88
and concept searching, 89
and file searches, 94
finding legal information with, 96–97
finding people with, 95
finding places with, 96
and human-based searching, 90–91
index of, 97
and keyword searching, 87
and metasearching, 89–90
and multimedia searches, 92–93
and newsgroup searches, 93–94
overview of, 85
and scholarly searching, 91–92
searching with, 114
and subject-oriented searching of directories, 86–87

SEARCH listserv command, effect of, 145

Search.com, features of, 90

secondary DNS servers, purpose of, 496

secret-key cryptology, overview of, 566

Section 508 of Rehabilitation Act of 1973. *See also* CSS design for accessibility; Web accessibility
(a) textual equivalents for nontext elements, 406–408
(b) synchronized alternatives for multimedia presentation, 408–409
(c) conveying color-coded information from context or markup, 409–410
coding according to, 429
(d) making Web pages readable without requiring style sheets, 409–410
(e) text links for active regions of server-side image maps, 410–411
(f) when to use client-side versus server-side image maps, 411
(g) table row and column headers, 412

(h) related table row and column headers, 412–413

(i) frame titling, 413–414

(j) avoiding screen flicker in the range of 2 Hz to 55 Hz, 414

(k) providing text-only page alternatives for noncompliant pages, 414

(l) describing scripts with functional text, 415

(m) applet and plug-accessibility, 415

(n) form elements, directions, and cues, 416

(o) skip navigation, 417, 425

(p) timed responses, 418

significance of, 405–406

sixteen rules of, 407

security

of browsers, 84–85, 113–114

of objects, 83–84

relationship to e-commerce, 180–181

risks associated with plug-ins, 80

security auditing and intrusion detection, implementing, 559–560

security issues

identifying, 575

network security threats, 551–552

physical access security, 551

user-level issues, 551

security of network data

and asymmetric cryptography, 567

and digital IDs in Microsoft Outlook, 569–571

and digital signatures, 567–569

and hash encryption, 567–569

and IPSec, 572

overview of, 566

and PGP (Pretty Good Privacy), 573

and PKI (public key infrastructure), 567

and secret-key encryption, 566–567

and SSL (Secure Sockets Layer) handshake protocol, 571

and symmetric cryptography, 566–567

and TLS (transport layer security) handshake protocol, 572

and VPNs (virtual private networks), 572

security risks, categories of, 550–551

security safeguards

applying, 575

defeating attacks, 558–559

firewall strategies, 560–561

Microsoft Security Newsletters, 556–557

security auditing and intrusion detection, 559–560

Windows Update Service, 557–558

SELECT statement, example of, 534–535

selection menus, creating in HTML forms, 310–312

self-extracting archives, overview of, 109–111

Serf instant storefront, setting up, 189–195

serif typeface, example of, 239

server names in URLs, explanation of, 62

server products, overview of, 508, 515

servers versus clients, 19

server-side databases

accessing, 543

and ADO (ActiveX Data Objects), 533

connectivity options for, 532

and OLE DB data sources, 533

providing Web access to, 522–526

and SQL (Structured Query Language), 534–536

server-side databases, providing Web access to, 542

server-side programming, explanation of, 308

service interruption, occurrence of, 551

services, identifying on computers, 512

servlets, purpose of, 525

Session Layer of OSI/RM, overview of, 450

SET listserv commands, effects of, 145

SET NOMAIL listserv command, effect of, 145

SET (Secure Electronic Transactions), overview of, 182

SFTP (Secure FTP) file transfers, making, 574. *See also* FTP (File Transfer Protocol)

"Share the Wealth of the Internet!" chain letter, significance of, 123

SHA-1 encryption algorithm, description of, 569

SHIFT-CTRL-R, replying to all e-mail senders with, 133

shipping overseas, relationship to trading internationally, 208–209

shopping. *See* online shopping

shopping carts, relationship to e-commerce, 177

SHOW STATS listserv command, effect of, 145

sidebar framesets, creating for résumés, 326–327

signatures, creating for e-mail, 134

SIGNOFF command, using with listservs, 144–145

silver, RGB code for, 282

SIM (Subscriber Identity Module), relationship to online payment processing, 187

Simply the Best Scripts, Web address for, 369

Singingfish, searching with, 93

single HTML tags, explanation of, 253

single-homed bastion firewalls, features of, 562

single-user licenses, overview of, 203

.sit filename extension, MIME and media types for, 507

site licenses, overview of, 203

skip navigation link, relationship to Web accessibility, 417

SKU (stock-keeping unit), significance of, 190

Slammer attack

and blocking traffic on port 1434, 553

effect of, 550

SLIP (Serial Line Internet Protocol) versus PPP (Point to Point Protocol), 56

smart card model, applying to processing payments online, 187

smart terminals, explanation of, 439

SMIL (Synchronized Multimedia Implementation Language), overview of, 392

smileys, relationship to Netiquette, 126

SMN (Streaming Media Network), overview of, 33

SMS (Short Message Service) messages, sending with ICQ, 155

SMTP (Simple Mail Transfer Protocol)

purpose of, 506

relationship to TCP/IP, 478

SNA (Systems Network Architecture), overview of, 453

SND file format, overview of, 104

SNMP (Simple Network Management Protocol), relationship to TCP/IP, 479

SOA (Start of Authority) DNS record type, purpose of, 497

SOAP (Simple Object Access Protocol), overview of, 184–185

social engineering attacks, significance of, 552

software, downloading from Internet, 108–111

spam, relationship to Netiquette, 122–123

<span> tags, using, 378–379

special characters, using in Web pages, 234

spell-checking e-mail, 138

spiders, purpose of, 501

SQL queries, creating, 536

SQL (Structured Query Language), using with server-side databases, 534–536

SSH (secure shell) protocol, using, 573

SSL (secure sockets layer) handshake protocol, overview of, 571

star topology, overview of, 446

Starpower, Web address for, 54

star-ring design, hybrid topology as, 446

stateful inspection, using with firewalls, 561

static versus dynamic routers, 482

static Web pages, definition of, 344. *See also* active Web pages; data-driven Web pages; static Web pages; top secret Web pages; Web pages

statistical multiplexing, relationship to Frame Relay, 459

STEP508 Web accessibility tool, features of, 428

Step-by-Step items
    Configuring Security Zones, 84–85
    Configuring Your E-mail Client, 129
    Downloading Audio and Video from the Internet, 103
    Downloading Images from the Internet, 101–102
    Downloading Text from the Internet, 98
    FTPing a File on a Legacy System, 166–167
    Searching Yahoo!, 86–87
    Sending and Reading Mail, 131–132
    for Windows Filename Associations for Internet Explorer, 75–76

STML (standard generalizable markup language), relationship to HTML, 254

storyboards, using in design stage of ADDIE, 196–197

STP (shielded twisted pair) cabling, features of, 464

stream ciphers, description of, 571

streaming media, overview of, 76–77, 507

streaming, overview of, 13–14, 77

string variables
    assigning values to, 350
    concatenating, 351–352
    definition of, 349

<strong></strong> tags, using on Web pages, 267, 354

Stuffit Expander, decompressing files with, 109

style classes and IDs, guidelines for creation of, 379–380

style sheets. *See* CSS (cascading style sheets)

subdomains and domains, overview of, 20–21

Submit buttons, coding for HTML forms, 306–307, 311

submit.html tutorial, following, 306–307

subnet masks, overview of, 487–488

subnet-directed broadcasts, explanation of, 486

SUBSCRIBE listserv commands, effects of, 145

sulfnbk.exe virus hoax, explanation of, 123–124

surfing, overview of, 64

SVCs (switched virtual circuits), relationship to Frame Relay, 459

.swf filename extension, MIME and media types for, 507

Switchboard search engine, finding people with, 95

switches, description of, 462

symmetric cryptography, overview of, 566

SYN floods attacks, effect of, 558

System 7.0 for Macintoshes, release of, 11

T

T1 and T3 services, explanations of, 460

tab-delimited data, explanation of, 527

table attributes, adjusting in Web pages, 280–282

table cells. *See also* cells and tables
    spanning rows and columns with, 287
    subdividing in Web pages, 285–287

table HTML tags, description of, 255

Table of Contents in Web pages, returning to, 264–265

table structure, indenting in Web pages, 284–285

<table></table> tags, using in Web pages, 256, 278–279

tables. *See also* HTML tables
    HTML tags for creation of, 276–278
    using in Web page layout, 276–278
    using in Web pages, 234
    of world's highest mountains, 282–284

tables and cells, coloring, 281–282

TAPI (Telephone Application Programming Interface), role in IP telephony, 35–36

targeting relationships, establishing for frames, 325–326

task analysis, role in in-house e-commerce systems, 196

tax forms, downloading from IRS Web site, 27

T-carrier systems, relationship to NAPs, 460–461

TCP (Transmission Control Protocol)
    overview of, 479
    split into TCP and IP, 8

TCP/IP (Transmission Control Protocol/Internet Protocol)
    and Application Layer protocols, 478–479
    configuring in PCs, 488–489
    development of, 7
    explanation of, 18

and IETF, 477

and Internet Architecture model, 476–477

and Internet Layer protocols, 480

as networking standard for Internet, 9

overview of, 19–20, 452, 513

and Transport Layer protocols, 479

<td></td> tags, using in Web pages, 256, 278–279

TDM (Time Division Multiplexing), relationship to T-carrier systems, 461

TEACH (Technology Education and Copyright Harmonization) Act, significance of, 203

teaching, impact of Internet on, 30

teal, RGB code for, 282

TEAS (Trademark Electronic Application System), Web address for, 207

Telecommunications Union, Web address for, 162

telecommuting, significance of, 24

TELENET, creation of, 7

television, impact of Internet on, 29

telnet
    logging onto legacy systems with, 163–165
    overview of, 171
    relationship to TCP/IP, 478
    setting local echo option in, 164

telnet clients, running, 164

telnet sessions, closing, 164

Ten Commandments of computer use, list of, 122

terminals, relationship to networking, 439

text, downloading from Internet, 98

text areas, creating in HTML forms, 310, 312

text editors, creating Web pages with, 223

text field input controls, coding for HTML forms, 304–305, 311

text file formats
    DOC and WPD, 100
    HTML (hypertext markup language), 99
    overview of, 98
    PDF (Portable Document Format), 100
    TXT (plain text), 99

text sizing, considering in Web pages, 239

text-to-speech conversion, overview of, 38–39

textual screen design, example of, 237

TFTP (Trivial File Transfer Protocol), relationship to TCP/IP, 478

.tga graphics format, description of, 101

Thicknet coaxial cable, features of, 464

ThinkPad laptop, introduction of, 11

Thinnet coaxial cable, features of, 464
three-tier Web application model
   components of, 522
   example of, 531
tiers, subdividing applications into, 440
.tif graphics format, description of, 101
tiled backgrounds, using in Web pages,
   240–241
Tile.Net directory, Web address for, 140
Times versus Arial font, 239, 422
title bar clock script, creating, 363–364
<title></title> tags, using in Web page
   résumés, 256–257
TLAs (three-letter acronyms),
   relationship to Netiquette, 126
TLDs (top-level domains)
   country codes for, 21
   examples of, 20
TLS (transport layer security)
   handshake protocol, overview of, 572
token ring standard
   development of, 10
   overview of, 457
tokens, role in ring topologies, 446
Tomlinson, Ray and first e-mail over
   network, 6
top secret Web pages, creating,
   540–541. *See also* active Web pages;
   data-driven Web pages; static
   Web pages; Web pages
top-level domains, examples of, 495
TopSecret database, creating, 530–531
TopSecret users, selecting, 536
toString() method, using in JavaScript
   clock project, 358
Tourbus listserv, subscribing to, 140
<tr></tr> tags, using in Web pages,
   256, 278–279
traceroute networking utility, using,
   490–491
trademarks
   overview of, 207
   regulating, 211–212
trading internationally
   language issues related to, 209
   and multiple currencies, 208
   overview of, 207, 212
   and shipping overseas, 208–209
transaction servers, overview of, 502
transactions
   filtering and logging with proxy
      servers, 499
   speeding up with EDI, 182
transition effects, example of, 384, 386
translation software, advisory about, 209
transparent images, creating for
   Web pages, 274–275. *See also*
   animated images; images
Transport Layer of OSI/RM,
   significance of, 450, 479
transport medium, significance of, 54–55

trapdoor attacks, effect of, 558–559
tritanopia, simulating, 423
Trojan horse virus
   definition of, 83
   description of, 554
   story of, 84
trunk cables, role in bus topology, 445
Try This! items
   Can You Find Middle C on an
      Image Map?, 67
   Conducting a Boolean Search, 88
   Create the World's Smallest
      Network, 494
   Creating a Sidebar Frameset for
      Your Résumé, 326–327
   Creating a TopSecret Database,
      530–531
   Creating an E-mail Signature, 134
   Creating More Screen Space, 71
   Creating Top Secret Web Pages, 541
   Detecting Unauthorized Services,
      554–555
   Discover Your NIC's MAC
      Address, 454
   Dynamic HTML Code
      Generator, 387
   Exploring Amazon.com's XML
      Web Services, 184
   Inspect Your Computer's
      Services, 512
   Inspecting Your Computer's
      Cookies, 374
   Installing ZoneAlarm, 564–565
   International Currency
      Converter, 208
   The Kennedy Moon Challenge
      Project, 393–394
   Linking Your Home Page to
      Your Résumé Page, 287–288
   Make a 10/100baseT Ethernet
      Cable, 466–467
   Make a Table of the World's
      Highest Mountains, 282–284
   Manipulating the URL Field, 69
   Pile Rocks with Absolute
      Positioning and z-index, 380–381
   Roll Your Own Image Map,
      318–319
   Rollover Effects, 367
   Selecting TopSecret Users, 536
   Subscribing to Listservs in Your
      Profession, 140
   Take WebEx for a Free Test
      Drive, 162
   Telnetting to the Weather
      Underground, 165
   Title Bar Clock Script, 363–364
   Update Your Browser, 61
   Using a Word Processor to
      Make a Web Page, 227

Using an E-mail Address Book,
   135–136
Virage VIR Patent, 39
Web Page Color Blindness
   Simulator, 424
twisted pair cabling, features of,
   464–465
.txt filename extension, MIME and
   media types for, 507
TXT (plain text) format, overview of, 99

U

UDDI (Universal Description,
   Discovery, and Integration),
   overview of, 183
UDP (User Datagram Protocol),
   relationship to TCP/IP, 479
.uk code, country associated with, 21
<ul></ul> tags, using in Web page
   résumés, 256, 260–261
UltimateTV service, features of, 42
unauthorized access
   detecting, 554–555
   occurrence of, 550–551
underlining, using on Web pages, 267
Unisys GIF patent, significance of, 206
UNIX operating system
   development of, 6
   and inetd, 509
   overview of, 444
   version 6 of, 7
   version 7 of, 8
   version 8 of, 10
unordered lists, using in Web page
   résumés, 260–261
Unsubscribe link, advisory about, 136
unwanted e-mail, dealing with,
   136–137. *See also* e-mail
URLs (Uniform Resource Locators)
   elements of, 62
   entering, 64
   linking to, 265
   manipulating, 68–69
   and Web pages, 63
.us code, country associated with, 21
USA Patriot Act, purpose of, 28
usability, considering in Web page
   design, 241–242
usemap attribute, applying to HTML
   image maps, 317
USENET newsgroups, 8–10.
   See also newsgroups
   and computer conferencing, 146
   explanation of, 146
   hierarchy of, 146–147
   name formats of, 146
user information, obtaining from
   HTML forms, 303
user-level security issues,
   overview of, 551

UTP (unshielded twisted pair) cabling, features of, 464–465
Uuencoding, overview of, 506

V

validated XML documents, explanation of, 389
valign attribute, effect of, 281
variables
 code analysis of, 350–351
 definition of, 348
 types of, 349
VBScript language
 creating ADO connection objects with, 533–534
 overview of, 83
 reading data from recordsets with, 538
 using to make decisions with logic, 540
VeriSign certificate authority, free trial offered by, 569–570
Veronica, searching with, 94
vertical frames, creating, 321
video, downloading from Internet, 103
video compression schemes, descriptions of, 106
video controls, using in Windows Media Player, 75
video formats
 AVI (audio/video interleave), 106
 MOV and QT, 106–107
 MPG, MPEG, and MPE, 107
 overview of, 106
 RM (Real metafile), 107
videoconferencing
 with CUseeMe, 160–161
 features of, 159
 overview of, 12–13, 170
videos, providing captions for, 393–394
Virage software for image recognition, features of, 39
virtual directories, relationship to Web servers, 504
Virtual Server 2005, release of, 14
viruses
 definition of, 83
 guarding against, 125
 and hacker process, 553–554
 relationship to Netiquette, 124–125
 safeguarding against, 110–111
 types of, 553–554
Vischeck, Web address for, 423
Visual Studio 2005, release of, 14
voice recognition, overview of, 38
VPNs (virtual private networks), overview of, 572

W

W3C color contrast algorithm, Web address for, 423
W3C (World Wide Web Consortium), Web address for, 16
WAI (Web Accessibility Initiative)
 significance of, 404–405
 Web address for, 428
WANs (wide area networks)
 creating, 470
 definition of, 454
 overview of, 458
WAP (Wireless Application Protocol), overview of, 73
WAPs (wireless access points), overview of, 461
.wav filename extension, MIME and media types for, 507
WAV (wafeform) format, overview of, 104
WCAG (Web Content Accessibility Guidelines), overview of, 405–406
Weather Underground, telnetting to, 165
Web
 creating new folders on, 334–335
 FTPing files to, 331–332
Web access, providing to server-side databases, 522–526, 542
Web accessibility. *See also* CSS design for accessibility; Section 508 of Rehabilitation Act of 1973
 definition of, 404–405, 429
 entitlement to, 405
 resources for, 428
 tools for assessment of, 430
Web accessibility assessment tools
 Bobby, 427
 LIFT, 427
 overview of, 426
 STEP508, 427
 WebKing, 427
Web application model
 components of, 522
 example of, 531
Web content, caching with proxy servers, 499
Web gateways, overview of, 505
Web logs
 explanation of, 17
 keeping through blogging, 152
Web Page color blindness simulator, 423
Web page creation strategies
 overview of, 222, 244
 using HTML editors, 223–225
 using HTML translators, 225–227
 using text editors, 223
 using WYSIWYG editors, 228–230
Web page design elements
 backgrounds, 233
 bookmarks, 233

borders, 235
frames, 234–235
headings, 231–232
horizontal rules, 231–232
images, 233
links, 234
lists, 232
named anchors, 234
overview of, 230–231, 244
paragraphs, 231
special characters, 234
tables, 234
Web page résumés
 analyzing layout of, 242–243, 245
 creating horizontal rules in, 261
 creating hypertext links to named anchor bookmarks in, 263–264
 creating lists in, 260–261
 creating named anchor bookmarks in, 262–263
 creating page title for, 257
 creating sidebar framesets for, 326–327
 creating white space in, 266
 HTML tags used in, 255–256
 identifying owners of, 265–266
 including bold text in, 267
 including mailto links in, 266
 inserting images into, 273–274
 inserting new headings in, 262
 italicizing text on, 267
 linking home pages to, 287–288
 linking to URLs in, 265
 overview of, 292–293
 returning to Table of Contents in, 264–265
 saving file for, 261–262
 saving pages for, 258
 starting page for, 256–257
 underlining in, 267
 using character attributes and word processors with, 266–267
 viewing in browsers, 259
 writing heading for, 257
 writing paragraphs in, 259–260
Web page screen design principles
 consistency, 242
 font selection, 238–239
 foreground versus background colors, 239
 layout, 236–238
 navigational icons, 240
 overview of, 236, 244–245
 photographic backgrounds, 240
 scrolling, 241
 text sizing, 239
 tiled backgrounds, 240–241
 usability, 241–242
Web pages. *See also* active Web pages; data-driven Web pages; static Web pages; top secret Web pages
 capturing images for, 270–271